The George Washington Collection

FINE AND DECORATIVE ARTS

AT

MOUNT VERNON

Merry Christmas to Ray and Sarah. May your world be decorative.
Love, Anne's Mom
Dec. 2006

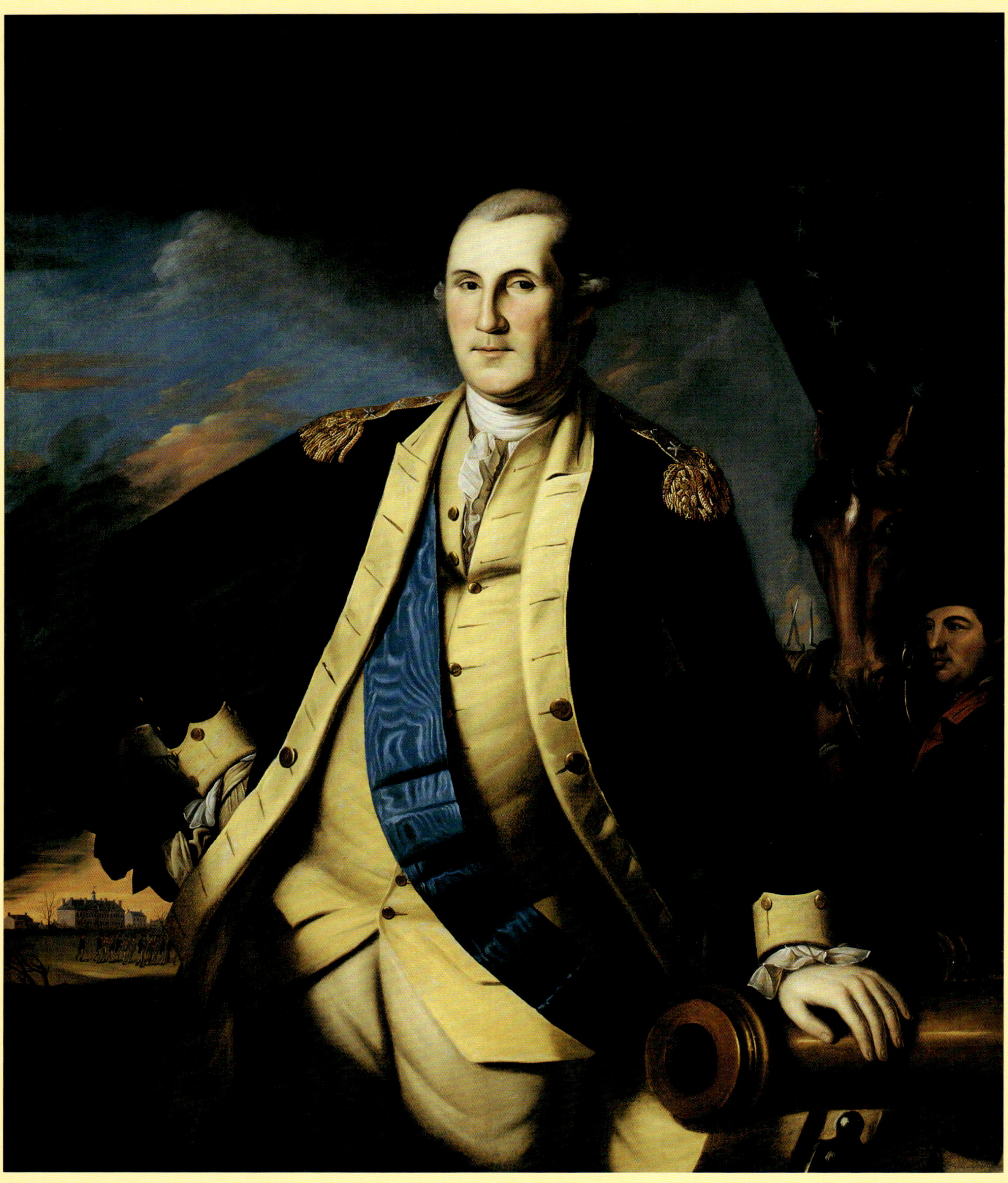

The George Washington Collection

FINE AND DECORATIVE ARTS AT MOUNT VERNON

CAROL BORCHERT CADOU

MOUNT VERNON LADIES' ASSOCIATION

HUDSON HILLS PRESS

MANCHESTER • NEW YORK

This publication marks the occasion of the opening of the Donald W. Reynolds Museum and Education Center at George Washington's Mount Vernon Estate and Gardens, Mount Vernon, Virginia, October 27, 2006.

First Edition

Copyright © 2006 Mount Vernon Ladies Association
All rights reserved under International and Pan-American Copyright Convention.
Except for legitimate excerpts customary in review or scholarly publications, no part of this publication may be reproduced or transmitted in any form or by any means, electronic or mechanical, including photocopying, recording, or information storage or retrieval systems, without written permission from the publisher.

Published in the United States by Hudson Hills Press LLC, 74-2 Union Street, Manchester, Vermont 05254.
Distributed in the United States, its territories and possessions, and Canada by National Book Network, Inc.
Distributed in the United Kingdom, Eire, and Europe by Windsor Books International.

Co-Directors: Leslie van Breen and Randall Perkins
Founding Publisher: Paul Anbinder
Editor: Fronia W. Simpson
Designer: Katy Homans
Production: Nerissa Vales
Indexer: Susan DeRenne Coerr
Proofreader: Richard G. Gallin
Production Manager: David Skolkin/Skolkin + Chickey, Santa Fe, NM

Color separations by Pre Tech Color, Wilder, Vermont
Printed and bound by CS Graphics Pte., Ltd., Singapore

Library of Congress Cataloging-in-Publication Data

Cadou, Carol Borchert.
The George Washington collection : fine and decorative arts at Mount Vernon / Carol Borchert Cadou.
p. cm.
Includes bibliographical references.
ISBN-13: 978-1-55595-268-6 (alk. paper)
ISBN-10: 1-55595-268-2 (alk. paper)
1. Decorative arts—Virginia—Mount Vernon (Estate) 2. Art—Virginia—Mount Vernon (Estate) 3. Washington, George, 1732-1799--Art collections. 4. Decorative arts—Private collections—Virginia--Mount Vernon (Estate) 5. Art—Private collections—Virginia—Mount Vernon (Estate) I. Title.
NK535.fi37 33 2007
708.155'291—dc22
2006016228

Contents

The Mount Vernon Ladies' Association

gratefully acknowledges the support of

DONALD AND NANCY DE LASKI

in making this publication possible.

Preface

It can be a burden as well as an honor to be a descendant in a famous family like the Washingtons. Family members who inherit objects sometimes feel they do not really own them but are merely caretakers for the American people of artifacts that sooner or later will find their way home.

In the case of George Washington, there is really only one place that he felt was home. His attachment to Mount Vernon was strong, and many aspects of the place reflect his taste in architecture, landscape design, and interior furnishings. And thank goodness, Washington was a meticulous record keeper. His inventory of the Mansion is extremely detailed and naturally becomes the wish list of Mount Vernon's curators.

Only a handful of original items were in the empty house when the first Regent and Vice Regents bought it in 1858 from Washington's great-great nephew, John Augustine Washington III (my great-great uncle). The contents were dispersed widely through a series of bequests, private auctions, and public sales that took place after Mrs. Washington died in 1802. Family members at the time realized that Washington's favorite chair, for example, or the bed in which he died would always be considered significant. Yet today curators crave almost anything the great man touched. Simple artifacts like the piece of coral he brought home from Barbados, or the little strip of paper he used to measure his slaves for hats, or his own well-used toothbrush are all now considered treasures.

That the Ladies of Mount Vernon have patiently collected thousands of original artifacts from a multitude of sources testifies to their determination to make the Mansion as authentic as possible. However, not everything associated with the life of Washington belongs in his Mount Vernon Mansion. During his eight years as commander in chief, and then eight more years as president, Washington continued to support the American economy by making purchases, large and small. Not all of these purchases made their way back to Virginia when Washington retired from public office. Fortunately, the Mount Vernon collection includes a range of these purchases, both those that returned with him and those that did not.

Most of these items do not belong in the Mansion, for reasons of authenticity, security, or environment. That is why the construction of a new state-of-the-art museum is important to those who love period objects. Now visitors will be able to see objects from just inches away, increasing their appreciation of Washington's taste in furniture, china, glass, silver, paintings, books, and on and on.

We all know that the objects that surround a person tell us about his personality. This is certainly true of Washington. He liked things that were stylish rather than old-fashioned, but never ostentatious. He appreciated fine craftsmanship, and his favorite pieces always were practical. He bought carefully, liked to find bargains, and, now and then, convinced himself that secondhand objects were perfectly fine.

Washington was detail oriented, even to a fault. He left little to chance. Thus everything that returns to Mount Vernon tells us a little more about its owner. Each year the collection at Mount Vernon grows and reflects a little better Washington's special sense of style, his keen interest in so many aspects of life, and his love for his new country.

Although Carol Borchert Cadou, the Robert H. Smith Senior Curator, has created an incredible overview of the fascinating objects currently residing at Mount Vernon, the collection will never be static. New items given to or bought by the Mount Vernon Ladies' Association add new bits to our understanding. Washington gathered his collection a few pieces at a time, and Mount Vernon's dedicated caretakers necessarily follow in his footsteps.

Particularly for a Washington family member this is truly exciting. But Washington is the Father of Our Country, we are all his family, and his home is a touchstone for all Americans. We all hope that, even as the collection grows and Mount Vernon's newly constructed underground museum is carefully tucked beneath a pasture, this unity will always endure.

JOHN A. WASHINGTON

Acknowledgments

This book could not have been realized without the assistance of numerous individuals, chief among them the past and present Regents and Vice Regents of the Mount Vernon Ladies' Association, who have labored for more than 150 years to preserve George Washington's private residence and to return to Mount Vernon those objects owned and used by our nation's first president.

The generous support of Donald and Nancy de Laski has provided the means for this publication that highlights a selected number of the objects preserved at Mount Vernon. We owe them a debt of gratitude for their wish to educate others about Washington's life and the objects he chose to furnish his material environment.

I am very grateful to Mount Vernon Executive Director James C. Rees IV and Director of Collections Linda Ayres for their strong support of this project and for their willingness to set aside precious time to review the manuscript.

The completion of this publication in time for the opening of the Donald W. Reynolds Museum and Education Center would not have been possible without the many hours devoted to it by Volunteer Research Assistants Royanne Chipps Bailey, Virginia Eisemon, and Ann D. Peel. They tirelessly organized, researched, and drafted material for inclusion in the catalogue entries. I deeply appreciate their involvement, support, and contributions.

Also at Mount Vernon, not only did Assistant Curators Gretchen Goodell and Christine Messing research and contribute to a number of catalogue entries, but they also graciously assumed and adeptly performed additional curatorial responsibilities so that I could devote time to complete this work. Dawn Bonner lent her keen eye and extensive knowledge of the Photo Archives and devoted many hours helping to identify appropriate images to complement the text and obtaining needed images and permissions. Director of Archaeology Esther White contributed valuable insights into the early years of Mount Vernon, kindly drafted an entry on excavated stoneware, and provided objects from the Archaeology Collection to give the reader a better understanding of plantation life at Mount Vernon. Librarian Barbara McMillan patiently guided me and the volunteers through research materials and archival holdings, generously sharing her time and knowledge. Research Specialist Mary V. Thompson graciously provided references and insights drawn from her broad understanding of primary source material, read the complete manuscript, and offered numerous helpful suggestions. Library Assistant Jennifer Kittlaus and Special Projects Manager John Rudder provided invaluable assistance and support, Intern Laura Liebert made numerous contributions through her research on the collection, and Conservators Flavia Perugini and Simona Christanetti ensured that each Washington object was brought to the best condition possible before being photographed. I am extremely grateful for the support provided by each one of these talented Mount Vernon colleagues.

For permission to include Washington objects held privately and in institutional collections, I thank Brian and Barbara Hendelson, the Smithsonian's National Museum of American History, Yale University Art Gallery, Arlington House, the Robert E. Lee Memorial, Fairfax County Circuit Court, the Brooklyn Museum, Washington and Lee University, and private lenders. A special word of appreciation needs to be expressed to Mary Troy at Arlington House, Lisa Kathleen Graddy at the Smithsonian's National Museum of American History, and Holly Bailey and Angelika Kuettner at Washington and Lee University for their assistance and collegiality.

At Colonial Williamsburg, a host of colleagues shared insights and expertise, including Linda Baumgarten, Tara Gleason Chicirda, Loreen Finkelstein, Leroy Graves, Ronald Hurst, Natalie Larson, and Robert Leath. At Winterthur Museum, Curators Donald Fennimore, Ronald Fuchs, and Ann Wagner kindly offered assistance identifying Washington porcelains and metals. Mary Cheek Mills at the Corning Museum of Glass provided much-appreciated insight into Washington's glass, and Susan Perdue at Monticello contributed valuable clarification on the writings of Thomas Jefferson. Scott Casper at the University of Nevada, Reno, offered helpful insight into the nineteenth-century Mount Vernon, and gemologist Richard Zemlo lent his expertise in identifying the stones in George and Martha Washington's personal articles.

For taking the time necessary to capture the Mount Vernon landscape, interiors, and collection at their best, I am grateful to all the photographers who contributed their talents to the images in this publication. In particular, I thank Gavin Ashworth, who made certain that his photographs do justice to the objects and to George Washington. For their assistance with photography preparations, thanks are due to Eleanor Breen, Julia Brennan, David Carpenter, Simona Christanetti, Sarah Holland, Christine Messing, John Payne, Flavia Perugini, and Joseph Sliger.

I am also very appreciative of Leslie van Breen and her talented team at Hudson Hills Press for their expertise and creativity that are reflected on each and every page of this book.

I would be remiss if I did not acknowledge those stewards and researchers of the Mount Vernon collection who have preceded me, both descendants and employees, for the foundation of material they have provided for understanding George Washington and his material world. We are indebted to them, and to the researchers and scholars at the University of Virginia who have labored for many years to provide us with the diaries and the papers of George Washington. Their hard work has made Washington and his world come alive.

For contributing to my understanding of American fine and decorative arts and the context in which they were created, I am indebted to Elisabeth Garrett, Wendell Garrett, Bruce Steiner, H. Barbara Weinberg, and the professors and curators of the Winterthur Program in Early American Culture, in particular, Gretchen Townsend Buggeln, J. Ritchie Garrison, Donald Fennimore, and Charles Hummel.

I am thankful for the support of family and friends throughout the writing of the manuscript, in particular, my husband, Christopher Cadou, whose understanding and encouragement were remarkable. My gratitude goes also to my parents, Donald and Mary Ellen Borchert, who instilled in me a love of learning at a very early age and who continue to inspire and guide me with their own quests to pursue "the examined life."

CAROL BORCHERT CADOU
Robert H. Smith Senior Curator
George Washington's Mount Vernon
Mount Vernon, Virginia

The George Washington Collection

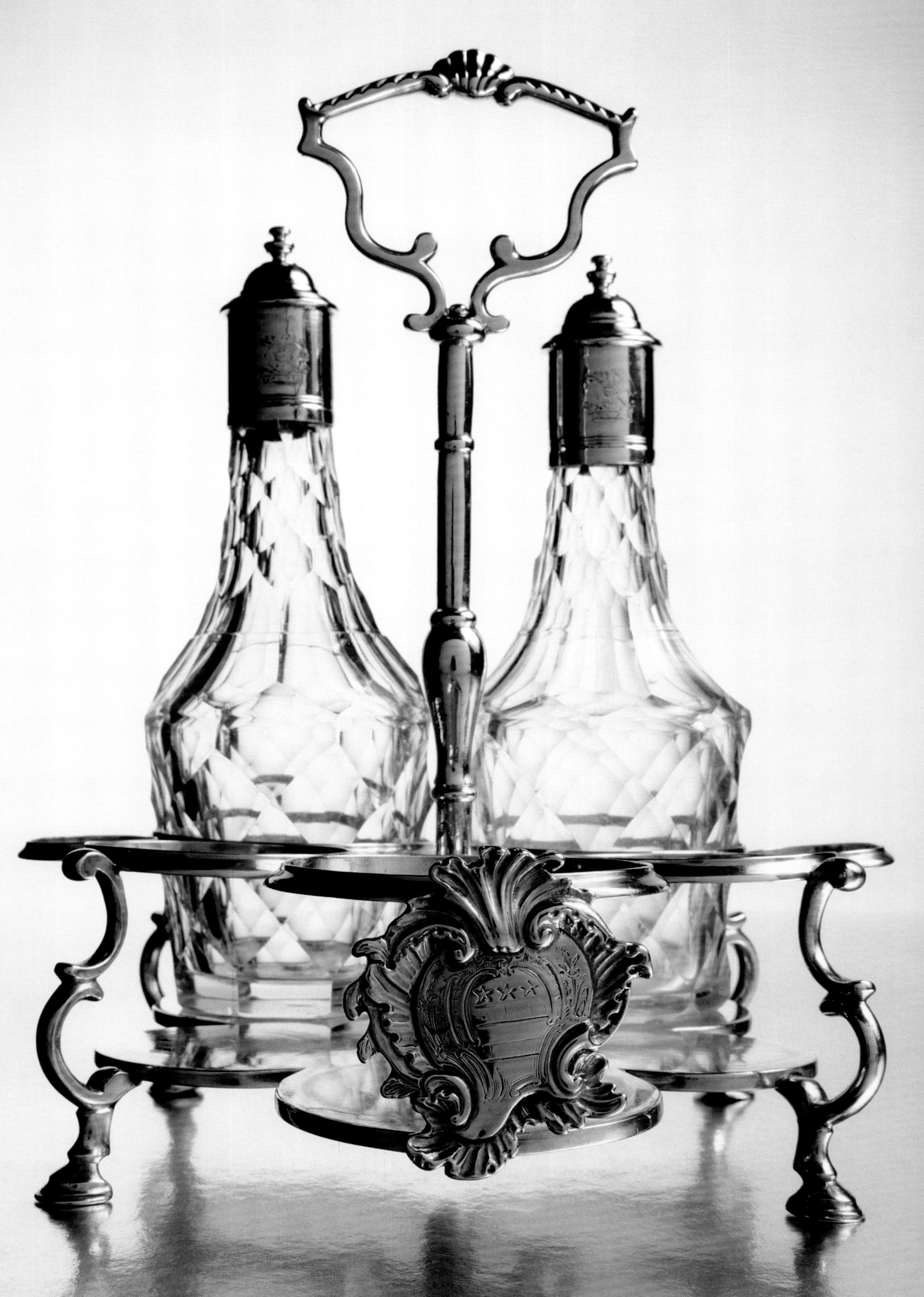

Introduction

George Washington has been recognized for more than two centuries as a figure worthy of study. Within his lifetime, biographers recorded the life and thoughts of this remarkable individual. Since his death in 1799, Washington has been the subject of countless publications, and scholars have devoted decades attempting to understand the "man behind the myth." Biographers have painstakingly researched and recounted the details of Washington's life, and several recent authors have addressed the social framework surrounding Washington and his decisions. Relatively few, however, have turned to material culture as a means to better understand our first president.

Material culture, broadly defined, is the study of human-made objects that speak of the culture in which they were created as well as the individuals who made and owned them. These artifacts can take the form of buildings as well as the paintings that hang on their walls, the furniture and household objects they contain, the clothing and jewelry worn by those who live and/or work in them, and the books or toys enjoyed by these individuals. Together, such human artifacts help us understand a people, a region, or an individual.[1]

George Washington was aware of the way in which the objects that surrounded him defined him. Personal possessions have long been a way by which human beings communicate with one another, conveying interests, education, political and social affiliations, as well as economic standing. For thousands of years, people have materially defined themselves by the objects they acquire, adorn themselves with, and place within their living spaces. George Washington was no different from his fellow eighteenth-century Americans in understanding that certain objects denoted gentility, sophistication, enlightenment, and wealth. Because Washington wanted to maintain a material appearance in accord with his professional and social position, he paid keen attention to the objects that surrounded him throughout his life. Additionally, he understood that how others perceived him could, if necessary, be manipulated through objects.

This book provides a window onto the artifacts that Washington lived with as a way of enriching our knowledge of him within the context of the eighteenth century. The discussion includes those objects used by Washington himself as well as articles owned and used by his wife, Martha Washington, by her children and grandchildren, and by the African American slaves who also formed what Washington considered to be his family. All of the objects selected for inclusion in this volume are preserved today at Mount Vernon, George Washington's private residence on the banks of Virginia's Potomac River, through the efforts of the Mount Vernon Ladies' Association.

The Association was founded in 1853 by Ann Pamela Cunningham to raise funds for the purchase of Mount Vernon from George Washington's great-great nephew John Augustine Washington III (figs. 1, 2). Because George Washington died without heirs, the estate passed to his nephew, Bushrod Washington, when Martha Washington died in 1802. Bushrod Washington and those to whom Mount Vernon passed

opposite: George Washington's silver cruet set (partial), MVLA

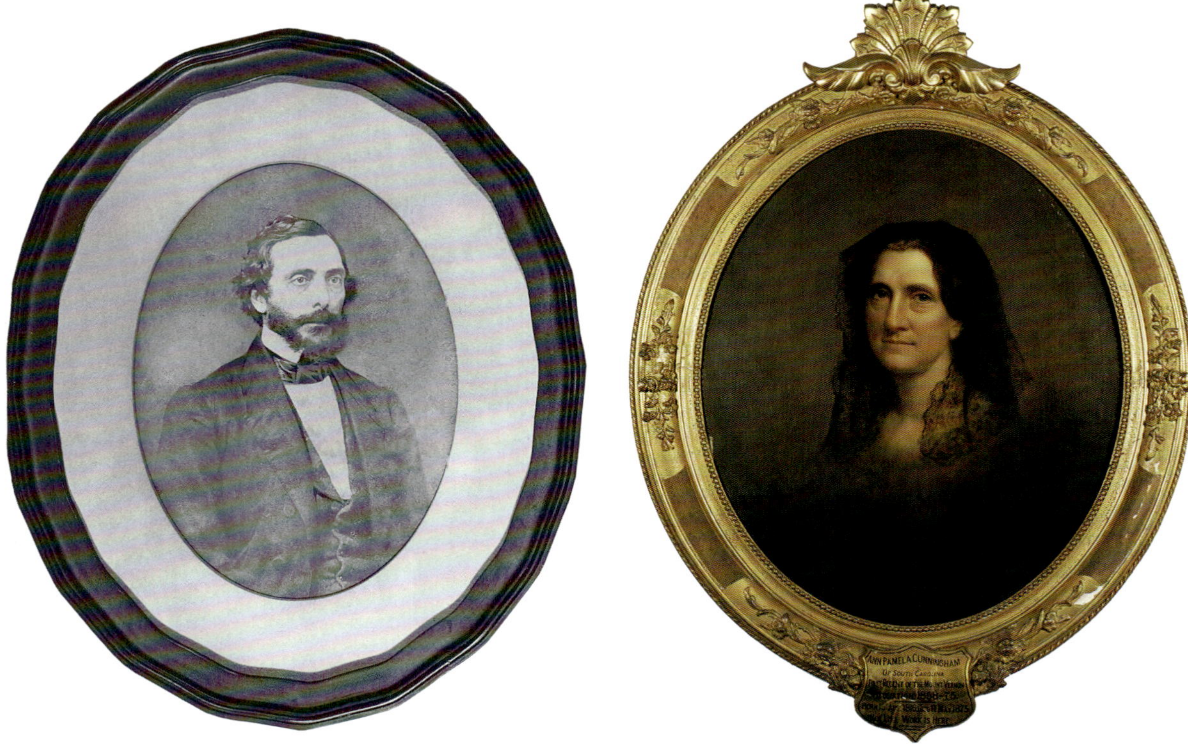

Fig. 1. John Augustine Washington III, the last Washington family member to own Mount Vernon

Fig. 2. Ann Pamela Cunningham of South Carolina, founder of the Mount Vernon Ladies' Association, by James Reid Lambdin, oil on canvas, 1870, MVLA

after him, inherited the dwelling owned by Washington, but not its contents. The contents of the house, therefore, were disbursed through bequests in the Washingtons' wills as well as through a series of public and private sales in 1802. Nonetheless, the house remained an attraction for scores of visitors each year who wished to pay their respects to the former general and president. By the time Ann Pamela Cunningham approached John Augustine Washington about the sale of the property, the Washington family resources to maintain the estate with its many callers was dwindling. In 1858 Mr. Washington signed a purchase agreement with the Ladies' Association, and Mount Vernon came into their possession in 1860.[2]

John Augustine Washington left behind a few articles that had remained at Mount Vernon since George Washington's lifetime: the terrestrial globe and bust of Washington in his study, leather fire buckets, pistol holders and pack bags that the general and president had used when away from Mount Vernon, and the key to the Bastille from the Marquis de Lafayette fixed to the central passage wall where Washington had placed it (fig. 3). Before the Association came into full ownership, Martha Washington's great-granddaughter Mary Anna Randolph Custis (Mrs. Robert E. Lee) arranged for the London harpsichord Washington presented to his wife's granddaughter Eleanor "Nelly" Parke Custis to be returned to Mount Vernon's back parlor.[3] In effect, however, the Association purchased an empty house that required furnishing and additional Washington-related objects to interpret it properly to the visiting public.

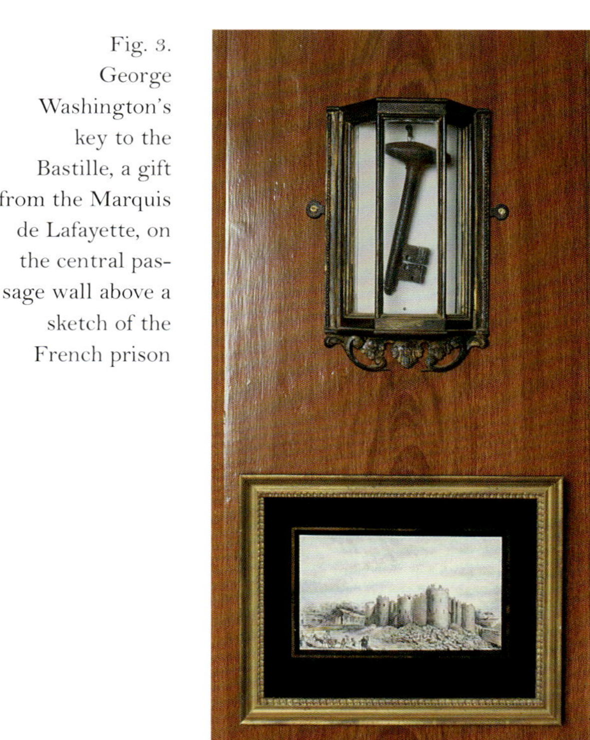

Fig. 3. George Washington's key to the Bastille, a gift from the Marquis de Lafayette, on the central passage wall above a sketch of the French prison

Cunningham had founded an association of prominent women drawn from across the United States. She served as Regent, or chair of the board of trustees, and each Vice Regent, or trustee, represented a different state in the Union. While their initial appeals were for funds to purchase Mount Vernon from the Washington

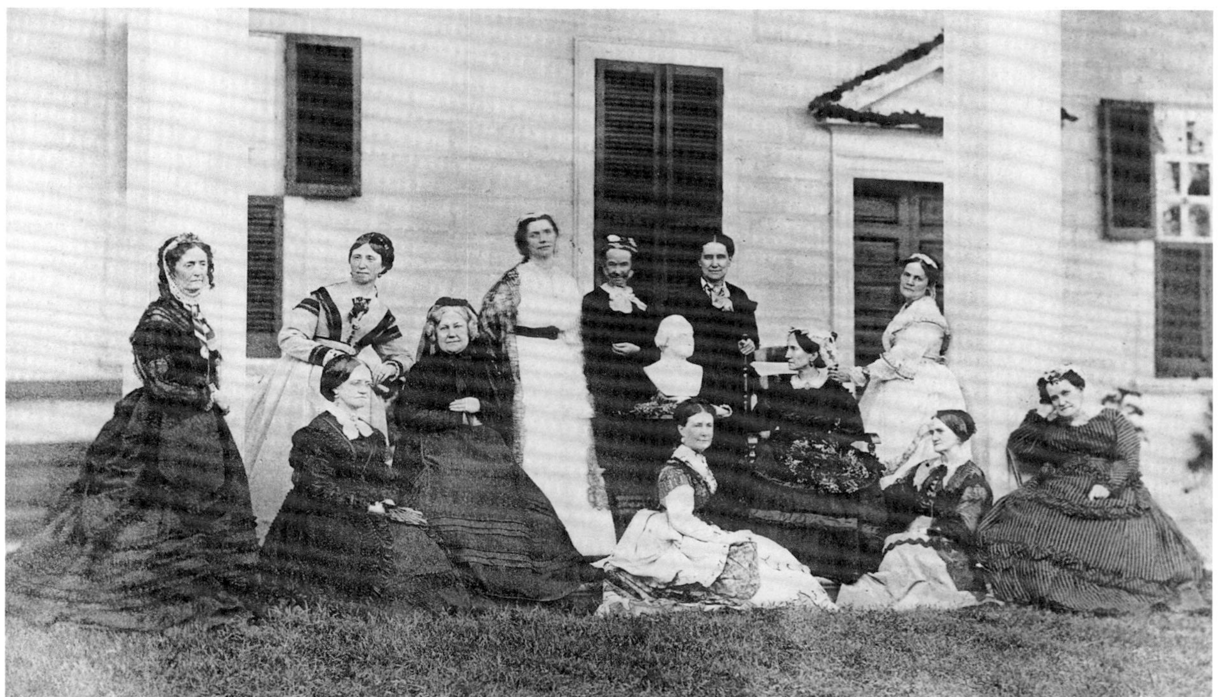

Fig. 4. Early Vice Regents of the Mount Vernon Ladies' Association on the East Lawn surround the treasured bust of George Washington by Jean-Antoine Houdon.

family, Cunningham and the Vice Regents now asked for help with the challenge of furnishing Mount Vernon. Donated objects included a brick from Washington's birthplace, buttons from his coat, and a needle case he supposedly used while encamped at Valley Forge. These relics were placed in cases throughout the house, but the rooms still lacked furnishings to convey the sense of Mount Vernon as the Washingtons' home (figs. 5, 6). In 1868 Nancy Wade Halsted, the Vice Regent for New Jersey (fig. 7), proposed that each of the Vice Regents from the original thirteen colonies select a room and furnish it with donations from her respective state. The idea took hold, and by 1870 the Vice Regents were encouraged by the progress they made. The Association secretary reported that the "furniture, carpets and antiquities [are] owing much of the cheerful appearance of the interior, once so desolate and forlorn."[4]

In addition to objects supplied by the Vice Regents' home states and those provided by patriotic citizens, descendants of Martha Washington contributed original furnishings and personal articles owned by the Washingtons that lent a feeling of authenticity to the rooms. By 1941 the house was overflowing with relics and furnishings of all varieties, and the Vice Regents decided to remove those objects they identified as being crafted after George Washington's death. Guided by the period room installations at the Metropolitan Museum of Art in New York (among others), the Association turned to George Washington's room-by-room estate inventory for clues to the proper furnishing of the individual spaces. While some objects were placed in storage or exhibited in the Relic House, others, like Rembrandt Peale's large and commanding equestrian portrait of George Washington, were donated to sister institutions (figs. 10, 11). During the 1950s and 1960s items continued to leave the house as original furnishings were acquired and those identified as inappropriate were removed.

The progress toward period-room interpretation was revolutionized in 1979 by the Association's bold decision to undertake scientific paint analysis. When the walls were returned to the bright colors and faux finishes George Washington enjoyed, Curator Christine Meadows implemented Mount Vernon's first formal furnishing plan. Objects deemed inappropriate or too difficult to see within the context of a period-room display remained in storage. A select few were placed on view in the small museum nestled among Mount Vernon's historic buildings that was open to visitors until 2005.

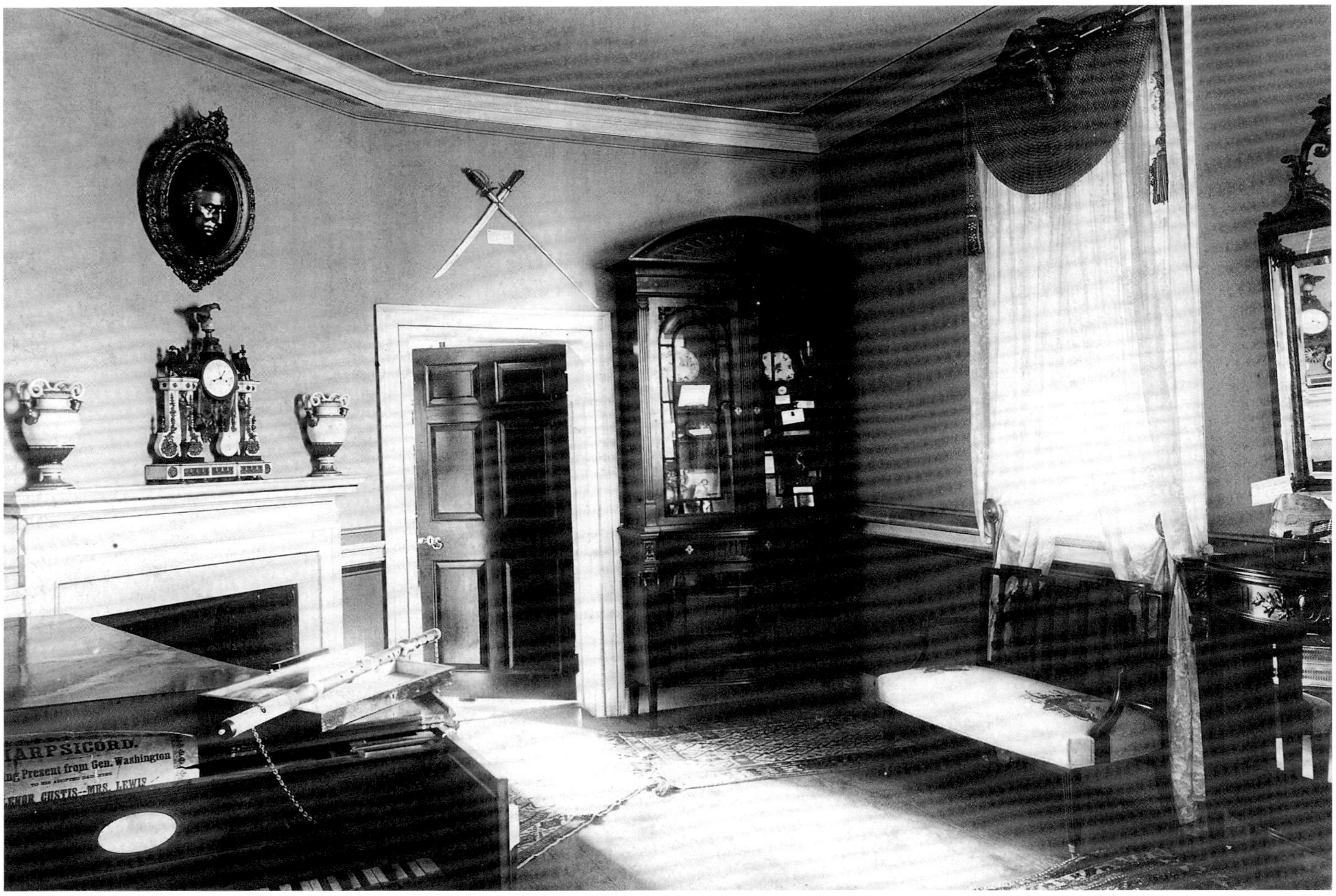

Fig. 5. (above) The Little Parlor furnished with Nelly Custis's harpsichord, a case of George Washington relics and two of his swords, 1889

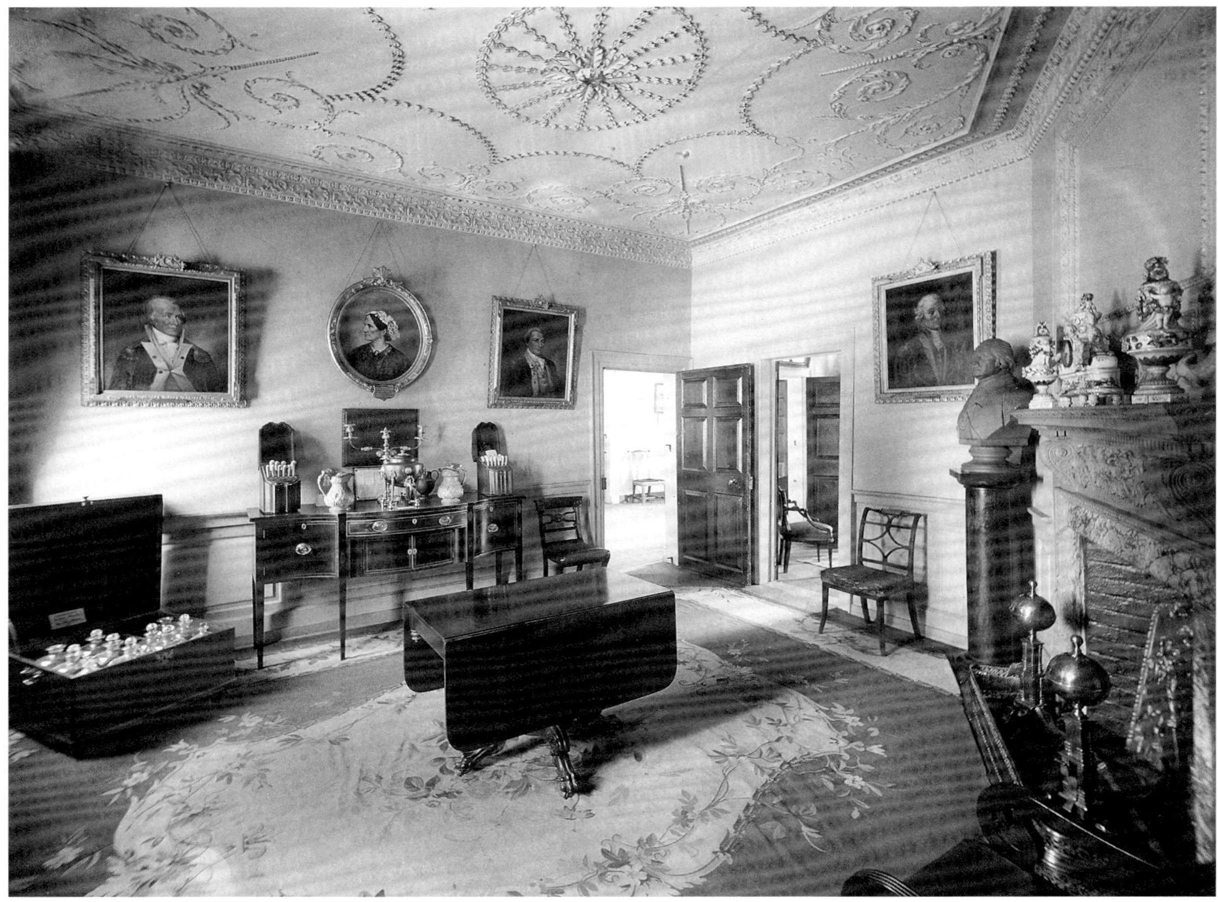

Fig. 6. The South Carolina Room (or Washington's Small Dining Room) included a portrait of Ann Pamela Cunningham and of some of the state's Revolutionary War heroes, ca. 1900.

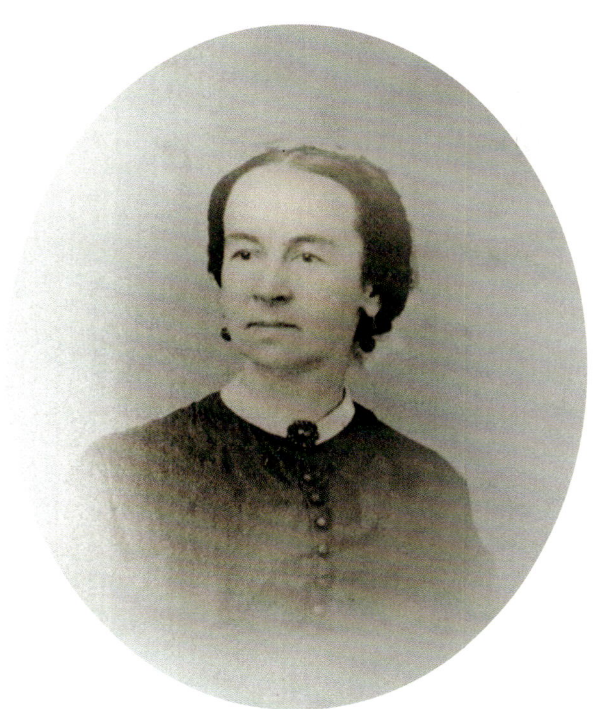

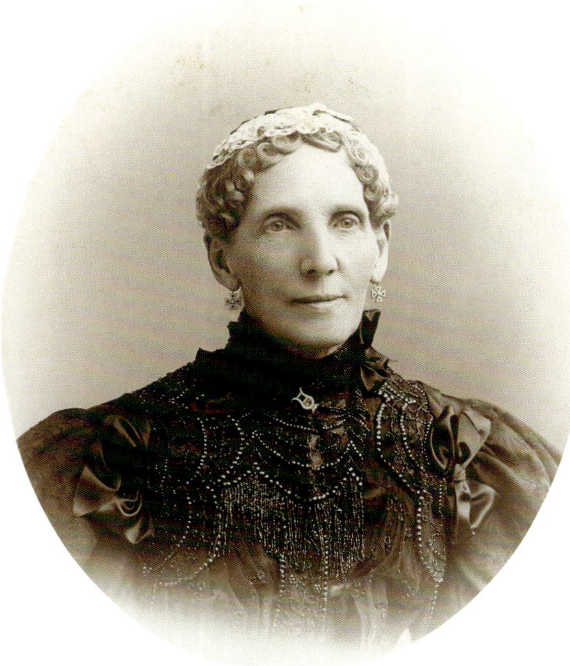

Fig. 7. (left) Nancy Wade Halsted, Vice Regent for New Jersey (1868–1891), proposed the adoption of Mansion rooms by Vice Regents in order to more fully furnish Washington's residence for the visiting public.

Fig. 8. Martha Washington descendant Mrs. George R. Goldsborough, Vice Regent for Maryland (1893–1904), contributed numerous original objects to the Association.

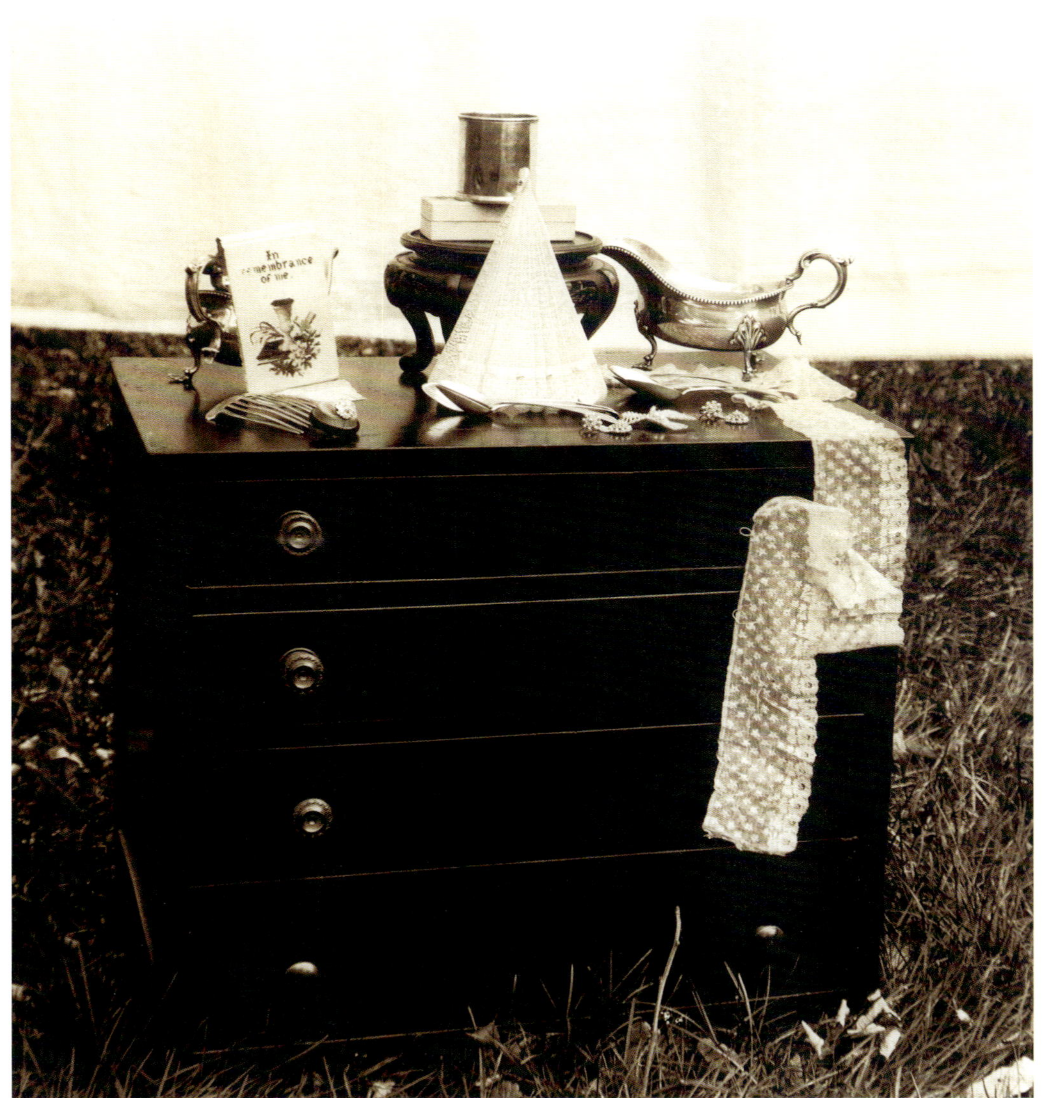

Fig. 9. Early photograph (taken by a Martha Washington descendant) of inherited Washington articles, many of which were subsequently returned to Mount Vernon (see cats. 93, 94)

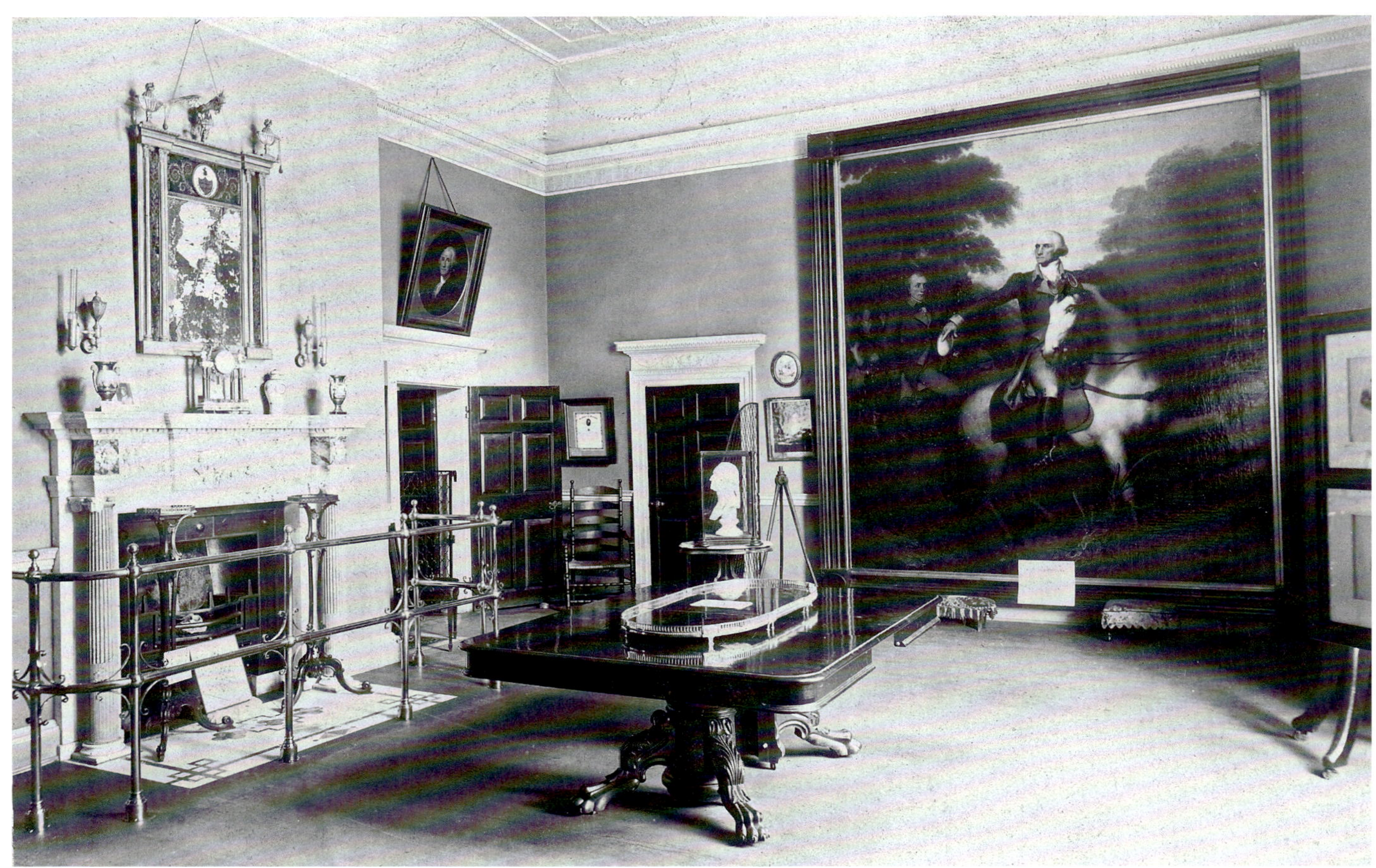

Fig. 10. (above) The large dining room, ca. 1900, before the 19th-century furnishings were removed and the donation of Rembrandt Peale's large-scale equestrian portrait to the Corcoran Gallery of Art

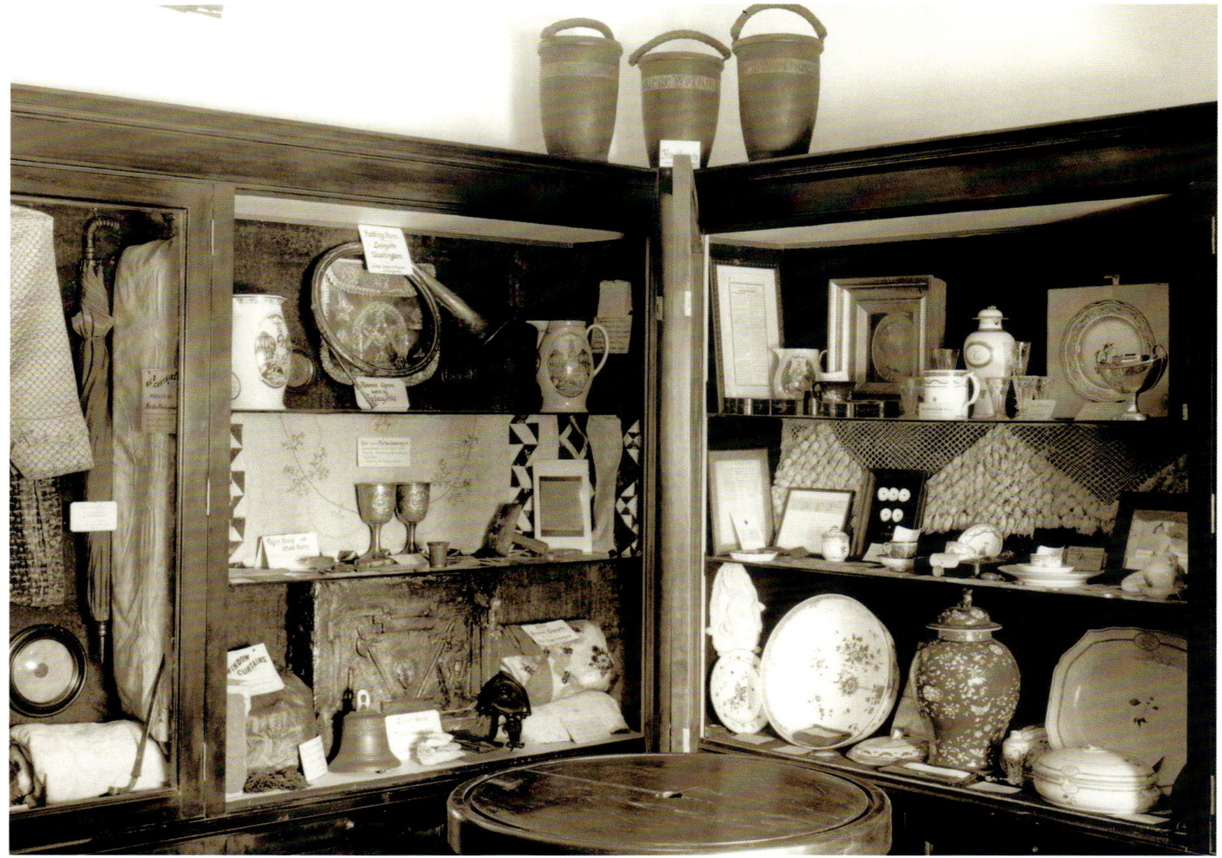

Fig. 11. The Relic House, ca. 1925, provided additional exhibition space for smaller-scale objects with Washington-related histories.

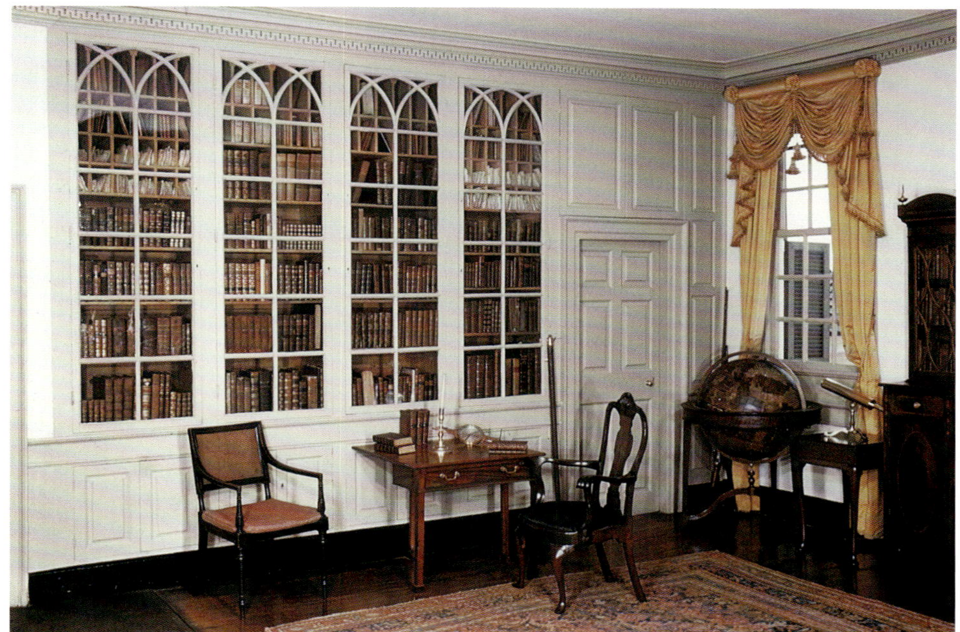

Fig. 12.
George Washington's study before paint analysis

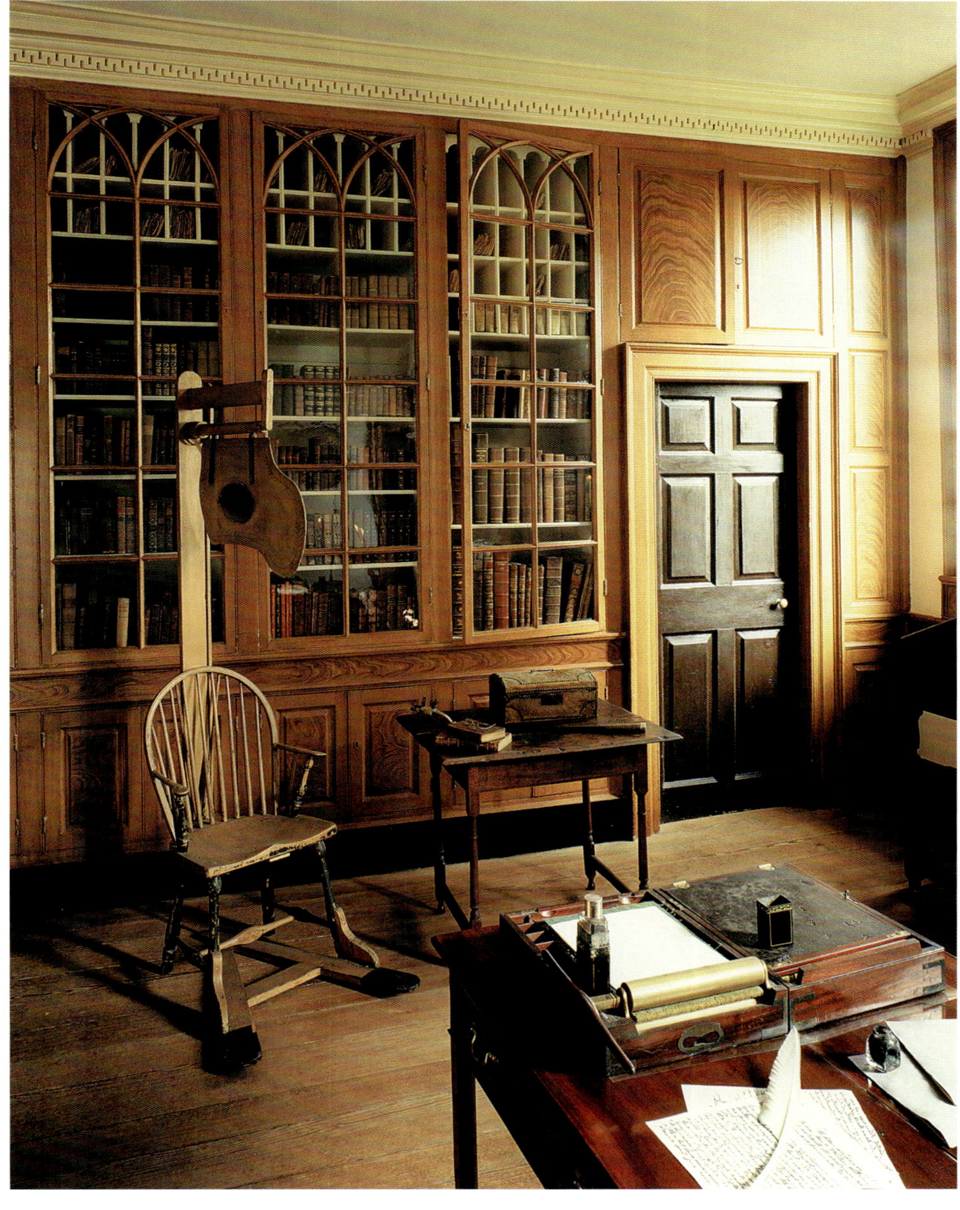

Fig. 13.
The study after paint analysis, the discovery and return of grained surfaces, and the introduction of a period fan chair similar to that owned and used by George Washington

Some of the objects that were removed from the house from the 1940s through the 1980s have remained in storage for decades. Others were hung on walls in administration buildings or were placed on exhibit at other institutions. The opening of the Donald W. Reynolds Museum and Education Center at Mount Vernon now brings together for purposes of exhibition the wide range of objects in the Mount Vernon collection, in order to examine these artifacts outside the context of the period-room display, and to consider George Washington and the objects that surrounded him in a new way. This volume focuses on a sampling of the objects in the Mount Vernon collection that are or will be on view in the new museum. Some are on display in the inaugural exhibits, while others are waiting in the wings for their turn. Many represent some of the first Washington items to enter the collection, while others are recent acquisitions or loans. This work is not, therefore, a definitive account of the objects owned or used by George Washington, nor is it a comprehensive look at the Mount Vernon collection. Rather, it is an introduction to Washington's possessions and the Mount Vernon collection through a selection of representative highlights that are or will be on exhibit in the new facility.

Other publications produced by the Mount Vernon Ladies' Association have looked at the collection: *General Washington's Swords and Campaign Equipment* (1944), *General Washington's Military Equipment* (1963), Kathryn C. Buhler's *Mount Vernon Silver* (1957), *Mount Vernon China* (1949 and 1962), Helen Maggs Fede's *Washington Furniture at Mount Vernon* (1966), Susan Gray Detweiler's *George Washington's Chinaware* (1982), Wendell Garrett's edited volume *George Washington's Mount Vernon* (1998), and James C. Rees' companion to Mount Vernon's traveling exhibition *Treasures from Mount Vernon: George Washington Revealed* (1999). All of these works have provided the public with insight into Mount Vernon's collection. This publication continues the collection focus in a slightly different way. Instead of concentrating on one medium or audience, it includes a panoply of objects owned and used by George Washington. It is intended for the interest and enjoyment of the wide range of visitors who come to Mount Vernon from diverse walks of life, who represent many nations, and who bring to the site a casual or focused interest in material culture. It is also for those who may not have the advantage of being able to walk where George Washington did: it is hoped they will learn about him through the many photographs of the exhibition objects and Mount Vernon included here. While this work aims to educate a broad audience about George Washington, it is nevertheless hoped that the essays and catalogue entries will provide insights for material culture researchers that will inspire them to explore further the life of George Washington and the collection at Mount Vernon.

The narratives and catalogue entries tell a story that is both familiar and somewhat new. The familiar is the account of an ambitious young man who rose in the ranks of colonial Virginia society to become the commander in chief of the Continental Army and the first president of the United States of America, the story of an American hero who did not allow his quest for distinction to mutate into the pride that has led all too many leaders throughout history to become despotic rulers, placing their personal aggrandizement above the common good. The new part of the story focuses on the objects that belonged to and were used by the nation's founding father, whether at home in Virginia, on the road during the Revolutionary War, or at the seat of government as our nation's first president.

It is a common misconception that Washington began to use objects to convey meaning during the presidential years, when he was charged with identifying and fixing the taste of the nation.[5] In fact, he had used possessions to define himself earlier, as a rising member of the Virginia gentry and throughout the Revolutionary War. The objects showcased in this book, therefore, are arranged chronologically to complement the familiar story of George Washington's life and career with the addition of the personal and household possessions he acquired over his lifetime.

Many of the artifacts have been part of the Mount Vernon collection for one hundred years or more. Others represent the continued quest of the Mount Vernon Ladies' Association to return to Washington's residence those personal and household objects owned and used by George and Martha Washington. The objects detailed in the afterword evidence the Association's commitment to enhance its collection of eighteenth-century objects with those that were fashioned to preserve the memory of George Washington and his family. Together, all of the objects contained in this volume serve to educate us about the life and legacy of George Washington and a man remembered as "first in war, first in peace, and first in the hearts of his countrymen."[6] As Elswyth Thane noted, however, "To understand George Washington, to *believe* him, one must come to Mount Vernon."[7] It is my hope that in addition to providing a portrait of Washington through material culture, this work will also inspire readers to visit the dwelling on the Potomac that served as George Washington's inspiration and residence for more than forty years.

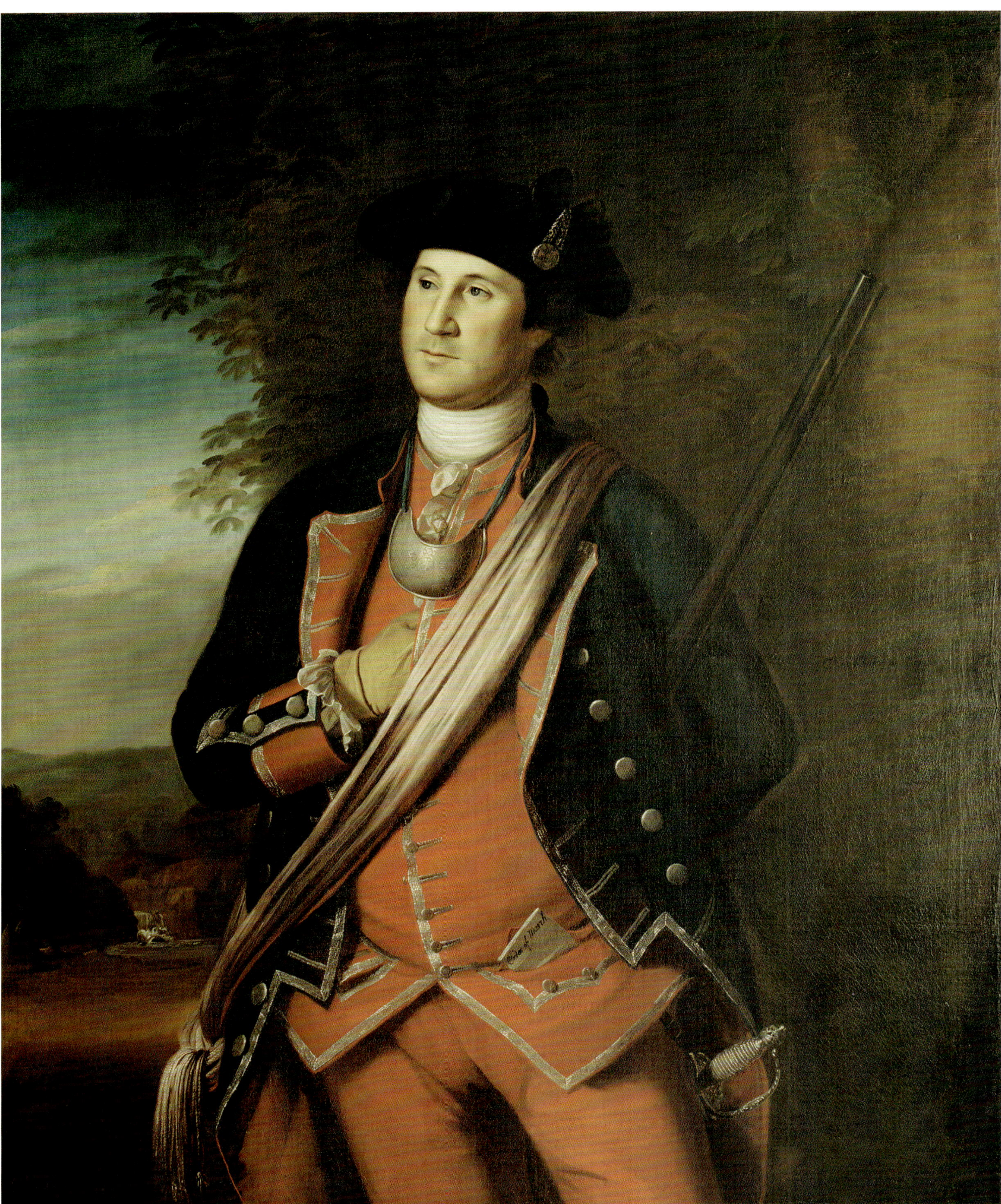
of March

CHAPTER ONE

At Home in Virginia George Washington's Rise to Planter 1732–1775

GEORGE WASHINGTON'S EARLY YEARS and those leading up to the American Revolution were marked by his ambition to distinguish himself among the social and political elite of the colony of Virginia. Through a series of calculated efforts, Washington bettered himself and his standing within the colony. By the time the colonies united in rejecting English rule, Washington was a leader in Virginia, poised to become a driving force on the national scene. Throughout these early years of aspiration, he paid particular attention to the objects with which he surrounded himself. Indeed, his correspondence to and from London agents provides a telling paper trail that reflects his desire to become a prominent member of the Virginia gentry. They demonstrate his keen observation of the material ways in which colonial elites defined themselves and his own efforts to emulate the gentry lifestyle through acquisitions.

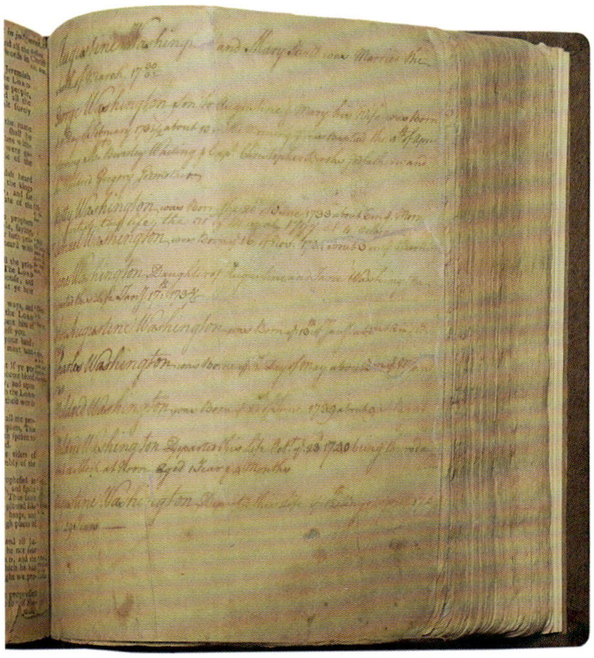

George Washington was born to Augustine and Mary Ball Washington at the family's Bridges Creek plantation.[1] The family Bible at Mount Vernon records his birth, on "ye 11th day of February 1731/32 about 10 in the Morning" and notes that he "was Baptised the 5th of April following" with "Mr. Beverley Whiting & Capt. Christopher Brooks Godfathers and Mrs. Mildred Gregory Godmother."[2] The infant son already had three older siblings by his father's first marriage, but he was the first of six children born to Augustine and Mary Ball (fig. 1).[3]

Fig. 1. Tipped-in page of the Washington family Bible at Mount Vernon on which is recorded the marriage of Augustine and Mary Ball Washington and the birth of their first son, George

opposite: *George Washington in the Uniform of a British Colonial Colonel*, painted in 1772 by Charles Willson Peale during a visit to Mount Vernon, Washington-Custis-Lee Collection, Washington and Lee University, Lexington, Virginia

In 1732 Virginia was a wealthy agricultural colony where planters cultivated primarily the cash crop of tobacco and modeled their legal and social structure after that of mother England. The Washington family had been established in Virginia for three generations, and Augustine was a respectable member of the colony's planter class. Before he could take his first steps, George was already socially superior to the majority of the Virginia population, composed, as it was, of indentured servants, convicts, and enslaved Africans. He was not, however, born into the most elite of planter families and would later devote great time and attention in an effort to advance his station beyond that of a second-tier Virginia farmer.[4]

By 1738 the family had settled at Ferry Farm across the Rappahannock River from Fredericksburg, Virginia. Family life was seriously disrupted five years later, when Augustine Washington died in 1743. Eleven-year-old George's portion of his father's estate included the 280-acre Ferry Farm and ten slaves.[5]

His older brothers, Lawrence and Augustine, were already married and settled with their wives at Mount Vernon and Wakefield plantations, respectively. George remained at home with his mother and younger siblings Betty, Samuel, John Augustine, and Charles.

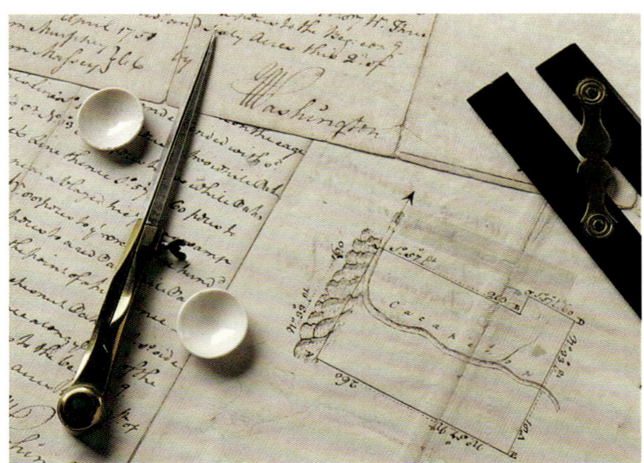

Fig. 2. George Washington's 1752 survey of William Naylor's acreage in western Virginia and some of the drafting instruments used during his early career as a surveyor, MVLA

Financial constraints prevented George from following in the footsteps of his father and older brothers, who had traveled to Appleby School in England for a formal education, instruction in gentry manners, and a view of the world outside the colonies. Nonetheless, his education progressed beyond reading, writing, and basic arithmetic, and he gained practical instruction in surveying and mathematics (fig. 2). He became familiar with the many legal documents needed by a planter to conduct business in Virginia, and he copied deeds, leases, and contracts that would assist him with the operation of his inherited lands. Moreover, Washington understood that a Virginia gentleman's education depended not only on these practical matters but also, and perhaps more so, on a knowledge of the conventions of etiquette and the social skills with which to express those conventions. Perhaps the most concrete manifestation of his desire to learn about proper conduct are the pages he copied from a book entitled *Rules of Civility and Decent Behaviour in Company and Conversation.* Although Washington later referred to his education as "defective," these early lessons undoubtedly helped him launch his career as a surveyor and provided him with the understanding essential for proper conduct in polite society.[6]

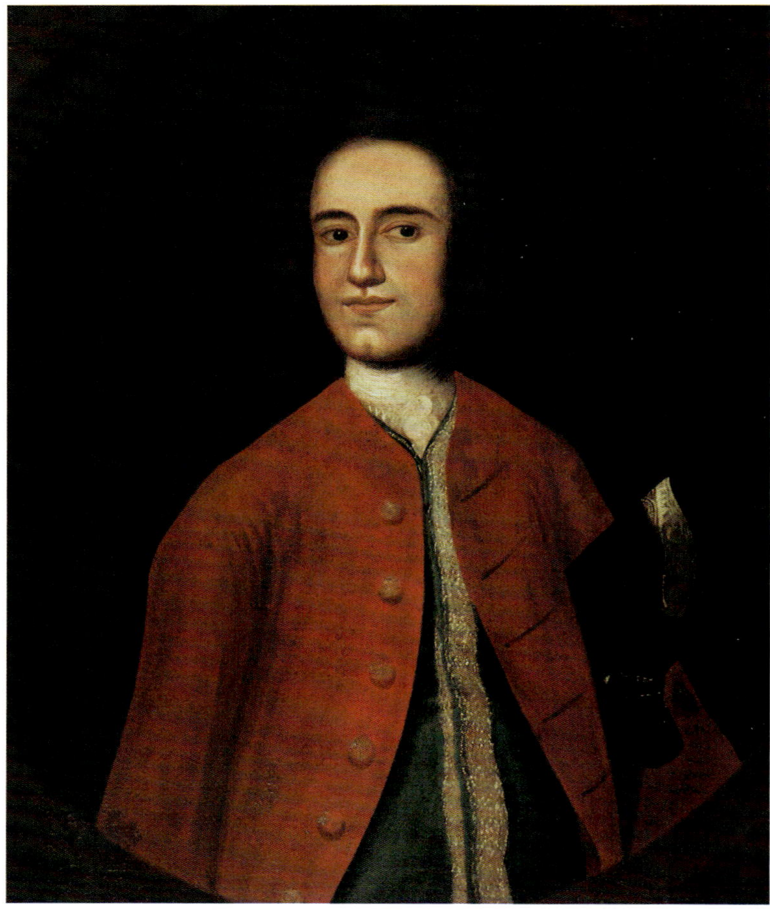

Fig. 3. Portrait of Lawrence Washington, George Washington's elder half brother and mentor, by an unknown artist, MVLA

Armed with his basic education in practical and social matters, Washington sought to escape the confines of a routine and rather austere life at Ferry Farm through a career at sea in the British navy. In his maritime aspirations, Washington was heavily influenced by his elder half brother, Lawrence (fig. 3), who had participated in the War of Jenkins' Ear with other Virginia troops under the command of Admiral Vernon during the Cartagena Campaign. Although he had Lawrence's approval and encouragement as he prepared to enter the navy, Washington was forced to abandon these ambitions in 1746 because of strong objections from his mother.

Finding life at home with his mother increasingly constricting, George spent much time at Lawrence's residence, Mount Vernon, named for his brother's former commanding officer. Washington was still a teenager in need of support and guidance, and Lawrence served as both an affectionate mentor and a father figure. In addition, Lawrence's marriage into the nearby Fairfax family of Belvoir plantation meant that Washington was exposed to the most elite segment of Virginia society and the possibility for a career and the advancement he sought.[7] William Fairfax welcomed the young George, and it was at Belvoir that he learned the social graces of the gentry and their pastimes, including dancing. In 1748 William Fairfax offered his son, George William, and also Washington the opportunity to survey some of the Fairfax lands on the south branch of the Potomac River.[8] Washington was eager to put some of the surveying techniques he had learned to use.

The venture to the frontier made a lasting impression on the youthful Washington. On the fifth day of his journey he was introduced to an altogether different manner of living, far removed from anything he had experienced to date. His diary of March 15, 1748, records:

> *Worked hard till Night & then returned to Penningtons we got our Suppers & was Lighted in to a Room & not being so good a Woodsman as the rest of my Company striped my self very orderly & went in to the Bed as they call'd it when to my Surprize I found it to be nothing but a Little Straw—Matted together without Sheets or any thing else but only one Thread Bear blanket with double its Weight of Vermin such as Lice Fleas &c. I was glad to get up (as soon as the Light was carried from us) & put on my Cloths & Lay as my Companions. . . . I made a Promise not to Sleep so from that time forward chusing rather to sleep in the open Air before a fire.*[9]

Washington's visit to Barbados with Lawrence three years later was equally educational. Lawrence went to the Caribbean in an attempt to ease his suffering from tuberculosis and hopefully to restore his health. The trip was significant for Washington in many respects. He witnessed the greater world of commerce and port cities that trafficked in goods from around the world. He also fell prey to a bout of smallpox, which caused him to remain in bed for part of his visit but which ultimately protected him from the virus that would later ravage his troops during the Revolutionary War. The trip was to be Washington's only venture outside North America, yet it was sufficient for him to grasp the role of the English colonial planter within the larger context of international commerce and social interaction.

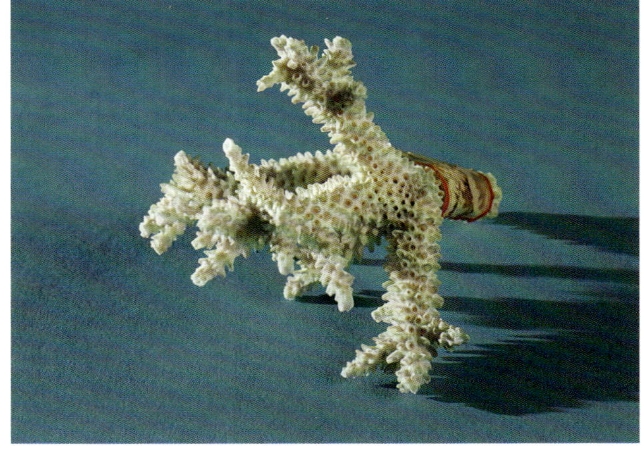

Fig. 4.
Coral, likely brought back by George Washington from Barbados, his only venture outside America. Purchased with funds donated by the Regent, Vice Regents, and Executive Director for the Mount Vernon Ladies' Association

Lawrence Washington's health was not improved by the climate of Barbados. He died in 1752, leaving Mount Vernon to his widow and infant daughter, and his post as district adjutant of His Majesty's colony of Virginia went to the twenty-one-year-old George. Washington's appointment in November 1752 gave him the rank of major as well as the regimental dress of the colonial militia. As a member of the militia with knowledge of Virginia's western frontier lands, Washington traveled in 1753 to the Ohio country on behalf of Virginia Governor Robert Dinwiddie with the order to deliver Dinwiddie's ultimatum to the French commander to abandon lands belonging to the British crown. The French had no intention of relinquishing the lands claimed by the British, however, and the ensuing disagreements and skirmishes led eventually to the French and Indian War.

When Washington returned from meeting with the French, he made the most of his trip across the mountains by presenting Governor Dinwiddie with his journal that was immediately published as *The*

Journal of Major George Washington, Sent by the Hon. Robert Dinwiddie, Esq; His Majesty's Lieutenant-Governor, and Commander in Chief of Virginia, to the Commandant of the French Forces on Ohio. To Which Are Added, the Governor's Letter, and a Translation of the French Officer's Answer.[10] This publication vaulted him suddenly onto the national and international scene, as its contents were included in London newspapers. Washington presented this account in an attempt to demonstrate his competence, with the hope of securing a formal British military commission. Military rank was particularly important to Washington because he lacked the bloodline or wealth to merit a social title. Military status seemed to be the quickest—and only—way of raising his standing within the rigid social structure of colonial Virginia.

Although Washington had served Governor Dinwiddie well and was becoming increasingly well known, he was still not granted the royal military commission he sought. Discouraged by treatment he felt was undeserved, Washington resigned his commission as colonel of the Virginia regiment in October 1754. He does not seem to have given up all hope of a military career, however. An invoice in his letter book dated October 23, 1754, lists articles Washington ordered in anticipation of continued military service to the Crown, including "1 Gold Shoulder Knott, 6 Yards gold Regim[ental] Lace, 24 rich gold Embroid[er]d Loops," one "Rich Crimson" military sash, yards upon yards of "plated gold Vellum," "gold wyre," gold thread, blue broadcloth, crimson velvet, four dozen each of "fash[ionable] gilt" coat and breast buttons, and a hat with gold lace (fig. 5).[11] These items constituted an impressive set of military regimentals that would have set Washington apart from other military personnel who did not have them. Although Washington was not able to put these symbols of military distinction to immediate use, the delay would not be long.

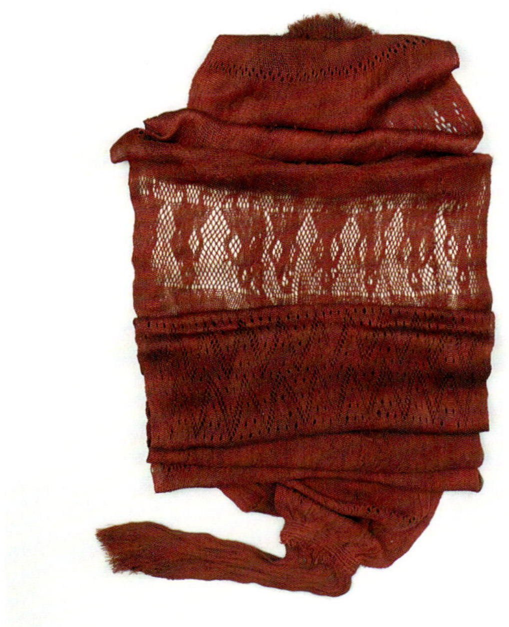

Fig. 5. George Washington's crimson silk military sash, possibly the one he received from London in 1754, MVLA

Turning his attention from the military and attempting to establish himself in the Virginia planter world, Washington leased Mount Vernon in December 1754 from Lawrence's widow and her new husband, George Lee. The annual rent was fifteen thousand pounds of tobacco. Included in the arrangement were eighteen slaves assigned to the land. A clause in the lease stipulated that the yearly rent would be reduced one thousand pounds of tobacco at the death of a male slave laborer, eight hundred pounds at the death of a female slave, and five hundred pounds of tobacco in the event of the death of "the Negroe man named Ceasar."[12] Despite the fact that his house and slaves were rented, Washington was well on his way to establishing himself as a member of the Virginia planter class.

He was just settling into Mount Vernon when General Braddock arrived in Virginia from England to help flush the French from the Ohio country. Braddock offered Washington a position as a volunteer aide-de-camp, thereby circumventing the touchy issue of formal commission and rank. In April 1755 George Washington was lured from Mount Vernon to join Braddock's forces. The campaign was a military disaster, culminating with Braddock's defeat and death at the Battle of Monongahela in July. For Washington, however, the expedition was a turning point in his career.

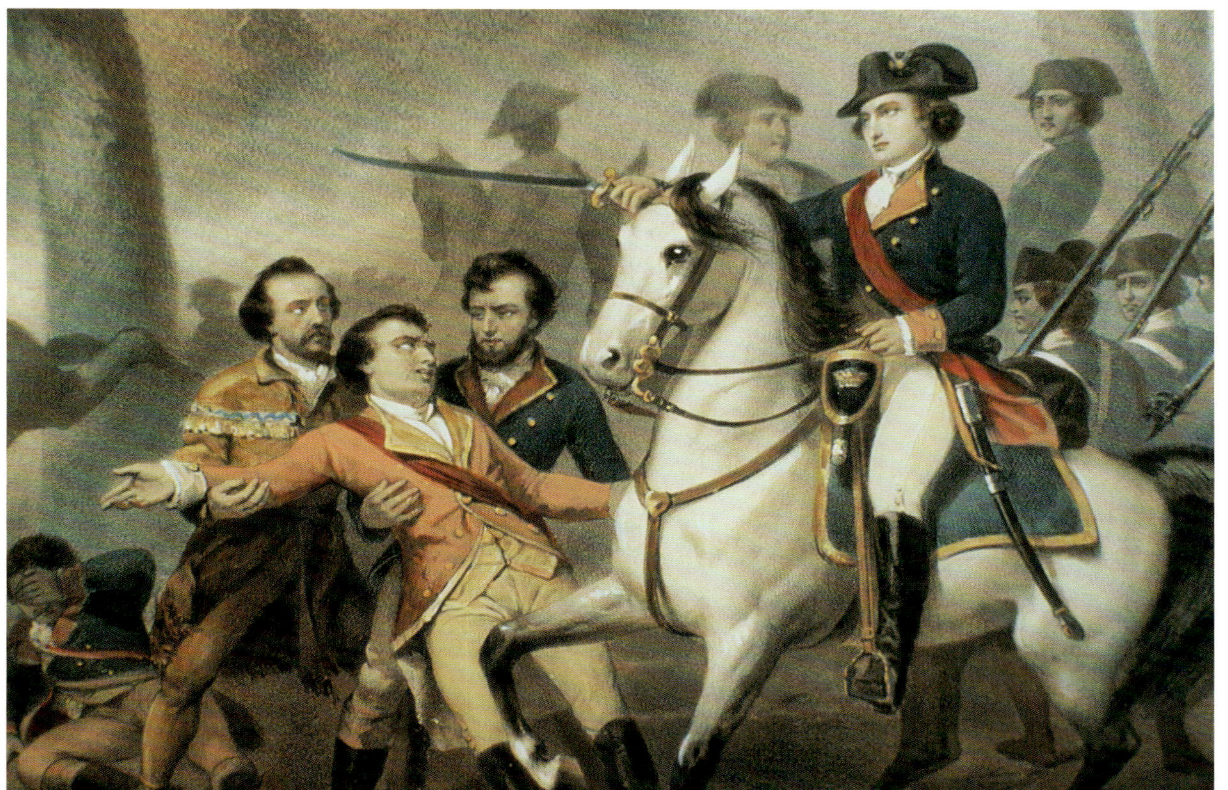

Fig. 6. George Washington at the scene of General Edward Braddock's defeat, *Battle of Monongahela, July 9, 1755*, published by M. Knoedler, Goupil & Co., 1854, Willard-Budd Collection, MVLA

In August 1755 the Virginia Assembly decided to create its own military force to protect the western border, and Governor Dinwiddie appointed George Washington "Colonel of the Virg[ini]a Regim[en]t & Commander in Chief of all of the Forces now rais'd & to be rais'd for the Defence of this H[is] Majesty's Colony."[13] Washington immediately embarked on his duties and also set about making certain he and his officers would be distinguished visibly. In his orders of October 6, 1755, Washington commanded that "Every Officer of the Virginia Regiment is, as soon as possible, to provide himself with an uniform Dress, which is to be of fine Broad Cloath: The Coat Blue, faced and cuffed with Scarlet, and Trimmed with Silver: The Waistcoat Scarlet, with a plain Silver Lace, if to be had—the Breeches to be Blue, and every one to provide himself with a silver-laced Hat, of a Fashionable size."[14] Washington did not comment on his own dress, but given the similarity of these specifications to the uniform he had envisaged for himself a year earlier, one can presume that Washington dressed as his officers did, with the exception that he wore gold lace instead of their silver.

Pleased with his long-awaited military appointment, Washington took the next step to signify his position in society. He established a connection with the London factor Richard Washington to facilitate the sale of his tobacco and the procurement of finished goods.[15] In his letter to the agent, George Washington requested London goods "with this only desire, that you will choose agreeable to the present taste, and send things good of their kind."[16] Wishing to outfit himself and two servants in a manner appropriate to his station, he requested "2 Compleat Livery Suits, 1 Sett horse Fur[n]iture, with livery Lace and the Washington Crest on the housing" with "trimmings and facings of scarlet" and "two Silver lac[e]d Hats." For himself, Washington ordered gold and scarlet as well as silver and blue sword knots, a fashionable gold-laced (or corded) hat, and Humphrey Bland's *A Treatise of Military Discipline*.[17] As commander of the Virginia forces, Washington would now appear on horseback in fine London-made regimentals while riding with two servants in Washington family livery. Although Washington never demonstrated a partic-

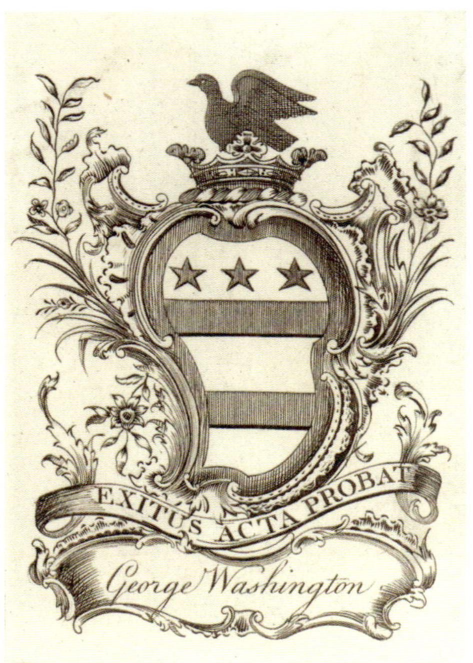

Fig. 7. George Washington's bookplate, including the Washington coat of arms and family motto, MVLA

ular interest in family ancestry, he was keen to use this opportunity to display the established family coat of arms, crest, and colors to suggest gentility (fig. 7).

Although Washington had been commissioned by the colonial governor of Virginia, he experienced difficulty in 1756 with British army officers not recognizing his rank and command of the Virginia forces. Seeking to rectify the situation, Washington rode with his liveried attendants from Fort Cumberland to Boston to discuss the matter with the British commander in chief of colonial forces, Governor William Shirley of Massachusetts. En route, he paused in Philadelphia for his first look at a large American city. There and all along the way he was regarded as the hero of the Braddock tragedy, and the *Boston Gazette* hailed his arrival in the city, "the Hon. Colonel Washington, a gentleman who has deservedly a high reputation of military skill and valor."[18] When Washington reached Boston, Governor Shirley directed him to take command at Fort Cumberland, but Shirley did not believe that the Virginia regiment should be absorbed into the British forces. Washington therefore found himself in the predicament of answering to the orders of any British commissioned officer. Despite this setback, Washington continued to serve the frontier lands and attempted to protect their inhabitants until he felt it safe enough to resign.[19] Recognizing the difficulty of establishing his place in society through military rank, he turned his mind to a future at Mount Vernon.

With an eye to positioning himself as a member of the Virginia planter gentry, Washington made plans from the frontier. Washington made lists of the items necessary to transform Mount Vernon into the

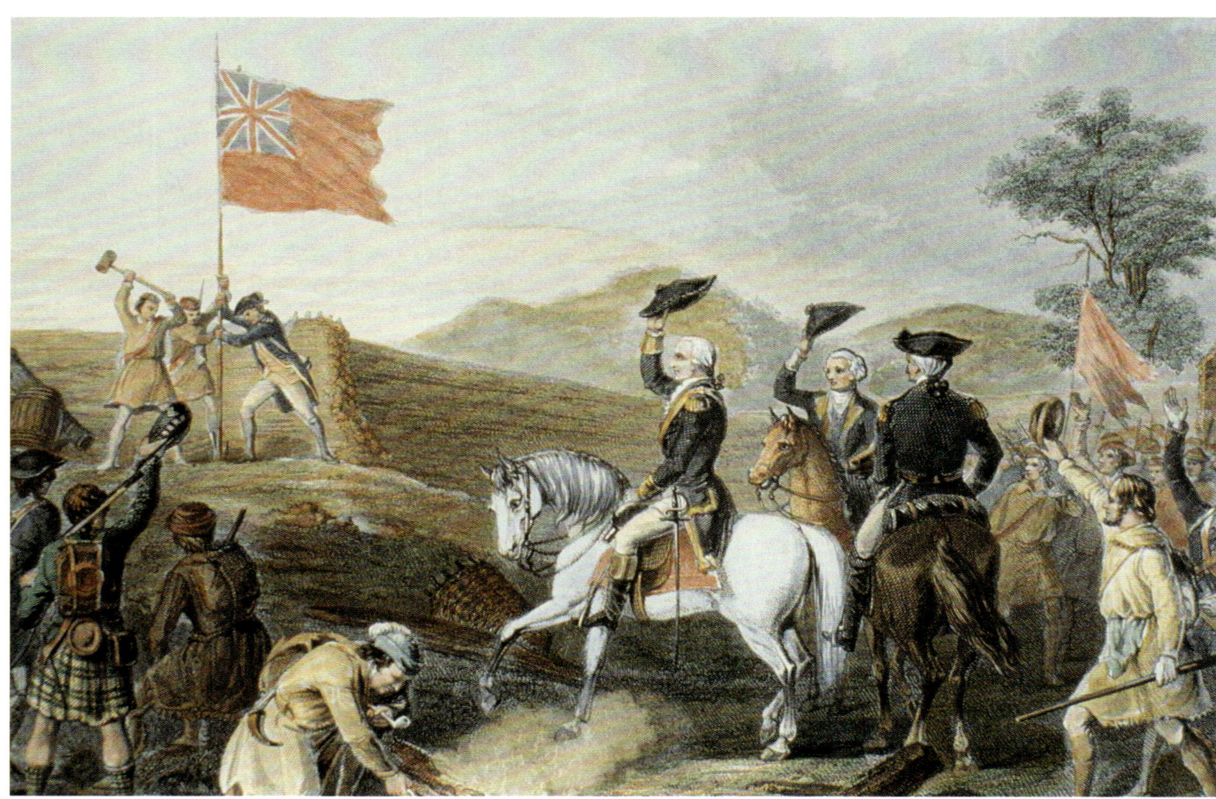

Fig. 8. In 1758 Washington captured the French Fort Duquesne for the Crown before resigning his commission and returning to Mount Vernon. *Washington Raising the British Flag at Fort Du Quesne*, engraving by T. B. Smith after J. R. Chopin, 1859, Willard-Budd Collection, MVLA

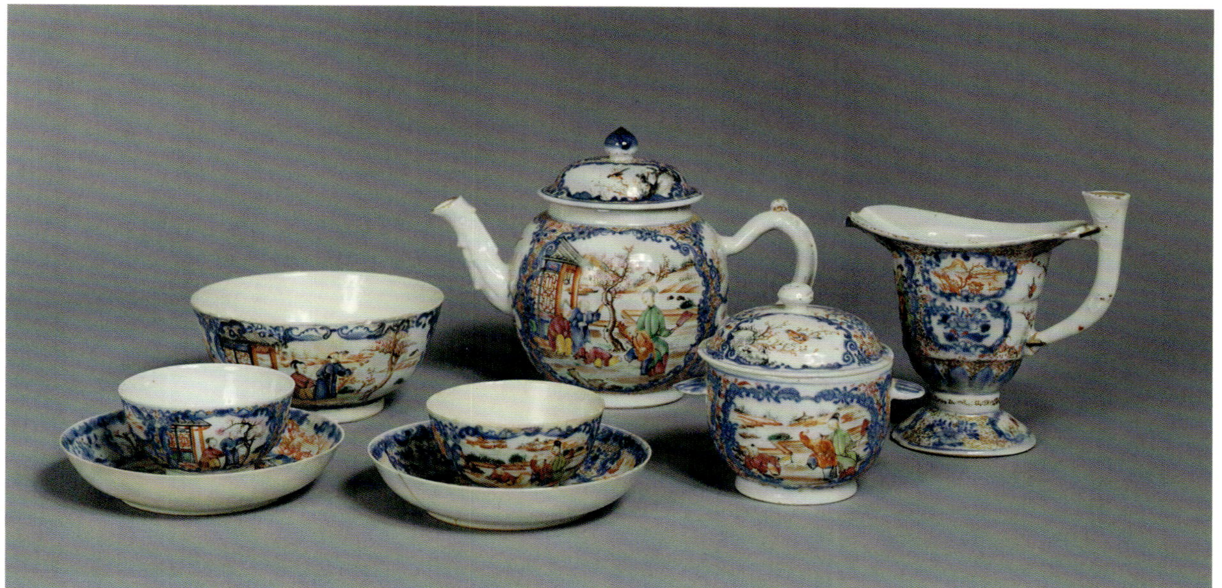

Fig. 9.
Chinese porcelain teawares, possibly among the pieces of "Fine Image China" Washington received from his London factor in 1757, MVLA

proper seat of an English colonial gentleman. Physically away from Mount Vernon, he relied on his friend John Carlyle of Alexandria and his brother-in-law Fielding Lewis to ship his tobacco to England. Against the profits from his crop, Washington specified that he expected to receive English goods, clarifying that "whatever Goods you may send me where the prices are not absolutely limited you will let them be fashionable—neat—and good in their several kinds."[20] The list of items Washington requested in 1757 from his posting at Fort Loudon included a marble chimneypiece, a "neat Landskip" (landscape painting) to be placed above the mantel, wallpaper for five of Mount Vernon's rooms, papier-mâché ceiling decorations for two rooms, and a mahogany dining table with "1 Dozn neat and strong Mahogany chairs."[21] By the end of the year, several large shipments of goods arrived that began to fill the rooms of Mount Vernon. The August shipment from Richard Washington included a mahogany bedstead with yellow silk and worsted wool damask hangings, complementing window curtains, Wilton carpets, and "fine Crimson and yellow Papers" for the walls. For dining, Mount Vernon received an assortment of Chinese export porcelain, "a Compleat sett Fine Image China," damask tablecloths and napkins, engraved wineglasses, decanters, and beer glasses, a silver cruet set, and silver-handled cutlery engraved with his crest (figs. 9, 10).[22] Another shipment in November included all of Washington's requested goods with notations from the factor that the mahogany chairs he had requested were in the "best gothick" style and that seats were "stufft in the best manner & coverd with horse hair." Washington was furnishing his house in a style befitting a Virginia planter, and he was also making certain that the items he purchased referenced the established Chesapeake gentry preference for the neat and plain aesthetic characterized by simply ornamented, elegant forms.[23] Whether "best London blade" knives or "a neat cruet stand and castors," Washington also requested that these items be engraved with the Washington crest or coat of arms, as he well understood that all one's appurtenances be appropriate to one's social station.

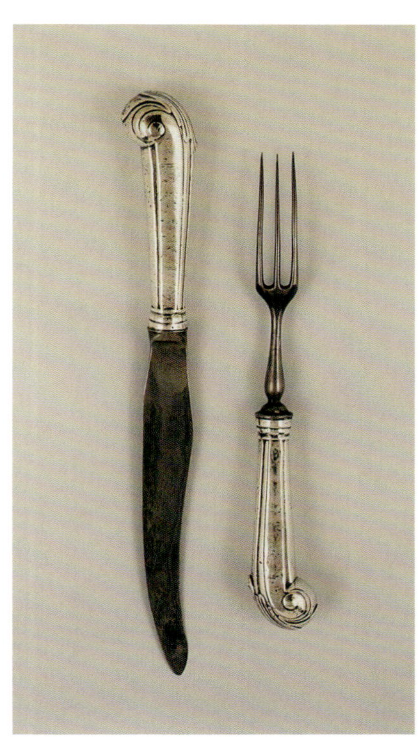

Fig. 10.
Silver-handled dinner knife and fork among those with "best London blade[s]" Washington ordered and received from London in 1757, Smithsonian's National Museum of American History, Behring Center

With his orders of 1757 and later ones, George Washington quickly grasped the operating system between colonial tobacco planter and English factor that favored the man in England. The planter shipped tobacco to the English factor who, for a commission, sold the tobacco, presumably at the best price that could be had. The factor then used the proceeds from the sale to purchase for the planter the goods the planter requested. The quality and prices of the items were left to the factor's discretion, and Washington and his contemporaries frequently complained that they were being sold second-rate goods at high prices instead of the most fashionable ones they asked for. All colonists, whether purchasing goods through factors or in shops in the colonies, were at the mercy of England for the manufactured goods the colonies were prohibited from producing.

Washington did not hesitate to voice his grievances over this flawed system. In the fall of 1757 Thomas Knox of Bristol sent Washington a set of the "finest white Stone plates" and all of the accompanying teapots, slop bowls, mustard pots, and butter dishes that were necessary for proper dining and entertaining.[24] Washington received the goods in January 1758 and wrote from Mount Vernon that he could not "help again complaining of the little care taken in the purchase: Besides leaving out one half, and the most material half too! Of the Articles I sent for, I find that the Sein is without Leads, Corks and Ropes which renders it useless—the Crate of Stoneware dont contain a third of the Pieces I am chargd with, and only two things broke—and every thing very high Chargd." Although he complained, Washington nonetheless directed Knox to procure for him a mahogany card table with playing cards and counters, fashionable "China Bowls from a large to a Midlg Size," fifty pounds each of Knox's best raisins, currants, and almonds, plus a cask of "best bottled Cyder."[25] Despite his grievances, Washington was wedded to the flawed planter-factor relationship to secure the fashionable finished goods he desired (fig. 11).

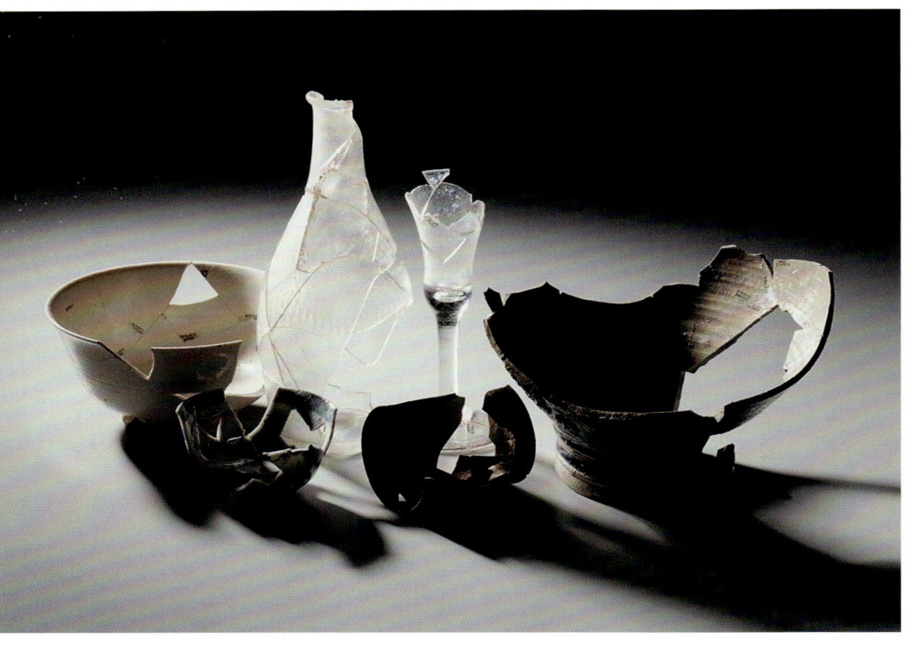

Fig. 11.
Early Mount Vernon glass, porcelain, and stoneware recovered by archaeologists

At the end of 1758 Washington declared the frontier safe for the moment, resigned his commission, and returned to Mount Vernon with his full attention fixed on becoming a first-class planter. He was elected to the Virginia House of Burgesses and focused on expanding the size of the estate and the number of its slaves, devoting both to the production of tobacco.[26] It did not occur to him to raise an alternative crop, as tobacco was the favored product of the elite planter class, and Washington succumbed to the thought that the quality of a man's tobacco determined his reputation. His pride was injured, however, when the poor Mount Vernon land could not produce the high quality of leaves grown at his contemporaries' plantations on the James, York, and Rappahannock rivers.[27]

The handsome young military celebrity at Mount Vernon did not remain very long either a lonely bachelor or a frustrated planter, however. On January 6, 1759, George Washington married Martha Dandridge Custis (fig. 12), the young widow of the wealthy Virginian Daniel Parke Custis. Martha Custis was twenty-seven years old with two small children, John "Jacky" Parke Custis, just four, and Martha "Patsy" Parke Custis, barely two (fig. 13). In addition to bringing a ready-made family to the marriage, the new

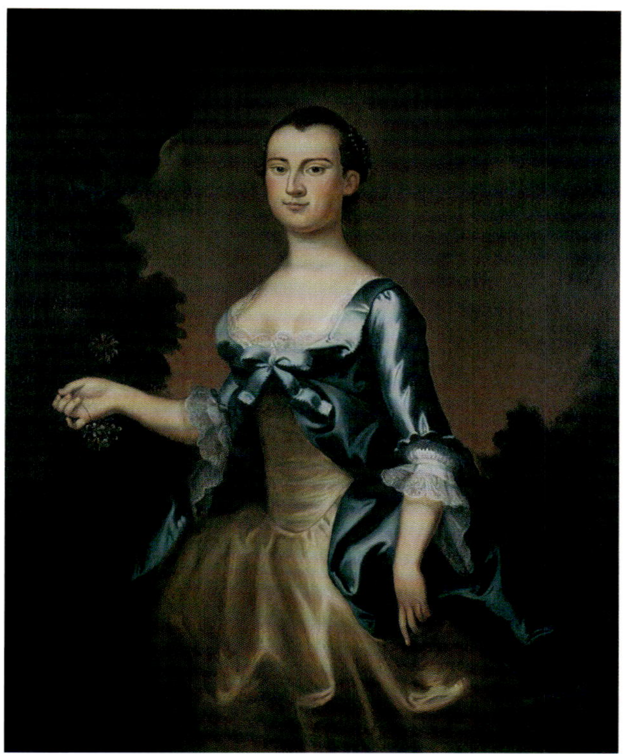

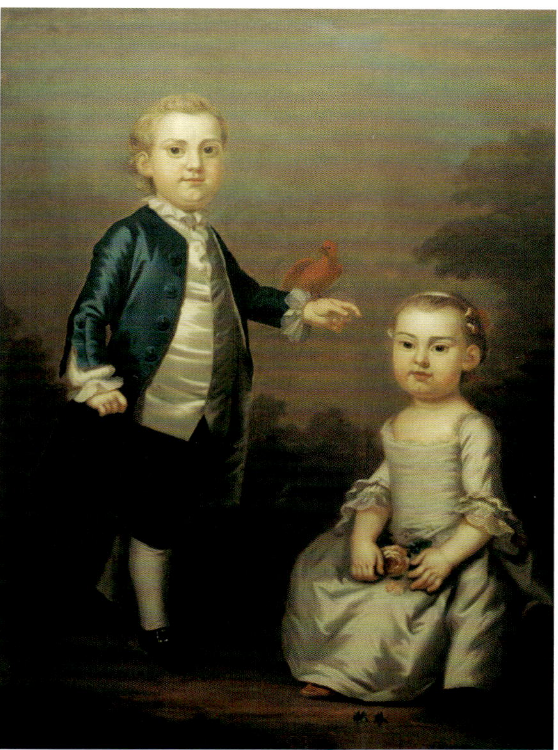

Fig. 12. *Martha Dandridge Custis*, by Adrian Lamb, after John Wollaston, just before her first husband's death and two years before her marriage to George Washington, MVLA

Fig. 13. *John Parke Custis and Martha Parke Custis*, painted in 1757 by John Wollaston, shortly before their mother's marriage to George Washington, Washington-Custis-Lee Collection, Washington and Lee University, Lexington, Virginia

Mrs. Washington brought a fortune in land, slaves, and currency that made her one of the richest women in the colony. In marrying the widow Custis, Washington gained access (with certain limitations) to one-third of the Custis fortune and guardianship of the remaining two-thirds that were in the possession of Martha's two children. His financial situation was now secure, and his social standing enhanced by the Custis association. Washington was free to grow accustomed to his place in society and to enjoy the activities of his position. As one scholar has noted, he spent the next sixteen years "perfecting the elegant lifestyle of a Virginia aristocrat."[28]

Washington promptly set about ordering for Mount Vernon those goods necessary to mark him as a member of the Virginia gentry. Martha's fortune enabled him to acquire the luxury goods that defined the planter elite and that he had no doubt envied from the time of his introductions to the homes of the Fairfaxes and their peers. He happily continued the relationship that the Custises had established with the London factor Robert Cary and Company. In May 1759 Washington wrote to Robert Cary and Company from Williamsburg, enclosing a marriage certificate and asked that "for the future please to address all your Letters which relate to the Affairs of the late Danl Parke Custis Esqr. To me, as by Marriage I am entitled to a third part of that Estate, and Invested likewise with the care of the other two thirds." He also ordered household goods from Cary. "I beg of you to send me by the first Ship bound either to Potomack or Rappahannock, as I am in immediate want of them," he wrote, specifying, "Let them be Insurd, and in case of accidents reshipd witht Delay."[29]

Washington's "immediately needed" items included "1 Tester Bedstead 7 1/2 feet pitch, with fashionable blew or blew and white Curtains . . . Window Curtains of the same for two Windows; with either Papier Mache Cornish to them or Cornish coverd with the Cloth" and additional upholstery "in order to make the whole furniture of this Room uniformly handsome and genteel." He also requested "1 Fashionable Sett of Desert Glasses . . . 4 fashionable China Branches, & Stands, for Candles . . . 6 Carving knives and Forks—handles of Staind Ivory and bound with Silver" (fig. 14). For himself, Washington ordered "1 Suit of Cloaths of the finest Cloth & fashionable Colour" and six pairs of "Men's neatest Shoes and Pumps."[30]

Washington received these goods in August and wrote for more in September. The September list was longer and included items for Mrs. Washington as well as for the house slaves. In addition to a light summer suit for himself, Washington ordered a host of laces, hose, and shoes for Mrs. Washington, and scarlet broadcloth, red shalloon, white buttons, white waistcoats, "course" hose, and shoe and knee buckles to place the house slaves in proper Washington-family-colored livery (fig. 15). For the house, Washington asked for eight busts: two "Furious Wild Beasts" and the military figures of Alexander the Great, Julius Caesar, Charles XII of Sweden, the king of Prussia, Prince Eugene of Savoy, and the Duke of Marlborough.[31] Cary was able to ship Washington's long list of requested goods with the exception of the six busts of military heroes. The busts were not to be had, and the retired Virginia colonel's wish to place himself amid images of these European greats remained unfulfilled.

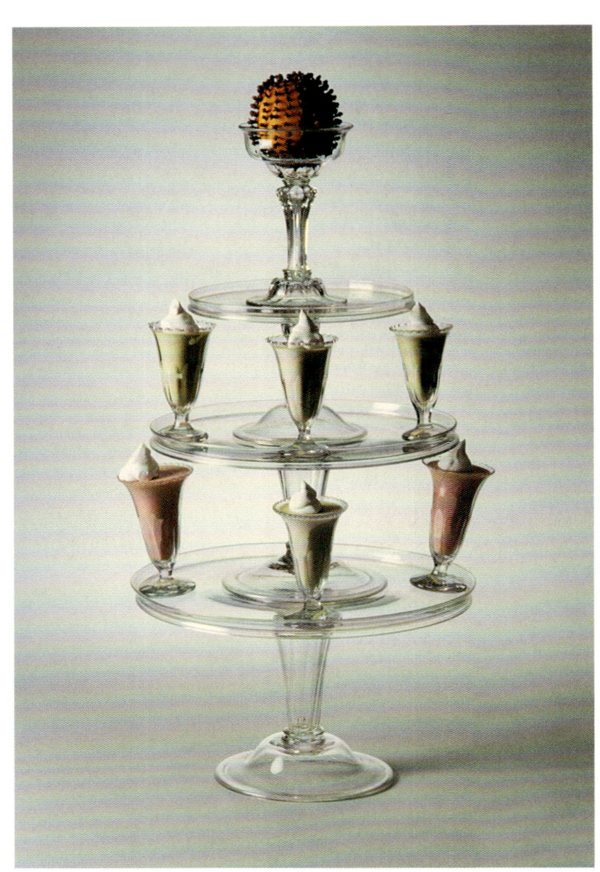

Fig. 14.
Set of tiered salvers, jelly glasses, and sweetmeat glass similar to the "Fashionable Sett of Desert Glasses and Stands" Washington received from London in 1759, MVLA

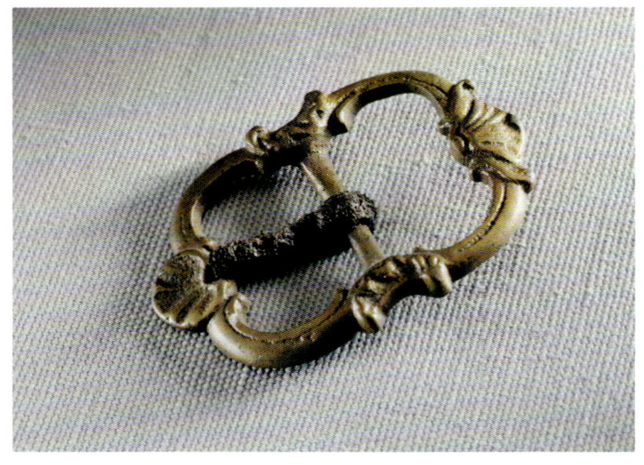

Fig. 15.
Excavated brass shoe buckle worn by one of the Washington slaves, MVLA

In addition to expanding and outfitting Mount Vernon, George Washington recognized his duty to his neighbors and the responsibility of the Virginia gentryman to participate in local government and society. Besides his seat in the Virginia House of Burgesses, Washington became a magistrate of the county court, a trustee of Alexandria, and a vestryman at his local Anglican parish, Truro. Washington's diaries record his time in Williamsburg attending the assembly meetings and socializing with his peers. Evenings were often spent in the company of the highest officials of Virginia, including the governor, and Washington came to know the interior of the Governor's Palace well. Other evenings were less grand, and Washington noted in his diary that he "Dined at the Speaker's and went to the Play—after wch. Drank a Bowl or two of Punch at Mrs. Campbells."[32] On occasion, he brought Martha, Patsy and Jacky with him to Williamsburg, where presumably they enjoyed the amenities of the larger city.

Although legislative work and agricultural pursuits required a great deal of Washington's time, he was able to enjoy the social life of a Virginia gentryman. His diary entries reveal a proclivity for hunting, and some months record fox, pheasant, or duck hunting nearly half the days. The Washingtons often dined with the Fairfaxes at Belvoir and attended plays and balls. George Washington became quite a connoisseur of the proper style a ball should have and in February 1760 noted in his diary attending one that did not meet his satisfaction:

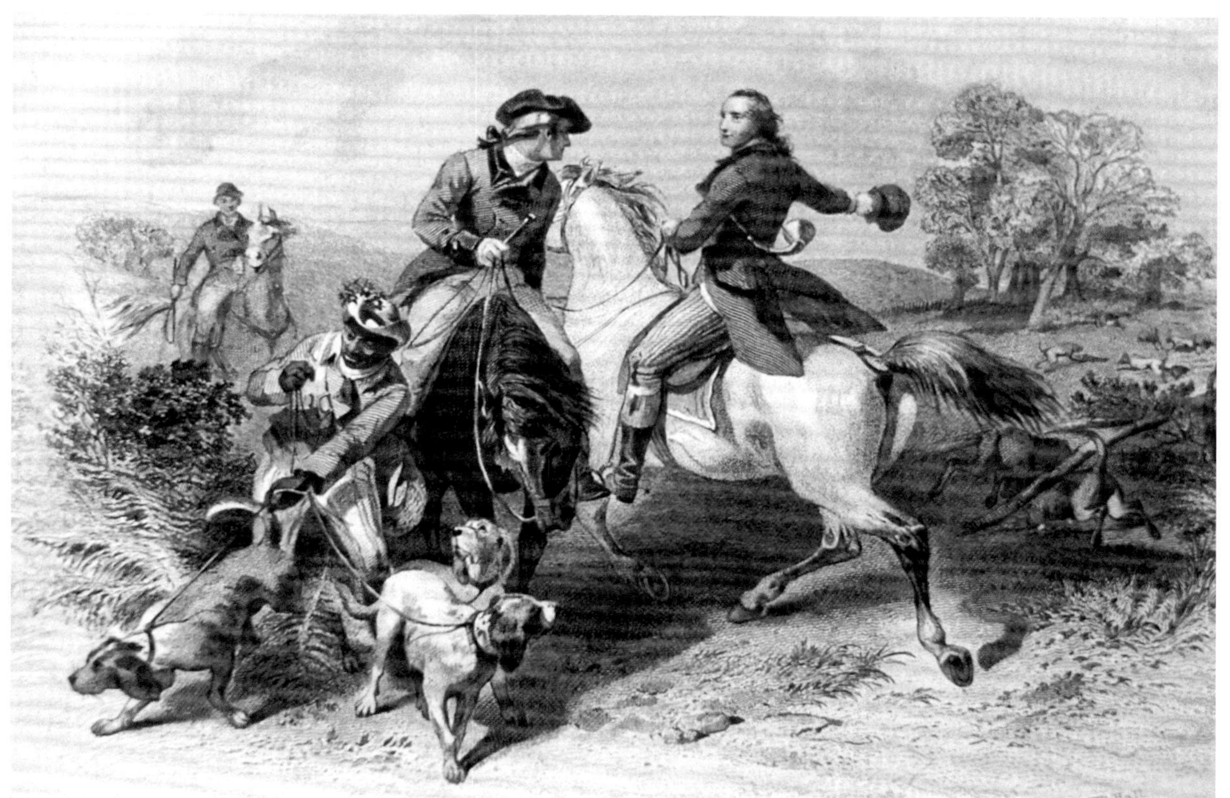

Fig. 16. George Washington enjoyed hunting and outdoor sporting events with other members of the Chesapeake gentry. "Washington and Fairfax—Field Sports," 19th-century engraving published by G. P. Putnam & Co., New York, Willard-Budd Collection, MVLA

> *Went to a Ball at Alexandria—where Musick and Dancing was the chief Entertainment. However in a convenient Room detachd for the purpose abounded great plenty of Bread and Butter, some Biscuets with Tea, & Coffee which the Drinkers of coud not Distinguish from Hot water sweetened. Be it rememberd that pocket handkerchiefs servd the purposes of Table Cloths & Napkins and that no Apologies were made for either. I shall therefore distinguish this Ball by the Stile & title of the Bread & Butter Ball.*[33]

George Washington enjoyed the material and social comforts of his position until he realized that he had quickly gone through much of the money from his wife's dowry as well as his own. Although he was not in the least neglectful in keeping proper track of accounts, the consignment system had caused him to run through his resources rapidly, and in 1761 he owed Robert Cary and Company almost two thousand pounds sterling. The indedbtedness did more than compromise Washington's finances: it was a potential indictment of personal misconduct. When Cary wrote of his concern over Washington's indebtedness in 1764, the planter responded with an emotionally charged letter insisting that "mischance rather than Misconduct hath been the cause of it."[34] Washington was very clearly vexed by the position in which the planter-factor relationship had placed him. As one scholar has noted, Washington "wanted to fill his estate with impressive English imports" but "could not tolerate being under another man's control."[35] Washington responded to the irksome constraints by altering Mount Vernon's farming and production priorities, and he diversified his crops in 1765 and 1766 to include wheat and corn. He also increased the number of weavers at Mount Vernon to encourage self-sufficiency and progressively moved psychologically away from England, the country he had "unquestionably considered the center and capital of his world."[36]

In 1767 tensions with England were exacerbated by the Townshend duties, which led Washington and his contemporaries in 1769 to draw up the Virginia Nonimportation Resolution. Washington had now taken his place among the elite planter group, and along with Peyton Randolph, Thomas Jefferson, and Patrick Henry, he protested the duties being levied on the colonies by encouraging a boycott of expensive imported British goods. He understood firsthand how the consignment system favored the English merchant, created a desire for and dependence on luxury household goods, and led to financial hardship. Washington explained to George Mason his support of nonimportation as well as his belief that adherence to the agreement needed to be widespread in order to be effective. He suggested that "those who live genteely & hospitably, on clear Estates . . . for how can I, *says he*, who have lived in such & such a manner change my method? I am ashamed to do it: and besides, such an alteration in the System of my living, will create suspicions of a decay in my fortune, & such a thought the world must not harbour."[37] In supporting the nonimportation agreement, and seemingly ridiculing those who would not adhere to it out of personal pride, Washington was eschewing the established material definitions of the Virginia elite. Nevertheless, it is difficult to avoid the conclusion that Washington was concerned about the appearance of his own fortune decaying and therefore supported widespread adherence to the nonimportation agreement.

After George Washington and his fellow members of the House of Burgesses voted to adopt a Virginia boycott of English manufactured goods, Washington wrote to Robert Cary and Company of his support of the resolution. With a list of items he wished Cary to supply, Washington noted:

> *if there are any Articles contain[e]d in either of the respective Invoices (Paper only excepted) which are Tax[e]d by Act of Parliament for the purpose of Raising a Revenue in America, it is my express desire and request, that they may not be sent, as I have very heartily enter[e]d into an Association . . . not to import an Article which now is, or hereafter shall be Taxed for this purpose. . . . I am therefore particular in mentioning this matter as I am fully determined to adhere religiously to it, and may perhaps have wrote for some things unwittingly which may be under these Circumstances.*[38]

The items Washington wanted included spices, buttons, needles, "sewing silk," and a few personal articles including "4 fine Ivory Combs" that were probably intended for Mrs. Washington. In lieu of fine porcelains from China, he requested an "Assortment of the most fash[ionabl]e kind of Queen's Ware," more than two hundred pieces ranging in form from "Oval Baking Dishes" and "large Fish Drainers" to "fluted Egg Cups" and "Shells for Pickles."[39] Queensware, or creamware, was the cream-colored earthenware produced in England and made popular in the 1760s by Josiah Wedgwood, and was not subject to taxation. In stipulating this fashionable but less expensive alternative to porcelain, Washington was adhering to the nonimportation agreement while supplying himself with wares that would demonstrate to all guests to Mount Vernon his political position on the issue of taxable English goods. In addition, these nontaxable goods were cheaper than taxable ones, a boon to Washington's indebtedness and that of his contemporaries. While none would have the courage alone to forgo English luxury goods (and thereby call their wealth into question), the gentry's adherence to eschewing taxable items allowed them to "transform their private fears over indebtedness into a public commitment to austerity."[40]

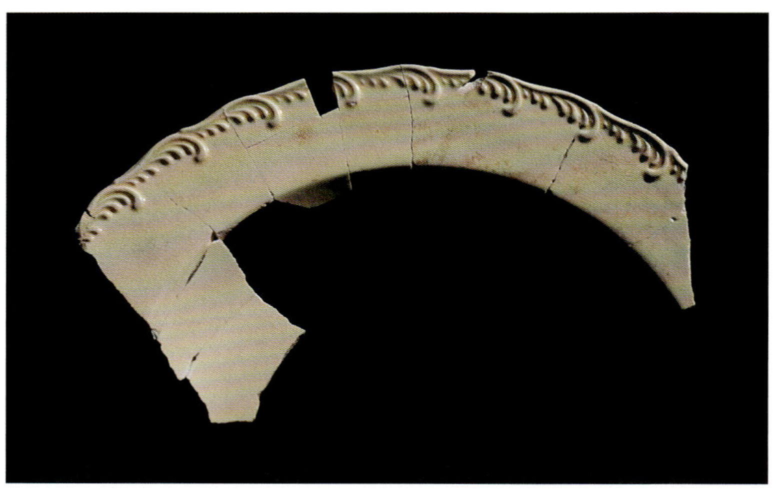

Fig. 17. Mended sherds of early Mount Vernon creamware excavated by Mount Vernon archaeologists

George Washington was a member of the Fairfax nonimportation committee, which scrutinized shipments into the port of Alexandria for compliance with the nonimportation agreements. In June 1771, for instance, he was called to Alexandria to inspect a shipment in which twelve hats were found to be unacceptable.[41] Owing to variances in enforcement, however, restrictions on imported goods were lifted the following month, and forbidden imports were limited to tea, paper, glass, and paint. In response, Washington forwarded to Robert Cary and Company a long list of goods that he had been avoiding earlier. He noted:

> *Our Association in Virginia for the Non-importation of Goods is now at an end except against Tea, Paper, Glass and Painters Colours of Foreign Manufacture: you will please therefore to be careful that none of the glass, Paper &ca contain[e]d in my Invoices are of those kinds which are subject to the duty Imposed by Parliament for the purpose of raising a Revenue in America.*[42]

The list included requests for numerous items of clothing and personal articles that had no doubt been desired for some time. They ranged from "2 p[ai]r Men's best buck Gloves with long fingers & to fit a large hand" and "a Very neat & fash[ionabl]e New Mark[e]t Sad[dl]e Cloth" for himself to "2 p[ai]r Womens purple kid Gloves" and "2 hands[ome] Gauze Caps for a middle aged Wom[a]n" for Mrs. Washington. Books were also on the list and included "Glasses Cookery," or Hannah Glasse's volume entitled *The Art of Cookery Made Plain and Easy*, and "A Prayr Book with the New Version of Psalms & Good plain Type—covd with red Moroco—to be 7 Inchs long 4½ wide, & as thin as possible for the great[e]r ease of carry[in]g in the Pocket" (fig. 18).[43]

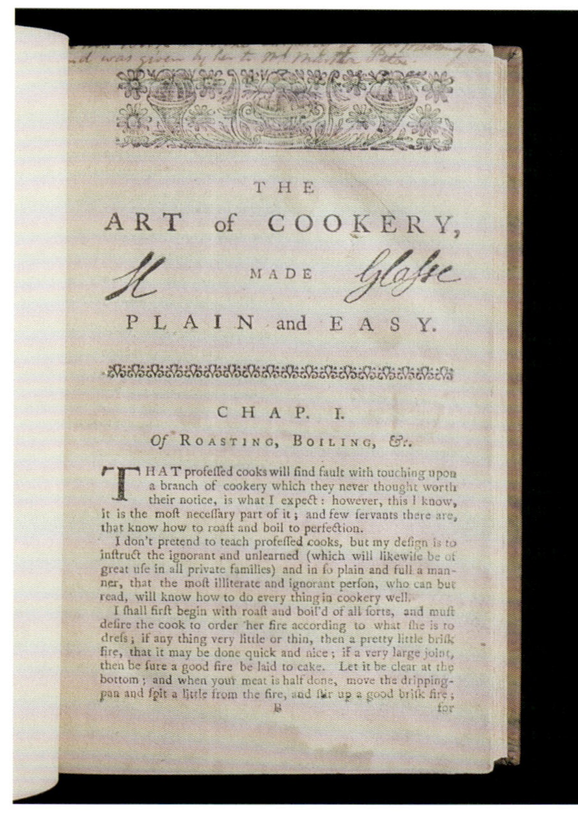
THE

ART of COOKERY,

MADE

PLAIN and EASY.

CHAP. I.

Of Roasting, Boiling, &c.

THAT profeſſed cooks will find fault with touching upon a branch of cookery which they never thought worth their notice, is what I expect: however, this I know, it is the moſt neceſſary part of it; and few ſervants there are, that know how to roaſt and boil to perfection.

I don't pretend to teach profeſſed cooks, but my deſign is to inſtruct the ignorant and unlearned (which will likewiſe be of great uſe in all private families) and in ſo plain and full a manner, that the moſt illiterate and ignorant perſon, who can but read, will know how to do every thing in cookery well.

I ſhall firſt begin with roaſt and boil'd of all ſorts, and muſt deſire the cook to order her fire according to what ſhe is to dreſs; if any thing very little or thin, then a pretty little briſk fire, that it may be done quick and nice; if a very large joint, then be ſure a good fire be laid to cake. Let it be clear at the bottom; and when your meat is half done, move the dripping-pan and ſpit a little from the fire, and ſtir up a good briſk fire; for

B

Fig. 18. Martha Washington's copy of Hannah Glasse's cookbook, *The Art of Cookery, Made Plain and Easy*, MVLA

Despite tensions with the mother country over the next few years, Washington continued to socialize with prominent colonial officials in Virginia, Maryland, and Pennsylvania. In this way he became acquainted with the material ways in which they defined their positions. When in Williamsburg, he attended meetings of the House of Burgesses and was welcomed to the palace by the royal governor. Washington noted in his diary entry of March 10, 1772, that he had "Dined and Spent the Evening at the Palace."[44] He also frequently traveled to Annapolis, Maryland, for horse races and was welcomed by prominent members of that city, including Maryland's royal governor. The Annapolis races were a highlight of the Chesapeake gentry's social season and included not only the races but also dinners, balls, and plays. Washington was among those invited to the governor's residence (Government House), recording in his diary in September 1771 that he "Dined with the Govr. And went to the Play & Ball afterwards."[45] The following October he recorded not only many nights dining and socializing at the governor's residence but also lodging with Maryland's highest royal official.[46] The two shared a keen interest in horse breeding and racing, and in March 1773 Governor Robert Eden returned the favor and visited Mount Vernon, where Washington assembled a group of gentlemen for socializing and hunting. When in Annapolis the following month, Washington dined and lodged with Eden at the governor's residence and paid his respects to the former royal governor of Maryland, Horatio Sharpe. Washington's enthusiasm for the gentlemanly sport of horse racing also placed him in contact with Pennsylvania's governor and elites

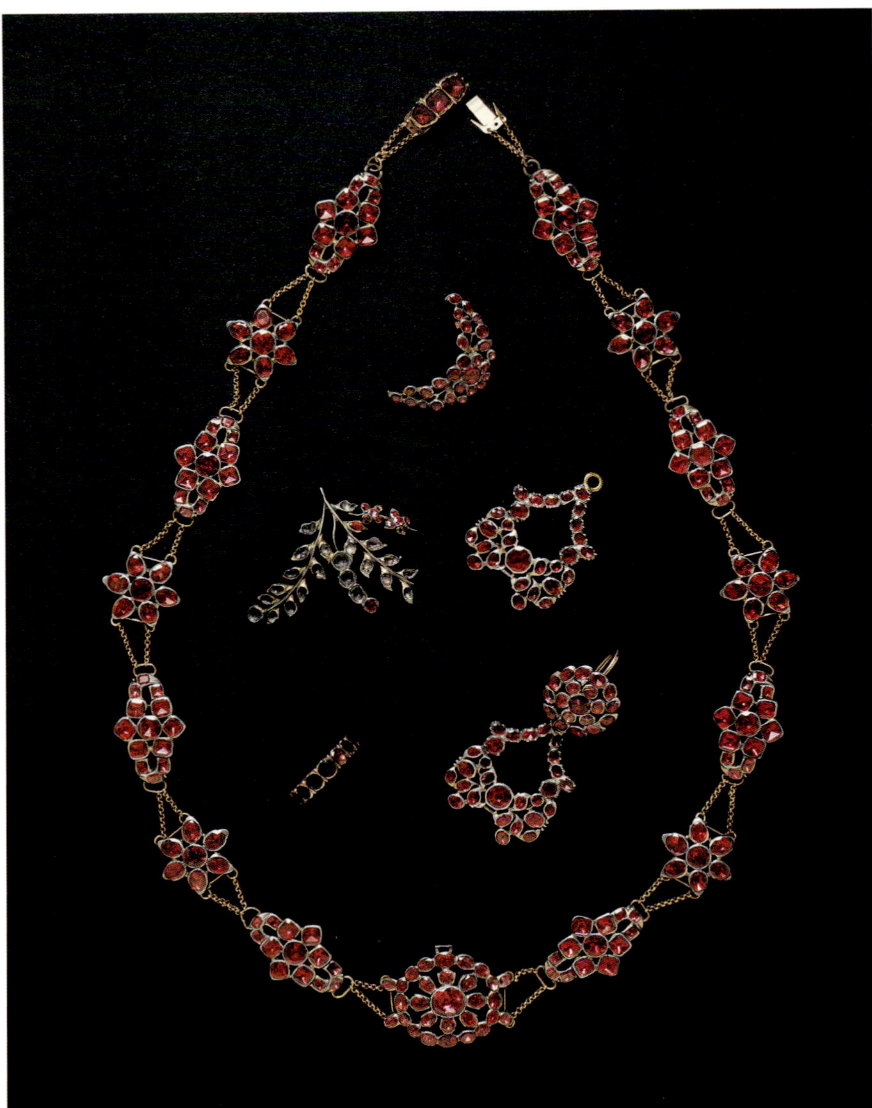

Fig. 19. Garnet jewelry worn by Martha Washington's daughter, Martha "Patsy" Parke Custis, before her death in 1773, MVLA

when he attended races in Philadelphia, dining and socializing with Governor Penn, president of the Jockey Club, and John Cadwalader, the club's vice president.[47]

In 1773 the Washingtons suffered the loss of Martha's daughter, Patsy, to what was likely epilepsy. George Washington recorded in his diary on June 19 that at "About five oclock poor Patcy Custis Died Suddenly."[48] The following day, he described in a letter to Burwell Bassett, a member of the family, "the distress of this Family" when Patsy "rose From Dinner about for Oclock . . . soon after which she was sized with one of her usual Fits, & expired in it, in less than two Minutes without uttering a Word, a groan, or scarce a Sigh." He continued, "this Sudden, and unexpected blow, I scarce need add has almost reduced my poor Wife to the lowest ebb of Misery, which is encreas'd by the absence of her Son."[49] Martha Washington sank into a period of deep mourning for her daughter, and Jacky Custis was recalled from school in New York so that she could have her one remaining child near her. A return to Mount Vernon also brought Jacky closer to his beloved Eleanor Calvert, and the two wed in February 1774.[50]

That same year, the changing political situation occasioned the permanent departure of the Fairfax family from Belvoir plantation. George William and Sally Fairfax returned to England, and George Washington suffered the loss of his close friends and neighbors as well as association with the household where he had come to know the elegance of the English aristocracy. With the Fairfaxes' return to England

and the sale of Belvoir's furnishings at auction, however, Washington was able to acquire some pieces to provide Mount Vernon with a bit of English grandeur, and he was by far the largest purchaser.

Tensions between Virginia and the mother country also reached a new height that year. Although Washington noted in his diary that he dined and spent the evening of May 25, 1774, at the Governor's Palace in Williamsburg, Governor Dunmore dissolved the assembly the following day. On May 27, George Washington and other members of the disbanded House of Burgesses met at the Raleigh Tavern in Williamsburg to boycott tea and other imports of the East India Company. Despite the attendance of Washington and his compatriots at a ball that evening to welcome Lady Dunmore, the governor's wife, a break from England and its royal traditions was in the air.[51]

In August 1774 George Washington was chosen as one of the delegates to represent the colony of Virginia at the First Continental Congress to be held in Philadelphia. The other Virginia delegates were Peyton Randolph, Richard Henry Lee, Patrick Henry, Richard Bland, Benjamin Harrison, and Edmund Pendleton. Life was about to change drastically for these men, and most of all for Washington. The second time the Continental Congress met, George Washington was unanimously elected commander in chief of the Continental forces in June 1775. The era of the relatively carefree planter was over.

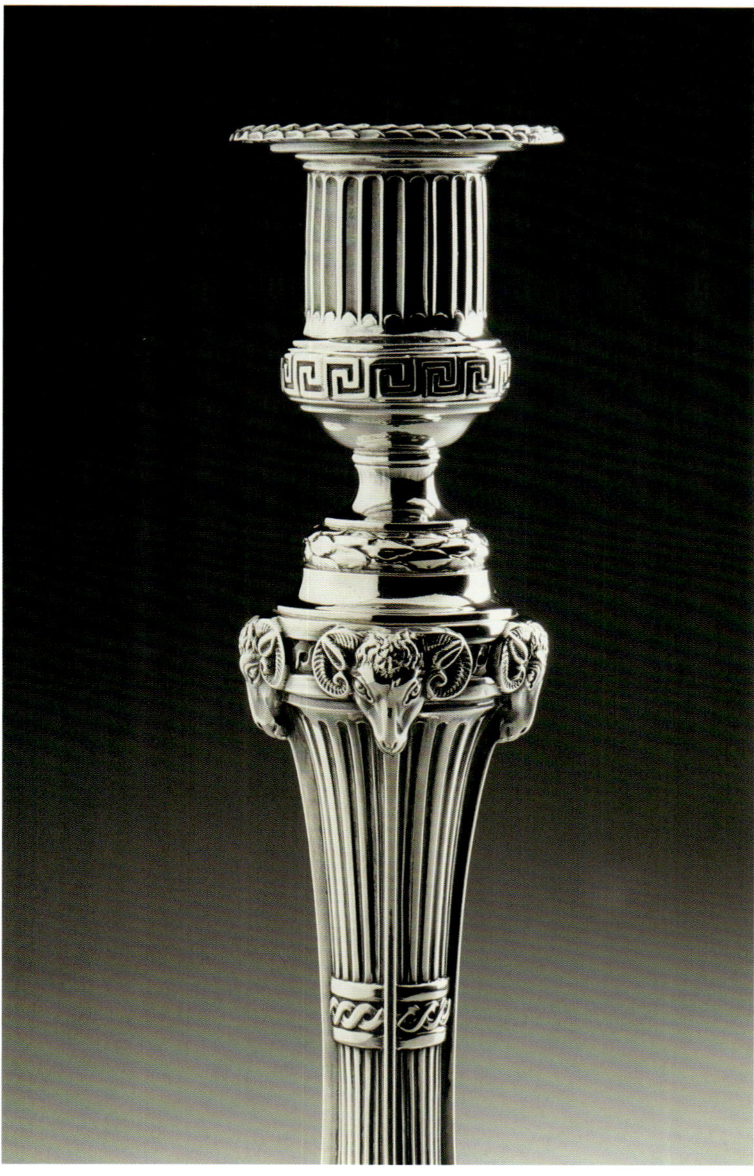

Fig. 20.
One of the silver-plated candlesticks among the large ensemble of London silver supplied to John "Jacky" Parke Custis the year of his marriage to Eleanor Calvert, MVLA

CAT. 1

Cruet Stand, Bottles, and Caster

Jabez Daniell (active ca. 1749–1774) and Samuel Wood (active ca. 1733–1773)
London, England, ca. 1757
Silver and glass, Stand H. 8", Bottles H. 6⅛", Caster H. 6⅜"
Gift of Mary Walker Lee Bowman and Robert E. Lee, IV, 1981
W-2518 (stand), W-2523/a&b (bottles), W-2526 (caster)

Cruet stands with casters and bottles provided a display of fashionable silver and glass on the eighteenth-century dining table. The set was sometimes placed in the middle of the table if there was no centerpiece, although the silver ensemble was primarily used to provide diners with condiments with which they could accent the meals on their plates according to individual taste. The bottles and casters held such substances as vinegar, oil, salt, pepper, sugar, and mustard powder. The stand secured the bottles and casters while serving as a vehicle for moving the condiments around the table.

George Washington's first order of London silver for Mount Vernon included a cruet stand with casters and bottles. In August 1757 he received "A Neat cruit stand & Casters" along with "2 best cut glass cruits."[52] The stand bears the maker's mark of the London silversmith Jabez Daniell and the date letter for 1757–1758. Daniell's silversmithing shop was located on Carey Lane, where he worked after concluding his apprenticeship to the silversmith Samuel Wood. The surviving caster of this set was made by Samuel Wood in 1736, three years before Daniell was apprenticed to him in 1739.[53] The weight of the silver noted in the invoice and the mention of only two glass cruet bottles suggest that the set originally comprised three silver casters, two bottles, and the stand. Two of the bottles remain with the stand, and the engraved griffins on the bottle caps agree with the engraving on the silver caster.[54] Although the cruet bottle caps are not marked with maker or year, the similarity of their finials to that on the Wood caster suggests that Wood contributed at least three of the five bottles and casters in the set.

Together, the bottles, caster, and stand are a fine example of midcentury Rococo silver. The cast and applied framework of the cinquefoil-shaped stand includes individual rings to secure the casters and bottles as well as places to rest the bottle tops when the contents of the bottle are being poured. The frame supports are cast C-scrolls atop double-pad feet, the bail handle is ornamented by a stylized scallop shell, and the frame is highlighted by a Rococo cartouche engraved with the Washington coat of arms. When placed on George Washington's dining table, this fashionable silver engraved with Washington family symbolism offered his guests a tangible reminder of their host's economic and social standing.

The ensemble remained in use at Mount Vernon until Martha Washington's death in 1802. In her will, Mrs. Washington bequeathed to her grandson, George Washington Parke Custis, "all of the Silver plate of every kind of which I shall die possessed."[55] Custis integrated the inherited Washington silver into his residence, named Arlington, overlooking the Potomac River. His daughter, Mary Anna Randolph Custis, married Robert E. Lee, and the two resided at Arlington. The strategic location of Arlington House and its reputation as the home of the commander of the Confederate forces made the dwelling vulnerable during the Civil War. Mrs. Lee evacuated Arlington House in May 1861, but she had already taken measures to protect the Washington silver from confiscation by the Union army. The silver was shuffled around Virginia, part of the time housed at the Virginia Military Academy, and on one occasion buried when the Union army marched through the valley of Virginia. After the war, the silver was returned to the Lee family and was in time divided among Mary and Robert E. Lee's seven children. In 1936 Martha Washington descendant Doctor George Bolling Lee placed his substantial collection of inherited pieces of Washington and Custis silver on loan to Mount Vernon, and in 1981 his children donated the collection to the Association.

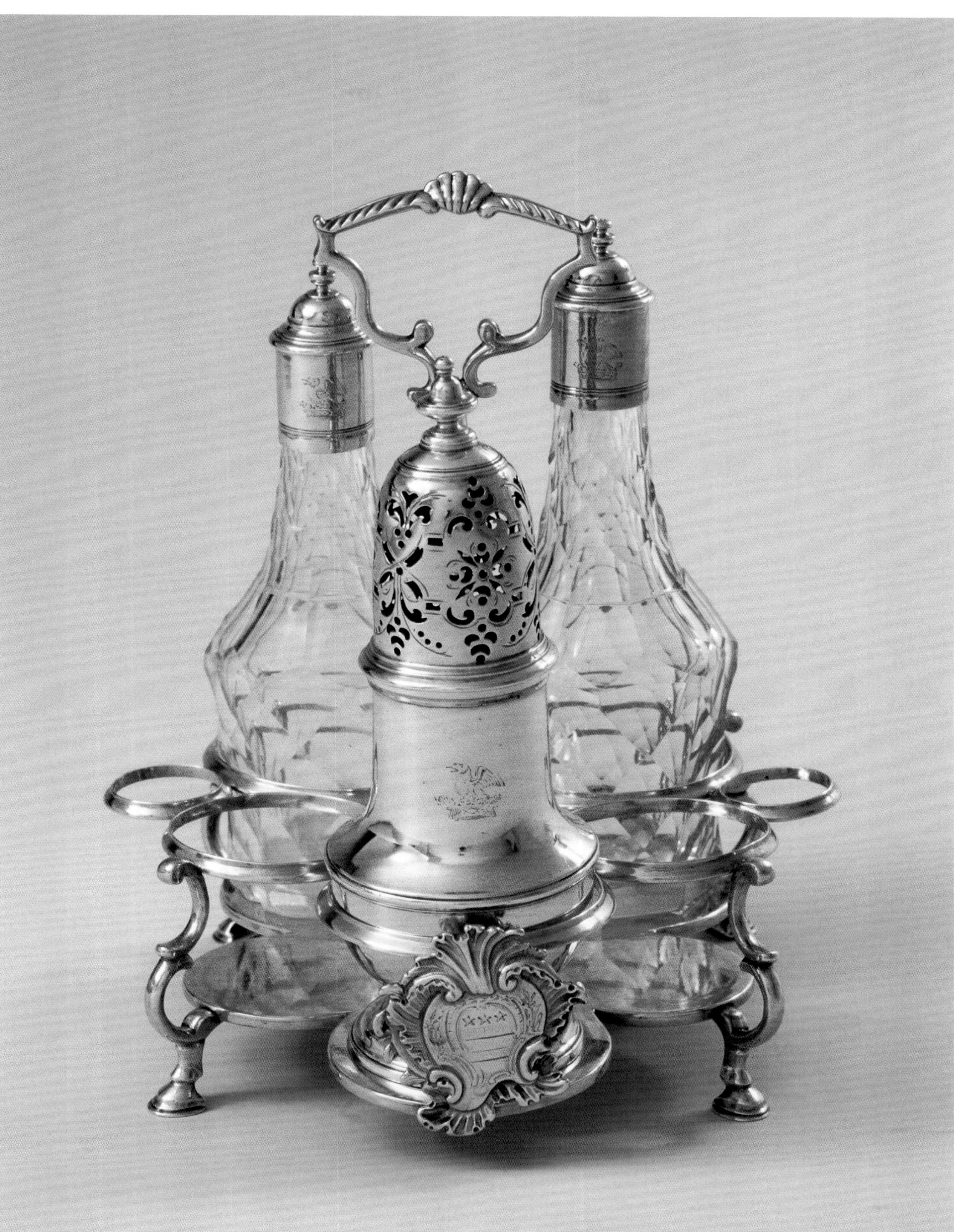

CAT. 2

Fork

Maker unknown[56]
London, England, ca. 1757
Silver and steel, L. 6½"
Gift of Mrs. William Henry Brown, 1891[57]
W-495/B

George Washington's 1757 shipment from London included numerous items necessary to outfit the young colonel's dining room. Among them were "2 Setts best Silver handle Knives & Forks best London Blades" at a cost of eleven pounds sterling, with a separate charge noted for the engraving of his crest on each piece.[58] Surviving examples of the cutlery confirm that the sets were of two sizes, likely for dinner and dessert. Examples at the Smithsonian's National Museum of American History, Behring Center are larger than the fork that survives at Mount Vernon, but all are of the same form with pistol-handled ends and engraved Washington griffins.

Washington's use of silver-handled cutlery demonstrated luxury at a time when those fortunate to have flatware pieces were generally satisfied with bone or wood handles. As the majority of people ate with knife blades, spoons, wood implements, and fingers, however, the use of any flatware service was a sign of an elite social and economic status in the Chesapeake until well into the second half of the eighteenth century.[59] Washington was no doubt aware of these distinctions, and his order of two sets of flatware that corresponded to particular courses of a meal reveals his desire to outfit his Mount Vernon table in accordance with the practices of the upper echelon of colonial Virginians. His inclusion of a Washington griffin on each knife and fork is a further distinction that would not have been lost on those dining with the young bachelor.

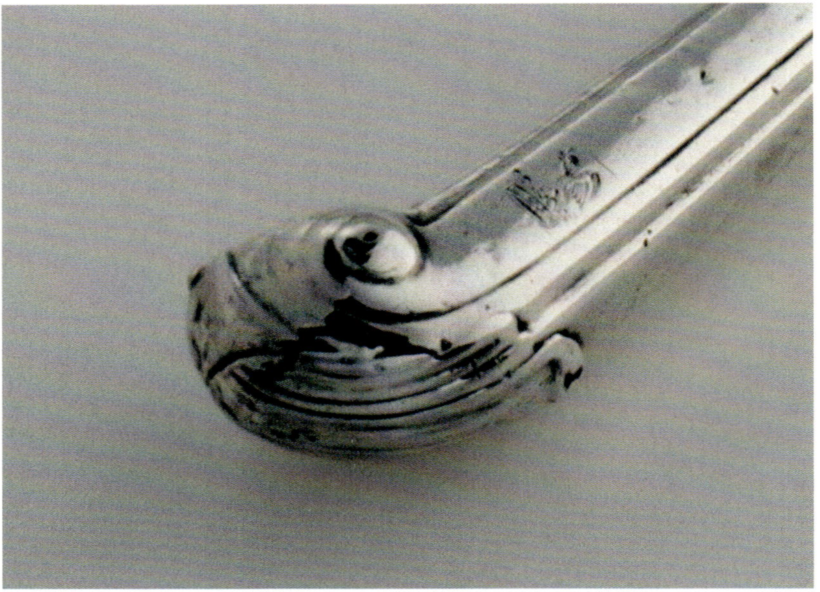

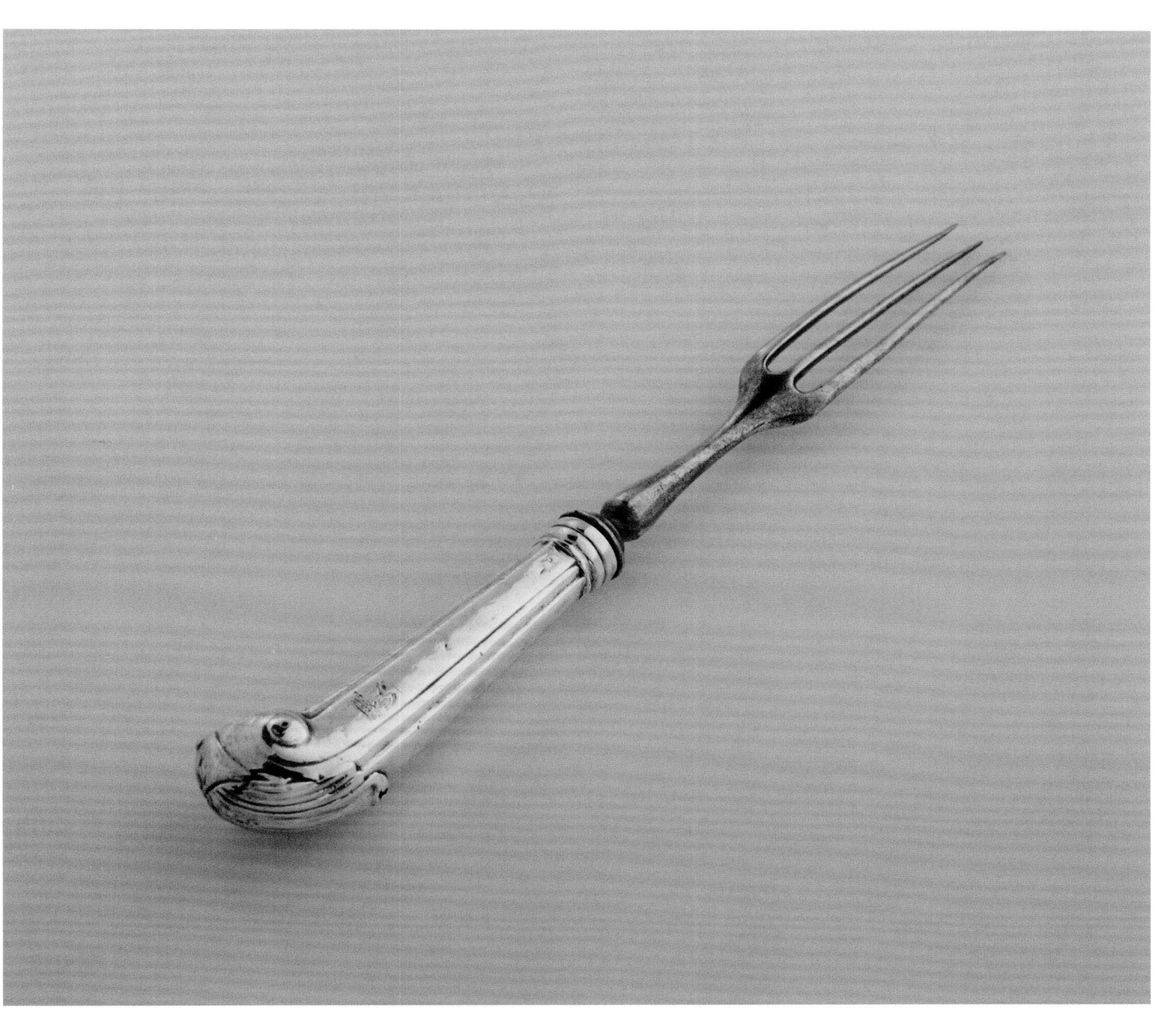

CAT. 3

Plate and Plate Sherds

Plate sherds (mended)
England, ca. 1757
White salt-glaze stoneware, H. 6½", L. 3½"
Mount Vernon Archaeology Collection (House for Families, 762/40E; 762/4 DELTA)

Plate
England, ca. 1757
White salt-glaze stoneware, DIAM. 9¼"
Purchase, 1992
M-3610

Beginning in the spring of 1757 George Washington placed orders to his English agents for "white stone" tableware, also known as English white stoneware. By December 1757 the first shipment arrived from Bristol, and the full set of white salt-glaze stoneware included "6 dozn finest white stone plates," along with "dishes, patti pans, mugs, tea pots, Slop Basons, butter dishes," and "mustard pots."[60] In the 1750s and 1760s the relatively inexpensive yet fashionable white-fired stoneware produced in England was the most widely used tableware in the American colonies, as it could be molded into a variety of specialized forms for use in dinner services and tea wares. In need of all kinds of tablewares for Mount Vernon, Washington ordered large quantities of stoneware for his bachelor household.

Complete examples of Washington's white salt-glaze stoneware do not survive, and invoices accompanying orders provide no details about the decoration of the stoneware used at Mount Vernon. Fragments recovered during archaeological excavations, however, confirm that his stoneware plates were press-molded and decorated with dot-star-diaper and basket panels separated by vertical scrolls around the rim. Press-molded plates, of which this excavated fragment is a period example, revolutionized the English ceramic industry. For the first time multiple pieces of pottery that were extremely consistent in size and decoration, using minimal skilled labor, could be easily manufactured. These characteristics allowed Washington to set an elegant and fashionable table relatively inexpensively. Initially chosen by the single George Washington, white stoneware was used and more ordered by the newly wedded couple throughout the first decade of their marriage.[61]

This plate fragment is probably from a sweetmeat or butter plate and perhaps corresponds to either Washington's initial order of white stoneware that included twelve butter plates or the dozen "white stone sweetmeat plates" he later received from Robert Cary and Company.[62] The decoration on the fragment includes all elements of the dot- star-diaper and basket motif. The hard white body was achieved through a combination of white clay and calcined flint, and the clear glaze was created by introducing common salt into the kiln during firing. The original small (6-to-8-inch) plate was one of at least two dozen that served multiple functions on the Washingtons' table during the main course or dessert.[63]

In July 1769 George Washington was eager to maintain the most fashionable table possible and placed the first known American order for Josiah Wedgwood's new creamware, or Queen's Ware.[64] As early as 1765, creamware was replacing white stoneware on English tables, and it is believed that Washington saw examples during a visit to Williamsburg. His request for "ye most fash^{e} kind of Queen's Ware"[65] was met with a complete service of more than 250 pieces, and when the new ceramic arrived, it supplanted the older white stonewares in daily use.

Archaeological evidence suggests that the outdated white stoneware plates were passed down to the slaves living in Mount Vernon's House for Families, the slave quarter adjacent to the main house. Archaeologists believe that slaves used the set of stoneware and ultimately discarded it, thereby accounting for the numerous fragments of white salt-glaze stoneware plates (including this example) that were found during archaeological excavations at the site.[66]

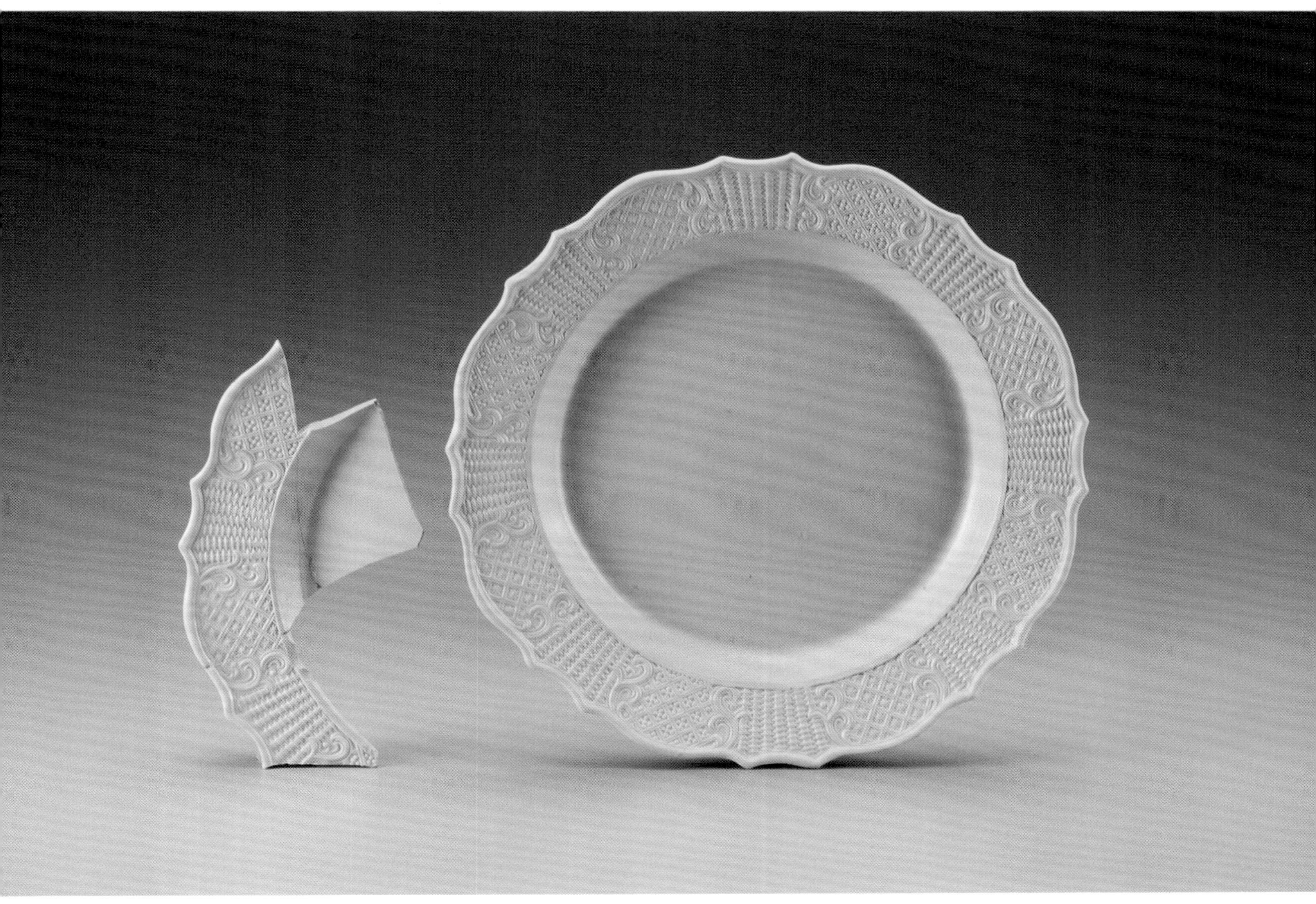

CAT. 4

Teapot and Lid

Jingdezhen, China, ca. 1755
Porcelain, H. 6⅜", W. 8¾"
Bequest of Miss Margaret B. Smith, to the memory of Henrietta Elizabeth Smith, grandniece of Martha Washington, daughter of Commodore John Dandridge Henley, and wife of J. Bayard H. Smith, Esq., 1910[67]
W-131/A

The consumption of imported Chinese tea was a mark of eighteenth-century gentility. Tea and the tea wares in which to serve and partake of Chinese tea constituted the bulk of any given East India Company shipment making its way to English and colonial shores. In the mid-eighteenth century, the height of elegance was to serve tea in highly prized, mysteriously translucent Chinese porcelain. Although the West had developed silver teapot forms, there existed an allure for porcelain, a medium the West had not yet perfected.

As soon as George Washington's mind turned to the furnishing of his newly rented Mount Vernon, he sought to equip it with proper tea wares. A "Compleat sett Fine Image China" was included with the goods he received at the end of 1757, and it was very likely the polychrome enamel (or *famille rose*) tea service that survives at Mount Vernon.[68] This teapot, the principal component of the service, likely dispensed for Washington's guests the Chinese Hyson tea frequently mentioned in his orders and invoices. Its globe-shaped body is decorated with polychrome vignettes of Chinese women and children framed by underglaze blue scrollwork and a gilded ground. Scenes of this nature on Chinese porcelains were popular in Europe and the colonies, and Washington was keeping pace with current tastes by including them on his tea table.

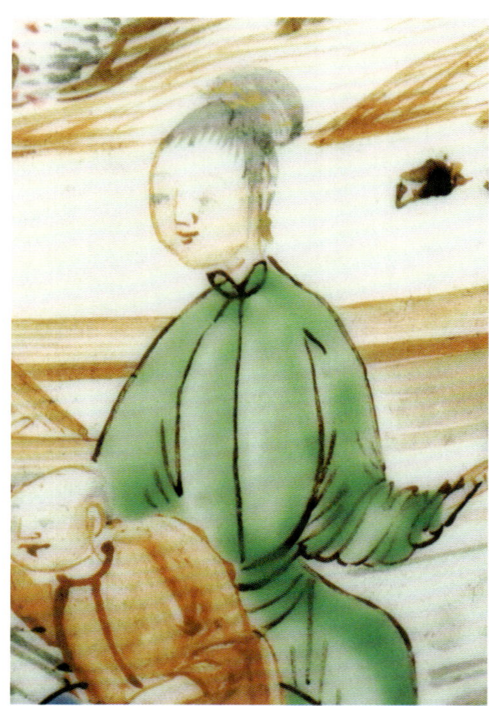

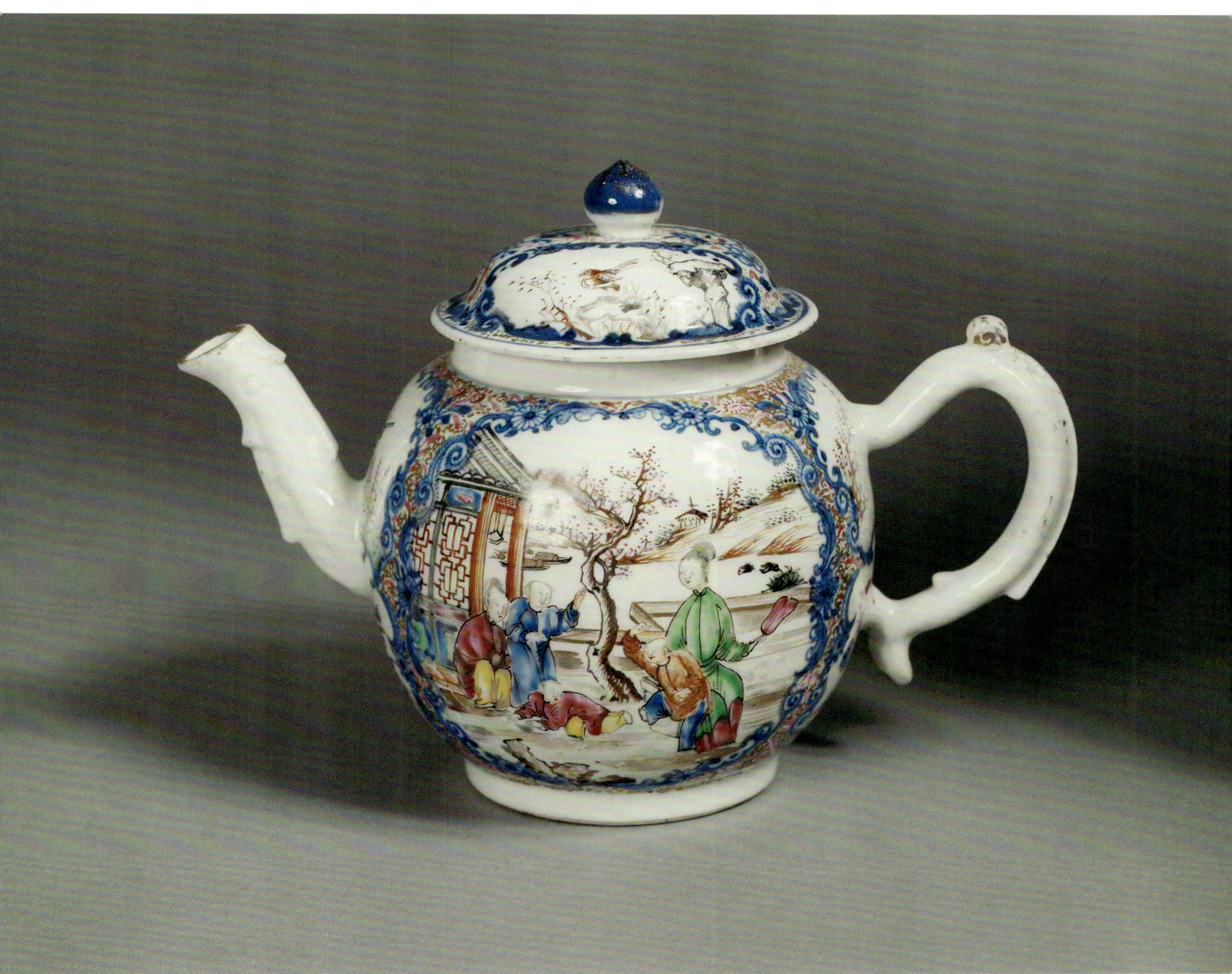

CAT. 5

Sugar Tongs

Robert Cox (active ca. 1752–1773)
London, England, ca. 1755
Silver, OL. 4½"
Gift of Mrs. Augustine Jaquelin Todd, Vice Regent for West Virginia, 1972
W-2616

The service and enjoyment of imported tea included the Western addition of sugar, which also necessitated the appropriate serving implement. Silver sugar tongs were the most elegant means by which to transfer pieces of sugar nipped from a larger cone into a teacup. This pair of sugar tongs was among the silver listed in the estate of Daniel Parke Custis, Martha Washington's first husband.[69] They were among the host of household goods she brought to Mount Vernon when she married George Washington, and which she used throughout their forty-year marriage.

The tongs are of scissor form and exhibit naturalistic detailing typical of Rococo English silver. The circular grips are secured to the central pivot by C-scrolls, and the stylized scrollwork arms terminate in shell bowls. The cast arms are secured by a circular pivot hinge onto which is engraved the Custis family crest. The interiors of both shell grips are stamped with the object's only marks, that registered to the London silversmith Robert Cox in 1755 and the lion passant.

Although Washington and the colonial elite sought silver and Chinese export porcelain tea wares in the 1750s and early 1760s, the acquisition of these luxury goods waned as England levied taxes on such imports against the colonies. In July 1774 the *Pennsylvania Gazette* published a poem entitled "A Lady's Adieu to her Tea Table":

> *Farewell the Tea Board, with its gaudy Equipage,*
> *Of Cups and Saucers, Cream Bucket, Sugar Tongs,*
> *The pretty Tea Chest also, lately stor'd*
> *With Hyson, Congo and best Double Fine.*
> *Fully many a joyous Moment have I sat by ye,*
> *Hearing the Girls tattle, the old Maids talk Scandal,*
> *And the spruce Coxcomb laugh at–may be–Nothing.*
> *No more shall I dish out the once lov'd Liquor,*
> *Though now detestable,*
> *Because I'm taught (and I believe it true)*
> *Its Use will fasten slavish Chains upon my Country,*
> *And LIBERTY'S the Goddess I would choose*
> *To reign triumphant in AMERICA.*[70]

As the poem suggests, George and Martha Washington likely stored these silver sugar tongs and other luxury tea wares until the upheaval surrounding English taxation had passed and they could again enjoy a proper cup of tea with their guests.

Following the Washingtons' deaths, the tongs were passed through a series of descendants of Eliza Parke Custis, Martha Washington's granddaughter, until the turn of the twentieth century. Eliza's great-great-granddaughter, Mrs. George R. Goldsborough,[71] presented the silver along with a box of Christmas candy to Miss Esther Cleveland, daughter of President and Mrs. Grover Cleveland. Mrs. Goldsborough's calling card carefully identified the gift as "Genl Washington's Sugar tongs (with his Crest) inherited by me from my Grandmother Eliza Parke Custis." The inscription was only partially correct. Although the tongs had been handed down through Eliza Parke Custis, the tongs bear the Custis crest rather than the Washington one. The mistake is a frequent one, for the Washington crest is a winged griffin seated on a coronet while the Custis crest is a wingless bird resting on a wreath.[72] The misidentification confirms, however, the melding of Custis and Washington silver articles that took place at Mount Vernon and use of the tongs by George Washington.

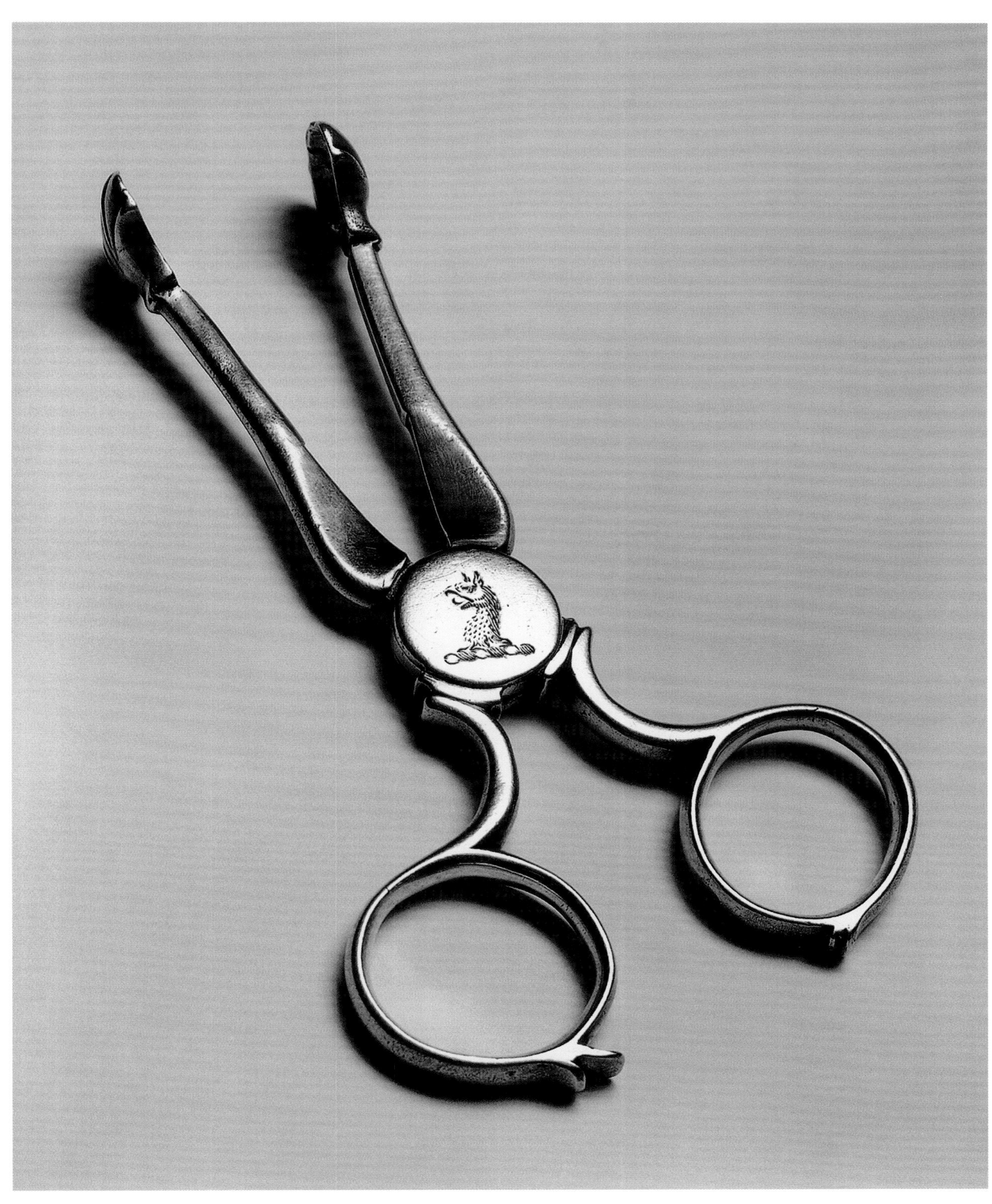

CAT. 6

Table Decorations

England, ca. 1755

Pair of Seasons

Porcelain, H. 4½"
Purchase, 1974, W-2649/A&B

Pair of Muses

Porcelain, H. 6"
Purchased with funds donated by the Melissa and David Dvorak Family, 2004, 2004.004.006/A&B

By the time George Washington and Martha Custis were married in 1759, it was a popular custom among the English and colonial elite to delight their guests with a dining table centerpiece consisting of molded sugar and almond-paste allegorical figures. These figures were placed in sugar-fabricated landscape scenes, lit by candles, and surrounded by fruits and elegant desserts to create a magical effect. Hosts and hostesses on both sides of the Atlantic supplemented the sugar decorations with more substantial glass or ceramic figures, and by midcentury English potteries such as Chelsea, Derby, and Bow were producing porcelain figures to be used in dessert scenes. The Chelsea pottery catalogue of 1756 advertised figures representing Africa, Europe, Asia, and America, as a few of their "many figures for a Desart."[73]

On May 1, 1759, just a few months after the Washingtons' wedding, George Washington wrote to the London firm of Robert Cary and Company requesting a host of tablewares for Mount Vernon. In addition to the "4 fashionable China Branches, & Stands, for Candles" Washington requested, Cary sent "1 pair Seasons, and 1 pair Music's figures" to accompany them.[74] Although Washington did not ask for the pair of Seasons and pair of "Music" figures, the gentlemen at Robert Cary and Company clearly thought they were a wise addition and procured them for the Mount Vernon table from Richard Farrer, a London china merchant, or chinaman.[75]

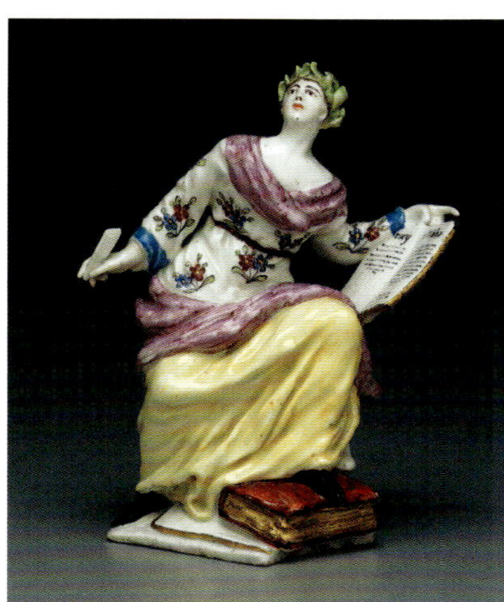

Fig. 1. A complete example of Clio, Muse of History, produced at the Bow manufactory in England. Photograph © 2006 Museum of Fine Arts, Boston

Possibly the product of the Derby or Chelsea factories, Spring and Summer are represented by a seated boy and girl each holding a basket of flowers. The bases are curved in the Rococo style popular at midcentury yet do not bear marks identifying the potter. Although the invoice refers to the complementing porcelains as "Music" figures, the pair represent two Muses manufactured at the Bow porcelain factory. Clio, the patron of history, is one of the nine Muses of Greek mythology. Although her head and significant portions of the figure no longer survive, an intact example of Clio in the Museum of Fine Arts, Boston, shows the porcelain figure as the Washingtons and their guests viewed her (fig. 1). She is seated with her left foot on a red book, holding open the *History of Wales* on to the right page of which is impressed "Clio." The other Muse, Euterpe, is the Greek mythological patron of tragedy or flute playing.[76] She holds a flute in her left hand while a mandolin and reed instruments lie at her feet.[77] When assembled on the Washingtons' table, the four figures added a touch of refinement with their references to faraway porcelain houses and Greek mythology.

The pair of Seasons came to light in the late twentieth century and were purchased for the Mount Vernon collection from the estate of Stephen Decatur in 1974. The "Music" figures were considered lost before they were discovered in the twenty-first century at the home of Betty Washington Whiting, a descendant of Nelly Custis Lewis. Like other objects cared for by Martha Washington's descendants, both Muses retained red and white paper labels affixed to the undersides of their bases reading *Washington Family*. The Muses were purchased for return to Mount Vernon at the auction of Miss Whiting's collection in January 2004. For the first time in more than two hundred years, George Washington's "1 pair Seasons" and "1 pair Music's figures" have been reunited.[78]

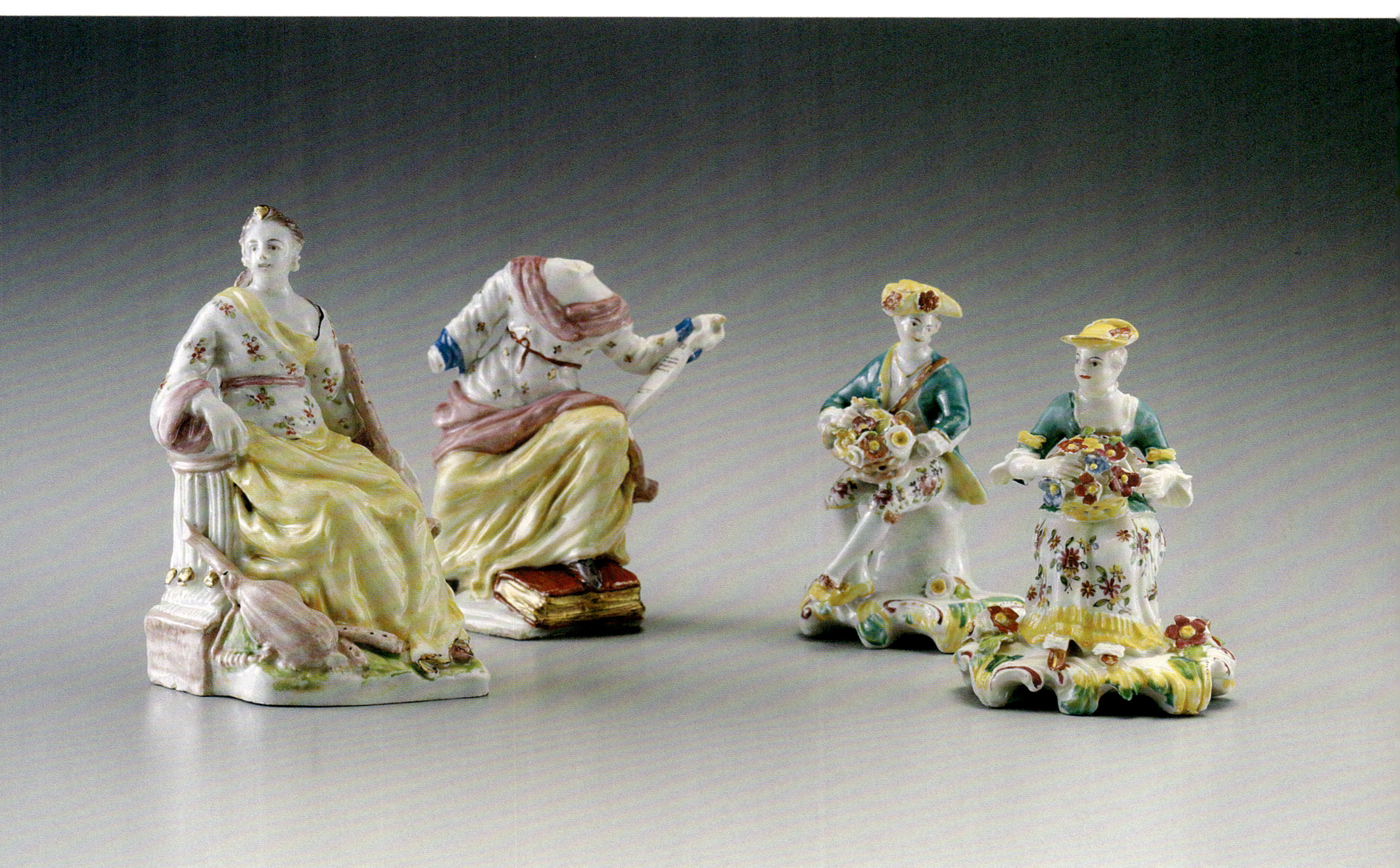

CAT. 7

Jelly Glass

Probably England, ca. 1755–1775
Colorless glass, H. 4½", W. 2¾"
Purchase, 1957[79]
W-2116

Writing from Williamsburg in May 1759, George Washington requested that Robert Cary and Company send him "1 Fashionable Sett of Dessert Glasses, and Stands for Sweet Meats Jellys &ca."[80] Three months later, Cary shipped to Washington "3 Salvers, 1 Top piece, 1 dozn Sullibub Glasses, 2 dozn Jellys, 1 dozn Sweet Meat ditto [glasses], [and] 2 dozn Baskets."[81] Together, this glassware formed what was one of the most stunning centerpieces of the day—a pyramid of round glass salvers displaying a variety of specialized glass forms containing an array of dessert delicacies.

A number of jelly glasses owned and used by George and Martha Washington survive, including this example that very well may be one of the two dozen mentioned in Cary's 1759 invoice. Its trumpet shape with flat knop and heavy base is accented with elaborate cut facets and petal-shaped rim. Similar jelly glasses are seen on Maydewell and Windle's London trade card of 1765 (fig. 1), although elaborately cut jelly glasses continued to be popular through the end of the eighteenth century.[82]

There were three dozen jelly glasses listed in Martha Washington's sweetmeat closet at the time of her death,[83] and the number of jelly recipes in her handwritten family cookbook suggests that jellies were a frequent dessert in the Washington household. Mrs. Washington's *Booke of Cookery* contains numerous recipes for making jellies using apples, quinces, plums, raspberries, and currants. Judging from the amount of hartshorne[84] shipped to the Washingtons in 1759 and 1760, however, it seems that the recipe "To Make Jelley of Harts Horne" was a favorite.[85]

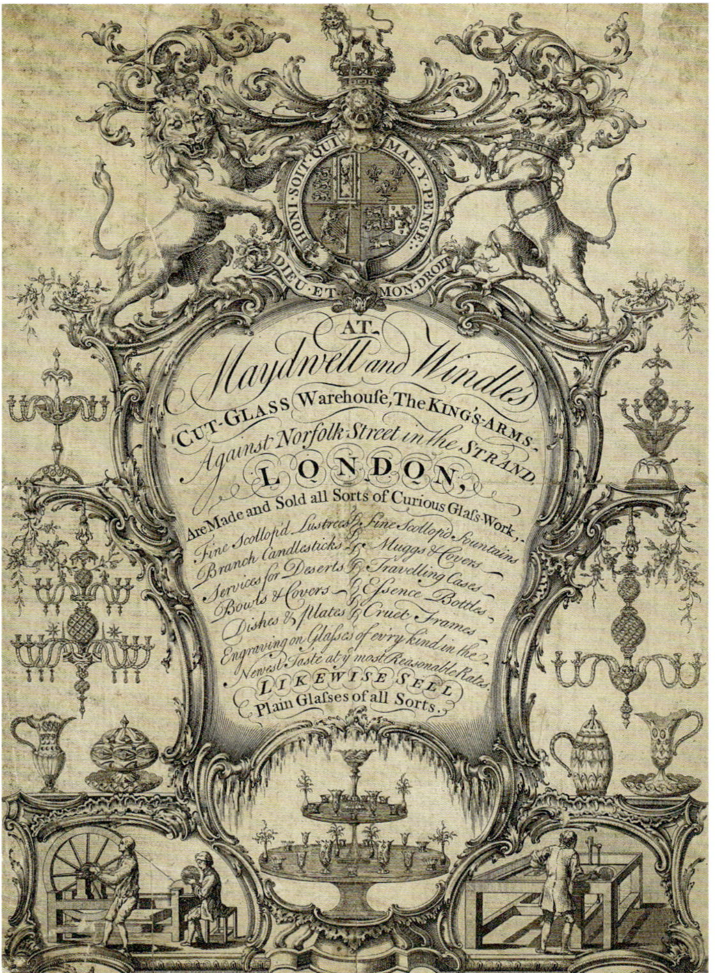

Fig. 1.
London glass houses, like Maydewell and Windle's, advertised salvers and jelly glasses. Courtesy of The British Museum

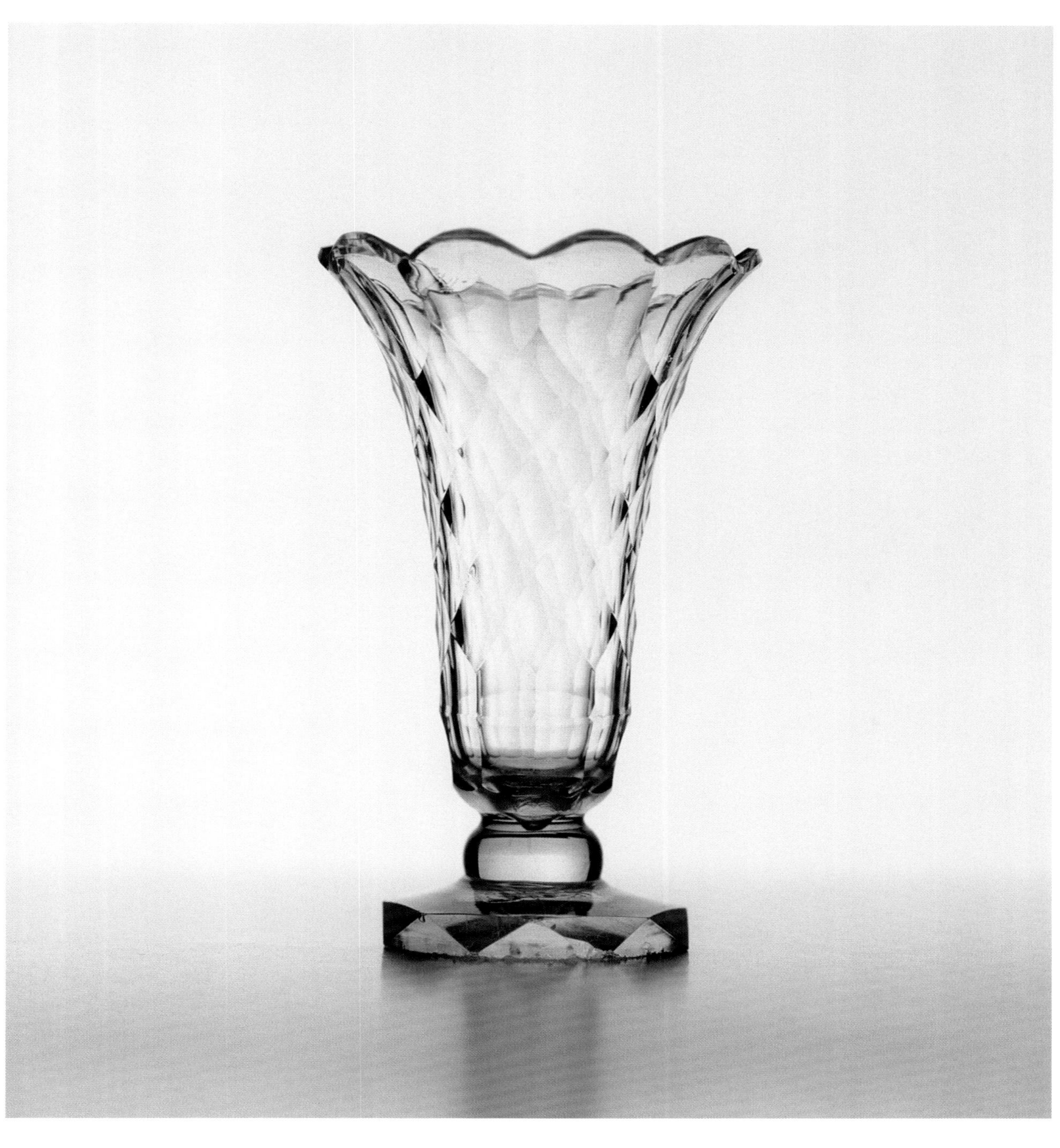

CAT. 8

Plate

Richard Cleeve (active ca. 1743-1760)
London, England, ca. 1759
Pewter, DIAM. 9⅞"
Purchase, 1959
W-2167

In the eighteenth century, pewter was a symbol of gentility. Pewter provided an advancement over wooden wares and yet was an alternative to the more costly silver. It could be cleaned and buffed to a reflective surface, and colonists who could afford it used pewter regularly.[86]

At the time George Washington ordered his pewter, literally tons of pewter wares were being shipped to the colonies. The finest of the imported English pewter was termed "hard metal." Hard metal pewter most resembled silver in appearance and received the distinction of a crowned "X" incised next to the maker's touchmark. This type of pewter also was the most expensive because its composition (tin and copper) did not include the softer lead. The surface of the pieces were also usually hammered after casting, making the wares additionally harder and stronger.

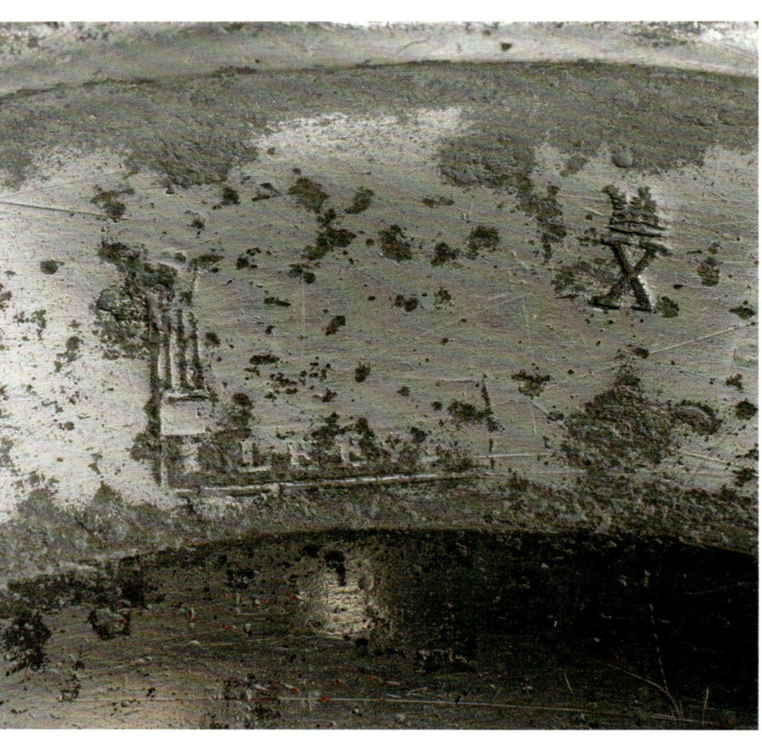

Washington, no doubt aware of this distinction, wrote to Robert Cary and Company on June 12, 1759, asking for "6 dozn large and best hard mettle Plates with my Crest engravd" as well as "2 dozn dishes of the same properly sorted, & sizd." Cary responded by shipping from London on August 6, 1759, goods secured from "Richd Cleeve—Pewterer" that included "2 dozn Superfine hard mettle dishes sorted" and "6 dozn very best Plates." Cleeve also charged for engraving ninety-six crests, per Washington's request that each item be identified with his symbolic griffin.[87] Washington received the total shipment, weighing 183 pounds, in November.

Although popular during the pre-Revolutionary years, pewter fell out of favor by the end of the eighteenth century as affordable ceramics made their way to American tables. By 1799 George Washington was probably using his early pewter purchases infrequently. The room-by-room inventory taken at the time of Washington's death lists "9 Pewter Plates . . . In the Kitchen," all valued at $1.50.[88] Thomas Peter, husband to Martha Washington's granddaughter Martha Custis Peter, purchased a number of kitchen goods at the sales held following Mrs. Washington's death in 1802, and this pewter plate was likely among the items he bought.[89]

This surviving plate from the 1759 order no longer retains a polished surface, but the Washington griffin is still clearly visible on the rim. On the reverse, the marks CLEEVE along with a crown and an "X" (detail) indicate Washington's purchase from Richard Cleeve of some of the finest available London pewter. Although Washington's guests likely did not see the marks noting its quality and origin, they certainly observed the griffin on the rim as a reminder of their host's status.

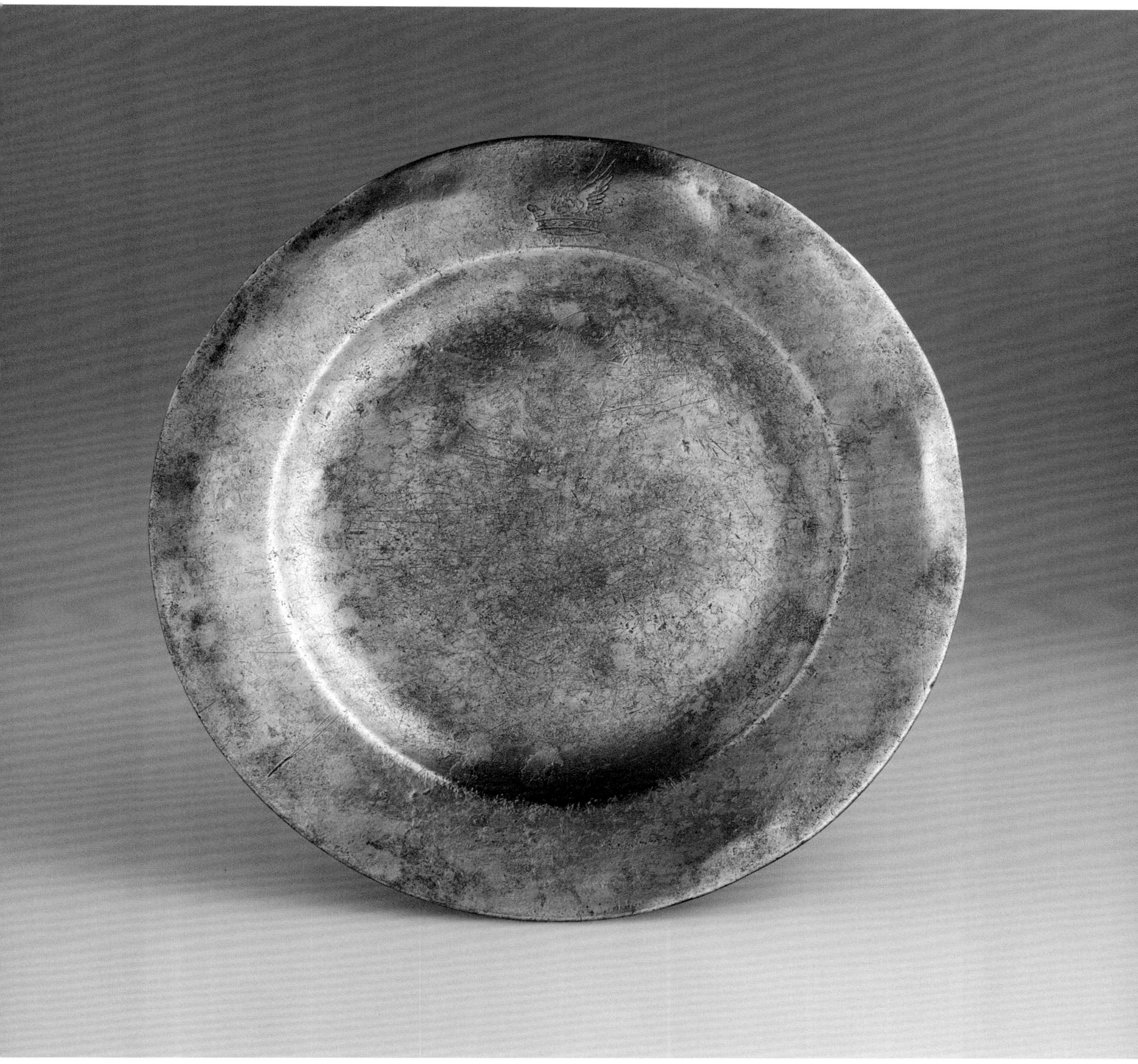

CAT. 9

Punch Bowl

Jingdezhen, China, ca. 1730–1750
Porcelain, H. 6⅜", DIAM. 15½"
Purchase, 1956[90]
W-2100

Eighteenth-century colonists shared with their English counterparts a fondness for a concoction of spirit, fruit, and spices called punch. The number and type of ingredients included in punch seems to have been a personal preference and one that was also determined by the season. Recipes for the drink are as varied as are the explanations for the word *punch* itself. Some suggest the word derives from the Hindi word for *five*, which became associated with the five main ingredients of punch—rum, water, lemons, sugar, and spices. Others suppose it refers to the casks—or puncheons—in which the principal ingredient, rum, was shipped from the West Indies.[91]

The fashion for punch led to the creation of equipage necessary for its enjoyment, and the punch bowl was the most necessary element of the ensemble. The punch concoction was usually mixed in the bowl and served from it with a ladle. In elite colonial residences, the punch bowl was of Chinese porcelain and the ladle of silver.

George Washington's first recorded receipt of a punch bowl appears in a 1758 invoice from Thomas Knox of Bristol, England, for "3 punch bowls" that were likely of the "white stone" or salt-glazed stoneware that formed the bulk of that shipment.[92] Washington later ordered and received porcelain examples including a "1 Gall[o]n Punch Bowl" and two quart punch bowls with "Nank[i]n[g] bord[e]r" from the London chinaman Richard Farrer in 1766.[93] The punch bowl pictured here was, however, probably among the porcelains Martha Dandridge Custis brought with her to Mount Vernon following her marriage to George Washington. Its exceptional quality is indicative of early eighteenth-century Chinese porcelains that were owned and used by the colonial elite, presumably the Custises included.

The bowl is a finely painted combination of rich polychrome enamels popular in the early and mid-eighteenth century, often referred to as *famille rose*. The carefully painted scenes of pheasants, hummingbirds, and peacocks amid chrysanthemums and peonies are typical of Chinese designs of the period. While the punch bowl form caters to the Western demand for serving a favored drink, the colors and designs represent a Chinese aesthetic not yet influenced by the West.[94]

Guests to Mount Vernon were frequently treated to punch, and Martha Washington's estate inventory lists eight "China Bowls" stored in the sweetmeat closet that may have been used for serving punch.[95] This example remained in use until the Washingtons' deaths and may even be the punch bowl the Polish visitor Julian Niemcewicz saw. Arriving at Mount Vernon one afternoon while George Washington was still attending to his farms, Niemcewicz recalled that he was not left alone long. Martha Washington "appeared after a few minutes, welcomed us most graciously and had punch served."[96]

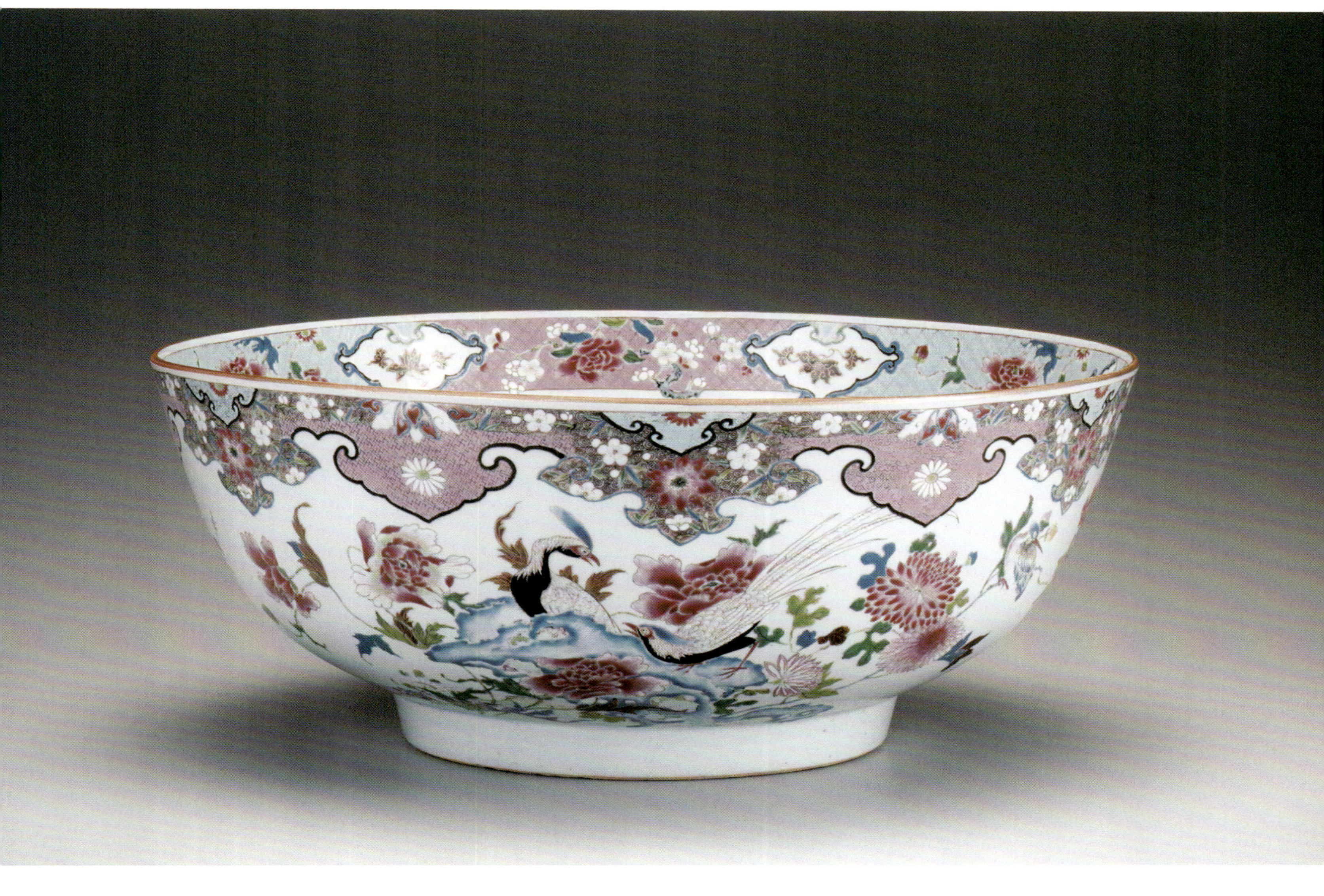

CAT. 10

Punch Strainer

Samuel Meriton I (active ca. 1739–1764)
London, England, 1750–1751
Silver, w. 6¼" Bowl DIAM. 9⁄16"
Gift of Mrs. Walter Gibson Peter, Jr., in memory of Agnes Peter Mott, 1975
W-2688

The service of punch necessitated proper punch equipment. Because fruit and spices were two of the five ingredients of punch, a strainer was necessary to cull the pulp and ground bits before they made their way to glass or cup. The Washingtons' punch strainer was of typical form for the period, with its shallow, circular raised bowl, the bottom of the body pierced with small holes drilled in geometric patterns, and cast scroll bracket handles attached to allow for the strainer to be suspended over a punch bowl or drinking vessel. Samuel Meriton, the likely silversmith, serviced London clientele and factors for people in the colonies. His shop was located at the sign of the acorn in Huggin Alley on Wood Street.[97]

The London stamped date mark of 1750–1751 suggests that the strainer was part of the Custis plate brought by Martha Washington to Mount Vernon from her first marriage.[98] A necessary implement of fashionable entertaining in any genteel colonial Virginia home, the strainer likely served both the Custis and Washington household guests partaking of punch and was used at Mount Vernon throughout the Washingtons' lifetimes. At the time of George Washington's death, it was probably among the 44 pounds 15 ounces of silver recorded as being "In the Closets &c under Frank's direction."[99] Frank, a house servant and slave, belonged to George Washington and served as a waiter. He was responsible for laying up foodstuffs and, as Washington's inventory evidences, overseeing the care of the family silver, including this strainer.[100]

Although Martha Washington bequeathed all of the family silver to her grandson, George Washington Parke Custis, it is evident that family members exchanged some of the inherited items after her death. Mrs. Washington's great-granddaughter Britannia Wellington Peter Kennon indicated that this strainer was given by G. W. P. Custis to his sister and Kennon's mother, Martha Custis Peter. The strainer bears the names of some of the Peter family members who treasured the Mount Vernon reminder. "G. W. Peter" is lightly engraved on the rim, and "BWK" is engraved on the bowl and handles. The strainer remained in the Peter family until its donation to Mount Vernon.

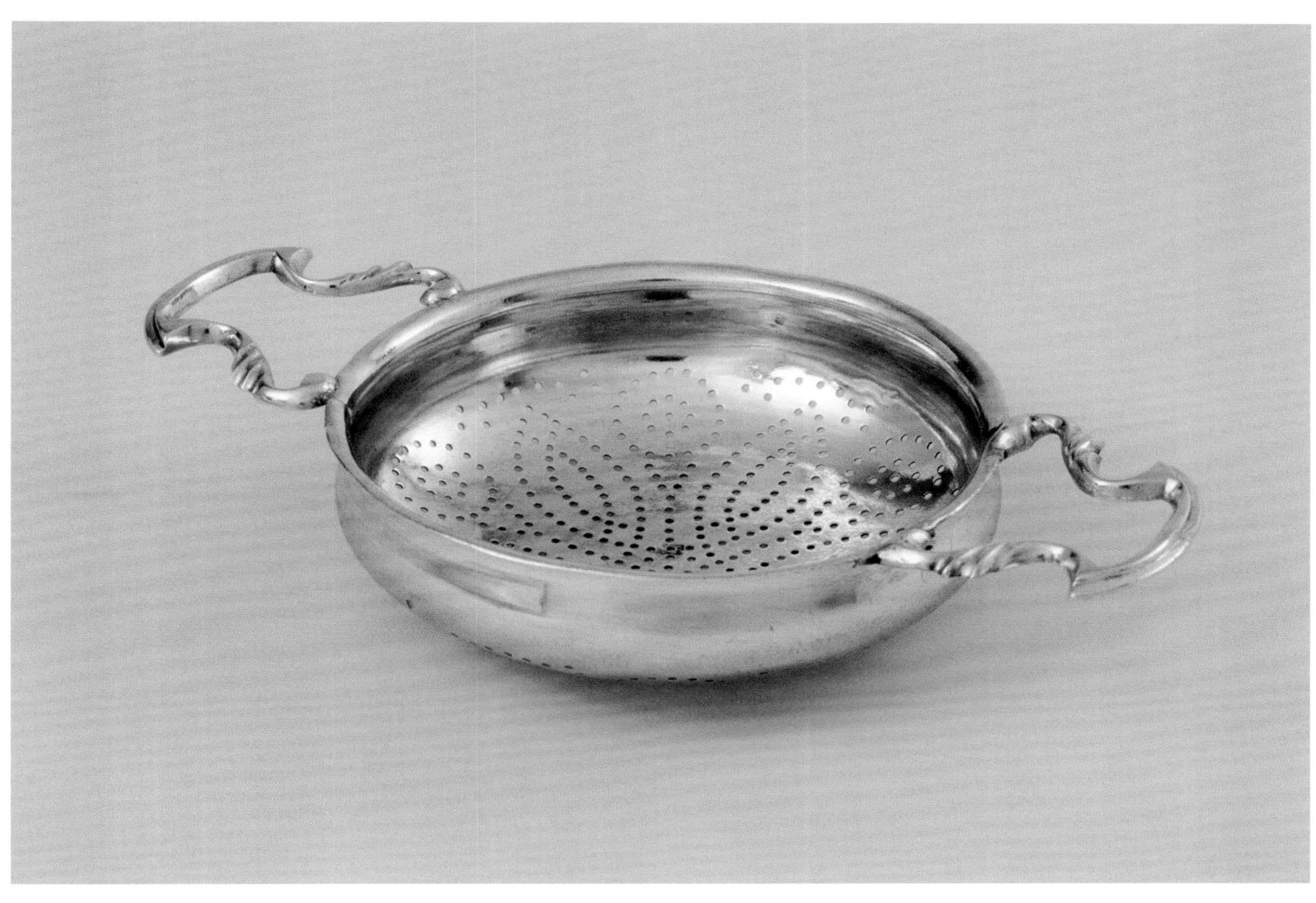

CAT. 11

Dessert Spoon

Thompson Davis (active ca. 1762–1764)
London, England, 1762–1763
Silver, L. 6¼"
Gift of Mrs. Gilpin Willson, Jr., 1965[101]
W-2458

On November 15, 1762, George Washington wrote from Williamsburg to Robert Cary and Company in London. Perhaps in response to items seen in the residences of his contemporaries and those he desired but could not locate in Williamsburg's shops, Washington enclosed a lengthy list of household items he wanted. Among the numerous articles of clothing, dry goods, and kitchen supplies, Washington requested two dozen "small Dessert Silver Spoons with my crest" and fourteen similar tablespoons (fig. 1). He noted that the fourteen tablespoons were to complement ten he already had, and that all of the spoons, in addition to two dozen knives and forks "with China handles," were to be placed in "neat Mahogany Cases for decorating a side board."[102]

Cary and Company shipped Washington's goods the following April, including "neat" mahogany knife boxes made by Philip Bell, porcelain-handled knives and forks supplied by Richard Weale, and silver spoons secured from the goldsmith John Payne.[103] Although supplied by Payne, the spoons bear the mark of the London silversmith Thompson Davis.[104] This dessert spoon is one of several dessert and tablespoons that survive in the Mount Vernon collection. The bowl is oval and elongated, and the rounded handle is upturned, with a midrib. The back of the handle is engraved with the Washington crest, a griffin seated on a coronet. Although the knives and forks are not known to survive, this dessert spoon offers a hint of the impact the cutlery must have had when placed on Washington's sideboard or used by his dinner guests.

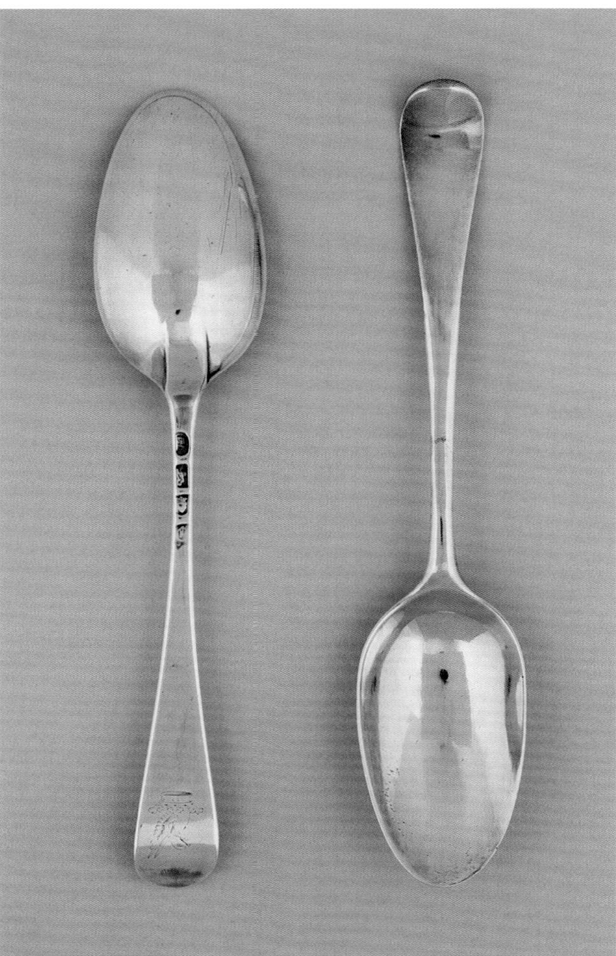

Fig. 1.
Silver tablespoons (left), stamped Thompson Davis, that complemented the dessert spoons shipped to Washington in 1763, MVLA

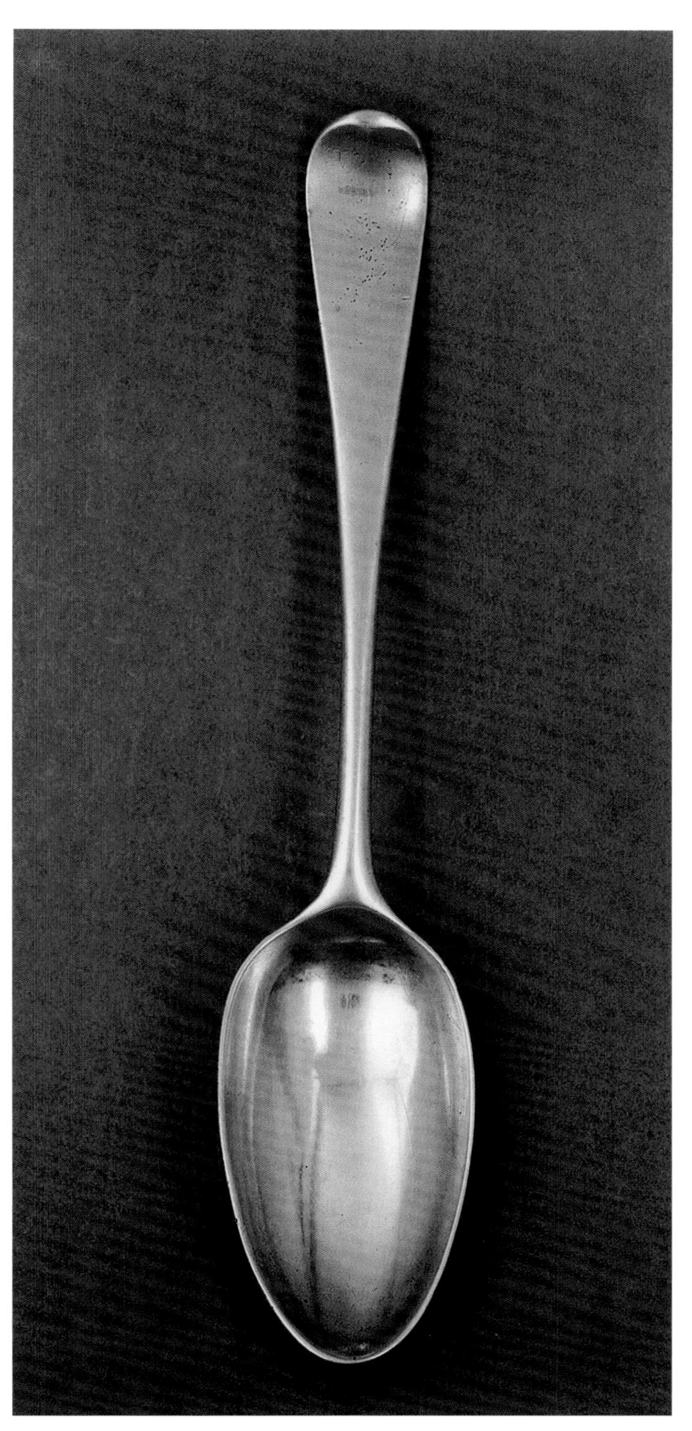

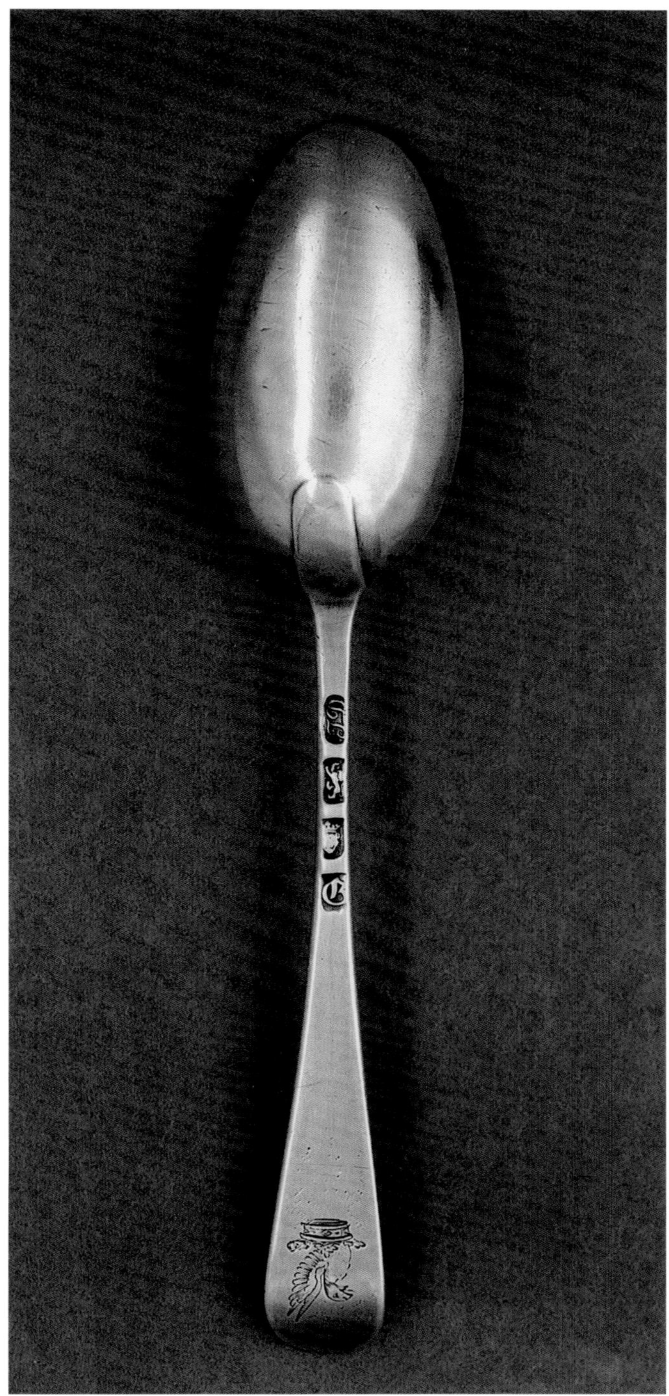

CAT. 12

Miniature Portraits

Martha Dandridge Custis Washington (1731–1802), 1772
Charles Willson Peale (1741–1827)
Watercolor on ivory, 2⅛ x 1¾"
Purchase, 1956
W-2102 /A&B

Martha "Patsy" Parke Custis (1756–1773), 1772
Charles Willson Peale (1741–1827)
Watercolor on ivory, 1⅝ x 1 3/16"
Purchase and partial gift of an anonymous donor, 2000
W-2355/A

John "Jacky" Parke Custis (1754–1781), 1772
Charles Willson Peale (1741–1827)
Watercolor on ivory, 1⅝ x 1 3/16"
Private Collection
W-2355/B

On May 18, 1772, George Washington recorded in his diary, "In the Evening Mr. Peale & J. P. Custis came to Mount Vernon." John "Jacky" Parke Custis, Washington's stepson, was studying in Annapolis and returned home with a young artist from that city, Charles Willson Peale.[105] Over the next few days, Peale worked on a large canvas of George Washington dressed as a Virginia colonel and three miniature portraits of Mrs. Washington, Jacky, and his younger sister, Patsy.[106]

Jacky is painted at age eighteen, a handsome young man with chestnut-colored hair dressed in a dark green coat with red collar and a finely embroidered waistcoat. Patsy is depicted at age sixteen, the year before her death. Despite her fragile health, Patsy appears as a beautiful young woman with rosy cheeks. Her black hair is laced with faux or real pearls, she wears a strand around her neck, and her mauve dress is trimmed in lace.

Washington recorded payments to Peale of thirteen pounds sterling for each of the children's miniatures, and the same amount for one of his wife, done at Jacky's request.[107] Peale's receipt to Washington confirmed that he painted "Mrs. Washington's Picture in Miniature for the use of Mr. Custis, and at his desire."[108] Martha Washington was forty-one years old at the time of the sitting, and the miniature is the earliest known depiction of her as Mrs. Washington.[109] Like Patsy, she is shown in a mauve-colored dress trimmed in lace, with real or simulated pearls woven into her dark hair and around her neck. With the addition of a veil secured in her hair and draped over her right shoulder, this portrait of Martha Washington stands apart as both the most elegantly detailed and, arguably, the most attractive of her portraits in miniature.

In 1780, Martha Washington sent all three miniatures to Charles Willson Peale to "have the three pictures set exactly alike—and all the same size." She wished to "have them for Braceletts to wear round the wrists" and requested that the settings be "neat and plain."[110] Peale complied, writing to Mrs. Washington that he had cut the miniatures to the same size, "moulded some of the best glass I could find . . . got a Lapidary to polish them," and sent them to a jeweler whom he had "begged . . . to take the utmost pains to set them neatly."[111] The portraits of Jacky and Patsy still retain the bracelet settings, with nine-strand loops on each side pierced to accommodate delicate gold chains.[112] The pair of miniature portraits were no doubt particularly meaningful to Martha Washington following Jacky's death in the fall of 1781.

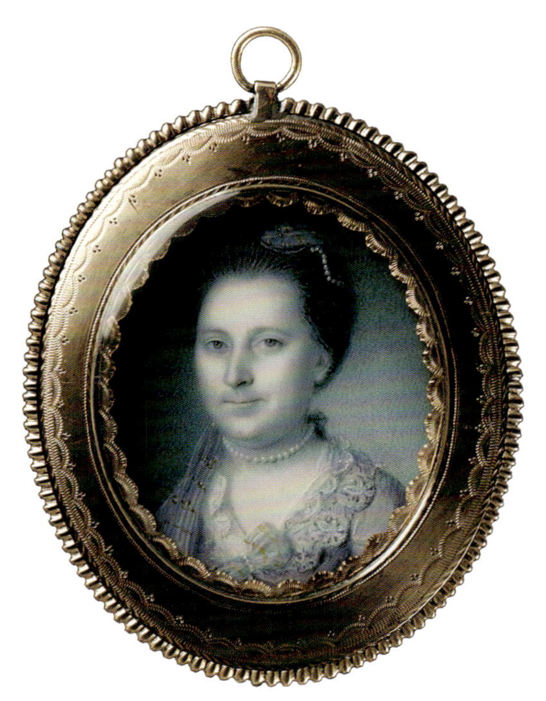

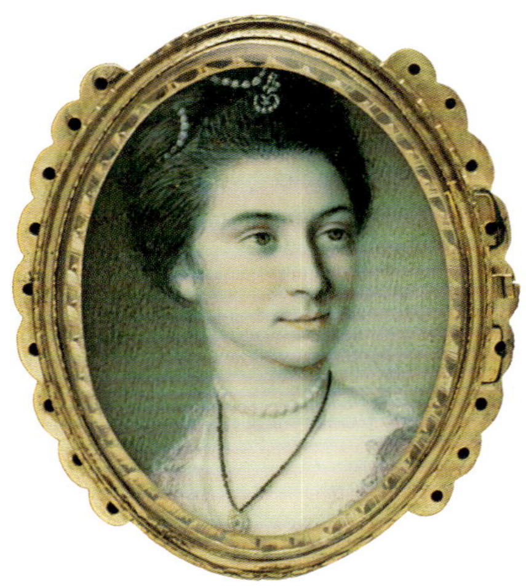

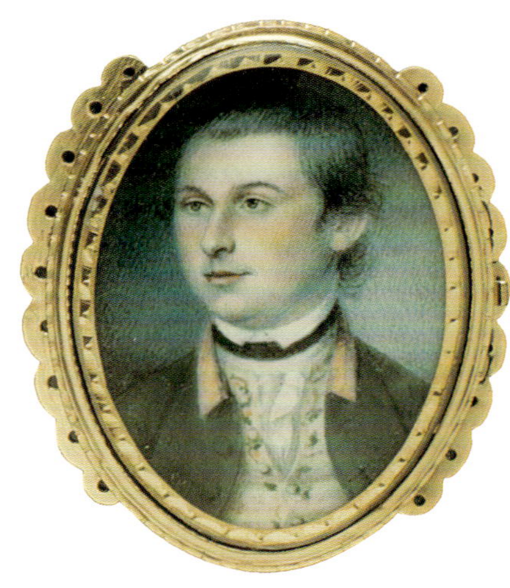

CAT. 13

Hot-Water Urn

Retailed and possibly manufactured by John Carter II (active 1769–1777)
London, England, 1774–1775
Silver, H. 21"
Purchase, 1932
Conservation courtesy of Mary V. Mochary
W-107

John "Jacky" Parke Custis, the surviving son of Martha Dandridge Custis Washington and stepson of George Washington, reached his majority and received control of his share of the estate of his late father in 1773. Despite George Washington's reservations concerning his age and education, the twenty-year-old Jacky married Eleanor Calvert the following year. This urn, embellished with the Custis arms, is part of a large suite of engraved silver dating from the wedding year and possibly ordered by Jacky to mark the occasion.[113]

The urn is marked by John Carter II, the proprietor of what must have been a successful London retail business. Carter was referred to in eighteenth-century trade directories as a *plateworker*, a term applied to those goldsmiths or silversmiths supplying the retail trade.[114] He used an unregistered maker's mark as a way to publicly brand and market his business's wares, and Carter's mark appears on several other Custis pieces. In all likelihood, Carter was not the actual maker of these items; one or several of Carter's employees, or journeymen, would have been responsible for their manufacture.[115] His business specialized in retailing salvers and candlesticks, both of which appear in the Custis suite with his marks. The salvers and other solid silver pieces were probably crafted in Carter's shop, while the silver-plated candlesticks were purchased from Sheffield makers and then overstruck with Carter's mark and resold.[116]

This hot-water urn was likely made in Carter's shop and stamped by him. The silversmith responsible utilized the popular classical style inspired by the recent archaeological excavations of Pompeii and Herculaneum. Characterized by symmetry and refined restraint, this style utilized classical Greek and Roman forms and motifs to great success.[117] The urn's silversmith combined these newly introduced Neoclassical elements with heavy embossed fluting associated with earlier English Baroque silver. The reeded, urn-shaped body rests on a trumpet pedestal supported by a plinth with four ball feet. The short C-scroll handles are attached at the beaded shoulder, the small, reeded, domed lid is crowned by an acorn finial, and an engraved cartouche of floral foliage encloses the Custis crest. These elements combine to make this piece among the most impressive survivals of the Custis silver, and it was no doubt noticed by those served tea by the newly married John and Eleanor Custis.

Placed on a tea table with other elements of proper tea equipage, the urn was used to dispense hot water into a teapot by means of a spigot.[118] The temperature of the water was maintained by heat radiating from a piece of hot charcoal, soapstone, or iron inserted into the reservoir before boiling water was poured into the body. Once the water was dispensed into the teapot, it mixed with the leaves of imported Chinese tea and became the fashionable beverage enjoyed by colonial Virginia's elite.

Shortly before his death in 1781, John Parke Custis drew up an inventory of his silver, presumably while at his Abingdon residence, and the hot-water urn is likely one of two "Tea Urns" itemized.[119] It is not known where the silver was kept immediately following Custis' death, but the hot-water urn was eventually used by the couple's only son, George Washington Parke Custis, at the residence he built overlooking the Potomac River and named Arlington House.

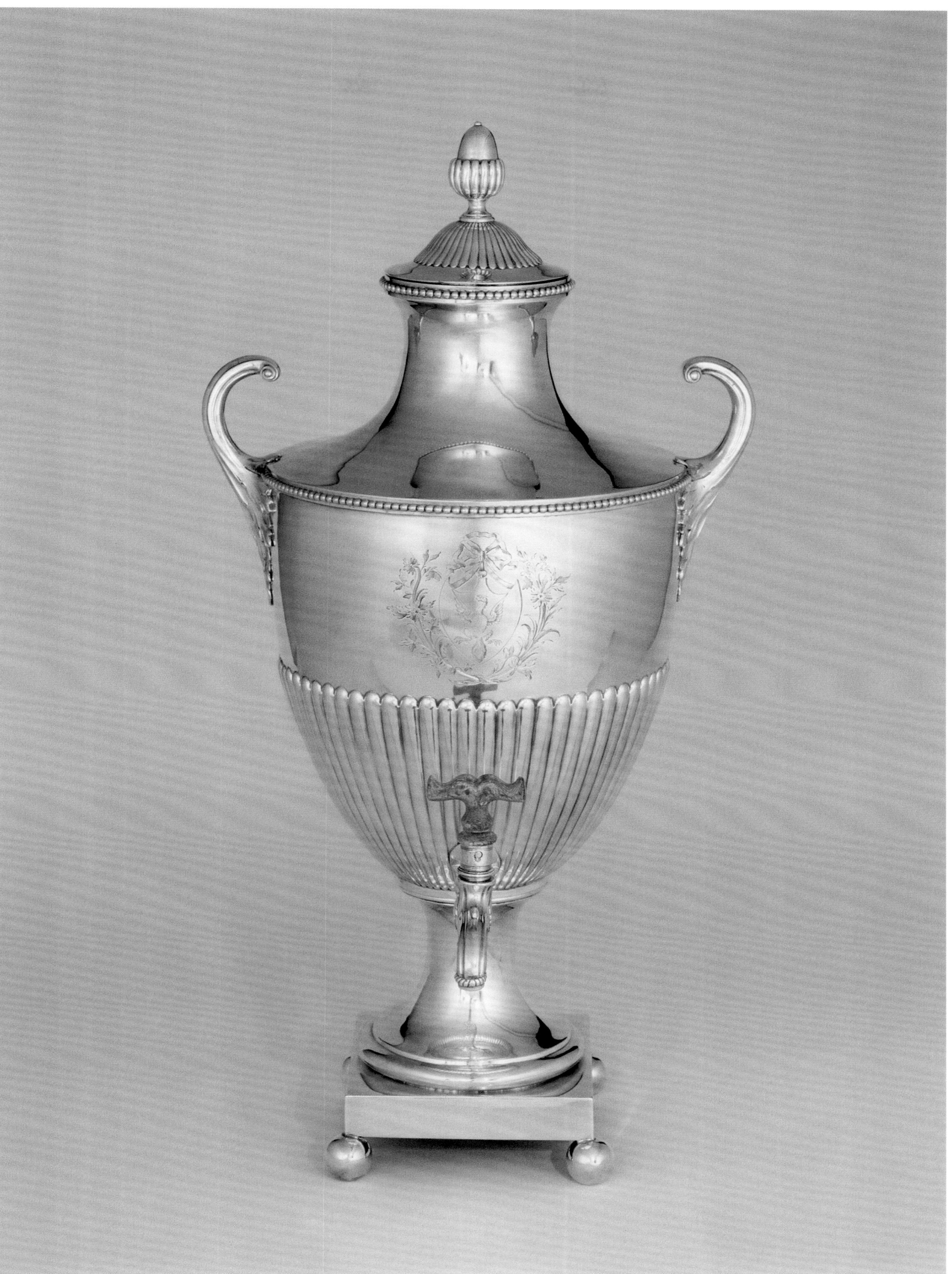

CAT. 14

Hunting Whip

John Amory (active 1775–1799) and John Johnson
New York, New York, ca. 1770
Leather, silver, horn, and natural fiber (possibly hemp), L. 22⅞", W. 1"
Gift of Francis A. Mead, via the American Red Cross Museum, 1944
W-1213

Many of George Washington's pre-Revolutionary interests and pastimes—from fox hunting to steeplechases—centered on horses. Understanding the necessity of outfitting oneself and one's horse in accordance with standards set by the gentry, Washington bought elegant articles of horsemanship ornamented with his crest or monogram.

Riding crops served a practical and ornamental feature of the riding equipage, and in 1765 Washington requested and received from London a "best whole Hunting Whip plated at the head & my name engraved thereon."[120] This similar example was crafted by the New York partnership of Amory and Johnson a few years later. The majority of the wood core[121] is enclosed within a double-ply natural fiber (possibly hemp), woven in a herringbone pattern. The grip is accented by silver braid wrapped in the small spiraling channels of horn and a silver ferrule with the engraved initials "GW" (detail). The sides of the ferrule are defined by two bands of engraved decoration that enclose the identification of the craftsmen responsible, "Amory and Johnson Makers New York." Washington must have purchased the riding crop before October 1775, for in that month John Amory advertised himself in the *New York Gazette* as a whip maker who "sells all sorts of the best and newest fashioned Horse-Whips . . . next Door to the Shop he formerly carried on that Business in, in the Company with John Johnson."[122]

Although Washington was soon occupied by other outlets for his excellent riding skills, the departure of the English gentry from Virginia certainly affected Washington's favorite pastimes. As a remembrance of years of shared experiences, Washington may have presented this riding crop to one of his many riding and hunting companions who returned to England on the eve of the Revolution. In 1939 Mr. Francis Mead donated the crop to the Canadian Red Cross in support of fund-raising efforts during World War II. Mead had coveted the crop when he saw it in the home of English relatives who identified it "as a remembrance of friendly relations" given by George Washington to one of the family's ancestors when they were leaving Virginia for England. As these relatives considered the crop to be "only a remembrance of a rebel," Mead returned the crop to North America to ensure its preservation. The Canadian Red Cross acknowledged the object's importance and transferred Washington's riding crop to the American Red Cross Museum in Washington, DC, which, in turn, returned it to Mount Vernon.

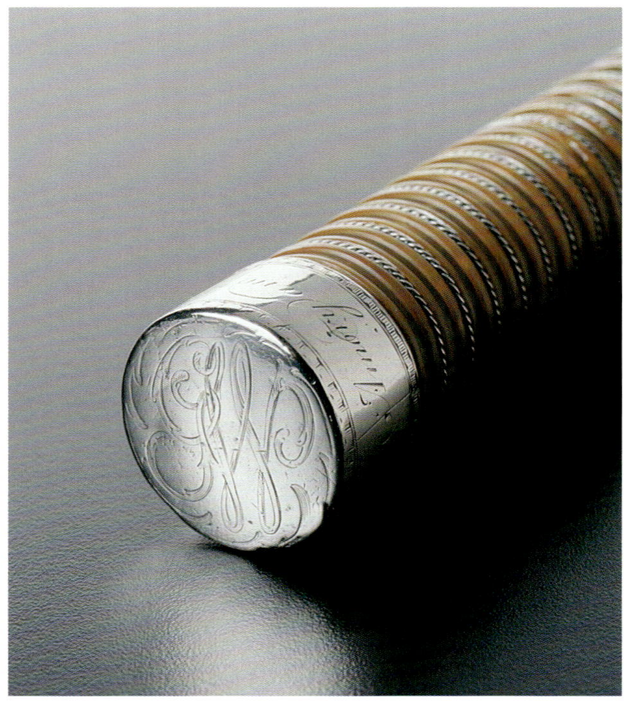

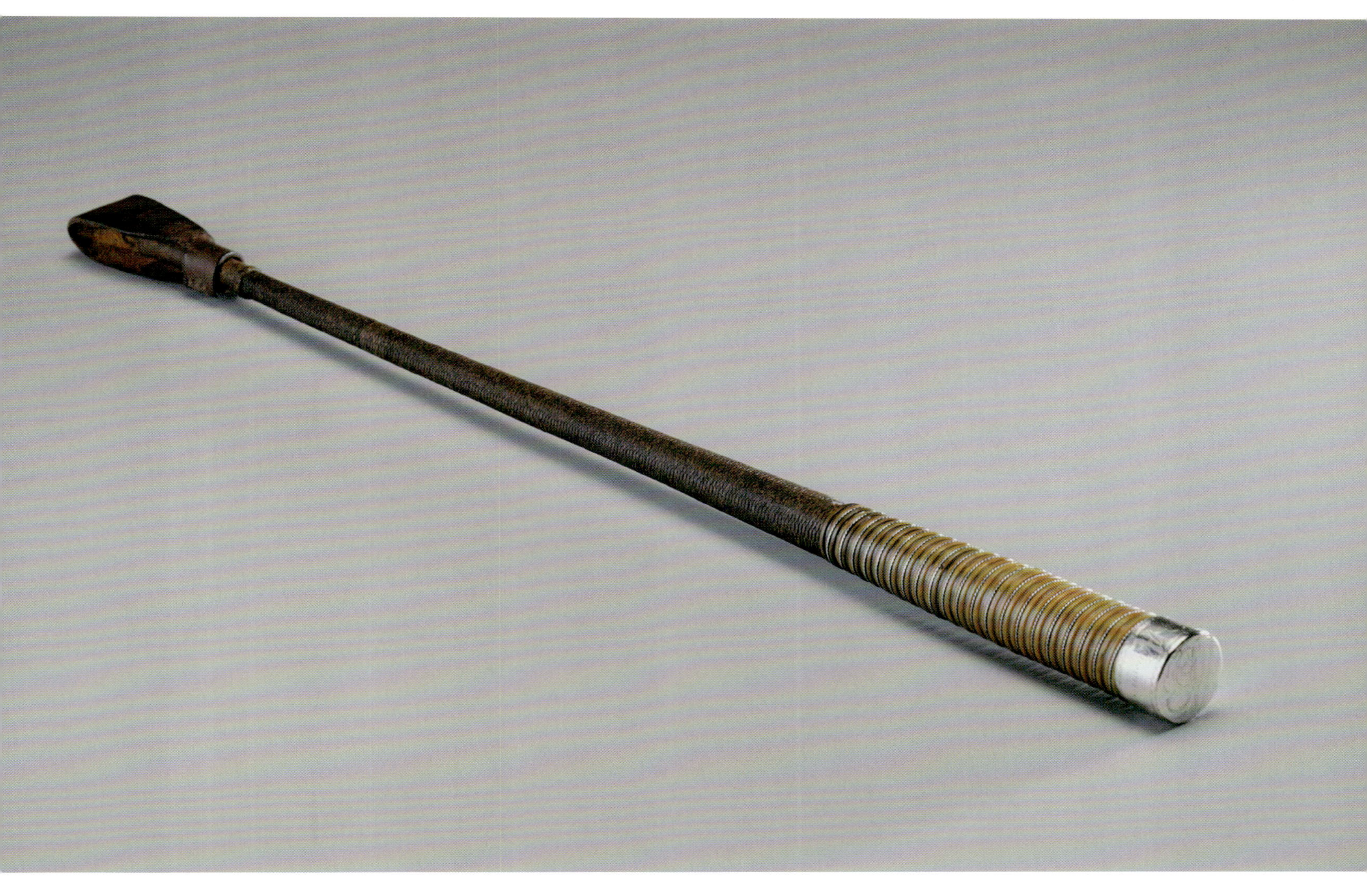

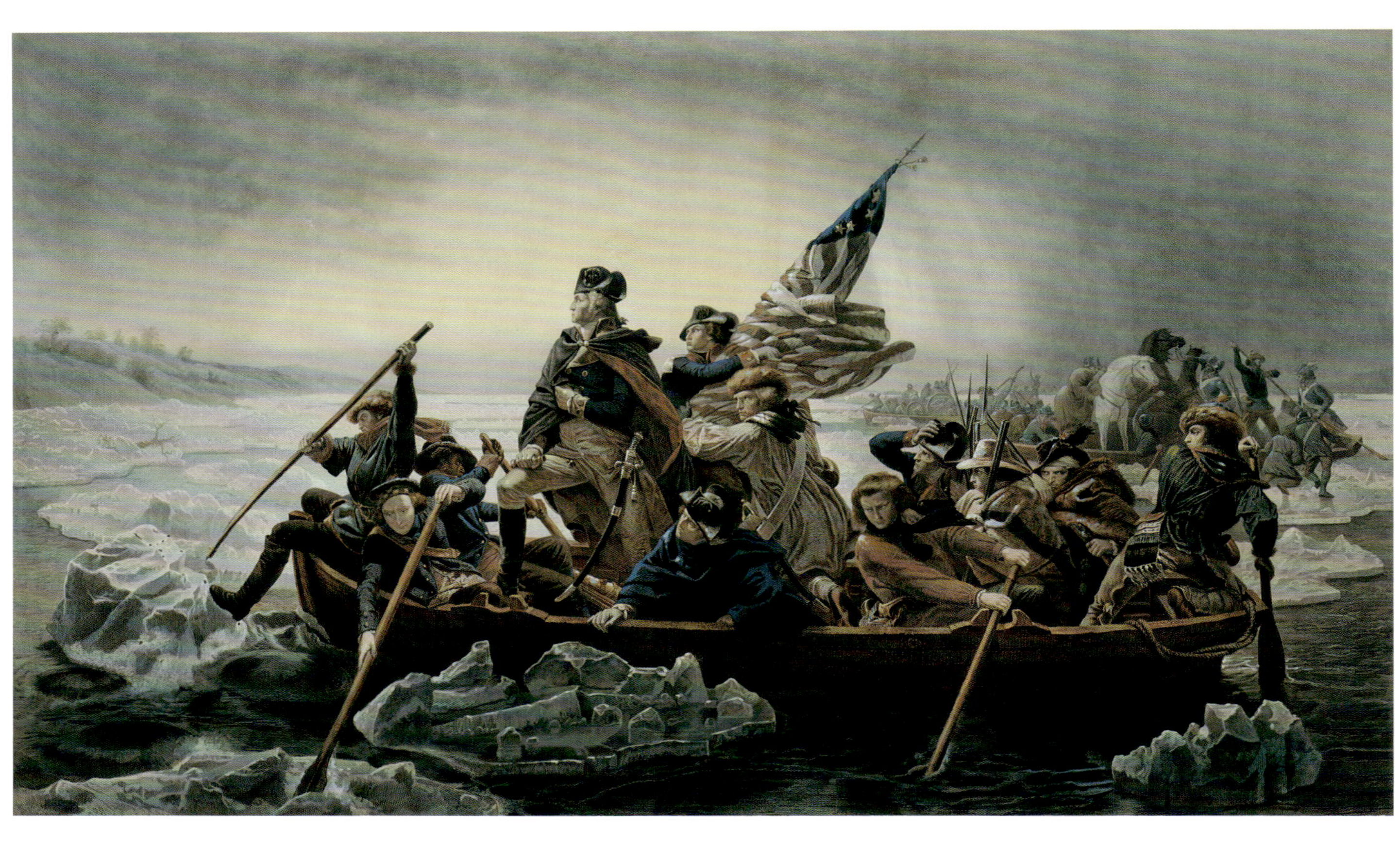

CHAPTER TWO

Taking Command
George Washington the General
1775–1783

WAR WAS ON THE LIPS OF MANY when the Second Continental Congress convened in Philadelphia on May 10, 1775. Word of the deadly altercation at Lexington and Concord between the British troops and the American patriots had traveled quickly, and George Washington attempted to sort through the myriad reports coming his way. He wrote to his longtime friend George William Fairfax, who had already returned to England, of the pending war. This was, perhaps, an attempt to ensure that Fairfax and his peers had a balanced view of the events in Massachusetts. Washington suggested that the events in Concord might convince the crown "that the Americans will fight for their Liberties and property," and he indicated that "unhappy it is though to reflect, that a Brother's Sword has been sheathed in a Brother's breast . . . the once happy and peaceful plains of America are either to be drenched with Blood, or Inhabited by Slaves. Sad alternative! But can a virtuous Man hesitate in his choice?"[1] Washington regrettably saw no alternative to bloody conflict, and many others shared his opinion.

Although the Continental Congress had not yet voted for an army, Washington quietly lobbied for the position of commander in chief. Conscious of the signals provided by outward appearances, he attended sessions of the congress in military uniform. His uniform was likely the blue and buff set of regimentals made for his service in the Fairfax Independent Company and could not have been overlooked in the sea of browns and grays worn by the other delegates.[2] Nor could the fact that Washington was the only man in the room with military experience. As John Adams noted, "Colonel Washington appeared every day in his uniform, and by his great experience and abilities in military matters, was of much service to all."[3] Although he would later protest that he did not feel up to the task, Washington's physical appearance and advance purchases of new pistol holders, a military uniform sash, and five "Military Books"[4] suggest he was preparing for the job despite any outward reservations.

Washington was unanimously elected commander in chief of the new Continental Army on June 15, 1775. He accepted the appointment on June 16:

> *I feel great distress from a consciousness that my abilities & Military experience may not be equal to the extensive & important Trust: However, as the Congress desire it I will enter upon the momentous duty, & exert every power I Possess In their service & for the Support of the glorious Cause. . . . I beg it may be remembered by every Gent[lema]n in the room, that I this day declare with the utmost sincerity, I do not think my self equal to the Command I am honored with.*[5]

Washington had accepted his command with a dose of eighteenth-century deference and modesty that was perhaps expected, yet his remarks were also likely an attempt to exonerate him from blame if any military maneuver should fail.

Voicing sadness at the prospect of being separated from Martha and Mount Vernon as well as his concern that the task was beyond him, Washington wrote to his wife, whom he affectionately called "Patcy."

opposite: George Washington led his troops across icy waters for a surprise attack and defeat of British and Hessian troops at Trenton. *Washington Crossing the Delaware,* engraved by Paul Girardet after Emanuel Leutze's painting, published by Goupil & Co., 1853, Willard-Budd Collection, MVLA

You may believe me my dear Patcy, when I assure you, in the most solemn manner, that, so far from seeking this appointment I have used every endeavour in my power to avoid it, not only from my unwillingness to part with you and the Family, but from a consciousness of its being a trust too great for my Capacity and that I should enjoy more real happiness and felicity in one month with you, at home, than I have the most distant prospect of reaping abroad, if my stay was to be Seven times Seven years. But, as it has been a kind of destiny that has thrown me upon this Service, I shall hope that my undertaking of it, is design[e]d to answer some good purpose. . . . it was utterly out of my power to refuse this appointment without exposing my Character to such censures as would have reflected dishonour upon myself, and given pain to my friends. . . . I shall rely therefore, confidently, on that Providence which has heretofore preserv[e]d & been bountiful to me, not doubting but that I shall return safe to you in the fall.[6]

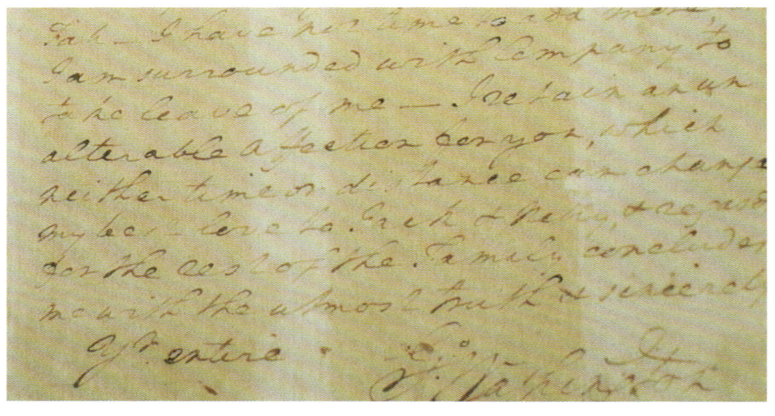
Sail— I have not time to add more, as I am surrounded with Company to take leave of me— I retain an unalterable affection for you, which neither time or distance can change my best love to Jack & Nelly, & regard for the rest of the Family conclude me with the utmost truth & sincerety Y[r] entire Go Washington

Fig. 1. On June 23, 1775, shortly before he left to take command of the Continental forces, George Washington wrote a letter to "My dearest," noting "unalterable affection" for his wife, Martha, MVLA

In the event he did not return safely, Washington enclosed a copy of his will.[7] Three days later, he began to equip himself with those articles necessary for the campaign ahead.

Declining any salary for his services, Washington asked only that his expenses be paid, which he knew would be considerable. His service during the French and Indian War acquainted him with the manner in which English gentlemen went to war, and he knew that that model needed to be followed in his own army. Washington understood the necessity of portraying his position, and that of the United Colonies, in an appropriate material fashion. To an observer, his Continental Army would have to appear as solidly professional as his English counterparts. Throughout the war, therefore, he kept in close correspondence with his quartermasters to place orders for items that would distinguish him as commander in chief and lend credibility to the colonies and the cause he represented.

Washington knew the British and European precedents for the objects associated with a commander's table and residences that bespoke gentility, even when encamped, or "under canvas," as it was called,[8] and made every attempt to equip himself in a manner that was in keeping with those models. Washington's orders for his table included an extensive array of ceramics, glass, silver, and linens. As one scholar has noted, "There was no lack of attention . . . to the appointments for the commander's table."[9]

Washington's expense records begin in Philadelphia in June 1775. Preparing to journey to Cambridge, Massachusetts, where he would join his troops, he sent his "Chariot & Horses back to Virginia" and purchased five horses as well as "a light Phaeton." For the phaeton (a light, four-wheeled, open carriage), he bought a double harness with brass ornaments from William Todd, as well as a host of items from the saddlers Christopher Binks, Elias Botner, and William Forbes.[10] Binks advertised that his saddlery was of "the neatest manner" and could be "supplied at the shortest notice, and on the most reasonable terms,"

Fig. 2. George Washington's trunk "No. 3" was one of many used to transport his belongings and papers during the Revolutionary War, MVLA

while Botner asserted that his leather goods were "made in the newest and neatest fashion," all of which was no doubt pleasing to Washington. With these items in hand, General Washington headed to Massachusetts, where the war was already under way.

When the Battle of Bunker Hill diminished any hope of a negotiated settlement, Washington focused on training troops and preparing for the months of war ahead. His purchase records for this time clearly demonstrate Washington's continuing effort to present himself as both a cultivated gentleman and a formidable military commander through his own clothing, the furnishings of his office and living quarters, and the garments of his servants. He turned to the partnership of William Vans and Nicholas Sparhawk of Salem for goods to supply the headquarters at Cambridge. A list of items shipped July 7, 1775, included thirty-four gallons of "West India Rum," a barrel of sugar, one box of lemons, a barrel of "old Spirits," and "12 doz. Lisbon wine." To these ingredients for punch Washington added four large tablecloths, eight "fine Napkins," four cases of knives and forks, and twelve silver spoons.[11] Washington relied again on Vans the following month to secure sundries including tea and a cask of Madeira. He purchased Madeira frequently throughout the war, and his repeated orders for tea wares indicate that both beverages were regularly consumed at the commander in chief's table. They spoke of a level of refinement that Washington no doubt recognized was necessary to provide the measure of gentility expected of his position.[12]

Washington established his first winter quarters at Cambridge, Massachusetts, outside Boston (fig. 3). As she did each winter during the war, Martha Washington traveled to be with her husband. Her son, John Parke Custis, and his wife, Eleanor Calvert, also joined the Washingtons in the large and comfortable house on Brattle Street that served as the commander in chief's headquarters. Built in 1759, the dwelling included office space for Washington, a drawing room, and a dining room for the comfort of his family and the entertaining of his officers and guests.[13] Accounts for the winter note the receipt of an assortment of white salt-glaze stoneware,[14] and entertaining differed little from the customary arrangements at Mount Vernon, with the exception that card playing and dancing were deemed unsuitable wartime amusements.[15]

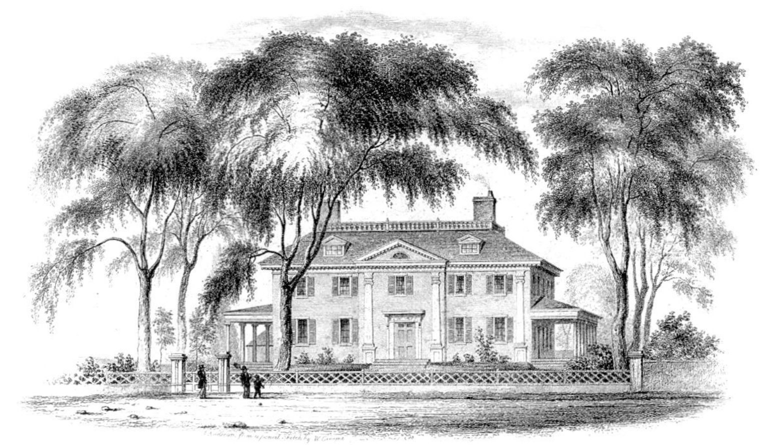

Fig. 3. George Washington's headquarters on Brattle Street in Cambridge, Massachusetts, MVLA

In February and March 1776 Washington prepared for his first full spring and summer of military campaigns. He wrote repeatedly from Cambridge to his military secretary in Philadelphia, Joseph Reed, for equipment needed for the road. He requested "a light traveling Waggon . . . with a secure cover, which might be under Lock and Key," and campaign furnishings that included eighteen camp stools, two folding tables, and "Plates & Dishes." Washington instructed Reed that when the articles were ready, he should "buy a pair of clever Horses, same color, hire a careful driver and let the whole come of at once," as Washington needed the items immediately. For reimbursement, Washington directed Reed to John Hancock for payment, as he had no doubt that "Congress must be sensible that I cannot take the field without Equipage."[16] The full list of items Washington requested as necessary field equipage is not known, but Reed's letters and several invoices survive to provide clues to the items amassed.

On March 15 Reed alerted Washington, "Most of your Camp Equipage will be completed this Week or the Beginning of next. . . . I hope when you see them they will prove agreeable. I have consulted

Oeconomy as much as I thought consistent with your Rank & Station. Most of our Workmen are such Strangers to these Things that they are very slow & tedious[,] two of the Tents are finished & the other just completed."[17] Reed had clearly done the best he could to supply Washington appropriately, despite the lack of experience American craftsmen had with fabricating military equipment. By the mid-eighteenth century, London craftsmen were well aware of what officers wanted to maintain comfort in the field. With the cessation of trade and denial of access to the imported goods from London, Reed was not able to buy tents and campaign furniture of the quality he might have wished, but he was able to outfit Washington to the best degree possible utilizing the talent he found in Philadelphia.

Reed turned to the upholsterer Plunket Fleeson to construct the tents that would serve as Washington's headquarters while in the field. Fleeson was an active member of the community and as early as 1769 had displayed his patriotic sentiments and salesmanship when he suggested that Philadelphians purchase his American-made wallpaper: "as there is a considerable duty imposed on paper hangings imported here, it cannot be doubted, but that every one among us, who wishes prosperity to America, will give a preference to our own manufacture."[18] By 1775 Fleeson was marketing gear to Americans ramping up for a conflict and advertised that he made and prepared "for sea or land, drums and colours, and other Military Instruments, of the most approved kinds."[19] Fleeson's high, patriotic standing in the Philadelphia community, as well as his specialty in military equipment, no doubt made him a favored choice for making Washington's camp equipage.

Fleeson's invoice records his construction of three tents for Washington—one noted as a chamber (or sleeping) tent, one "large Dining Marque," and one "large Baggage Tent." They were made of "red striped . . . Flanders ticken [ticking]," "Canvis for Skirting," and "guard lace" for trim. For the dining tent, Fleeson supplied eighteen walnut camp stools with wool moreen upholstery ornamented with brass nails and three walnut "Camp Tables." His inclusion of three packing cases for the tents and dining furnishings suggests that all the pieces could be easily disassembled for compact storage and efficient transportation.[20]

Other Philadelphians helped furnish Washington's camp table. The silversmith William Hollingshead sent "2 Cases Knives and forks, 2 Doz Camp cups, ½ Doz Coffee cups, [and] 2 half pint camp cups" from his shop located on the corner of Arch and Second streets.[21] Joseph Stanbury supplied glass saltcellars and vinegar cruets,[22] and Benjamin Harbeson supplied "1 Nest of Camp Kettles," tin canisters, a dozen "Oval tin Dishes" that were likely used for serving, and 45 tin plates.[23] All of these wares were relatively lightweight and would have served Washington well while in the field.

It is not clear if Washington used heavier ceramics and porcelains while under canvas; they may have graced his table only during his winter or more lengthy encampments, being stored when not in use. Those purchased that spring included an extensive assortment of ceramic tablewares with some noted as "Earthen" and others as "China," presumably a mixture of creamware and Chinese export porcelain. Besides dozens of varying sizes of earthenware plates, the specialized forms included pitchers, pudding dishes, sauceboats, jelly cups and saucers, a fruit basket, a mustard pot, and "fluted bowls." Chinese porcelain tea and dinnerwares included teapots, sugar dishes, milk pots, two sets of "large burnt china cups & saucers," a set of "large china" (a large set of china), and "2½ setts large china cups & saucers." Washington also purchased wineglasses, a pair of cut-glass salts, three fruit baskets, a "Japan sugar canister," and a variety of items for the bedchamber including chamber pots and water guglets.[24] Washington was certainly ready to entertain properly, and it is likely that these wares accompanied him and were in use until he placed another significant order of table ceramics three years later.

Fig. 4. George Washington's military equipment and tent furnishings, as exhibited in Mount Vernon's 1999 exhibition "Treasures of Mount Vernon"

In July 1776 Congress approved Richard Henry Lee's resolution, "That these United Colonies are, and

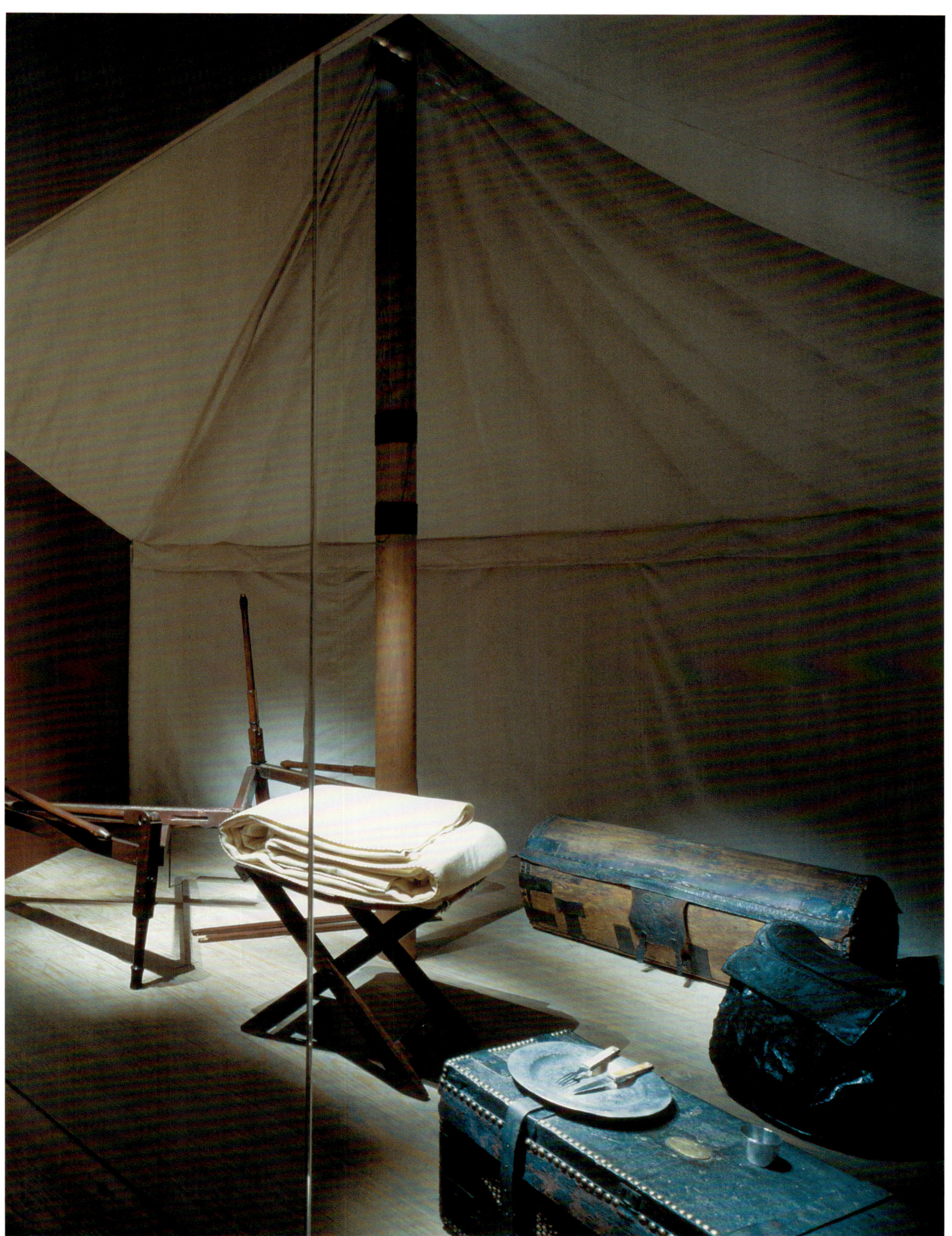

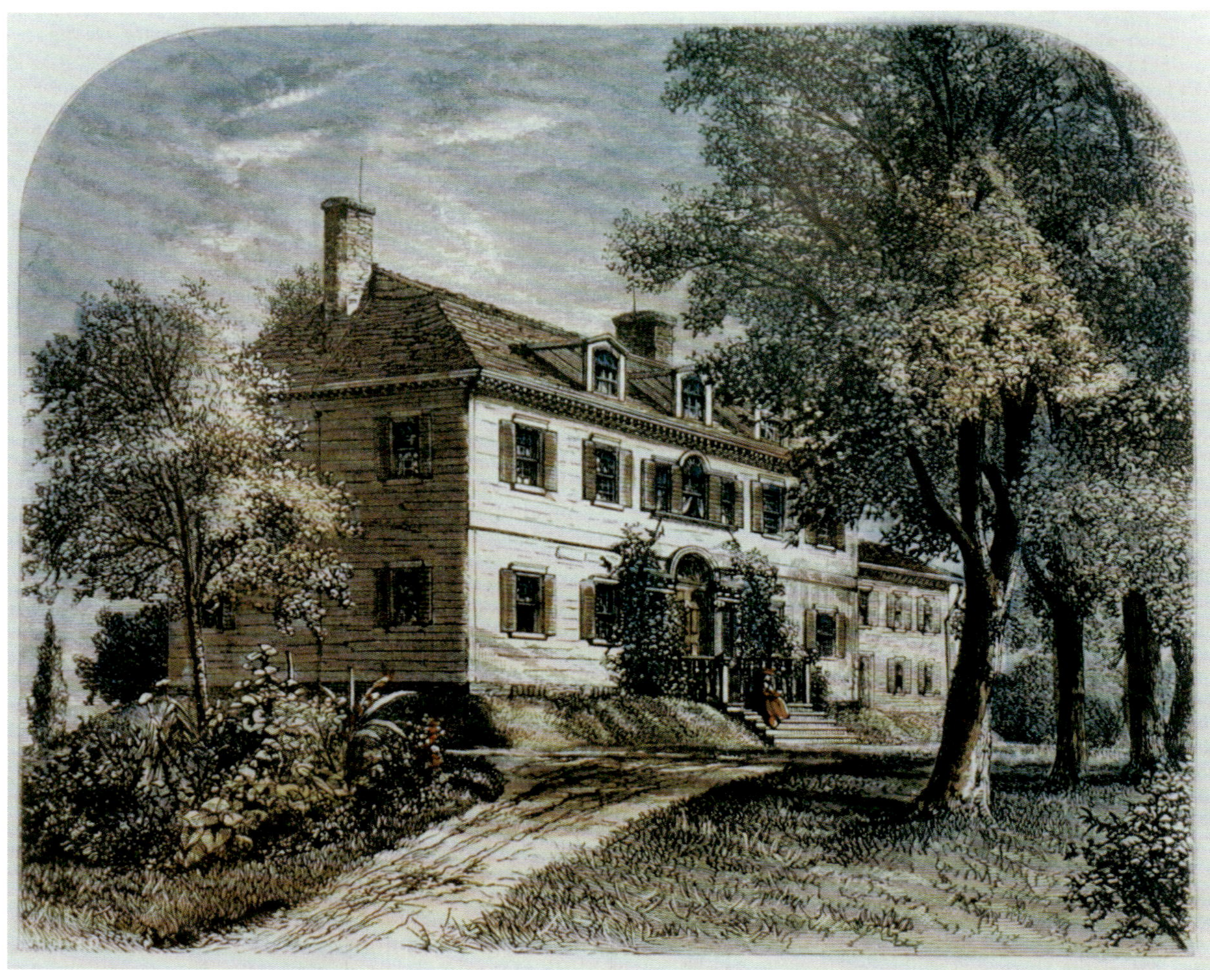

Fig. 5. George Washington's Headquarters at Morristown, New Jersey, engraver unknown, *Appleton's Journal,* vol. 12, no. 280 (August 1, 1874), Willard-Budd Collection, MVLA

of right ought to be, free and independent States, that they are absolved from all allegiance to the British Crown, and that all political connection between them and the State of Great Britain is, and ought to be, totally dissolved."[25] On July 4 the delegates officially adopted the Declaration of Independence, drafted by Jefferson and a select committee, and word traveled quickly to George Washington and his troops.

That summer, the English general Sir William Howe launched his campaign against New York and nearly won a decisive victory. Howe did not press his advantage, however, and Washington was able to withdraw his troops, and by November he had retreated through New Jersey and crossed the Delaware River into Pennsylvania. General Howe and his troops took to their winter quarters with some of the despised Hessian mercenaries posted at Trenton, New Jersey. In the December attack made even more famous by Emanuel Leutze's painting *Washington Crossing the Delaware,* Washington and his troops won a surprise attack on the Hessians followed by a victory a few days later at Princeton. These two successes were certainly needed by the Continental Army as both sides went into winter quarters—Washington's in Morristown, New Jersey (fig. 5).

During his Morristown encampment, Washington's correspondence provides not only a glimpse of those who surrounded him during the war besides his family and officers but also confirmation of Washington's desire to present himself as a proper gentleman and a commanding military leader. He wrote to Captain Caleb Gibbs in Philadelphia for assistance in procuring a housekeeper as well as a man with experience as a steward or "Butler in a Gentlemans Family." He also requested livery for his slave Will and servant John who attended the household and specified that the garments be in the Washington family colors, "lined with red Shalloon" with "a bit of red Cloth for capes, or Collars to them."[26] Even as Washington

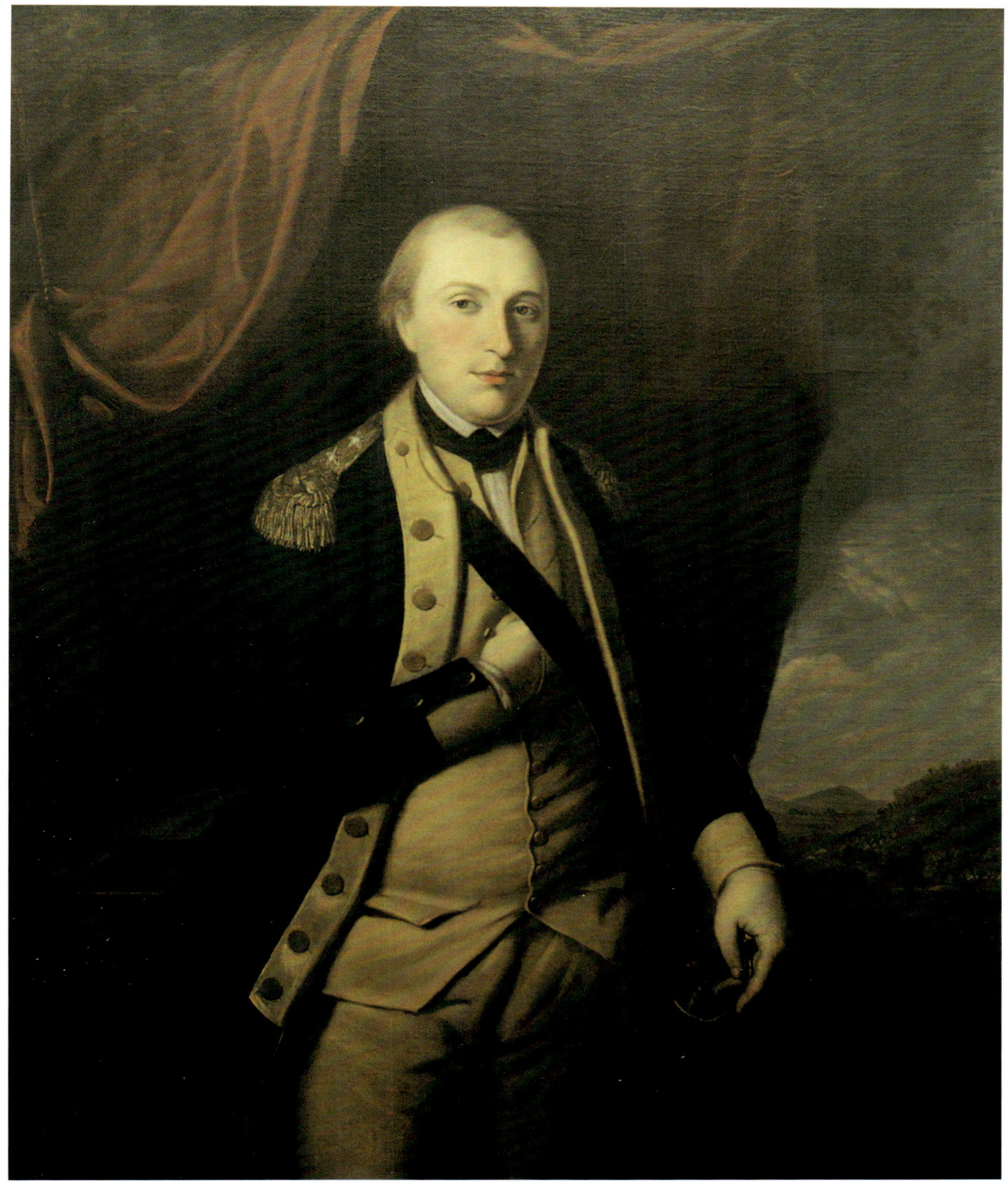

Fig. 6.
The introduction of French assistance brought the young Marquis de Lafayette, who served as General Washington's aide-de-camp. *Marquis de Lafayette*, 1779, by Charles Willson Peale, Washington-Custis-Lee Collection, Washington and Lee University, Lexington, Virginia

was providing staff for his headquarters and encampments to ensure operations would run smoothly and his guests would be properly cared for, he was drawing a distinction between his military role and that of a private gentleman. The servants and slaves were to be those requisite to a gentleman's household. To make the point clear to those admitted to Washington's quarters, the slaves were dressed in his family colors of red and white.

The conflicts of 1777 focused on the Brandywine and New York, which concluded with the surrender of General Burgoyne at Saratoga and the introduction of France's support for the colonies. With the city of Philadelphia occupied by the British, who made it their winter quarters, Washington settled his troops at Valley Forge, Pennsylvania, for what would become a famously trying winter of deprivation, hunger, and desertion. Although Washington and (for the most part) his generals lived outside the encampment that Benjamin Rush described as "dirty & stinking" full of "dirty & ragged" men, Washington's situation was not one of comfort and abundance.[27] After her arrival, Martha Washington described Washington's headquarters at the Isaac Potts House, a small two-story stone dwelling: "The General is in camped in what is called the great Valley on the Banks of the Schuykill officers and men are chiefly in Hutts, which they say is tolerable comfortable; the army are as healthy as can well be expected in general—the Generals apartment is very small he has had a log cabben built to dine in which has made our quarter much more tolerable then they were at first."[28]

The quartering at Valley Forge was no doubt softened by the presence of Mrs. Washington and other women, who provided a degree of normalcy and gentility. Their presence lifted the spirits of at least one Frenchman, Pierre Étienne Du Ponceau, an aide-de-camp of Baron von Steuben. Du Ponceau noted:

> *The situation of our Army, during the dismal winter that we spent at Valley-Forge, has been so often described. . . . Suffice it to say that we were in want of provisions, of clothes, of fodder for our horses, in short of everything. . . . In the midst of all our distress, there were some bright sides to the picture, which Valley-Forge exhibited at the time. Mrs. Washington had the courage to follow her husband in that dismal abode; other ladies also graced the scene. Among them, was the lady of General Greene, a handsome, elegant, and accomplished woman. Her dwelling was the resort of the foreign officers, because she understood, and spoke the French language, and was well versed in French literature. There were also Lady Stirling, the wife of Major General Lord Stirling; her daughter Lady Kitty Alexander . . . and her companion Miss Nancy Brown, then a distinguished belle. There was Mrs. Biddle, the wife of Colonel Clement Biddle. . . . They often met at each other's quarters, and sometimes at General Washington's, where the evening was spent in conversation, over a dish of tea or coffee. There were no levees or formal soirees; no dancing, card-playing, or amusement of any kind, except singing. . . . I soon learned the favorite English songs, and contributed my share to the pleasures of the company. Thus the time passed, until the beginning of May, when the news of the French Alliance burst suddenly upon us.*[29]

The following year, Washington and his troops were quartered at Middlebrook, New Jersey, and the contrast between it and Valley Forge could not have been more striking. Celebrations of the one-year anniversary of the French alliance were marked by a ball hosted by General Henry Knox, where people danced all night.[30] Washington, always pursuing the model of a cultivated gentleman and general, wrote from Middlebrook to his deputy quartermaster general, John Mitchell, in Philadelphia, complaining:

> *My Plates and Dishes, once of Tinn, now little better than rusty iron, are rather too much worn for delicate stomachs in fixed and peacable quarters, tho they may yet serve in the busy and active movements of a Campaign. I therefore desire that you will send me a sett of Queens China if to be had; not less I conceive, than what follows of each article will do—*
>
> *2 large Turennes*
> *3 dozn. Dishes, sized*
> *8 dozn. Shallow Plates*
> *3 dozn. Soup Ditto*
> *8 Table drinking Mugs*
> *8 Ditto Salts. And some pickle plates*
>
> *The whole to be very carefully packed. I also desire you will send me Six tolerably genteel but not expensive Candlesticks all of a kind and three pair of Snuffers to them.*

Washington also wanted to know "how many Table Cloths you sent to me at different times and by whom. No more than Seven ever came to my hands."[31] Although Mitchell initially told Washington that he would not be able to procure the creamware, he was eventually able to do so despite the inflated wartime prices of English imports.[32]

Perhaps dining from the creamware, one dinner guest noted on February 26, 1779, "The table was elegantly furnished, and the provisions ample, but not abounding in superfluities. . . . In conversation, his excellency's expressive countenance is peculiarly interesting and pleasing; a placid smile is frequently observed on his lips, but a loud laugh, it is said, seldom, if ever escapes him. He is polite and attentive to each individual at table, and retires after the compliments of a few glasses."[33] With the sounding of thirteen cannons, Monsieur Gérard, the French minister, and Don Juan Marailles, of Spain, arrived at the camp at Middlebrook.[34] For their benefit, a review of the army was presented, and James Thacher recorded the scene in his military journal:

> *The whole of our army in this quarter was paraded in martial array in a spacious field, and a stage was erected for the accommodation of the ladies and gentlemen spectators. At the signal of thirteen cannon, the great and splendid cavalcade approached in martial pomp and style. . . . Having arrived on the field of parade, the Commander in Chief, with the foreign ministers, and general officers, passed in front of the line of the army. . . and took seats with Mrs. Washington, Mrs. Green[e], Mrs. Knox, and a number of other ladies who had arrived in their carriages. The army then performed the field manoeuvres and evolutions, with firing of cannon and musketry.*[35]

At Middlebrook, Washington also received Native Americans in a similar fashion. Thacher's brigade "paraded for the purpose of being reviewed by General Washington and a number of Indian chiefs. . . . His Excellency, with his usual dignity, followed by his mulatto servant Bill, riding a beautiful grey steed." Washington deemed "it good policy to pay some attention to this tribe of the wilderness, and to convince them of the strength and discipline of our army, that they may be encouraged, if disposed to be friendly, or deterred from aggression, if they should become hostile to our country."[36] Washington was clearly aware of the need to maintain appearances and order for a broad audience, and Thacher's descriptions of camp at Middlebrook offer a portrait of his success in this arena.

For the summer of 1779, Washington was encamped at West Point, New York. He established his headquarters in a house that was built before 1749 by John Moore, a prominent New York merchant. It must have been a substantial dwelling, for it was called Moore's Folly and noted on maps as such.[37] Although thirty years old by the time it served as Washington's headquarters, the house was likely still in good shape and appropriate for a general. Writing to apprise two ladies of the conditions they would encounter when joining him for dinner in August 1779, Washington noted:

> *Since our arrival at this happy spot, we have had a Ham (sometimes a shoulder) or Bacon, to grace the head of the table; a piece of roast Beef adorns the foot; and, a small dish of Greens or Beans (almost imperceptible) decorates the center. When the cook has a mind to cut a figure . . . we have two Beefstake-Pyes, or dishes of Crabs in addition, one on each side the center dish. . . . Of late, he has had the surprising luck to discover that apples will make pyes; and it's a question if, amidst the violence of his efforts, we do not get one of apples instead of having both of Beef. If the ladies can put up with such entertainment, and will submit to partake of it on plates once tin but now Iron; (not become so by the labor of Scowering) I shall be happy to see them.*[38]

Fig. 7.
For his camp table, George Washington ordered silver spoons engraved with the Washington family griffin from the Philadelphia silversmith Richard Humphreys. MVLA

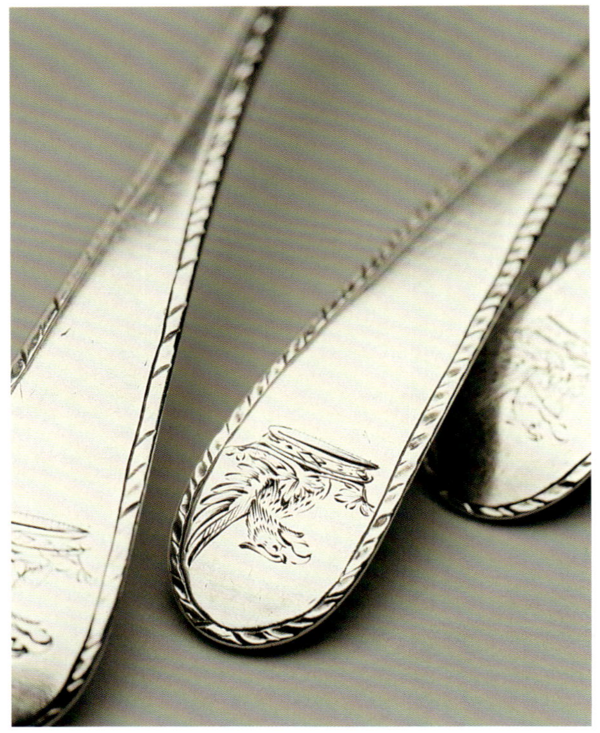

Washington's description of the tin plates was probably an exaggeration, unless he did not have with him the costly set of creamware he had purchased for wartime entertaining earlier that year.

Also while Washington was at West Point, the Frenchman Louis-Philippe, Comte de Ségur, visited the camp and noted: "At his table thirty people sat everyday. These meals, according to the English and American custom lasted several hours and ended with many toasts, most of them to the independence of the United States, to the King and Queen of France [and] the success of the allied armies. . . . Almost always when the table had been cleared and only cheese and bottles were left upon the table, the reunion went on into the night."[39] Another French officer, François Marbois, described the meal he had on arriving at Washington's West Point headquarters on September 12, 1779:

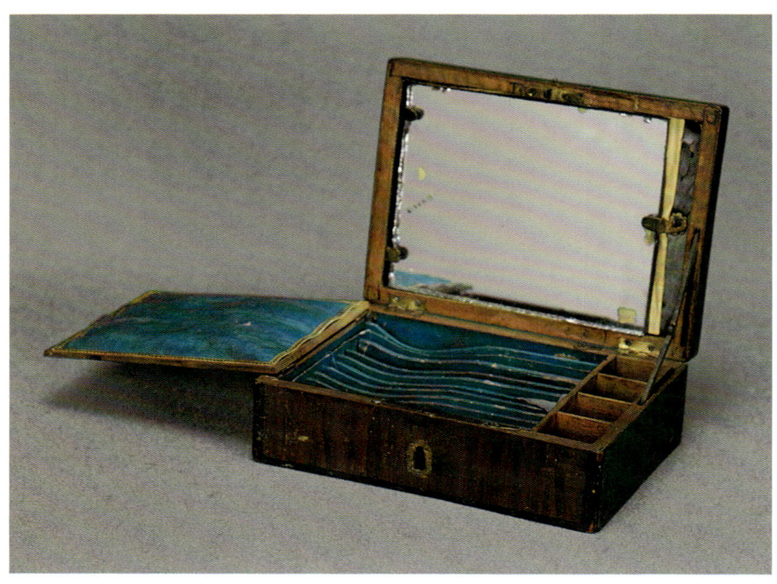

Fig. 8.
George Washington's portable shaving "case for razors," supposedly the one used by him during the Revolutionary War and possibly the one he asked for in January 1781, MVLA

During dinner the conversation touched on the great things which the Americans had done. All the generals and the higher officers were there. It was interesting to see this meeting of these warriors, each of them a patriot renowned for some exploit, and this military meal, served in a tent in the midst of the apparatus of arms, in the heart of the former possessions of our enemies, to a French minister and officers, was to all of us a memorable novelty. . . . The river was being driven back by the tide, and the waves came right up to the tent-pins, where they broke with a solemn roar. A few steps away from us musicians played military and tuneful French airs. The banks and the forests of the mountain answered long to the cannon shots fired to the health of the King and Queen [of France], and the opposite bank shone with the fires which the soldiers had lighted.[40]

Washington was essentially conducting diplomacy and holding state dinners while on the road. From the descriptions of these French officers, his attention to the details of these entertainments had their intended effect.

In January 1781 George Washington made preparations from his winter quarters in New Windsor, New York, for what would be the last season of conflict in the war. Among the items he would need for traveling, the general requested Colonel Laurens to bring him several things, including "A traveling Razor case with every thing compleat; to be strong, portable, and compendius" (fig. 8), as well as "A vest pocket reconnoiterer, or Telescope. A very small case of pocket Instruments containing a Scale, dividers &ca." and

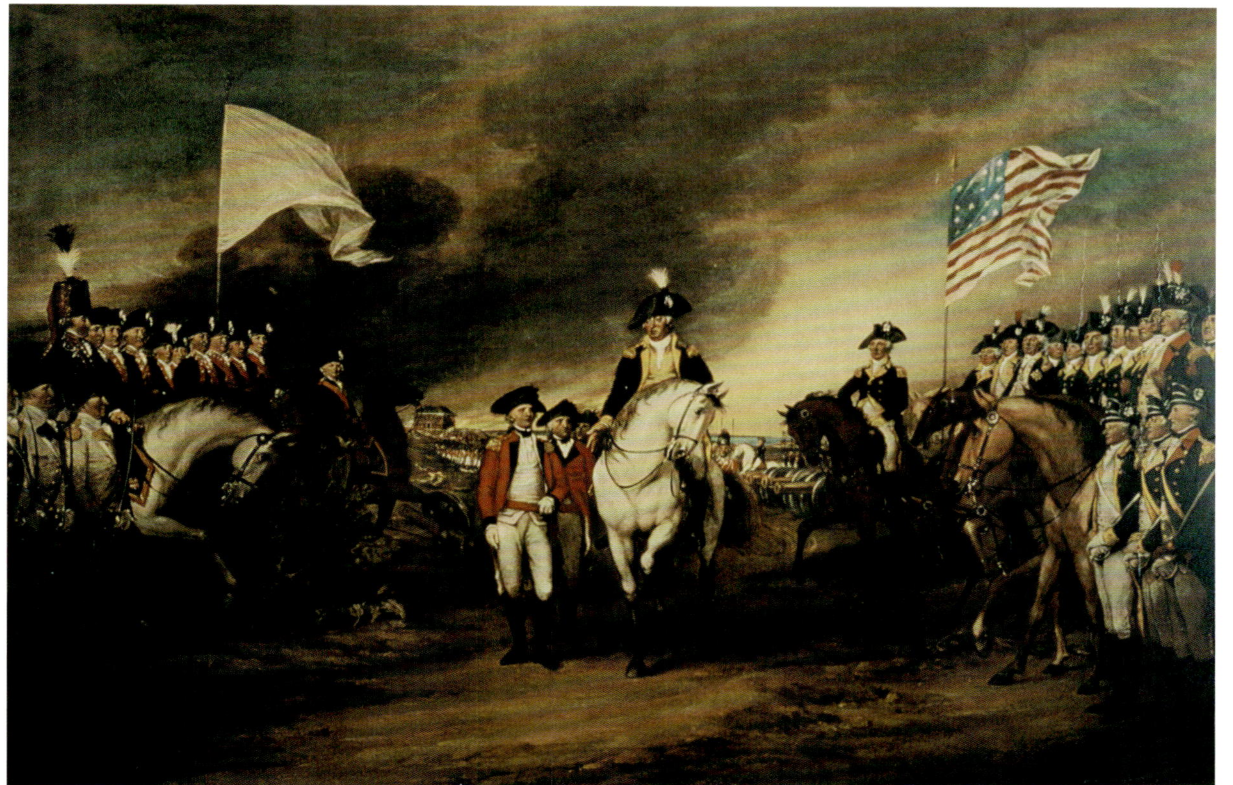

Fig. 9. British General Cornwallis surrendered to George Washington at Yorktown, Virginia in 1781. *Cornwallis Surrender at Yorktown [October 19, 1781]*, engraver unknown after John Trumbull, unknown date. Willard-Budd Collection, MVLA

"A good Sadle, bridle and furniture (excluding Pistols) fit for a republican General." For entertaining, the general requested "2 Dozn. Dishes sized 4 dozn. Soup and 8 dozn. Shallow Plates of Tin or something very light for the Field."[41] A few short months later, Washington rode southward to his homeland of Virginia. General Cornwallis had marched his army to Virginia, and the American and French forces prepared to unite against him. Although desperate to attack the British at New York, Washington succumbed to the Comte de Rochambeau's urging and agreed to strike at Yorktown, Virginia. The decision was to have lasting consequences, as he joined with Lafayette's and Comte de Grasse's troops there. By October 17 Cornwallis asked for terms of surrender, and although it did not appear clear to Washington at the time, the war was essentially over.

John Parke Custis joined him during the siege of Yorktown. There he contracted camp fever and became so ill that his mother, wife, and oldest daughter rushed to his side. He died on November 5, 1781. Martha Washington had now lost both her children, and grief consumed her. She continued, however, to travel to her husband's encampments and to serve as hostess to his military family as the final movements of the war played out.

In July 1782 Washington was encamped at Newburgh, New York. Perhaps with the knowledge that he would soon be receiving a string of foreign visitors, Washington was eager to entertain with his set of creamware in a style appropriate to his station. He wrote to Deputy Quartermaster Colonel Samuel Miles in July complaining that he had expected tureens, salad dishes, plates, soup plates, and salts but had received instead an odd assortment and fewer pieces.[42] Still awaiting his creamware, Washington again wrote to Miles in August, enclosing a duplicate of his previous letter, "as I have neither received the Articles ordered, nor an acknowledgement of my Letter. . . . I have requested the Secretary at War to let one of the Gentlemen in his Office put this into your own hands."[43] With that type of delivery, Miles quickly received the letter, and he responded immediately, saying that he had been out of town for more than six weeks owing to poor health. Miles offered Washington his apologies, noting:

Fig. 10. George Washington's headquarters at Newburgh, New York, RP-47, 3273, MVLA

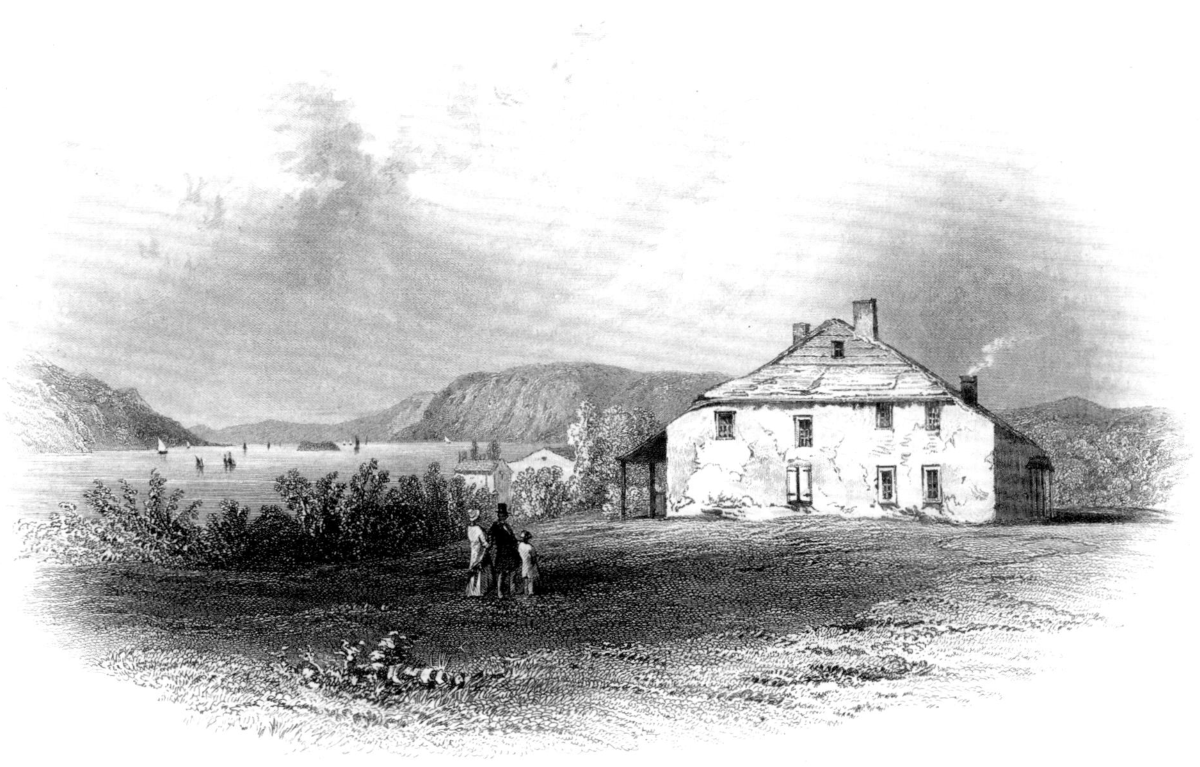

> *I am exceedingly sorry that there was any mistake respecting your Crockery ware, & must take, at least part of the blame to myself. . . . I did not send for them till some days after your Excellency left the City . . . and did not compare them with the invoice, but ordered them to be packed ready for transportation, whenever they should be called for. . . . On receipt of your Excellencies letter, inquiry was immediately made respecting the deficiency, and it appeared that Don Francino had an entertainment a day or two after you left the City & that his Stewart had made use of these dishes, plates &c and had also lent part of them to the Minister of France's Stewart. They are, however, I am informed, all returned and forwarded except one dozn. Plates.*[44]

George Washington did not write again to Miles, presumably because the general received his creamware shortly thereafter but was none too pleased.

In March 1783 Washington received unofficial news at his Newburgh headquarters that the peace treaty ending the war had been signed. While awaiting official word, he continued to host a great number of visitors. One of them, George Bennet of Jamaica, shared a meal with the Washingtons and about fifteen officers. He later recalled, "The dinner was good, but everything was quite plain. We all sat on camp-stools and there was nothing to be seen about the house but what any officer in the army might likewise have in his. Mrs. W., was as plain, easy and affable as he was, and one would have thought from the familiarity which prevailed here, that he saw a respectable private gentleman dining at the head of his own family."[45] Indeed, the officers with whom Washington had shared meals during the war had become very much his family. And, even at the end of the war, Washington was maintaining those appearances of hospitality and refinement that he deemed so necessary.

Official news of the peace treaty, signed in Paris on September 3, reached Washington and his army on November 1, 1783. Shortly thereafter he delivered the joyous news that all troops "shall be considered as discharged from the service of the United States."[46] After a pause in New York, where he bade farewell

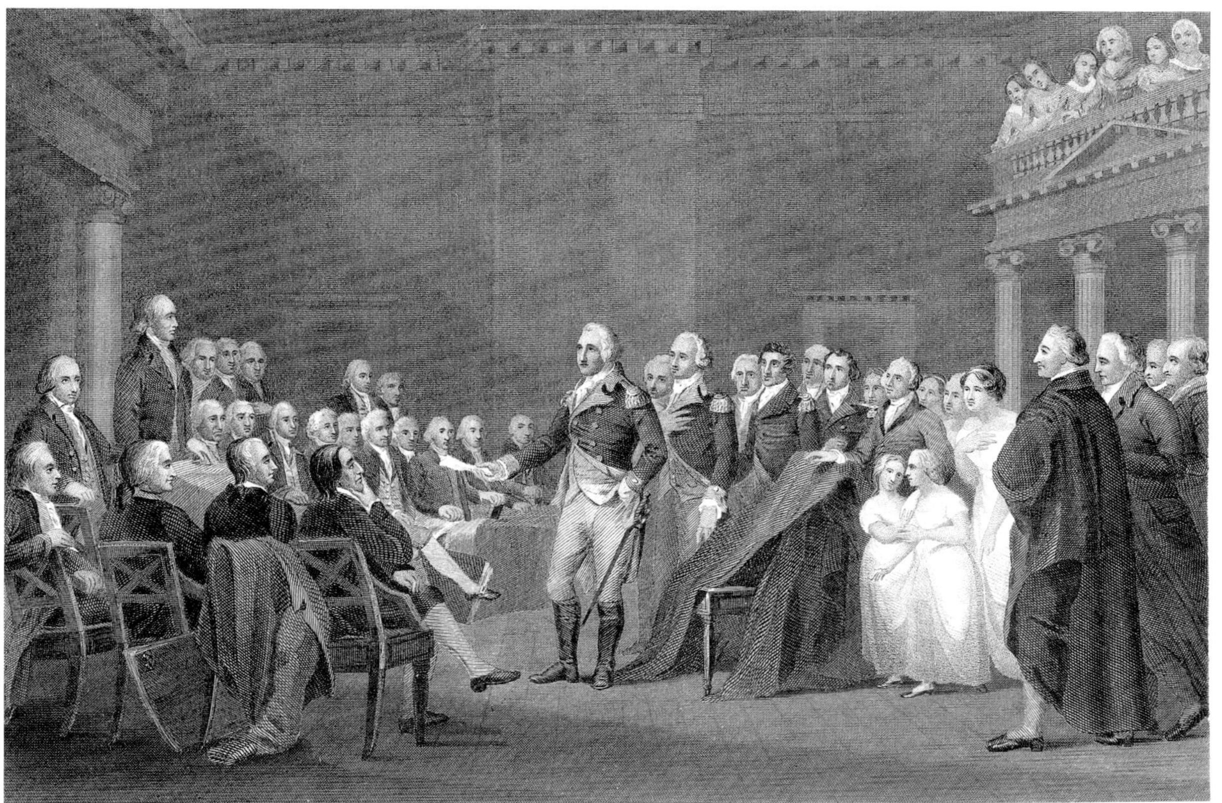

Fig. 11.
In 1783 George Washington resigned his military commission as commander in chief to the civil authority of Congress at the Annapolis State House. RP-751, Print 4994, MVLA

to his officers at Samuel Fraunces's tavern, Washington rode to Annapolis, Maryland, where Congress was convened. On December 23, 1783, George Washington resigned his commission before Congress, declaring himself "Happy in the confirmation of our Independence and Sovereignty, and pleased with the oppertunity afforded the United States of becoming a respectable Nation, I resign with satisfaction the Appointment I accepted with diffidence. . . . Having now finished the work assigned me, I retire from the great theatre of Action."[47] The war was at last concluded, and Washington rode directly to Mount Vernon for his first Christmas at home in eight long and trying years.

CAT. 15

Field Bed

England or America, ca. 1770–1780
Beech, iron, and brass, H. 48", W. 72", D. 35¼" (open)
Gift of Miss Birdie Washington in memory of her mother, Mrs. N. D. B. Washington, 1921[48]
W-473

George Washington, like his English officer counterparts, enjoyed the benefits of campaign furniture while in the field. Campaign furniture was similar to its household equivalents, with the exception that it could be easily assembled, disassembled, stored in traveling cases, and moved around with a certain degree of ease. The furnishings not only offered the comforts of home, but they assisted with preserving rank and distinction.[49] Serving a basic need of any officer, the field bed (or tent bed) was a crucial component of any assemblage of campaign furniture.

English cabinetmakers produced field beds from the early part of the eighteenth century, and prominent furniture makers such as Thomas Chippendale, George Hepplewhite, and Thomas Sheraton were well aware of the officer's demand to be outfitted properly during military campaigns. As Sheraton noted, "In encampments, persons of the highest distinction are obliged to accommodate themselves to such temporary circumstances, which encampments are ever subject to. Hence every article of an absolutely necessary kind, must be made very portable, both for package, and that such utensils should not retard rapid movement, either after or from the enemy. The articles of cabinet work used in such services, are therefore, each of them required to be folded in the most compact manner that can be devised; yet this is to be done in such a way as that when they are opened out, they will answer their intended purpose."[50]

Furniture makers met the need for high-quality campaign furniture with designs that were published along with their domestic furniture.[51] Suggested designs for elegant, canopied field beds appeared in Chippendale's 1762 *Gentleman and Cabinet-Makers Director* and, when fully dressed, would have appeared as elegant as those in elite interiors of the period.[52] Although similar in overall appearance to beds for domestic use, Chippendale noted that the hangings and other "Furniture of . . . these Bedsteads is made to take off, and the laths are hung with Hinges, for the convenience of folding up."[53]

In October 1775, shortly after assuming command of the Continental Army, George Washington secured "a Field Bedstead & Curtains, Mattresses, Blankets etc. etc." for the sum of twenty-two English pounds.[54] The expense was considerable, and no doubt much of it was for the costly imported hangings and bedding. With its purchase, however, Washington was following the established mode of English gentility while at war and in the field.

This field bed is perhaps the one Washington purchased in 1775.[55] It represents eighteenth-century ingenuity in meeting the demands of portability and economical use of space. Folded into a small bundle, it could be easily dismantled and moved. The bedstead has four tapering posts, turned legs, and folding side rails. The iron hinges and hooks provide stability for the folding side rails, and a removable central rail (now missing) was mortised into the side rails for additional support to the frame. The rabbeted side rails retain nail hole evidence of the original sacking bottom that provided a foundation for the mattresses and bolsters. When assembled for use, curtains that provided privacy for sleeping hung from the tester (now missing) and the four tall posts. When placed in the sleeping tent supplied by Plunket Fleeson, this bedstead would have fulfilled the need for comfortable, portable, stylish furniture while in camp.

Following the Revolution, Washington returned to Mount Vernon and placed the majority of his wartime wares in storage. At the time of his death in 1799, it appears that the only items of campaign furniture still in use were half a dozen folding camp stools listed in the servant's hall. His estate inventory also notes eighteen trunks of varying sizes and form and four "Traveling Chests" in one of the third floor storage rooms in the Mansion. Additional trunks, pack saddles, leather canteens, old holsters with "fringed leather housings," and "2 bags and 2 leather valices cont[ainin]g Markee Tents, &c" are listed as present in the Mount Vernon storehouse.[56] This camp bed was likely among those objects in storage and may have been part of the items grouped in the storehouse with Washington's sleeping tent.

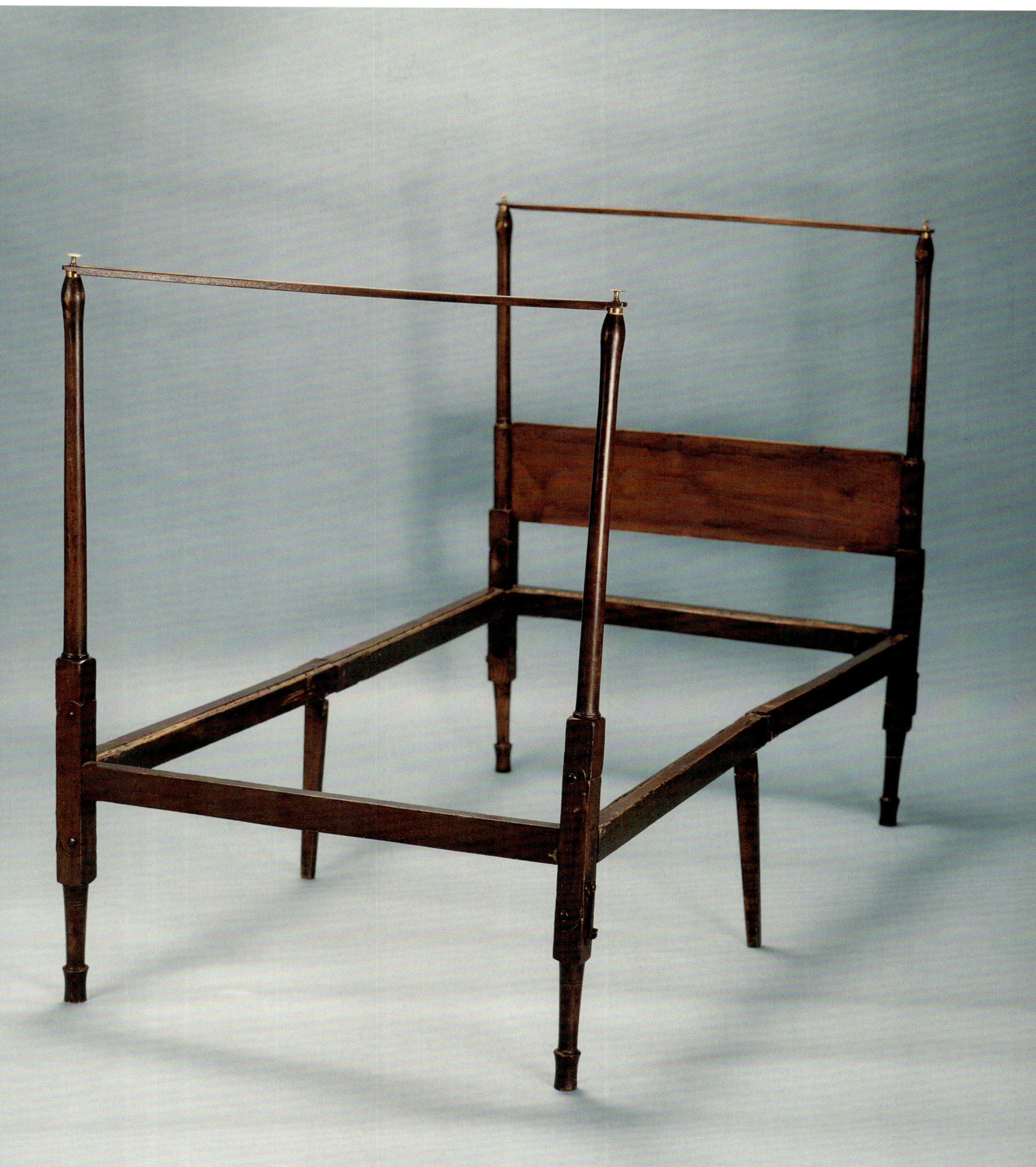

CAT. 16

Pistol Holders

England or America, ca. 1775–1785
Leather, linen, and wool, Holster L. 13¾", W. 4¾"; Housing L. 19", W. 10½"
Transferred to the Mount Vernon Ladies' Association through the generosity of John Augustine Washington, III, 1860
W-349/A&B

George Washington paid keen attention to the appearance of his horse furniture and repeatedly requested the best and most fashionable items. Pistol holders were part of that equipage, and Washington's correspondence contains frequent mention of repairs to and orders for them.[57] These examples consist of two parts: a leather holder and a fabric housing. The holder is made of heavy black leather, and its tubular shape with a flared top is designed to easily receive a pistol. The arrow-shaped fabric housing is made of linen and wool with a trim of one-inch-wide red-and-white cut velvet livery lace that follows the contour of the housing.[58]

It was important to Washington that his pistol holders were fashionable as well as suited to his saddle. His order in 1771 to the London factor Robert Cary and Company requested "Holsters, or Covers for a pair of Pistols (about 12 Inches long straight Measure, which I have by me) to fit the Saddle order'd in my last," with the specification that the holsters were "to be in the newest Taste & handsome."[59] It is not surprising, then, that while Washington was in Philadelphia in June 1775, waiting for the Second Continental Congress to appoint him commander in chief, he took the opportunity to have his pistol holders "covered," or upholstered. While it is impossible to determine if these holders were those Washington bought just before his appointment as commander in chief, Washington family tradition suggests that they were used by him during the Revolution.[60] His practice of using his Washington family colors of red and white throughout the war, seen in the red-and-white livery lace on these examples, certainly offers the possibility that they rested against his saddle while he commanded the Continental Army.

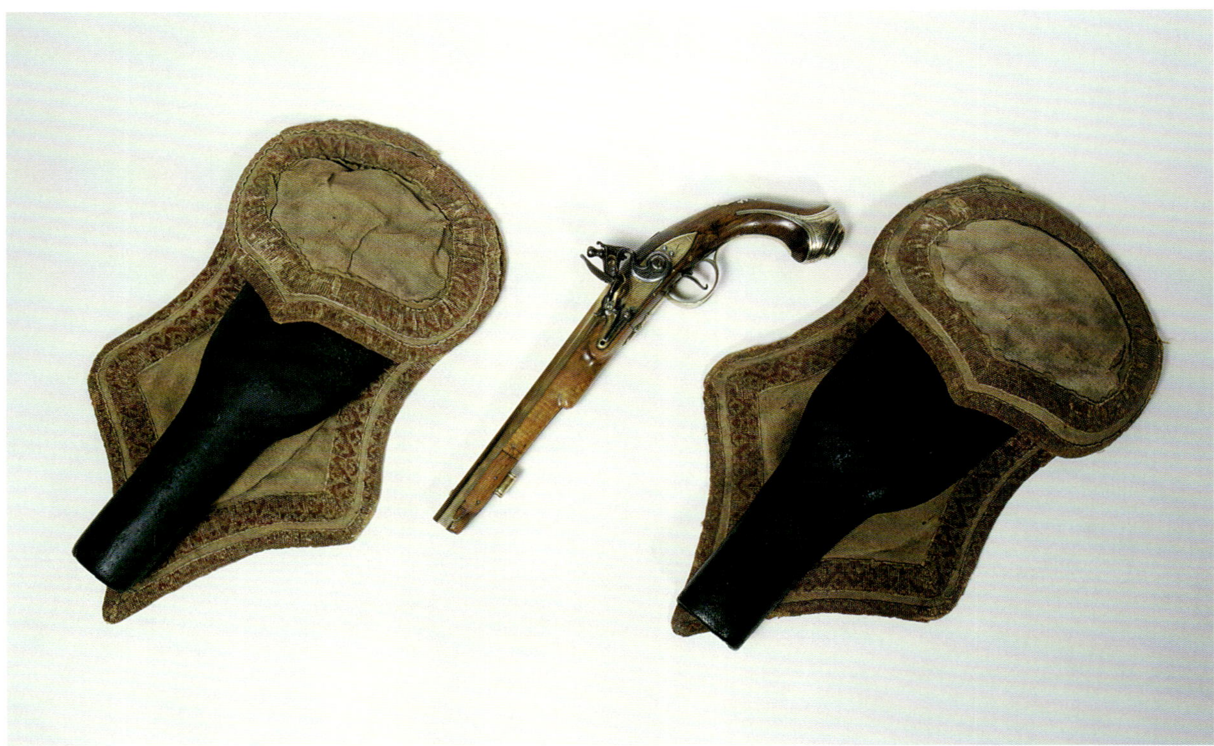

CAT. 17

Telescope

Henry O. Pyefinch (ca. 1739-1790)
London, England, ca. 1775
Mahogany and brass, L. 33" (closed 10½"), DIAM. 2¼"
Gift of Mrs. Jefferson Davis, 1899
W-644

Telescopes were crucial to George Washington's ability to monitor enemy troop movements and the battlefield landscape during the war. It is therefore not surprising that telescopes are frequently mentioned in his wartime correspondence, as Washington purchased, lent, and borrowed telescopes according to the need at hand.

In 1776 the New York legislature procured for Washington a telescope for which he was "extremely obliged" and hoped "to employ it for the Valuable purposes you designed It."[61] That telescope was probably larger than one of "Dolands best pocket Telescopes"[62] Washington requested in 1778, or the "vest pocket reconnoiterer"[63] he sought in 1781. All of the telescopes were no doubt of English manufacture, including the "pretty good one" Washington sent to Major General John Sullivan so that the general could communicate with him via signal fires.[64]

This example was made by Henry Pyefinch of London, whose shop was located at 67 Cornhill.[65] It opens into four mahogany sections defined by brass bands, and the brass sleeve at the viewing end is engraved "Pyefinch / Cornhill / London." The eye lens has a small shutter and the distant lens is protected by a screwed-on brass cover. In his will, Washington identified it as one of the telescopes he used during the Revolution. Washington left to "the acquaintances and friends of my Juvenile Years," Lawrence and Robert Washington, each "one of the Spy-glasses which constituted part of my equipage during the late War," indicating that he thought the telescopes would "be useful where they live."[66] This telescope is the example inherited by Lawrence Washington and through a series of bequests came into the possession of Jefferson Davis, president of the Confederacy. Following her husband's death in 1899, Mrs. Davis presented the telescope to Mount Vernon.

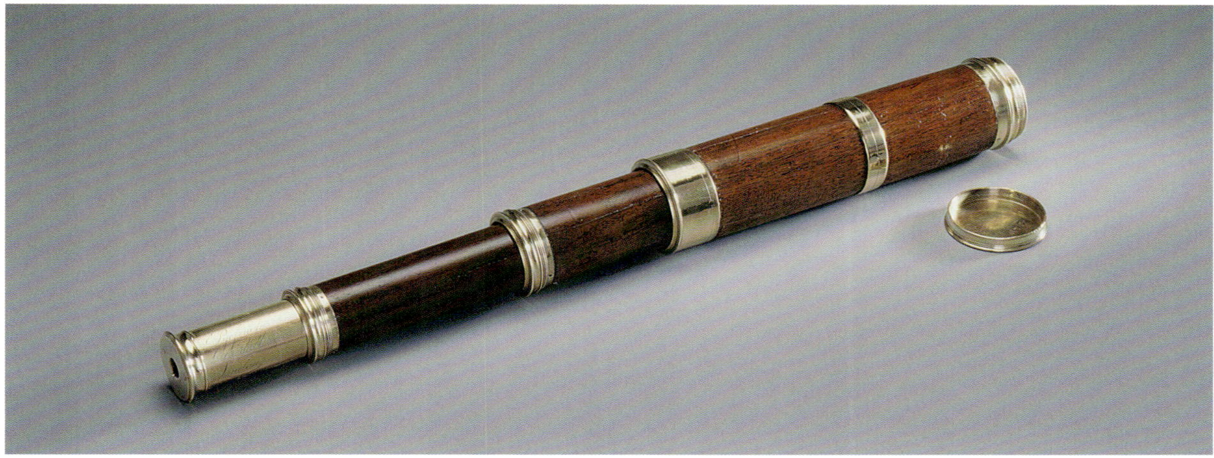

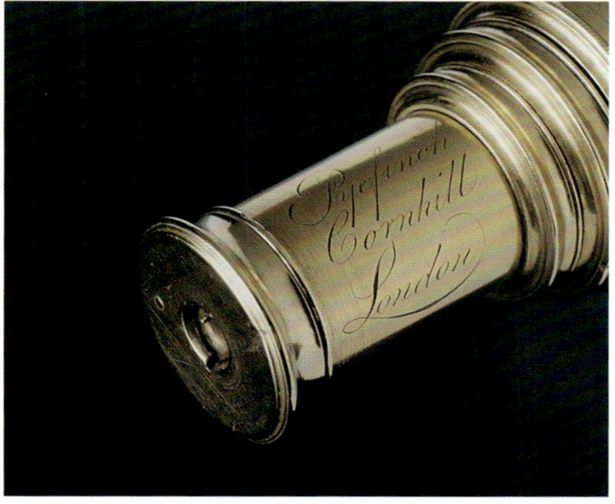

CAT. 18

George Washington (1732–1799)

1776

Charles Willson Peale (1741–1827)
Philadelphia, Pennsylvania
Watercolor on ivory, 1 11/16" x 1 3/8"
Purchase, 1920
W-460

Charles Willson Peale painted numerous large-scale portraits of George Washington, but in July 1776 his attention focused on a miniature in watercolor. Martha Washington commissioned the portrait of her husband, and Peale's diary for July 26 notes that he "began a miniature of Gen. Washington."[67] The general was unable to sit for the portrait, being at the front. Accordingly, Peale used as his model a three-quarter-length canvas of Washington that he had painted a few weeks earlier at the request of John Hancock.

The general is shown in his blue military uniform with buff-colored facings and waistcoat. The waistcoat differs from that in Peale's other portraits of Washington by the addition of the floral embroidery, although it is similar to the waistcoat in the miniature portrait of John Parke Custis the artist made four years earlier. Washington's shoulders were narrowed so that his gold-washed epaulettes could be seen, and the royal blue sash that identified him as commander in chief is raised so that it, too, could be included.

Peale completed the miniature portrait on August 4 and delivered it to Mrs. Washington.[68] Although she ventured each winter to George Washington's winter headquarters, the war years included lengthy periods of separation. This miniature, small enough to fit in the palm of her hand, must have provided comfort to Martha Washington during her husband's absence.

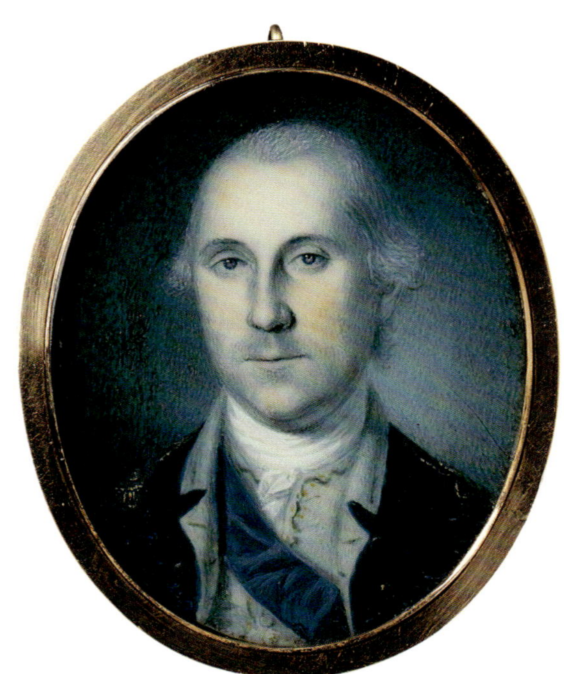

CAT. 19

George Washington after the Battle of Princeton

1780

Charles Willson Peale (1741–1827)
Philadelphia, Pennsylvania
Signed, dated, and inscribed lower right: CWPeale pinx:[t] 1780 at Phi:[a]
Oil on canvas, 51" x 39"
Bequest of Miss Jane J. Boudinot, 1925
H-17

Despite George Washington's triumphs at the battles of Trenton and Princeton and his army's success in clearing New England, New Jersey, and Pennsylvania of hostile forces, at the beginning of 1779 the outcome of the Revolutionary War remained uncertain. Nonetheless, these victories and the recent French alliance provided the Continental Congress and the nation with a new sense of confidence. When Washington was called by Congress to Philadelphia, the Supreme Executive Council of Pennsylvania (the governing body of that colony) commissioned Charles Willson Peale to paint a full-length portrait of Washington for its council chamber. Washington, who was first painted by Peale at Mount Vernon in 1772 and several times thereafter, sat for the portrait from January 20 to February 1, 1779. The resulting canvas, heavily imbued with symbolism, depicted the victorious general on the battlefield at Princeton, with the college's Nassau Hall in the background. The painting was an immediate success, and Peale was flooded with orders for replicas. Private citizens and foreign dignitaries alike requested copies of the canvas, as Europeans sought an image of the colonial general who had beaten the well-equipped and well-trained British forces. For the first time, American paintings crossed the Atlantic Ocean to hang in the residences of European nobility.[69]

This example was commissioned by Elias Boudinot of New Jersey, a statesman, friend, and fellow officer of Washington.[70] Boudinot's three-quarter-length version of the full-scale painting shows Washington in the foreground dressed in his buff and blue uniform complemented by the light blue sash identifying him as commander in chief. He stands at ease with his left hand resting on a cannon, with Princeton in the background. Known for his realism, Peale captured Washington's confident and serene calm that were among his notable battlefield qualities.

In 1889, the centennial of George Washington's inauguration in New York as the country's first president, the portrait was exhibited at the Metropolitan Opera House. It descended in the Boudinot family until its donation to the Mount Vernon Ladies' Association in 1925.

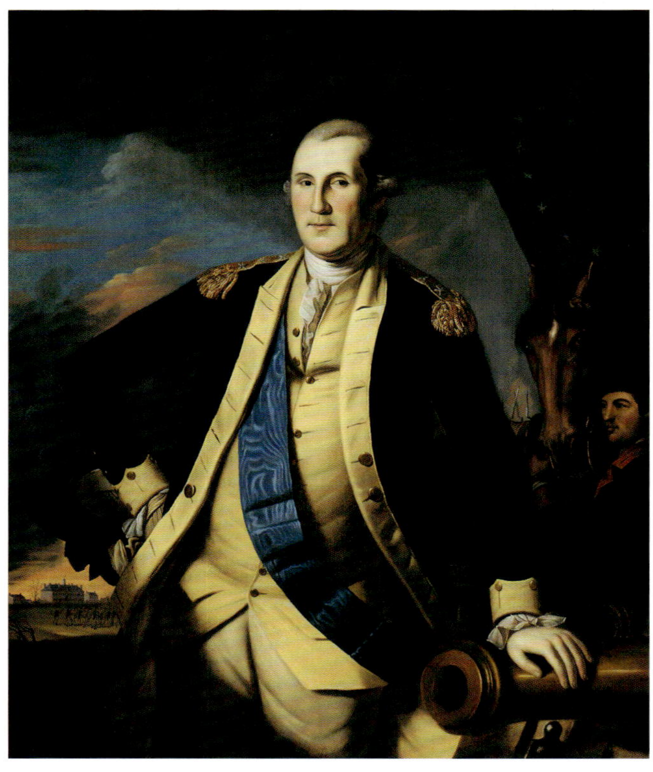

CAT. 20

Trunk

America, ca. 1778
Leather, wood, iron, and brass, H. 12", W. 27⅜", D. 12"
Purchase, 1949
W-1513

Throughout the Revolution, George Washington patronized saddlers for trunks in which to store and transport his belongings.[71] Most were of leather, fitted with reinforcement straps, and identified by a brass or copper plate on to which his name was engraved. This trunk may be one of the two "proper Camp Trunks, with Straps &ca"[72] Washington requested in 1778, and perhaps one of "4 Black Leather Campaign Trunks with Leather Straps" mentioned in a June 1781 inventory of articles left in the charge of Richard Varick, Washington's recording secretary. The oval brass plate engraved "GEN.L WASHINGTON / NO 4" on top of the lid (left detail) indicates that this trunk was part of a series of at least four in number.[73] Brass nails also decorate the plain black leather cover. With straps and a lock for added security, this sturdy ironbound example of Washington's luggage was designed to withstand much travel and hard use.

In June 1780 Washington, on the field and at a "Camp near Springfield," specifically mentioned this trunk to Major Caleb Gibbs:

> *A Trunk of mine No 4 (which the inclosed Key will open) is not more than half filled. I intend to have completed the package with my Bed blankets, but on enquiry, found they had been sent down to the Marquis [Lafayette] (which I am sorry for, as I hardly expect to see them again, or much dirtied if I do). —Under these circumstances I wish you to fill the Trunk No 4 with the best of those blankets which were drawn from the public stores as well for the purpose of preventing injury from the loose state they are now in, as to secure some coverings for me against the Winter. —The remainder of those Blankets I would also have detained subject to my order* only *as there may be in the course of the Campaign & our intercourse with our allies, occasion for them. Pray send us (if it is not already done) such things as are necessary for our tolerable comfort & convenience at this place & nothing more.*[74]

Washington's attention to the details of packing his belongings is typical, as is his insistence on minimal items while on the road.

Three years later, at the conclusion of the war, Washington again paid particular heed to his trunks and their contents when he wrote from Newburgh on June 18, 1783, to request trunks "for the purpose of Transportating my Books of record and Papers with safety." He specified, "I want Six strong hair Trunks well clasped and with good Locks. If such are to be had you will oblige me by the purchase of them. . . . Should you be able to procure the Trunks which I have required in the body of this letter, I should be glad to have a Label (in brass or Copper) containing my name, and the year on each."[75] Once again, Washington's specifications for his luggage are indicative of the meticulous attention he gave to the details of his belongings.

When Washington returned to Mount Vernon after the war, his trunks were stored in the Mansion garret and the storehouse. Several were preserved by Washington family members, including Martha Washington's granddaughter, Eliza Parke Custis. "GEN[L] WASHINGTON / NO 4" was cared for by Eliza, who evidently had it mended and repaired in Georgetown during the second quarter of the nineteenth century. A paper label affixed to the interior lid advertises "John Lutz High Street, Georgetown District of Columbia" (right detail).[76] John Lutz probably worked on the trunk in the 1820s or 1830s, and the plain woven linen interior as well as many of the leather repairs, replaced tacks, hinges, and locks are likely his work. Eliza perhaps commissioned Lutz to make repairs to the trunk to preserve it as much as its contents. When the trunk entered the Mount Vernon collection, it contained numerous articles of clothing belonging to George and Martha Washington as well as a pair of Washington's famous dentures.

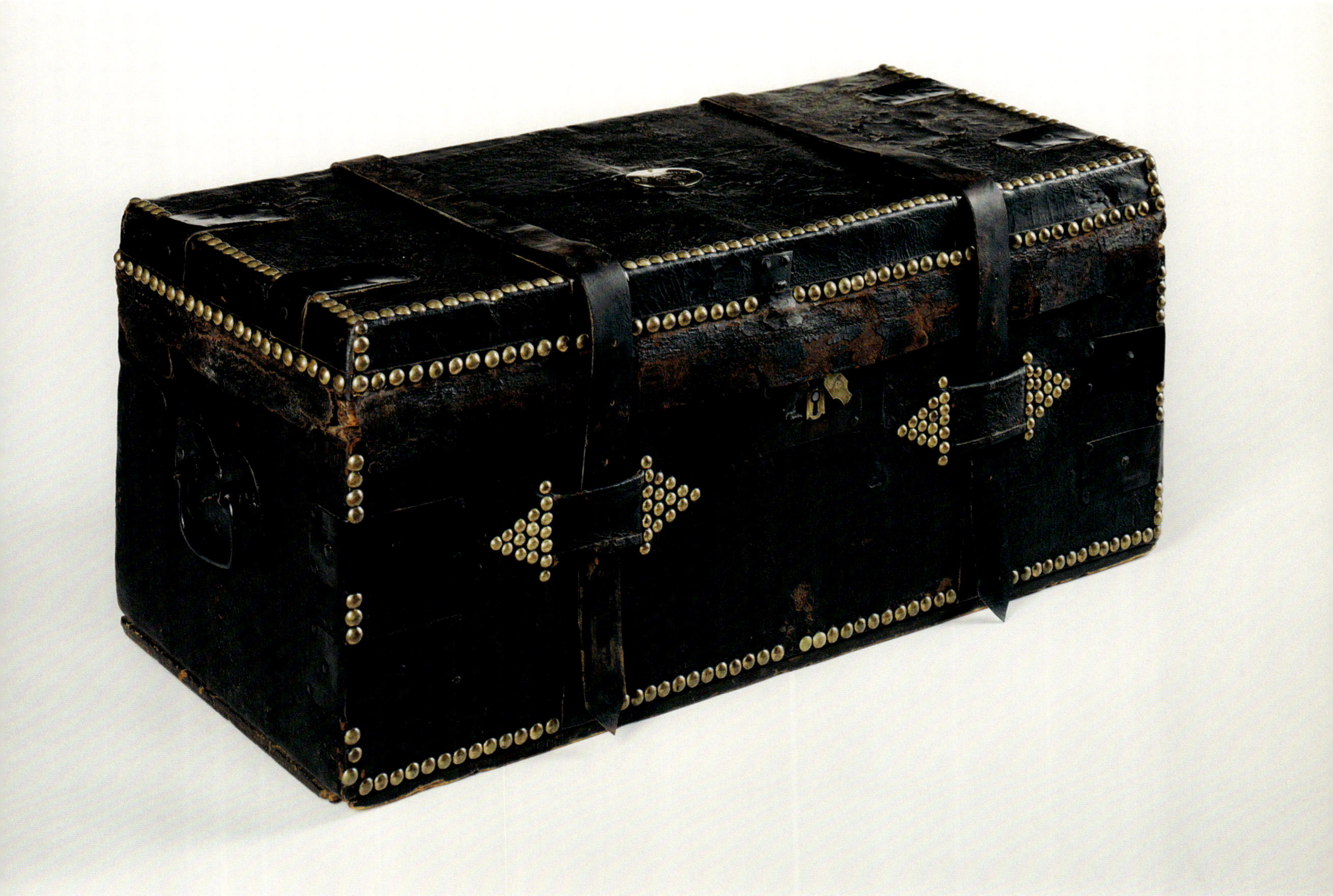

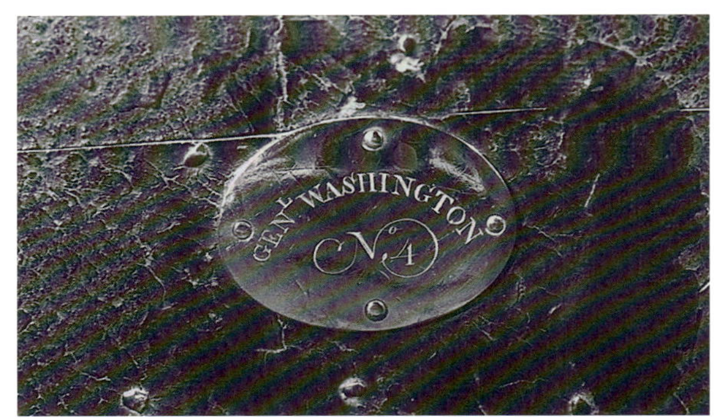
GENL WASHINGTON
No 4

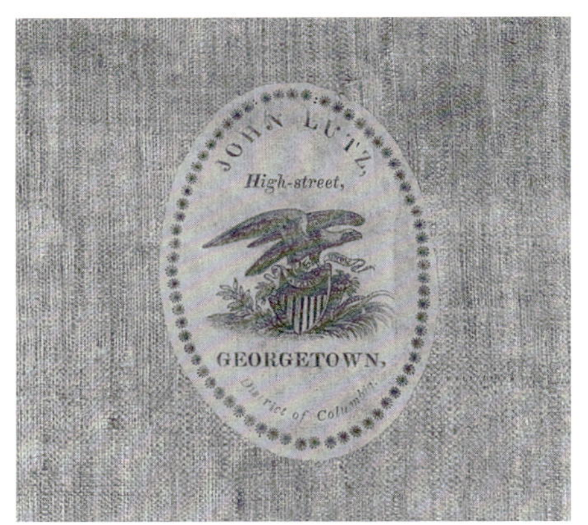
JOHN LUTZ,
High-street,
GEORGETOWN,
District of Columbia

CAT. 21

Spurs

England or America, ca. 1775
Silver, L. 5⅜", W. 2 11/16"
Gift of Miss Aimee Lamb and Miss Rosamond Lamb, 1952
W-1912

Paintings of George Washington often highlight the general's silver spurs fitted to his boots. Washington was certainly attentive to this detail of riding equipment and requested fashionable examples when ordering them. While encamped in New Windsor, New York, for the winter of 1780–1781, Washington turned to Assistant Quartermaster General Charles Pettit when he wanted a new set of fashionable silver spurs.

From Philadelphia, Pettit complied, noting,

> *As Your Excellency was pleased to mention* fashionable *spurs, I took some pains to enquire, amongst the Gentlemen of fashion, for the reigning taste of the day, but with less success than I expected, as I could not find any standard for it, nor that their ideas agreed with each other. I found, however, that the late prevailing mode of connecting the strap & spur by a chain, was generally rejected; and that a plain spur was most generally approved; I therefore sought for the best plain pattern I could find ready made, the time not admitting of getting a pair made by a new direction.*[77]

When he received the spurs, Washington wrote to Pettit, "Your choice of Spurs is very agreeable to my taste."[78] Washington may already have been aware of this new fashion, as the type of spurs described in this correspondence is remarkably similar to this pair that Washington presumably relinquished at Valley Forge three years earlier.

With clean lines and a simplicity of ornament, this pair of silver spurs could very well be described as "plain." The silversmith responsible for crafting them is not identified by a maker's mark, and they were perhaps part of the ready-made goods supplied to the colonies by English makers who specialized in silver spurs and other riding equipment.[79] Each spur is fitted with a steel rowel, and an engraved inscription on the interior side reads: "Presented to Lieut. Thomas Lamb, by Gen[l]. Washington's taking them from his own Boots, while giving his orders to Lieut. Lamb, at Valley Forge in Jan[y]. 1778, to proceed to Boston, for Supplies for the Army."

First Lieutenant Thomas Lamb served at Valley Forge where the winter conditions were harsh and supplies scarce. Lieutenant Lamb volunteered to ride to Boston to obtain needed supplies. According to the inscription, Lamb received the silver spurs from George Washington to accomplish this mission, as he had none of his own. Unfortunately, when he was near Boston Lamb's horse stumbled at night on a rope that was stretched across the road. Lamb was able to deliver Washington's message, but his injuries prevented further active duty in the army and he was discharged in 1779.[80]

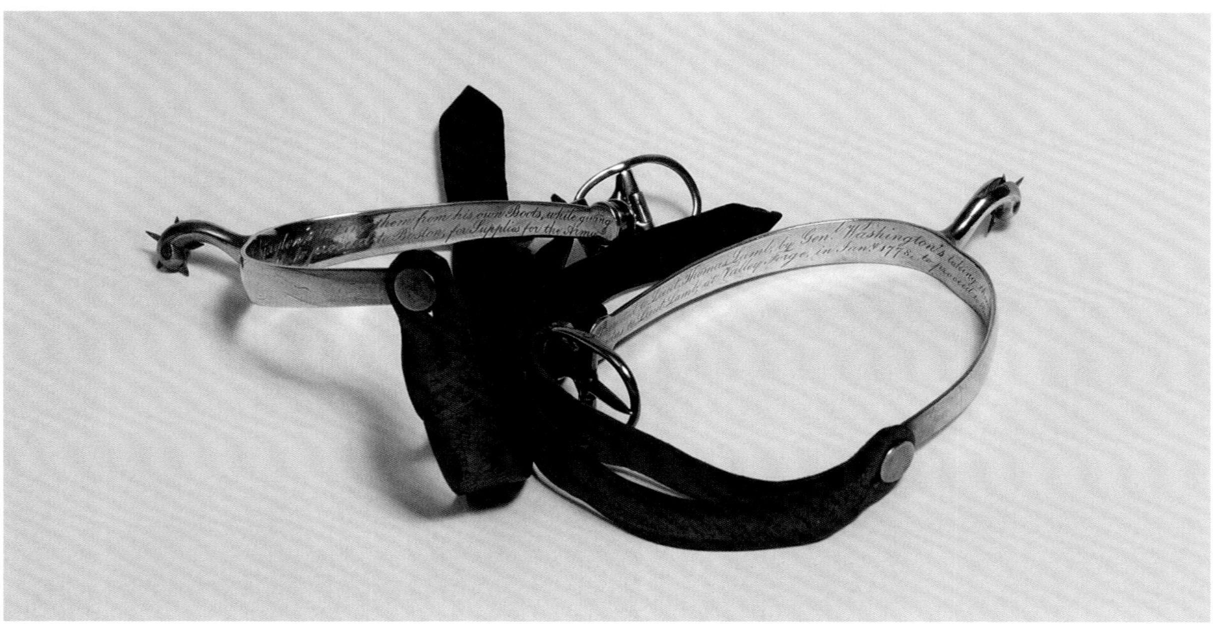

CAT. 22

Waste Bowl

Niderviller, France, ca. 1782
Porcelain, H. 4⅜", DIAM. at rim 8"
Purchase, 1978[81]
W-2322

While George Washington was encamped at Newburgh in 1782, waiting to receive official word of the war's end, Mrs. Washington returned to Mount Vernon. That summer, French land troops passed near Mount Vernon on their way north from Yorktown. Through Baron Ludwig von Closen, Martha Washington extended a dinner invitation to several of the French officers, including the Comte de Custine-Sarreck. Custine had served under Generals Rochambeau and Washington at Yorktown.[82] Mrs. Washington must have remembered him fondly, for von Closen recalled that "Madame Washington begged me to write for her to M. le Comte de Custine," in order "to invite him and all the officers of his corps to do her the honor to dine with her the next day."[83]

In advance of dinner, Custine sent ahead a porcelain tea and coffee service made specifically for the Washingtons at his Niderviller factory in France.[84] It is unknown how many pieces the service originally contained, but the survivals offer an elegant array of forms and designs.[85] Each is decorated with a version of the decorative borders the factory produced and a prominently displayed "GW" monogram surmounted by a wreath of roses and nestled in a cloud. Von Closen noted that Mrs. Washington was delighted with the gift and "expressed her appreciation to him [the count] in the most gracious manner."[86] Writing from Newburgh several days later, Washington added his gratitude for "a present of elegant China, which, as the product of your own Estate, I shall consider as of inestimable value knowing, as I do, the favourable Sentiments which accompanied it."[87]

This waste bowl, used as a receptacle for the dregs of the teacup and its rinsing, is a beautifully preserved example of the Custine porcelain service. Its pure white body is almost without flaw, and the gilded lip and foot rim frame the enamel border design and graceful floral swags. The underside is marked in enamel with inverted letters "C" and "No. 29," the latter referring to the company's number assigned to the border design.[88] Given the variety of designs present on the Washingtons' service, the tea and coffee wares served as a remarkable range of factory talent, and perhaps also as an intentional display of Niderviller's capabilities.

Gifts of porcelain were common between the French aristocracy and Americans who traveled to Paris. The porcelain presented to the Washingtons is, however, the only known instance of eighteenth-century French porcelain specifically crafted for an American recipient.[89] Although Custine was a victim of the guillotine in 1793, his compassion for the American cause of liberty and his friendship with the Washingtons lives on through the many survivals of his elegant porcelain gift in the Mount Vernon collection.

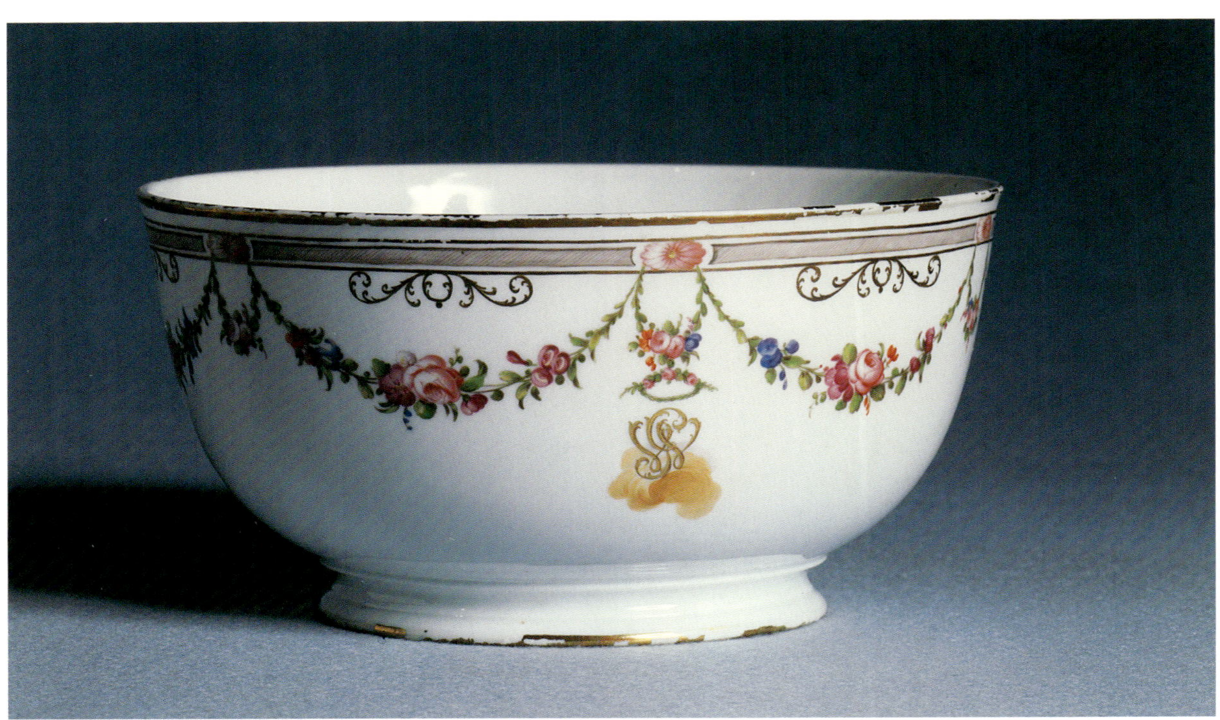

CAT. 23

Trunk

John Sunnocks
Philadelphia, Pennsylvania, ca. 1775–1790
Leather, wood, iron, and linen, H. 19½", W. 35", D. 19½"
Gift of Mrs. Wilfred Mustard, 1928[90]
W-368

Despite rough and often dangerous traveling conditions, Martha Washington ventured each year to her husband's winter quarters and was at his side through much of the Revolutionary War. She customarily traveled by carriage, packing her personal articles into leather-covered wood trunks. Eliza Parke Custis, Mrs. Washington's granddaughter, identified this trunk as one used during the Revolution, and a note she pasted inside the lid interior recalls: "It was that in which the cloaths of my Sainted Grandmother Mrs. Washington were always pack'd by her own hand when she went to visit, & spend sometime with the General, wherever the Army were in quarters. I have stood by it as she put in her cloaths sadly distress'd at her going away—& oh how joyfully when she returned did I look on to see her cloaths taken out, & the many gifts she always brought for her grandchildren!"[91]

The ironbound leather trunk is studded on the lid and sides with decorative brass nail heads. A leather skirt attached to the lid overhangs the bottom and provides added protection between lid and base. The linen lining, perhaps originally printed in blue or purple, has faded to brown, and the trim, likely dark red leather when new, has darkened with age. At the time it left the craftsman's shop, however, the trunk was certainly a handsome article of luggage, quite elegant for traveling and visiting.

A printed label affixed to the interior of the lid identifies the maker as "John Sunnocks, Trunk-Maker, from London" (detail). Sunnocks operated a shop in Philadelphia at 40 Chestnut Street, where he made and sold "all Sorts of Trunks . . . for traveling either by Sea or Land."[92] George Washington's household account book for expenses during the presidency notes payments to Sunnocks "for a traveling trunk for the Presidents Phaeton" and "two Trunks per Acct."[93] Given the large volume of material the Washingtons bought in Philadelphia, and their patronage of Sunnocks in the 1790s, it is possible that the Washingtons purchased trunks from Sunnocks during the Revolution as well as the presidency. Eliza Custis (1776–1831) recalled from her childhood a similar trunk her grandmother used on trips to war encampments. Whether this trunk was that used by Mrs. Washington during the Revolution or during the presidential years, Eliza Custis's recollections serve as a reminder of the personal sacrifices and many long journeys Martha Washington made to be at her husband's side throughout the Revolutionary War.

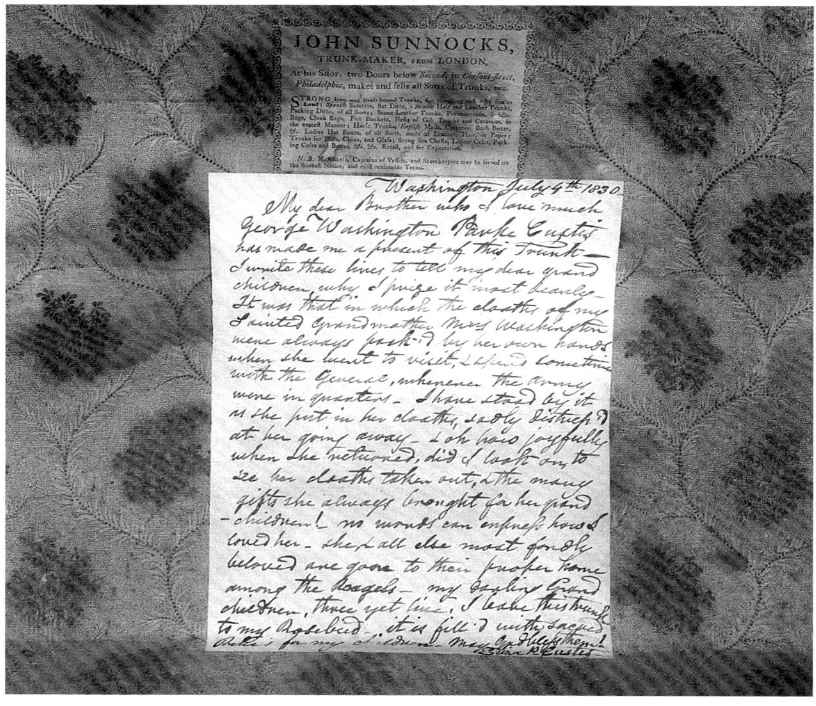

JOHN SUNNOCKS,
TRUNK-MAKER, FROM LONDON,
At his SHOP, two Doors below *Second*, in *Chesnut-street*, *Philadelphia*, makes and sells all Sorts of Trunks, *viz.*

STRONG Iron and Brass bound Trunks, for travelling either by Sea or Land; *Spanish* Sumters, flat Ditto, common Hair and Leather Trunks, Packing Ditto, of all Sorts; Stout Leather Trunks, Portmanteaus, Saddle-Bags, Cloak Bags, Fire Buckets, Nests of Gilt Trunks and Caravans, in the neatest Manner; Horse Trunks, *English* Mails, [illegible], Bath Boxes, &c. Ladies Hat Boxes, of all Sorts, made of Leather, Hair, or Paper; Trunks for Plate, China, and Glass; strong Sea Chests, Liquor Cases, Packing Cases and Boxes, &c. &c. Retail, and for Exportation.

N. B. Merchants, Captains of Vessels, and Storekeepers may be served on the shortest Notice, and most reasonable Terms.

Washington July 4th 1830
My dear Brother who I love much
George Washington Parke Custis
has made me a present of this Trunk—
I write these lines to tell my dear grand
children why I prize it most dearly—
It was that in which the cloaths of my
Sainted Grandmother Mrs Washington
were always pack'd by her own hands
when she went to visit, & spend sometime
with the General, wherever the Army
were in quarters— I have stood by it
as she put in her cloaths, sadly distress'd
at her going away— & oh how joyfully
when she returned, did I look on to
see her cloaths taken out, & the many
gifts she always brought for her grand
-children!— no words can express how I
loved her— she & all else most fondly
beloved are gone to their proper home
among the Angels— my darling Grand
children, three yet live. I leave this trunk
to my Rosebud— it is fill'd with sacred
relics for my children— May God bless them!
Eliza P. Custis

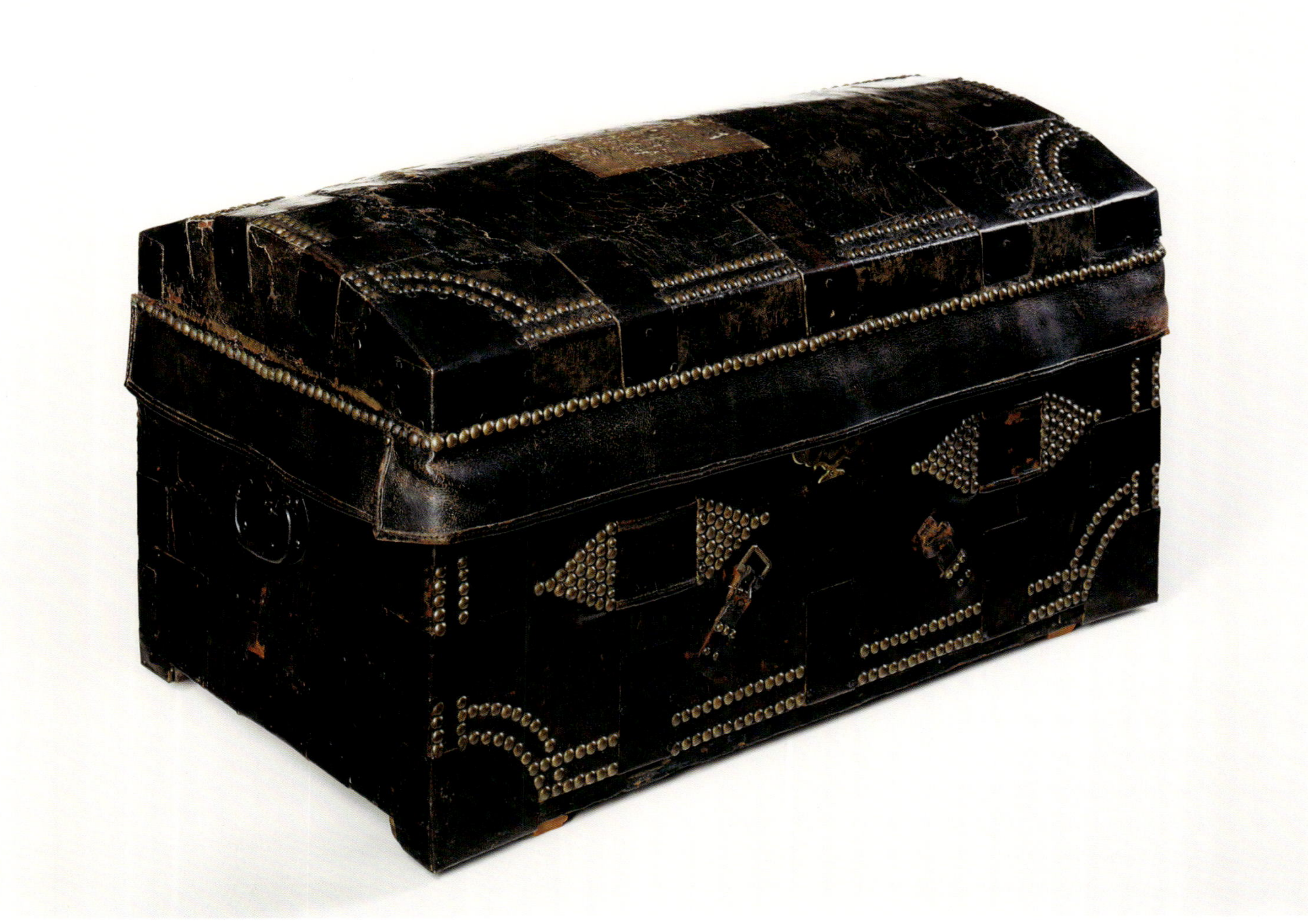

CAT. 24

George Washington

ca. 1779

Jean-Baptiste Le Paon (ca. 1738–1785)
France
Oil on canvas, 25¾" x 21⅜"
Purchased with funds donated by Mr. and Mrs. Guerin Todd, Mr. and Mrs. Donald L. Segur, Mrs. Lyle C. Roll, Mrs. Samuel M. V. Hamilton, Pendleton Woolen Mills, Mrs. C. Lalor Burdick, and Mrs. Richard Alexander, 1992
M-3660

George Washington's reputation as a dashing American general fighting for the noble cause of liberty was known throughout Europe from the earliest days of the American Revolution. The citizens of France, perhaps more than any others, were fascinated by Washington, presumably because of their considerable interest and involvement in disentangling the American colonies from the grip of the British Empire. Fictitious images of Washington circulated until the late 1770s, when the first accurate images of him were seen in the form of paintings and prints based on Charles Willson Peale's 1776 life portrait commissioned by John Hancock (fig. 1).[94] This portrait, by the French painter Jean-Baptiste Le Paon, was undoubtedly based on a version of the Peale portrait.

The Marquis de Lafayette traveled to France in January 1779 to raise money for the Continental Army, bringing with him a version of the Peale portrait and thereby providing the likely means by which Le Paon saw an accurate depiction of Washington.[95] One of the earliest and best-known French engravings showing a truthful image of Washington, by Noël Le Mire in 1780, supports this supposition, for it bears an inscription stating that it was based on Le Paon's painting after a portrait in the possession of Lafayette (fig. 2).

Much as Peale had done, Le Paon painted Washington facing forward, shoulders slightly to one side, wearing his blue and buff Continental Army uniform. In contrast to Peale's three-quarter-length portrait that shows the city of Boston in the background, Le Paon simplified the composition to bust length with an essentially blank background.[96] The general's typical light blue sash disappears in Le Paon's version, and his simple white collar is replaced by a French-style collar with a dark cravat. Although an accomplished artist and principal painter for the Prince de Condé,[97] Le Paon was known primarily for his epic battlefield scenes, and his only other known portrait shows Lafayette at Yorktown with his servant James. In 1782 Le Paon's portrait of Washington was exhibited to the Parisian public at the Salon de la Correspondance, leading many in France to comment with great surprise on the youthfulness of so great a military hero as Washington.[98]

This painting was owned initially by Le Paon's patron, the Prince de Condé, after which it descended in the French royal family to King Louis-Philippe (1773–1850).[99] On the reverse of the canvas the king's inventory mark and the stamp of his private residence, Château d'Eu, are visible, while the inventory number "370" appears on the front of the canvas. After King Louis-Philippe's art collection was sold, this portrait was owned privately until its purchase for the Mount Vernon collection in 1992.

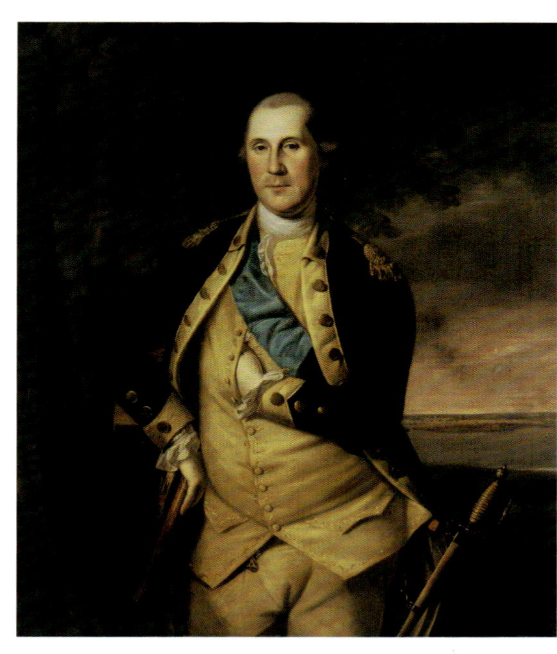

Fig. 1. John Hancock's portrait of George Washington by Charles Willson Peale provided the inspiration for numerous prints and paintings that circulated in Europe during the late 1770s. Brooklyn Museum, 34.1178, Dick S. Ramsay Fund.

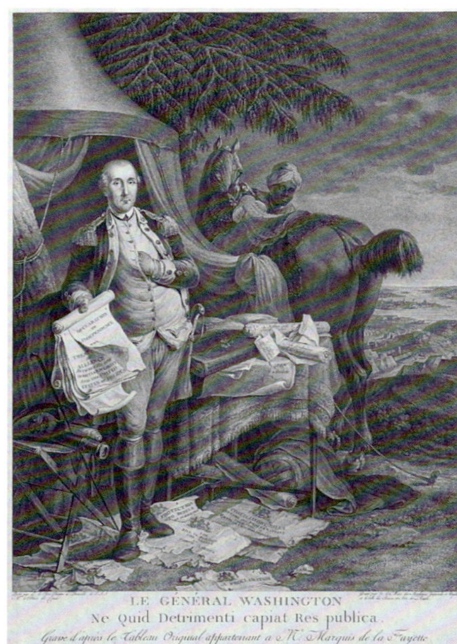

Fig. 2. The French engraver Noël Le Mire based his work on Jean-Baptiste Le Paon's portrait of George Washington, creating one of the earliest and most accurate engraved portraits of Washington to circulate in Europe. MVLA

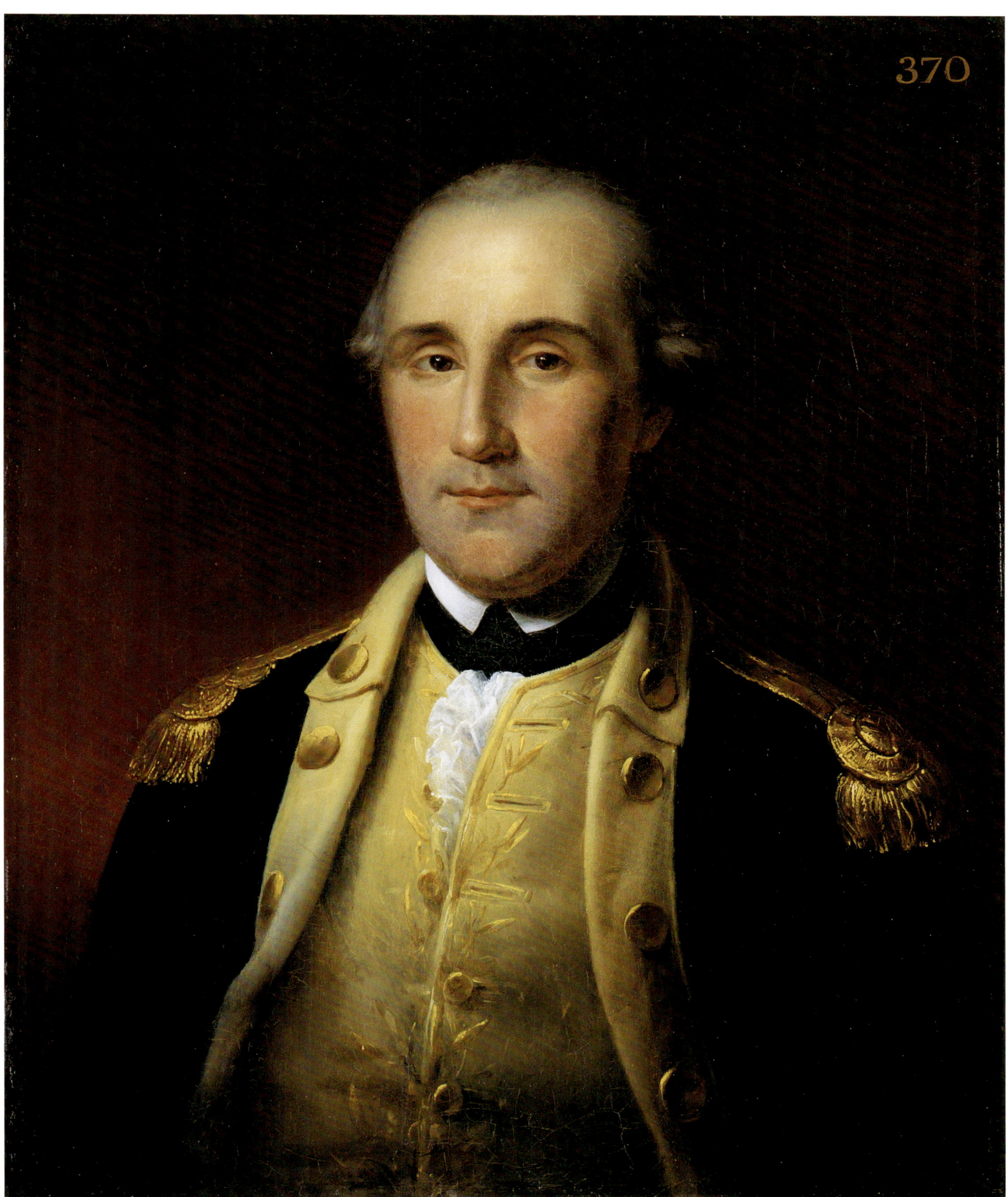
370

CAT. 25

Camp Cups

Richard Humphreys (1749–1832)
Philadelphia, Pennsylvania, 1780
Silver, H. 3½", DIAM. at rim 3¼"
Private Collection
W-2754/A&B

Throughout the Revolutionary War, George Washington demonstrated a preference for drinking and serving from silver camp cups when in the field. Three Philadelphia silversmiths supplied him with forty-six of the elegant vessels. The first "2 Doz Camp cups" and "2 half pint camp cups" were supplied by William Hollingshead in March 1776.[100] The following year, in August 1777, Edmund Milne made "12 Silv^{r} Camp Cups" from "16 Silv^{r} Doll^{s}" for Washington's table.[101] Perhaps Washington's best-known camp cups, however, were fashioned by Richard Humphreys in 1780 and include this pair.

Richard Humphreys served as an apprentice to Bancroft Woodcock in Wilmington, Delaware, and was advertising his own work as a goldsmith in that city in 1771.[102] In 1772 Humphreys assumed the practice of the Philadelphia silver- and goldsmith Philip Syng, "a few doors below the Coffee House," where he sold "a NEAT and GENERAL ASSORTMENT of GOLD and SILVER WARE."[103] By the time he fashioned Washington's camp cups, Humphreys could be found "at the [sign of] the Coffee Pot on Front Street."[104]

In June 1780 Clement Biddle called on Humphreys and bought for General Washington "Half a Doz^{n} Large Camp Cups" and "2 Small d^{o} [ditto]," each engraved with Washington's signature griffin.[105] Two years later, the Marquis de Chastellux paused at Washington's encampment at Verplanck Point and recalled a restorative drink he had from one of the general's camp cups:

> *I had suffered severely from an ague, which I could not quit of, though I had taken the exercise of a hard trotting horse. . . . The General observing it, told me he was sure I had not met with a good glass of wine for some time, an article then very rare, but that my disorder must be frightened away; he made me drink three or four of his silver camp cups of excellent Madeira at noon, and recommended to me to take a generous glass of claret after dinner, a prescription by no means repugnant to my feelings, and which I most religiously followed. I mounted my horse next morning and continued my journey to Massachusetts, without ever experiencing the slightest return of my disorder.*[106]

After the war, Washington's silver camp cups returned with him to Mount Vernon. This pair became the property of George Washington Parke Custis, Martha Washington's grandson, who inherited a majority of the Washingtons' silver.[107] From Mount Vernon the cups went to Custis's home, Arlington House, and were sketched by Benson Lossing during his visit there in the mid-nineteenth century (fig. 1). Custis's only child, Mary, the wife of Robert E. Lee, preserved the cups during the Civil War and later passed them on to one of her children. In addition to the two large camp cups by Richard Humphreys that survive at Mount Vernon, one of Humphreys' "2 Small" cups is part of the Mabel Brady Garvan Collection at the Yale University Art Gallery, and two of Edmund Milne's cups are in the collection of the Los Angeles County Museum of Art.[108]

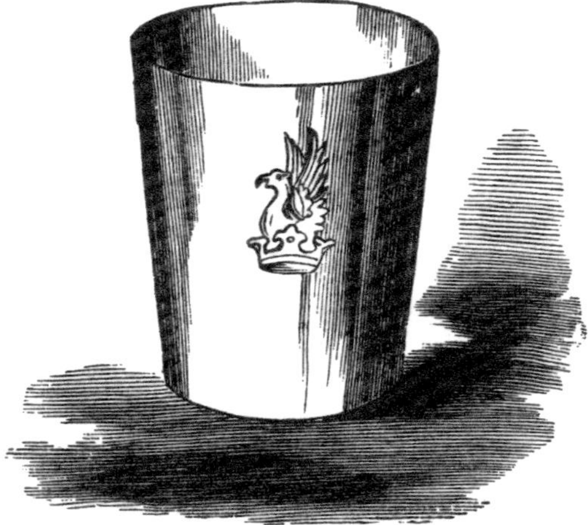

SILVER CAMP-GOBLET.

Fig. 1.
One of George Washington's silver camp cups used during the war, sketched by Benson Lossing at Arlington House prior to 1859 and published in his book *Mount Vernon and Its Associations*

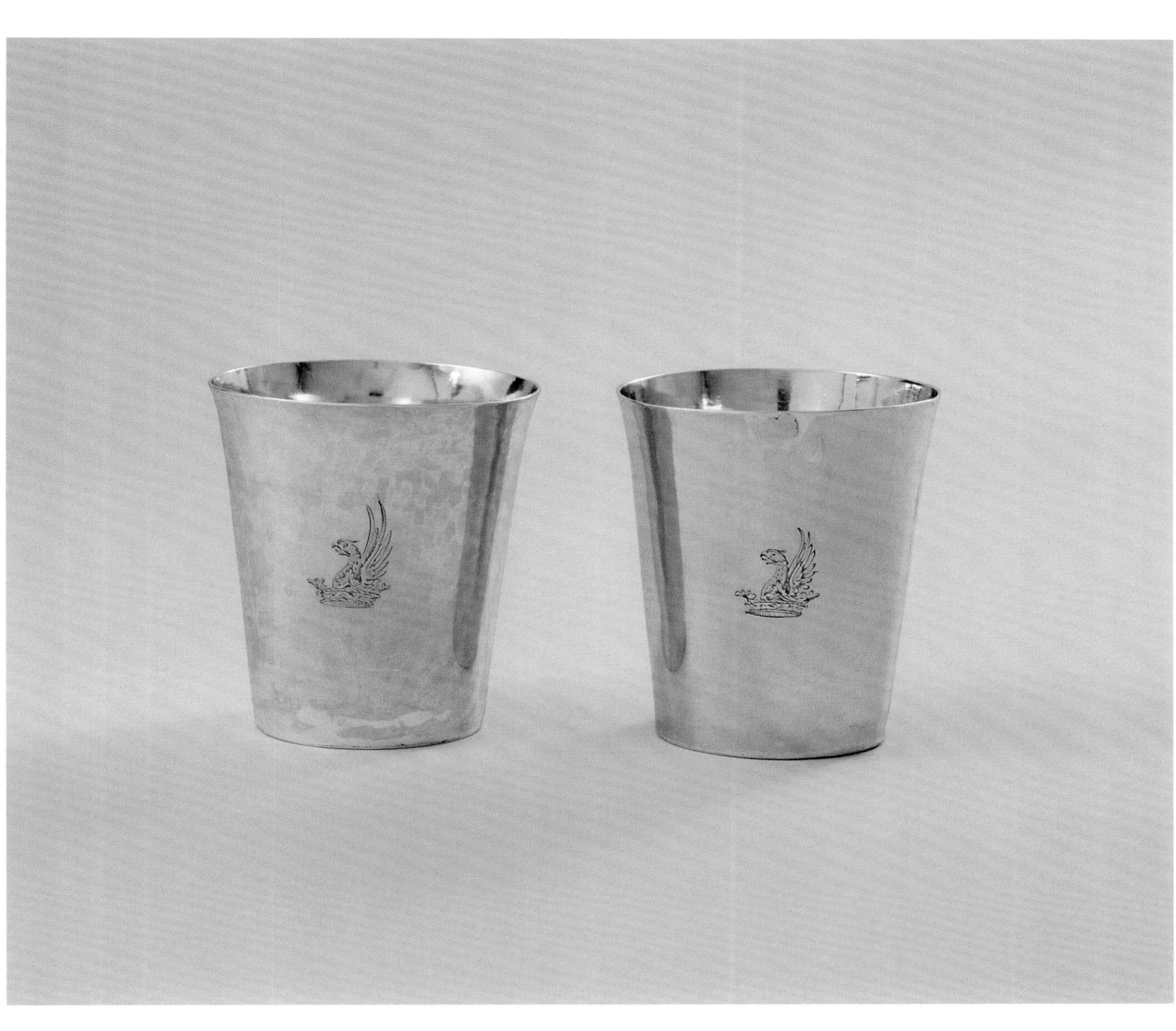

CAT. 26

Tablespoons

Richard Humphreys (1749–1832)
Philadelphia, Pennsylvania, 1780
Silver, L. 9", W. 1⅞"
Gift of Mary Walker Lee Bowman and Robert E. Lee IV, 1981
W-2535/A&D

When looking for proper silver spoons for George Washington's camp table, it is not surprising that Colonel Clement Biddle turned to the Philadelphia silversmith Richard Humphreys. Humphreys was supportive of the war cause and had fashioned a silver hot-water urn in 1774 for members of the First Continental Congress to present to Secretary Charles Thompson.[109] In June 1780 the silversmith supplied Biddle with "2 Doz[e]n Table Spoons" for the general's table, in addition to six large and two small camp cups.[110] Although supporting written documentation is lacking, it is possible that Humphreys also crafted three smaller-sized spoons for Washington during the Revolution. Surviving table-, dessert, tea-, and salt spoons in the Mount Vernon collection bear Humphreys' mark (detail) and exhibit the same bright-cut engraving and Washington's signature griffin.

These examples are among the two dozen tablespoons made by Humphreys for Washington in 1780. Round-tipped shafts are attached to elongated oval bowls, and the handles are ornamented with bright-cut engraving and the Washington crest. The bright-cut edge decoration, achieved by removing silver with a graver, creates a small facet that twinkles as it catches the light. This form of decoration, characteristic of early Federal period American silver,[111] appears on numerous examples of Washington's flatware and was perhaps favored by him for the sparkle it brought to a dining table lit by flickering candles.

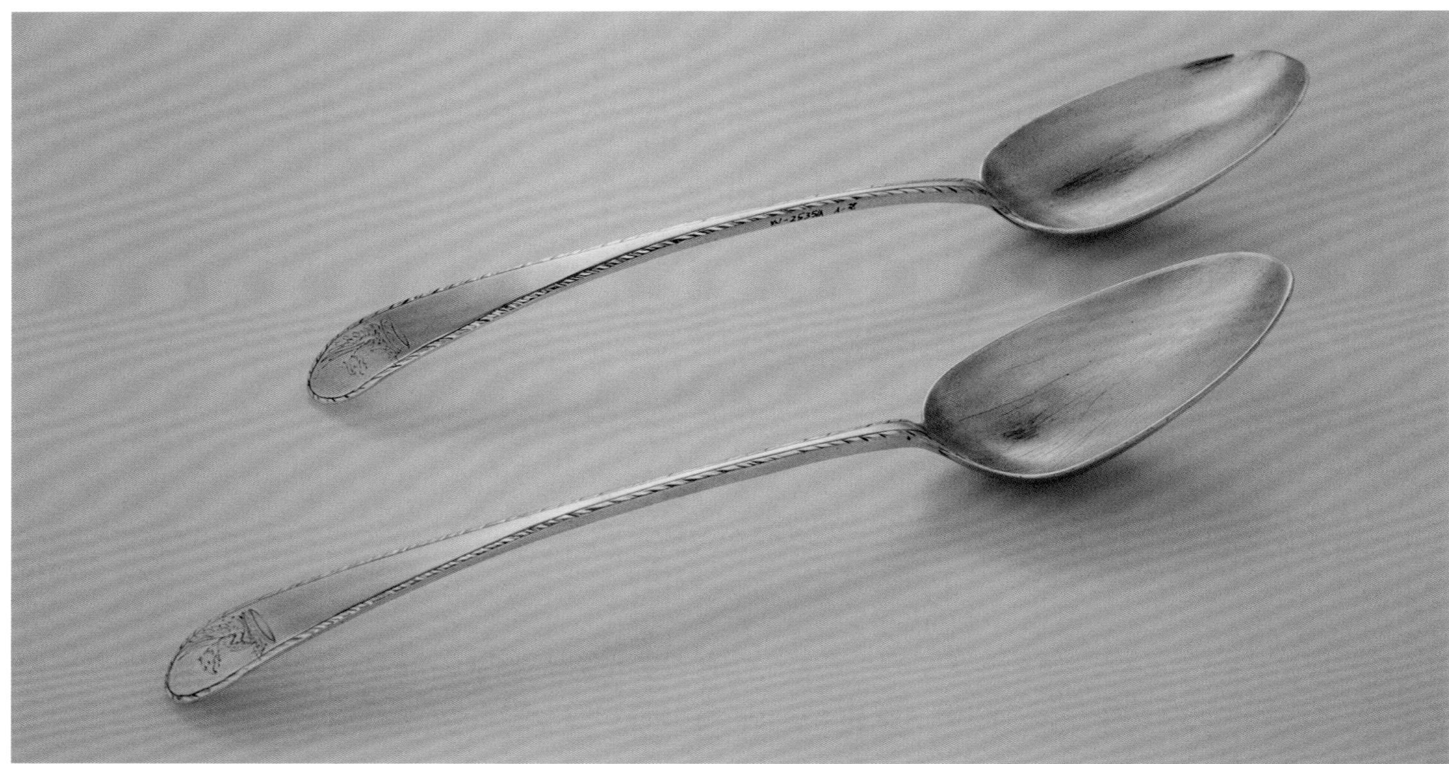

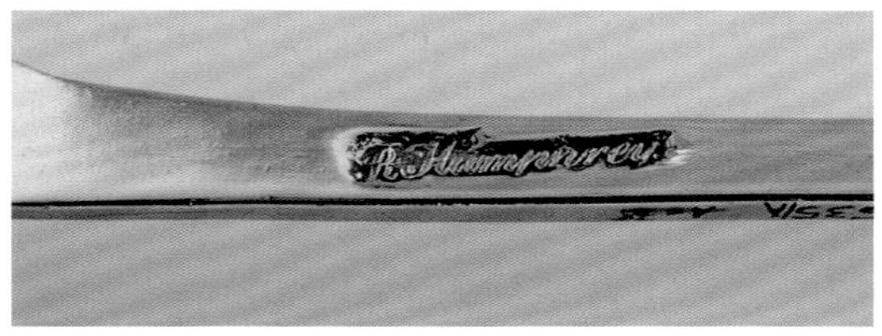

CAT. 27

Ladle

Andrew Billing (1743–1808)[112]
Fishkill, New York, ca. 1782
Silver, L. 12⅛", DIAM. of bowl 3¼"
Gift of Mary Walker Lee Bowman and Robert E. Lee IV, 1981
W-2524

As George Washington awaited word of the official end to the war at his Newburgh headquarters, he attended to the engraving of a cannon for presentation to the Comte de Rochambeau. The French general had commanded the largest French military contingent at the Battle of Yorktown, leading to the defeat of the British forces on October 19, 1781. Congress lacked funds to pay the French for their invaluable military services, however, and therefore quickly passed a resolution, "That two pieces of the field ordnance, taken from the British army . . . be presented by the commander in chief of the American army, to Count de Rochambeau; and that there be engraved thereon a short memorandum," to thank Rochambeau for "the illustrious part which he bore in effectuating the surrender."[113] Months passed, however, without a formal presentation, and Washington apologized to Rochambeau, explaining his "difficulty in getting the engraving properly executed."[114]

While at Newburgh, Washington turned to the local silversmith Andrew Billing, and Billing completed the engraving by December 1782.[115] Washington perhaps requested the silversmith to craft this ladle for him while he was engraving the cannon. Throughout the war, Washington patronized a variety of silversmiths in furnishing his camp table with appropriate silver serving pieces and flatware, and this ladle is in perfect keeping with his earlier purchases. Its long bright-cut-edged handle is similar to the tablespoons the Philadelphia silversmith Richard Humphreys supplied to Washington. And, like Humphreys' spoons and camp cups, Washington's signature griffin is engraved on the handle (detail). The deep circular bowl served those at Washington's wartime table, and later at Mount Vernon. It was among the silver at Mount Vernon when the former general died and was bequeathed to Martha Washington's grandson, George Washington Parke Custis.[116]

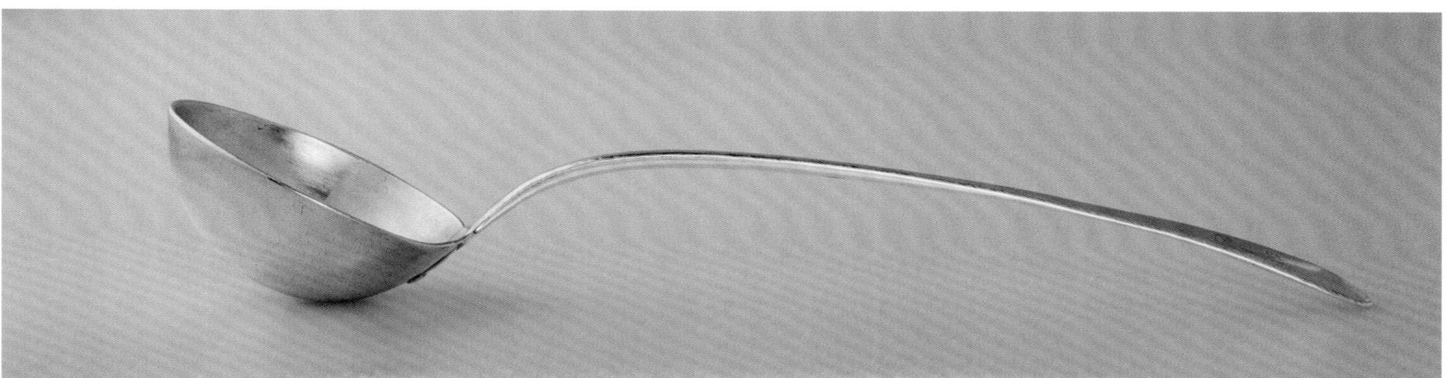

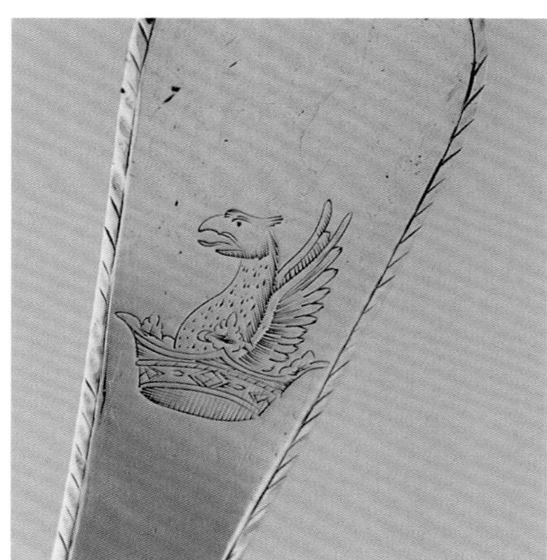

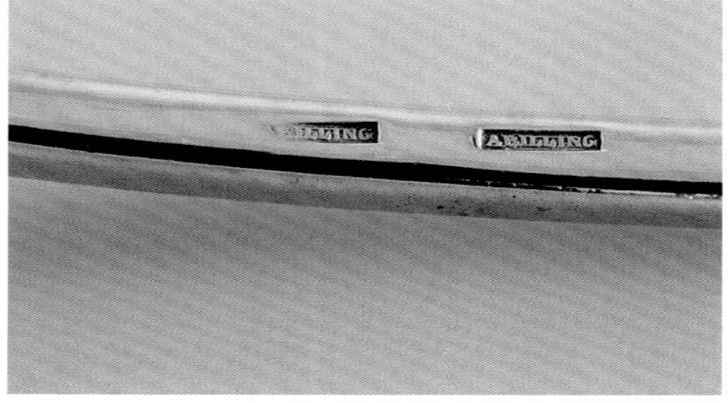

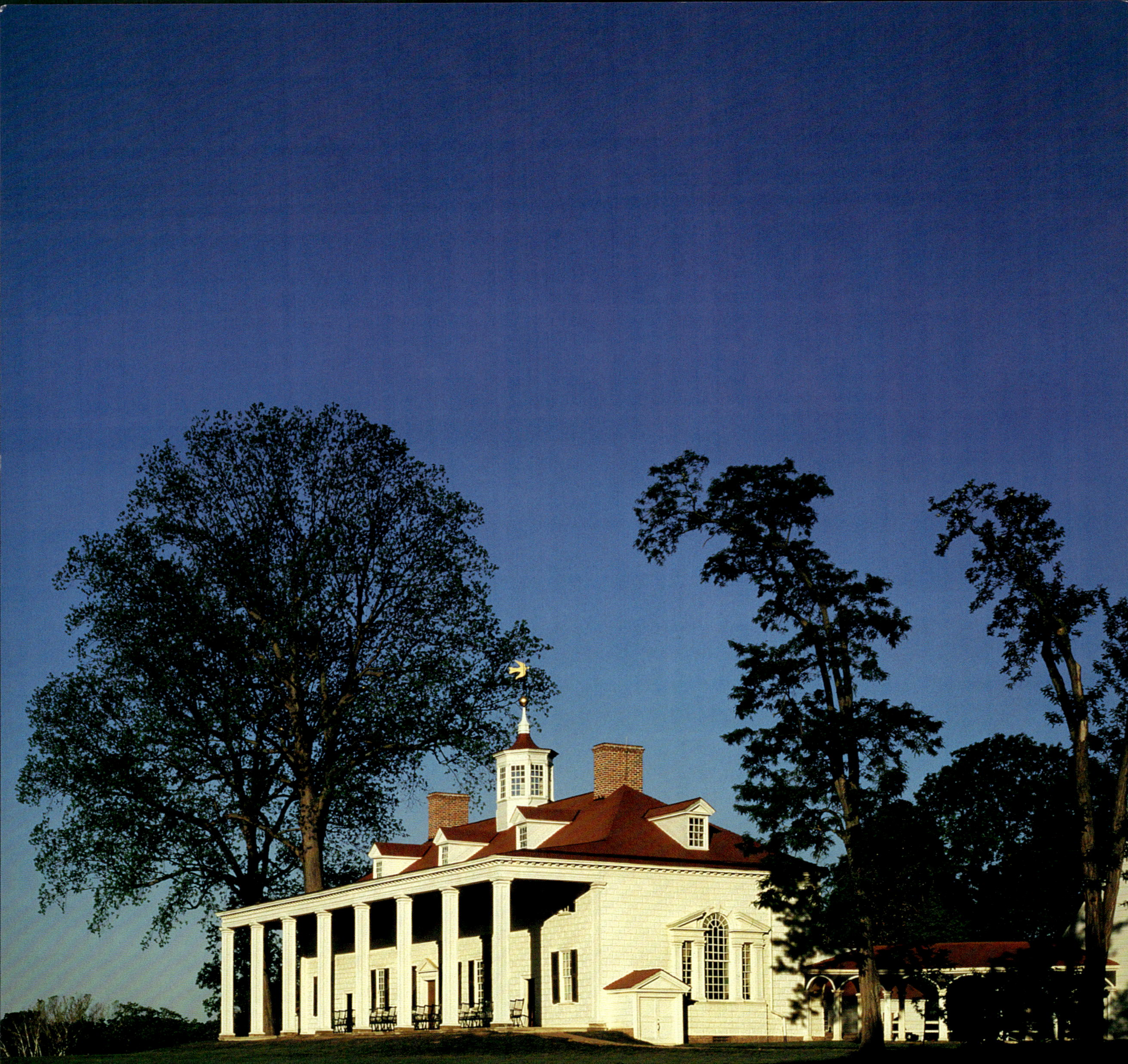

CHAPTER THREE

Cincinnatus Returns Home
George Washington the War Hero
1783–1789

WITH THE CONCLUSION OF THE REVOLUTIONARY WAR, George Washington rose to unprecedented fame among his fellow colonials, now Americans. His refusal to be named king and his return to Mount Vernon prompted comparisons to the famous fifth-century B.C.E. Roman patriot, statesman, and general Cincinnatus. The Roman, who responded to the Senate's request to serve as commander in chief, speedily defeated Rome's enemies, then resigned his position, having held it for less than a month and returned to the joys of his farm. Visitors flocked to Virginia to pay their respects to the retired general as Washington resumed work on his Mount Vernon estate, attending to the Mansion's interior appointments and his treasured farms. He focused on family and friends, agriculture and navigation. When Robert Hunter of London visited Mount Vernon in November 1785, he observed that Washington's "greatest pride now is, to be thought the first farmer in America."[1] In the 1750s and 1760s Washington had sought entry into the elite planter class of Virginia through his use of Mount Vernon. Now at home, he sought to perfect the life of the gentleman-farmer.

Even before his arrival at Mount Vernon, Washington planned the constellation of objects he wished to surround him in retirement. After announcing the cessation of hostilities between America and England in April 1783, he waited out the remaining months of the year until final word of a peace treaty arrived. He used to good advantage the "listless state"[2] of waiting he described to the Marquis de Lafayette by ordering those articles necessary and appropriate for the residence of a victorious general in retirement.

Preparing to entertain his Mount Vernon guests properly, Washington wrote to Clement Biddle in Philadelphia to secure one dozen tablecloths "for the common sized square tables . . . long enough to cover two Tables,"[3] and to Daniel Parker in New York for wine with appropriate drinking vessels. Washington had a clear idea of the type of glass he wanted for Mount Vernon and wrote to Parker:

> *If there are Wine and Beer Glasses (the latter of the same shape but larger in size) exactly like those which Mr. Fraunces brought to Orange Town, of which I have the perfect recollection, I should be glad . . . to get Six dozn. Or more of the first, and three dozn. Of the latter with as many Water Glasses, together with one dozn. And half neat quart decanters, and as many Water Bottles for Table use.*[4]

Washington specified, "If there are none of the kind of Glasses here described, (which pleased my fancy) to be had, I would buy none; as I may have an opportunity of endulging my taste in another kind at Philadelphia (as I return home) upon as good terms as the New York Markets afford." In the same letter Washington requested "a neat and compleat sett of blue and White Table China" and wished to know "what Goods, for family use, are very low in New York, and if they are to be had cheaper, than Goods of the same kind and quality, at Philadelphia."[5] Clearly the retiring general retained his desire for fashionable and quality goods, yet continued to demonstrate his established trait of thrifty stewardship of financial resources.

For the meals to be served on his newly ordered blue-and-white Chinese export porcelain, Washington

Fig. 1. (opposite) View of Mount Vernon and the expansive East Lawn

sought to take advantage of the British evacuation of New York to engage an experienced cook. Writing again to Parker, he requested "a good Cook, German I should prefer . . . who has understanding in the business, who can order, as well as get a dinner, who can make dishes, and proportion them properly, to any Company which shall be named to him in the amount of 30." While also suggesting that the candidate should possess "honesty, sobriety and good temper," Washington noted that locating such a person should not be difficult, inasmuch "as the army as well as many Genteel Families are now upon the point of leaving New York."[6]

Although Parker had turned to the tavern keeper Samuel Fraunces for assistance, he was unable to supply Washington with the complete set of blue-and-white china requested, but he was able to provide 205 pieces of Chinese export in assorted form and design.[7] Washington's nephew Bushrod, then in Philadelphia, likely was able to supplement the porcelain service, while at the same time finding for his uncle other furnishings and necessities for Mount Vernon entertainments. Washington requested of Bushrod:

> *Let me beg of you to make enquiry of some of the best Cabinet makers, and at what price, and in what time, two dozen strong, neat and plain, but fashionable, Table chairs (I mean chairs for a dining room) could be had; with strong canvas bottoms to receive a loose covering of check, or worsted, as I may hereafter choose . . . I will go further, and ask you to enquire at what prices the several kinds of French and other wines (Madeira excepted, of which I have enough) of good quality, can be bought. . . . give me the prices also for imported Nuts and Fruits of different kinds . . . also of olives, Capes Oil, Anchovies, & ca. . . . I wish also that you would enquire, if there is any blue and white table china, to be had in settes and the price.*[8]

To furnish Mount Vernon, Washington's preference for neat, plain, and fashionable items of quality remained dominant. On his return to Virginia, he continued to acquire such furnishings from the leading craftsmen of New York and Philadelphia.

At Mount Vernon just in time for Christmas 1783, Washington settled back into private life. As he oversaw the refining of the architectural and interior details of his residence and the proper maintenance and prosperity of his estate, Washington enjoyed the serenity of being a gentleman-farmer. He wrote to the Marquis de Lafayette:

> *I am become a private citizen on the banks of the Potomac, and under the shadow of my own Vine and my own Fig-tree, free from the bustle of a camp and the busy scenes of public life. . . . I am not only retired from all public employments, but I am retiring within myself; and shall be able to view the solitary walk and tread the paths of private life with heartfelt satisfaction. Envious of none, I am determined to be pleased with all; and this, my dear friend, being the order of my march, I will move gently down the stream of life until I sleep with my fathers.*[9]

Washington was—as he said—retiring within himself. Keenly aware of his family's tendency to a short life span, the retired general felt his own death could not be far ahead, and he was determined to spend his remaining years peacefully at Mount Vernon.

In the spring of 1784 he traveled to Philadelphia for the first meeting of the Society of the Cincinnati, the hereditary organization formed of American and French officers, over which he presided as its first president. While there, he asked Biddle to forward to Mount Vernon samples of blue and green wallpaper, "paupier-Maché and gilded borders,"[10] and "a dozn. and a half of Windsor Chairs,"[11] quite possibly for tak-

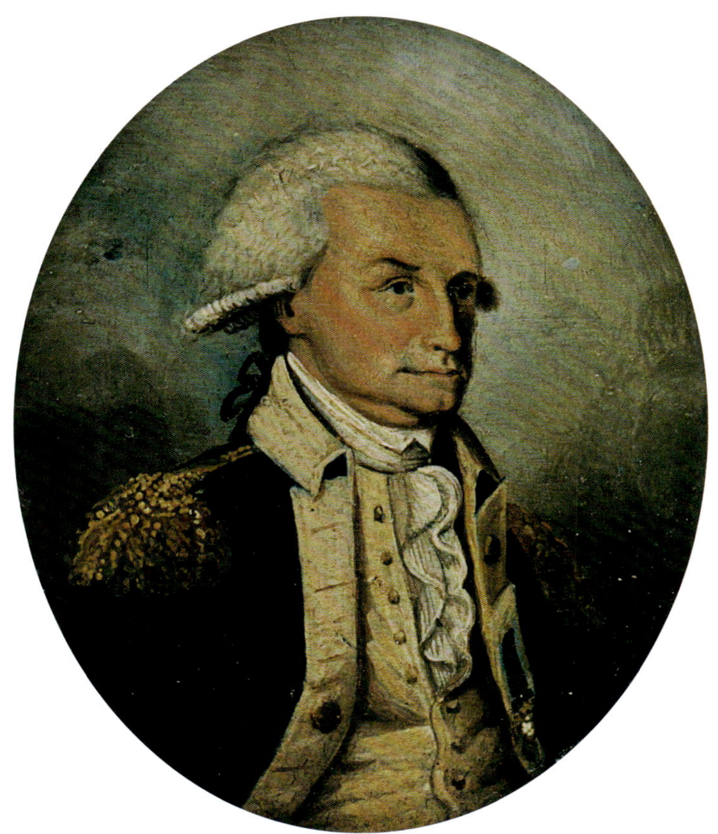

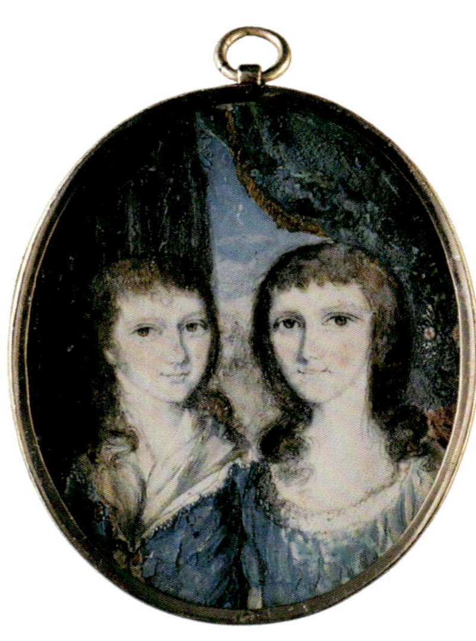

Fig. 2.
Edward Savage's portrait of George Washington in military uniform wearing his badge of the Society of the Cincinnati, MVLA

Fig. 3.
Miniature portrait of Martha Washington's grandchildren, George Washington Parke Custis and Eleanor Parke Custis, who resided with the Washingtons following their father's death, MVLA

ing in the Potomac River breezes from the piazza he was perfecting. The Windsor chairs were among the last of the tablewares and furnishings Washington purchased for the next few years. Following his return to Mount Vernon, Washington's orders to Biddle continued and were filled with requests for materials necessary for the repairs, additions, and renovations he was undertaking on the Mansion, as well as articles like flax spinning wheels to make Mount Vernon as self-sufficient as possible.

Although both George and Martha Washington were now more than fifty years of age, they experienced a renewed family life at Mount Vernon. Without children from their own marriage and following the deaths of both Patsy and Jacky, the couple helped Jacky's widow to raise her two youngest children, Eleanor Parke Custis and the general's namesake, George Washington Parke Custis (fig. 3). As in their early married life together, some twenty-five years earlier, the home of George and Martha was filled with the sounds and laughter of two young children. The Washingtons also welcomed Fanny Bassett, Martha Washington's niece, who, since her mother's death, had spent time with a multitude of relatives before finding a home at Mount Vernon. These young people provided a blended, but happy, state of domesticity for the retired general and his wife.

In late 1784 the Marquis de Lafayette, whom Washington regarded as an adopted son and member of the family, visited Mount Vernon. Artists and historians have provided a wealth of imagery and speculation about the appearance of Washington and Lafayette and the topics of their discussions during this three-week visit (fig. 4). Certainly, Washington must have served as a sounding board and mentor as only a "father" can, while Lafayette considered the application of revolutionary ideals to his home country of France. Lafayette's visit to Mount Vernon was undoubtedly a highlight of Washington's first year of retirement. Shortly before Lafayette's departure, Washington penned letters to the Frenchman's family that were likely hand-carried by the Marquis. To Lafayette's wife, the Marchioness, he offered, "We restore him to you in good health, crowned with wreaths of love and respect from every part of the union."[12] To

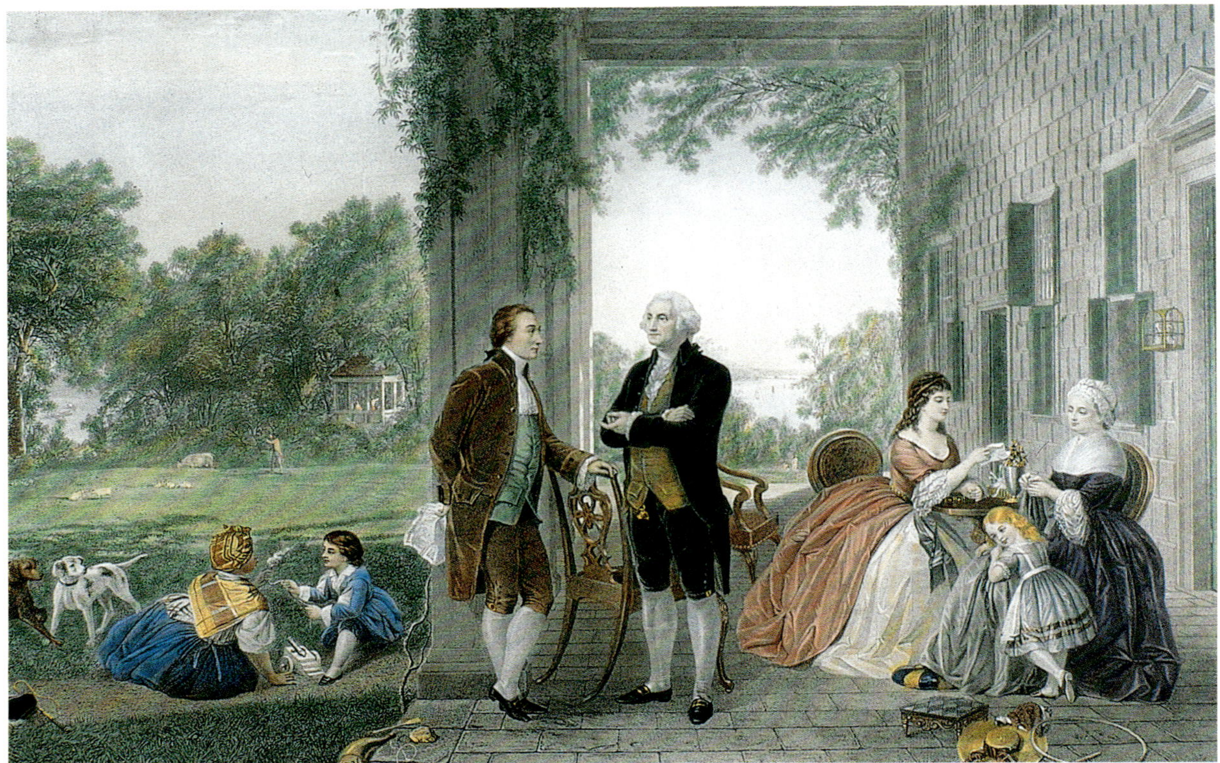

Fig. 4. Military companions, like the Marquis de Lafayette, joined those traveling to Mount Vernon to pay their respects to Washington in the postwar years. *Washington and Lafayette at Mount Vernon, 1784,* engraving by Thomas Oldham Barlow, 1860, after the painting by Thomas Prichard Rossiter and Louis Rémy Mignot, 1859. Willard–Budd Collection, MVLA

Lafayette's daughter, Washington wrote, "Her papa is restored to her with all the good health, paternal affection and honors her tender heart could wish. He will carry a kiss to her from me, (which might be more agreeable from a pretty boy) and give her assurances of the affectionate regard with which I have the pleasure of being her well wisher."[13] Although Washington corresponded with Lafayette throughout his life, their meeting at Mount Vernon in 1784 was their last.

Washington relished the opportunity to devote time to making Mount Vernon a stately and productive farm. The famous precedent of the Roman military leader who returned to his farm was not lost on many. As one visitor observed, "You have often heard him compared to Cincinnatus: the comparison is doubtless just. This celebrated General is nothing more at present than a good farmer, constantly occupied in the care of his farm and the improvement of cultivation."[14]

Washington's diary entries recount his routine surveys of his land, his attention to the trees, plantings, and gardens surrounding the house, and his attempts to create a pleasing house and garden. On one venture "in search of Elm & other Trees for my Shrubberies," Washington "went to Belvoir and viewed the ruined Buildings of that place."[15] The dwelling had been ravaged by fire in 1783, and Washington found it "scarcely worth repairing." The experience of returning to a spot that had offered so much joy before the Revolution, now in such visible ruin, was almost more than Washington could bear. He wrote to his old friend George William Fairfax, now in England, that "Belvoir is no more! I took a ride there the other day to visit the ruins—& ruins indeed they are. . . . In a word, the whole are, or very soon will be a heap of ruin. When I viewed them—when I considered that the happiest moments of my life had been spent there—when I could not trace a room in the house (now all rubbish) that did not bring to my mind the recollection of pleasing scenes; I was obliged to fly from them; & came home with painful sensations & sorrowing for the contrast."[16] Washington did not dwell on the past, however, but focused on his plans for Mount Vernon.

The work on his "New Room," or the north addition to the Mansion, continued. He indicated to Samuel Vaughan, an Englishman who had recently immigrated to Philadelphia, that he needed a mantel

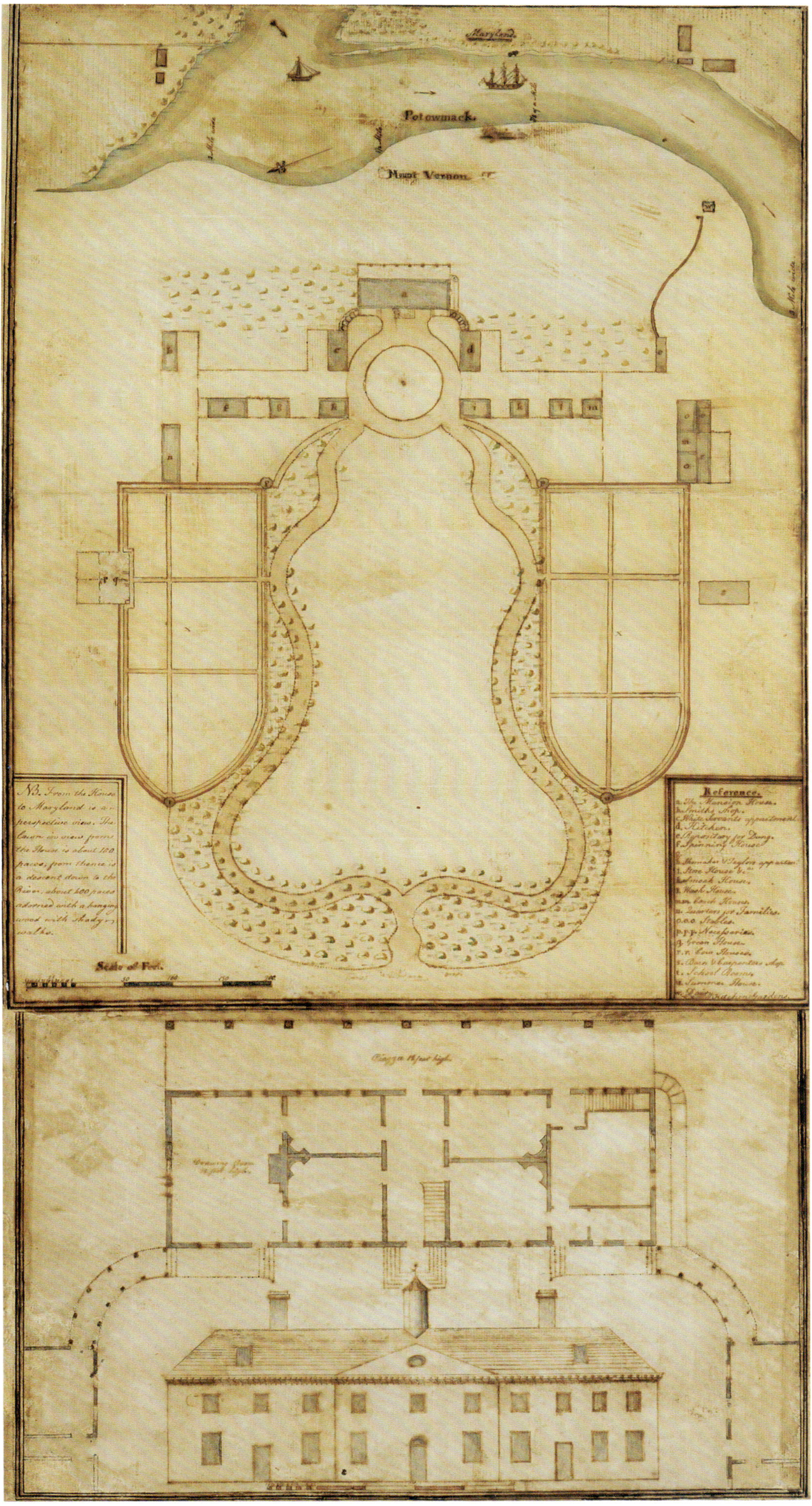

Fig. 5. Samuel Vaughan carefully drew a plan of the Mount Vernon estate during his 1787 visit that remains one of the best sources for understanding Washington's layout of buildings and gardens. MVLA

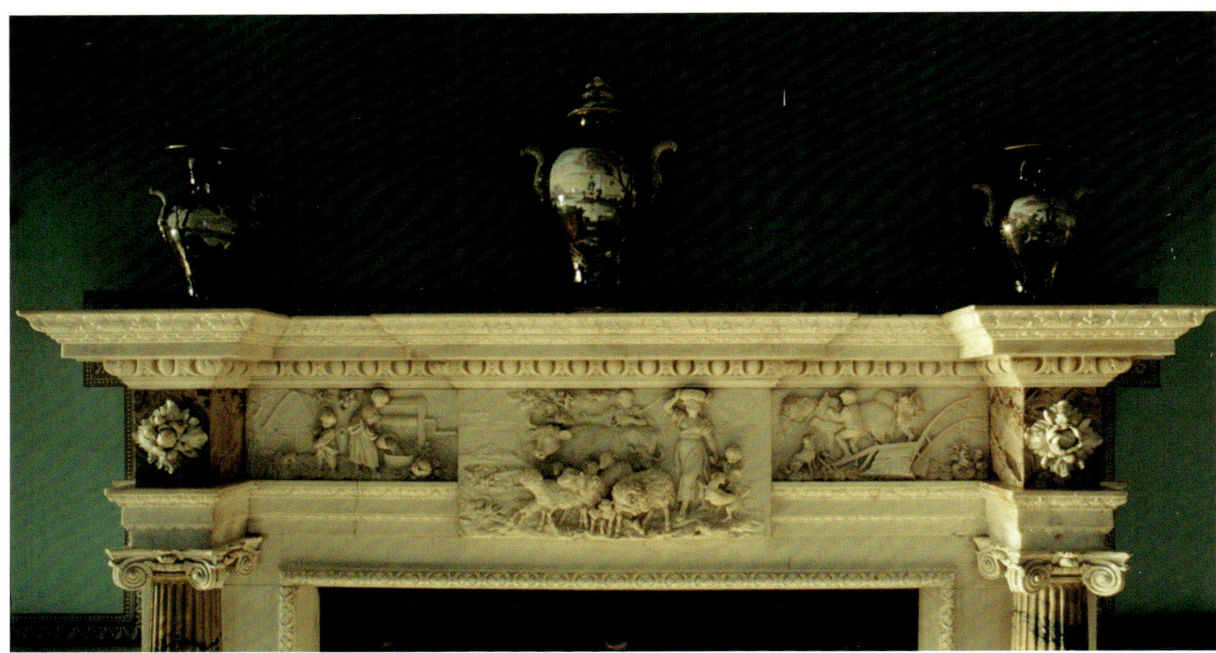

Fig. 6. Marble chimneypiece and Worcester porcelain mantel vases in the "New Room," or large dining room at Mount Vernon, gifts to George Washington from Samuel Vaughan, MVLA

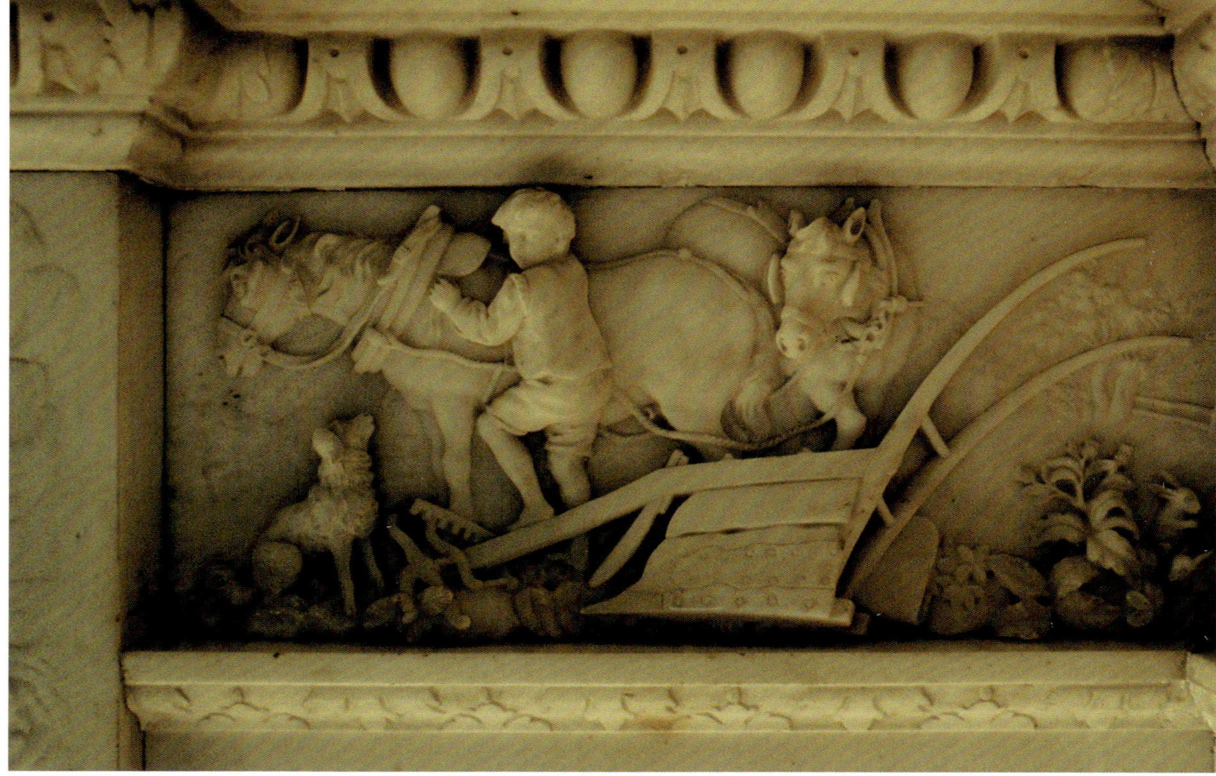

Fig. 7. Detail of the agricultural scenes in the marble chimneypiece Vaughan presented to Washington, MVLA

for the room. Vaughan responded by forwarding one from his own residence, Wanstead, back in England. Washington, though humbled by Vaughan's generosity, nonetheless delighted in the addition to his dining room. He wrote to Vaughan in February 1785 to inform him "that the Chimney piece is arrived, & by the number of Cases (ten) too elegant & costly by far I fear for my own room, & republican stile of living."[17] Although Washington may have had doubts about the suitability of the marble chimneypiece for his new dining room, he surely approved of the carved agricultural detailing that was obviously appropriate for a Cincinnatus figure (figs. 6, 7).

The frequent interruption of his attention to Mount Vernon by those coming to see, speak with, or

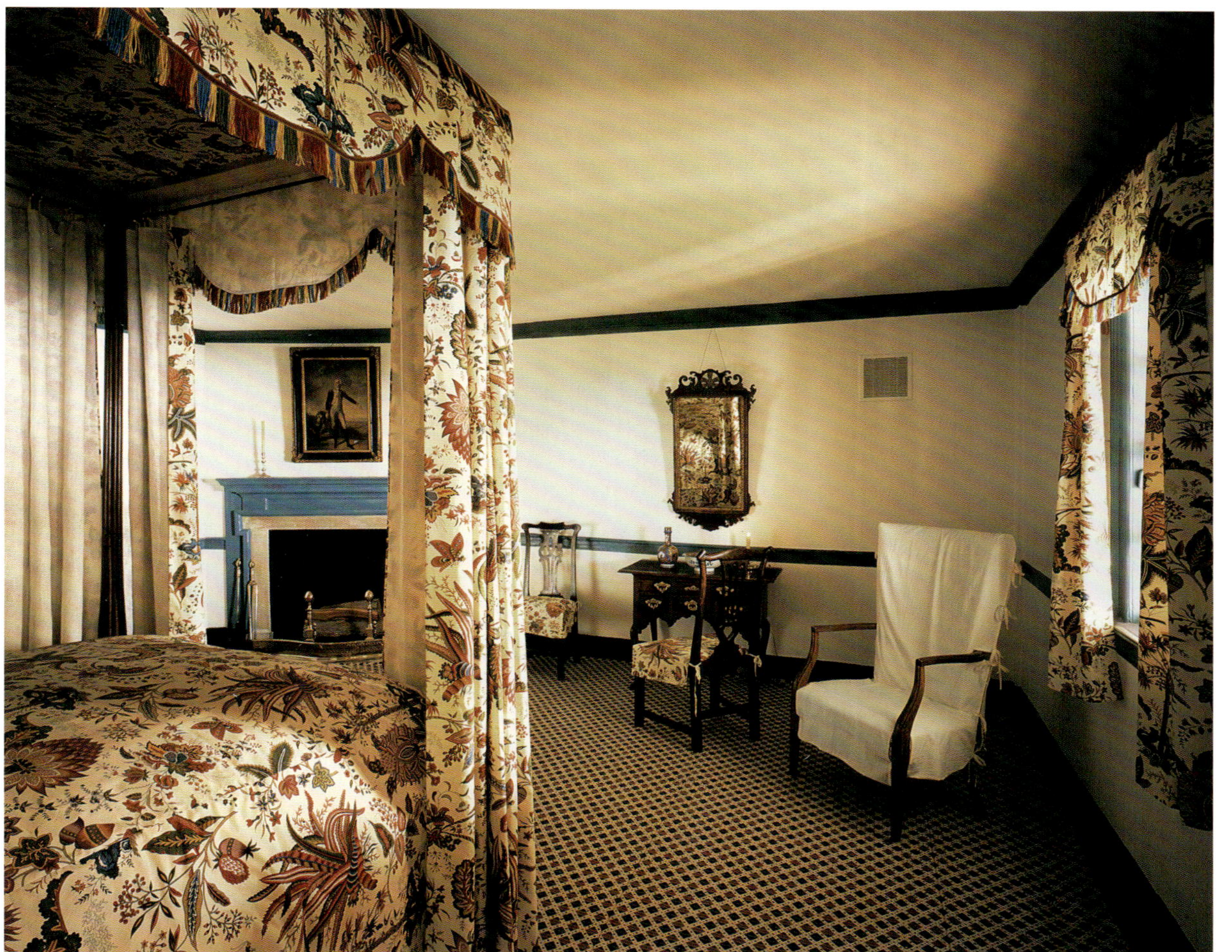

Fig. 8.
Mount Vernon bedchamber used by the Washingtons' numerous overnight guests, perhaps including the Marquis de Lafayette, MVLA

dine with the former general, however, rendered Washington's retirement not so quiet as he would have liked. When the Chevalier de la Luzerne visited Mount Vernon, the Frenchman noted, "After having seen him on my arrival in this continent, in the midst of his camp and in the tumult of arms, I have the pleasure to see him a simple citizen, enjoying in the repose of his retreat the glory which he so justly acquired. . . . He dresses in a gray coat like a Virginia farmer, and nothing about him recalls the recollections of the important part which he played except the great number of foreigners who come to see him."[18] Hundreds came to pay their respects and to glimpse the man who had defeated mighty England. Many, such as Elkanah Watson, had served with Washington during the Revolution. Watson recorded:

> *I had feasted my imagination for several days on the near prospect of a visit to Mount Vernon, the seat of Washington. No pilgrim ever approached Mecca with deeper enthusiasm. . . .The first evening I spent under the wing of his hospitality, we sat a full hour at table, by ourselves without the least interruption after the family had retired. I was extremely oppressed with a severe cold and excessive coughing, contracted from the exposure of a harsh winter journey. He pressed me to use some remedies, but I declined doing so. As usual after retiring, my coughing increased. When some time had elapsed, the door of my room was gently opened; and on drawing my bedcurtains, to my utter astonishment, I beheld Washington himself, standing at my bed-side with a bowl of hot tea in his hand. I was mortified, and distressed beyond expression. This little incident, occurring in common life with an ordinary man, would not have been noticed; but as a trait of the benevolence and private virtue of Washington, it deserves to be recorded.*[19]

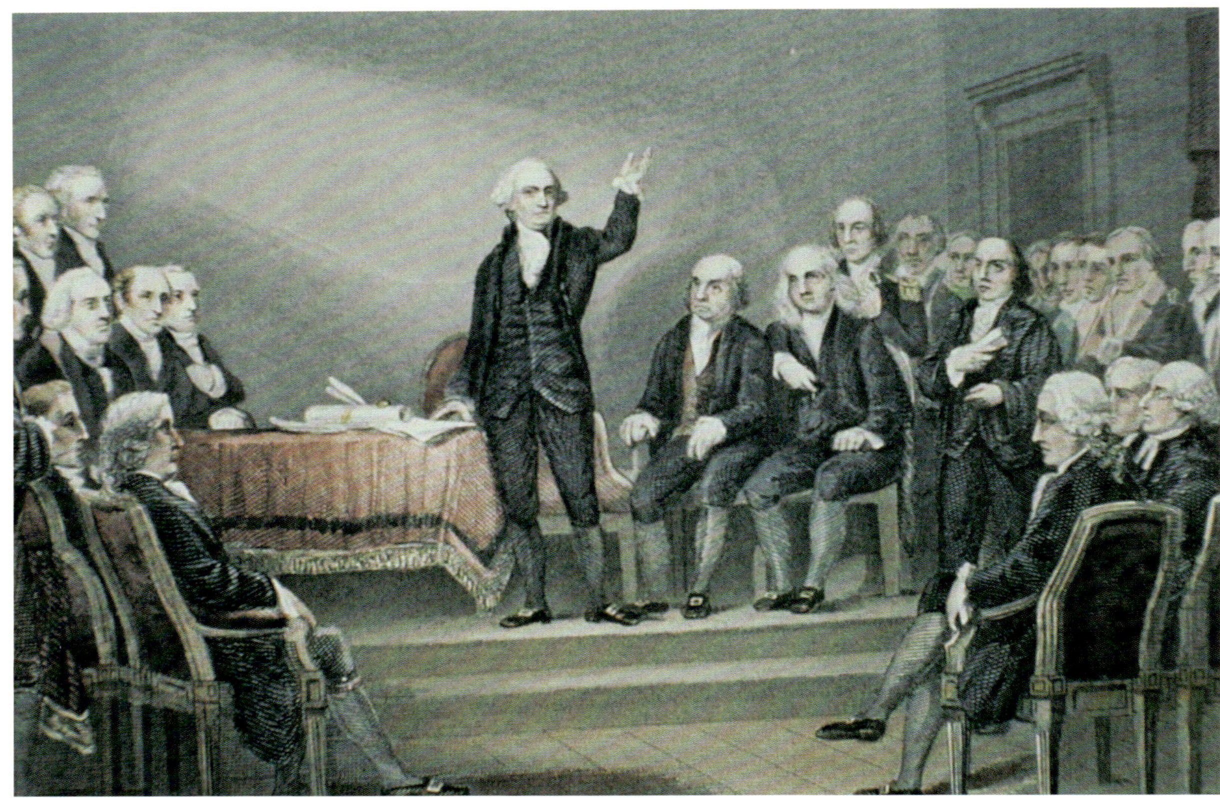

Fig. 9. Delegates unanimously selected George Washington to preside over the Constitutional Convention in 1787. Engraving published by Virtie & Co., ca. 1850, Willard-Budd Collection, MVLA

Washington was certainly gracious and hospitable to his guests and may well have enjoyed their company and the news they brought. Yet with the departure of a host of guests and family members on June 29, 1785, Washington recorded on the following day what must have been one of the more pleasing experiences of his retirement. He wrote, "[I rode] to my Hay field at the Meadow—from thence to my Dogue run and Muddy hole Plantations and dined with only Mrs. Washington which I believe is the first instance of it since my retirement from public life."[20]

In addition to the frequent admirers and well-wishers who made their way to Mount Vernon, friends wrote to tell the general of the admiration in which he was held around the globe. Reflecting on his tours through Europe, the Marquis de Lafayette declared, "Where Ever I went, my dear General, I Had the pleasure to Hear Your Name pronounced with that Respect and enthusiasm which altho' it is a matter of course, and I am so used to it, never fails to Make My Heart glow with Unspeakable Happiness."[21] Despite the urging of Lafayette and others, Washington could not be tempted away from Mount Vernon to travel to Europe to enjoy this fame. As he explained to Adrienne, the Marchioness de Lafayette, "The noon-tide of life is now passed with Mrs. Washington & myself, and all we have to do is to spend the evening of our days in tranquility, & glide gently down a stream which no human effort can ascend."[22] Others were aware of Washington's decision, as Robert Hunter noted in his travel diary: "And though solicited by the King of France and some of the first characters in the world to visit Europe he has denied them all and knows how to prefer solid happiness in his retirement to all the luxuries and flattering speeches of European courts."[23] If Washington would not venture to Europe, then Europe would go to Mount Vernon in the person of one of Europe's finest sculptors. In October 1785 the French sculptor Jean-Antoine Houdon delayed his modeling of Catherine the Great of Russia to cross the Atlantic for the purpose of taking George Washington's likeness. As scholars have noted, Houdon's visit to Mount Vernon at the encouragement of Americans and Europeans abroad prompted Washington to consider seriously the place he would hold in history.[24]

In 1787 Washington needed to look after his mother, who was failing in health and finances. He had arranged to rent her farm and set her up in a house in Fredericksburg, Virginia, near his sister, Betty Lewis. Mary Ball Washington, however, seemed unable to care for herself and her household. Washington, accordingly, encouraged her to live with one of her children. While willing to welcome her at Mount Vernon, Washington noted, "I am sure, and candour requires me to say it will never answer your purposes, in any shape whatsoever—for in truth it may be compared to a well resorted tavern, as scarcely any strangers who are going from north to south or from south to north do not spend a day or two at it."[25] Washington's mention of Mount Vernon as a "well resorted tavern" as a reason to dissuade his mother from selecting his home as her residence is a poignant reminder of the number of visitors that continued to make their way to his door.

That same year, Washington was called to the Constitutional Convention, where he was unanimously elected its president (fig. 9). Being president prevented him from participating in the discussions that were often highly charged, a situation that kept Washington's powerful influence from swaying opinion. His presence in the room lent dignity and gravitas to the proceedings, and his interaction outside the discussions enhanced relations between the diverse group of delegates. Known to a large number of the delegates from geographically dispersed colonies, Washington was able to facilitate their interaction through social engagements, suppers, and entertainments. Once the Constitution was drafted, Washington was the first to sign before it was sent to the states for ratification. For many, it was enough for them to know that he had presided over the crafting of the document and that his signature was first.[26]

Washington was back at Mount Vernon when word came that enough states had ratified the Constitution of the United States to make it a working document. He knew that his election to the role of president would soon follow. Without a hint of campaigning, Washington remained at Mount Vernon while the Continental Congress hammered out the details of the new government in Philadelphia. On February 4, 1789, the Electoral College unanimously elected George Washington the first president of the United States.

CAT. 28

Society of the Cincinnati Table and Teawares

Teapot with Lid	Covered Cup	Jingdezhen, China, ca. 1784	Tureen and Cover	Plate
H. 5⅛", W. 9½"	H. 3½", W. 3"	Porcelain	H. 5", W. 7¼"	DIAM. 9½"
W-1436/E	W-1436/C	Purchase, 1944	W-1436/H	W-1436/K

While George Washington spent the spring and summer of 1783 waiting for a formal declaration of peace and making preparations for retirement at Mount Vernon, so did his officers. In April Major General Henry Knox[27] circulated a letter from West Point to suggest that his fellow officers form a society of the American and French officers who had served in the cause for American independence.[28] The intent of the society was the maintenance of the relationships made during the war, so that officers could meet "from time to time, to recall the scenes of thrilling interest, in which they had mutually shared, and at the same time, of creating a fund for the relief of their indigent members."[29] The name, the Society of the Cincinnati, was inspired by the legendary fifth-century B.C.E. Roman Lucius Quinctius Cincinnatus, who left his plow to defend Rome in battle and returned to his farm at the conclusion of his military duty. The society's emblems were to reflect the union of America and France in a blue-and-white ribbon from which was suspended a bald eagle proclaiming the motto of the society—Omnia relinquit servare Rempublicam (He leaves all behind to protect the state)—and within an oval medallion a figural scene of Cincinnatus' return home.[30]

George Washington approved of the Society of the Cincinnati, and, like the Roman general to whom he was being compared, his thoughts focused on a return to the land. Once at Mount Vernon, Washington sought a porcelain service like that described in an announcement in the Baltimore *Advertiser*, which displayed "the Arms of the Order of the Cincinnati."[31] He wrote to now retired Lieutenant Colonel Tench Tilghman,[32] then in Baltimore, of his interest in the ship *Pallas*, "immediately from China," whose contents were being sold "at public Venue." Washington asked Tilghman to secure for him some items, but only "if *great bargains* are to be had," including "A Sett of the best Nankin Table China . . . With the badge of the Society of the Cincinnati, if to be had."[33] This sale of recently imported fashionable Chinese wares did not yield great bargains, and Tilghman reported the goods were "so extravagantly high, that you might have bought them cheaper out of any store in Town."[34] Although Tilghman made no purchases for Washington, the general was supplied with a service through the efforts of Colonel Henry "Light-Horse Harry" Lee the following year.

In July 1786 Henry Lee was attending the meeting of the Continental Congress in New York when he wrote to George Washington, "If you should be in want of a new set of china it is in my power to procure a very genteel set, table & tea—what renders this china doubly valuable & handsome is the order of the eagle engraved on it in honor of the Cincinnati—it has upwards of 306 pieces and is offered at the prime cost, 150 dollars."[35] Washington at once responded that he was "much obliged" to Lee for this news and requested that the porcelain be immediately purchased and shipped to Alexandria.[36] That October, Washington acknowledged to Lee his receipt of the porcelain at Mount Vernon, noting, "The China came to hand without much damage; and I thank you for your attention in procuring & forwarding of it to me."[37]

Washington's service, which included breakfast, table, and tea wares, numbered 302 pieces, each decorated in overglaze enamel with the insignia of the Society of the Cincinnati held by the allegorical winged figure of Fame (or Pheme), the mythological goddess of fame and report.[38] The underglaze blue Fitzhugh border places the porcelain among the best quality and most stylish of Chinese export porcelains making their way to American shores at the time.[39] Of the extensive service, approximately 130 pieces are known to survive in private and public collections. Relatively few of these survivals are tea wares, however, and the teapot at Mount Vernon is believed to be the sole extant example.

The Society of the Cincinnati porcelain was in use at Mount Vernon by the Washingtons until Martha Washington's death in 1802. Her will specified that George Washington Parke Custis should have the general's "Set of Cincinnati tea and table China,"[40] and Custis took the service to his residence overlooking the Potomac, Arlington House. In 1859 the author and Washington enthusiast Benson Lossing published an engraving of some of the pieces of the service that survived at Arlington House (fig. 1).[41] Soon afterward, during the Civil War, the dwelling was occupied by Union troops, eager to take over the home of Custis's son-in-law, Robert E. Lee. Like many of the Washington objects at Arlington House, the Society of the Cincinnati porcelain was removed to the United States Patent Office in Washington, D.C., and, after years of efforts on the part of the Lee family, restored to Mary Lee by President William McKinley.[42]

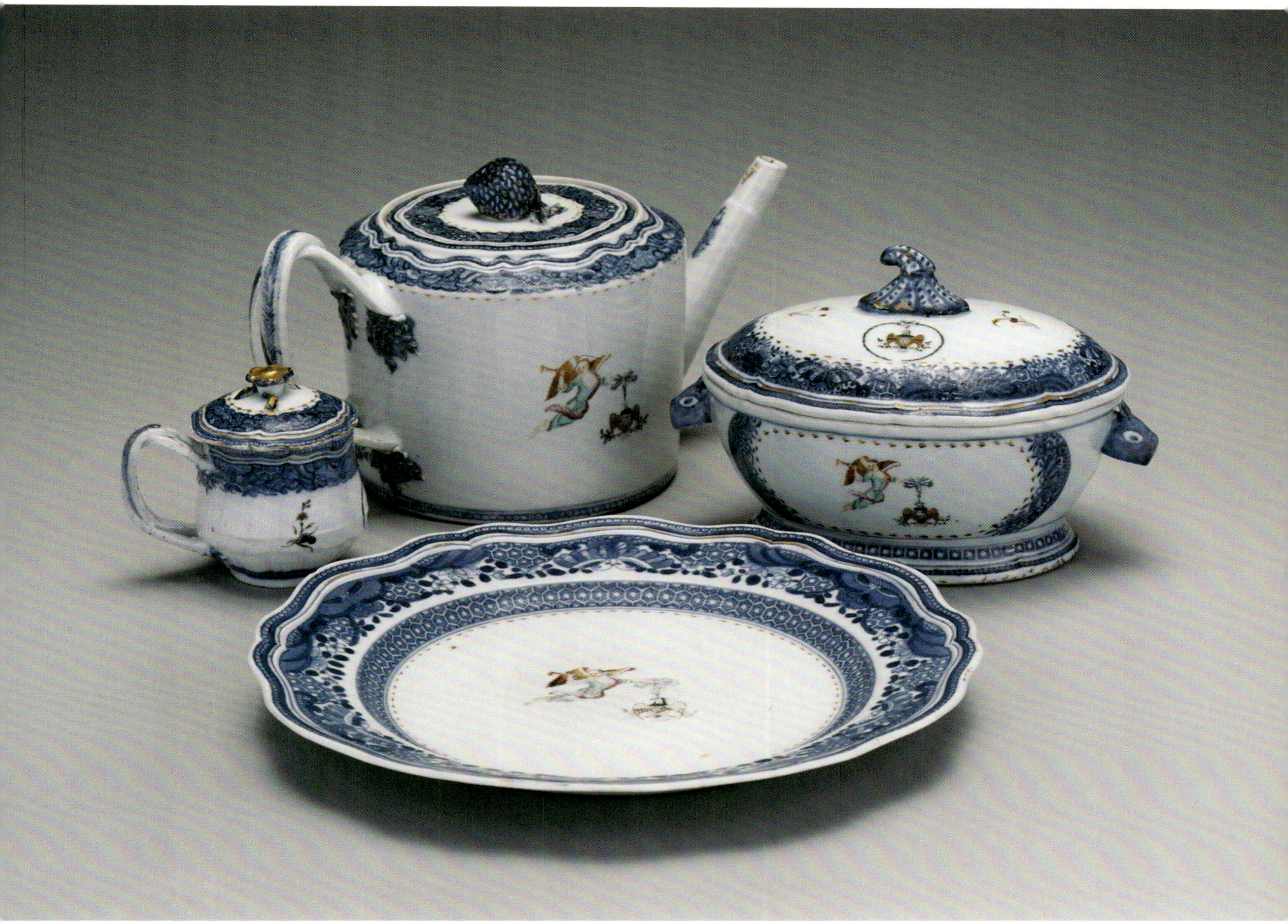

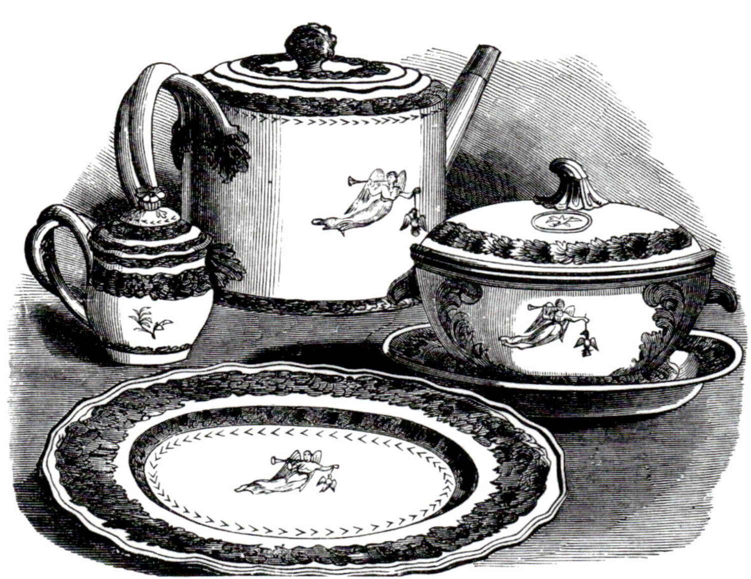

Fig. 1.
Assemblage of Society of the Cincinnati porcelain as sketched by Benson Lossing at Arlington House and published in his *Mount Vernon and Its Associations*, 1859, MVLA

CAT. 29

Platter

Jingdezhen, China, ca. 1770–1780
Porcelain, L. 13", W. 9⅛"
Purchased by the A. Alfred Taubman Fund, 2001
2001.008

In the fall of 1783, a few weeks before returning to Mount Vernon, George Washington tried to buy a blue-and-white Chinese export porcelain table service to take the place of the earthen creamware service he had ordered before the Revolution. He sent word to Daniel Parker in New York and his nephew, Bushrod Washington, in Philadelphia that the "neat and compleat sett of blue and White Table China" should include "Not less than 6 or 8 dozn Shallow [plates] and a proportionable number of Deep and other Plates, Butter Boats, Dishes and Tureens."[43] To Bushrod, Washington felt the need to add, "As you are young in this business, take some mentor as a guide to your enquires."[44]

Parker asked the New York tavern keeper Samuel Fraunces to help locate the porcelains Washington wanted. Although Fraunces was not able to find a complete set for Washington, he was able to amass a mixed assortment of 205 pieces, including tureens of two sizes, butter boats, salad dishes, "Flatt," soup, dessert, and fruit plates, as well as "27 Dishes."[45] Platters were not mentioned on Parker's invoice, and this example may be part of the "27 Dishes" noted that were likely of different sizes and design.

This platter is a slightly smaller version of an example in the Smithsonian Institution's collection.[46] The central landscape scene and ornate border are well rendered in handpainted underglaze cobalt blue and feature common elements of the Chinese design vocabulary such as the weeping willow tree, pagoda, and butterflies. It was still in use at the time of George Washington's death in 1799, and Martha Washington referred to it as part of the "blew & white china in common use"[47] when she willed it to her granddaughter, Eleanor "Nelly" Parke Custis Lewis. Nelly kept the memories of George and Martha Washington alive at her nearby home, Woodlawn Plantation, and frequently shared her inheritance with friends and relatives who called on her there. In August 1839 Nelly presented this platter "to her much esteemed friend Mr. Samuel Whitall," with a note that identified it as "imported by Genl G Washington either before, or immediately after the War of Independence."[48]

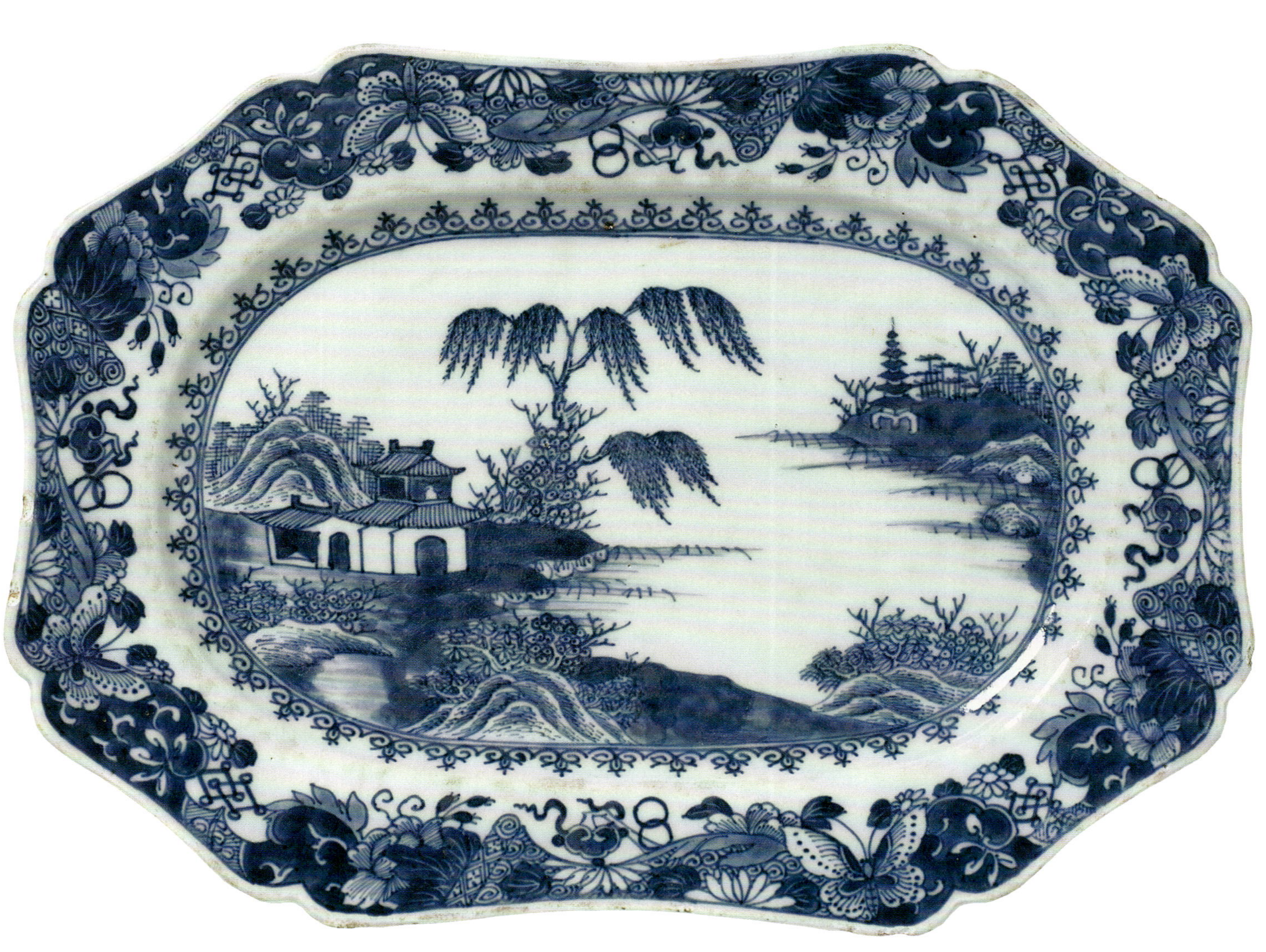

CAT. 30

Cream Pail and Ladle

Pail
England, ca. 1784
Silver plate, H. 6¼", DIAM. 3⅜"
Purchase, 1992
W-3653

Ladle
England, ca. 1784
Silver plate, L. 5½"
Purchase, 1975
W-2669

In addition to asking Bushrod Washington to investigate the availability of dining chairs and blue-and-white Chinese porcelains in Philadelphia, George Washington also asked if his nephew could discreetly ascertain if silver-plated wares were fashionable and therefore appropriate purchases for Mount Vernon. He wrote to Bushrod:

> *I wish to know, without having it known for whom the enquiry is made; and that is, whether French plate is fashionable and much used in genteel houses in France and England; and whether, as we have heard, the quantity in Philadelphia is large, of what pieces it consists, and whether among them, there are Tea urns, Coffee pots, Tea pots, and other equipage for a tea table.*[49]

"These enquiries you may make in behalf of a friend," Washington instructed his nephew, "without bringing my name forward, 'till occasion (if a purchase shou'd happen) may require it."[50] Now that the imported beverage could again be enjoyed, the retiring general wished to secure proper tea wares for Mount Vernon, and he wanted them to be fashionable, like those utilized in the "genteel" residences across the Atlantic.

Bushrod must have responded that "French plate," or silver-plated tea wares, were in fashion but not readily available in Philadelphia, for while in New York shortly after the British evacuation, Washington purchased "many pieces of the plated Ware"[51] and requested Daniel Parker to have additional pieces sent from London. In April 1784 the London firm of Joy and Hopkins shipped the plated pieces Parker had ordered for Washington, including a tea (or hot-water) urn, two teapots, one coffeepot, an inlaid mahogany tea board (or tray) and a tea caddy, and two pairs of "sug^r^ & cream pails with Ladles & Glasses."[52]

This cream pail with ladle, part of the London wares supplied by Joy and Hopkins, are good examples of the new silver-plate technology that made silver items more broadly affordable. They are crafted of the double-sandwich form of Sheffield plate developed about 1770, in which a sheet of copper is placed between two sheets of silver. The resulting combination of base metal and silver was worked by silversmiths in the same manner as a sheet of solid silver. The pail's raised urn-shaped body and trumpet foot, ornamented with beaded rims and chased floral garland, represent the new Neoclassical taste. The beading is continued on the ladle, and both bear Washington's signature griffin. The pail's delicate pierced work provides a glimpse of the cobalt blue glass liner, a contrast that must have been pleasing when seen on the Washingtons' tea table.

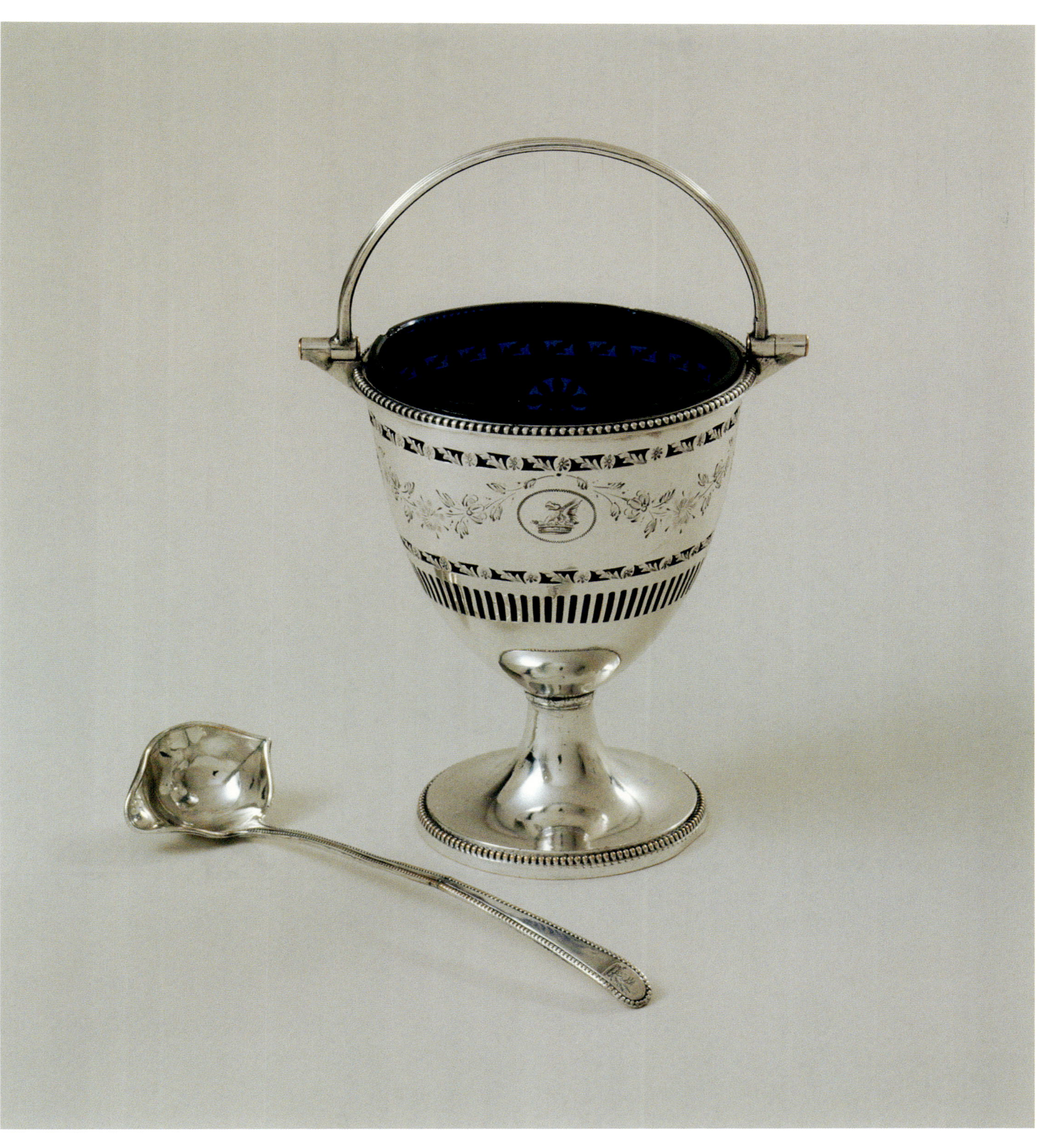

CAT. 31

Bread Basket

England or France,[53] ca. 1784
Silver plate, OH. 11½", W. 14⅜"
Purchase, 1981
W-2801

George Washington also wrote to Paris for the Marquis de Lafayette's assistance in acquiring silver-plated wares necessary to equip his Mount Vernon table properly. He apologized for putting Lafayette to the trouble of securing the goods for him, suggesting that he had turned to his protégé "because I do not incline to send to England (from whence I formerly had all my goods) for anything I can get upon tolerable terms elsewhere." Washington further noted that he had "no correspondence with any Merchants or artisans in France," and that, even if he did, the Marquis was much better aware of "our customs, taste and manner of living in America."[54]

Washington's list of requested plated ware included "every thing proper for a tea-table," as well as four salvers for wineglasses, a dozen saltcellars, a dozen candlesticks, eight "Bottle Sliders" (fig. 1), half a dozen "Large Goblets," "a Cross of Stand for the centre of the Dining table, a Sett of Casters, for holding, oil, Vinegar, Mustard &ca," and "Two Bread-baskets, middle size."[55]

This bread basket is one of two that arrived at Mount Vernon from Lafayette in the spring of 1784.[56] Exhibiting neoclassical design elements, the oval body is heavily pierced and engraved with rows of leaves enclosing wheelwork flowers connected by swags and is supported by a pedestal of closely spaced pierced reeding. A large bail handle is hinged to the sides so that Washington's guests could easily circulate and take bread from this fashionable addition to the dining table.

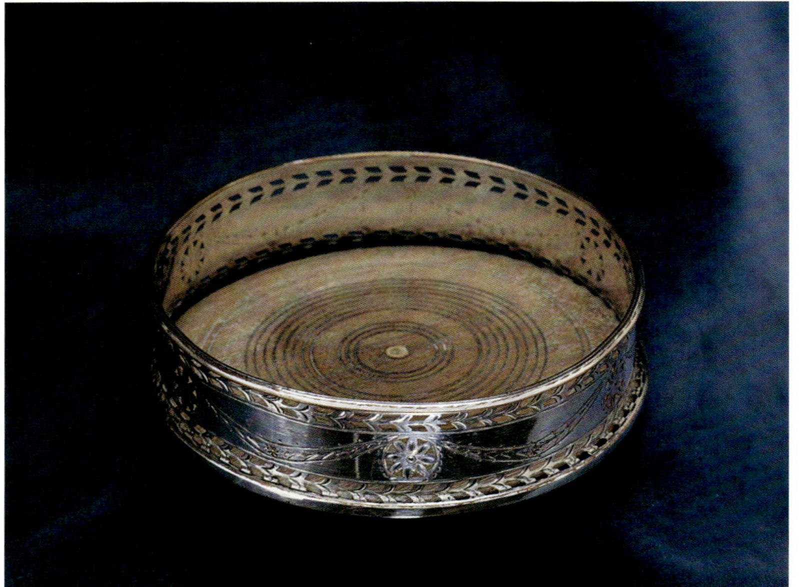

Fig. 1. One of the eight silver plate "Bottle Sliders" (or wine coasters) included in Lafayette's shipment, MVLA

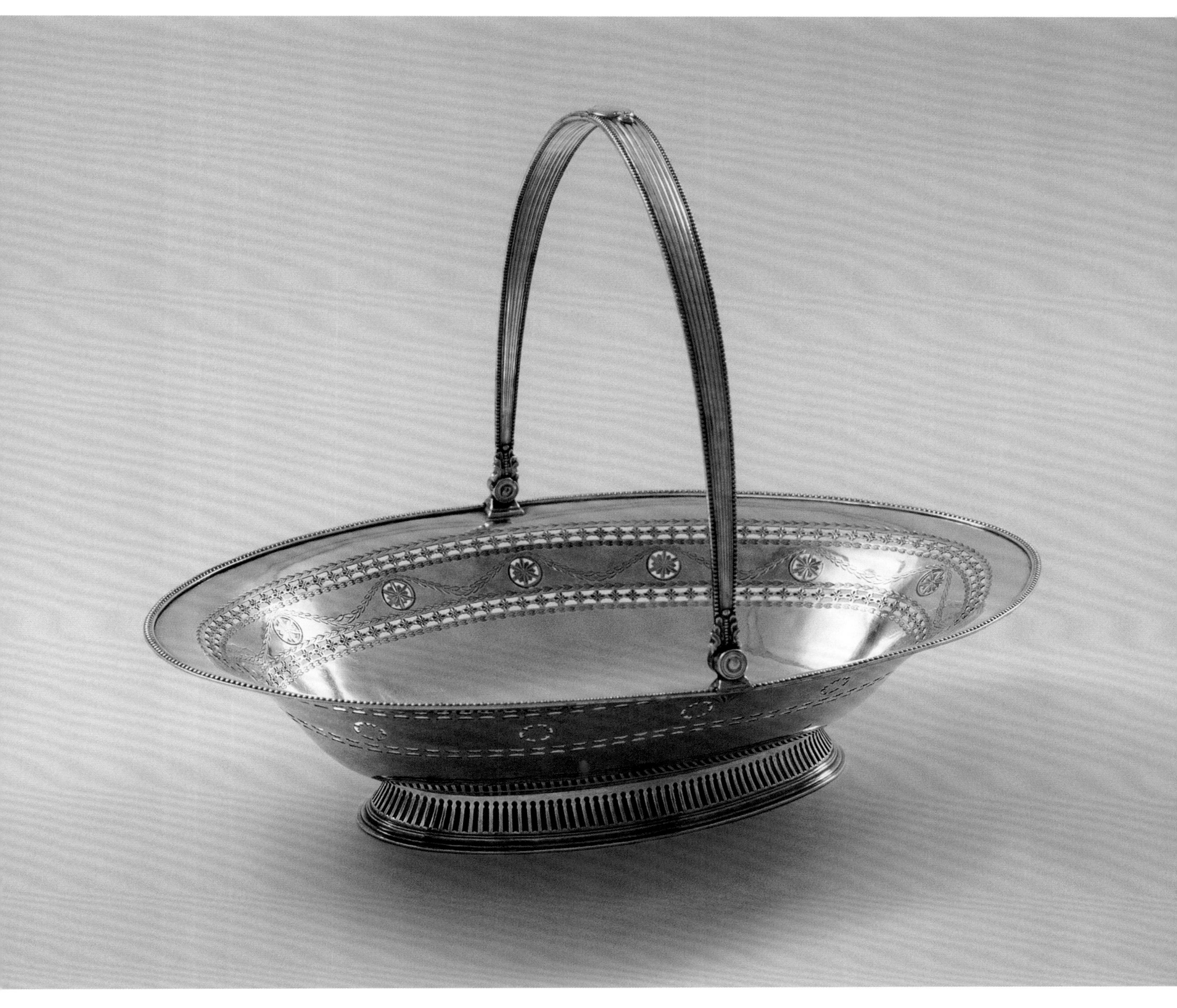

CAT. 32

Coffeepot

Joseph Anthony, Jr. (1762–1814, active 1783–1810)
Philadelphia, Pennsylvania, ca. 1783
Silver, H. 14¼"
Gift of Mary Walker Lee Bowman and Mr. Robert E. Lee IV, 1981[57]
W-2517

Turkish traders introduced the coffee bean to Europe and Great Britain in the mid-seventeenth century, that is, at nearly the same time that Chinese tea and Mexican chocolate arrived on British shores. The English public first encountered coffee as a beverage in local coffeehouses, the commercial gathering places for businessmen. In time, coffee made its appearance in affluent English and colonial residences and created the need for new domestic serving vessels.[58]

Coffee was enjoyed regularly at Mount Vernon, and as early as 1758 George Washington was buying ten pounds of the "best" Turkish coffee for himself and his guests.[59] It is not surprising, then, that while in Philadelphia and en route to Mount Vernon, the general's thoughts turned to the most elegant means for serving coffee to those who would call on him once he was at home. On December 13, less than two weeks before resigning his commission, Washington noted the purchase of this "Silvr Coffee Pot"[60] in his cash memorandum. Perhaps for use with the coffeepot, he wrote three weeks later from Mount Vernon to Philadelphia that "a Barrl. of good Coffee might be sent me by the first Vessel bound for the Port of Alexandria."[61]

Washington's coffeepot is an excellent example of Rococo silver and is stamped "J. Anthony" twice on the bottom by its maker, the Philadelphia silversmith Joseph Anthony, Jr. (detail).[62] The raised body of the pear (or double-bellied) form rests on a pedestal foot ornamented with a gadrooned border, and the double-domed lid is accented by a gadrooned rim with a bell-shaped finial. The double-scroll wood handle and leaf-capped S-curved spout balance the form and contribute to the naturalistic Rococo detailing. The retiring general paid an additional three dollars to have the Washington family coat of arms engraved in a Rococo cartouche on the coffeepot, and it no doubt became a stately and elegant part of George and Martha Washington's postwar entertaining.

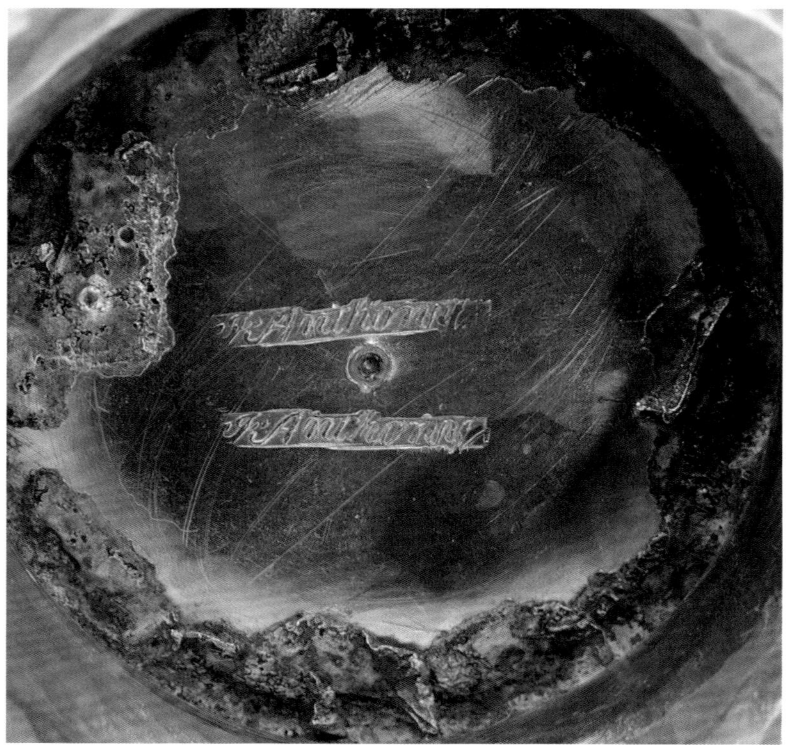

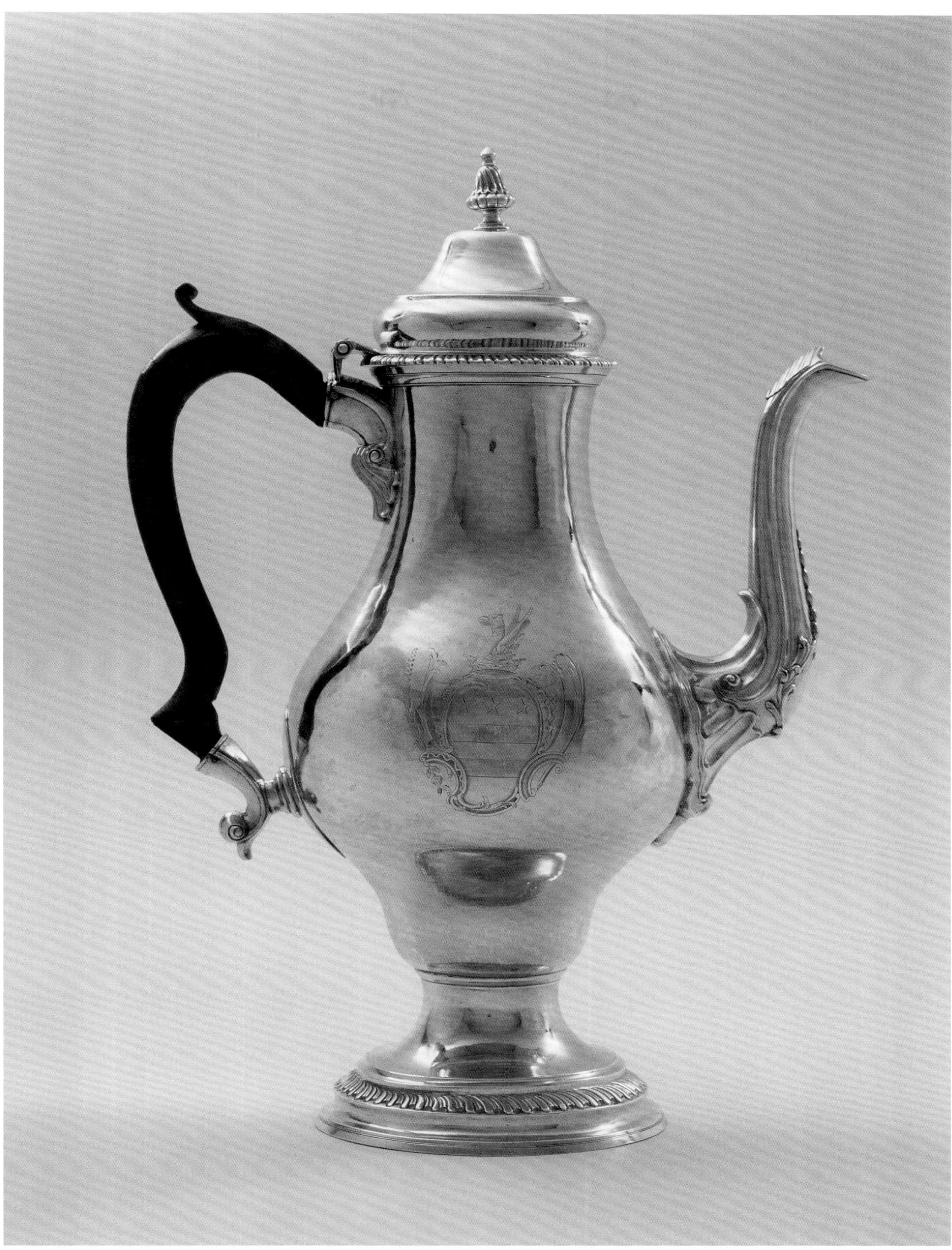

CAT. 33

Salver

Probably Philadelphia, ca. 1783
Silver, DIAM. 11½"
Gift of Mary Walker Lee Bowman and Robert E. Lee IV, 1981
W-2515

When Washington retired, he had a great interest in properly outfitting Mount Vernon with silver and silver-plated wares. Although he had requested the Marquis de Lafayette to help him in the acquisition of silver-plated items, including "Two large Salvers, sufficient to hold twelve common wine glasses, each" and "Two smaller size . . . for 6 wine glasses, each,"[63] Washington seems to have seized the opportunity to acquire the salvers in solid silver in Philadelphia and Alexandria, Virginia. This large salver was likely purchased by Washington in Philadelphia when en route to Mount Vernon; he also bought a coffeepot from Joseph Anthony, Jr. (cat. 32). Once he had returned to Virginia, Washington probably turned to the Alexandria silversmith Edward Sanford to produce two smaller salvers modeled on the larger example. His accounts list payment in March 1784 to Sanford "for mak^{g} Silver salvers,"[64] and two surviving examples patterned after the larger Philadelphia salver may be linked to this entry (fig. 1).[65]

This large salver is attributed to Philadelphia based on comparable examples produced by the city's silversmiths. The similarity of its cast and applied border to those fashioned by Richard Humphreys offers the possibility that it was crafted in Humphreys' shop. Washington's signature griffin crest, centered on the salver, is engraved in the same manner as those placed on the camp cups and spoons supplied by Humphreys several years earlier. The stylized shell-and-gadrooned border together with the salver's claw-and-ball feet makes it a fine example of American Rococo silver. It was an elegant vehicle for conveying wineglasses to the Washingtons' guests.

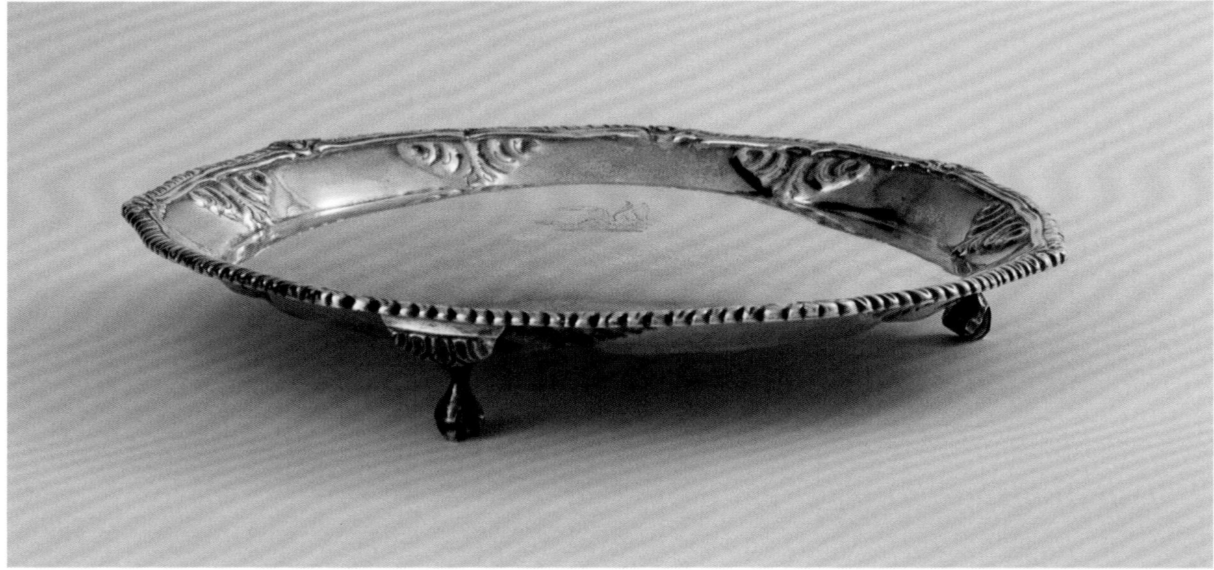

Fig. 1. (right) One of two silver salvers attributed to Edward Sanford of Alexandria and likely based on Washington's larger Philadelphia example. Private collection

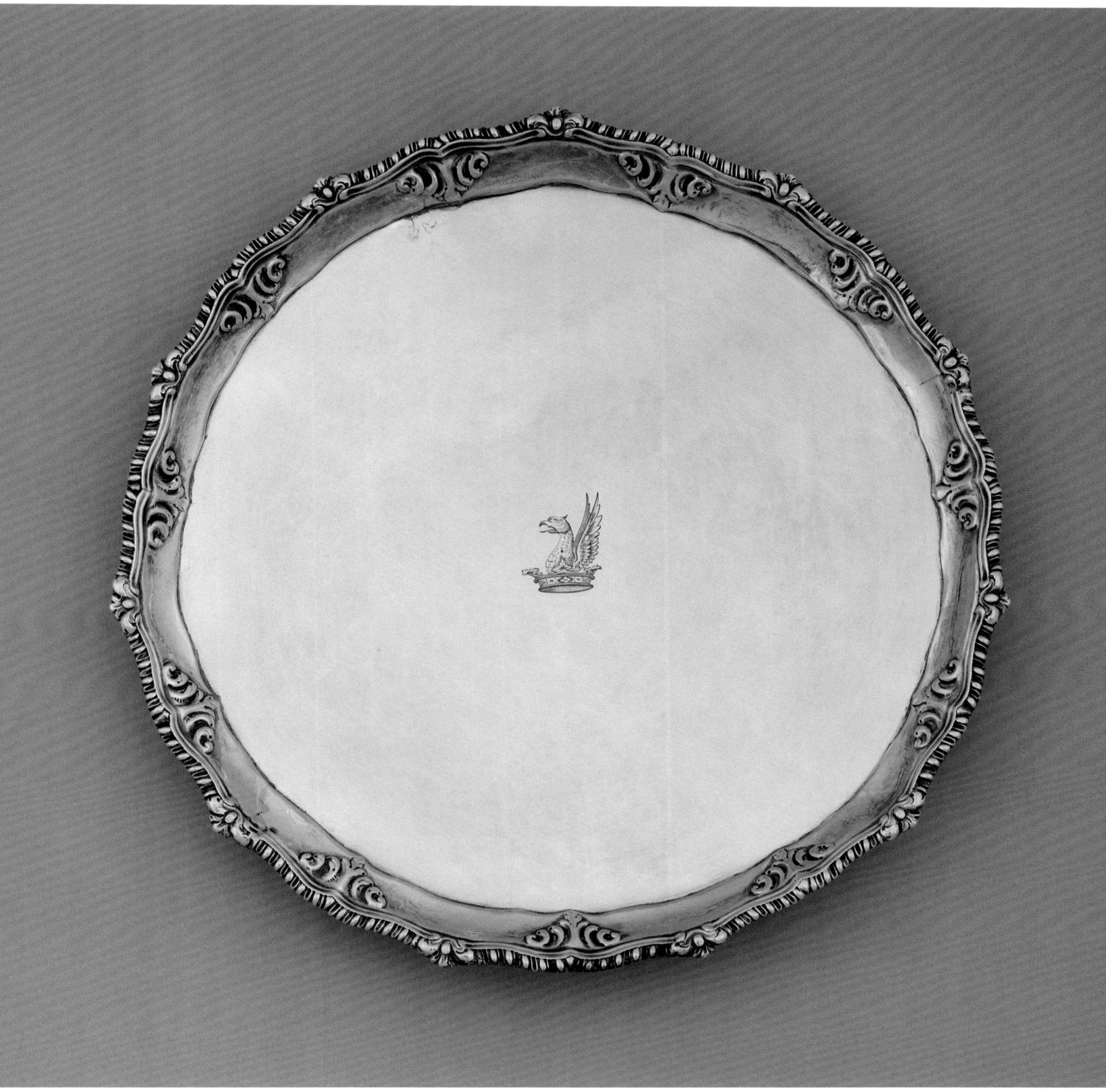

CAT. 34

George Washington

1785

Jean-Antoine Houdon (1741–1828)

Low-fired clay, H. 22"

Signed and dated on proper right shoulder: Houdon F. 1785

Transferred to the Mount Vernon Ladies' Association through the generosity of John Augustine Washington, III, 1860

W-369

In December 1784 Benjamin Franklin and Thomas Jefferson were in Paris considering an appropriate sculptor to undertake a statue of George Washington for the Virginia Capitol in Richmond. Jefferson wrote to Washington, "I find that a Monsr Houdon of this place possesses the reputation of being the first statuary in the world . . . and is so enthusiastically fond of being the executor of this work that he offers to go himself to America for the purpose of forming your bust from the life, leaving all his business here in the mean time."[66] Jefferson advised that if Franklin agreed with the selection of Jean-Antoine Houdon as the sculptor to portray Washington, "we shall send him over, not having time to ask your permission & await your answer" and trusting that Washington would take time "to transmit to posterity the form of the person whose actions will be delivered to them by History."[67]

The following September, Franklin wrote from Philadelphia to tell Washington that Houdon had arrived in that city and that he was soon to visit Mount Vernon. He noted that he himself had just arrived from France, "a Country, where the Reputation of General Washington runs very high, and where every body wishes to see him in Person, but being told that it is not likely he will ever favour them with a Visit, they hope at least for a Sight of his perfect Resemblance by means of their Principal Statuary Mr. Houdon." Franklin further noted that he understood "there is no Prospect of your coming hither."[68] Indeed, Washington could not be tempted to leave Mount Vernon for the acclaims of Europe or even Philadelphia unless the nation required it.

Houdon's arrival at Mount Vernon on October 2, 1785, rousing a sleeping household, must have been dramatic, for Washington recorded in his diary the arrival of the sculptor and three assistants, "After we were in Bed (about Eleven Oclock in the evening)."[69] Over the next two weeks, Houdon accompanied Washington on his normal routine in order to select the pose and expression that best defined the general. The sculptor apparently chose Washington's expression after observing the general's indignant look over the high price quoted to him on a pair of horses.[70] On October 6 Houdon began work on this clay bust, which he modeled with the assistance of detailed measurements of Washington. Likely created as a model for the larger sculpture, the bust was perhaps fired in the Mount Vernon kitchen bake oven.

Four days later, Houdon began work on a plaster life mask of Washington. Washington was fascinated by Houdon's "process for preparing the Plaster of Paris."[71] Eleanor Parke "Nelly" Custis, Martha Washington's granddaughter living at Mount Vernon, recorded her recollection of the day Houdon laid the plaster on Washington's face:

> *I was only six years old at the time, and perhaps should not have retained any recollection of Houdon & his visit, had I not seen the General as I supposed, dead, & laid out on a large table cover'd with a sheet. I was passing the white servants Hall & saw as I thought the Corpse of one I consider'd my Father, I went in, & found the General extended on his back on a large table, a sheet over him, except his face, on which Houdon was engaged in putting on plaster to form the cast. Quills were in the nostrils. I was very much alarmed until I was told that it was a bust, a likeness of the General, & would not injure him.*[72]

On October 17, 1785, Houdon departed Mount Vernon, leaving the clay bust with Washington and returning to France with the life mask and Washington's measurements that would assist him in sculpting the larger version for the Virginia State Capitol.[73]

Washington placed Houdon's work in his study, where it remained for fifteen years, until after his death. His estate inventory in 1800 lists it as "1 bust of General Washington in plaister from the life," with the substantial evaluation of $100.[74] It was apparently worth far more, however, to those assembled at Mount Vernon in 1802 for its sale, inasmuch as Bushrod Washington paid $250 to own the lifelike image of his uncle and retain it at Mount Vernon.[75] Through several generations of Washington family owners and the estate's purchase by the Mount Vernon Ladies' Association, Houdon's bust of George Washington has remained at Mount Vernon. Said by friends and relatives to be the most accurate likeness of George Washington ever created, and as a work of the master sculptor Houdon, this clay bust is arguably the most precious object in the Mount Vernon collection.

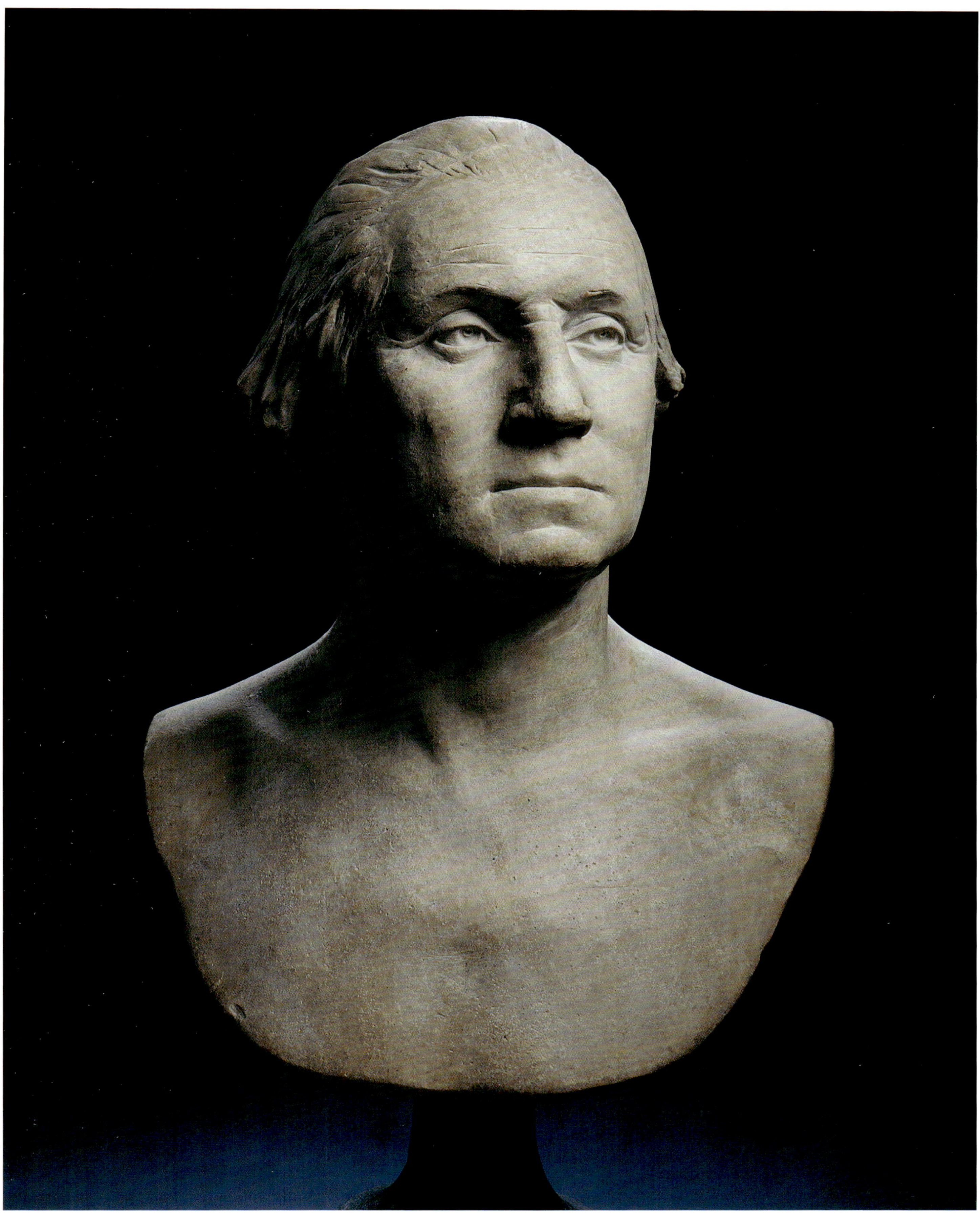

CAT. 35

Weathervane

Joseph Rakestraw (c. 1735–1794)
Philadelphia, Pennsylvania, 1787
Copper, iron, lead, OH. 42¼", OW. 35"
Signed and inscribed: PAC / Philadelphia Copper / J. Raikstraw
Transferred to the Mount Vernon Ladies' Association through the generosity of John Augustine Washington, III, 1860
W-2492

During the summer of 1787 George Washington presided over the Constitutional Convention held in Philadelphia. Although he participated in the events and discussions surrounding the convention, Washington's mind frequently turned to his retirement and Mount Vernon. He was working on a cupola to adorn the Mount Vernon roofline and asked the Philadelphia architect Joseph Rakestraw to construct a weathervane.[76] Washington wrote to George Augustine Washington, his nephew who managed Mount Vernon in his absence, for dimensions and drawings to enable Rakestraw to make the weathervane to the correct proportion.[77] On July 20 he shared with Rakestraw his idea for the weathervane: "I should like to have a bird (in place of the Vain) with an olive branch in its Mouth—the bird need not be large (for I do not expect that it will traverse with the wind and therefore may receive the real shape of a bird, with spread wings)."[78]

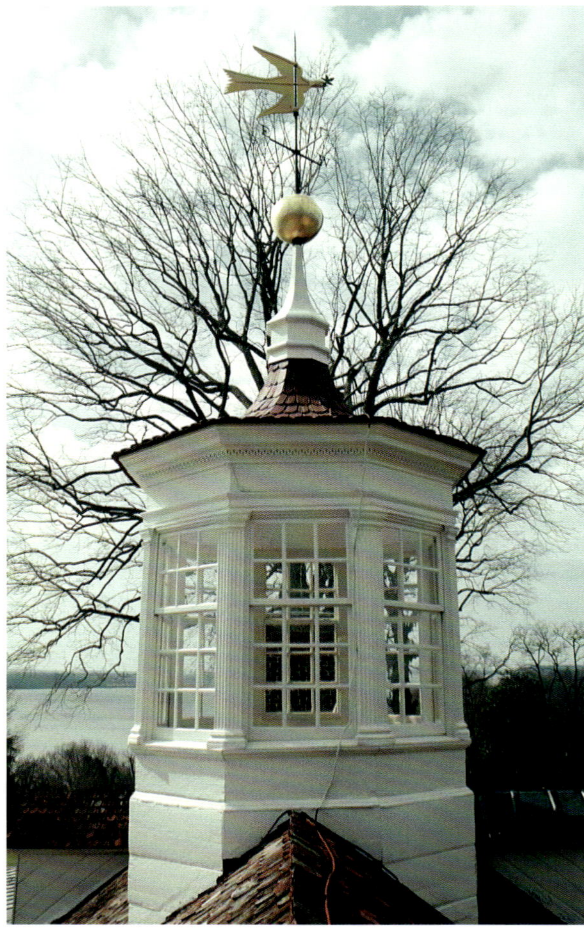

Washington's dove of peace weathervane atop Mount Vernon's cupola

Rakestraw used copper bound with iron strips to fashion the dove's body, one piece of iron for the bill and olive branch, and lead for the dove's head, in order to balance the body's weight. Rakestraw's bill for crafting the weathervane was just over twenty-four pounds, and Washington recorded payment on August 10, 1787.[79] The general lost no time in shipping his new acquisition to Mount Vernon and wrote to George Augustine Washington on August 12 that a number of items, including the weathervane, were en route by water via the *Dolphin.* He sent specific installation instructions with the object, noting that it must be painted properly: "the bill of the bird is to be black, and the Olive branch in the mouth of it, must be green."[80]

Washington's desire to crown his residence with a dove holding an olive branch in its beak referred to ancient Greek and Early Christian symbolism, which used the dove and olive branch as references to peace.[81] Drawing on classical iconography, Washington's dove symbolized domestic peace for the new nation and reminded all of the many visitors winding their way up Washington's path of the classical ideals that inspired the founding of America.

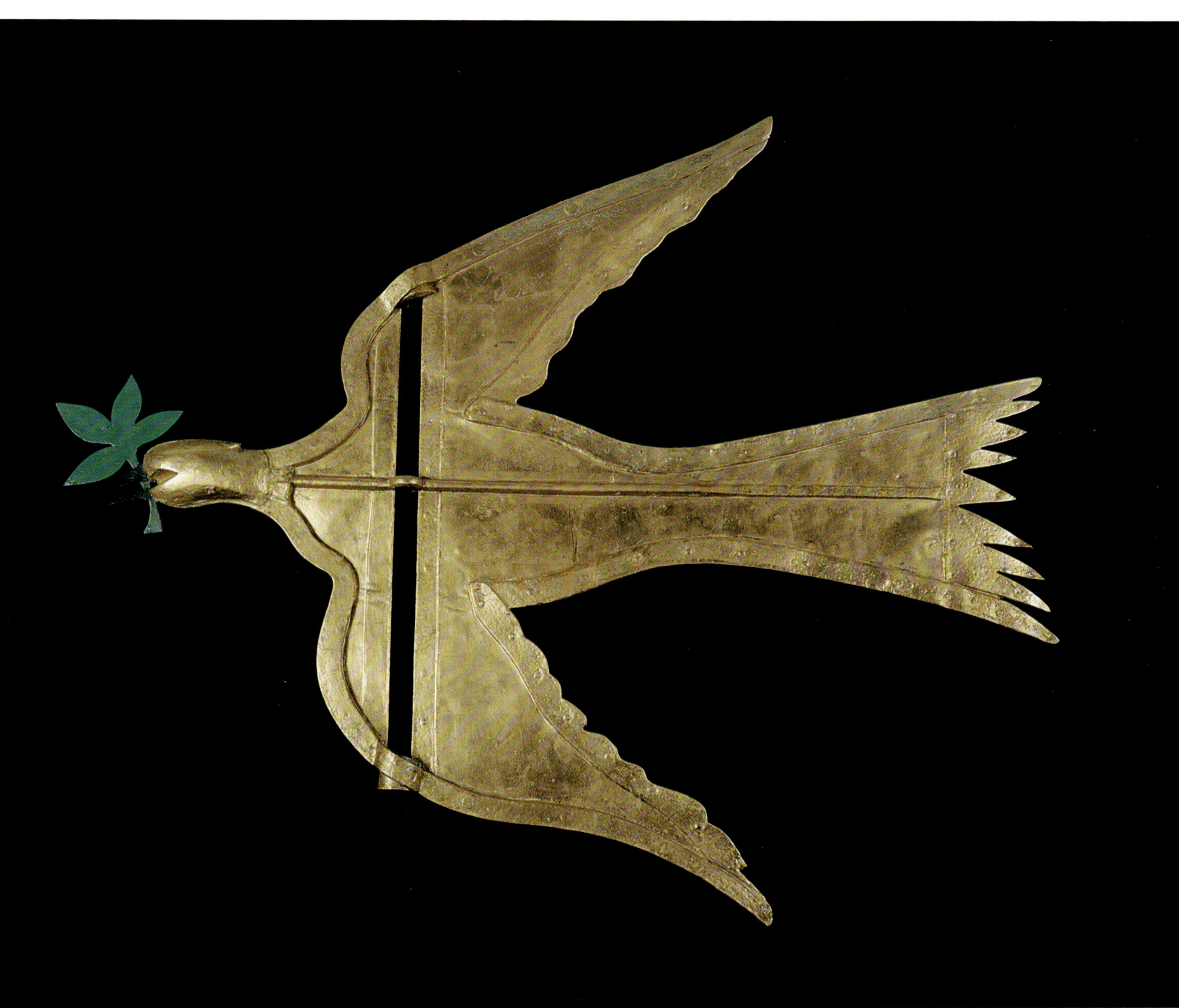

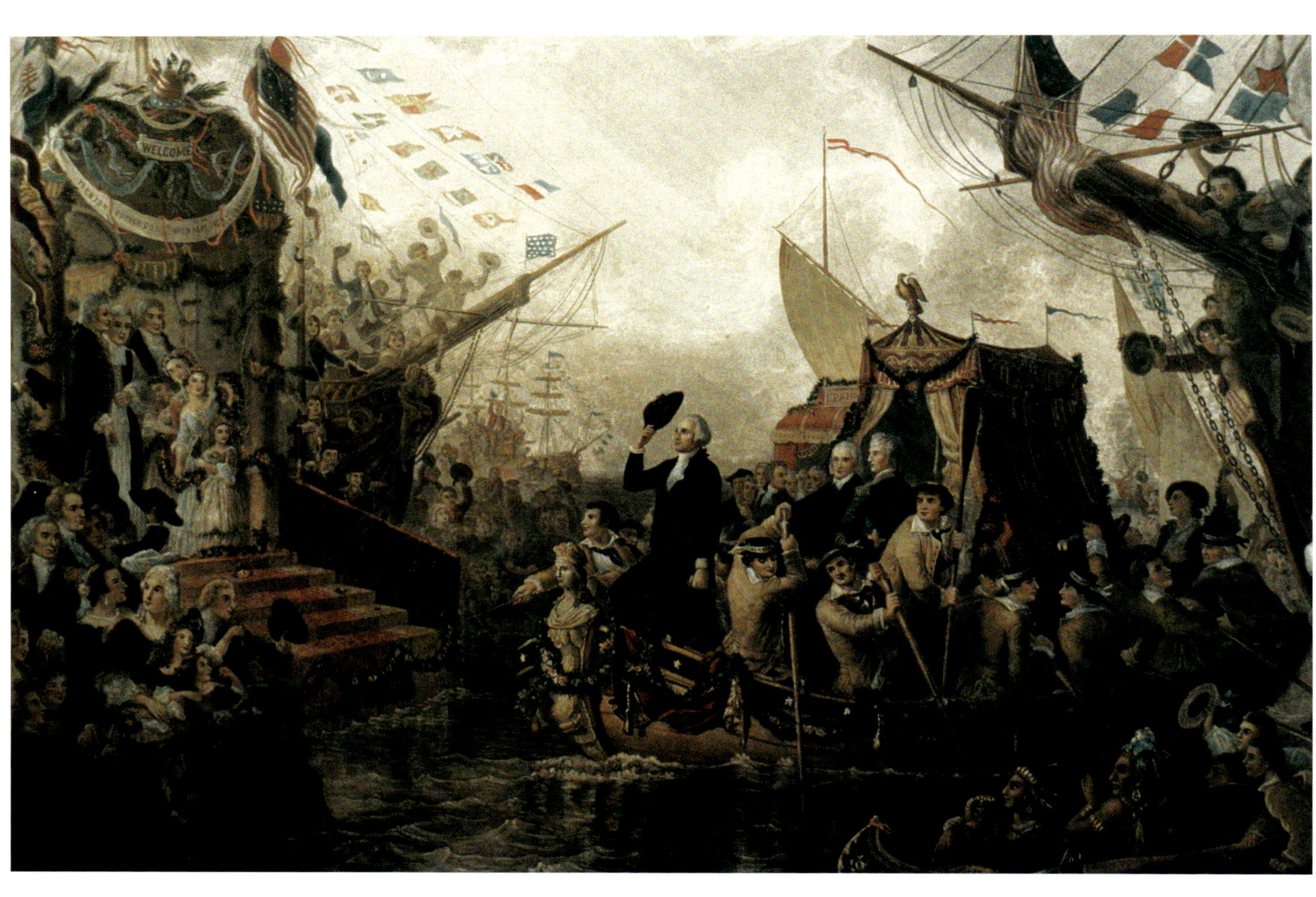
WELCOME

CHAPTER FOUR

The Presidency
George Washington Defines the Role
1789–1797

ON APRIL 14, 1789, GEORGE WASHINGTON WAS ENJOYING DINNER at Mount Vernon when Charles Thomson, Secretary of Congress, arrived with the news that the retired general had been elected the first president of the United States. Two days later, Washington departed for New York, the new nation's capital. He went with seeming reluctance, noting his "adieu to Mount Vernon, to private life, and to domestic felicity . . . with the best disposition to render service to my country in obedience to its calls, but with less hope of answering its expectations."[1] The president-elect was well aware of the challenges that lay before him and the expectations of those who could think of no other individual capable of uniting the country and leading it forward. Martha Washington did not immediately accompany her husband. Noting her own concern over his election to her nephew John Dandridge, she informed him that "the General is gone to New York,—Mr. Charles Tompson came express to him, on the 14th—when, or wheather he will ever come home again god only knows,—I think it was much too late for him to go in to publick life again, but it was not to be avoided, our family will be deranged as I must soon follow him."[2] Although they both went with trepidation, the presidency offered a return to public service for both George and Martha Washington and the opportunity to define the roles of president and first lady for a nation and generations to follow.

En route to New York, Washington was greeted at every stop along the way with fanfare and overwhelming appreciation for his service to the country during the Revolution and his commitment now to lead his fellow countrymen into the next phase of their journey of nationhood. He reached New York on April 23, and one week later, on April 30, 1789, George Washington was inaugurated the first president of the United States at Federal Hall (fig. 2). The French minister, Éléanor-Françoise Élie, Comte de Moustier, wrote to his government of the event and offered a portrait of Washington:

> *Nature, that has conferred on him the art of governing, seems to have endowed his figure, which has nothing in common with the other Americans. He has the soul, look, and figure of a hero united in him. Born to command, he never seems embarrassed at the homage rendered him, and he has the advantage of uniting great dignity with great simplicity of manner.*[3]

As the nation's first president, Washington was entrusted with the establishment of the office and the definition of its role in government and in society. The challenge was complex, for it was incumbent on Washington to project a solid and strong leader (and thereby government) while avoiding any appearance of a monarchy. He had rejected the title and role of king when it was suggested to him, and he now needed to demonstrate to his fellow Americans and the world that his conviction against a monarchy was sincere. He must have felt the pressure acutely, for he related to one family member that "the eyes of America, perhaps of the world, are turned to this government; and many are watching the movements of all those who are concerned with its administration."[4]

opposite: George Washington was greeted with fanfare on his eight-day trip from Mount Vernon to New York for his inauguration. *First in Peace, Representing the Arrival of General George Washington at the Battery, New York, April 23, 1789,* engraving published by James Tyroler, 1867, Willard-Budd Collection, MVLA

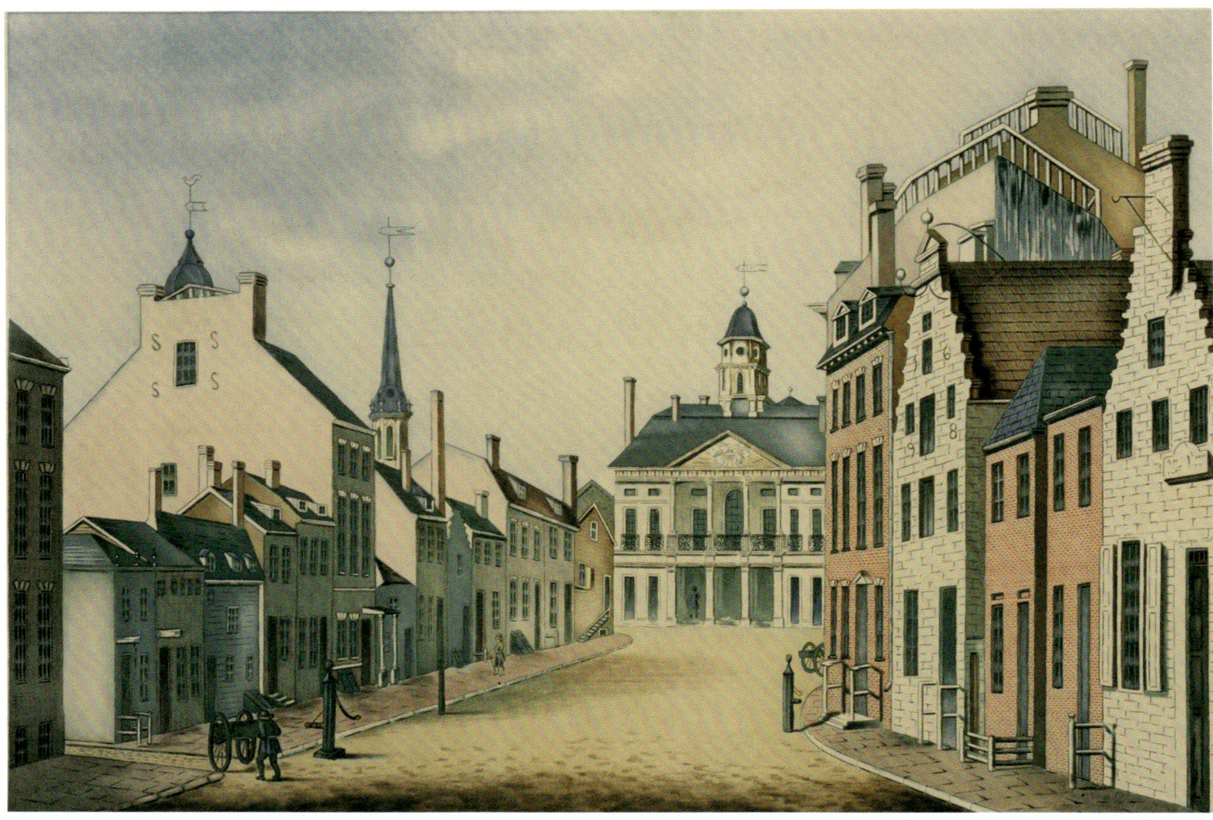

Fig. 2.
On April 30, 1789, George Washington was inaugurated the first president of the United States on the balcony of Federal Hall. *A View of the Federal Hall of the City of New York*, aquatint by Sidney L. Lucas, after John Joseph Holland, Willard-Budd Collection, MVLA

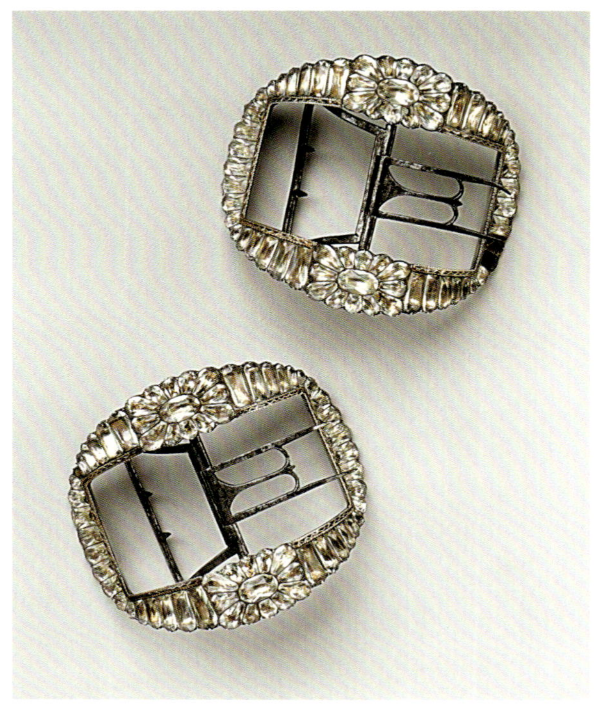

Fig. 3.
A pair of gentleman's shoe buckles set with paste (artificial) stones, worn to one of the many inaugural celebrations in honor of George Washington, MVLA

With every step, Washington was defining how a nation, founded on republican ideals, functioned in the world and outwardly defined itself. From the use of his own slaves in Washington family livery at the executive residence, to his theater box "elegantly fitted up and distinguished by the arms of the United States,"[5] the new president outwardly represented the nation's ideals in the appearance of his domestic and public settings. Washington wished to respect public opinion and "to conform to the public desire and expectation, with respect to the style proper for the Chief Magistrate to live in,"[6] yet he was uncertain of what that style might be. Over the next several years, Washington sought advice from other founding members of the new government, as well as friends and those interested in the proper style for the president and the new nation. In the three executive residences Washington inhabited during his two terms, he paid particular attention to the details of furnishing the spaces so that they would reflect what he felt best defined the new American presidency.

Congress assisted by securing and outfitting the first executive residence. In preparation for Washington's arrival in New York, Congress leased 3 Cherry Street from Samuel Osgood for $845 per year, and a joint resolution of the Senate and House of Representatives on April 15, 1789, directed Osgood

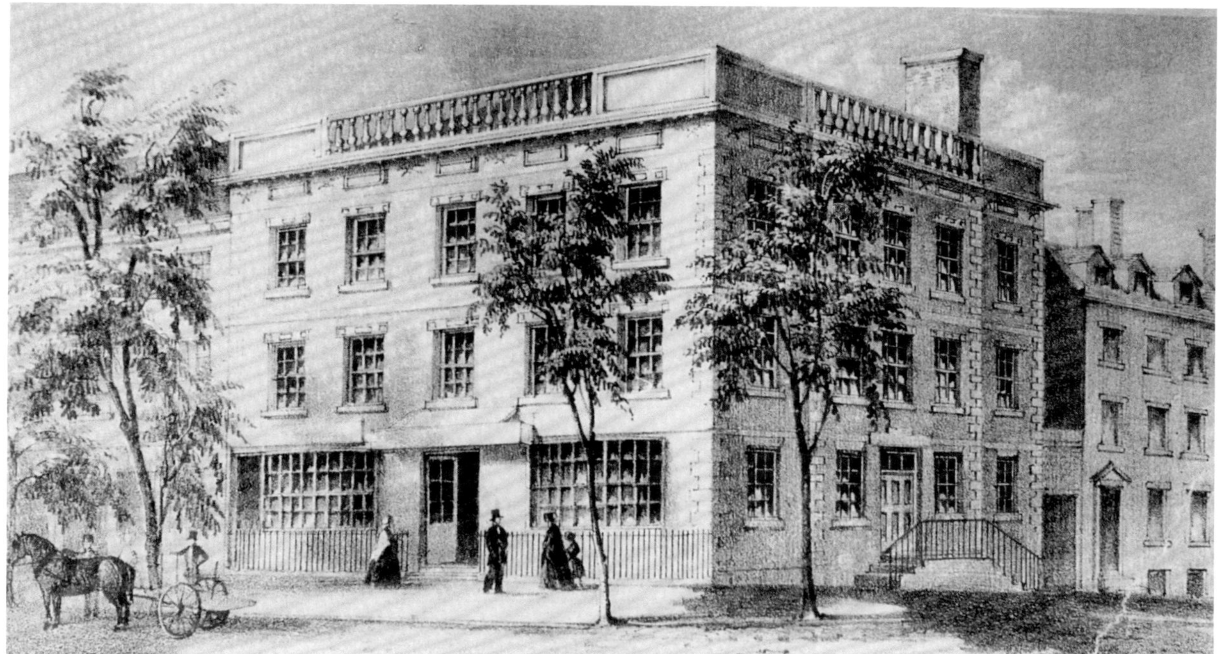

Fig. 4.
No. 3 Cherry Street, the first presidential residence, lithograph by G. Hayward from *Valentine's Manual*, 1853, Collection of the New York Historical Society

to put the house "and the furniture thereof, in proper condition for the residence and use of the President of the United States."[7] The house was cleaned, repaired, and altered to expand one of the drawing rooms sufficiently to accommodate presidential entertaining (fig. 4).

To furnish the residence, Osgood turned to New York craftsmen and retailers. Berry & Rogers, William Buckle, and Ephraim Brasher each supplied close to £300 of silver and silver plate. J. & N. Roosevelt provided £204 of Chinese porcelain and silver plate, James Chrystie contributed £281 worth of "Glass and Queens Ware [creamware]," and William Williams supplied glassware totaling £127. Window and bed hangings from Henry Tenbroek cost £292, and Thomas Burling billed for £463 worth of mahogany furniture. By far the largest charge was that for upholstery work provided by John Brower, totaling £945. In all, Congress spent just over £5,671 to repair and furnish the Osgood house in a manner befitting the president.[8] Although it was an enormous expense, Congress clearly recognized the important role the surroundings of the president would play when the residence was opened to domestic and foreign visitors.

Sally Robinson, a young woman from Philadelphia, described to a friend the transformation of her uncle's former house into one with "every room furnished in the most elegant manner":

> *I went the morning before the General's arrival to look at it. The best of furniture in every room, and the greatest quantity of plate and china I ever saw; the whole of the first and second stories [walls are] papered and the floors covered with the richest kinds of Turkey and Wilton carpets. . . . There is scarcely anything talked about now but General Washington and the Palace.*[9]

Despite the substantial expenditure to refurbish the house and Sally Robinson's description of it as "the Palace," the dwelling was likely comparable to elite New York households of the late eighteenth century. With only fifteen days between Congress's resolution and Washington's inauguration, the articles furnished for the residence were no doubt those that retailers and craftsmen had readily available, and few were custom-made. A contemporary observer recalled that the house was perfectly appropriate for the first president:

[It] partook of all the attributes of our republican institutions, possessed at the same time that degree of dignity and regard for appearances, so necessary to give to our infant republic, respect in the eyes of the world. The house was handsomely furnished the equipages neat, with horses of the first order; the servants wore the family liveries; and, with the exception of a steward and housekeeper, the whole establishment differed but little from that of a private gentleman.[10]

Crafting a residence to give the infant republic respect in the eyes of the world was quite an undertaking, yet Washington understood its necessity and addressed the challenge continuously throughout his presidency. Adhering to the philosophical premise of the new nation, he sought to avoid any appearance of an American aristocracy or court culture.

Washington also understood the need for properly entertaining those who called on him. Statesmen, former soldiers, and foreign dignitaries all "crowded to the seat of the general government, all anxious to witness the grand experiment that was to determine how much rational liberty mankind is capable of enjoying, without that liberty degenerating into licentiousness."[11] The steady stream of visitors to the executive residence increased and became inordinately distracting. Washington wrote,

Gentlemen, consulting their own convenience rather than mine, were calling from the time I rose from breakfast, often before, until I sat down to dinner. This, as I resolved not to neglect my public duties, reduced me to the choice of one of these alternatives, either to refuse them altogether, *or to appropriate a time for the reception of them.*[12]

Washington chose the second alternative by establishing regular days and times for the public to call on him and Mrs. Washington. Every Tuesday afternoon, Washington received male callers from three until four o'clock in the afternoon. The reception was a formal series of gentlemanly introductions and greetings, perhaps the president's attempt to affirm the gravity of the office he held, since as one person noted, Washington "understood himself to be visited as the *President* of the United States and not by his own account."[13]

Dinners for members of Congress and other important government offices were held on Thursday. The Pennsylvania Senator William Maclay attended one Thursday and declared it "a great dinner & the best of the kind ever I was at," although he also suggested "it was the most solmen dinner" he ever attended, with "not an health drank [and] scarce a word said, until the Cloath was taken away . . . then the President filling a Glass of Wine with great formality drank the health of every individual by name round the Table."[14] Maclay also seemed irritated at the dinner conversation and classical knowledge of Vice President John Adams' son-in-law, "who mentioned, how *Homer* described Aeneas leaving his Wife and carrying his father out of flaming Troy, he had heard somebody, (I suppose) witty on the Occasion—but if he had ever read it he would have said *Virgil*." Washington was perhaps equally dissatisfied with the conversation at these dinners his position mandated, for Maclay recorded, "The President kept a fork in his hand when the Cloath was taken away I thought for the purpose of picking nuts . . . but played with the Fork striking on the Edge of the Table with it."[15]

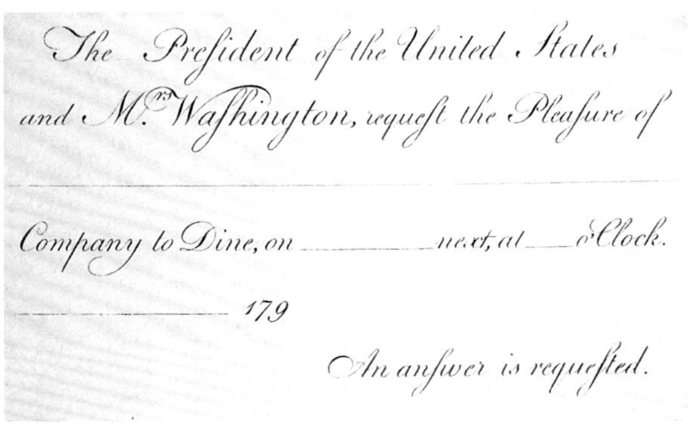

The Preſident of the United States and Mrs. Waſhington, requeſt the Pleaſure of

____

Company to Dine, on ________ next, at ___ o'Clock.

___________ 179

An anſwer is requeſted.

Fig. 5. Guests invited to dine at the executive residence received engraved invitations from the president and Mrs. Washington. MVLA

The levees held by Mrs. Washington every Friday evening were less formal affairs for ladies and gentlemen, and the president seems to have been more relaxed on these occasions. Abigail Adams described to her sister the routine:

> *The form of Reception is this, the servants announce & Col. Humphries or Mr. Lear, receives every Lady at the door, & Hands her up to Mrs. Washington to whom she makes a most Respectfull courtesy and then is seated without noticeing any of the rest of the company. The Pressident then comes up and speaks to the Lady, which he does with a grace dignity & ease, that leaves Royal George far behind him. The company are entertained with Ice creams & Lemonade, and retire at their pleasure performing the same ceremony when they quit the Room.*[16]

Mrs. Adams attended the event in August 1789, when the cool refreshment of ice cream and lemonade must have been pleasing on what was likely a warm summer evening. The menu changed with the seasons, and other refreshments served included tea, coffee, cakes, and candies.[17]

As Washington established the manner in which the presidential household would operate, he also had an opportunity to reflect on some of the purchases made for him by Congress. Osgood and those who had assisted him had performed admirably, quickly working to secure goods readily available for the presidential residence. Since Washington understood the important role tablewares played in communication and had paid a great deal of attention to his dining table and dining spaces throughout his life, his mind automatically turned to orchestrating an ensemble of tablewares appropriate to the type of entertaining he had established. Ceramics listed in the congressional purchases included "China," presumably a service of Chinese export porcelain for formal entertainments, and "Queensware" or creamware, like that Washington had procured for Mount Vernon before the Revolution and later for his camp table, probably for family and informal use. Washington supplemented these ceramics with his newly acquired Society of the Cincinnati porcelains[18] and asked his secretary, Tobias Lear, to help him find a proper centerpiece for formal dinners.

In an attempt to locate Washington's requested centerpiece, or plateau, Lear wrote to Clement Biddle in Philadelphia: "The President is desireous of getting a sett of those waiters, salvers, or whatever they are called, which are set in the middle of a dining table to ornament it. . . . Mr. Morris and Mr. Bingham have them, and the French & Spanish Ministers here, but I know of no one else who has."[19] Washington had clearly seen a set of the fashionable plateaux and wished to keep pace with those, including his European colleagues, who had them. Biddle responded and shipped examples available to him, but as Lear relayed, "The President thinks those Ornaments will not answer the purpose as the two sets are not made to Join each other and neither separate are large enough for his table." Lear expressed the president's thanks but indicated, "The President has been much indisposed, for a week past with a fever and a tumor on his thigh."[20] Washington's illness had been quite serious, yet his attention to the plateau sent by Biddle is testimony to his concern for proper tablewares. When he had recovered, Washington took the matter into his own hands and asked the Philadelphia statesman Gouverneur Morris for help in acquiring the set of plateaux, as well as porcelain table ornaments, silver-plated wine coolers, and newly designed lighting fixtures patented by Aimé Argand. At his own expense, Washington was complementing those tablewares and furnishings supplied by Congress with additions he felt were necessary to provide respect for the young republic.

Although the Osgood house was the best available residence in New York at the time of Washington's inauguration, its location eventually proved inconvenient and its size too small for the president's household, which included family, secretaries, servants, and slaves. When the Comte de Moustier, the French

Fig. 6.
The presidential dining table offered a mixure of French and English porcelains, silverplate, and glassware.

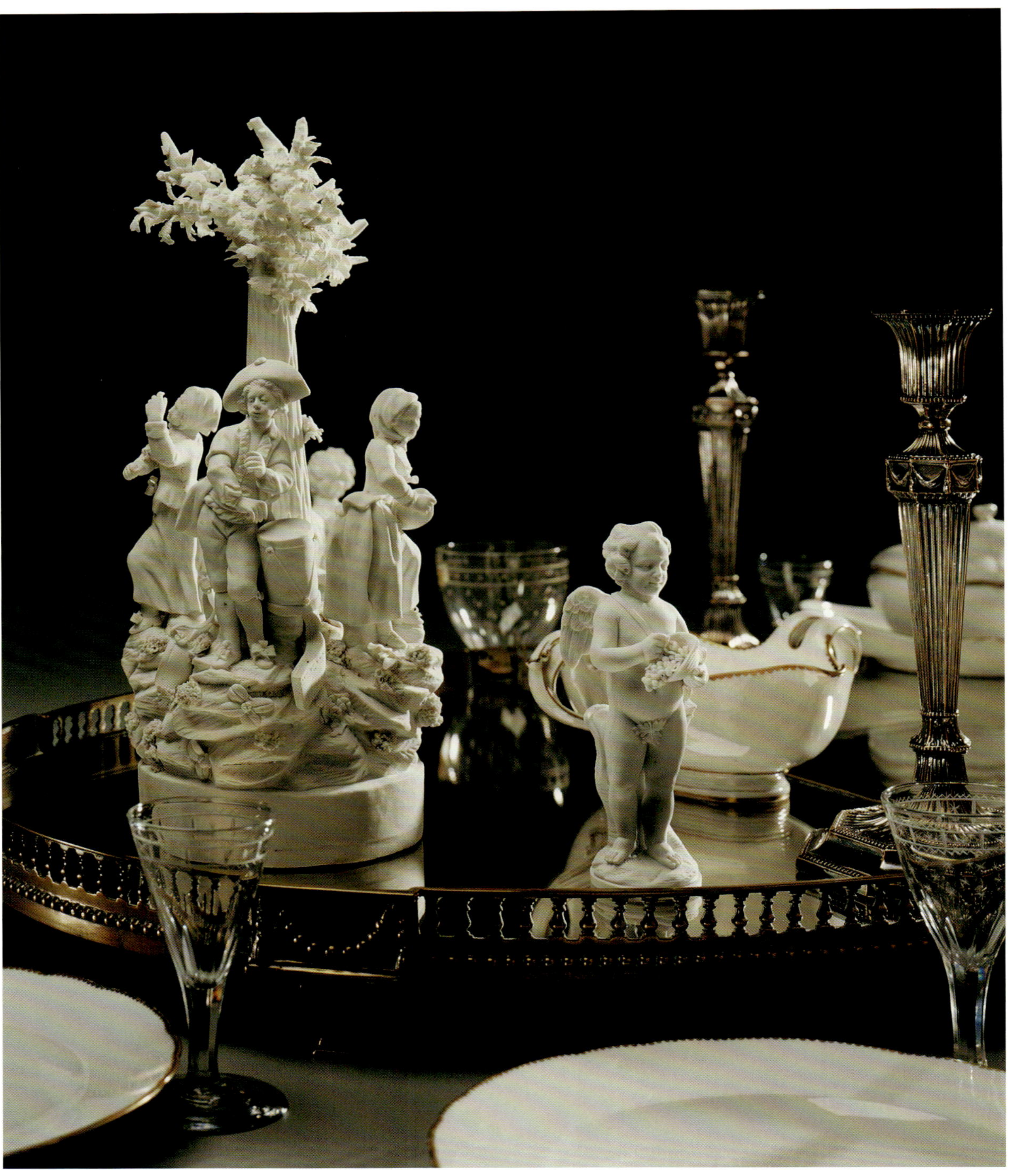

minister to the United States, was recalled to France in October 1789, Washington seized the opportunity to lease the Frenchman's former residence on lower Broadway that was owned by Alexander Macomb. In February 1790 the executive mansion moved from the Osgood house at 3 Cherry Street to the Macomb house at 39–41 Broadway. A much larger dwelling, the Macomb house had two drawing rooms and a number of additional spaces that needed to be furnished.

In working out the details of the move, Alexander Macomb indicated to Tobias Lear that Washington "could speak for any part of the furniture" that the Comte had brought with him.[21] The American appetite for French goods at this time was considerable. Washington had not benefited from travels to France as had Benjamin Franklin and Thomas Jefferson and had never before had the opportunity to purchase French furnishings on this scale. He was certainly very pleased with the chance to acquire items that had been suit-

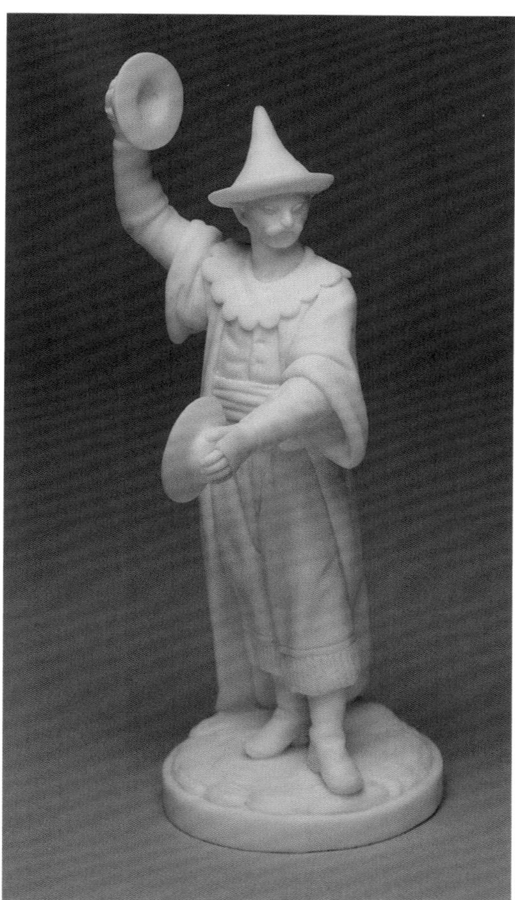

Fig. 7.
Cymbal player bisque table ornament produced at the Niderviller porcelain factory in France and supplied by Gouverneur Morris for the presidential dining table, MVLA

able for the leader of the French delegation, already in situ in the new residence, and presumably at a price that reflected the savings of transatlantic shipment and a little wear. Washington recorded in his diary that he had "fixed on some furniture of the Ministers (which was to be sold & was well adapted to particular public rooms)."[22] The purchases included a suite of green silk upholstered French furniture with matching green silk window curtains, mahogany "buffets" for what would be the state dining room, a pair of large gilt looking glasses, a writing desk for Mrs. Washington, a dressing table for the president, and a large elegant French porcelain table and dessert service (figs. 8, 9).[23] Washington was very attentive to all details of the installation of the new residence, including a "Carpet of the best kind" with "A Pea-Green ground with white or light flowers or spots" to complement the French furniture.[24] In what could have been seen as a criticism of Congress's ability to provide proper lodgings for the first president, Washington was utilizing his own sense of how the residence should appear, supplementing those furnishings already procured by Congress and sent from the Cherry Street residence with those he purchased privately.

In the spring of 1790 the first shipment of goods from Gouverneur Morris arrived from Paris. With it, Morris conveyed his notion about the tone or style he felt appropriate to the executive residence. Morris opined:

> *I think it of very great Importance to fix the Taste of our Country properly, and I think your Example will go very far in that Respect. It is therefore my Wish that every Thing about you should be substantially good and majestically plain; made to endure. Nothing is so extravagant in the Event as those Buildings and Carriages and Furnitures and Dresses and Ornaments which will want continual Renovation. Where a Taste of this kind prevails, each Generation has to provide for itself whereas in the other there is a vast Accumulation of real Wealth in the Space of half a Century.*[25]

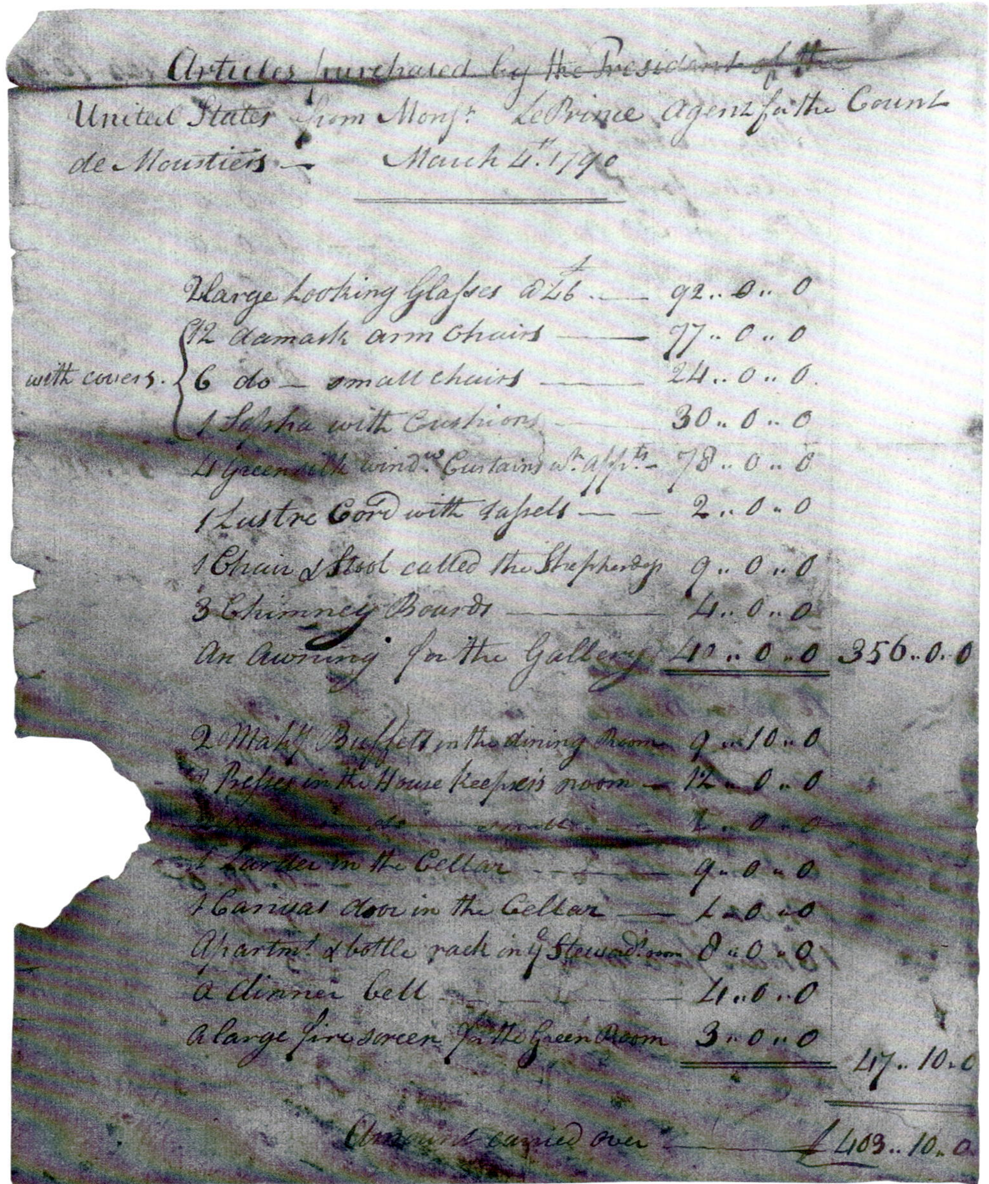

Articles purchased by the President of the United States from Monsr. Le Prince agent for the Count de Moustiers — March 4th. 1790

	2 large Looking Glasses @ £26 —	92..0..0	
with covers.	12 damask arm Chairs —	77..0..0	
	6 do — small chairs —	24..0..0	
	1 Sopha with Cushions —	30..0..0	
	4 Green silk wind.w Curtains w.t app.ts —	78..0..0	
	1 Lustre Cord with tassels —	2..0..0	
	1 Chair & Stool called the Shepherds	9..0..0	
	3 Chimney Boards —	4..0..0	
	An Awning for the Gallery	40..0..0	356..0..0
	2 Mahy. Buffets in the dining Room	9..10..0	
	2 Presses in the House keeper's room —	12..0..0	
	[illegible] do — small —	[illegible]..0..0	
	1 Larder in the Cellar —	9..0..0	
	1 Canvas door in the Cellar —	1..0..0	
	A partitn. & bottle rack in ye Steward's room	8..0..0	
	A dinner bell —	4..0..0	
	A large fire screen for the Green Room	3..0..0	47..10..0
	Amount carried over —		£403..10..0

Fig. 8. List of articles purchased privately by George Washington for the presidential residence from Comte de Moustier, MVLA Archives, acc. no. W-1310/a

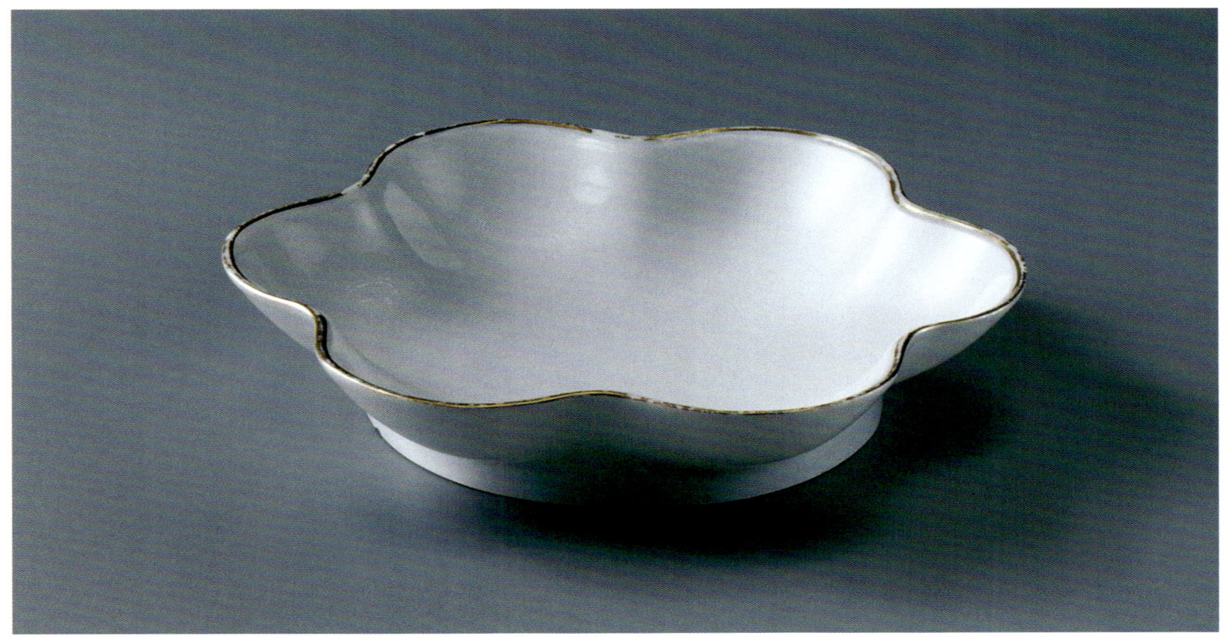

Fig. 9. Scalloped serving dish from Washington's French porcelain service, made at the Angoulême factory. Purchased with funds donated by the Friends of the Collections, MVLA

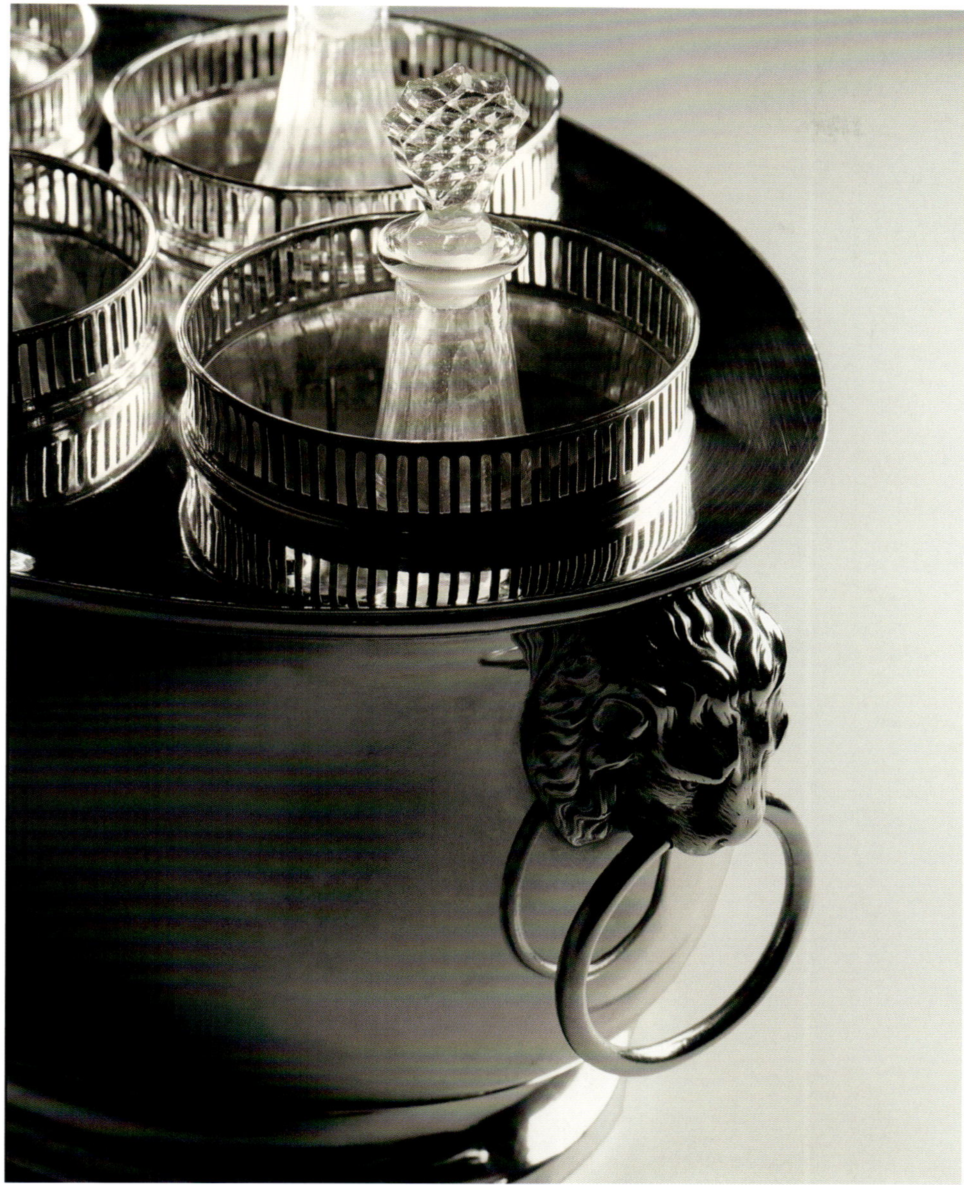

Fig. 10.
One of Washington's silver-plated four-bottle wine coolers ordered for holding glass decanters of wine served during the dessert course, MVLA

Morris clearly had a vision of the American taste he wanted Washington to establish and assisted the president with purchases that he thought reflected an enduring classical aesthetic rather than a passing fashion. It is not surprising that the first items Morris shipped to Washington retained "a noble Simplicity and as they have been fashionable above two thousand years, they stand a fair Chance to continue so during our Time."[26]

Washington was just settling into the new residence when Congress decided to shift the nation's capital to Philadelphia for the next ten years while preparations were made to transfer the capital to the new Federal City (Washington, DC). When locating a proper Philadelphia residence for the president proved challenging, Senator Robert Morris offered his house for the purpose (fig. 11).[27] In September 1790 Washington wrote to his secretary, Tobias Lear, of the selected residence. He considered it "the best Single house in the City; yet without additions, it is inadequate to the commodious accommodation of my family."[28] Washington wrote in detail to Lear of the required improvements that were to be undertaken after Morris vacated the house and while Washington was enjoying some time at Mount Vernon. Lear efficiently negotiated the necessary repairs and the move of the furnishings from New York to Philadelphia. From his home in Virginia Washington directed the proper placement of furnishings. There was no detail

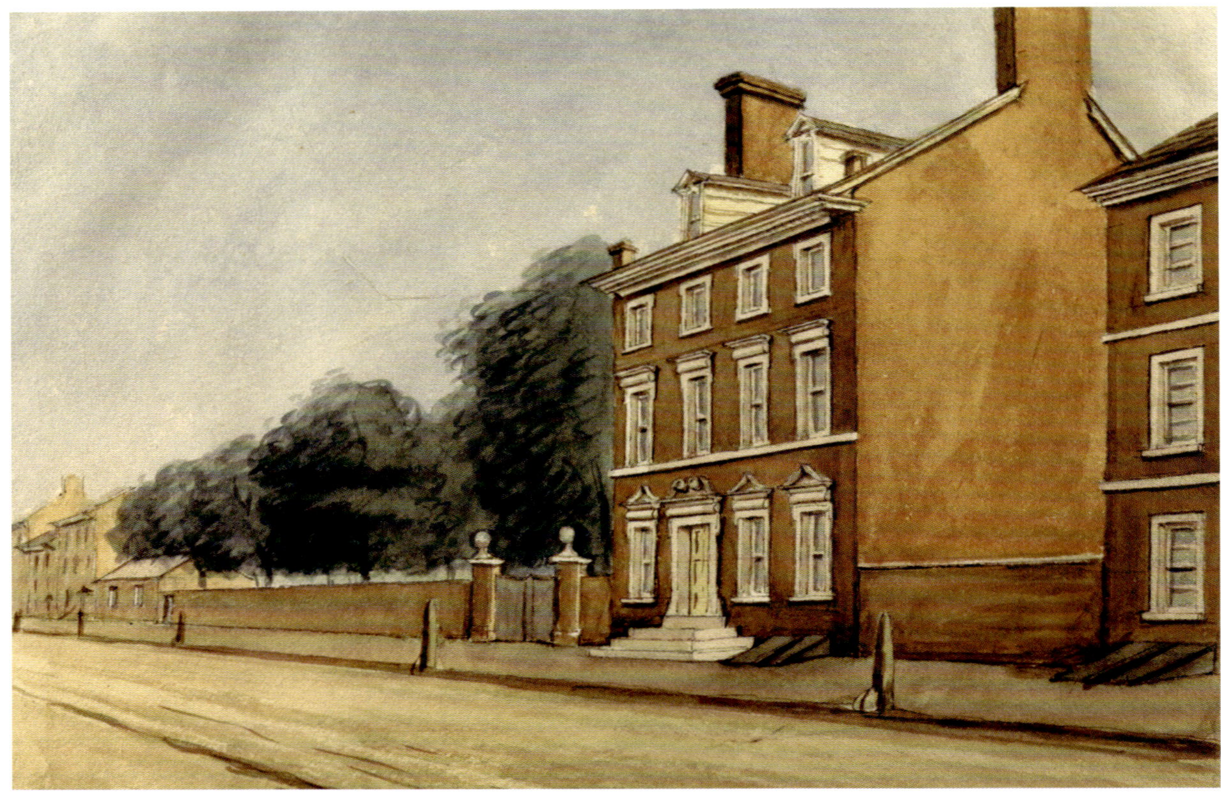

Fig. 11. George Washington's executive residence in Philadelphia, the home of Robert Morris on High Street. Robert Morris House, watercolor on paper, W. L. Breton (Print Bb 862 B756 #9). The Historical Society of Pennsylvania

too small for his attention. On the subject of adapting the curtains from the New York residences to the windows in Philadelphia, he wrote to Lear, "Whether the Green which you have, or a new yellow Curtain, sho[ul]d be appropriated to the Stair case above the Hall, may depend upon your getting an *exact* match in colour &ca of the latter. For the sake of appearances one w[oul]d not, in instances of this sort, regard a small additional expense."[29] Washington was clearly determined that this residence, like those he had inhabited in New York, would be appropriate for the nation's highest-ranking official.

Although Washington had attended to the details of furnishing the executive residence in a manner he felt befitted the office of president, he was very much prepared to leave it behind when his first term in office expired. With political disputes abounding as his colleagues wrestled with domestic and international issues facing the new nation, however, Washington remained the single individual capable of holding the differing parties together. He was elected by the Electoral College to a second term as president on February 13, 1793. Throughout the difficult first four years and those of his second term, Washington, plagued by ill health, political squabbling, and often harsh criticism, was no doubt comforted by the presence of Martha Washington and grandchildren Eleanor "Nelly" Parke Custis and George "Washy" Washington Parke Custis. From the outset, the children must have offered a welcome (if not comic) relief for the president. Martha Washington described Nelly as "a wild little creature . . . [who] spends her time at the window looking at carriages &c passing by which is new to her."[30] By the end of the presidency, however, Nelly had matured to the point that Washington encouraged the young woman's musical talents with gifts of elegant London-made instruments (fig. 12).

In 1797, as Washington prepared to leave the presidency and return home to Mount Vernon, he meticulously drew up a list of all public furniture procured for presidential use by Congress and all private objects he had purchased throughout his presidential years. He carefully itemized the furniture, silver, stoves, andirons, knives, and forks, but not the linens, china, and glassware. Of these, the president noted that "they have been worn out, broken, stolen and replaced (at private expense) over & over again"

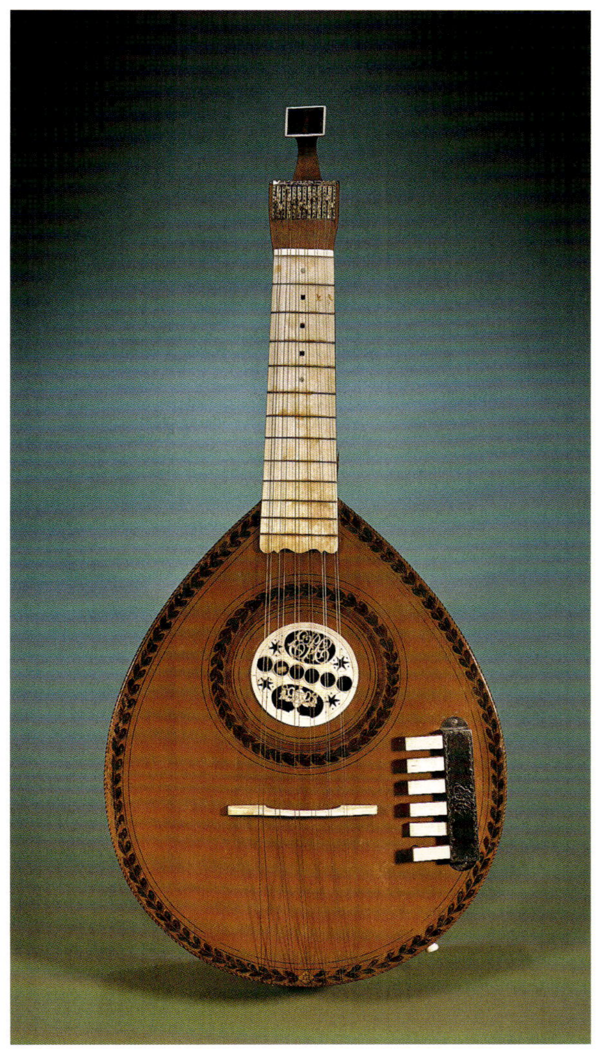

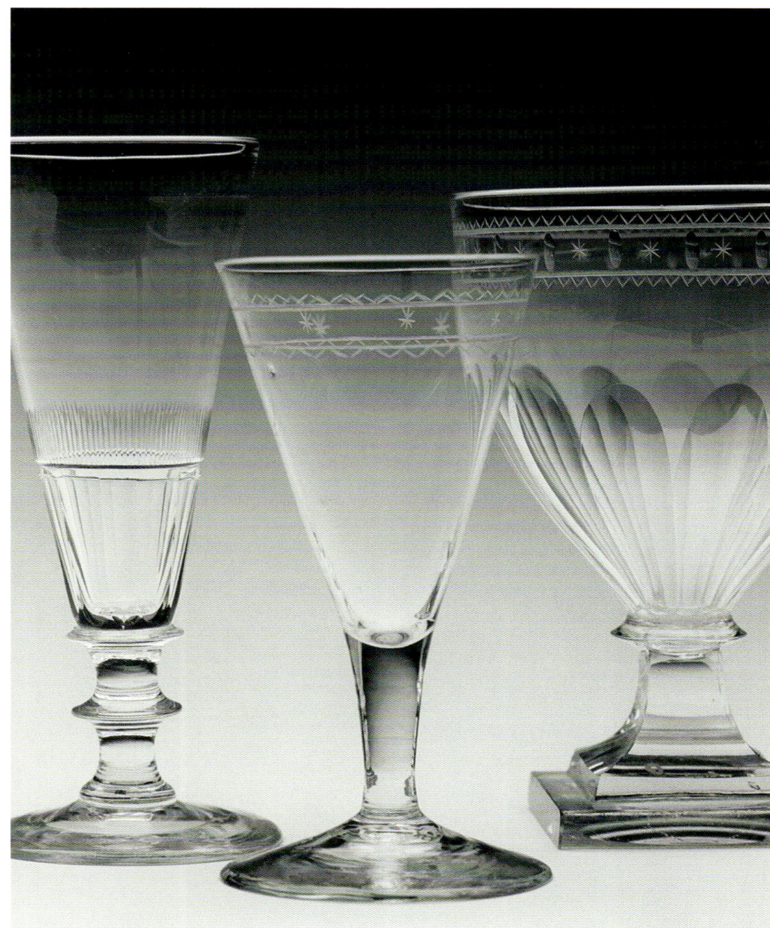

(fig. 13).[31] He offered to sell some of the personally acquired furnishings to incoming President Adams. Adams declined, however, and Washington sold or took to Mount Vernon many of the furnishings he had selected and purchased for the residence.

Washington left the presidency with great fanfare and what must have seemed a series of unending entertainments in his honor. When rumors circulated that Martha Washington's levee on February 17, 1797, would be her last, scores turned out to produce what Washington noted in his diary as "a Very crouded drawing Room."[32] Five days later, Washington recorded that he "Went in the evening to an elegant entertainmt. Given on my birth night."[33] The "elegant" evening was preceded by a day of events held to honor Washingotn's birthday that included the pealing of bells and the firing of cannon. The Washingtons gave their last formal presidential dinner on March 3, as the new president, John Adams, was inaugurated at noon the following day. On March 9, a day in which Washington recorded that the wind changed to the northwest and "blew very hard & turned very cold," the former general and president left Philadelphia to head home to Mount Vernon. The small "family" party included Mrs. Washington, Nelly Custis, and the Marquis de Lafayette's son named in his honor, George Washington Motier Lafayette.[34] On their way south, the party was greeted by scores of well-wishers in each state and city. In Baltimore, as in many other locations, they were "Met & escorted into town by a great concourse of people."[35] On March 15, Washington was eager to reach Mount Vernon. He did not pause in Alexandria to receive the additional public accolades of his neighbors but pressed on to arrive home by dinnertime.[36]

Fig. 12. (above left) Eleanor "Nelly" Parke Custis's English guitar, made by Longman and Broderip of London, with a delicately pierced ivory panel incorporating her initials. Smithsonian's National Museum of American History, Behring Center

Fig. 13. (above) At the end of his presidency, Washington noted that he had replaced broken glassware "over and over again" at his own expense. MVLA

CAT. 36

Side Chair

Philadelphia, Pennsylvania, ca. 1775–1785
Mahogany, yellow pine, and white cedar, H. 38¾", W. 23¾", D. 21½"
Purchased with funds donated by the Friends of the Collections, 1999
W-4116

Congress purchased all of the mahogany furniture needed for the first executive residence from the New York cabinetmaker and retailer Thomas Burling. Burling was a logical choice, as he had recently placed himself in the position of a furniture retailer, selling the works of other craftsmen. In March 1787 the *Daily Advertiser* notified its readers that "Thomas Burling Cabinet and Chair maker, at the Sign of the Chair . . . has opened a Ware Room of Mahogany and other Furniture, on a more extensive plan than heretofore; and for the convenience of strangers and others, who may resort to or settle in this city, he means to keep an assortment where they may be supplied on the shortest notice."[37]

Of the sixty-eight mahogany chairs purchased from Burling, this example is perhaps one of those listed as "plain."[38] Carving on the chair is limited to the front ball-and-claw feet, and the fluting on the stiles and the beading on the seat frame are simple and subtle. This modest display of the Philadelphia craftsman's abilities may be due to the chair's export for a New York market, as well as the maker's hesitancy to invest heavily in carving and detailing on a speculative product sent to a retailer. Although the craftsman who supplied the chair to Burling is unknown, his expert eye and hand are evident in the chair's successful synthesis of Chippendale designs and the Gothic tracery of the splat that constitutes the chair's focal point.

The chair's Chippendale, rather than Federal, style suggests the continued acceptability of older fashions in the early republic even when they were mixed with newer Neoclassical forms. It is difficult to determine the specific room in which this chair was placed and the newer forms beside which it would have been compared. At the time of George Washington's retirement in 1797, however, it could very well have been one of the many mahogany chairs upholstered with yellow damask in the second-floor drawing room.[39]

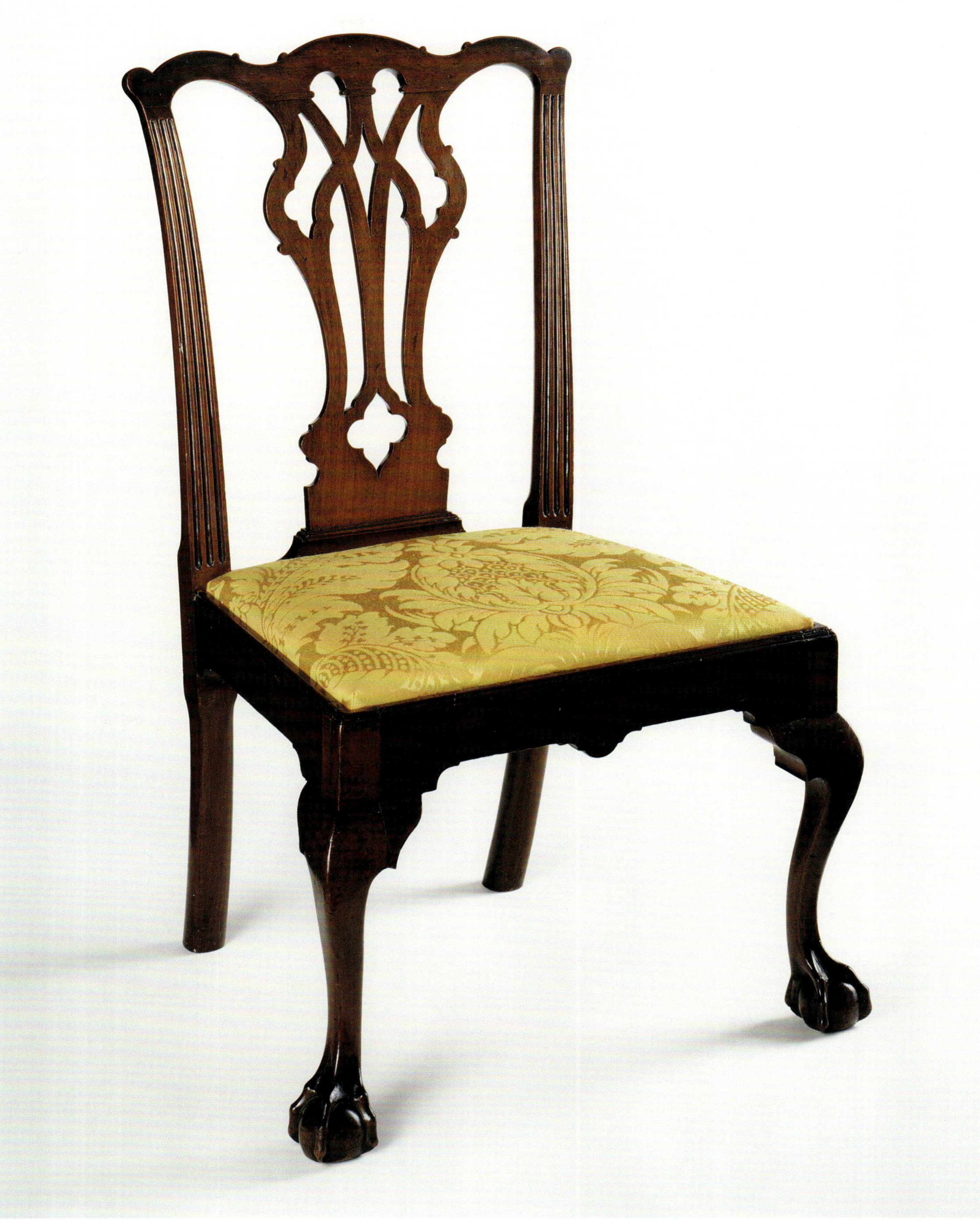

CAT. 37

Side Chair

Probably Philadelphia, Pennsylvania, ca. 1770–1790
Walnut, cedar, and pine, H. 38½", W. 21½", D. 19⅞"
Carved into front slip-seat rail: "M C III"; into front seat rail: "II"
Gift of Colonel Frank M. Etting, 1886
W-259

When Thomas Burling quickly supplied the first executive residence with sixty-eight mahogany chairs,[40] necessity required that he mix chairs of different styles and perhaps regions. This side chair is one of a set of walnut chairs that retain a history of being used in George Washington's presidential household. A carved numeral "II" in the front seat rail and "M C III" in the front slip-seat rail identify the chair as part of a set, and those that survive with the same history bear identical carvings.[41] Given the large number of chairs Burling delivered in 1789 and the speed with which he supplied them, it is possible that walnut could have been mistaken for mahogany by those assembling the order and preparing the invoice. Alternatively, the chairs could have been later supplements to those procured from Burling at the beginning of Washington's first term. When Washington concluded his presidency in Philadelphia, he made a detailed list of all the items that Congress had supplied for his use and those he had purchased privately. Among the chairs furnished by Congress, he listed seventy side chairs, ten of which were not specifically identified as mahogany.[42] Other furnishings noted on Washington's 1797 inventory were added as the residence moved, and it is quite possible that these walnut chairs were among those additions.

The construction of the chairs, especially the exposed side rail tenoned through the rear seat rail, suggests that the chairs were crafted by a Philadelphia cabinetmaker. The chair's plainness is enhanced by the fluid movement of the serpentine crest rail and vase-shaped splat. The cabriole legs are simple, with unadorned knees and trifid feet. While the chairs could have been used in several rooms in the Philadelphia executive residence, their current upholstery in crimson silk damask reflects that which was used in the state dining room. There were approximately three dozen dining chairs in the room to accommodate the large parties of thirty or more guests who ate with the president. Crimson silk damask curtains hung at the large bow window at one end of the room, and the dining chairs in the room were likely upholstered en suite.[43]

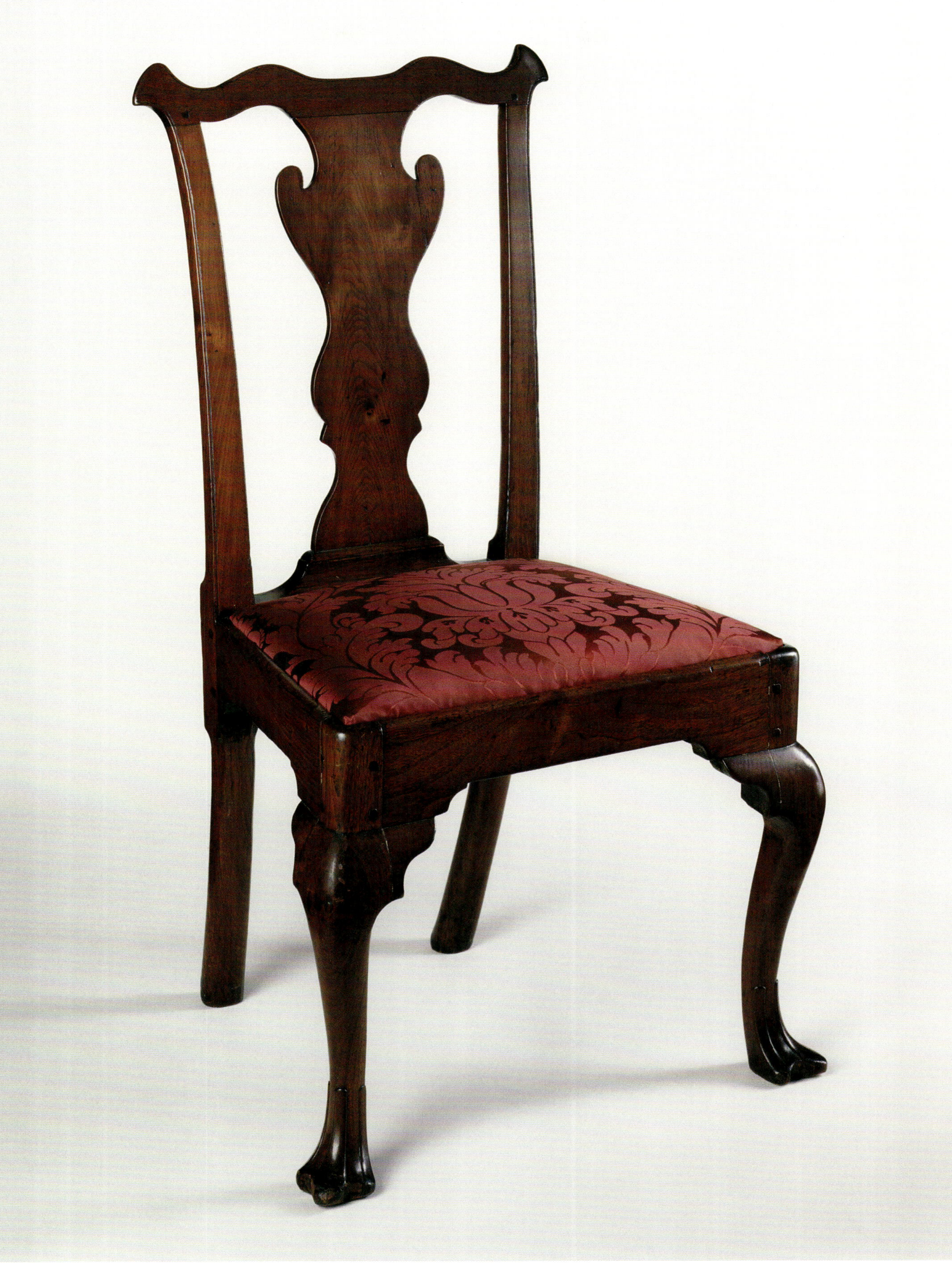

CAT. 38

Plateau

France, ca. 1789
Silver plate and mirrored glass, three rectangular center sections, each H. 1½", W. 24", D. 17¼";
two half-circular end sections, each H. 1½", W. 24", D. 17¼"
Gift of Mrs. George R. Goldsborough, Vice Regent for Maryland, 1895[44]
W-105 /A–C

By the end of the eighteenth century, a plateau (mirrored set of trays) running the length of the dining table was among the most fashionable forms of table decoration.[45] George Washington had seen the form in the residences of the French and Spanish foreign ministers[46] and asked Gouverneur Morris to help secure one for the presidential dining table. Writing from New York to Morris in Paris, Washington requested:

> *Will you then, my good sir, permit me to ask the favor of you to provide and send to me by the first ship bound to this place or Philadelphia, mirrors for a table . . . the mirrors will of course be in pieces that they may be adapted to the company (the size of which I mean) the aggregate length of them may be ten feet—the breadth two feet—the frames may be plated ware or anything else more fashionable but not more expensive.*[47]

Morris found and forwarded the desired "mirrors for a table." Assembled into an elongated oval, they formed an architectural frame in silver that served as the ideal backdrop for candlesticks, porcelain ornaments, and vases of flowers enhanced by reflected candlelight.

This rectangular center portion and two semicircular ends are part of the original nine-piece set that graced the presidential table.[48] The silver-plated outer edges support a continuous, beaded, pierced gallery with turned balusters between miniature parapets decorated with festoons. The frame rests on grooved, tapered feet, and the upper surface is lined with mirrors. In its Neoclassical detail, the plateau is reminiscent of the delicate metalwork characteristic of the British architect Robert Adam (1728–1792), whose influence in America was at its height during Washington's presidency.[49]

The placement of the plateau and its accompanying ornaments on the presidential table did not escape the comment of Washington's guests. The Massachusetts congressman Theophilus Bradbury spent much of a letter describing the centerpiece:

> *Last Thursday I had the honor of dining with the President in company with the Vice-President, the Senators, the Delegates of Massachusetts and some other members of Congress, about 20 in all. In the middle of the table was placed a piece of table furniture about six feet long and two feet wide, rounded at the ends. It was either of wood gilded or polished metal, raised about an inch with a silver rim round it like that round a tea board; in the center was a pedestal of plaster of Paris with images upon it, and on each end figures, male and female of the same. It was very elegant and used for ornament only.*[50]

After the presidency, Washington returned to Mount Vernon with his Parisian ensemble, where it melded well with the Neoclassical detailing of the large dining room and no doubt continued to delight those gathered around it.

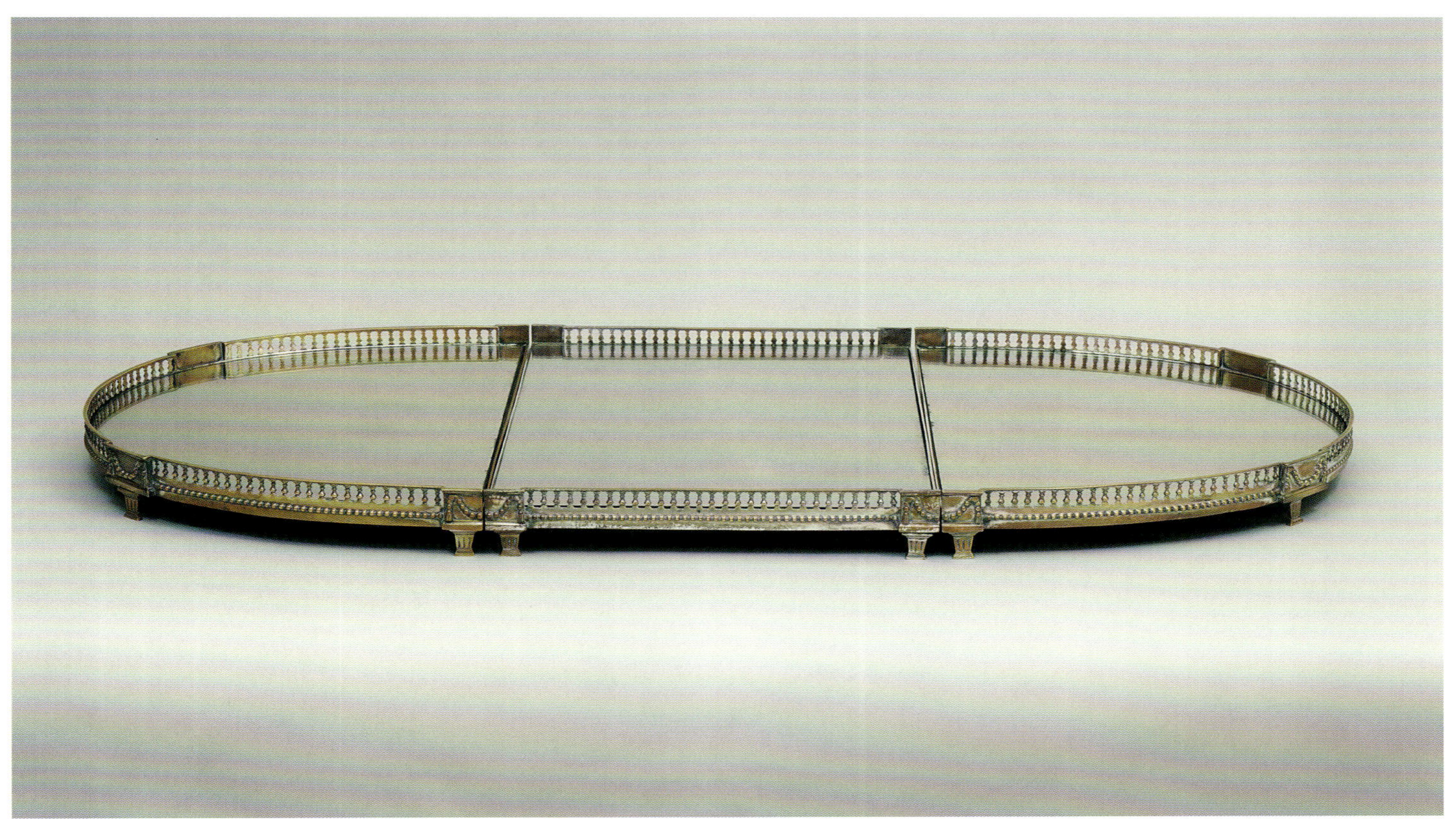

CAT. 39

Figural Group of Venus and Cupids

Angoulême factory, France, ca. 1789
Biscuit porcelain, H. 15¼", W. 12⅞"
Purchase, 1957
W-2133

George Washington's appeal to Gouverneur Morris in October 1789 for a set of "mirrors for a table" included the request for "neat and fashionable but not expensive ornaments for them—such as will do credit to your taste."[51] Washington wanted porcelain ornaments, and Morris found them at the Angoulême manufactory salesrooms in Paris.[52] He shipped them from France in January 1790, noting that he could have supplied Washington less expensively with "a Number of pretty Trifles," but the cost of packing and transportation would have been more than the ornaments, and their effect on the presidential table would not be in keeping with what he presumed Washington wished.[53] Morris had taken the liberty to buy costly ornaments, but he felt they would evince "a noble Simplicity" that had been "fashionable above two thousand years,"[54] and would be suitable for the executive residence table. Despite the additional expense and Washington's concern for exhibiting any kind of conspicuous consumption, the president was very well pleased with Morris' initiative. He thanked Morris for his attention to detail, noting that the ornaments were not only well packed and arrived safely, but "are very elegant—much admired—and do great justice to your taste."[55]

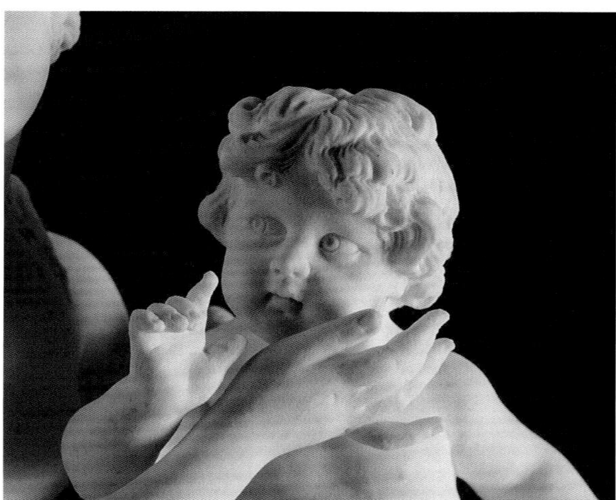

This group of Venus and cupids is one of three classically inspired ensembles, two vases, and twelve figures sent by Morris. All were fashioned of unglazed biscuit porcelain in figures and forms that referred to the political ideals of ancient Greece and Rome. The pure white body of this Venus with two cupids (detail) suggests the cool white marble of antique sculptures. The classical subject and appearance blended perfectly with the founding principles of the new nation.

Morris included three large glass covers for the groups. He noted that "the three Groups . . . may serve both for ornaments to the Chimney Piece of a drawing Room (in which case the Glasses will preserve them from the Dust & Flies) or for the Surtout." When the groups were to be placed on the surtout, or set of plateau, for large entertainments, Morris suggested that "the large Group will be in the Middle the two smaller ones at the two Ends the Vases in the Spaces between the three and the Figures distributed along the Edges or rather along the Side."[56]

When the government and executive residence moved from New York to Philadelphia in the fall of 1790, Washington took great care to give instructions on the proper movement of the fragile biscuit table ornaments. Once in Philadelphia, Washington's secretary, Tobias Lear, made certain that the delicate figures were protected in the new residence Lear suggested that to reduce the risk of breakage of the large groupings, including Venus and her cupids, "it would not be improper to let the large images stand on the Side-Boards in the Dining Room. The Glasses which cover, will preserve them from the dust, and prevent the delicate parts from being touched. They will likewise be an ornament to the Room."[57] After serving as an ornament in the presidential dining room, this Venus group returned with the Washingtons to Mount Vernon, where it continued to educate, inspire, and delight dinner guests.

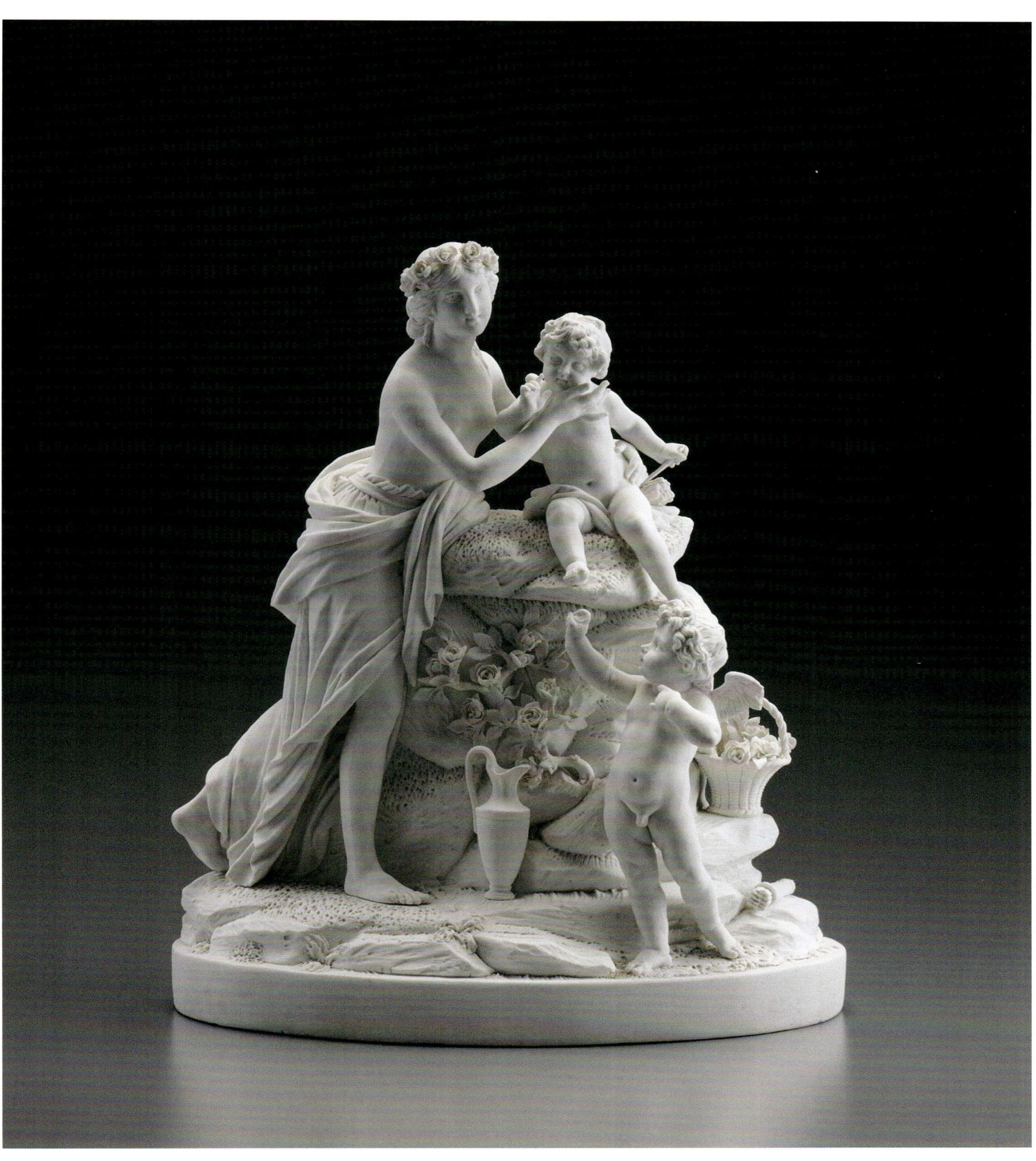

CAT. 40

Wine Cooler

England, ca. 1789
Silver plate, H. 10½", W. 21", D. 12½"
Gift of Miss Edith McHenry, 1972
W-2618

Among the goods George Washington asked Gouverneur Morris to buy for him in either England or France were "handsome and useful Coolers for wine *at* and *after* dinner" of silver plate.[58] Washington knew how he wanted the coolers to be constructed and the number of wine decanters they should hold. He declared himself in need of

> eight *double ones (for Madeira and claret the wines usually drank at dinner) each of the apertures to be sufficient to contain a pint decanter, with an allowance in the depth of it for ice at the bottom so as to raise the neck of the decanter above the cooler—between the apertures a handle is to be placed . . . [and] For the wine* after *dinner* four *quadruple coolers will be necessary each aperture of which to be of the size of a* quart *decanter or quart bottle for four sorts of wine—These decanters or bottles to have ice at bottom, and to be elevated thereby as above—a central handle here will also be wanting— . . . The reason why I prefer an aperture for every decanter or bottle . . . is that whether full or empty the bottles will always stand upright and never be at a variance with each other.*[59]

The instructions for Morris were clear. The president wanted wine coolers of two different sizes, each to contain a varying number of decanters in different sizes. The ensemble was intended to serve several functions, cooling the wine, moving it easily around the table, and providing order to the table. In addition, Washington stressed, "One idea however I must impress you with and that is in whole or part to avoid extravagance. For extravagance would not comport with my own inclination, nor with the example which ought to be set."[60]

Morris was not able to find any wine coolers ready-made in London that matched Washington's specifications. He wrote to alert the president, "Nothing of this Sort has ever yet been executed here except in a coarse and clumsy manner in lacquered Ware."[61] He therefore took Washington's specifications to a London craftsman who used them to generate what Morris deemed a "very elegant" design in silver plate as opposed to solid silver (or plate). Morris acknowledged, "I own that considering the Simplicity of the Workmanship I have been much tempted to have them made of Plate, but upon considering well your Letter I could not venture what would have looked so much like Extravagance."[62] Washington received them in November and thanked Morris for the "elegant" articles, noting his pleasure at the inclusion of glass decanters,[63] yet he confided some reservations to his secretary Tobias Lear.

Washington was at Mount Vernon waiting for the Philadelphia residence to be put in order when he received Morris' bill for the silver plate. He wrote to Lear to authorize payment of the bill, complaining that "the prices of the plated ware exceeds—far exceeds the utmost bounds of my calculation." Nonetheless, Washington indicated that he was satisfied Morris had "done what he conceived right."[64] Noting that the coolers were useless in cold weather and that those with space for four bottles were "too unwieldy to pass; especially by Ladies," Washington asked Lear to contract with a Philadelphia silversmith to make two lightweight frames that would each hold four glass decanters. Washington suggested the silversmith model the frames on the coolers sent by Morris, and that they be crafted "immediately" and in "a handsome fashion."[65]

When Washington concluded the presidency, he had used only two of the larger four-bottle coolers. These, along with four of the two-bottle coolers, went to Mount Vernon with him. Two of the four-bottle and three of the two-bottle coolers were left in Philadelphia under the care of Washington's secretary of war, James McHenry. Washington asked McHenry to keep one of the two-bottle coolers "as a token of my friendship and as a remembrancer of it."[66] He also directed McHenry to offer the same to fellow cabinet members Secretary of State Timothy Pickering and Secretary of the Treasury Oliver Wolcott. Of the two unused four-bottle coolers, Washington requested one to be forwarded to Alexander Hamilton as a gift from the retired president and the other to be sold.[67]

James McHenry purchased this four-bottle wine cooler, to complement the two-bottle cooler he received as a gift from Washington. Its simple and elegant elliptical shape is ornamented by applied lion-mask bail handles. The removable lid is fitted with four pierced collars to highlight the quart decanters placed in the fitted silver wire baskets suspended within. The side bears an engraved inscription identifying the cooler as one of those in use in the presidential household and later sold when Washington returned to private life. The cooler remained with James McHenry's descendants until May 1972.

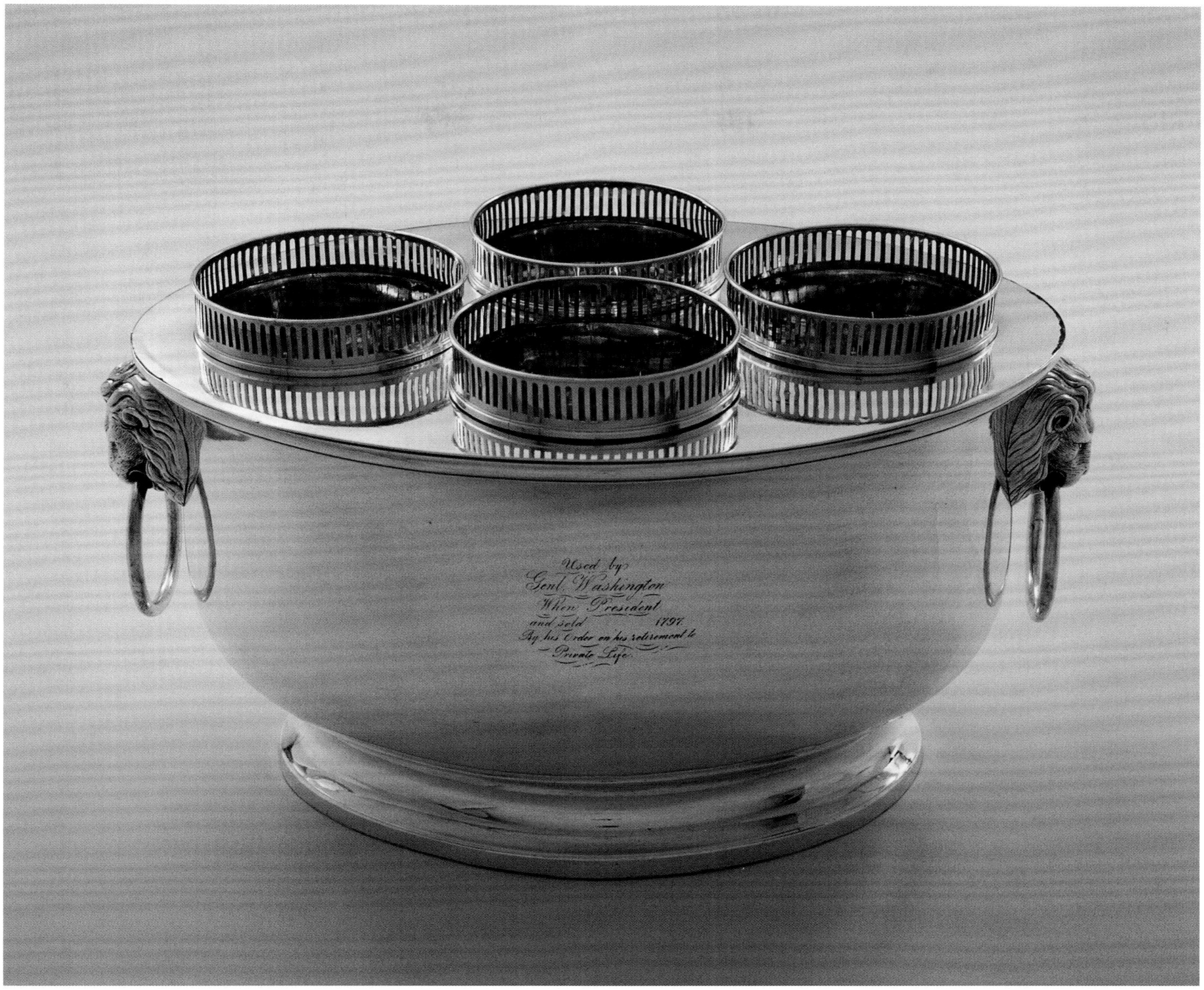

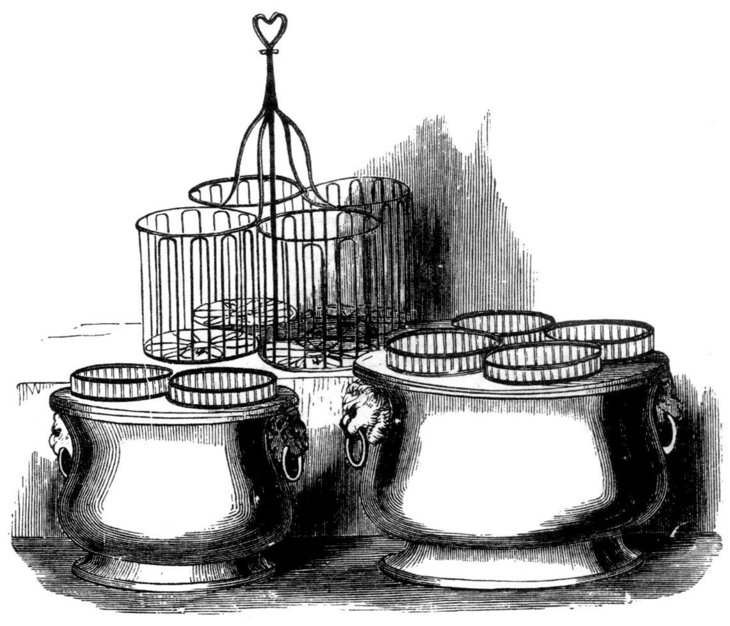

WINE-COOLERS AND COASTER.

At left: Washington's two- and four-bottle wine coolers, and the frames he had fashioned for circulating glass decanters at the presidential dining table, sketched and published by Benson Lossing, 1859

CAT. 41

Side Chair

Jean-Baptiste Lelarge (1744–1802)[68]
Paris, France, ca. 1785
Beechwood, H. 35⅜", W. 18⅛", D. 16½"
Purchase, 1932
W-217/B

When the French minister to the United States, the Comte de Moustier, was recalled to France in the fall of 1789, George Washington not only took the occasion to transfer the executive residence to that vacated by de Moustier, but he also availed himself of the opportunity to purchase a sizeable quantity of the Frenchman's furnishings. The Comte had brought a number of French luxury goods with him when he assumed his American post, but he did not take all of them back to France. Washington joined his contemporaries in their fascination with and preference for French furnishings and was delighted at the prospect of acquiring those being relinquished by de Moustier.

The itemized list of Washington's purchases from the Comte de Moustier survives in the Mount Vernon Archives and notes his acquisition of "12 damask armchairs," "6 ditto [damask] small chairs," and one sofa.[69] The suite of furniture traveled with the president to the Morris house in Philadelphia, where Washington added to the ensemble six chairs and two stools purchased from the French émigré craftsman George Bertault.[70] They were all placed in the drawing room immediately above the state dining room, where the green silk window hangings complemented the "Green floured damask" furniture. When Washington retired in 1797, he decided that the French furnishings in the green drawing room were among those articles that should be sold instead of accompanying him to Mount Vernon.[71] He offered them to incoming President Adams and then sold them at auction when they were declined.[72]

This Louis XVI–style side chair is likely one of the "small chairs" Washington purchased from the Comte de Moustier. Stamped by the French cabinetmaker Jean-Baptiste Lelarge, the chair's molded frame, carved rosette blocks, and tapering-stop, fluted legs are typical of French furniture produced in the third quarter of the eighteenth century. Evidence of the original principal upholstery fabric, noted by Washington as green flowered damask does not survive. Recent conservation efforts, however, revealed fragments of the plain-woven green-and-white checked linen that originally upholstered the chair's back.[73]

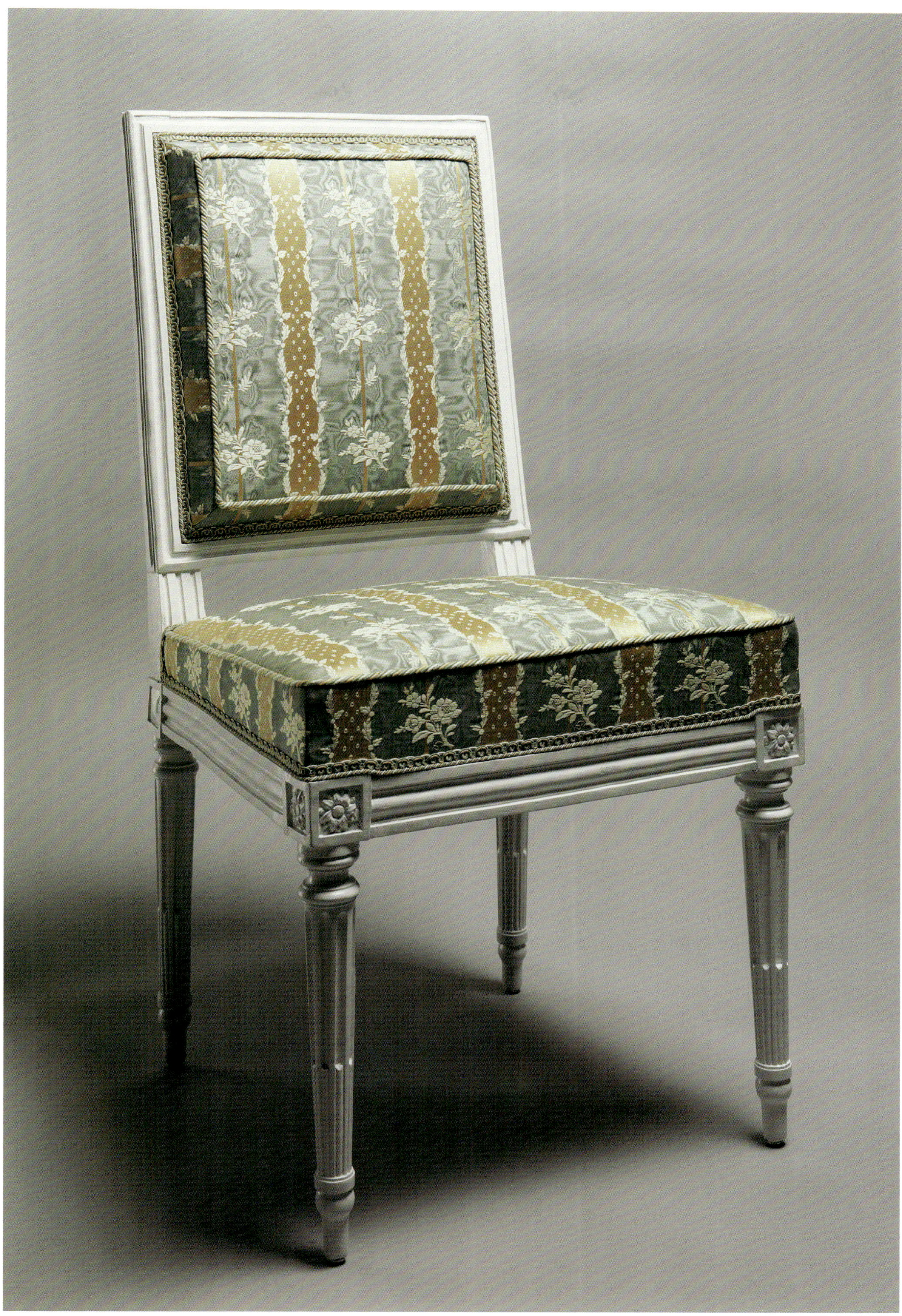

CAT. 42

Sugar Bowl and Milk Jug

Sèvres factory, France, ca. 1780

Sugar Bowl and Cover
H. 4½", W. 4¼"
Gift of Madeline Blakey Street, 1955
W-2025/A&B

Milk Jug
H. 4⅞", W. 5⅜"
Brian and Barbara Hendelson Collection
IL2004.005.014

Perhaps the best known of George Washington's purchases from the Comte de Moustier is the white-bodied, gilt-rimmed porcelain service associated with his presidency. The 309 pieces were assembled from the French porcelain factories of Sèvres, Angoulême, and Nast. They included dozens of soup and dinner plates as well as a host of specialized forms including iceries and ice-cream pots, egg dishes, and flowerpots. For the service of tea and coffee, there were cups and saucers as well as sugar dishes and cream pots.[74] With a simple and elegant Neoclassical aesthetic, the pieces matched Washington's preference for neat and plain while offering fashionable French porcelain with subtle reference to ancient white marble statuary and republican ideals.

The dinner, dessert, coffee, and tea wares in the service included this milk jug and sugar bowl from the French porcelain manufactory at Sèvres, which catered to the demand for tea and coffee wares with the production of specialized forms. The milk jug facilitated adding milk to coffee or tea (more of it to the latter), and the covered sugar bowl contained refined white sugar for the sweetening of the often bitter beverages.[75] The jugs were produced in three sizes and introduced in the 1750s as a *petit pot à lait à 3 pieds.*[76] The bulbous jug form rests on three branchlike feet, with curvilinear detailing provided by the shaped spout and rim and crabstock handle. The sugar bowl was similarly produced in more than one size, beginning in the 1750s, and remained in production into the 1780s.[77] Referred to as a *pot à sucre Bouret,* the cylindrical form rests on a footed base, and the domed lid is ornamented with a globular knop resting in foliage. The pure white bodies of the pieces demonstrate the purity of the clay and the skill of the potter in averting imperfections during the firing process. The only overglaze decoration is the gilding on the rims, feet, handle, and knop.

After the presidency, Washington brought the French porcelain service to Mount Vernon, where he continued to use it in retirement. At the sales following Martha Washington's death, the service was divided and sold to her granddaughters Eliza Parke Custis Law, Martha Parke Custis Peter, and Eleanor Parke Custis Lewis.[78] Whereas the sugar bowl returned to Mount Vernon through a descendant of Martha Custis Peter, the cream pot descended in the family of Eleanor Parke Custis Lewis until its recent purchase and subsequent loan to the Association. After more than two hundred years, the two pieces have been reunited to offer a portrait of the refined porcelains that graced Washington's table.

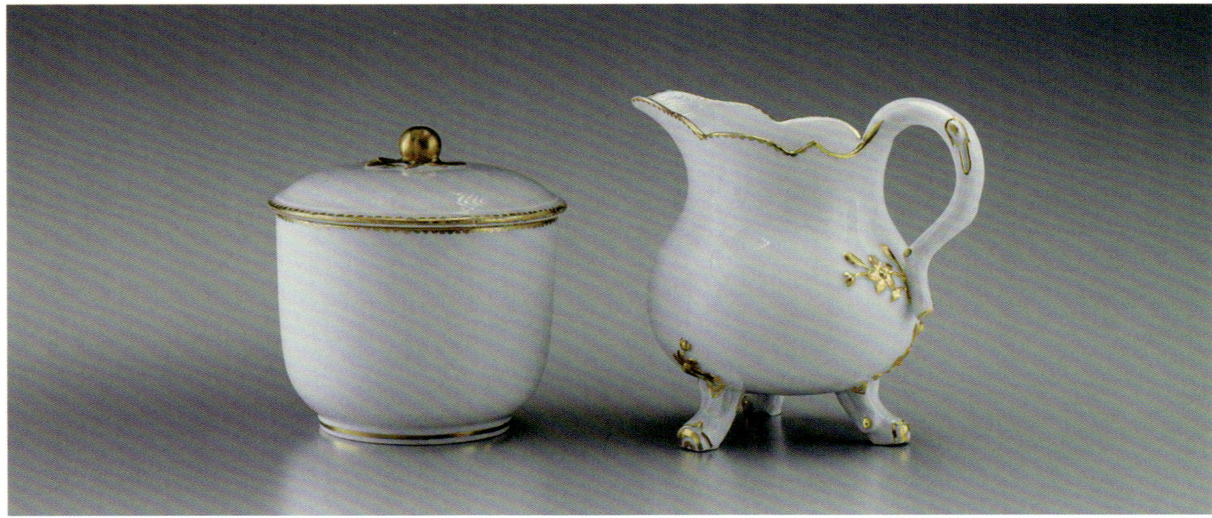

CAT. 43

Covered Cup and Saucer

China, ca. 1795
Porcelain, H. 5", Saucer DIAM. 6"
Gift of Mrs. Francis P. Garvan, 1948
W-1497/A-C

On April 24, 1796, the Dutch merchant Andreas Everardus van Braam Houckgeest sailed into the port of Philadelphia aboard the *Lady Louisa.* "A Box of China for Lady Washington" was among the Chinese treasures the merchant brought with him from work and travel through that country. Van Braam (as he was called) had done very well in the Dutch East India Company and now intended to make the new United States his home.[79] A gift of Chinese porcelain for the First Lady no doubt seemed an appropriate gesture, and the merchant designed an elaborately decorated service for Martha Washington.[80]

This covered cup and saucer is one of the few survivals of Van Braam's gift. The central gold sunburst contains Martha Washington's initials within a laurel wreath and above a ribbon scroll reading "DECUS ET TUTAMEN AB ILLO." A new translation of this phrase provides a better understanding of the additional symbols in the design. The translation, "[Our Union is our] Glory, and [our] Defense against Him," suggests Van Braam's strong belief in the unity of the colonies that formed the United States as well as his scorn of their former ruler, King George III.[81] This central medallion is surrounded by an unbroken chain of green enamel links naming all of the then fifteen states. A blue serpent biting its tail, a symbol of eternity, serves as the border design. In its beautiful overglaze enamel and gilt decoration, Martha Washington's porcelain embodied meaning imbued by Van Braam's carefully considered symbolism that was not likely lost on presidential guests.

Mrs. Washington took the porcelain to Mount Vernon, and at her death bequeathed "the set of tea china that was given me by Mr. Van Braam" to her grandson George Washington Parke Custis.[82] The only porcelains that survive from the service are two-handled covered cups with saucers, plates, and a sugar bowl.[83] Given the use of covered cups for drinking chocolate and the service of the beverage at Mount Vernon, it is entirely possible that Martha Washington used Van Braam's tea china for serving tea as well as warm chocolate.

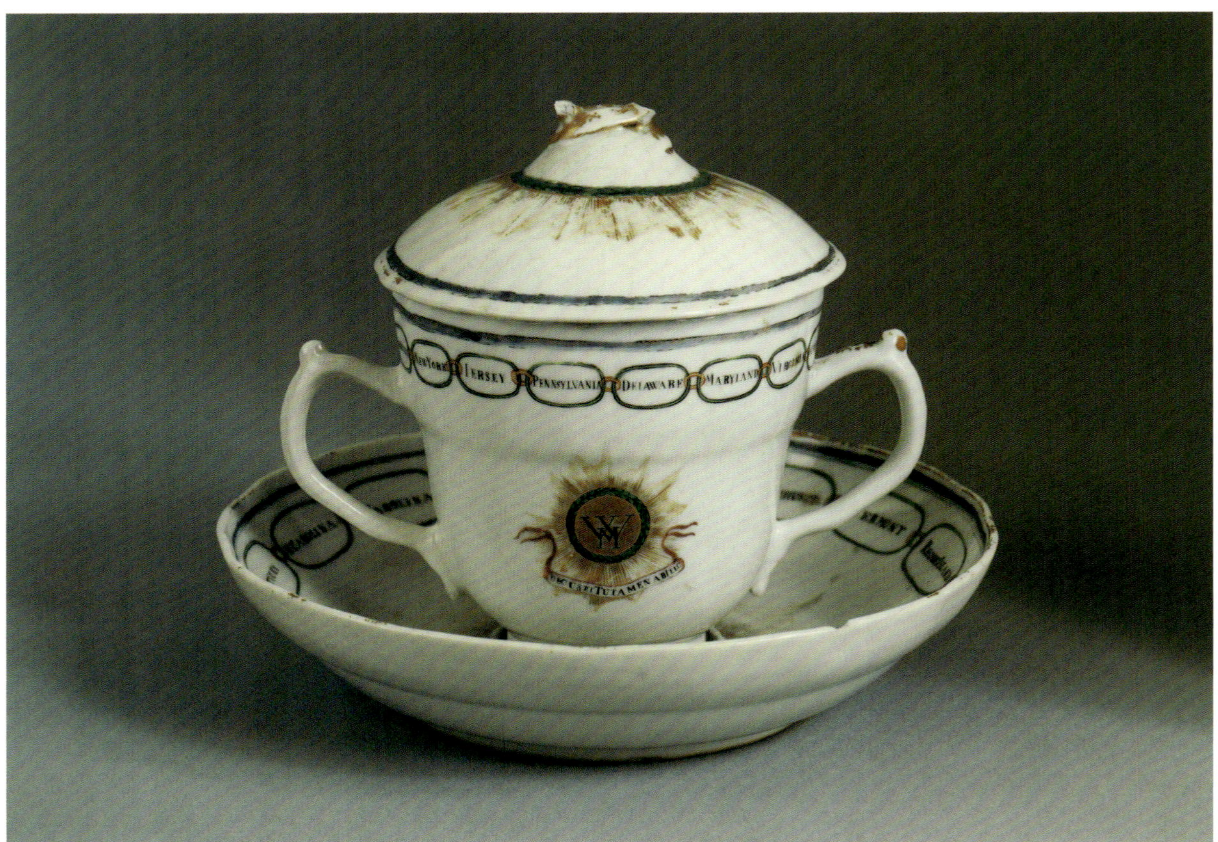

CAT. 44

Argand Lamp

England or France, ca. 1790
Silver plate, base, H. 6", W. 9"
Purchase, 1949
W-1545

After moving into the New York residence vacated by the Comte de Moustier and purchasing a host of furnishings from the departing French minister, George Washington continued to outfit the executive residence with French items. On March 1, 1790, the president wrote to the Philadelphia statesman Gouverneur Morris, then in Paris, for assistance in purchasing Argand lamps (what he called "patent lamps"), similar to those in Robert Morris's Philadelphia residence. Washington requested "fourteen (of what I believe are called) Patent lamps, similar to those used at Mr. R. Morris's, but less costly—two to three guineas a piece, will fully answer my purposes."[84] Washington's interest in the lamps was twofold, to acquire devices that would stylishly light the executive residence and to avail himself of a new technology.

The Argand lamp was the first significant advance in lighting technology since the prehistoric oil lamp was improved on by the Greeks and Romans,[85] and Washington's letter to Morris evidences an understanding of the significance of this innovation. He noted, "These lamps, it is said, consume their own smoke—do no injury to furniture—give more light—and are cheaper than candles."[86] Washington's words also demonstrate his practicality, with concern for protecting costly imported textiles and reducing candle expenses. Morris responded from London, with a touch of trepidation, on May 3, 1790, "I have bespoke the Lamps you desired and at about the limited Prices. They are as handsome as those Prices would admit of but in a different style from those of Mr. Morris's which cost a great Deal more. These will however be I beleieve as useful but not quite so ornamental."[87] Washington's restriction of spending "two or three guineas" per lamp had clearly presented Morris with a challenge, but Morris' concern that they answer the president's request must have been alleviated by Washington's letter in December 1790. The president acknowledged his gratitude to Morris for the lamps: "The articles are elegant, and I am perfectly satisfied with the price of them."[88]

This urn-shaped lamp, one of the fourteen sent by Morris, combines the new Neoclassical style with recent silver-plating technology. The overall urn shape with applied scroll handles reflects the forms and detailing of ancient Greece and Rome that were inspiring the West. The use of silver-plated copper to construct the lamp allowed for its lower cost and availability to a wider clientele. Whether placed on a table or wall bracket, the lamp no doubt served as a pleasing reference to republican taste and technological advancements for those entertained by the president.

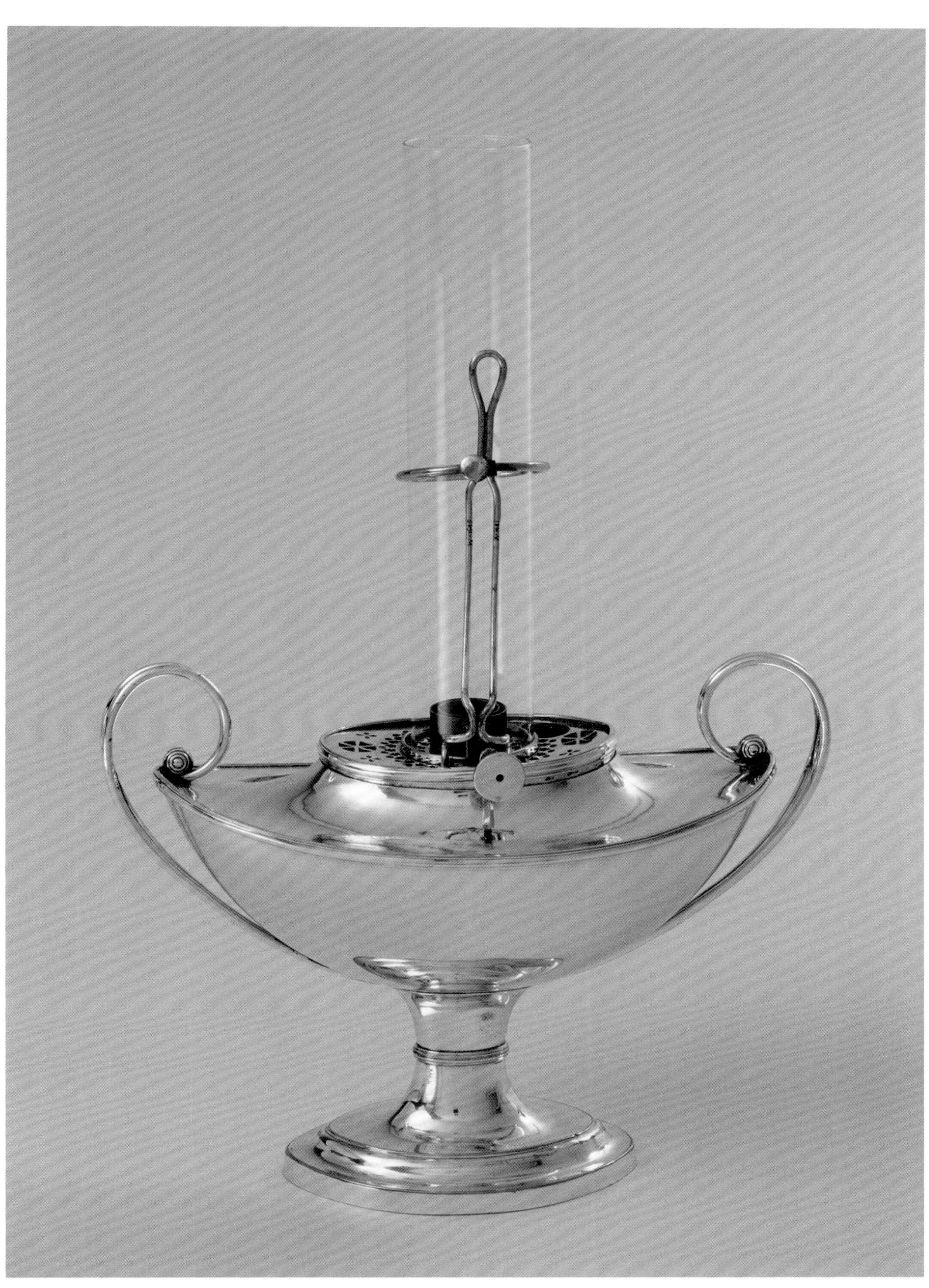

CAT. 45

Argand Wall Lamp

England or France, ca. 1790
Base metals and glass, H. 15⅞", W. 8½", D. 9"
Purchase, G. Freeland Peter, Jr., Collection, 1956
W-2169

In addition to the elegant silver-plated Argand lamps George Washington requested for the executive residence, he also wished Gouveneur Morris to procure for him "a dozen other patent lamps for the Hall, Entries, and Stairs of my house" that were of "a more ordinary sort."[89] By August 1790 the lamps were on their way to Washington, and by December of the same year they were being used to brighten the halls and stairways of the presidential house.[90] These "patent" lamps were among the earliest lamps of the Argand design to be brought to America and at the time represented a revolutionary concept in brighter, more economical, and more convenient household lighting.[91]

A Swiss chemist, Aimé Argand (1750–1803) had invented the first scientifically designed illumination in the early 1780s, when he was summoned to Montpellier, France, to assist vintners with a new distillation process. Needing better light for his studies, Argand devised a lamp that permitted a draft to supply oxygen to the inside of the flame as well as the outside.[92] With the wick enclosed in a glass chimney, the air current improved combustion and created a brighter and hotter flame that was nearly smokeless.[93] Refused financial support to bring his new lamp into commercial production in France, Argand succeeded in obtaining a patent for the lamp in England on March 12, 1784: hence Washington's reference to a "patent lamp."[94]

This example of the "more ordinary sort" of Argand lamps used in the executive residence was for mounting on a wall. The painted oval reflector is fitted with segments of mirrored glass and contains an oil reservoir accessed by a decorative pineapple knob. A small tube connects the reservoir to the tubular wick burner enclosed in a glass chimney. An oval plate fixed to the face of the burner reads "Ami Argand" in reference to the inventor. Argand turned to the Englishmen William Parker and Matthew Boulton to make his lamps, and it is possible that Washington's were a product of this partnership. The innovation of the lamps was so profound, however, that they were quickly copied and sold in England and France without Argand's permission.[95]

Argand-type lamps quickly rose to popularity among those who could afford them. They were adjustable, burned cleanly, and produced ten to twelve times the amount of light as a candle. The drawback was the expense involved for the lamp itself and then for the amounts of oil necessary for its use. Spermaceti oil (oil from the sperm whale) was prized because it burned cleanly and with little odor. With demand for it high after the invention of the Argand lamp, the oil commanded high prices. Despite the cost, Washington clearly enjoyed the fashionable technology. He secured additional Argand lamps from Philadelphia silversmiths and took all of his lamps to Mount Vernon when he retired. In his 1797 list of public and private purchases for the executive residence, Washington referred to this wall-mounted variety as "oval Japan," or japanned, in reference to the original surface that imitated Japanese and Chinese imported lacquerware.[96] After George and Martha Washington's deaths, the lamp descended in the family of Martha Custis Peter, Martha Washington's granddaughter, and is the only surviving example known of the original dozen.

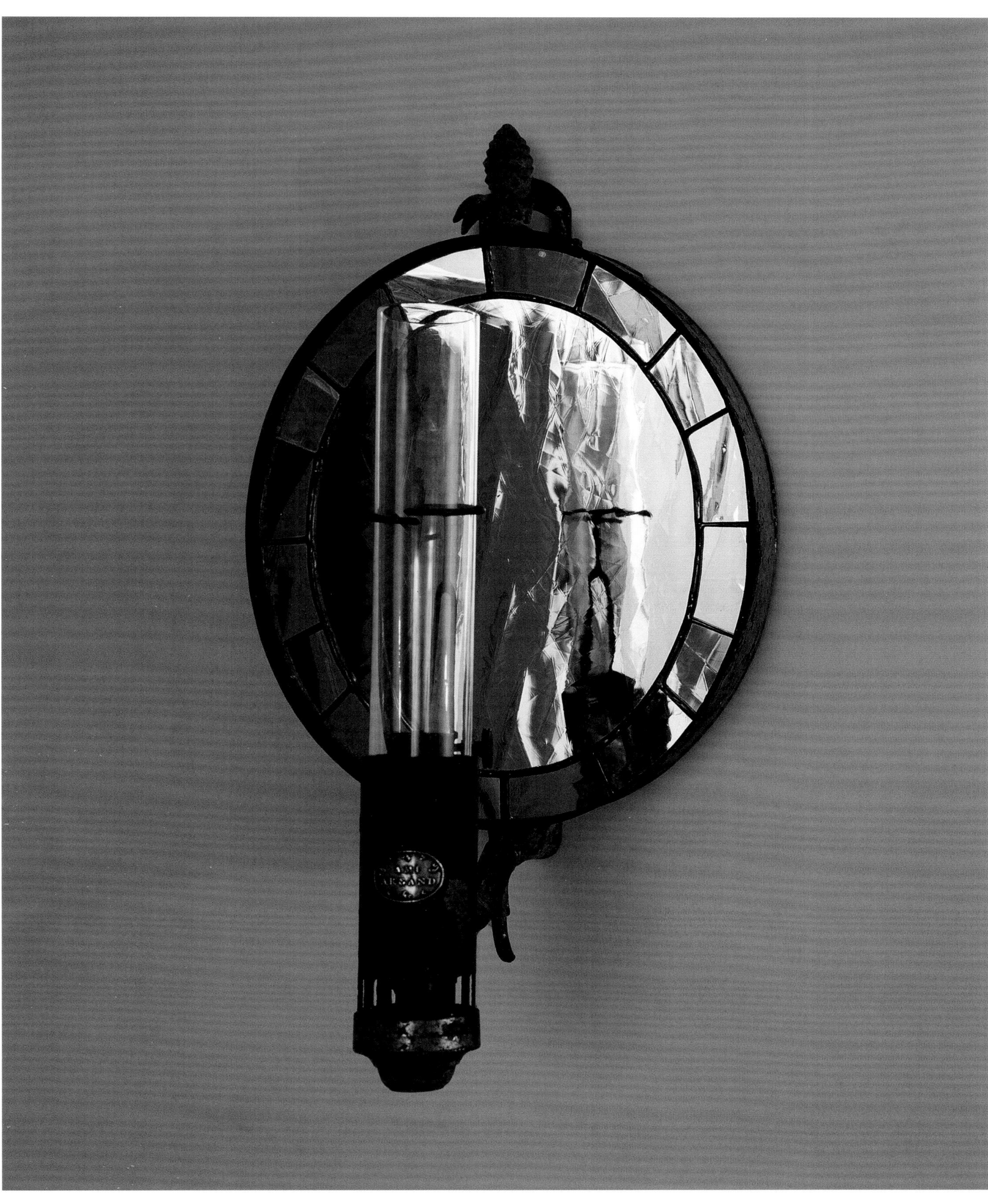

CAT. 46

Armchair

Thomas Affleck (1740–1795)
Philadelphia, Pennsylvania, ca. 1790–1794
Mahogany and red oak, H. 36", W. 25", D. 20¼"
Gift of Dr. and Mrs. Joseph E. Fields, 1991
H-3552

In 1790, just one year into George Washington's presidency, the seat of government moved from New York to Philadelphia, the executive residence was transferred to the Robert Morris House, and a new Congress Hall was built to house the Senate and House of Representatives. The Philadelphia cabinetmaker Thomas Affleck was selected to craft the seating furniture for Congress Hall and provided sixty-five "Elbow Chairs" (or armchairs) for the House of Representatives, twenty-seven for the Senate (one of which was likely for the Senate Secretary), and forty-five additional chairs when the building was refurbished in 1793.[97]

The choice of Thomas Affleck to make chairs for the House and Senate matched an expert craftsman with the challenge of establishing the style most appropriate for the legislative bodies overseeing the formation of the newest experiment in democracy. The chairs Affleck produced were a departure from his earlier work, which demonstrated a pronounced influence of English pattern books and were characteristic of the Rococo style fashionable among Philadelphia's prewar colonial elite.[98] Instead, they embraced the Neoclassical aesthetic, preferred by President Washington and his contemporaries, which emphasized graceful restraint and classical lines.

The armchairs were uniform with the exception of upholstery, black leather for the House chamber and "red Morocco" leather for the Senate.[99] All were accented by decorative brass tacking. This example was likely in the original House of Representatives chamber, as a small fragment of black leather was revealed in recent conservation work. The frame is primarily mahogany, with square upholstered seat and back, and upholstered arms that project from the back to gently curved supports detailed with simple carved beading on the front face. The straight, square front legs have similar carved beading, while the back legs are slightly curved and chamfered.

After the nation's capital was moved to the new Federal City (Washington, DC) in 1800, Affleck's Congress Hall armchairs remained in storage in Philadelphia until the early years of the nineteenth century, when the Senate chamber chairs were sent to the new Pennsylvania state capital in Lancaster and the House chamber chairs were dispersed through gift and sale.[100] Some of the chairs were brought together in Philadelphia at the time of the 1876 centennial. Others were highlighted during the Marquis de Lafayette's final tour of America in 1824–1825, a year marked by remembrance and renewed interest in the American Revolution and the early years of the republic. At that time, this chair and others of its kind developed the erroneous designation "Signers' Chairs," presumed to be those used by signers of the Declaration of Independence in 1776.[101] This chair was displayed for a number of years in the Philadelphia museum of William H. Long and afterward auctioned in New York.[102]

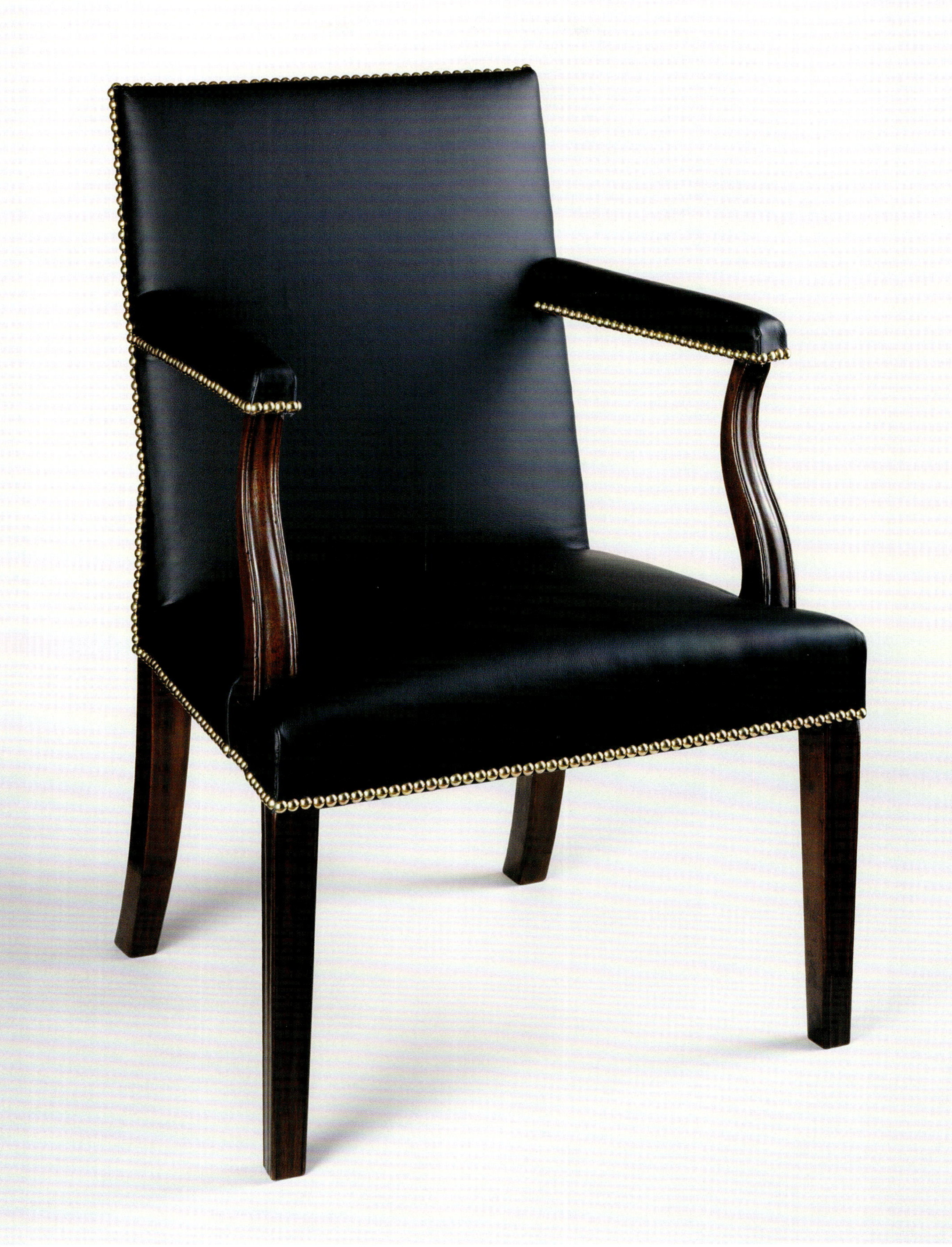

CAT. 47

Tray

Ephraim Brasher (1744–1810)
New York, New York, 1790
Silver, H. 2", W. 24½", D. 17"
Purchase, 1932
W-32

In July 1790 Tobias Lear corresponded on behalf of Washington with the Philadelphia merchant Clement Biddle to procure silver waiters needed for presidential entertaining. After Biddle provided the price of available waiters in Philadelphia, Lear wrote from New York that "Silver Waiters can be had here of Warranted silver and best workmanship at 13/10 per oz. this currency, which is lower than with you, [and] we shall therefore have them made here."[103] Lear was perhaps referring to the silver and workmanship of Ephraim Brasher, who operated his silversmithing business on Cherry Street, just a few doors down from the executive residence.[104]

That September, Brasher sold the president "two Silver Waiters" and two "Tea" trays.[105] The waiters were likely intended for the service of wine and other beverages in stemmed glasses, while the trays held tea wares. Although the words *waiter* and *tray* are often interchanged, this example of Brasher's work was likely one of the tea trays he supplied to Washington.

Crafted in the Neoclassical style, the elliptical tray is ornamented simply by an applied beaded border. The two upturned scroll handles are secured to the sides with stylized acanthus leaves that recall the naturalistic detailing popular several years earlier. Brasher marked the tray twice between the handle returns on both sides, leaving no doubt as to which New York silversmith was responsible for the elegant and stylish object.

The silver waiters and tea trays George Washington purchased from Ephraim Brasher remained in use at the conclusion of the presidency, and all were likely taken back to Mount Vernon. This tray and its mate were part of the silver inherited by George Washington Parke Custis at Martha Washington's death in 1802.[106] The two silver waiters, presumably also marked by Brasher, remain unlocated.

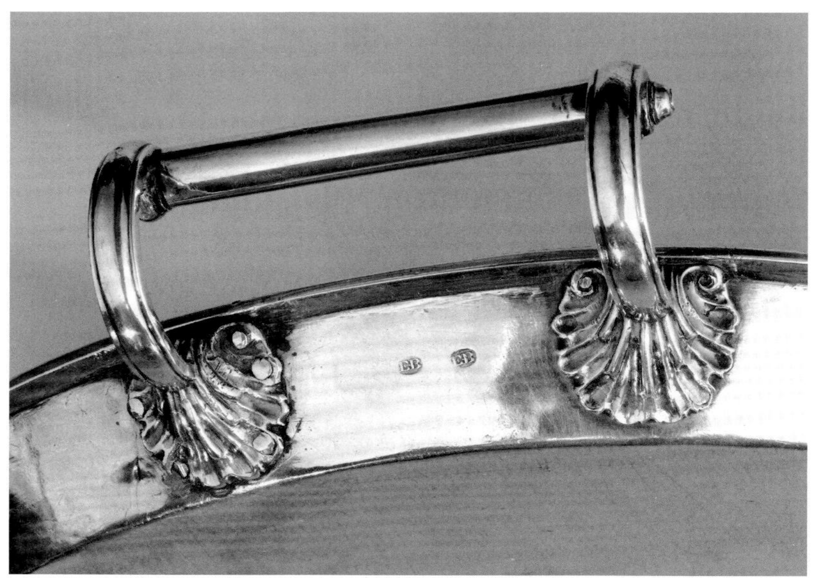

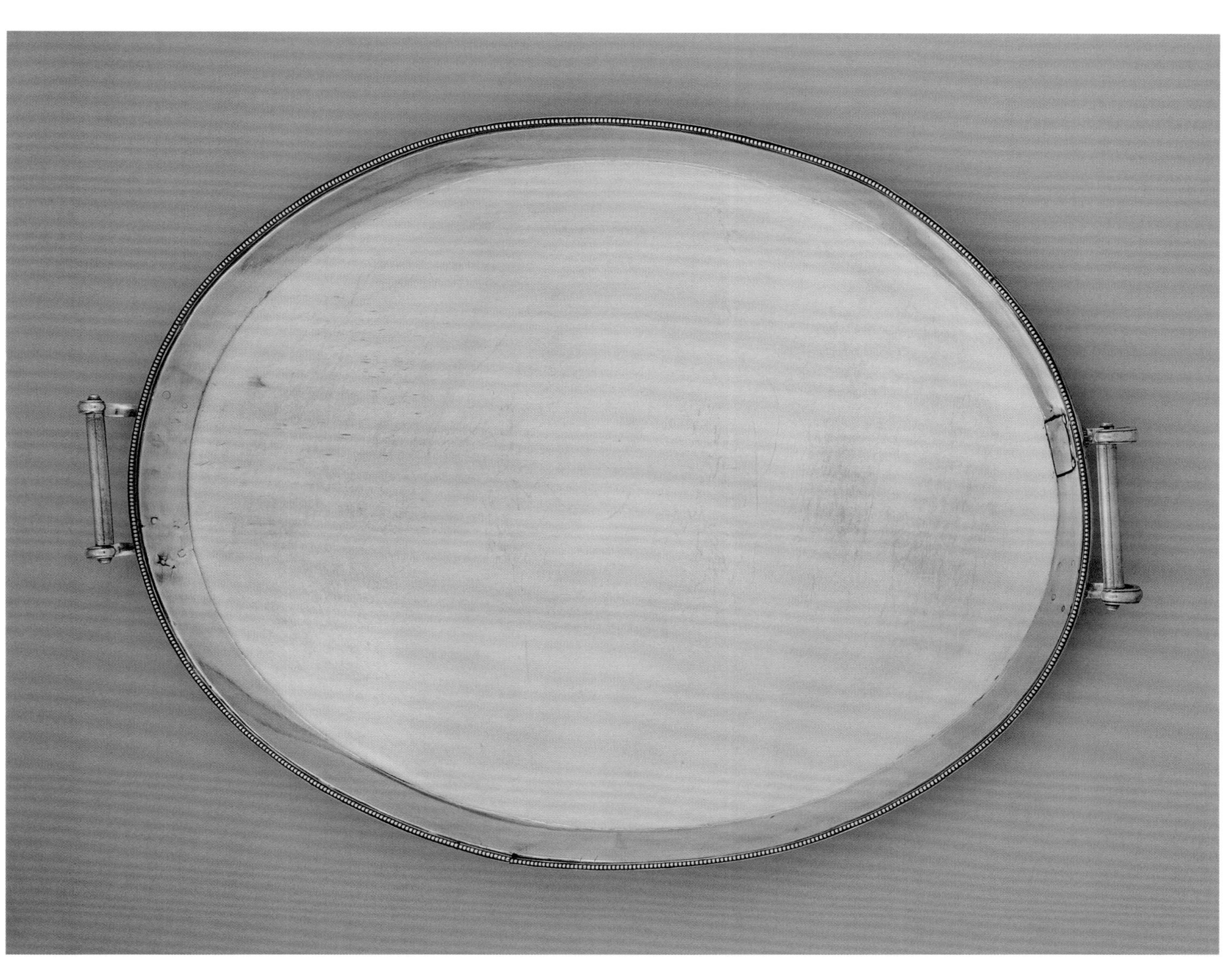

CAT. 48

Decanter and Wineglasses

Probably European, ca. 1785–1795
Colorless glass, Decanter: H. 11½", DIAM. 4"
W-2108/A&B
Glasses: H. 4⅝"; 4¼"
W-2117/A; W-2117/B
Purchase, 1957

In 1797, as Washington was leaving Philadelphia at the end of his second term, he made an inventory of the presidential furnishings purchased publicly and those he had bought with his own funds. He noted that he considered the glassware his own, inasmuch as it had been broken and replaced repeatedly at his own expense.[107] This decanter and these wineglasses were likely among the pieces of glass purchased during the presidency to escape breakage and were taken to Mount Vernon when Washington retired.

Stylistically appropriate for the presidential years (1789–1797), the decanter and glasses are decorated with patterns of wheel-engraved stars and banding prevalent among the neoclassically inspired glasswares produced in England and Bohemia at the end of the eighteenth century. The decanter's barrel shape became popular about 1780, as did its flanged lip, applied faceted neck rings, and cut flutes encircling the base.[108] The trumpet-shaped wineglasses are similarly engraved from the rim to the cut fluting that accents the bowls and stems.

This glassware offered multiple ways of fulfilling the Washingtons' entertaining needs. The decanter could be filled with wine, its colorless nature allowing the host to identify any undesired sediment before serving, and used for dispensing the fermented beverage into glasses at the dining table. Or it could hold and offer beverages such as beer, distilled liquors, and punch. The glasses might hold Washington's favorite Madeira or even be used to serve soft-boiled eggs.[109] Regardless of the beverage or food they served, this decanter and glasses offered the Washingtons' guests an elegant imported and fashionable vehicle for enjoying their hosts' well-known hospitality.

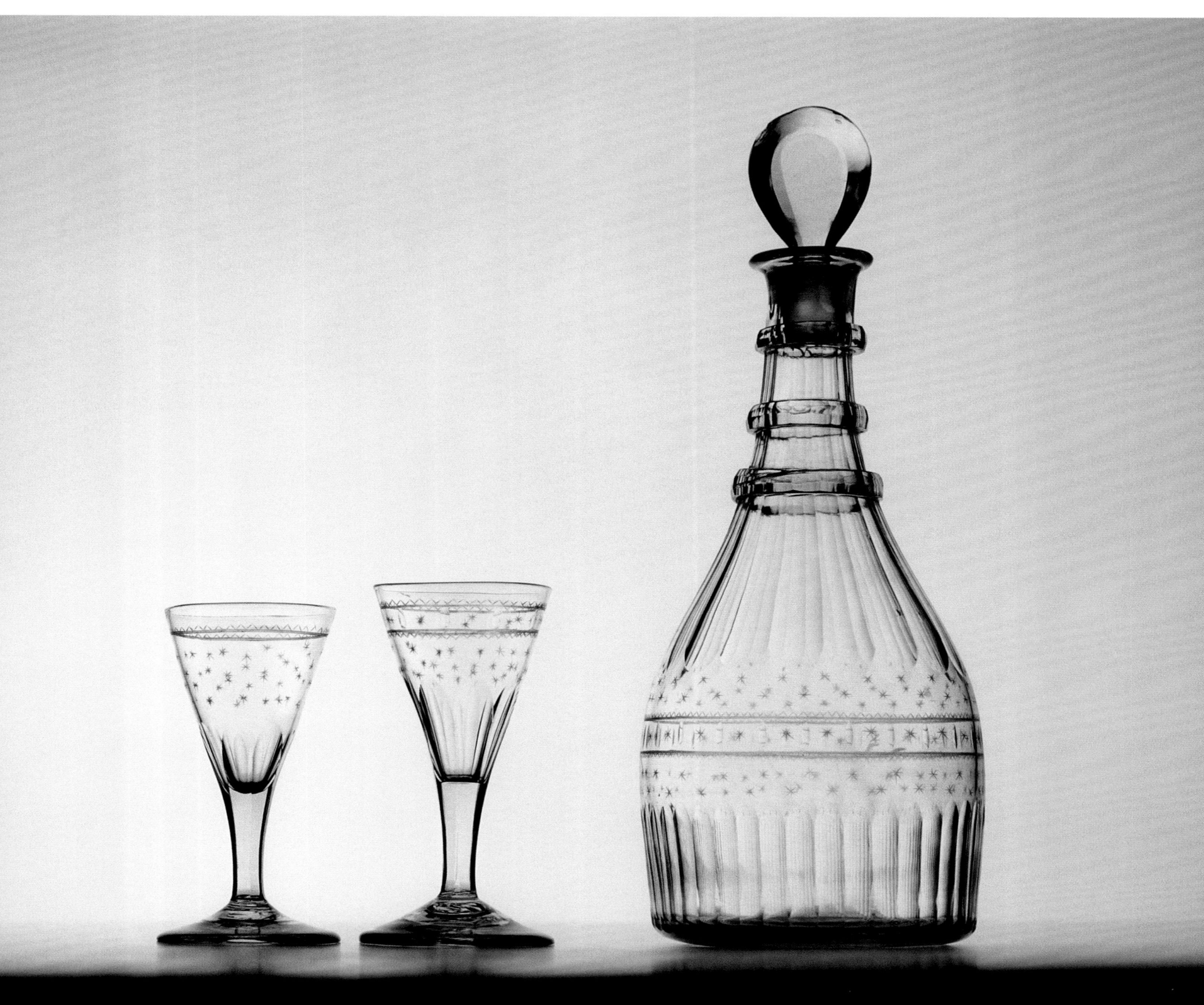

CAT. 49

Sword

Solingen, Prussia, ca. 1795
Steel, brass, copper, and gold, OL. 39½" 4¼", Blade L. 33¾" 4¼", W. 1¾" 4¼"
Gift of Miss Alice L. Riggs, Col. E. F. Riggs, the Rev. T. L. Riggs and Miss Jane A. Riggs,
Vice Regent for the District of Columbia, 1924
W-85

As president, George Washington attracted worldwide attention and admiration, often receiving gifts that spoke of his successful military past. In the fall of 1796 Washington received a sword that puzzled him. Writing to John Quincy Adams from Philadelphia on September 12, 1796, Washington requested Adams's assistance in understanding how and why the sword had come into his possession. He relayed:

> *Some time ago . . . I read in some gazette . . . announcing that a celebrated artist had presented, or was about to present to the President of the United States a sword of masterly workmanship, as an evidence of his veneration &c. &c. I thought no more of the matter afterwards, until a gentleman with whom I have no acquaintance, coming from and going to I know not where, at a tavern I never could get information of, came across this sword (for it is presumed to be the same) pawned for thirty dollars; which he paid, left it in Alexandria, nine miles from my house, in Virginia with a person who refunded him the money and sent the sword to me. This is all I have been able to learn of this curious affair. The blade is highly wrought, and decorated with many military emblems. . . . If, Sir, with this clew you can develop the history of this sword, the value of it; the character of the maker, and his probable object in sending it; it would oblige me.*[110]

The following February, John Quincy Adams replied from The Hague that he had been able to trace the sword to a workman from Solingen named Alte who had commissioned it with the intention of presenting the sword to George Washington.[111] At roughly the same time, Washington received a letter from Theophilus Alte of Solingen. Alte explained that with a "natural inclination to a free country," he had selected America for his son, Daniel, and had sent with him a sword to present to Washington, "as the only man I know in this world who acted in an uninterested manner for the happiness of his country."[112] In addition to asking Washington for the protection he hoped the president would offer his son, Alte wrote to confirm the safe arrival of both Daniel and the sword. Ten months later, Washington received another plea from Alte for information regarding his son's fate, in which Alte speculated that his "inexperienced and very timid" son "has fallen into some malicious hands" and neglected his father's counsel.[113] Although the mysterious fate of Daniel Alte was not resolved in Washington's correspondence, the beautifully wrought sword he brought to America remains a testament to the precise workmanship of Solingen artisans and the high Prussian esteem for George Washington.

The hilt is of gilt brass, and the leather-covered grip bound with copper wire that was originally likely gilded as well. The steel blade is heavily ornamented with gilded, engraved, and hammered designs on both sides. Floral motifs highlight and frame symbols of freedom, and George Washington is named and depicted as a soldier standing astride a conquered lion and unicorn (detail). The German inscription reads: "VERTILGER DES DESPOTISM BESCHUTZER DER FREIHEIT BEHARRLICHER MANN NIMM VON MEINES SOHNES HAND DIES SCHWERD ICH BITTE DICH Theophilus Alte Zu Solingen" (detail) (DESTROYER OF DESPOTISM, PROTECTOR OF FREEDOM, STEADFAST MAN, TAKE FROM MY SON'S HANDS THIS SWORD, I PRAY THEE Theophilus Alte at Solingen).[114] Even without the inscription that renders the object so important to American history, the sword is an excellent example of the exquisite design and precise workmanship of the Solingen craftsmen known throughout Europe for their steel weapons.

After George Washington's death, this sword was among those bequeathed in his will to his nephews and selected by George Steptoe Washington, son of the general's brother Samuel.[115] It descended in the Washington family until its sale after the Civil War and gift to Mount Vernon in 1923, where it continues to recall the global veneration for our nation's first president.

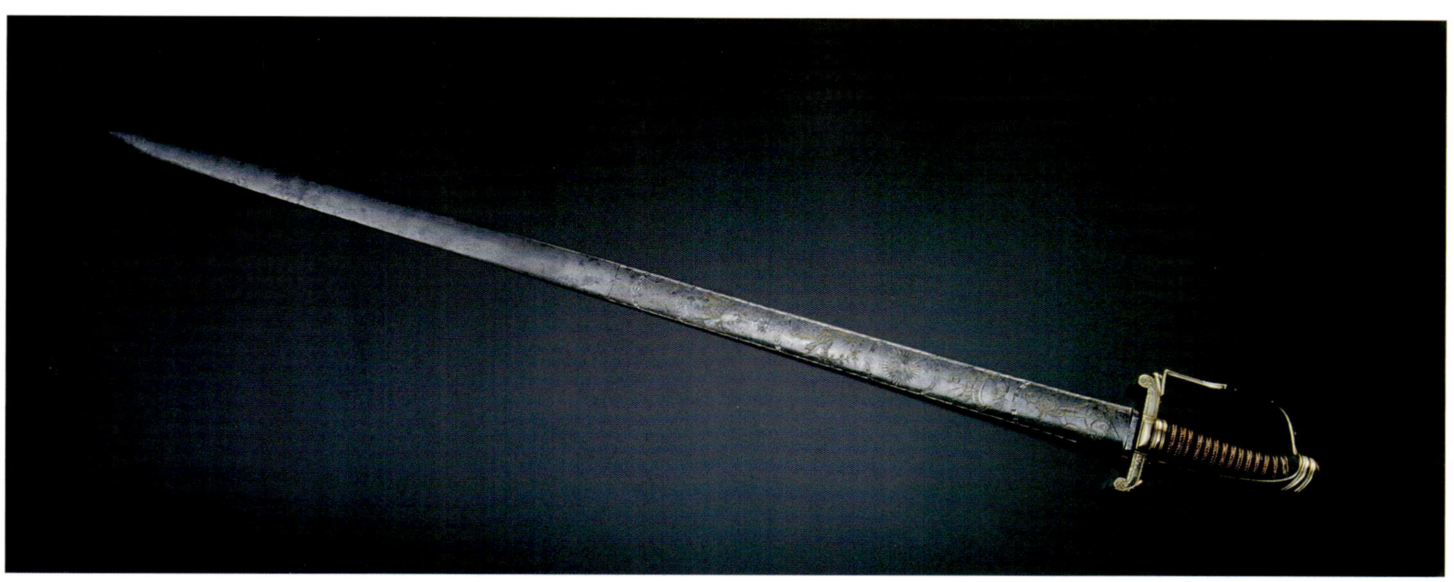

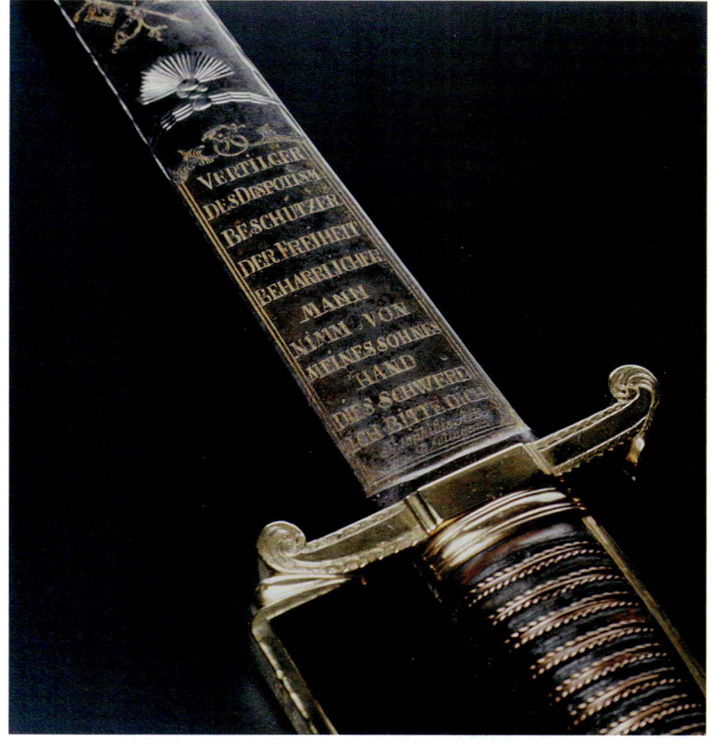
VERTILGER
DES DESPOTISM
BESCHUTZER
DER FREIHEIT
BEHARRLICHER
MANN
NIMM VON
MEINES SOHNES
HAND
DIES SCHWERD

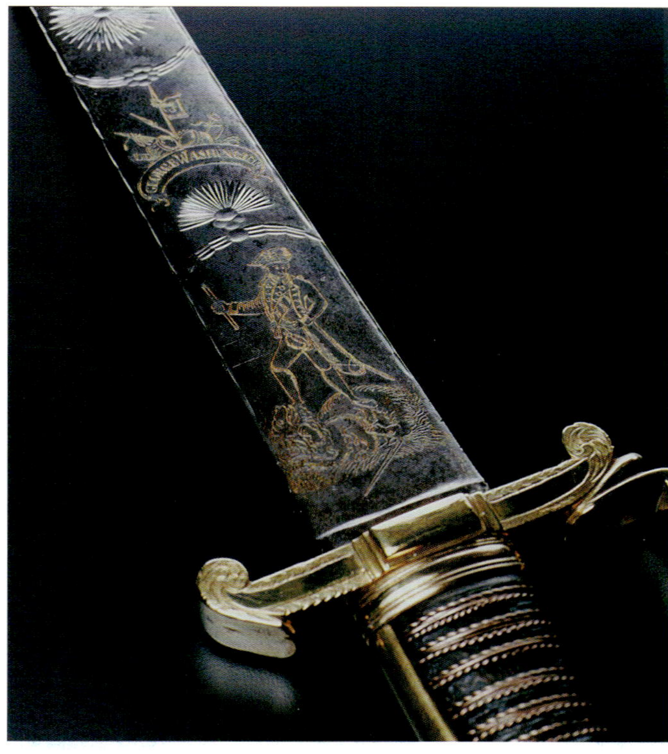

CAT. 50

Candlesticks

Probably England, ca. 1795
Silver plate, H. 10½", W. 3⅞"
Bequest of G. Freeland Peter, Jr., 1991
W-3549/A–D

Despite his new interest in Argand lamps, George Washington varied his purchases of lighting devices to include numerous silver-plated candlesticks to illuminate the executive residence. His list of "Plated-Ware" acquired during the presidency notes large, oval, small, plain, flat, and even "Spangle" varieties.[116] Washington purchased this pair from the Philadelphia silversmith Rowland Parry in 1796, and they are noted in his account book with payment of twenty-five dollars on May 30 to "Row'd Parry for 2 pr. Octagonal plated Candlesticks."[117] Parry had recently dissolved his silversmithing partnership with James Musgrave,[118] perhaps to undertake the retail sale of silver-plated items such as these.

The candlesticks are fitted with removable bobeches for easy cleaning and wax removal and represent the latest Neoclassical fashion. The overall fluting of the base, shaft, and cup is defined by beading and ornamented with acanthus leaves and swagging. When placed on the presidential dining table, they would have harmonized with Washington's classically inspired table ornaments, porcelain, and glassware.

After the presidency, the candlesticks continued to be used in the Washington household at Mount Vernon. At the time of George Washington's death they may have been one of four pairs of silver-plated "high candlesticks" listed in the estate inventory.[119] Although the silver and plated ware at Mount Vernon were willed to George Washington Parke Custis and Eleanor Parke Custis Lewis at the time of Mrs. Washington's death, this pair descended in the family of granddaughter Martha Custis Peter. One candlestick from the matching pair also descended in the Peter family, and a pair with slightly larger dimensions and less crisp detailing descended in the line of granddaughter Eliza Parke Custis. The survival of at least five silver-plated octagonal candlesticks and the variations demonstrated by the latter pair suggest that Washington may have preferred their design to others and acquired additional examples.[120]

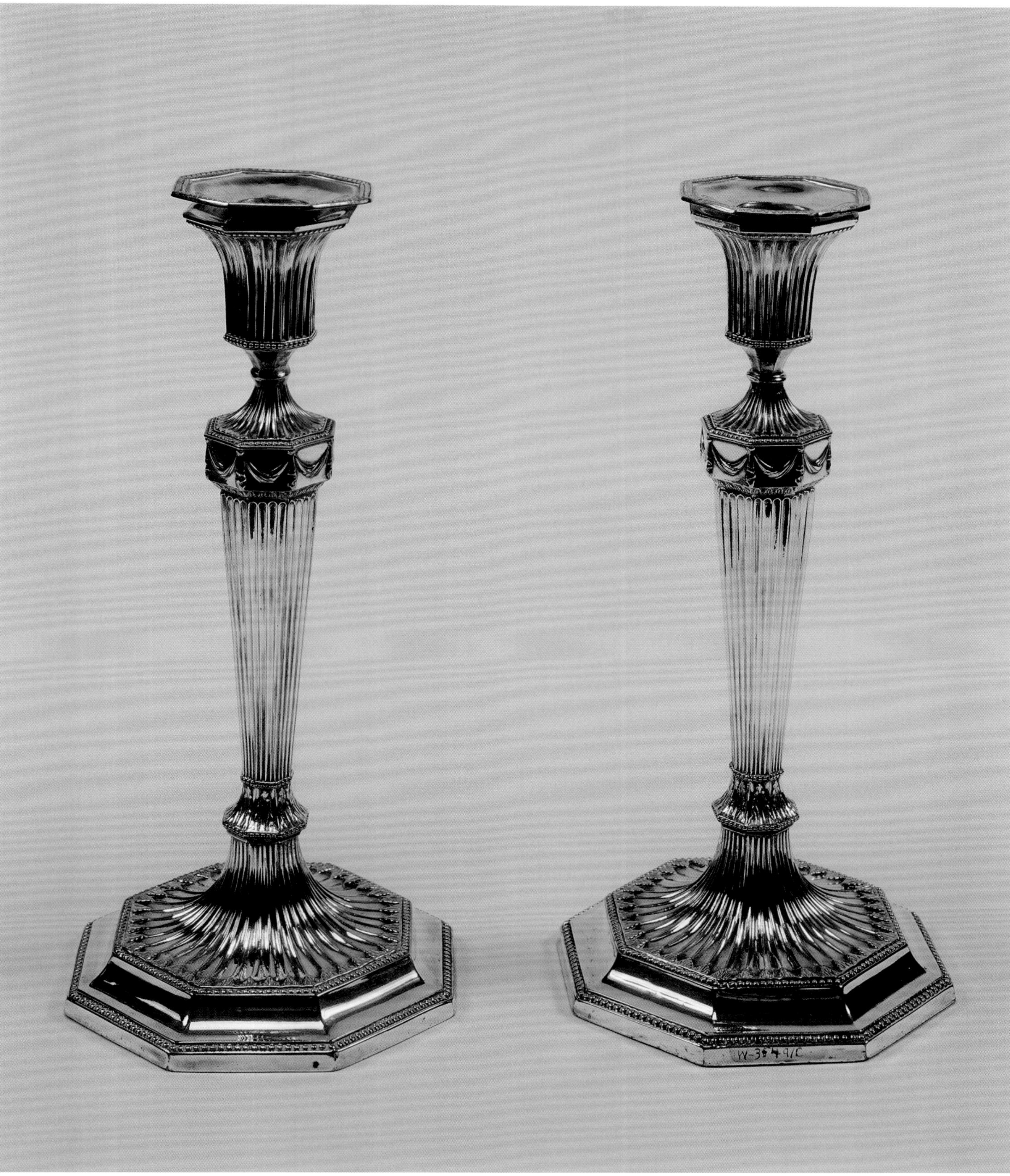

CAT. 51

Fire Buckets

Peter Abel
Philadelphia, Pennsylvania, 1797
Leather and hemp, H. 13", DIAM. 9"
Transferred to the Mount Vernon Ladies' Association through the generosity of John Augustine Washington, III, 1860
W-403

Fires were serious threats to life and livelihood in eighteenth-century cities, and fire buckets were a necessary item in fighting fires until more advanced equipment was developed. Made of tanned hides carefully sewn together to ensure watertight seams, fire buckets had a typical capacity of three gallons. When filled with water, they could be used to put out small residential fires or tossed into the street to assist the fire brigade in extinguishing larger fires. The names of the fire bucket owners were sometimes placed on the buckets to ensure their return to the proper household, like those supplied to George Washington during his presidency.[121]

In March 1797 Washington purchased "6 fire buckets" for nineteen dollars, all of which survive in the Mount Vernon collection.[122] Each black leather bucket is slightly tapered and has a leather-covered rope bail handle. The exterior is decorated with "George Wafhington" painted in black on a white band. The stamp "P.ABEL" on the bucket bottom identifies the maker as the shoemaker Peter Abel.[123] On several of the buckets, a paper label still identifies the retailer who sold Abel's work as William Jones, a saddle, harness, and trunk maker in Philadelphia (detail).[124]

After the presidency, Washington took his fire buckets to Mount Vernon. At the time of his death in 1799, they are listed among the articles in the servants' hall, where they stood ready to extinguish any fires that threatened the Mansion and its dependencies.[125] Unlike many items that were disbursed following the Washingtons' deaths, the buckets have remained at Mount Vernon.

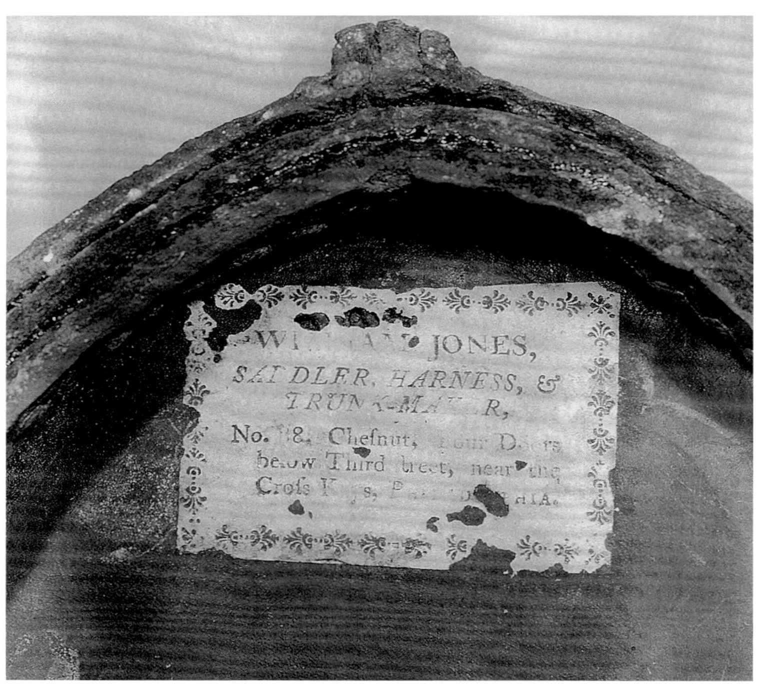

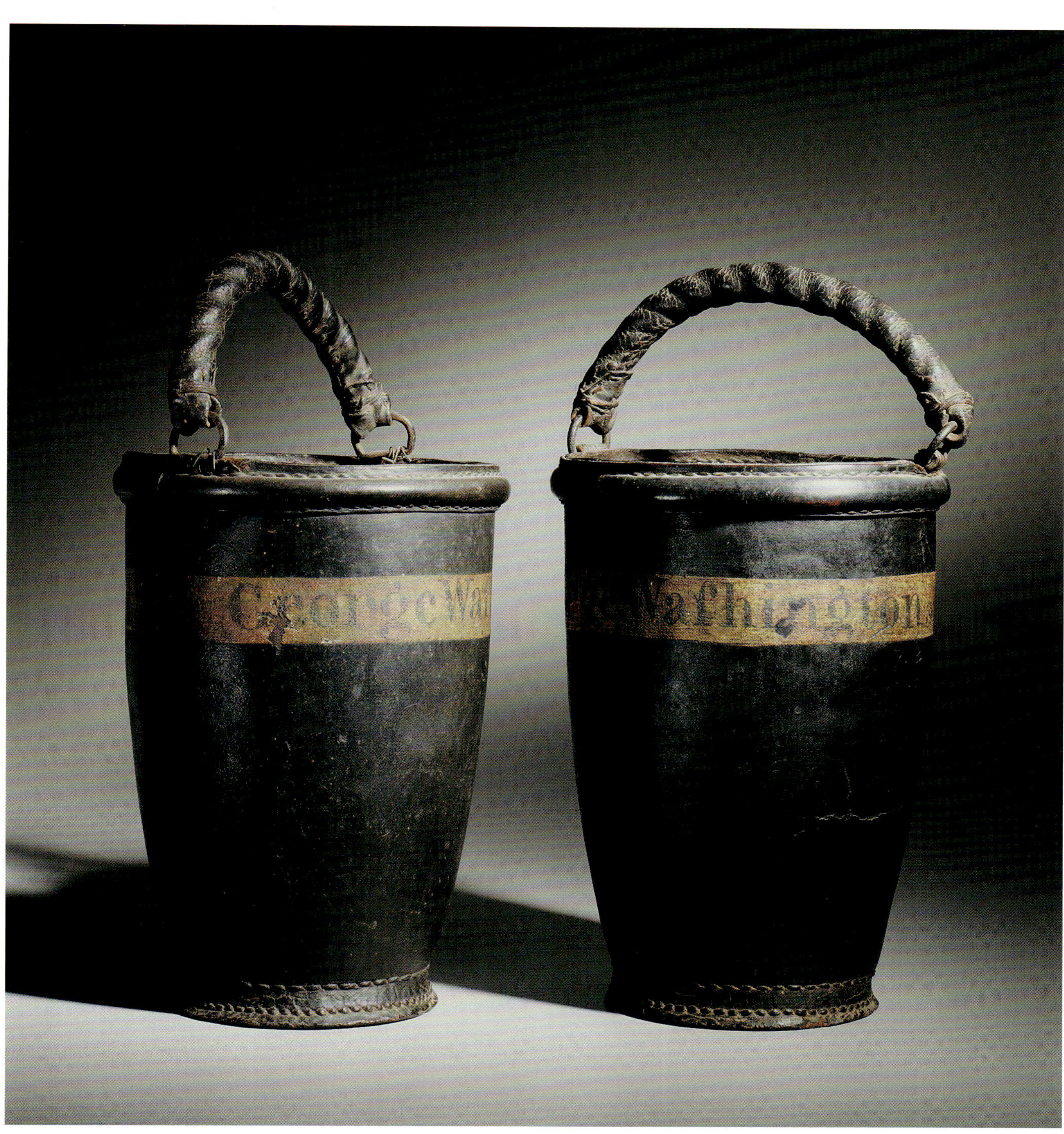
George Wa
Wafhington

CAT. 52

George Washington (1732–1799)

ca. 1804
Gilbert Stuart (1755–1828)
Oil on canvas, 30 x 25"
Gift of Miss Caroline H. R. Richardson,
through her sister, Mrs. Tobias G. Richardson, the Vice Regent for Louisiana, 1904
H-4

When Gilbert Stuart put brush to canvas during George Washington's presidency, he painted the image most recognized today. Stuart wanted to paint Washington, for he expected that he could make a "fortune" on images of the Revolutionary War hero and American leader.[126] At the time the president sat for Stuart, the artist apparently tried to relax his sitter, offering, "Now, sir, you must let me forget that you are General Washington and that I am Stuart, the painter," to which the president responded, "Mr. Stuart need never feel the need for forgetting who he is and who General Washington is."[127] After Stuart's initial portrait of Washington, he made more than one hundred copies for American and European patrons eager to own an image of the illustrious sitter.[128] They were of three types: a waist-length Vaughan version showing the right side of Washington's face; an Athenaeum variant displaying the left side; and a full-length Landsdowne example. The artist promised to give Martha Washington the original canvas of the Athenaeum portrait used to make the copies but unfortunately never kept his word.[129]

This Athenaeum-type portrait was purchased from Stuart by George Beck, a landscape artist whom Washington patronized, for Major Alexander Parker of Lexington, Kentucky. The canvas shows Washington dressed in a black velvet suit with a white lace jabot at his neck and his powdered hair pulled back into a queue ornamented by a sawtoothed ribbon rosette. His lips appear swollen and his mouth uncomfortable, owing to a new set of ill-fitting dentures. For a person conscious of the impression made by his outward appearance, it would likely displease our nation's first president to know that the likeness taken at a moment of discomfort would become the best known. Indeed, the image was widely circulated through Stuart's copies as well as by painters, engravers, and lithographers who copied the original work.[130] Stuart's painting became, and remains, "the household Washington of the world."[131]

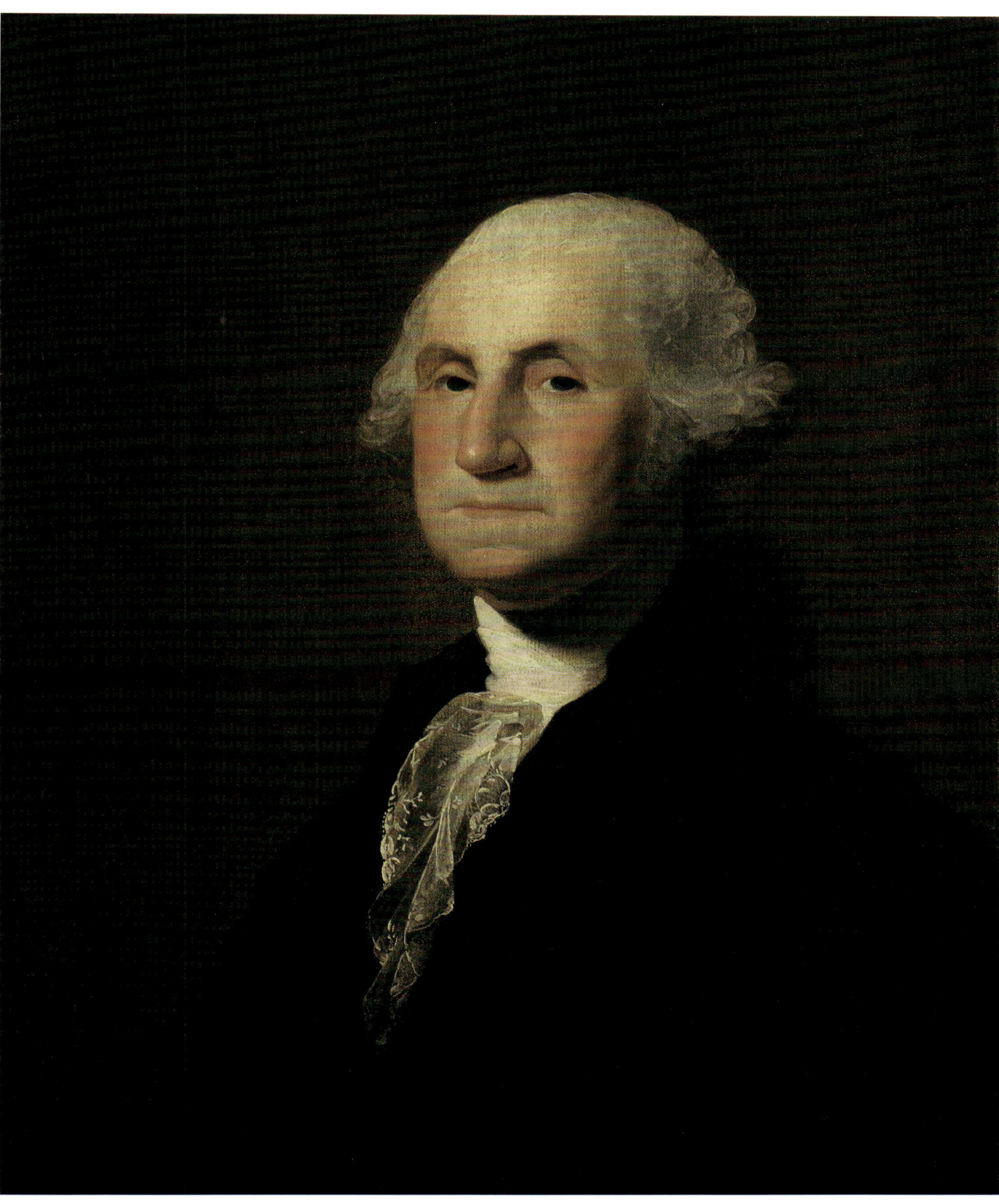

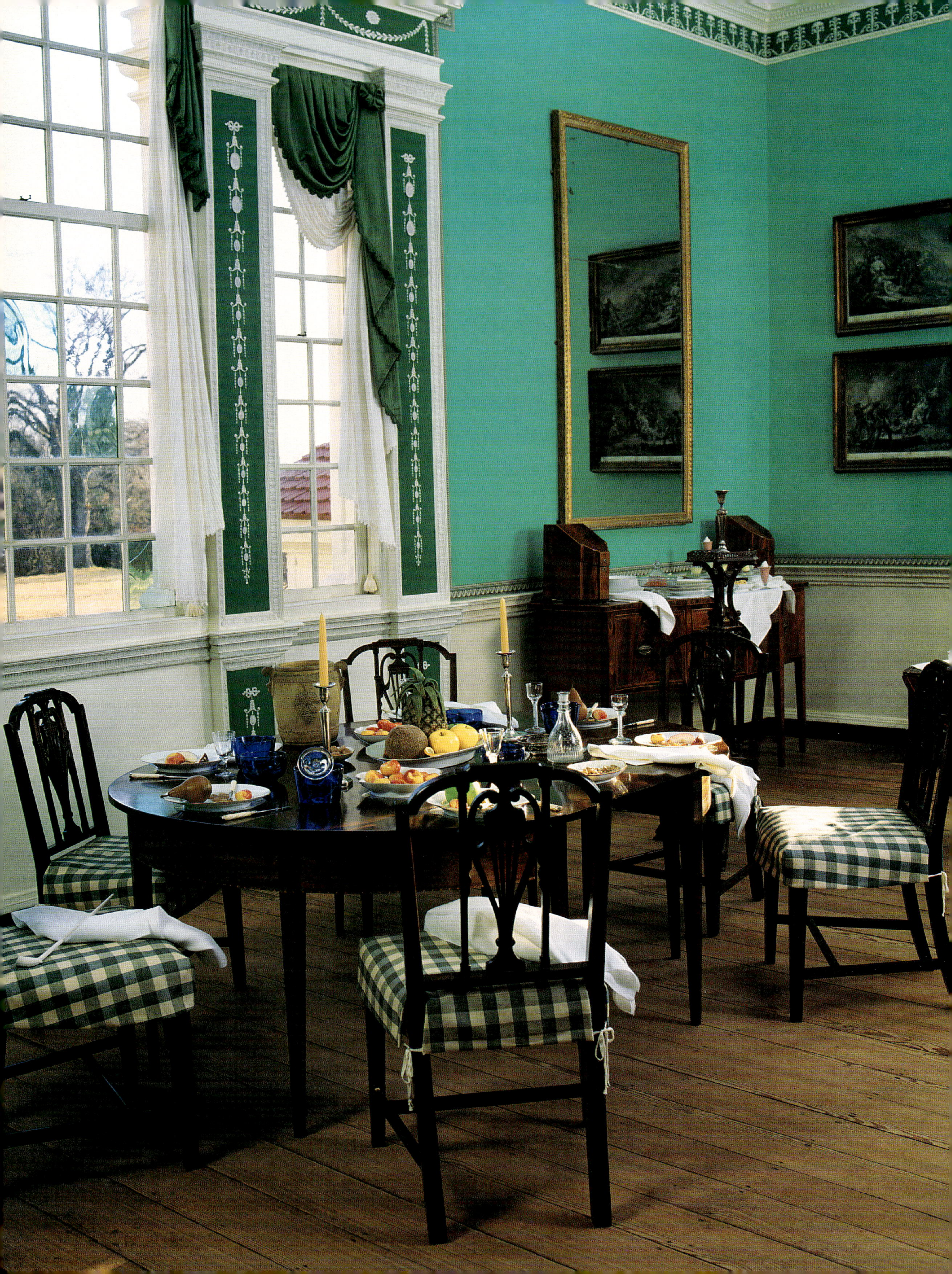

CHAPTER FIVE

George Washington's Final Retirement to Mount Vernon

1797–1799

IN 1797 GEORGE WASHINGTON ONCE AGAIN BECAME A PRIVATE CITIZEN and retired to Mount Vernon. After eight long years as president, he was able to return to the estate and farms and devote himself to its management and family life. The objects that surrounded Washington in the final two years of his life represented a lifelong interest in the details of interior appointment. From his early years as an aspiring member of the Virginia gentry, through his time as the nation's highest official, Washington had accumulated worldly goods that told of his varied interests, concern for appearance, and enduring preference for the best goods available without being ostentatious. After forty years of purchases, Washington had amassed a substantial collection of objects from East Asia, England, France, and America. When assembled at Mount Vernon in the final years of his life, they presented a perfect means for understanding Washington's economic, social, and national standing, as well as his characteristic regard for economy and quality. In addition, their examination affords insight not only into the variety of pursuits George and Martha undertook throughout their lives but also into the lives of the extended family of servants and slaves who worked for them.

During his last weeks as president, Washington was thinking of retirement and the finishing touches and improvements he would make to Mount Vernon. He made lists of the objects bought with public and private funds for the executive residence, selecting those private purchases he wished to take to Mount Vernon. Looking ahead to completing the furnishing of his new large dining room, Washington acquired two Neoclassical sideboards and twenty-four mahogany dining chairs from the Philadelphia cabinetmaker John Aitken (fig. 1). In addition to household furnishings, Washington was taking home "twenty four plow plates," a "bundle" of fruit trees, "one ton of Iron," and "four bundles" of nail rods for farming, gardening, and the improvement of his estate.[1] While these items formed the large shipment of articles traveling by water from Philadelphia to Mount Vernon aboard the sloop *Salem*, the Washingtons took their silver with them in their carriage by land.[2]

En route to Mount Vernon, the family stopped at an inn in Elkton, Maryland, where Washington took a moment to write to his secretary, Tobias Lear, still in Philadelphia. The retired president asked Lear "to provide for me as usual new Carpeting as will cover the floor of my blue Parlor. That it may accord with the furniture it ought to have a good deal of blue in it." Indicating that he would prefer a Wilton carpet (a fashionable and expensive English import), Washington also noted that "a suitable border if to be had, should accompany the Carpeting."[3] Perhaps he consulted with Mrs. Washington after writing Lear, for Washington again penned a letter to Lear when he reached Baltimore. He reiterated his request for a carpet for Mount Vernon's west parlor, specifying "that as the furniture was blue, the ground or principal flowers in it ought to be blue also," and his preference for "Wilton Carpeting" if it "was not much dearer than Scotch" (or ingrain) carpeting. In this second letter, Washington also relayed that "Mrs. Washington

Fig. 1. (opposite) A fruit and nut course in the large dining room, where Washington placed his newly acquired chairs and sideboards crafted by the Philadelphia cabinetmaker John Aitken

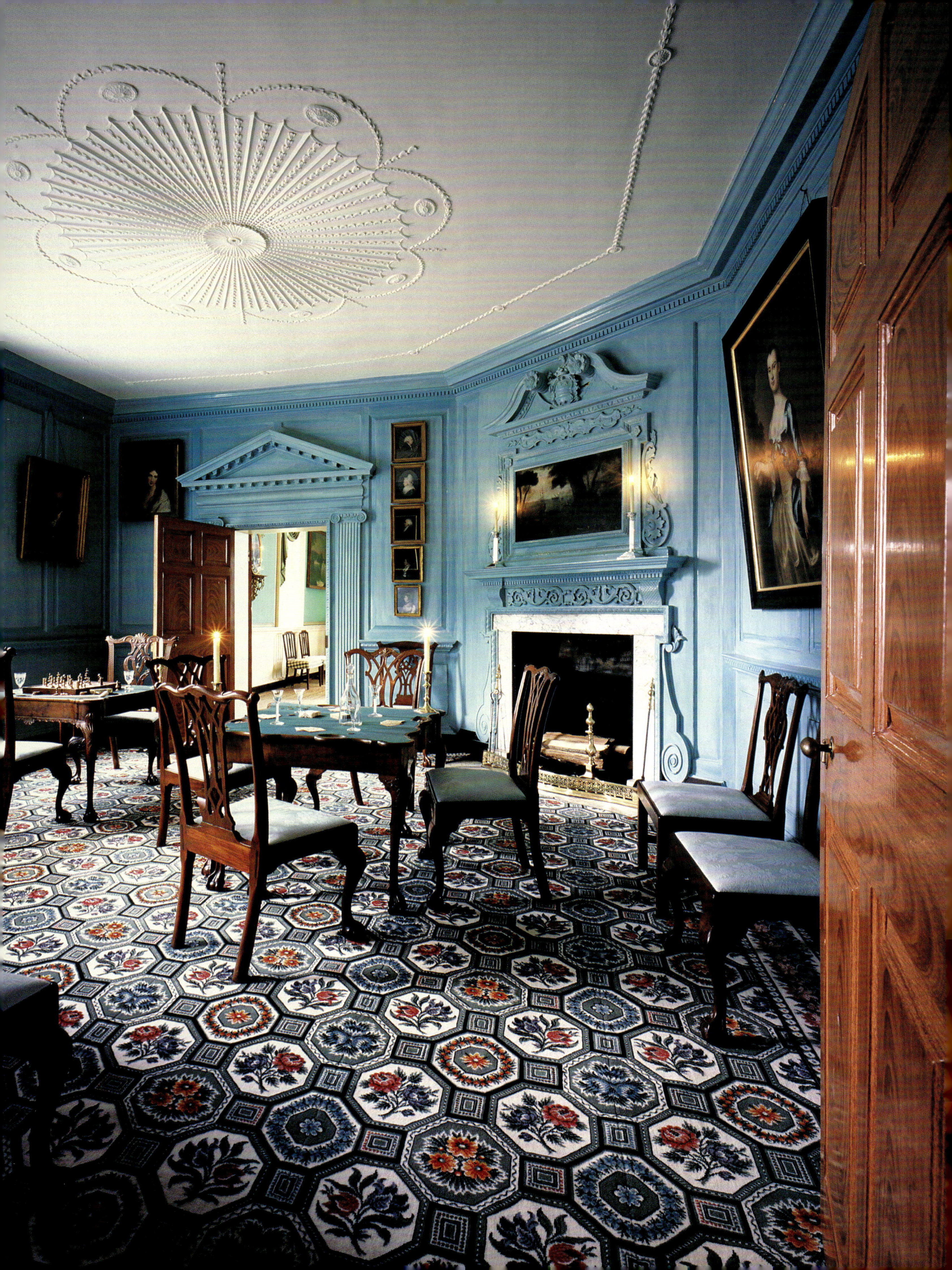

says there is a kind different from both much in use (Russia) if not dearer or but little more so than the former I would have it got."[4] Washington was clearly not retiring from his efforts to acquire the best and most fashionable items for his rooms at Mount Vernon, nor was he deviating from his consistent wish to secure furnishings at a reasonable price.

Fig. 2. (opposite) Washington's west (or blue) parlor, outfitted with a Wilton carpet that accords with his 1797 order

Once back at Mount Vernon, Washington was at last able to devote himself to the long-awaited repairs of his estate: "I find myself almost in the situation of a New beginner, so much does my houses and everything about them, stand in need of repairs."[5] By April Washington declared himself to be "already surrounded by Joiners, Masons, Painters, &ca,"[6] and moving forward with the interior repairs needed. He put the finishing touches on the large dining room, or "New Room," as the Washingtons called it, and added items acquired during the presidency: landscape paintings by George Beck and William Winstanley, looking glasses likely made by Joshua Reynolds, and dining chairs and sideboards supplied by John Aitken. From the room's graceful Adamesque composition ornament to the white-bodied Neoclassical porcelains on the table, this room depicted the ideals and prevailing fashion of the young republic.

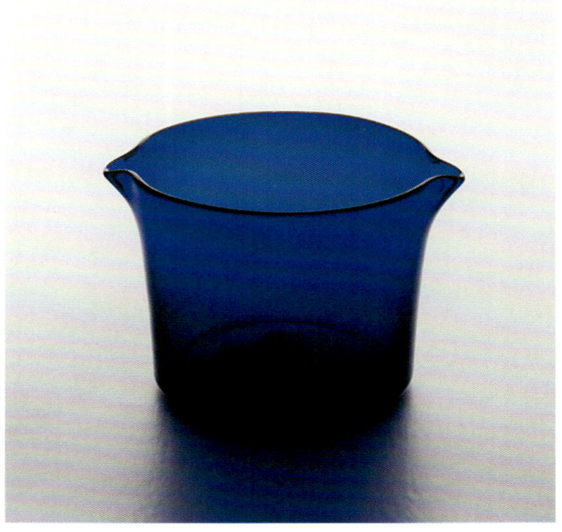

Fig. 3. One of Washington's cobalt blue glass rinsers, used by dinner guests to rinse their wineglasses between courses, MVLA

Although cash poor, and needing to borrow money, Washington continued to repair and improve Mount Vernon, to support extended family members, and to entertain the many guests who called on him. Washington wrote to Secretary of War James McHenry of his daily activities:

> *I begin my diurnal course with the Sun; that if my hirelings are not in their places at that time I send them messages expressive of my sorrow for their indisposition; then having put these wheels in motion, I examine the state of things further; and the more they are probed, the deeper I find the wounds are which my buildings have sustained by an absence and neglect of eight years; by the time I have accomplished these matters, breakfast (a little after seven Oclock, about the time I presume you are taking leave of Mrs. McHenry) is ready. This over, I mount my horse and ride round my farms, which employs me until it is time to dress for dinner; at which I rarely miss seeing strange faces; come, as they say out of respect to me. Pray, would not the word curiosity answer as well? . . . The usual time of sitting at Table; a walk, and Tea, brings me within the dawn of Candlelight; previous to which, if not prevented by company, I resolve, that, as soon as the glimmering taper, supplies the place of the great luminary, I will retire to my writing Table and acknowledge the letters I have received; but when the lights are brought, I feel tired and disinclined to engage in this work, conceiving that the next night will do as well: the next comes and with it the same causes for postponement, and effect, and so on.*[7]

As this letter evidences, the retired president had returned after eight long years to his beloved Mount Vernon only to be faced with repairs, a host of unfamiliar guests, and his desk filled with letters sent by those not making the journey to communicate with him in person. Instead of enjoying well-deserved relaxation and a slowing of pace, Washington had found an almost overwhelming amount of work, with his ability to get tasks done compromised by the frequent respects paid to him by callers.

Amid the constant flow of both invited and unexpected guests arriving daily at his door, Washington

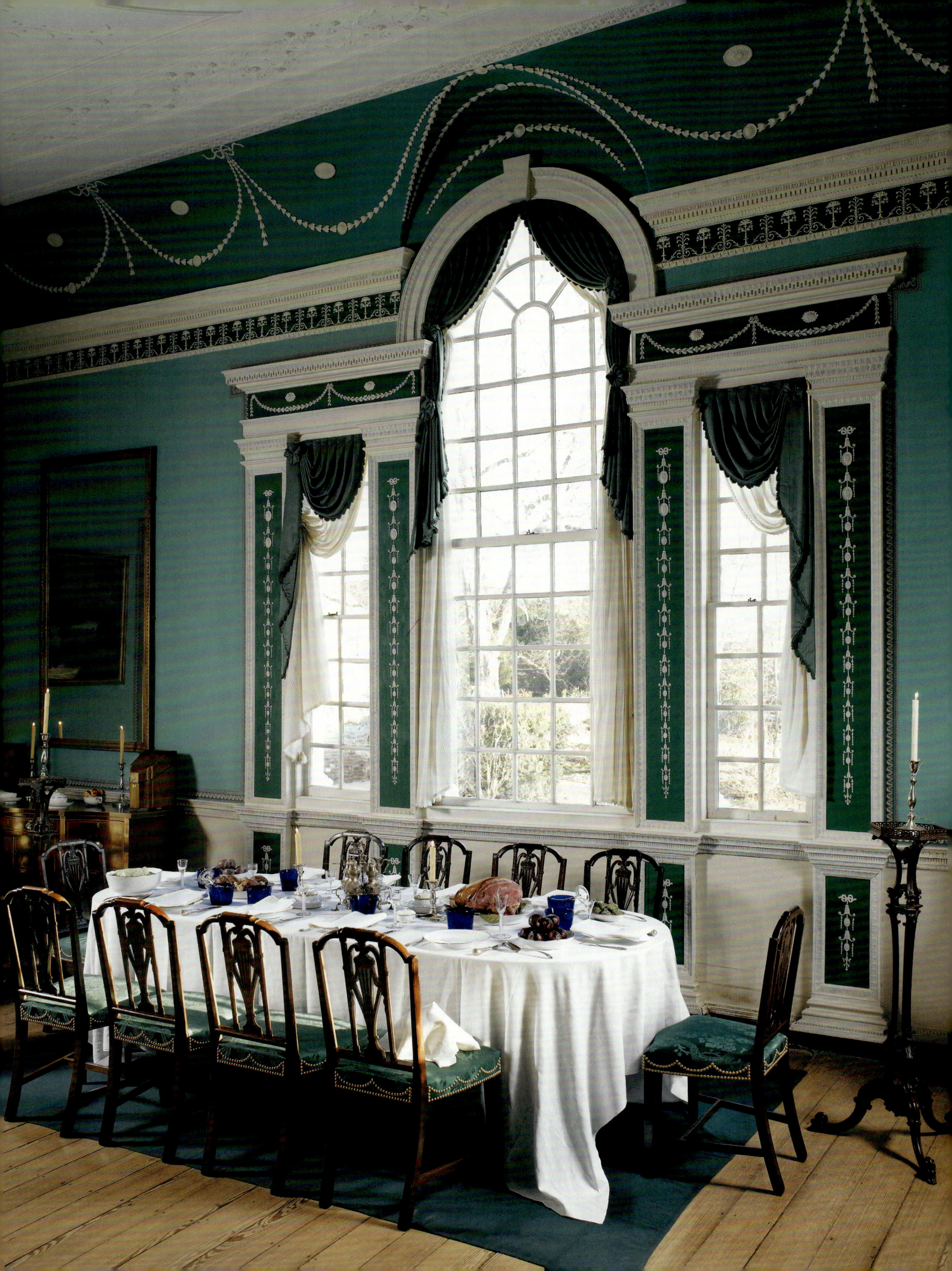

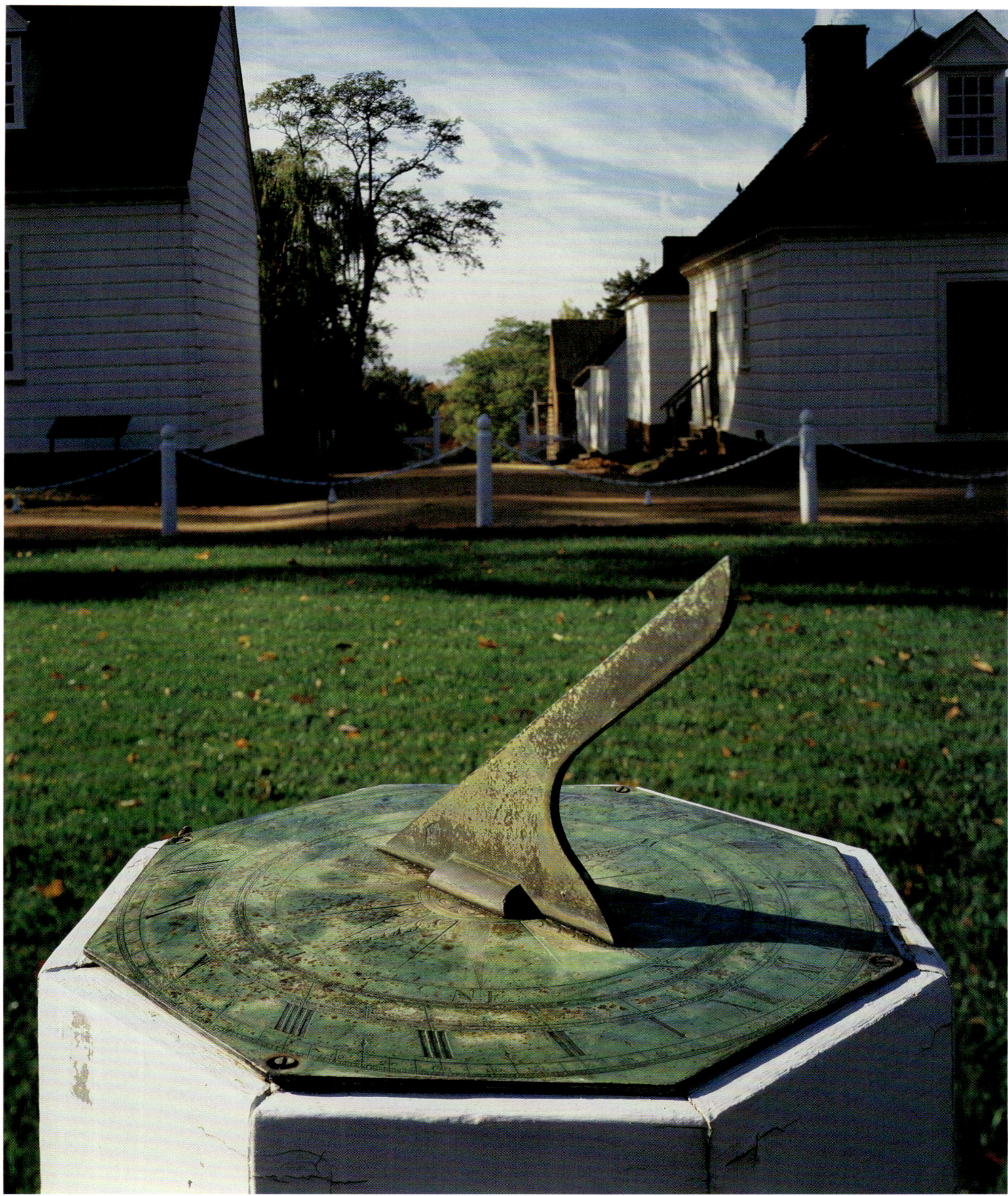

Fig. 4. (opposite) George Washington placed many of his presiential purchases in Mount Vernon's large dining room.

Fig. 5. Washington's sundial in the west front circle, with a view to the South Lane dependencies, was centrally located for all to view the hour.

understood the societal standards he was expected to meet as former president and member of the Virginia gentry. Conscious of this social standing and its embedded implications, Washington fulfilled his role of proper host despite any misgivings he may have felt when visitors called on him out of "curiosity." When Amariah Frost of Milford, Massachusetts, stopped at about one o'clock one June afternoon in 1797, he discovered that "[t]he General was out on horseback viewing his labourers at harvest." Hospitality was extended to Frost, however. He and his companions enjoyed "rum punch brought to us by a servant," while awaiting Washington, who "received us very politely." Frost was, of course, invited to join Washington's dinner table and declared it a "very good" one, at which was served "a small roasted pigg, boiled leg of lamb, beef, peas, lettice, cucumbers, artichokes . . . puddings, tarts, etc." Washington kept Frost and his other

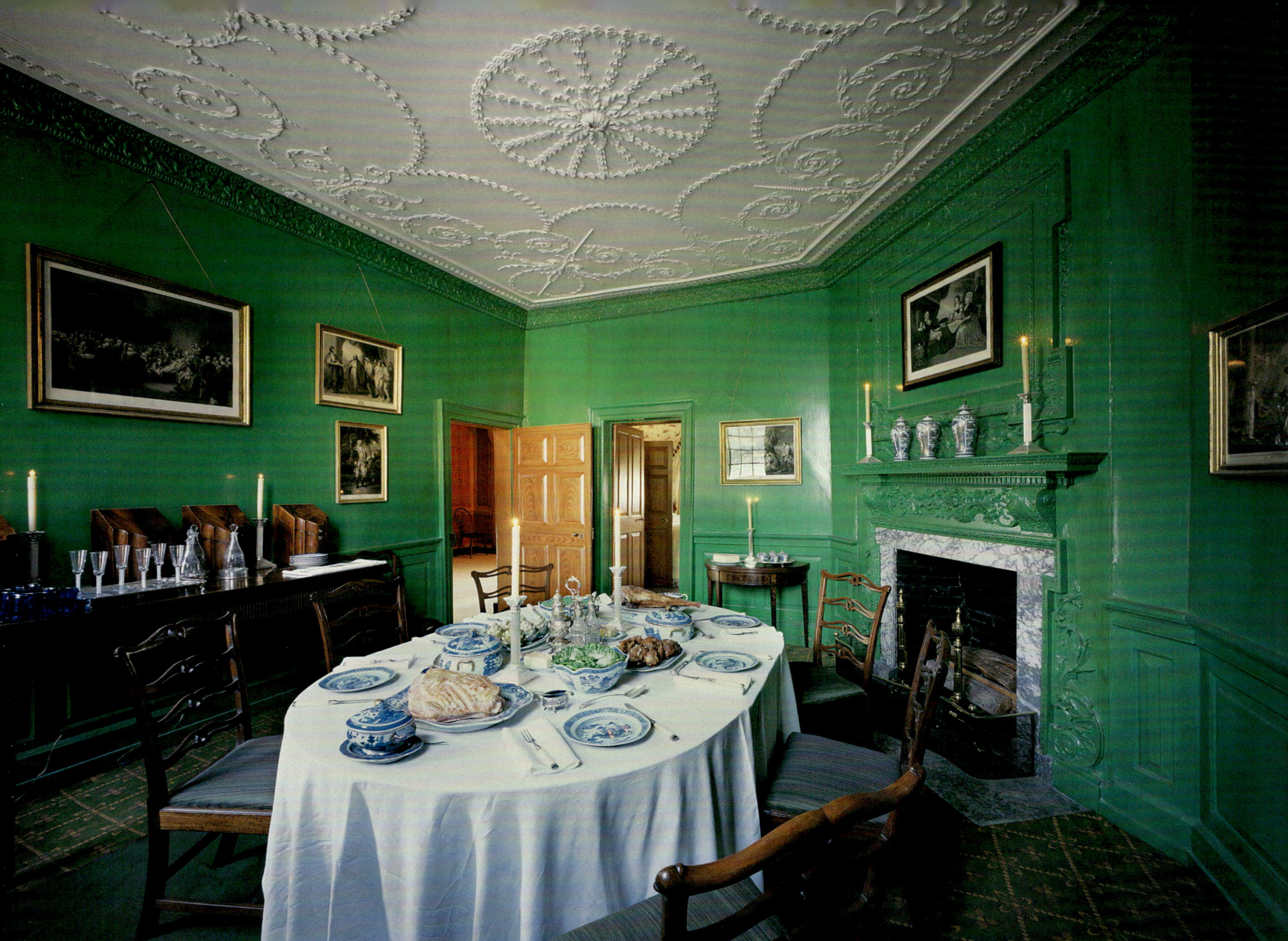

Fig. 6. The small dining room, used for meals when a smaller number of people were in attendance

Fig. 7. (opposite) Washington's two-story piazza, furnished with Windsor chairs, offered a commanding view of the Potomac River and a spot to catch cooling breezes.

guests in conversation with discussion of current events and those in Frost's home state of Massachusetts in particular. At the conclusion of the meal, Washington raised his wineglass in a toast to "All Our Friends," despite his recent introduction to some at the table.[8]

In the role of consummate host, Washington was required to keep up conversation with visitors, which must from time to time have proved challenging. One afternoon, while taking in the view from his piazza, Washington may have attempted a bit of humor when he was joined by Thomas Perkins. Perkins recalled that

> *a toad passed near to where I sat conversing with Gen. Washington; which led him to ask me if I had ever observed this reptile swallow a fire-fly. Upon my answering in the negative, he told me that he had; and that, from the thinness of the skin of the toad, he had seen the light of the fire-fly after it had been swallowed. This was a new, and to me a surprising fact in natural history. I need not remark how deeply I was interested in every word which fell from the lips of this great man.*[9]

Only trying to be hospitable and share a few moments on his piazza with a guest, Washington likely had no idea that his remarks about a toad and a firefly would be so revered as to be recorded for posterity.

In July 1797 Washington commented to Tobias Lear that "unless some one pops in, unexpectedly—Mrs. Washington & myself will do what I believe has not been done within the last twenty Years by us,—

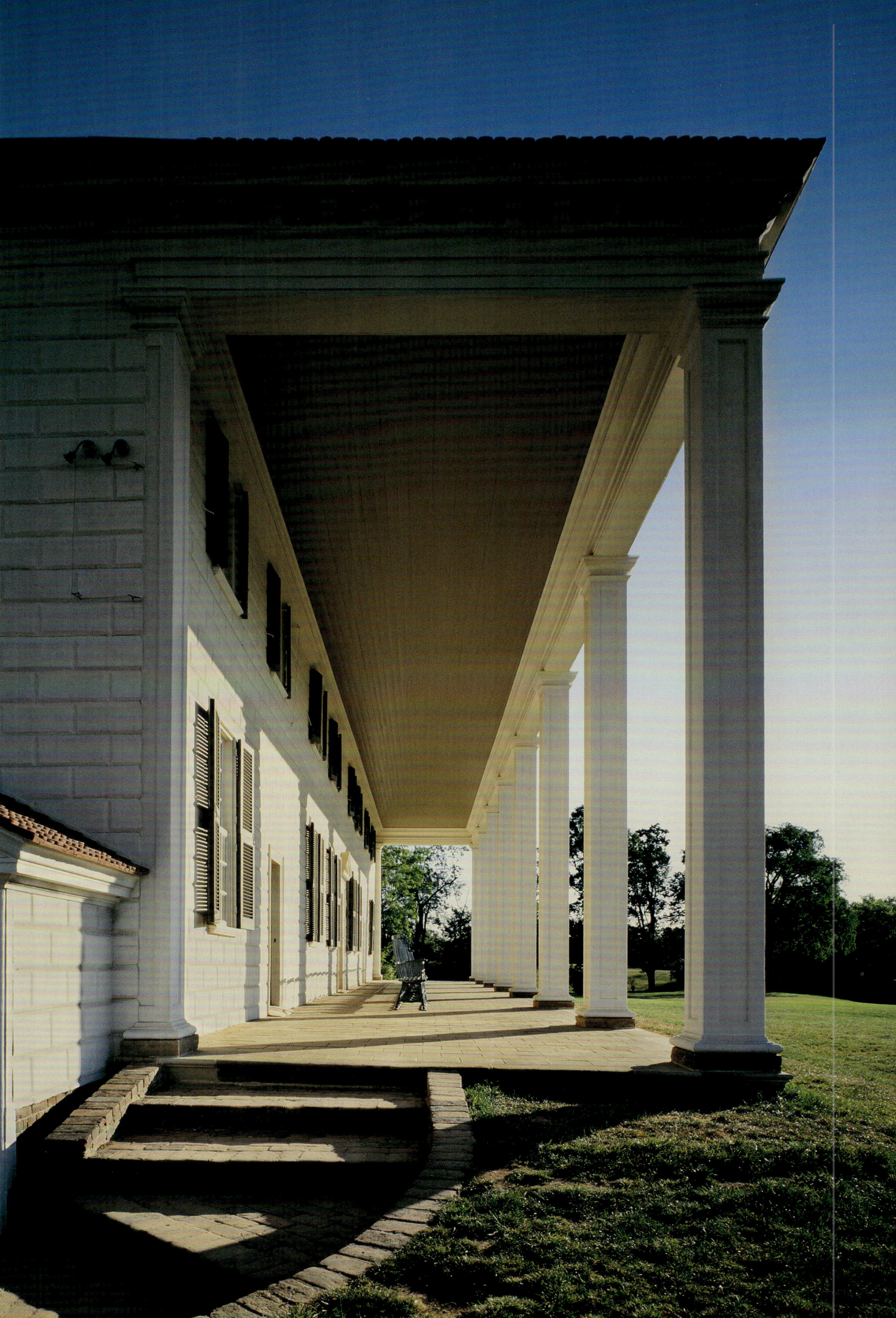

Fig. 8. The little (or back) parlor, often used for musical entertainment and the enjoyment of tea

that is to set down to dinner by ourselves."[10] The seemingly unending stream of visitors was taking its toll on Washington, and by August 1797 he found that entertaining such large numbers of people was tiring. He understood that guests expected a certain level of hospitality, and he had always accommodated guests with the best possible. He therefore sought a gentleman to help with the evening entertainments and turned to his nephew Lawrence Lewis, suggesting that,

> *As both your Aunt and I are in the decline of life, and regular in our habits, especially in our house, of rising & going to bed; I require some person (fit & proper) to ease me of the trouble of entertaining company; particularly of Nights, as it is my inclination to retire (and unless prevented by very particular company, always do retire) either to bed, or to my study, soon after candle light.—In taking these duties, (which hospitality obliges one to bestow on company) off my hands, it would render me a very acceptable Service.*[11]

Lewis agreed to the unpaid position and entered the household, although it is unclear what functions he actually fulfilled.

Admirers and well-wishers continued to flock to Mount Vernon, many recording their visits and providing some of the best accounts of Washington and his estate in this, the final chapter of his occupancy. In 1798 Julian Niemcewicz of Poland visited Mount Vernon and described Washington's "New Room" as "a large salon that the [General] has recently added . . . [as] . . . the most magnificent room in the house."[12] He was very pleased with all that he found at Mount Vernon, noting, "In a word the garden, the plantations, the house, the whole upkeep, proves that a man born with natural taste can divine the beautiful without ever having seen the model. The Gl [General] has never left America. After seeing his house and his gardens one would say that he had seen the most beautiful example in England of this style."[13] Through careful attention to detail, Washington's aspiration to effect the appearance of an English country house had succeeded. And to Niemcewicz, as well as other visitors, Washington gave no hint of the strain he felt from entertaining so many guests. As the Polish gentleman recalled, "Since his retirement he has led a quiet and regular life. He gets up at 5 o'clock in the morning, reads and writes until seven. He breakfasts on tea and cakes made from maize; because of his teeth he makes slices spread with butter and honey. He then immediately goes on horseback to see the work in the fields; . . . he returns at two o'clock, dresses, goes to dinner. If there are guests, he loves to chat after dinner with a glass of Madeira in his hand."[14]

On July 4, 1798, the retired general and president attended the celebration of the anniversary of the Declaration of Independence in Alexandria, an occasion that must have impressed him with all that had been accomplished in twenty-two years. One week later, Secretary of War James McHenry arrived at Mount Vernon with a letter from President Adams, asking Washington to serve as commander in chief of armies raised to defend the United States should the tension with France worsen into military conflict. Although weary from public life, Washington accepted the call and once again stood ready to serve his country if needed. While in Philadelphia in the late fall of that year attending to his renewed military duties, Washington received word that Nelly Custis and his nephew Lawrence Lewis had become fond of one another. He took steps to become Nelly's formal guardian so that he could authorize her marriage. As a compliment to him, Nelly selected Washington's birthday, February 22, to be the wedding day. On that day, Washington recorded in his diary that "Miss Custis was married ab[ou]t Candle light to Mr. Law[renc]e Lewis."[15]

The fall of 1799, their last together, appears to have been a happy one for the Washingtons at Mount Vernon. Lawrence and Nelly Lewis were married and living with them, and Nelly was about to deliver

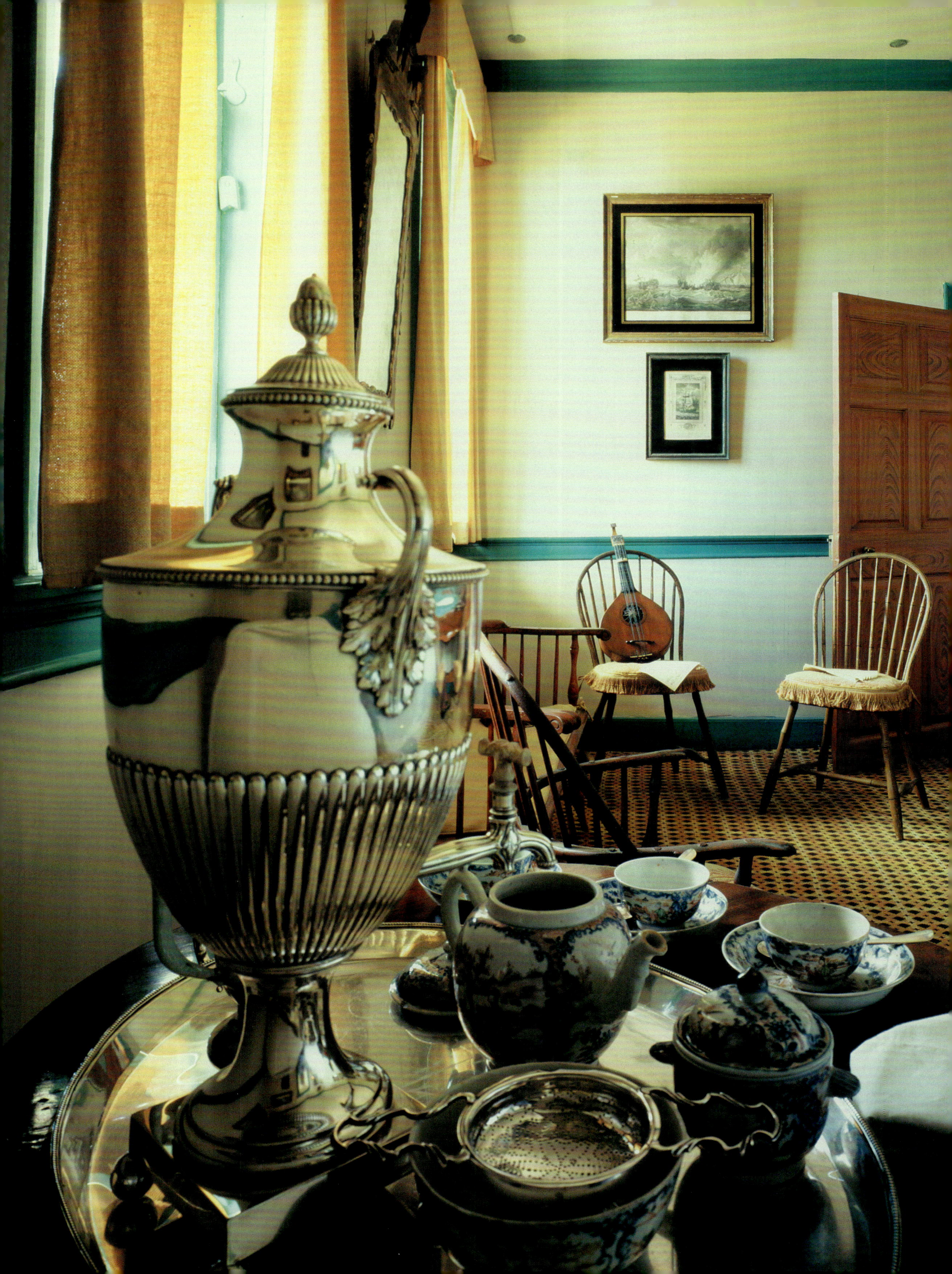

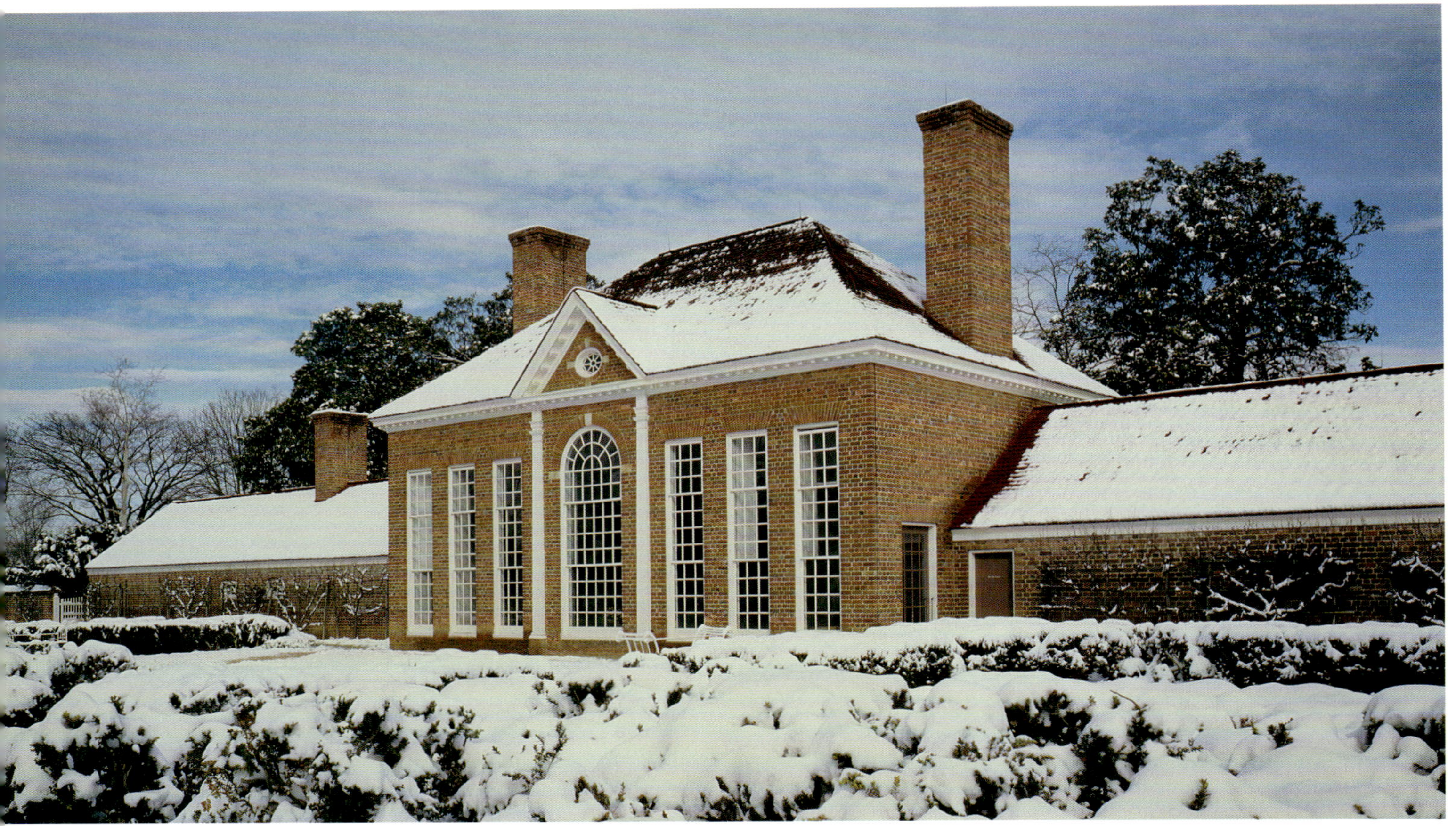

Fig. 9. Mount Vernon's greenhouse offered a warm enclosure for growing tender and exotic plants throughout the winter. The original structure burned in 1835 and was reconstructed based on George Washington's original plans.

Fig. 10. (opposite) The Washingtons' bedchamber, dominated by the dimity-hung bedstead ordered by Martha Washington, where the former general and president died on December 14, 1799

Martha Washington's first great-grandchild. Longtime friends from Richmond, Edward and Betsy Carrington, visited in November, and Mrs. Carrington was delighted to see the couple enjoying retirement, "when but a year since they were forced to forego all the innocent delights which are so congenial to their years and tastes, to sacrifice to the parade of the drawing-room & the Levee."[16] Mrs. Carrington had accurately divined that the Washingtons were happier at home in Virginia than being the focus of national and world attention in the presidential residence. Indeed, Washington had said while president, "I can truly say I had rather be at Mount Vernon with a friend or two about me, than to be attended at the Seat of Government by the Officers of State and the Representatives of every Power in Europe."[17]

On December 12, 1799, George Washington rode, as usual, to his farms to inspect winter activities, noting in his diary, "About 1 oclock it began to snow—soon after to Hail and then turned to a settled cold Rain."[18] The bad weather delayed Washington's return home, and, already late for dinner, he ate without changing clothes despite a neck that "appeared to be wet" and snow "hanging upon his hair."[19] Next day heavy snow prevented him from taking his usual ride. Although he complained of a sore throat, he "went out in the afternoon into the ground between the house and the river to mark some trees, which were to be cut down in the improvement of that spot."[20] His hoarseness increased that evening, and during the night he woke Mrs. Washington, who observed that he could hardly speak and was breathing with great difficulty. Despite his discomfort, Washington did not wish his wife to leave their bed to call for help lest she catch cold herself. When day broke on December 14, Washington received the attention of doctors, slaves, and servants. All attempts to save his life were in vain, however, and the illustrious general, president, and founding father died shortly after ten o'clock that night. Seated at the foot of the bed, Martha Washington said, "'Tis well . . . all is now over; I shall soon follow him; I have no more trials to pass through."[21]

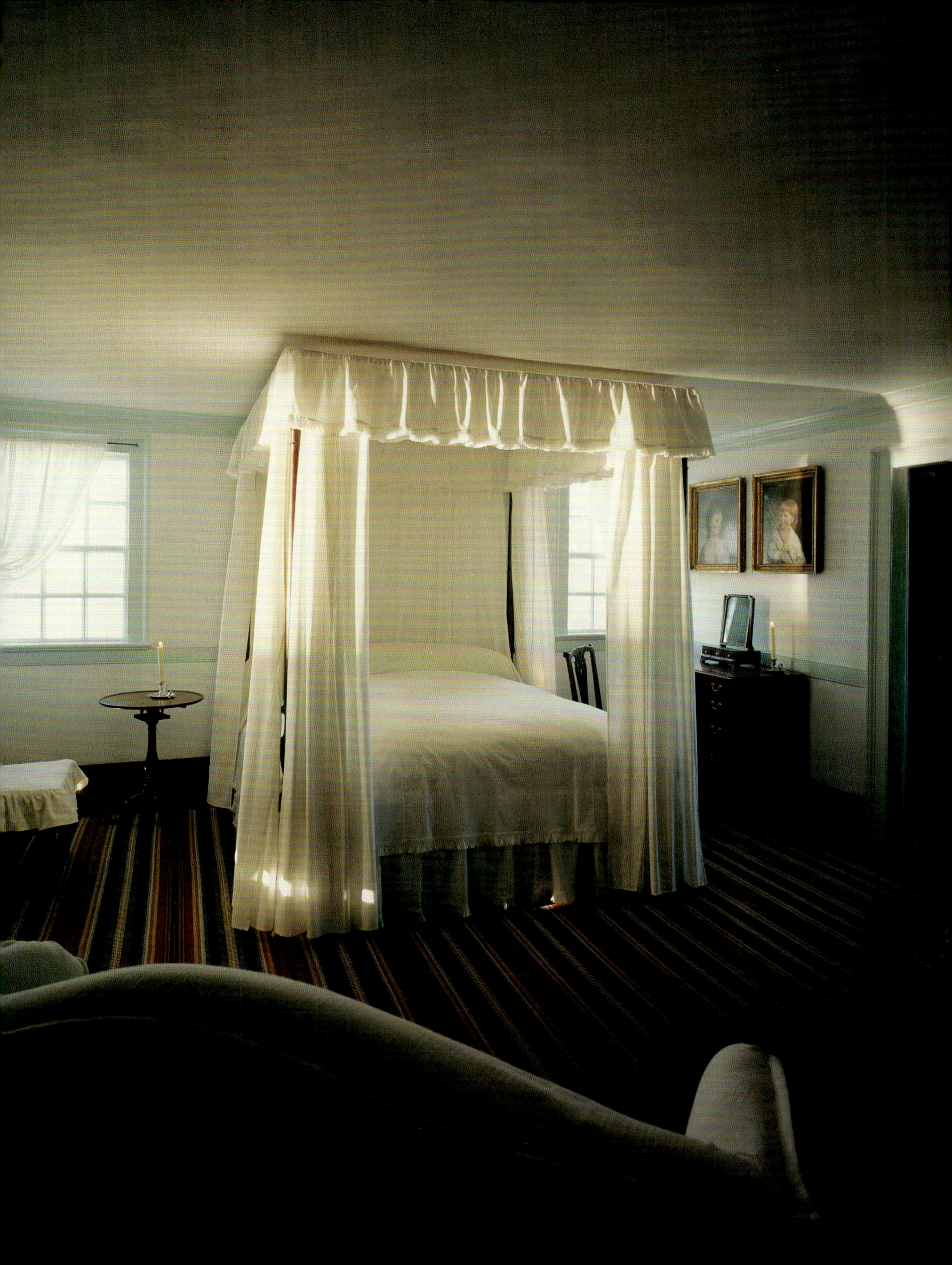

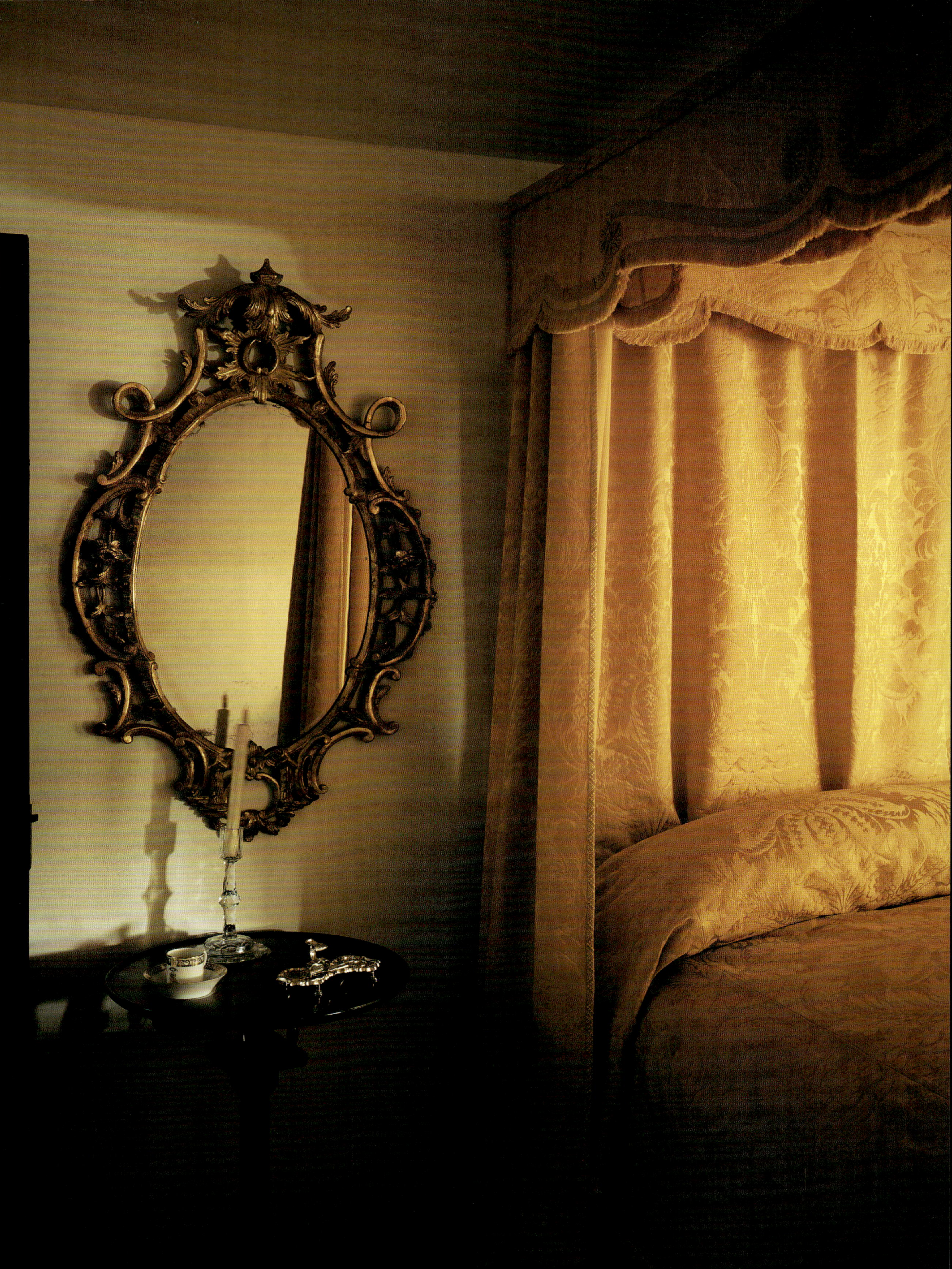

When George Washington's will was read, it left to his "dearly beloved wife," Martha Washington, "the use, profit and benefit of my whole Estate, real and personal, for the term of her natural life."[22] On her death, it was Washington's "Will & desire that all the Slaves which I hold in *my own right,* shall receive their freedom."[23] Although Washington "earnestly wished" the emancipation of the slaves during his wife's lifetime, he was concerned "on account of their intermixture by Marriages" with those she had inherited from her first husband.[24] After an unsuccessful attempt on Martha Washington's life (presumably by slaves), George Washington's slaves were freed in 1801.

Unwilling to enter again her husband's study or the bedchamber where he died, Martha Washington used for the remaining years of her life one of Mount Vernon's third-floor garret bedchambers (fig. 11). The room's furnishings dated largely to the prewar period and recalled the happy years of the Washingtons' early marriage. Although surrounded by grandchildren and great-grandchildren, Martha Washington's thoughts were with her husband, and she followed him on May 22, 1802. She joined her husband in the Washington family tomb overlooking the Potomac River. The Washingtons had enjoyed full lives that concluded, as they no doubt wished, at Mount Vernon. After spending the majority of his most productive years serving his country away from Mount Vernon, Washington had returned to his beloved estate, of which he claimed: "No estate in United America is more pleasantly situated than this. It lyes in a high, dry and healthy Country 300 miles by water from the Sea, and . . . on one of the finest Rivers in the world."[25]

Fig. 11. (opposite) View of the third-floor garret chamber where Martha Washington resided following her husband's death

CAT. 53

Side Chair

Attributed to John Aitken (active ca. 1775–1800)
Philadelphia, Pennsylvania, ca. 1797
Primarily mahogany, H. 37 7/16", W. 20 5/8", D. 18 3/4"
Purchase, 1998
Conservation courtesy of Mrs. John F. Bookout III, Vice Regent for Texas,
in honor of Mrs. Richard W. Call, former Vice Regent for California
W-2820

As George Washington concluded his second term as president, he made plans to return to Mount Vernon and complete the furnishing of his recently added two-story dining room.[26] In February 1797 Washington paid the Philadelphia cabinetmaker John Aitken just over four hundred dollars "for two doz[en] chairs & 2 sideboards," which the retiring president shipped to Mount Vernon that March for placement in the "New Room," as the Washingtons called it.[27] Aitken advertised that he carried on a "cabinet and chair manufactory," where he sold "chairs of various patterns, some of which are entirely new, never before seen in this city, and finished with an elegancy of stile peculiar to themselves and equal in goodness and neatness of workmanship to any ever made here." He also stated that the case furniture he sold was "finished in the completest and newest taste now prevailing in this city" and that he offered it "on the most reasonable terms."[28] Newest fashions, "neatness of workmanship," and reasonable terms were all appealing to Washington and perhaps influenced his selection of Aitken as the craftsman to contribute to the furnishing of Mount Vernon.[29]

The chairs were of the latest Neoclassical fashion, closely resembling plates from *The Cabinet-maker and Upholsterer's Drawing-book*, a book first published in London in 1793 by the English furniture designer Thomas Sheraton. As demonstrated by this example, a carefully carved and pierced urn-shaped splat provides the chair's focal point and is framed by beaded stiles and an arched crest rail. The side, rear, and serpentine front seat rails all bear evidence of the original decorative brass tacking pattern that highlighted the seat's perimeter and accented the original green upholstery fabric.[30] Raised on tapered legs defined by string inlay, the chair offers a combination of overall Neoclassical form with a design vocabulary that characterized the style. When placed in Mount Vernon's New Room, or large dining room, the chairs mirrored the Neoclassical detailing of the room's architectural elements and composition ornament, and reconfirmed Washington's selection of a classicizing aesthetic as that most appropriate for the new nation.

After George Washington's death in 1799, the twenty-four side chairs remained in the New Room at Mount Vernon as part of the household furnishings left to Martha Washington for use during her lifetime.[31] At her death in 1802, Mrs. Washington willed to her granddaughter Eleanor "Nelly" Parke Custis Lewis "twelve chairs with green bottoms" from the room "to be selected by herself."[32] The remaining Aitken chairs were disbursed through the sale of Mount Vernon furnishings not specified in bequests, at one of which "Doctor Weems" purchased twelve chairs for sixty dollars. This chair, one of those purchased by Dr. John Weems, suggests that some (if not all) of the chairs Weems bought in 1802 were those produced in the Philadelphia shop of John Aitken for George Washington.

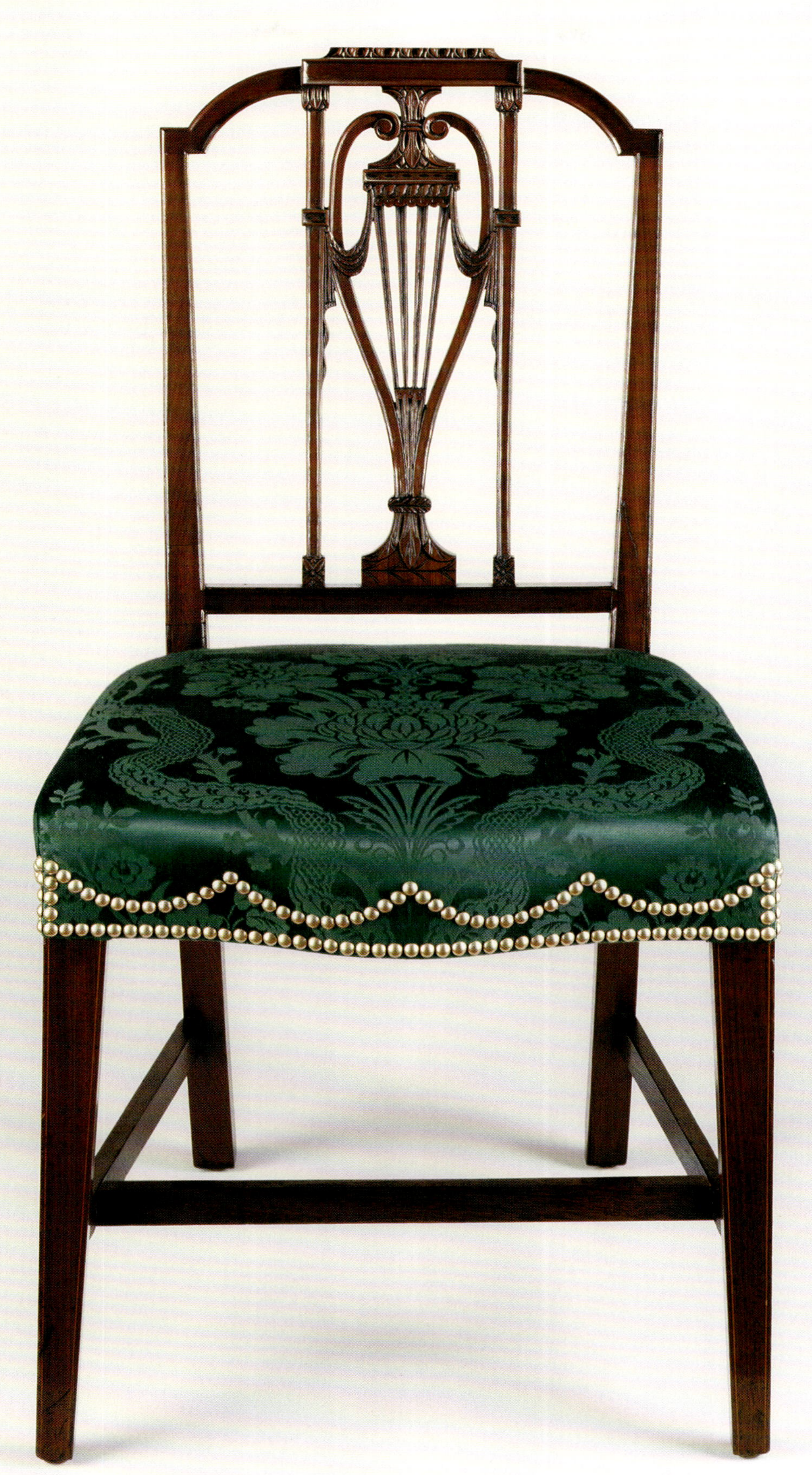

CAT. 54

Terrestrial Globe

Dudley Adams (1762-1830)
London, England, 1789–1790
Globe: laid paper, papier-mâché, gesso, and wood lathe, DIAM. 28"
Stand: mahogany and brass, H. 34", DIAM. 35⅞"[33]
Transferred to the Mount Vernon Ladies' Association through the generosity
of John Augustine Washington, III, 1860
W-166

Following the Revolution, George Washington resumed asking for goods to be supplied from London by the successor to Robert Cary & Company, Wakelin Welch & Son. A few months after assuming the presidency, Washington wrote to Welch & Son "to send me by the first vessel, which sails for New York, a terrestrial globe of the largest dimensions and of the most accurate and approved kind now in use."[34] The eighteenth century witnessed a rapid increase in the demand for and production of both terrestrial and celestial globes, as interest grew in the natural sciences and those parts of the world just being charted. Although globes were often sold in celestial and terrestrial pairs, Washington asked for only the landed variety. As a former surveyor, he was keenly interested in cartography, and his request for a terrestrial globe may have combined his curiosity about newly charted lands with an attempt to place the new nation in his charge within the greater context of its international community.

Wakelin Welch & Son turned to London's leading globe maker to fill Washington's request, reporting to the president, "One Adams here is Suppos'd to be the first optician we have, he purposes to made the Terrestial Globe upon the New & approv'd method, it may take up two Months to Compleat & that will be as early as a Conveyance may offer, for after this Vessell none is expected to Sail before February."[35] Dudley Adams, the man to whom Welch & Son referred, was the son of the late George Adams (1709-1772), the most important globe maker of the era and instrument maker to both George III and Captain James Cook.[36] Washington was probably already aware of Adams's expertise, for his library contained George Adams's 1766 *Treatise Describing and Explaining the Construction and use of New Celestial & Terrestial Globes*.[37]

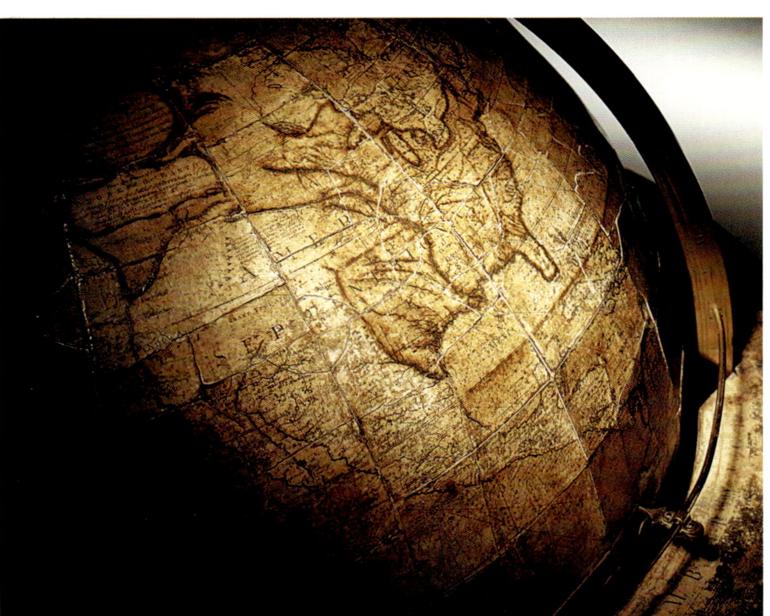

The crafting of Washington's globe did, indeed, take Adams several months, and it was not shipped from London until February 1790. The total cost was just over twenty-seven pounds, and Welch & Son noted, "Mr. Adams presumes, as no Care on his part, has been wanting in the making the Globe in the most accurate manner, that it will be found to answer your Expectation."[38] Presumably it did, for Washington shipped the globe to Mount Vernon at the conclusion of his presidency, for use in his private study.

The globe's map is largely in Latin, although later discoveries are added in English. Captain Cook's voyages are traced, and the most recent date is that which records the explorer's death in "Owyhee" (Hawaii) in 1779. Of the two labels, one is in Latin (portions of which are now indecipherable). The other, in English, reads: "A New and most Correct GLOBE of the EARTH Laid down from the latest Observations of the most Judicious Astronomers Navagators & Travellers—By Jon. SENEX, FRS, Now made &c Sold by D. Adams only with all the latest discoveries &c West Gate of Charing Cross London." The hollow sphere is supported by a mahogany and brass stand that allows it to rotate (detail).

When Martha Washington died in 1802, Thomas Jefferson sought unsuccessfully to purchase the globe for his collection. Since its inheritance by Bushrod Washington, the globe has remained at Mount Vernon, leaving the property only on rare occasions when conservation work has required it.

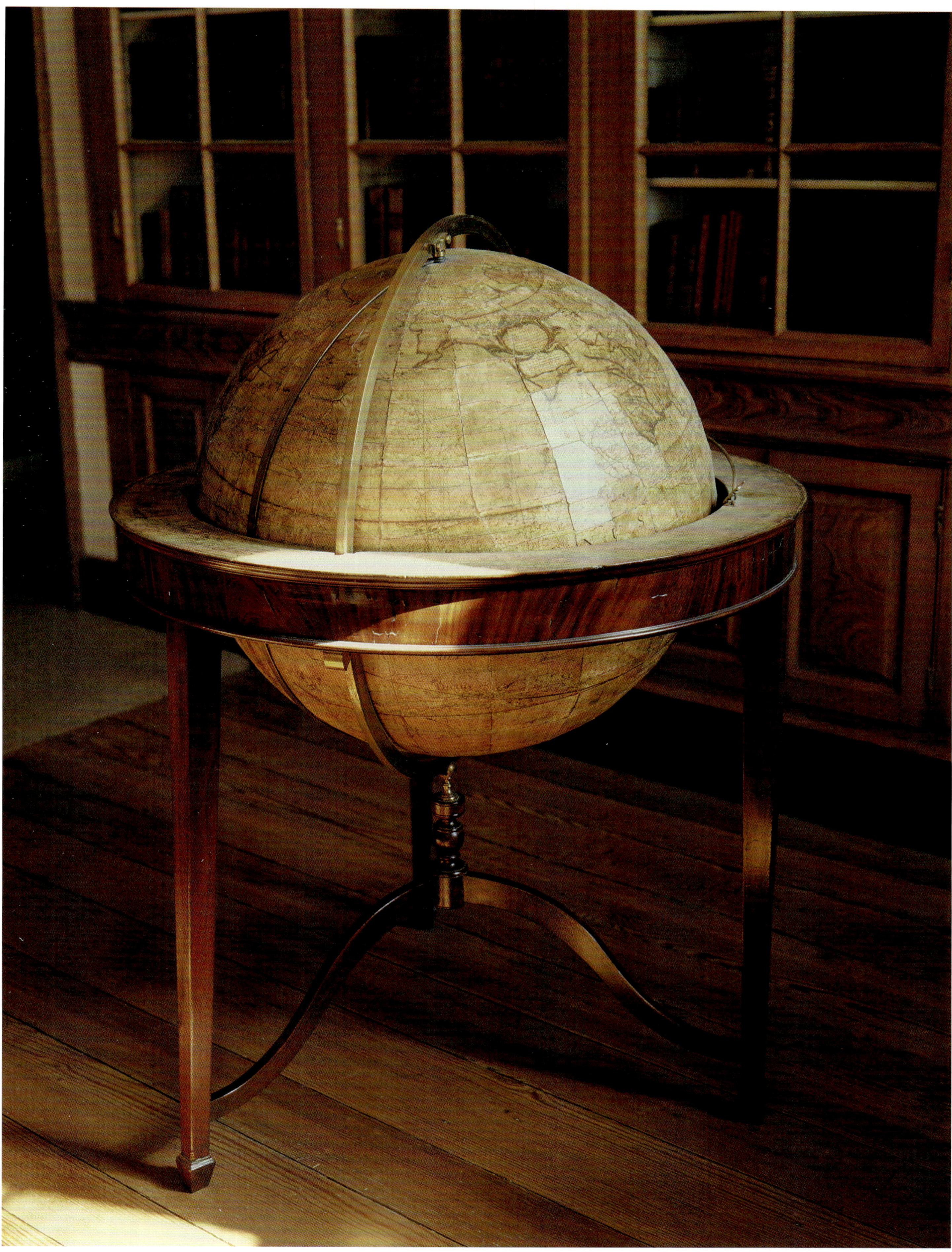

CAT. 55

Dressing Table

France, ca. 1760–1780
Mahogany, fir, marble, and glass, H. 29", W. 37⅜", D. 21"
Purchase, 1905
W-202

Éléanor-Françoise Élie, the Comte de Moustier, was appointed as the French minister to the United States in 1787. He arrived in the new nation's capital of New York in January 1788 with his sister, the Marquise de Brehan, and established residency at the Macomb house located at 39 Broadway.[39] George Washington lived nearby at the executive residence on Cherry Street until de Moustier and his sister returned to Paris in 1789. In addition to relocating the presidential household to the Macomb house, Washington took the opportunity to purchase many of the furnishings left behind by the departing Parisians.[40] He paid nineteen pounds for this "drissing table," which he used throughout the presidency and shipped to Mount Vernon at the time of his retirement.[41] Washington placed the dressing table in his private study, where he bathed, dressed, and spent several hours each morning attending to his correspondence and affairs.

Rectilinear and symmetrical with sleek, elegant lines, the dressing table exemplifies the return to classical design principles that occurred during the latter half of the eighteenth century. Crafted in the Louis XVI style, the table could serve as either a writing desk or a dressing table. The hinged top is fitted with a mirror that opens to reveal a marble surface appropriate for shaving and bathing articles. Four locking drawers offer storage for dressing or writing articles when not in use, and the table is raised on cylindrical, tapered, and fluted legs fitted with brass and mahogany casters that facilitate its movement.

At his death in 1799, George Washington bequeathed his "large shaving & dressing Table" to friend and extended family member Doctor David Stuart.[42] It descended in Stuart's family until its return to Mount Vernon in 1905. Today, it serves as a reminder of Washington's continued interest in securing neat and plain, yet fashionable, furnishings and his prevailing preference for economy.

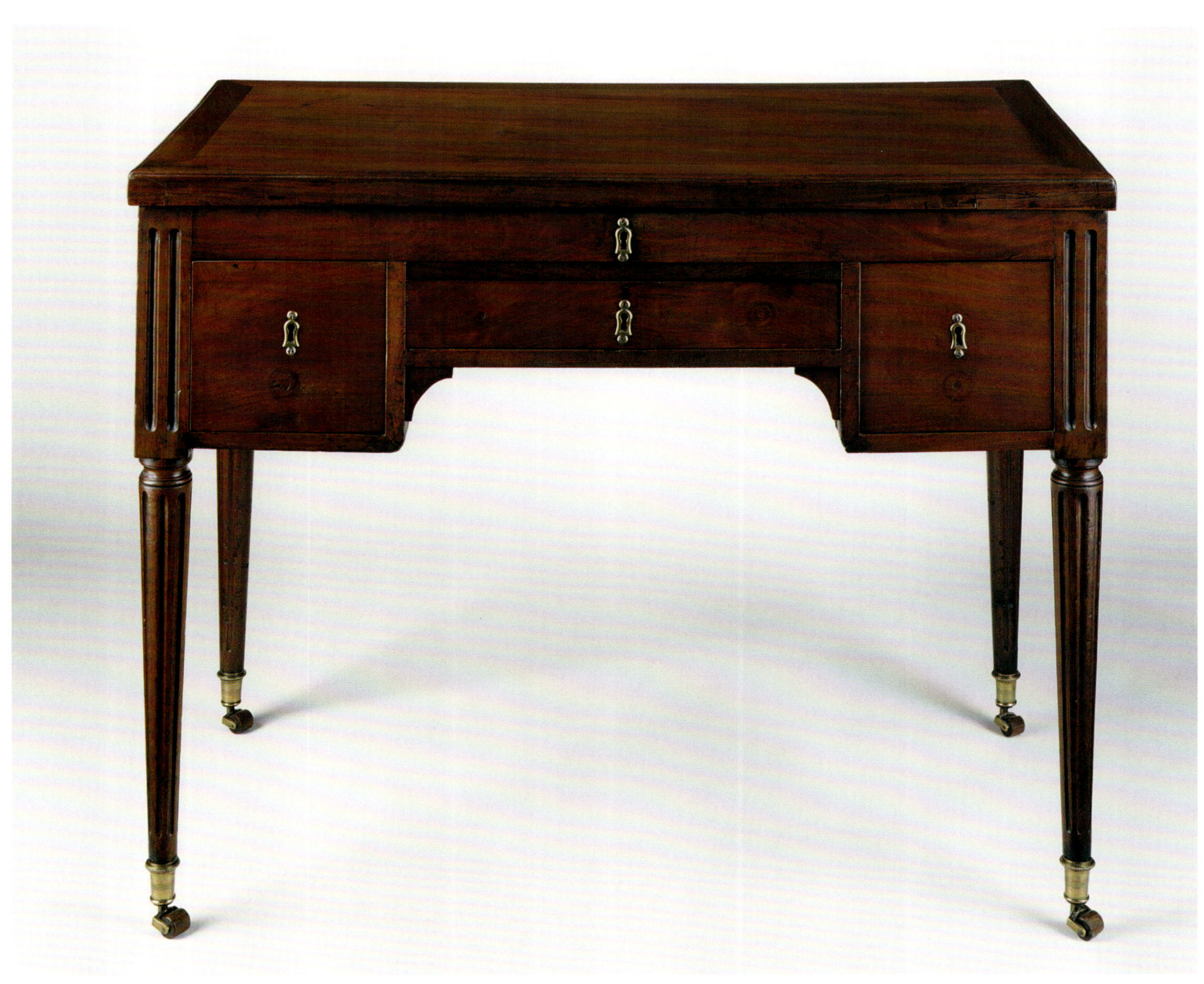

CAT. 56

Wash-Hand Glasses

Probably England, ca. 1780–1790
Cobalt-colored glass, H. 3⅜", DIAM. 4¾"
Purchase, 1957
W-2107/A&B

Whether resting on small individual plates or alone, wash-hand glasses (or finger bowls)[43] embellished the eighteenth-century dining table while fulfilling very specific functions. They contained either plain or rose water and were used by diners for rinsing soiled fingers between courses. Wash-hand glasses also served another not quite so genteel function, when, following the dessert course, diners could rinse their mouths with water from the bowls and then expectorate it back into the same bowl. Wash-hand glasses were not widely used in America, however, and among those like the Washingtons who did use them, the custom of mouth rinsing never became popular.[44]

Because it was all too easy to view the dirty water following hand or mouth rinsing through colorless glass, manufacturers provided bowls of decorated or colored glass to disguise the unappetizing sight. At the end of the eighteenth century, the New York merchant Frederick Rhinelander sold imported English blue, purple, and opaque white Bristol wash-hand glasses, some molded with designs.[45]

The Washingtons followed the preference for colored wash-hand glasses and, like others who entertained often, maintained a good supply of them. Martha Washington's estate inventory of 1802 recorded "28 blue glass bowls" in the "Sweet Meat Closset."[46] These two glass bowls were likely among the twenty-eight in storage with other glassware and ceramics on the third floor of the Mansion. The globular blown bowls are simple and elegant in form, with the only decoration the cobalt added to the glass batch to produce their deep blue color. Their very dark blue was often referred to as Bristol blue and was known for its extremely dense quality.[47] With so much care taken to present a neat and fashionable assemblage of tablewares, George Washington must have appreciated the opacity of Bristol blue when guests rinsed their fingers while dining at Mount Vernon.

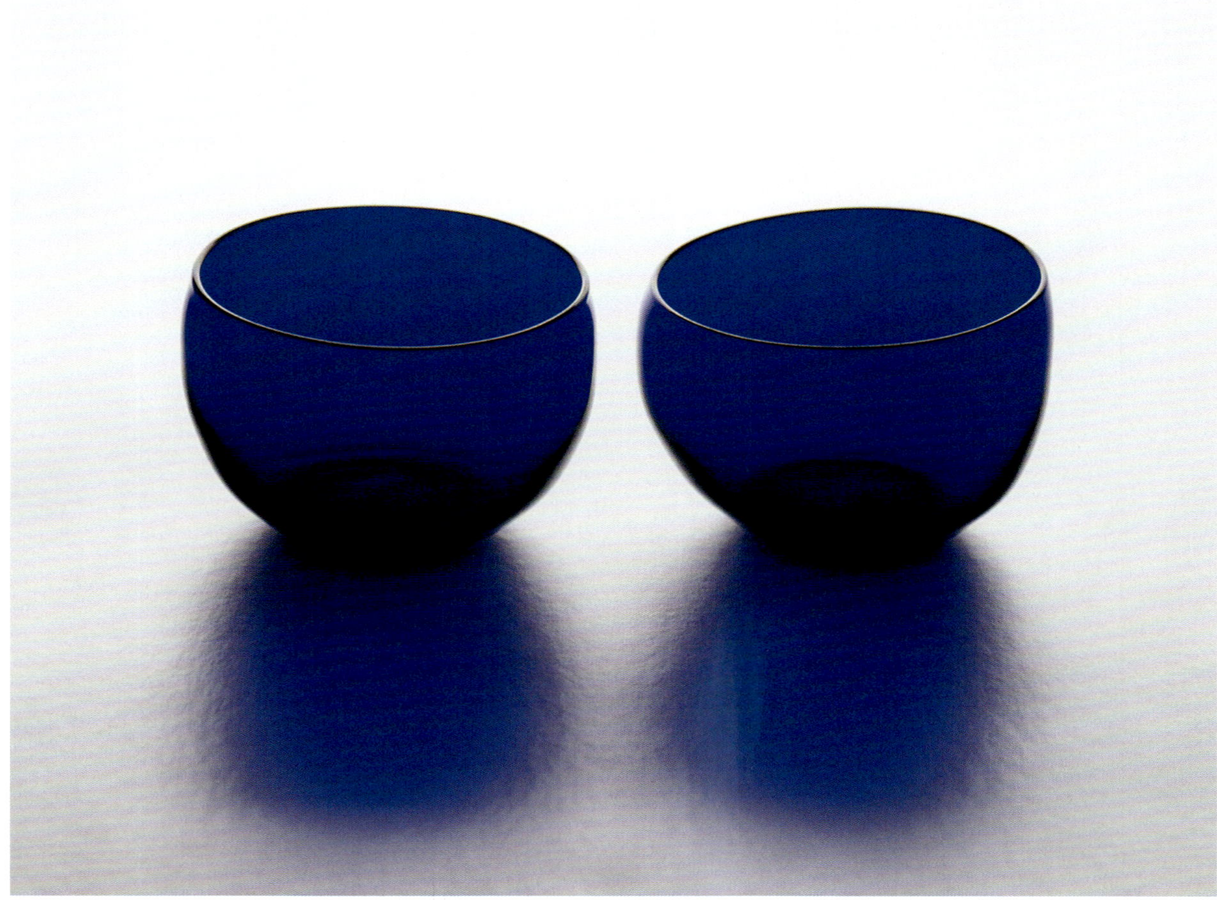

CAT. 57

Saltcellar and Spoon

Cellar
Probably England, ca. 1780–1790
Glass, L. 4¼", W. 3⅜", H. 1⅞"
Purchase, 1957
W-2111

Spoon
Richard Humphreys (1749–1832)
Philadelphia, Pennsylvania, ca. 1780
Silver, L. 3⅞"
Stamped: RH
Gift of Mary Walker Lee Bowman and Robert E. Lee IV, 1981
W-2532

Salt was a key condiment on the eighteenth-century dining table, and specialized forms were developed for its use. The saltcellar evolved from a large common salt often placed in the center of the table to a series of smaller shared and individual salts placed within easy reach of diners. George Washington purchased not only a variety of silver, ceramic, and glass saltcellars but also appropriate silver spoons by which he and his guests could transfer salt from the vessels to their individual plates.

Glass saltcellars offered a noncorrosive surface and were particularly popular in America during the second half of the eighteenth century.[48] When Washington ordered silver-plated salts in 1783, he requested that they be fitted "with glasses in them."[49] He likely purchased this glass saltcellar after the Revolution when trade resumed with England and new glass forms decorated with cutting became available to the American consumer. The boat-shaped cellar is raised on an applied circular foot, the sides are decorated by double swag engraving, and the rim is defined by a scalloped cut edge.

This salt spoon was fashioned by the Philadelphia silversmith Richard Humphreys, who also provided Washington with two dozen similar tablespoons in June 1780.[50] The round bowl and feather edge decoration are similar to English-made examples,[51] and Washington's engraved griffin here is like that placed on a host of his silver tableware (detail).

After the dispersal of Mount Vernon tablewares following Martha Washington's death, the glass saltcellar (along with several matching examples) descended in the family of granddaughter Martha Parke Custis Peter, while the salt spoon (and its mates) went to grandson George Washington Parke Custis and his heirs. Reunited at Mount Vernon, they assist in understanding the importance salt held on George Washington's dining table and his attention to its proper service.

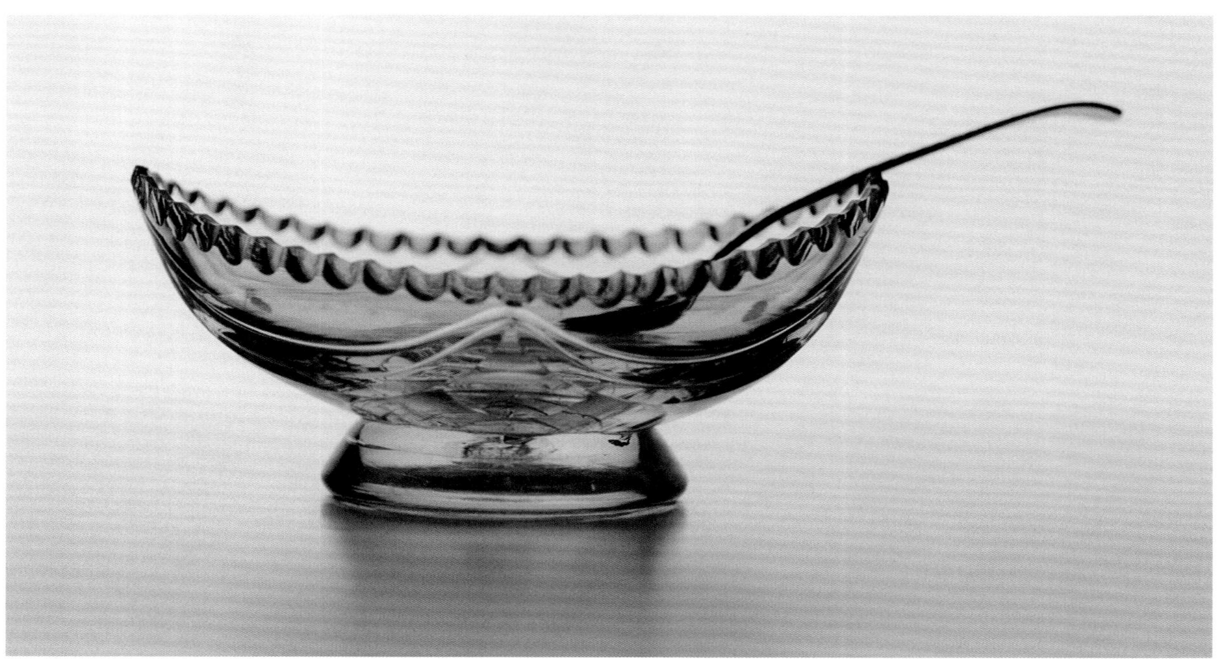

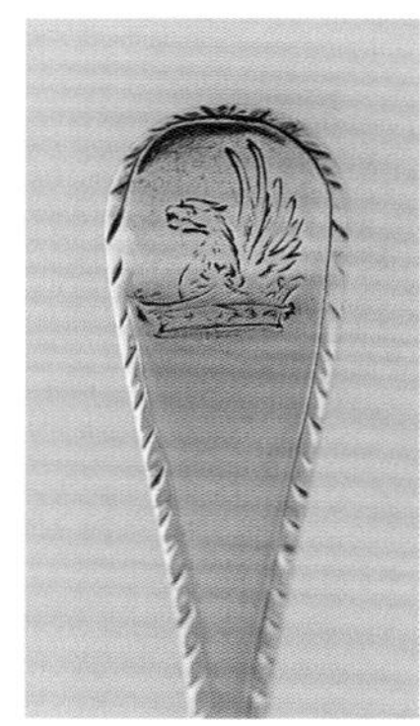

CAT. 58

Punch Ladle

Adam Lynn (1775–1835)
Alexandria, Virginia, ca. 1797–1799
Silver and ebony, L. 13⅝", W. 4½"
Gift of Mrs. Richard B. Tucker in memory of Mrs. Maria Washington Tucker, 1964[52]
W-2450

When the Polish visitor Julian Niemcewicz arrived at Mount Vernon in 1798, he discovered that George Washington was making his routine inspections of his farms. Martha Washington, however, "appeared after a few minutes, welcomed us most graciously and had *punch* served. At two o'clock the Gl [General] arrived mounted on a gray horse, he shook our hand, dismounted, gave a cut of the whip to his horse which went off by itself to the stable. We chatted a little; then he went off to dress and we to see the interior of the house."[53] Niemcewicz described what was a frequent occurrence at Mount Vernon during the Washingtons' final years of retirement, the arrival of unexpected guests in need of refreshment and hospitality. Mrs. Washington assisted her husband in welcoming those who came, offering on this occasion a sip of punch perhaps served from this ladle.

The silver bowl is stamped on the underside as the work of the silversmith Adam Lynn, engraved with Washington's signature griffin on its exterior, and fitted with a curved ebony handle. Lynn was an Alexandria, Virginia, gold- and silversmith and engraver who advertised goods ranging from recently arrived London jewelry and shoe buckles to coffeepots and cream pots that were presumably of his own hand.[54] Lynn's father was certainly known to Washington, for he had served with the general in the Continental Army and was a fellow member of the Society of the Cincinnati.[55] When Washington retired from public life and returned to Virginia, he may well have turned to Lynn as the son of a fellow officer or as a talented local silversmith as he outfitted Mount Vernon with wares needed for entertaining his many visitors.

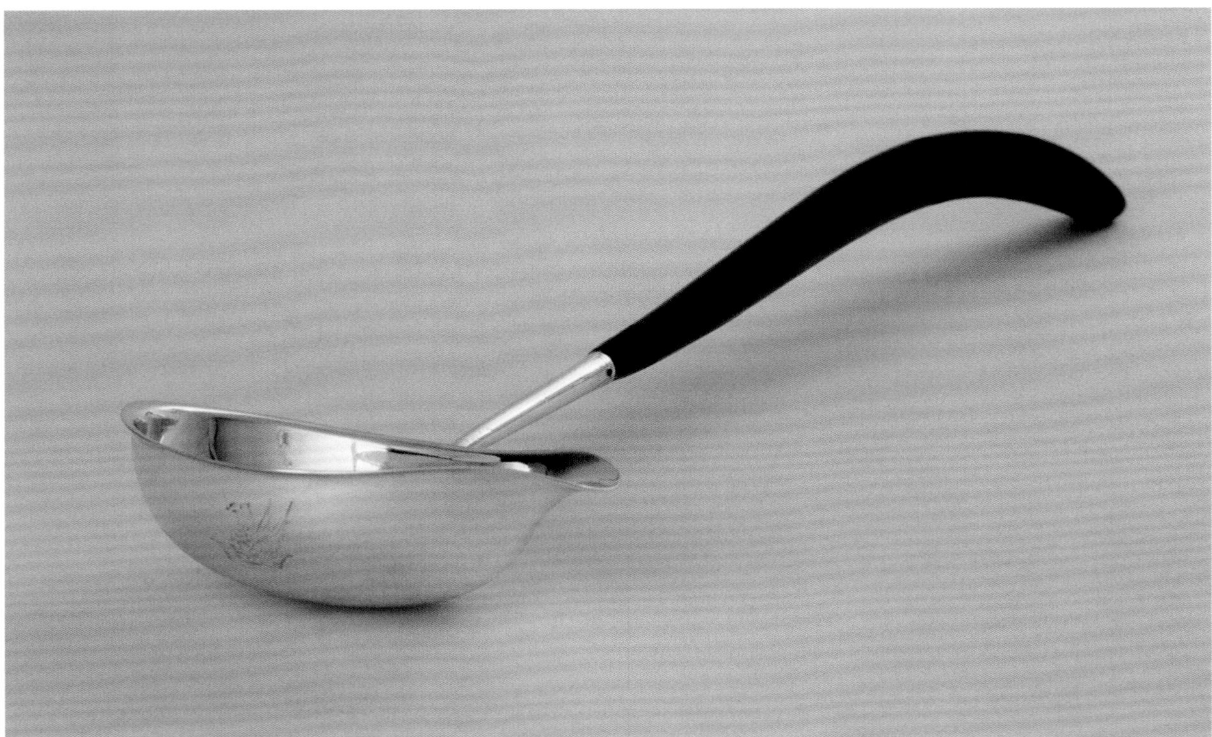

CAT. 59

Flowerpot

Jingdezhen, China, ca. 1760–1780
Porcelain, H. 9¾", W. 14"
Purchase, 1986[56]
W-2329

George Washington completed his greenhouse in 1787, shortly before he was called by his country to assume the presidency. When he returned to Mount Vernon, he was able once again to devote himself to his experiments of growing exotic plants and fruits in the warmth of a glass and brick enclosure. In addition to lemons, limes, and oranges, Washington grew aloe, coffee, and palm trees, perhaps bringing specimens to the main house for family and guests to enjoy.[57]

This Chinese export porcelain flowerpot may have been one of "5 China flower pots" listed in the "front Parlor" and valued at fifty dollars in Washington's estate inventory.[58] The hexagonal body is decorated with underglaze cobalt blue landscape and river scenes, and the piercings of the openwork stand are highlighted by underglaze blue brushstrokes. A circular drainage hole in the bottom center suggests that the flowerpot once was used to hold potted examples of Washington's botanical specimens. If placed in the Prussian blue painted front parlor, the flowerpot would have offered the room an exquisite complement of Chinese artistry.

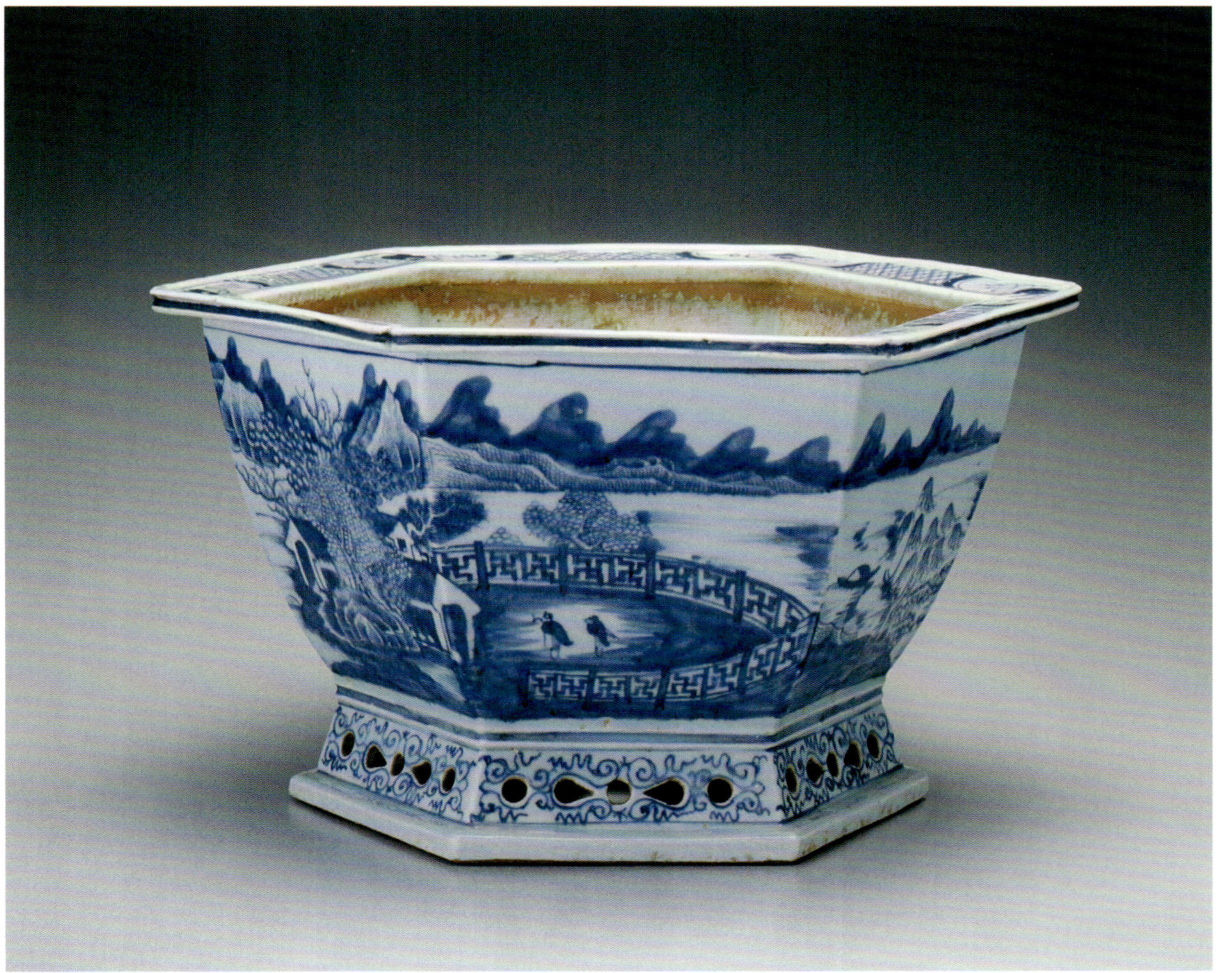

CAT. 60

Saucepan and Cover

Probably England, possibly America, 1750–1800
Copper, iron, and tin, H. 7⅝", DIAM. at base 10", Handle length 6"
Bequest of G. Freeland Peter, Jr., 1991
W-3550/A&B

Saucepans made of iron or copper were staple tools in well-stocked eighteenth- century kitchens, and midcentury recipes recommended them "primarily for the sweating of small groups of ingredients or the making of rich butter-based sauces."[59] Used in the Mount Vernon kitchen by slave cooks and scullions, copper saucepans were used to prepare the large variety of dishes expected on the eighteenth-century table, and the Washingtons' in particular. Nathan, an enslaved cook belonging to George Washington, and Lucy, one of Martha Washington's slaves who was married to the butler Frank, worked in conjunction with a staff of maids, stewards, and scullions to prepare and serve elegant dishes for the Washingtons, their family, and guests.[60] In planning their retirement from public life and return to Virginia, Martha Washington observed that "there are always two persons, a man and woman, in the Kitchen; and servants enough in the house for all needful purposes."[61]

With the typical flat bottom, bulbous shape, and close-fitting cover, this copper saucepan features a single curled iron handle attached to the body with three copper rivets, as well as dovetail seaming running vertically under the handle and around the perimeter of the underside. The interior of the saucepan and lid were lined with tin, a common practice with copper cookware, using either a powder that could be brushed onto the prepared surface or a liquid that could be swirled around the interior and the excess poured off.[62] A cookbook in Martha Washington's library advised readers to "take great Care the Pots or Sauce-pans, and Covers be very clean, and free from all Grease and Sand, and that they be well tinned, for fear of giving . . . any brassy Taste."[63] While the tin lining would have maintained the taste of the foods cooked in the vessel (as well as avoiding the food poisoning now known to be connected to cooking in copper utensils), it wore off quite quickly under heavy use and would have been frequently reapplied.[64] During the Washingtons' stay in Philadelphia during the presidency, for example, Thomas Bradley was paid "for tinning kitchen utensils" on August 31, 1793, and again less than nine months later.[65]

Alexandria and Philadelphia merchants of the period offered large quantities of imported copper cookware for ready sale, and Washington's cash memoranda book for 1797 through 1799 indicates various "sundries" purchased in these nearby port cities.[66] In Alexandria, James Hendricks and Company, at the corner of Pitt and King streets, advertised "copper sauce-pans and tea-kettles,"[67] while "Sundry Sorts of Goods" were offered at the store of Adam Foulke in Philadelphia, including "large and small sauce pans cullenders, fish kettles, [and] large and small camp kettles."[68]

At the time of George Washington's death, three copper saucepans were in use in the kitchen, with three more of the iron variety in storage "Up the Kitchen Stairs."[69] Washington stipulated in his will that Martha Washington should inherit the "household & Kitchen furniture of every sort & kind, with the liquors and groceries which may be on hand at the time of my decease; to be used & disposed of as she may think proper."[70] Descending through the family of granddaughter Martha Parke Custis Peter of Tudor Place before returning to Mount Vernon, the copper saucepan and cover were likely part of the purchases made by Thomas Peter in 1802 following Martha Washington's death.[71]

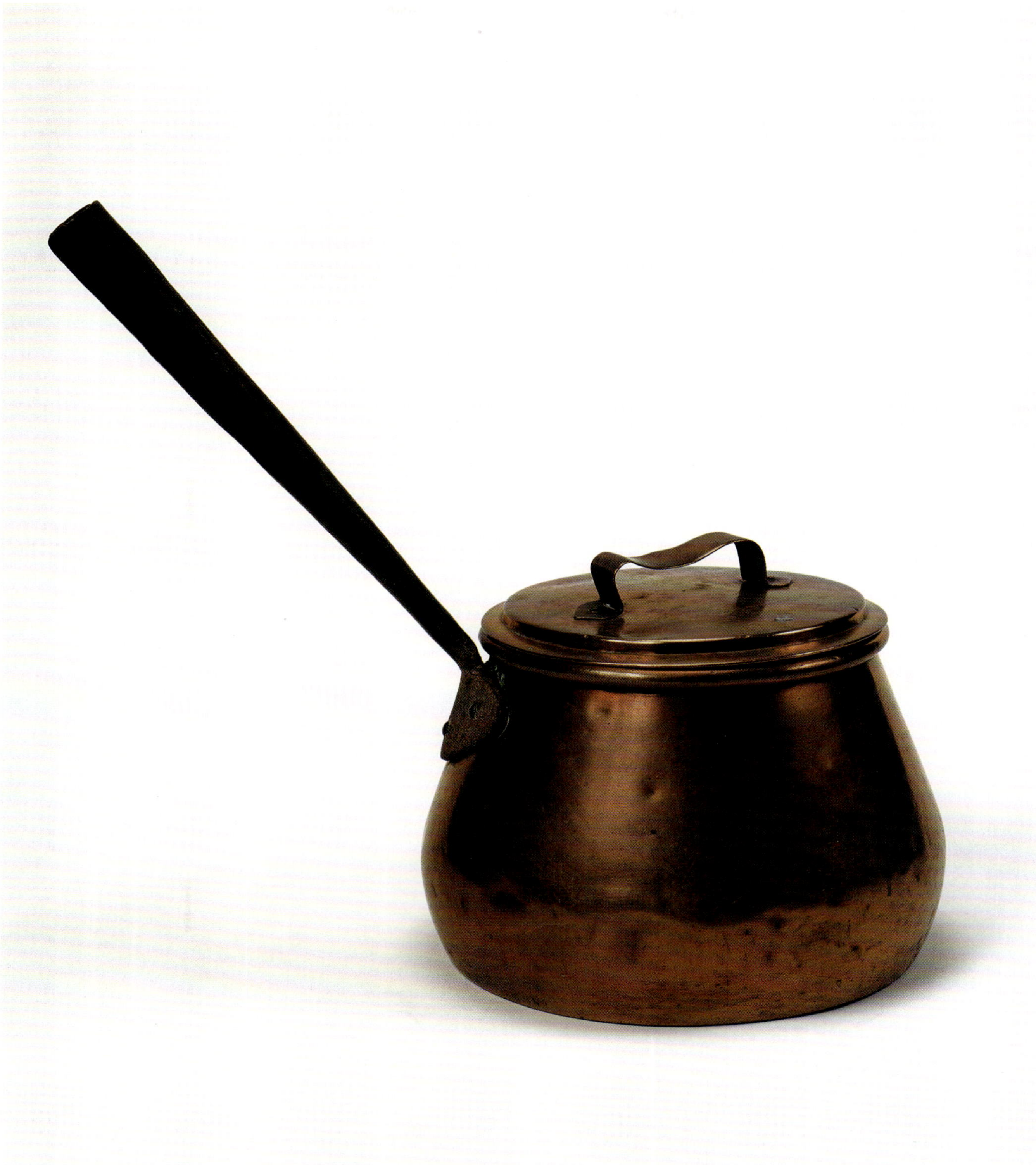

CAT. 61

Beaker Vase

Jingdezhen, China, ca. 1775–1790
Porcelain, H. 10"
Purchased with funds contributed by an anonymous donor, 2004
2004.04.01

This recently discovered Chinese export porcelain beaker vase was originally paired with another beaker and three baluster-shaped vases with lids to complete the five-piece *garniture-de-cheminée*, or garniture set, that likely decorated one of George and Martha Washington's fireplace mantelshelves at Mount Vernon.[72] The 1797 price list of an unidentified American porcelain trader describes these types of porcelains as "Jars & Tumblers for ornaments to a Chimney, 6 to 18 inch high, 5 in a sett."[73] Popularized by the Dutch in the seventeenth century, these purely decorative porcelain forms were displayed widely during the eighteenth century throughout Europe and America. Arrayed on mantels, tables, or wall shelves or exhibited in cabinets and wall niches, these fashionable Chinese ceramics signaled wealth and worldly sophistication. Elizabeth and James Canby of Wilmington, Delaware, owned a nearly identical set,[74] and it is not surprising that George Washington also wanted the exotic decorative porcelains at Mount Vernon.

The beaker vase, like its other original four components, is decorated with underglaze cobalt blue in one of the best-known Chinese export designs known as *Two Birds*.[75] In a river scene framed by scrolled borders and floral motifs, two birds fly above pavilions and willow trees. This underglaze-blue painted riverscape is highlighted by overglaze gilding that adds further elegance to the idyllic Chinese scene.

George and Martha Washington received numerous shipments of Chinese export blue and white porcelains from London, New York, and Philadelphia.[76] It is difficult to know when the garniture set came to Mount Vernon, but it was perhaps recorded in 1802 as the "5 China Jarrs" in the "Front Parlour" or the "5 blue & White Jars" in the "Sweet Meat Closset."[77] At Martha Washington's death, she willed "all the blew and white china in common use" to her granddaughter Eleanor Parke Custis Lewis.[78] The garniture was included in this bequest, and this beaker vase descended to Nelly's great-great-granddaughter, Betty Washington Whiting, until its purchase and return to Mount Vernon.

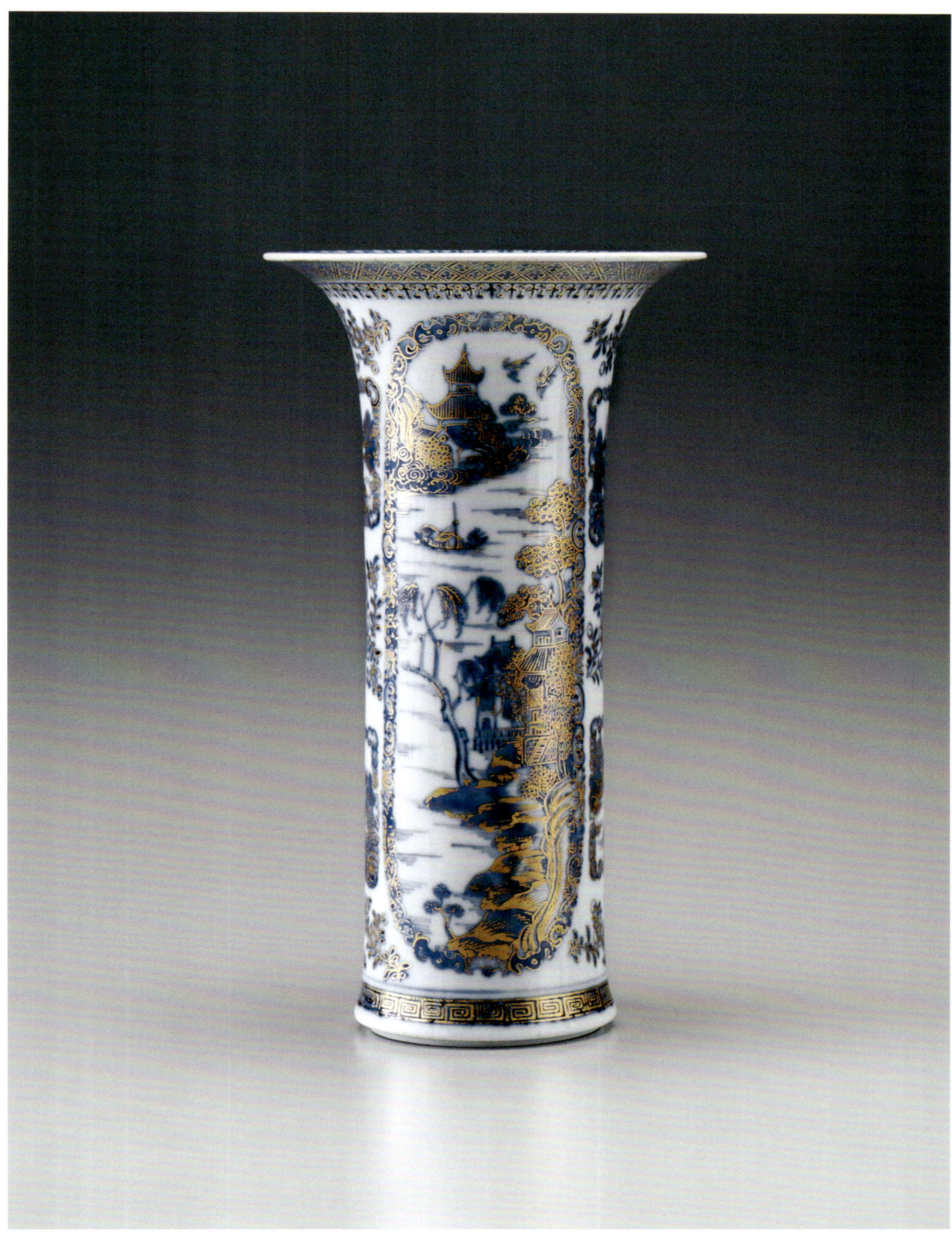

CAT. 62

Guglet and Basin

Jingdezhen, China, ca. 1760–1780
Porcelain, Guglet H. 9¾", W. 5"; Basin H. 3⅞", DIAM. 10⅜"
Purchase, 1985
W-2325/A&B

Chinese export porcelain guglets (or bottles) and wash basins were ubiquitous in elite colonial residences, and George Washington's estate inventory lists them in nearly every bedchamber. The guglet, or long-necked vessel for holding water, received its name from the "gug-gug-gug" sound it made when water was poured into a basin.[79] The pair was part of the eighteenth-century bathing ritual that emphasized cleanliness of one's face and hands. This guglet and basin could be any one of those itemized in Washington's inventory as a "wash bason & pitcher" or "bason & bottle" in the second-floor bedchambers at Mount Vernon.[80] These rooms were used by family members as well as by the many guests making their way to Mount Vernon in Washington's retirement. As forms made by the Chinese for the Western market, the guglet and basin were familiar objects to Washington's guests, although imported porcelain examples like these were not commonplace.

The bright polychrome decoration of the porcelain is usually termed Mandarin, in reference to the Chinese official (mandarin) depicted in the scenes. The rich blue underglaze decoration includes cell-diaper bands, typical of Mandarin design, along the rim of the basin and neck of the guglet. Overglaze enamel decoration of iron red, green, brown, pink, and yellow offers typical Mandarin color and drama to the scenes framed by blue scrollwork and iron red diaper ground.

George Washington purchased so many porcelain guglets and basins that it is difficult to determine when he secured this particular pair. They were, however, in use at Mount Vernon during his later retirement years and continued to serve the Washingtons and their guests until Mrs. Washington's death.[81]

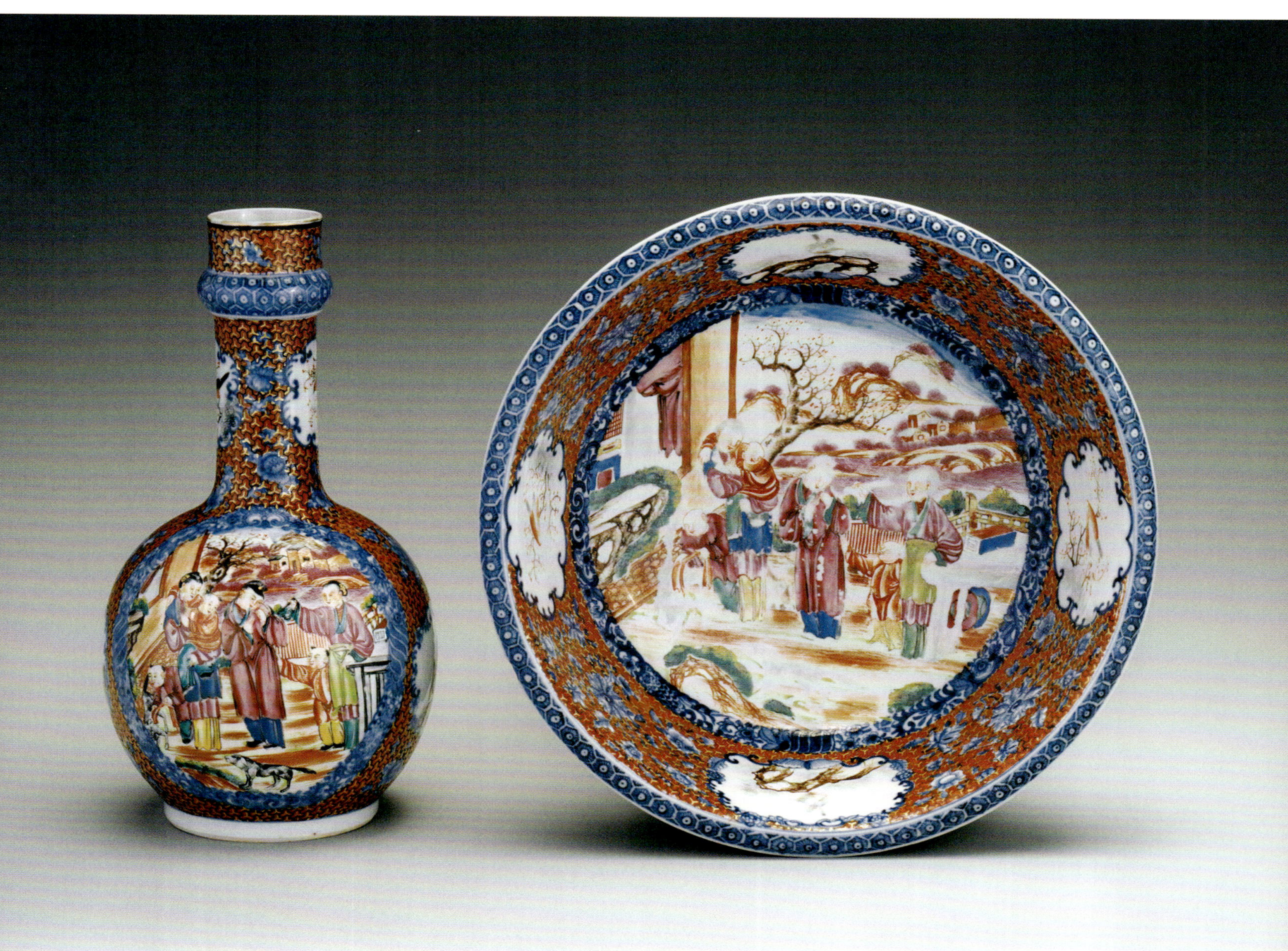

CAT. 63

Breakfast Table

Possibly Thomas Burling (1746–1831)
Probably New York, New York
Mahogany, tulip poplar, pine, and lightwood inlay, H. 28 3/16", W. 19 3/4" (closed), D. 30 3/8"
Private Collection
W-2660

In the fall of 1789 George Washington made two personal purchases from the New York cabinetmaker and retailer Thomas Burling, a large writing desk for himself and this breakfast table for Martha Washington.[82] Several months earlier, Burling had supplied several "inlaid" articles of furniture for the executive residence, including a "best Inlaid Tea Table" and an "Inlaid Breakfast Table."[83] Mrs. Washington may have found these examples of the latest Neoclassical styles pleasing and wanted one for herself.

The table exhibits the decorative inlays and veneers found on other examples of Burling's work from this period,[84] and it is quite possible that Martha Washington's table was crafted in Burling's workshop rather than simply being sold through his retail operation. The oval mahogany top measures thirty-seven inches wide when fully open and is ornamented by a simple beaded molding on the sides. It rests above two drawers, one functional and one false. The tapering legs are highlighted by descending bellflower inlay and terminate in a band of stepped inlay above casters.

At the conclusion of the presidency, Washington listed the table as among the "Private Cabinet work" he purchased for the excutive residence,[85] and it went with the Washingtons to Mount Vernon. It is not clear in which of the many rooms the table was placed, but a watercolor by Benjamin Henry Latrobe suggests it was used outdoors when the Washingtons enjoyed tea on the piazza (fig. 1).

George Washington Parke Custis purchased the table at the sale of furnishings after his grandmother's death in 1802.[86] It was recorded at his home, Arlington House, by Benson Lossing in 1853 and remained there until its removal to the United States Patent Office in 1862, when Arlington was occupied by Union soldiers. The table was part of an exhibition of Washington relics at the 1876 centennial and was transferred to the Smithsonian Institution in 1883. It was not returned to the Lee family until 1901.

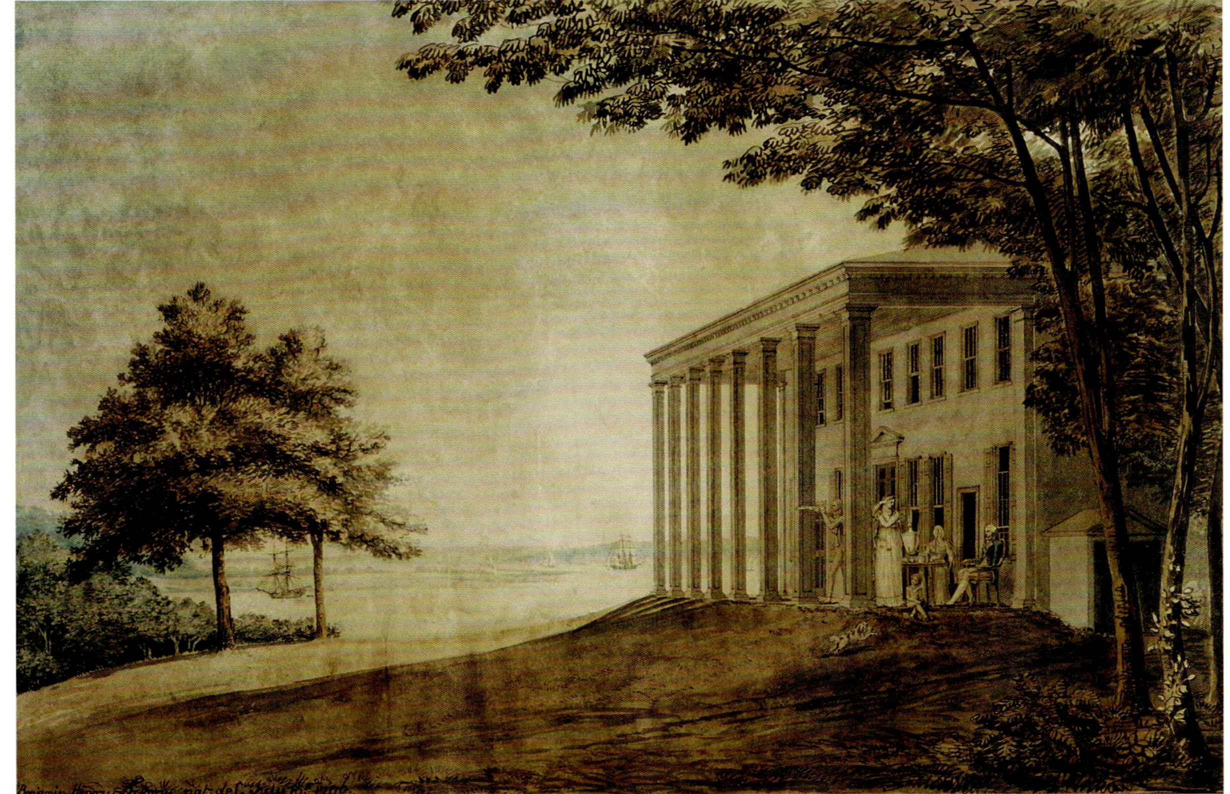

Fig. 1. Watercolor by Benjamin Henry Latrobe, rendered in the summer of 1796, recorded the Washington family enjoying tea on the piazza from a breakfast table relocated to the breezy outdoor space. Courtesy of Louise and Brad Mentzer

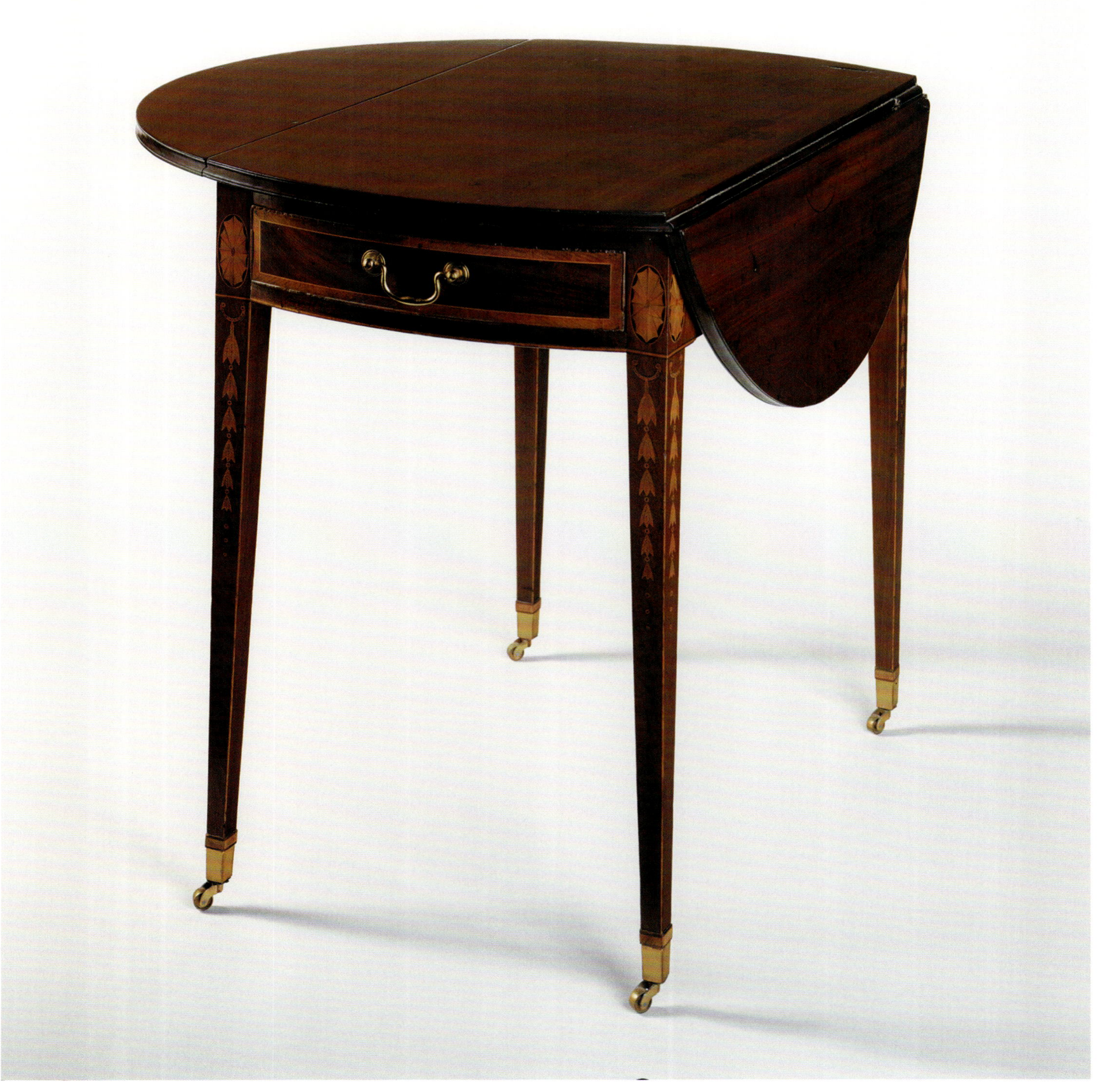

CAT. 64

Chair Cushion

Martha Washington
Eastern United States, ca. 1765–1802
Linen, wool, and silk, H. 2", W. 15¾", D. 18½"
Purchase, 1960
W-2173

In 1765 thirty-four-year-old Martha Washington decided to cross-stitch canvas bottoms for some of the chairs at Mount Vernon and alerted her husband to those materials she would need. In October George Washington requested London agent Robert Cary and Company to send:

> *Canvas for one dozn. Chair bottoms—neither course nor fine—but of a middle size*
> *Dark shades of yellow worsted for working cross Stitch—viz.*
> *1¾ lb. of the first and Second colour*
> *1½ lb. of the third and fourth*
> *1¼ lb. of the fifth*
> *3 lb of the sixth*
> *¾ of a pound of the Seventh—and*
> *¾ of the eigth and to be silk—the rest all worsted*[87]

Cary and Company turned to the London upholsterer Philip Bell, and the needed supplies were shipped from England in March, arriving in Virginia in July 1766. They included "11 lb. fine yellow worst[e]d of diff[eren]t Shades to Work cross Stitch," "12 Oz. floss Silk," and "12 Y[ar]ds yellow Canvas."[88] Over the next thirty-six years, Martha Washington carefully stitched onto the canvas, using wool and silk, a repeated scallop shell design that was, quite possibly, of her own creation (detail).[89]

From the oversight of domestic routines at Mount Vernon to accompanying her husband during the Revolutionary War, Martha Washington experienced numerous demands on her time, which interrupted her work on these chair seats. On June 2, 1794, nearly thirty years after beginning them, she wrote from Philadelphia to her niece Fanny Bassett Washington, who was living at Mount Vernon: "When the President comes down I beg you will get the key of my closet if you have not get it and send me the two bags that has my worked chear Bottoms in, as I intend to have them made into some thing if they are not spoiled and Eaten up with the moth."[90]

A few weeks later, Mrs. Washington again wrote to Fanny on the subject of the canvas work:

> *I dont recolect whether I put the needles that I worked the cross stitch with in the bag with the chare covers if they are not I dont know whare to derect you to find them—if they are to be found I beg you to send them to me in a letter will be as ready as any way—I dont believe any needles of the kind is to be got hear and I shall want them—I intend to set about my chear and get them done if these that are worked is good for any thing I shall soon have them done.*[91]

The chair canvases, however, were not to be done "soon," and Martha Washington completed the last one shortly before her death in 1802.

While they may have originally been intended to upholster chair slip seats, the canvases were ultimately made into chair cushions that may very well have been in use in Mount Vernon's back, or little, parlor. When Joshua Brookes visited Mount Vernon in February 1799, he noticed, "The sitting parlor, a small back room with the chimney in the corner" contained "yellow bottom windsor chairs."[92] The hard wood seats of these chairs perhaps prompted Martha to make them more comfortable by outfitting them with her cross-stitched cushions. One of the white dimity slipcovers made for the cushions survives and offers the possibility that the largely wool cushions were protected from insects by the cotton material during the warm Virginia summer months.

After Martha Washington's death, it appears that her twelve shell-patterned chair cushions were divided among her three granddaughters. Of the six examples that survive in the Mount Vernon collection, four were returned through descendants of Eliza Parke Custis Law, one from a descendant of Eleanor Parke Custis Lewis, and this example from a descendant of Martha Custis Peter.[93] The cushion's scallop shell design, worked in red worsted on a yellow worsted ground, references the Rococo shell motifs popular in the mid-eighteenth century that decorated furniture and silver flatware handles. The original yellow worsted wool casing that complemented the canvas work and enclosed the cushion's stuffing remains intact, as does some of the silk tape applied to the seam. The hand-knotted multicolor silk fringe attached to the front face of the cushion and portions of the tape that once secured the cushion to seat spindles or stiles also survive. Together, they offer a rare documented example of Martha Washington's needlework, her design aesthetic, and original upholstery at Mount Vernon.

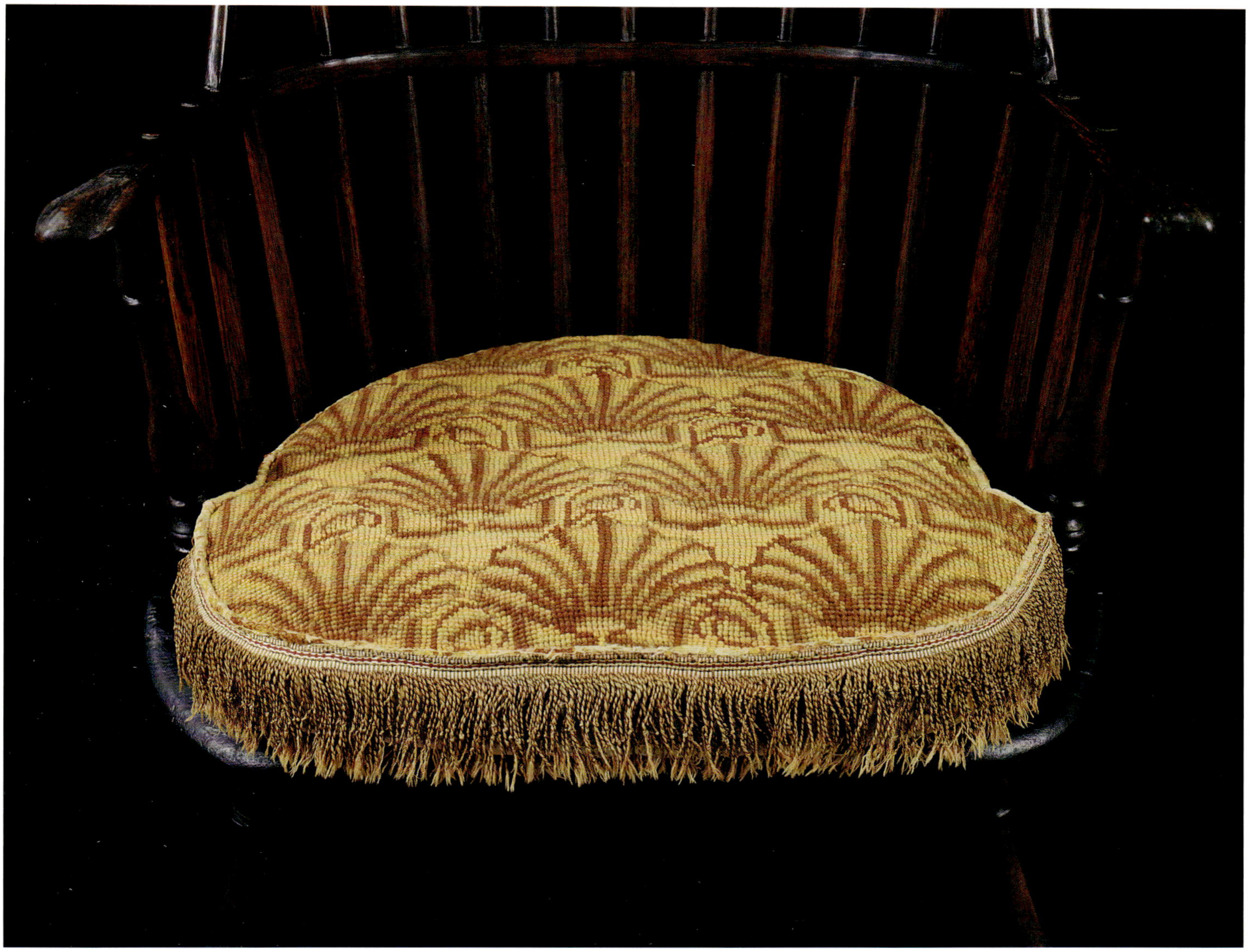

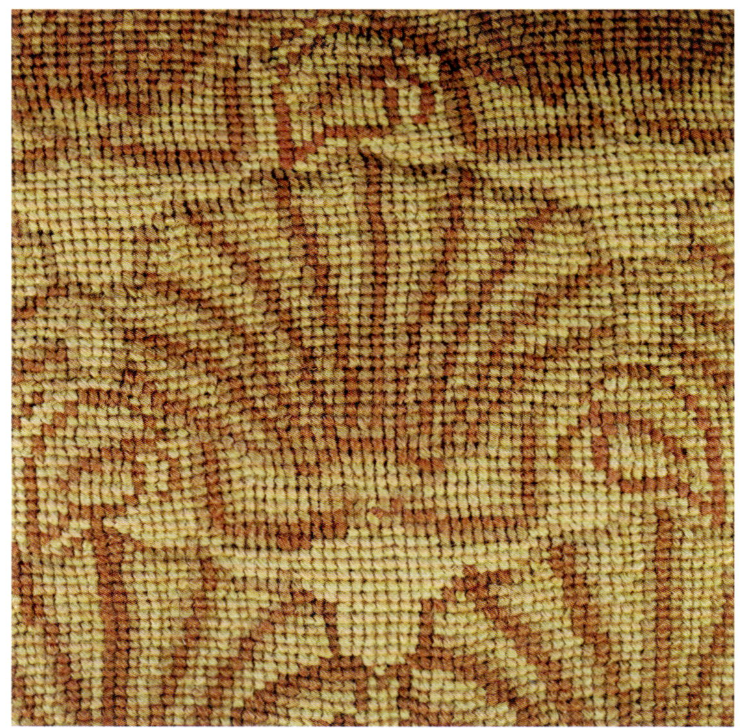

CAT. 65

Rule

Probably England, 1760–1800
Boxwood, W. 4½", L. 1¼"
Gift of Mary Means Huber, 2004
2004.017

Useful for mathematical calculations and composing scale drawings, small scales or rules were common tools in European and American households. Incised with decorative detailing early in the eighteenth century, their form and size had become more functional by midcentury. Usually made of brass, silver, ivory, or boxwood, these rules were smaller in size—4½ to 6 inches long—and were often included in a small case of instruments.[94] Imported English and French cased sets of drawing instruments were widely available from merchants in America by the mid-eighteenth century and incorporated a combination of related tools, including pencils, dividers, and protractors.

Such boxed sets of instruments were readily available to George and Martha Washington. On King Street in Alexandria, Virginia, William Hartshorne and Company offered for sale a variety of goods, including "neat sets of mathematical instruments,"[95] while John Sparhawk of Philadelphia provided "cases of ploting Instruments" to his customers as well as "brass Protractors; [and] ivory and brass Paral'el Rules."[96] The Washingtons owned numerous sets of these small boxed instruments, and the list of items sold following Martha Washington's death in 1802 included "one box plotting instruments," "a case with a rule," and "a box of instruments,"[97] and this rule was likely originally part of a larger set of mathematical or drafting instruments.

Although short, this common boxwood ruler, inscribed and inked with inches, equal part divisions, diagonal scales, and decimals, would have allowed a variety of calculations to be made in combination with protractors and dividers (detail). A surveyor in his youth, George Washington was no doubt skilled at utilizing the varied scales inscribed on this rule for plotting points on a map and crafting detailed drawings. Well versed in current scientific discoveries, Washington obtained for his library articles that, at his death, included maps and charts, as well as an "Ansons voyage round the world" and "Columbus's discovery."[98]

Martha Washington, an avid seamstress and knitter, may well have used such a tool while laying out needlework patterns and making exacting measurements of expensive textiles. A note accompanying the rule in the hand of her granddaughter Eliza Parke Custis Law draws this connection, for it identifies the object as the "Box rule from the writing desk of my lamented grandmother."[99] Instructive literature of the time advised that ladies' workbaskets should include rules or scales to aid in the intricate calculations necessary for detailed needlework and the making of garments, tasks that Martha Washington, like many of her contemporaries, practiced with great regularity.[100]

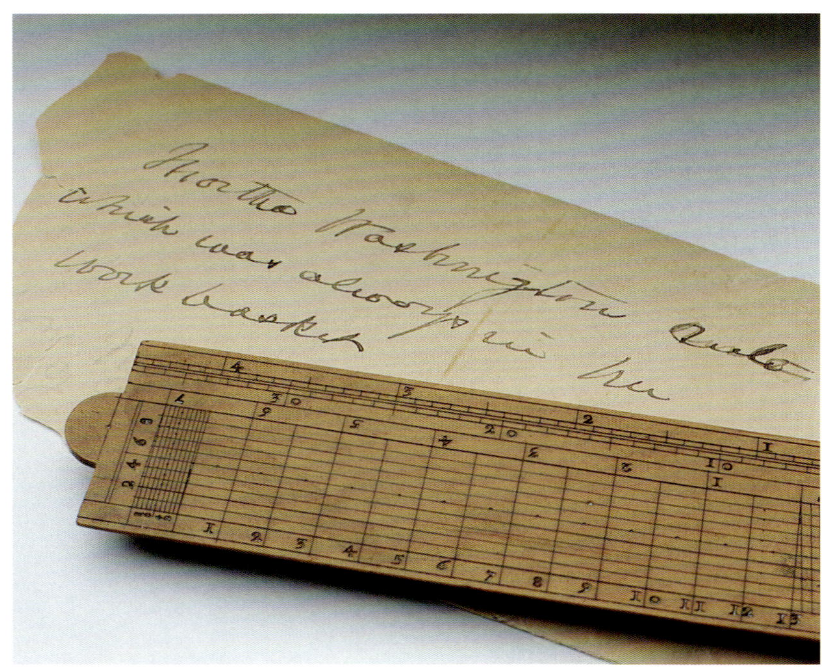

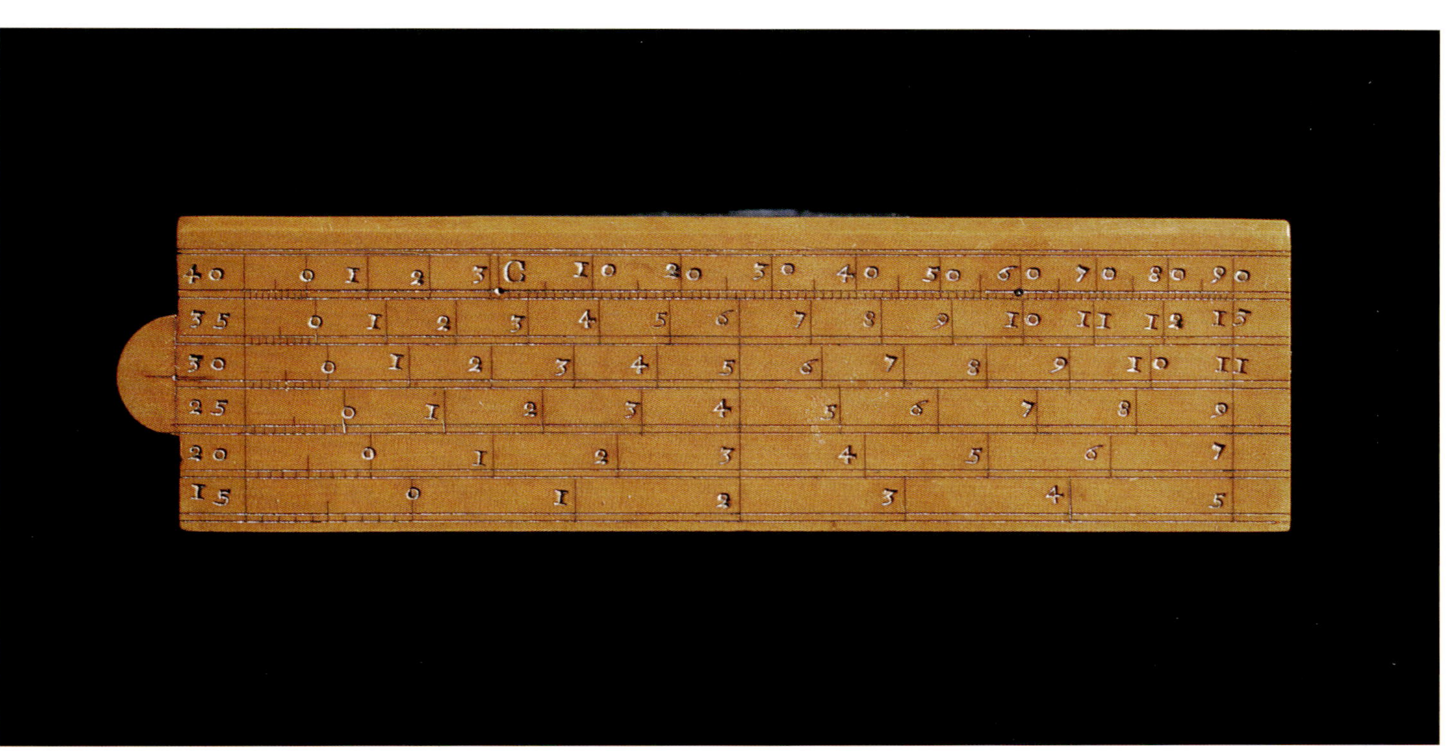

CAT. 66

Pinking Iron and Plank

Pinking iron
England or America, 1750–1800
Iron, L. 3⅞"
Purchase, 1958
W-2141

Plank
England or America, 1750–1800
Lead, L. 14", W. 6⅞"
Purchase, 1960
W-2168

Pinking irons, or "pinks," were used to finish the edges of fabrics in lieu of hemming, as well as to provide decorative embellishments for garments. For those who could afford the luxury in the mid-eighteenth century, gowns and other clothing featured trimming that was pinked into scalloped shapes and punched with ornamental patterns.[101]

To achieve this decorative detailing, "the textile was folded and positioned under the cutting edge of the pinking iron. The pinking tool was struck with a mallet, cutting down through the layers of fabric."[102] A plank of wood or lead placed under the fabric allowed the mallet to be struck sharply. The marks left behind by pinking irons on this thick lead plank are evidence of this practice.

Records of purchases during her lifetime indicate the wide variety of fabrics Martha Washington bought for her fashionable gowns. Although professional dressmakers were available in such cities as New York and Philadelphia, Martha Washington also relied on the skills of her house staff for sewing tasks. Experienced house slaves such as Charlotte and Oney Judge (Martha's maid) hemmed and made trims for garments and caps and most likely would have been familiar with the practice of pinking fabrics. George Washington noted that Oney, in particular, "was handy and useful to her [Martha Washington] being perfect Mistress of her needle."[103] Evidence for the reliance on slave labor for such tasks is also found in a letter from Martha Washington to Fanny Bassett Washington, who was overseeing Mount Vernon during the presidency: "I sent by Hercules some rufles for my little Boys bosom which I beg you will make Charlot hem—and ship them ready to sew on."[104]

Useful for a variety of trims as well as leatherworking tasks, pinking irons were sold in sets of different sizes and shapes. The pinking iron in the Mount Vernon collection, bearing the maker's marks "IK" and "K—GHT" along its length, is one of five that descended in the family of Martha Parke Custis Peter of Tudor Place with the history of having been used at Mount Vernon.[105] These pinking irons and their accompanying lead plank may have been part of the "Kitchen furniture" or "sundries" purchased by Martha Peter's husband, Thomas, at the estate sale of Martha Washington's belongings in 1802.[106] They, like many of the objects identified and preserved at Tudor Place, retain paper labels corresponding to the itemized list of original Mount Vernon furnishings prepared by Martha Washington's great-granddaughter Britannia Wellington Peter Kennon.[107]

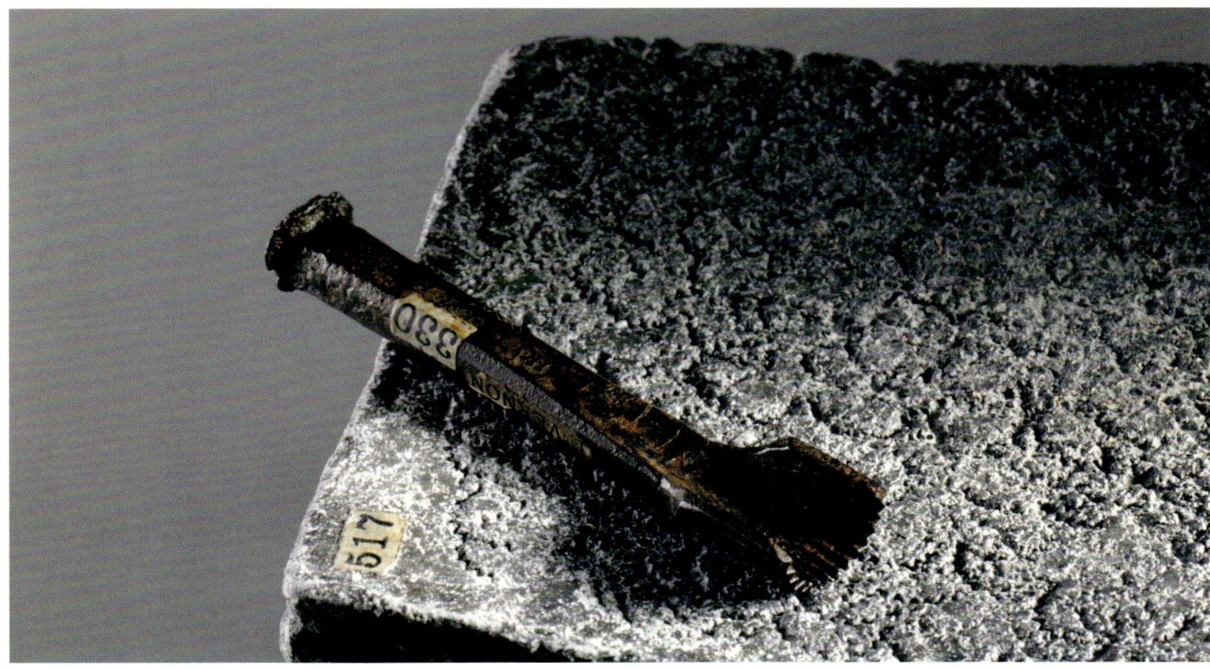

CAT. 67

Tackle Box and Fishing Hook

Probably England, ca. 1760–1790
Principally iron, Box L. 4⅛", W. 2¾", H. ¾"; Hook L. 3¼", W. 1¼"
Gift of Mrs. A. W. Bryan, 1958[108]
W-2201

In addition to fox and duck hunting, George Washington enjoyed the sport of fishing. Throughout his life, he recorded on the pages of his diary moments spent with rod and line. As a young man in Barbados, Washington "catched a Dolphin at 8 . . . a Shark at 11"; the Dolphin "was dressed for Dinner."[109] During the prewar years at Mount Vernon, Washington recorded "Fishing along towards Seridine Point" and days in which he "Went in the Evening a fishing with my Brothers Sam[ue]l & Charles."[110] After the war, when the Constitutional Convention was adjourned in July 1787, Washington joined Gouverneur Morris in a fishing expedition "in the vicinity of Valley-forge to get Trout."[111] Later, when he made his tour of the northern states as president, Washington passed a fort in Portsmouth Harbor, New Hampshire, where he was "saluted by 13 Guns," and "Having Lines . . . Proceeded to the Fishing banks a little with out the Harbour and fished for Cod."[112] While he was president, one of his fishing expeditions was recorded in the *Pennsylvania Packet.*

> *Yesterday afternoon the President of the United States returned from Sandy Hook and the fishing banks, where he had been for the benefit of the sea air, and to amuse himself in the delightful recreation of fishing. We are told he has had excellent sport, having himself caught a great number of sea-bass and black fish.*[113]

One likes to think the retired president also enjoyed a few quiet days fishing once he retired to Virginia.

Regardless of year or location, Washington likely carried with him a small tackle box that included fishing hooks, lines, and floats. In November 1762 he requested from London "A Fishing Case for the Pocket—properly furnished with Lines &c."[114] This pocket-sized tackle box, or one very similar, may have been sent in response. Included with the painted metal case are two lines, two floats, and an assortment of iron fishing hooks, many of which likely represent replacements over time. The fishing hooks differ in size and construction, but some retain the mark of the talented blacksmith who wrought them. On the head of these hooks, "IS" identifies the maker who likely had little idea that his or her work would be owned by America's first president (detail).[115]

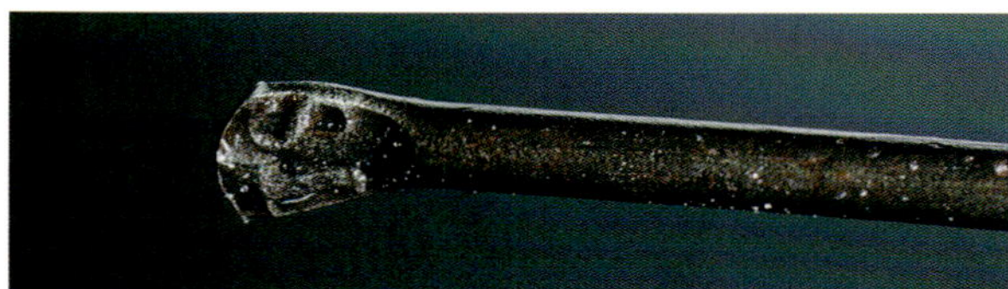

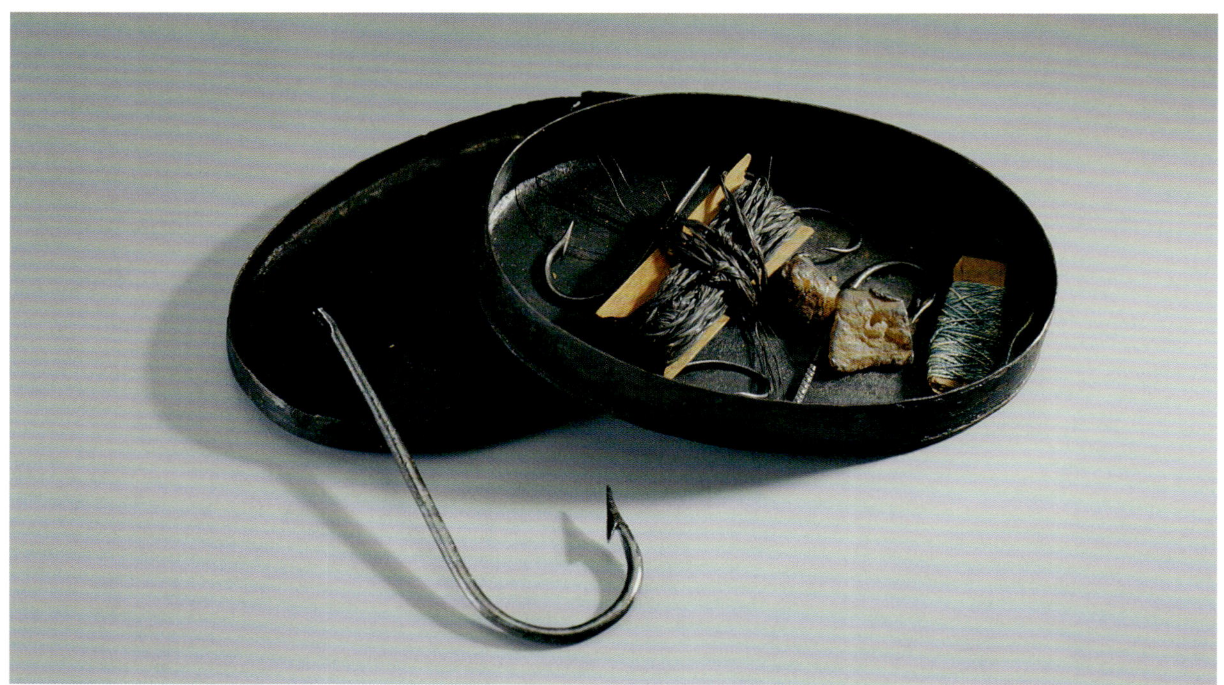

CAT. 68

The East Front of Mount Vernon

ca. 1787–1792

The West Front of Mount Vernon

ca. 1787–1792

Attributed to Edward Savage (1761–1817)
Oil on canvas, each 21⅞ x 35½"
Bequest of Helen W. Thompson, 1964
H-2445/A&B

Although these two paintings never hung at Mount Vernon, their importance is difficult to overestimate. As the earliest known views of the house and grounds, they not only served as an inspiration to others who would paint George Washington's estate, but they are the only eighteenth-century eyewitness paintings that record the Washington family and both the east and west facades of the Mansion buildings and grounds in the same year. The identity of the artist has been debated for decades, but Edward Savage is the most likely candidate.

Washington was first introduced to Savage in 1789 when the artist painted the president for Harvard University[116] and may have become reacquainted with the artist when both men were in Georgetown, South Carolina, in April 1791.[117] On his way north, Savage may have paused at Mount Vernon, making sketches that would later become the basis of these two canvases. Over the course of twenty-two years, Savage exhibited paintings entitled *A West View of Mount Vernon* and *A North-East view of Mount Vernon, Painted on the spot.*[118] While the artist of these unsigned works cannot be confirmed, the architectural details and figures represented in them suggest that Savage painted them.[119]

This pair of paintings provide two very different views of Mount Vernon. *The West Front* is a domestic scene peopled with the Washington family, guests, and slaves. George and Martha Washington walk with Nelly Custis. George Washington Parke Custis stands with two hounds and one of the general's aides (or perhaps Pierre-Charles L'Enfant, the engineer who brought Washington the first plans for the new Federal City that summer). A gardener and assistant walk toward the flower garden, a female slave heads to the kitchen, and a horse drawn carriage rounds the circle. In contrast, *The East Front*, devoid of people, depicts the bucolic setting of the main house, its many outbuildings, and the brick ha-ha wall and white wood fence that kept deer and other animals from the expansive green of the East Lawn.

The paintings record a number of details that help determine when they were created. The dove of peace weathervane included in both views was added to the Mansion's cupola in 1787 and provides the earliest date they could have been rendered. The slate-colored roofs on the greenhouse and dependency buildings were repainted a Spanish brown color in 1792,[120] and the paddock to contain deer was removed that year. In the summer of 1792 Washington wrote, "I have about a dozen deer (some of which are of the common sort) which are no longer confined in the Paddock which was made for them but range in all my woods and often pass my exterior fence."[121] By 1794 the uncontained deer kept nibbling at the plantings on his property, and Washington eventually declared, "I am at a loss therefore in determining whether to give up the Shrubs or the Deer!"[122]

The East Front of Mount Vernon and *The West Front of Mount Vernon*, therefore, were painted sometime between 1787 and 1792. The range corresponds with the time in which Edward Savage could have visited the Washingtons, and his later paintings suggest him as the likely artist. Whoever the painter, this blend of a historic recording of Mount Vernon's details with an artful rendering of its landscape provides an invaluable portrait of life on the estate in the years following the Revolution that undoubtedly served as inspiration for future artists who helped to make Mount Vernon part of a national consciousness.

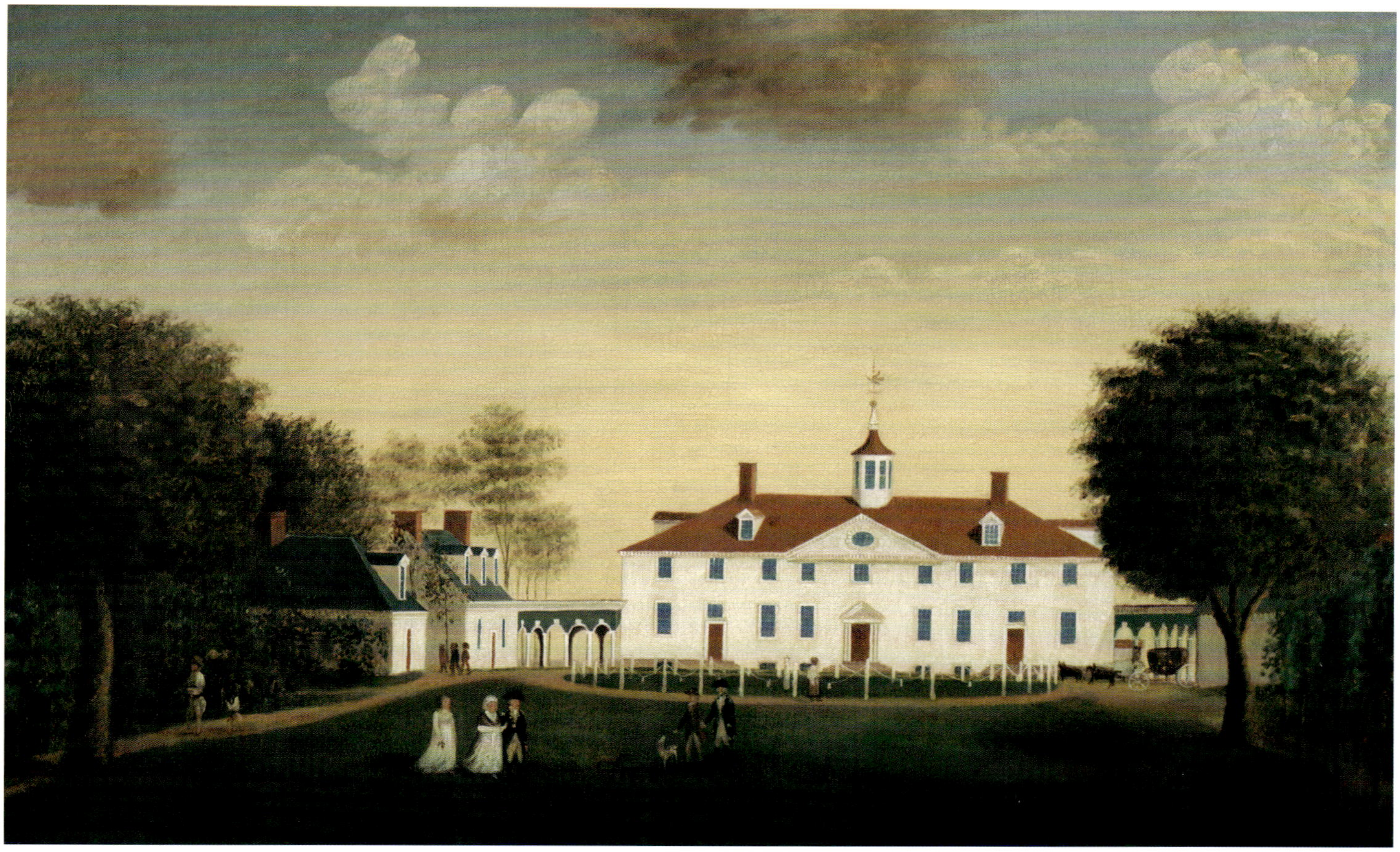

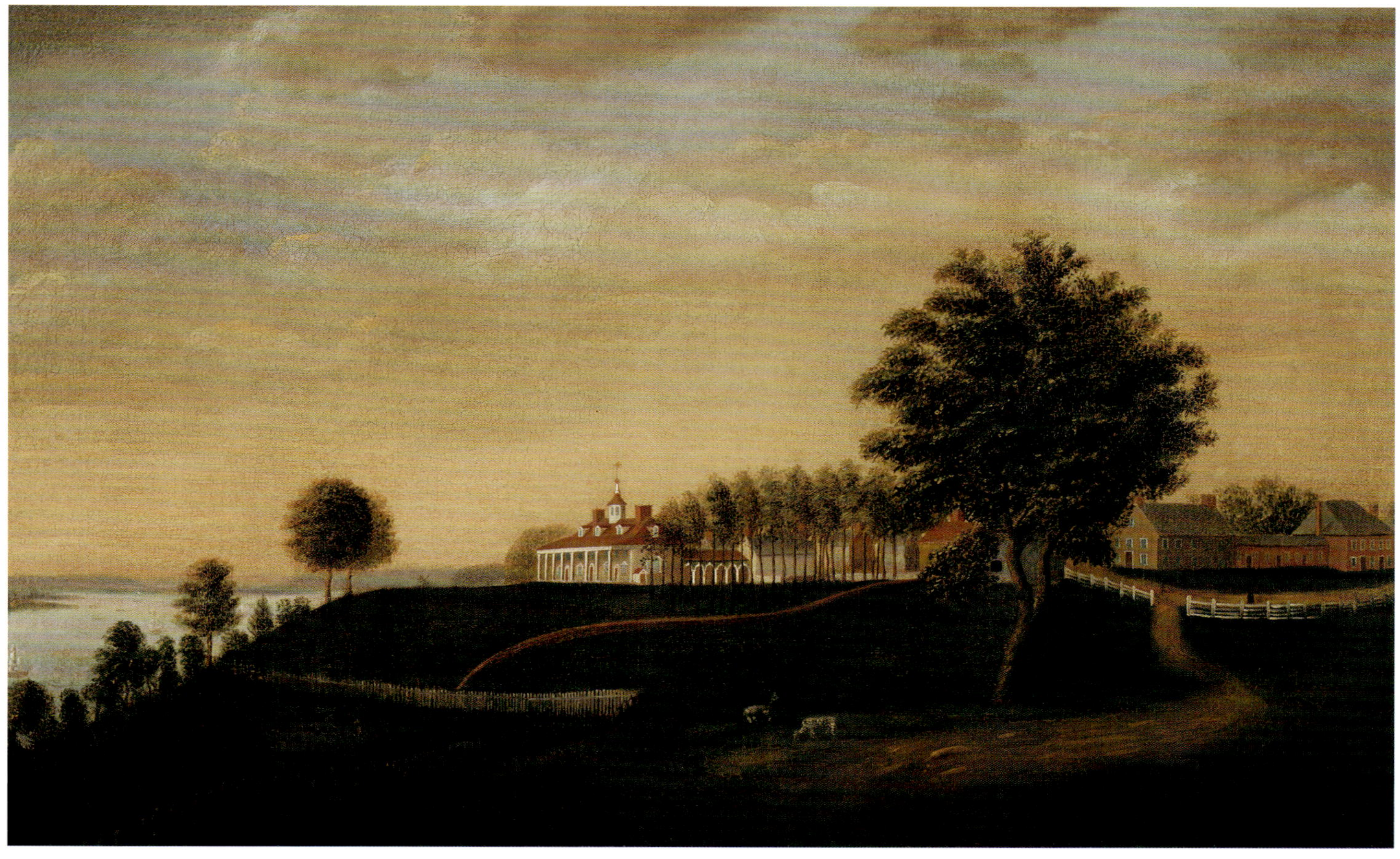

CAT. 69

Sundial

Probably England, ca. 1765–1785
Brass, H. 6¼", DIAM. 11¾"
Gift of Miss Annie Burr Jennings, Vice Regent for Connecticut, 1938
W-715

George Washington maintained a lifelong interest in the weather and time. He recorded the weather daily in his diary and was known for his punctuality. The Congressional Chaplain, the Reverend Ashbel Green, once noted that, "In private, as well as in public, his punctuality was observable. . . . At his dinner parties he allowed five minutes for the variation of time pieces, and after they were expired he would wait for no one." When guests arrived late, "His only apology was, 'sir, or Gentlemen, we are too punctual for you;' or in pleasantry, 'Gentlemen, I have a cook, who never asks whether the company has come, but whether the hour has come."[123]

In eighteenth-century America, sundials were the most accurate and widely available instruments for telling time.[124] Washington likely had an example in place some years before he paid Charles Turner for mending his "Dial" in 1770.[125] Washington perhaps knew Turner from the sundial he had supplied for the Alexandria courthouse yard and may have bought from him this example.[126] Washington placed this dial on a white painted wood post in the center of the circular grass lawn in front of the west entrance to the Mansion. It was a visible reminder of the hour for the Washingtons, their guests, and the slaves who daily rounded the circle in the course of their chores. In 1785 the retired general recorded in his diary that he "began to set my turned Posts in the Circle,"[127] as he enhanced the surroundings of the sundial with a circle of posts linked by chains ornamented with iron drops.

Because sundials relied on the sun's rays, their accuracy depended on the proper calibrating of the hour and minute marks on its face and the appropriate angle of the dial's gnomon (vertical shadow maker). Although Turner or another American craftsman could have made this sundial, it retains no visible maker's mark and could also have been an English export adjusted to accommodate Mount Vernon's location. The octagonal brass face is engraved with a central circular design comprising an eight-pointed star radiating outward to points identified as north, south, east, west, northeast, southeast, southwest, and northwest. The Roman numerals I to XII surround the gnomon to identify the hour, and an outer ring of engraved minute markers delineate portions of the hour.

After leaving the Washington family in the mid-nineteenth century, the sundial was located, purchased, and returned to Mount Vernon by the Association's Vice Regent for Connecticut, Annie Burr Jennings. After nearly two years of researching the proper placement and support for the object, the Ladies installed the sundial at their spring meeting in 1939. On April 30, "at about eight o'clock, immediately after dinner, Council reassembled around the sun dial and watched with much interest Mr. Williams' alignment by the north star."[128] George Washington's sundial had returned home.

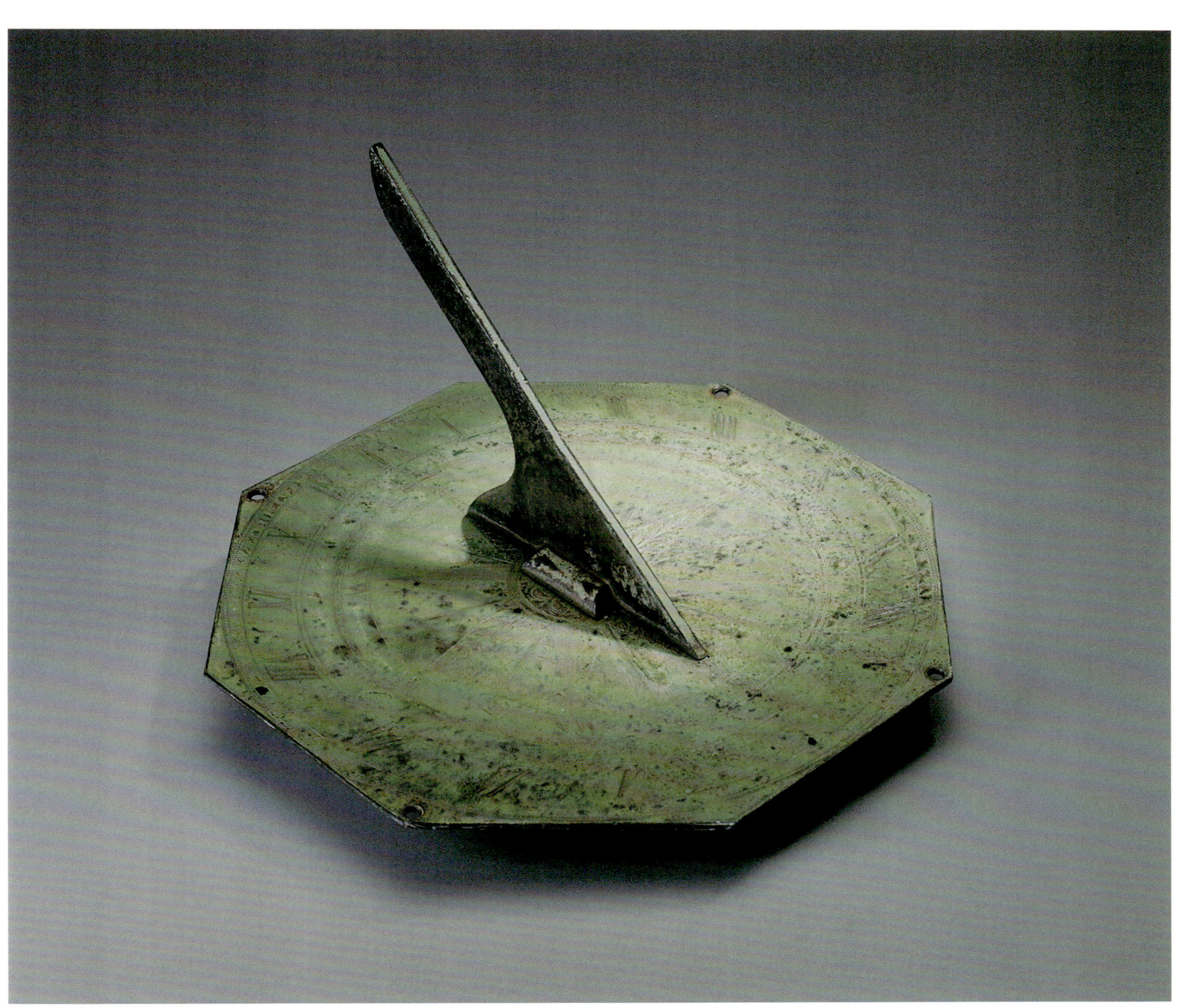

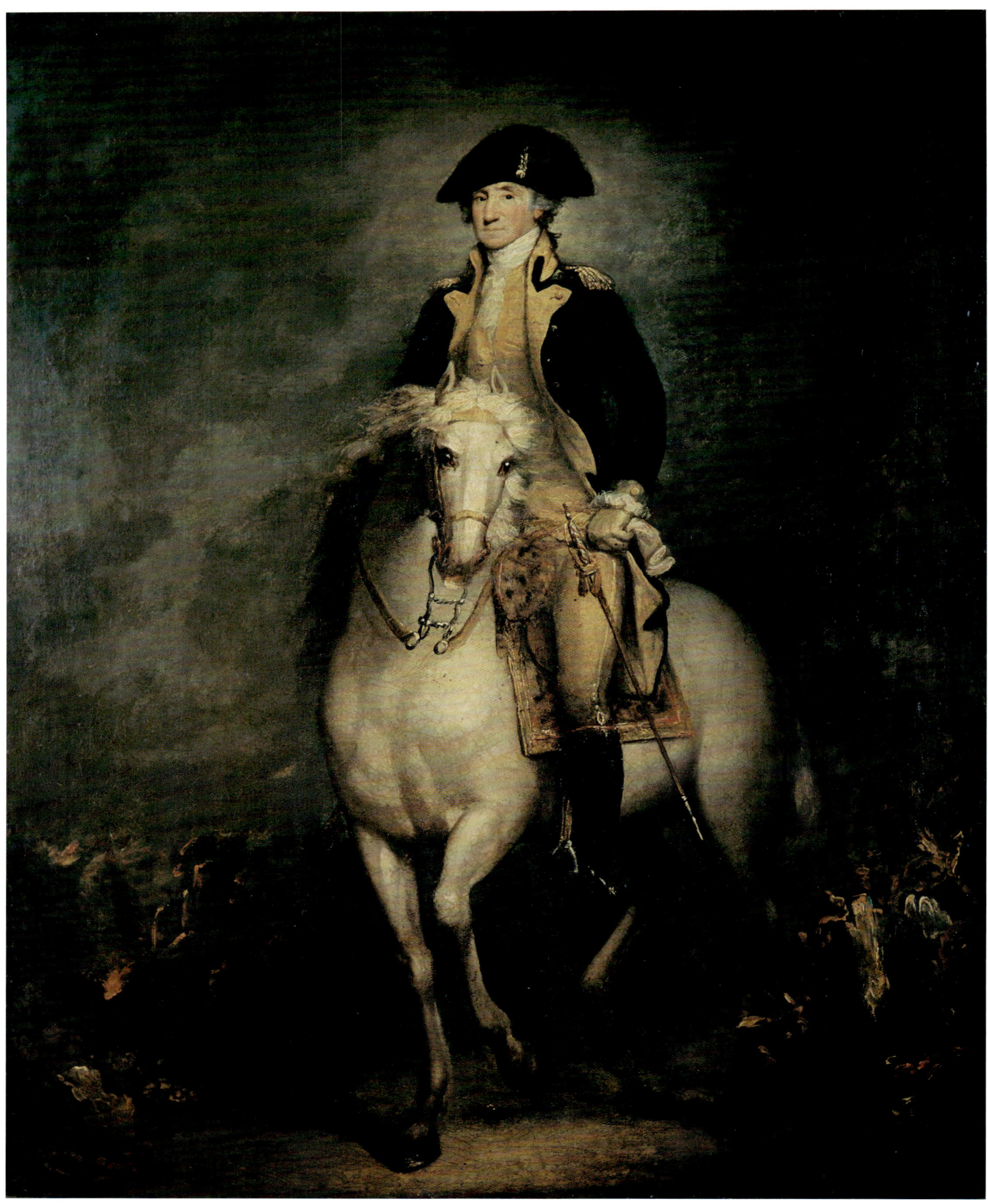

CHAPTER SIX

Silver Swords to Silk Waistcoats The Personal Style of George Washington

THROUGHOUT HIS LIFE, NOT ONLY DID GEORGE WASHINGTON pay close attention to those objects that filled his living, dining, and entertainment spaces, but he also gave thoughtful consideration to the personal articles he wore and carried. From his military and presidential attire to the garments he wore when riding around his Mount Vernon farms, Washington was attuned to the details of dress. His practicality and abhorrence of ostentation steered him toward the neat and plain aesthetic that also guided his selections in furnishings. At the same time, Washington understood the role his appearance played in conveying to others his social, economic, and political status. With great care, the Virginia planter, commander in chief, and president chose articles that defined the position he held at each stage in life.

As a teenager, George Washington already took note of the type and number of clothing articles in his possession. In 1748, as he headed for the south branch of the Potomac River to survey some of the Fairfax lands, Washington listed in his diary the clothing he carried with him. His "Memorandum of what Clothes I Carry into Fairfax" recorded a razor, nine shirts, six linen waistcoats, one cloth waistcoat, six bands, four neck cloths, and seven caps.[1] At approximately the same time, Washington spelled out in considerable detail the instructions for a coat he wanted to have made. He specified that it was to be

> *a Frock with a Lapel Breast[,] the Lapel to Contain on each side six Button Holes and to be about 5 or 6 Inches wide . . . in Length to come down to or below the bent of the knee[,] the Waist from the armpit to the Fold to be exactly as long or Longer than from thence to the Bottom[,] not to have more than one fold in the Skirt[,] and the top to be made just to turn in and three Button Holes[.] the Lapel at the top to turn as the Cape of the Coat and Bottom to Come Parrallel with the Button Holes[.] the Last Button hole in the Breast to be right opposite to the Button on the Hip.*[2]

Apparently, Washington had seen or owned a similar garment and now wished to imitate it. The young surveyor's close attention to the details of clothing illustrates his concern for appropriate appearance that would remain with him his entire life.

Ten years later, Washington was placing clothing orders with his English factors. A bachelor aspiring to become a member of the Virginia gentry elite, Washington wished his clothing not only to reflect current fashion in London but also to declare his connections and his planter status. He was often dependent on his factor, however, to guide him in the prevailing fashion. In 1758, for instance, he asked Thomas Knox of Bristol to forward "two pair of Work[e]d Ruffles at a guinea each pair—if work[e]d Ruffles should be out of fashion send such as are not."[3]

With his economic and social standing changed by his marriage to Martha Dandridge Custis in January 1759, Washington ordered clothes that were consonant with his roles as an established planter, a member of the Virginia gentry, and the head of a household. In addition to the fine porcelains and silver he requested in the first years of marriage, Washington wrote to London for garments made of some of the best textiles available. In September 1760, for example, he ordered four pairs of breeches from Charles Lawrence, one each of "Crimson Velvet, black silk, black Ditto [silk] worsted," and "light coloured silk

Fig. 1. (opposite) Washington paid close attention to the details of military dress and distinction, offering a commanding figure on horseback. *George Washington*, attributed to Rembrandt Peale, ca. 1830, MVLA.

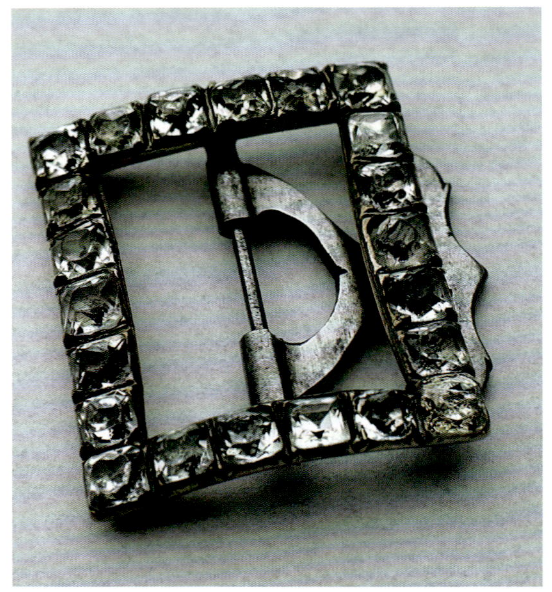

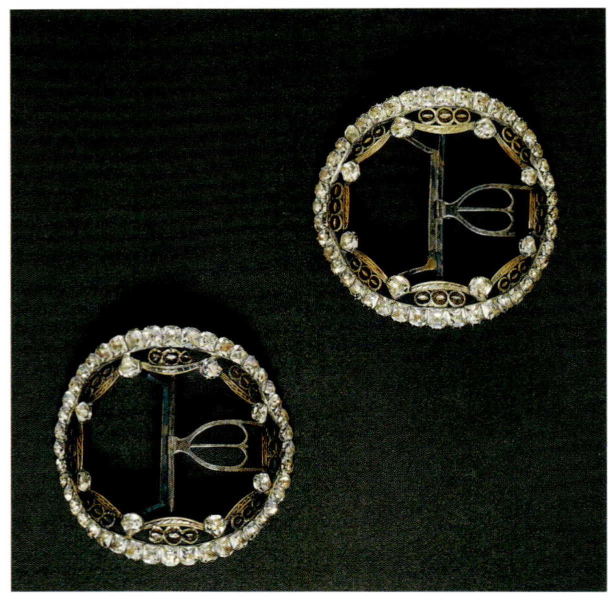

Fig. 2. (left) Paste buckle used by George Washington to fasten the knee bands of his breeches, MVLA

Fig. 3. (right) George Washington's paste (artificial) stone shoe buckles, Courtesy of the Yale University Art Gallery, de Lancey Kountze Collection

Shag."[4] Washington also made clear that he expected his orders would result in a particular style. When requesting "a genteel suit of cloathes made of superfine broad cloth," he specified that the material was to be "handsomely chosen,"[5] and when writing to London for "a suit of handsome cloth cloathes," noted, "I have no doubt but you will choose a fashionable colored cloth as well as a good one and make it in the best taste."[6]

The articles of clothing he sought were in perfect keeping with the attire expected of a Virginia gentleman. Appearance was important, but Washington did not lose sight of the utility and durability of his garments. When he asked Robert Cary and Company for "a new Market Great Coat with a loose hood to it made of Blew Drab or Broad Cloth," Washington stipulated that it should be made "according to the present taste" as well as "of such Cloth as will turn a good Shower of Rain."[7] In footwear, Washington also blended practicality with the current fashion. When enclosing his "Measure for Boots" in a letter to John Didsbury in London, Washington requested two pairs: "one of which made of stout strong Leather for Winters use, the other pair to be light and thin for Summer." He also asked for "two pair of real turn[e]d Pumps and four pair of neat, but at the same time strong Shoes."[8]

Washington's orders to London for his clothing also contained repeated complaints about ill-fitting garments, a situation that must have been disconcerting for a person so attuned to proper appearance. In October 1761 Washington was frustrated with the inability of his tailor to cut and sew his clothing to the measurements and specifications sent. In writing to his London factor, he proposed a solution:

> *I have hitherto had my Cloathes made by one Charles Lawrence in old Fish Street but whether it be the fault of the Taylor, or the Measure sent I can't say but certain it is my Cloathes have never fitted me well. I therefore leave the choice of the Workman to your care. . . . I enclose a Measure and for a further Insight I don't think it amiss to add that my stature is six feet; otherwise rather slender than Corpulent.*[9]

In addition to allowing his agent to select an appropriate tailor, Washington also placed his trust in the Londoner's taste: "As they are designed for Wearing Apparel for myself I have committed the choice of them to your fancy, having the best opinion of your taste."[10] While leaving the selection of "a handsome Suit of Cloth Cloaths, for Winter Ware," one for Summer, "A fashionable Cloke," and "Two best Beaver Hatts" to the discretion of this Londoner, Washington nevertheless added words that indicated his contin-

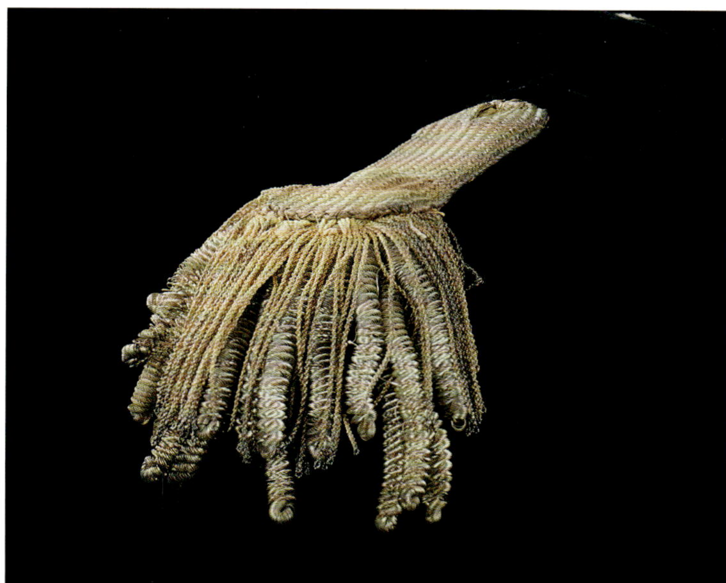

Fig. 4.
One of George Washington's gold epaulettes that distinguished him as commander in chief, Courtesy of the Brian and Barbara Hendelson Collection

ued concern for dignified appearance without ostentation: "I want neither Lace nor Embroidery; plain Cloathes with a gold or Silver Button (if worn in genteel Dress) is all that I desire."[11] Clearly displeased with his tailor despite the careful instructions sent in earlier correspondence, Washington authorized his factor to select a new tailor. He also relinquished the choice of his clothing's material, cut, and style to the London factor he trusted would outfit him in "genteel Dress."

In military as well as civilian attire, George Washington outfitted himself in a manner that spoke of his rank, political sentiments, and ambition. In 1774 a body of Virginia gentlemen organized themselves into the Fairfax Independent Company and elected George Washington commanding field officer. He acquired a full set of regimentals in the chosen dress of the new corps—"a regular Uniform of Blue, turn'd up with Buff; with plain yellow metal Buttons, Buff Waist Coat & Breeches, & white stockings."[12] The company's selection of blue and buff was symbolic. They were the colors of the English Whig party with whom American colonists felt themselves aligned against the ruling Tory party in power.[13] Washington's blue and buff regimentals were sewn by his indentured tailor, Andrew Judge, and accented by his purchase of "an Officer's sash," gorget, and epaulettes.[14] Washington likely wore this newly made uniform and its accoutrements throughout the meeting of the Second Continental Congress, when his attire alerted his fellow representatives of his political sentiments, military experience, and—presumably—his ambition to be commander in chief.

With his unanimous election as commander in chief in June 1775, Washington not only set about securing the equipment necessary for camp life, but he also purchased those articles of clothing that would lend distinction and credibility to his position. Before leaving Philadelphia to assume his command in Massachusetts, he paid the tailors John Galloway sixteen pounds and John Cotringer more than six pounds for clothing that likely included a new set of regimentals.[15] Washington kept to the colors of the Fairfax Independent Company and specified that as commander in chief, his uniform was to consist of "a blue coat with yellow buttons and gold epaulettes (each having three silver stars); linings cape and cuffs of buff; in winter buff vest and breeches; in summer a white vest and breeches of nankeen."[16]

The following month, Washington's attire made an impression on the military surgeon James Thacher, who recorded in his journal: "His excellency was on horseback, in company with several other military gentlemen. It was not difficult to distinguish him from the others; his personal appearance is truly

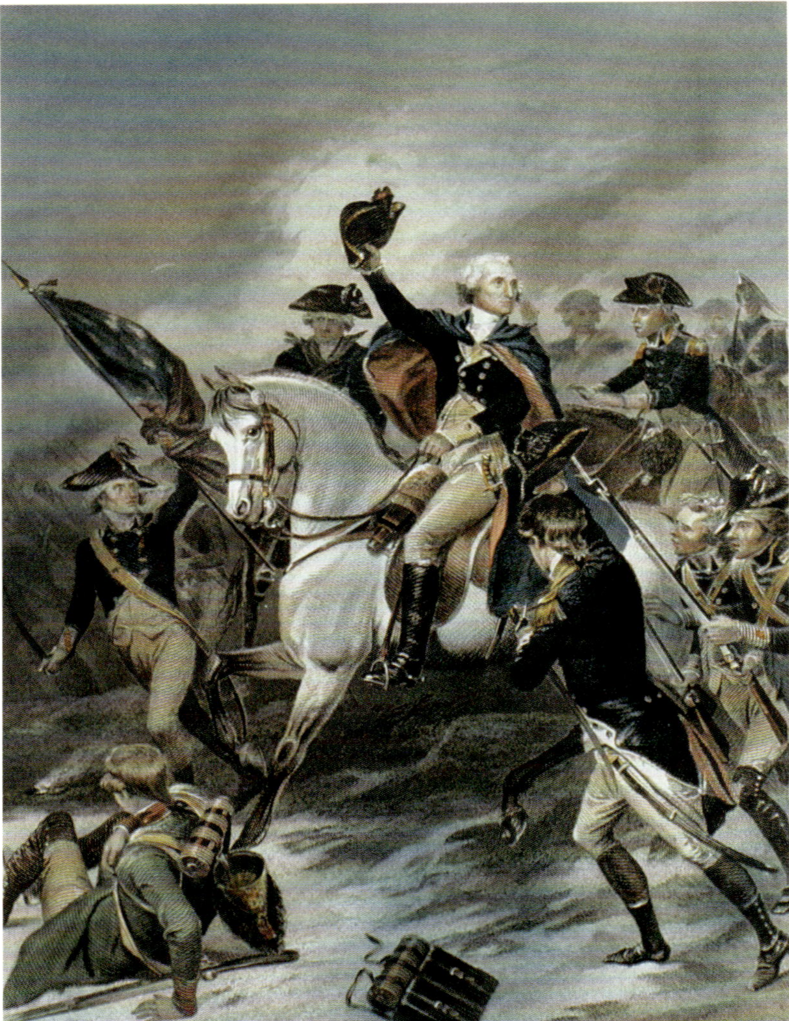

Fig. 5.
Washington at the Battle of Princeton [January 3, 1777], engraver unknown, published by Louis Kurz, Chicago, Illinois, ca. 1911, Willard-Budd Collection, MVLA

noble and majestic . . . his dress is a blue coat with buff-colored facings, a rich epaulette on each shoulder, buff under dress . . . an elegant small sword; a black cockade in his hat."[17] Clearly, Washington, who understood the symbolic nature of dress and its power to communicate, had not missed the opportunity to impress on his troops a general's power and superiority through his attire.

In July 1775 Washington, cognizant of the ability of attire to communicate, instituted a means by which the officers and soldiers could be identified using colored ribbands (or sashes). Washington's orders indicated that the commander in chief was to be identified "by a light blue Ribband, worn across his breast, between his Coat and Waistcoat. The Majors and Brigadiers General by a Pink Ribband worn in the like manner. [and] The Aids-de-Camp by a green ribband."[18] By 1779, however, it seems Washington rarely (if ever) wore his blue sash. That year the French officer François Marbois noted of his encounter with Washington: "His uniform is exactly like that of his soldiers. Formerly, on solemn occasions, that is to say on days of battle, he wore a large blue sash, but he has given up that unrepublican distinction."[19]

At the end of the war, Washington waited at his Newburgh, New York, encampment for official word of the peace treaty. Although he knew a conclusion to the conflict was in sight, Washington sought to keep up his appearance and was keen to obtain new clothes. He wrote to the New York merchant Daniel Parker for "as much superfine Buff Cloth (not of the yellow kind) as would make me a Vest Coat Breechs, and facings to a Coat; and . . . as much Buff-Silk Shag as would line a Coat and Vest Coat."[20] In March Washington had to renew his order, for he had been sent white lining material instead of buff. He wrote to Parker, clar-

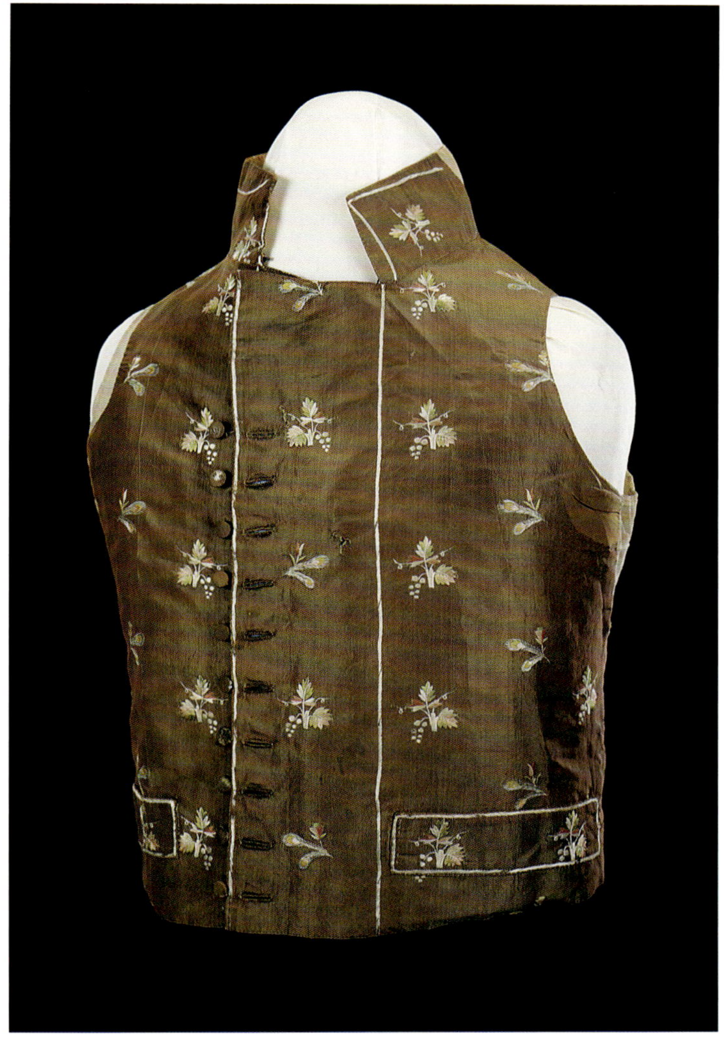

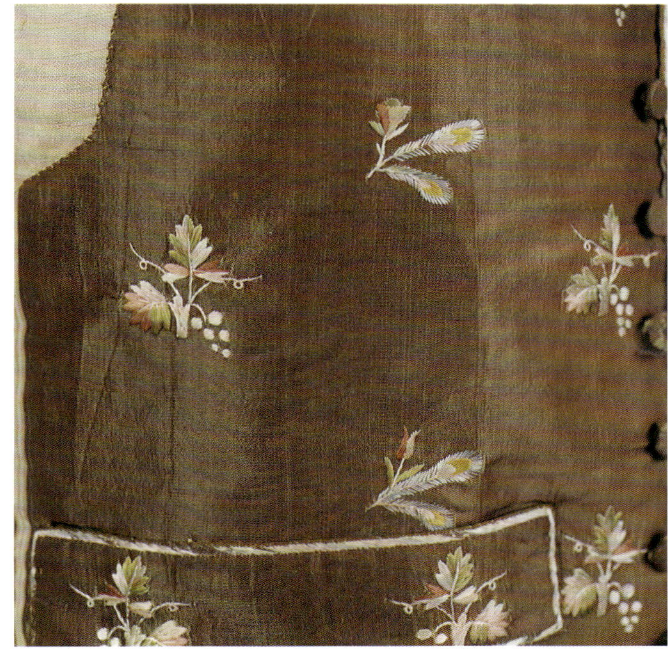

Fig. 6.
George Washington's green silk embroidered waistcoat of the 1780s, later refashioned by descendants, MVLA

Fig. 7.
Detail of the colorful embroidery that embellished Washington's green silk waistcoat, MVLA

ifying the color: "I shall thank you therefore to bring me a *Buff* lining of *any kind* from Philadelphia, sufficient for a Coat and Vest-Coat."[21] In addition, the general indicated, "If a pair of French Epauletts (gold) could be had, I would thank you for bringing me a pair; I do not want them of the largest and richest kind; because it is for a frock Coat they are intended. . . . Such as you will probably see upon Count de Dillon or any *Field* Officer in the French Service are the kind I would prefer."[22] Although Washington would no doubt have preferred to have received an international visitor in his new clothing, the Jamaican George Benet seemed charmed that April when he found the General in older garments. Benet wrote of Washington:

> *In his dress he was perfectly plain—an old blue coat faced with buff, waist-coat and britches of the latter, seemingly of the same age, and without any lace upon them, composed his dress. His shirt had no ruffles at the wrists, but of very fine linen. . . . His hair is a little grey and combed smoothly back from the forehead and in a small queue—no curls and but very little powder to it. Such is the man; but his character I cannot presume to describe—it is held in the highest veneration over the whole Continent.*[23]

Washington retired his buff and blue uniforms when he returned to the life of a Virginia planter. When Robert Hunter, Jr., called on him at Mount Vernon in 1785, he found the former general "neatly dressed in a plain blue coat, white cassimere waistcoat, and black breeches and boots, as he came from his farm." After changing for dinner, "the General came in again, with his hair neatly powdered, a clean shirt

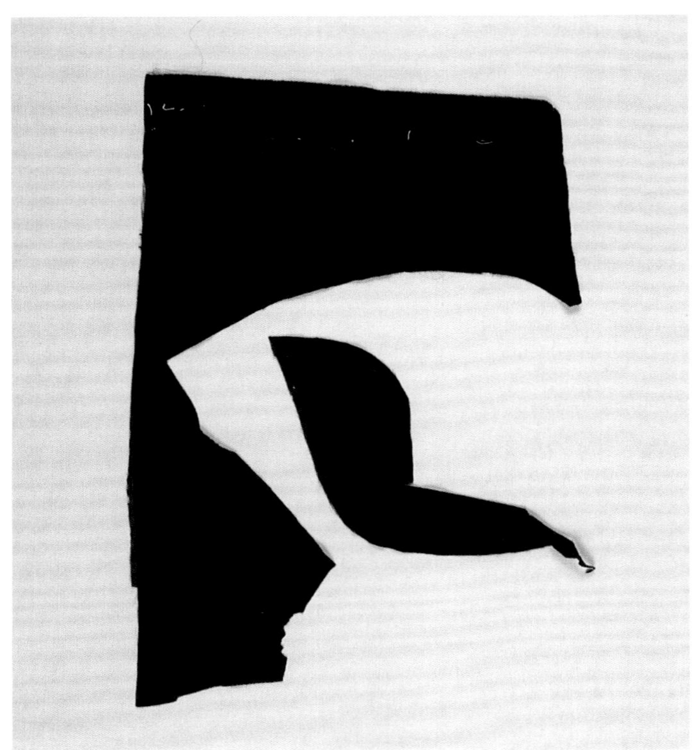

Fig. 8. Black velvet fragments from one of George Washington's suits worn during the presidency, MVLA

on, a new plain, drab coat, white waistcoat, and white silk stockings."[24] His neat and plain attire was not always without color, however, and included costly European textiles sent from admirers abroad. When in Philadelphia for the Constitutional Convention in the summer of 1787 and seeing no end to his staying there, Washington wrote to Mount Vernon for more clothes and requested "my Blew Coat with the Crimson collar and one of those made of the Cloth sent me by the Spanish Minister—to wit that without lapels, & lined with white Silk."[25]

When elected president two years later, Washington, as usual, was quick to understand the task of defining his new status through attire. As was the case in his selections for furnishings for the executive residence, he sought to avoid European court precedents. Washington made certain his official dress conveyed the message of an elegant and sophisticated young nation. At the same time, Washington took advantage of his position to advocate for support of American manufacturing, including wearing to his inauguration a suit of brown wool from the Hartford Woolen Manufactory in Connecticut. As he wrote to Daniel Hinsdale, "I shall always take a peculiar pleasure in giving every proper encouragement in my power to the manufactures of my Country."[26]

In addition to goods supplied from Connecticut, Washington patronized the merchants, tailors, milliners, and seamstresses of New York and Philadelphia for attire suitable for a head of state. Washington's quest for appropriate clothing is evident in a series of acquisitions. In the fall of 1789 Hercules Mulligan supplied "14½ y[ar]ds Velvet for a suit of clothes for the President" at a cost of £29.[27] To keep the Washingtons warm their first winter in New York, the merchant Lot Merkel provided "fur Cloaks for the Preside^{t} and Mrs Washington" at a cost of more than £42.[28] To complement his coat, breeches, and waistcoats, Ann Ball of New York made shirts,[29] while in Philadelphia, Mrs. Clark supplied 28½ yards of "Cotton for Shirts for the President,"[30] and Mrs. Emerson was paid for "ruffling" them.[31] To cover his calves, merchants and tailors supplied dozens of pairs of "silk stockings," "silk hose," "raw silk hose," and "bl[ac]k silk hose."[32]

William Sullivan, who attended one of the weekly levees held at the executive residence, described the routine and Washington's appearance.

> *At three o'clock, or at any time within a quarter of an hour afterward, the visitor was conducted to . . . [the] dining room, from which all seats had been removed for the time. On entering, he saw the tall manly figure of Washington clad in black velvet; his hair in full dress, powdered and gathered behind in a large silk bag; yellow gloves on his hands; holding a cocked hat with a cockade in it, and the edges adorned with a black feather about an inch deep. He wore knee and shoe buckles; and a long sword, with finely wrought and polished steel hilt, which appeared at the left hip; the coat worn over the sword, so that the hilt, and the part below the coat behind, were in view.*[33]

Washington's appearance, so described, evokes respect and a sense of dignity appropriate for the president of the new nation. His use of the power of attire to communicate seems to have served him well.

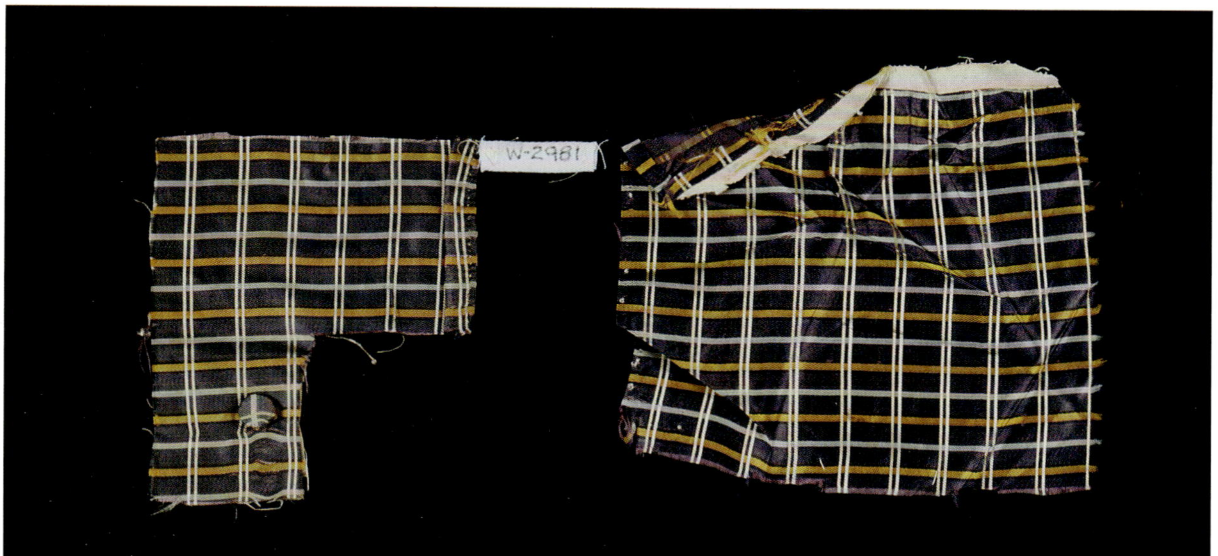

Fig. 9.
Fragments from a purple and yellow plaid silk waistcoat worn by George Washington, later cut so that pieces could be distributed to descendants and admirers, MVLA

From the recollections of Walter Buchanan, Washington's godson, it is clear that for the formal receptions when he functioned as president Washington dressed differently from the way he did when he was at home in the executive residence. Washington's godson recalled the difference when he went to dine at the executive residence one Saturday:

> *The general's coach . . . was sent as usual on a Saturday for me to dine. . . . I found him and lady in the back dining room, and after a little he disappeared, shortly thereafter making his appearance in full dress, black silk-velvet chapeau, and elegant steel-hilted dress sword. A servant soon approached him and the general followed him to the stoop . . . before which were congregated a number of gentlemen to whom Washington . . . addressed a few words. . . . The company then came into the house, and were served with cakes and wine. On their departure the general again retired and came down to dinner in his usual costume of pepper-and-salt colored clothes.*[34]

As president, Washington performed his duty to uphold the office he held by dignifying it with elegant attire. When at ease around family, however, he returned to a simple manner of dress.

In summary, Washington's clothing reflected a moderately conservative outlook. He preferred good-quality, well-made items that were stylish yet understated and well suited to the different stations of planter, commander, and statesman. He kept pace with fashion but was not enslaved by its dictates. Washington's perspective on changing styles is reflected in his advice to his nephews. To George Steptoe Washington he counseled, "a conformity to the prevailing fashion in a certain degree is necessary; but it does not from thence follow that a man should always get a new Coat, or other clothes, upon every trifling change in the mode, when perhaps he has two or three very good ones by him. A person who is anxious to be a leader of the fashion, or one of the first to follow it will certainly appear in the eyes of the judicious men, to have nothing better than a frequent change of dress to recommend him to notice."[35] To Bushrod Washington, the future heir to Mount Vernon, Washington advised, "Do not conceive that fine Clothes make fine Men, any more than fine feathers make fine Birds. A plain genteel dress is more admired and obtains more credit than lace and embroidery in the Eyes of the judicious and sensible."[36] It was in commenting on his wife's preferences in clothes, however, that Washington probably summarized best his own perspective: "her wishes coincide with my own as to simplicity of dress and everything which can tend to support propriety of character without partaking of the follies of luxury and ostentation."[37]

CAT. 70

Small Sword

London, England, ca. 1767–1768[38]
Silver and steel, L. 41"
Gift of John Pierpont Morgan, Sr., 1909
W-84

The small sword, a popular form of weaponry, was considered part of an eighteenth-century gentleman's formal attire, being worn for dress and ceremonial occasions.[39] George Washington was eager to obtain one in September 1757, and he complained to his London factor that the fulfillment of his request for a "Small Sword of 8 or 10 Guin[ea]s price" was a year overdue. Two months later, probably before Washington's letter reached London, he received "a fine strong silver pierced Boat Shell two edg'd Sword Silver & gold gripe" accompanied by "Green Silk Hussar" and "red Morocco" belts and buckles.[40]

This sword is similar in style and type to that Washington received in 1757 and likely was used as Washington's best sword when purchased ten years later. Made in London, it was fashioned by two craftsmen; the cutler (or blade maker) who wrought the steel blade, and the silversmith who worked the hilt (or handle). The blade is a three-sided form known as the colichemarde type and is etched with elaborate scrollwork decoration at its base. The hilt is formed of a grip wrapped with silver wire and ornamented by an oval shell guard, quillons, knuckle guard, and pommel of cast, pierced, and faceted silver that were originally gilded (detail). The two colors of gold employed in the silversmith's work are in keeping with the eighteenth-century fashion for men's "jewel-like accessories for civilian attire."[41]

Charles Willson Peale included the sword in his 1772 portrait of Washington when he depicted the retired Virginia colonel in military uniform. Washington may also have worn this elegant accessory when he resigned his commission as commander in chief in Annapolis in 1783 and six years later when he was inaugurated the first president of the United States. It is one of "7 Swords & 1 blade" listed in his study at the time of Washington's death in 1799,[42] and one of five he bequeathed to his nephews. In his will, Washington provided that each nephew should select a sword but noted, "These Swords are accompanied with an injunction not to unsheathe them for the purpose of shedding blood, except it be for self defence, or in defence of their Country and its rights; and in the latter case, to keep them unsheathed, and prefer falling with them in their hands, to the relinquishment thereof."[43] George Lewis selected this dress sword as a remembrance of his uncle, and it remained with his descendants until its purchase and donation to Mount Vernon in 1909.

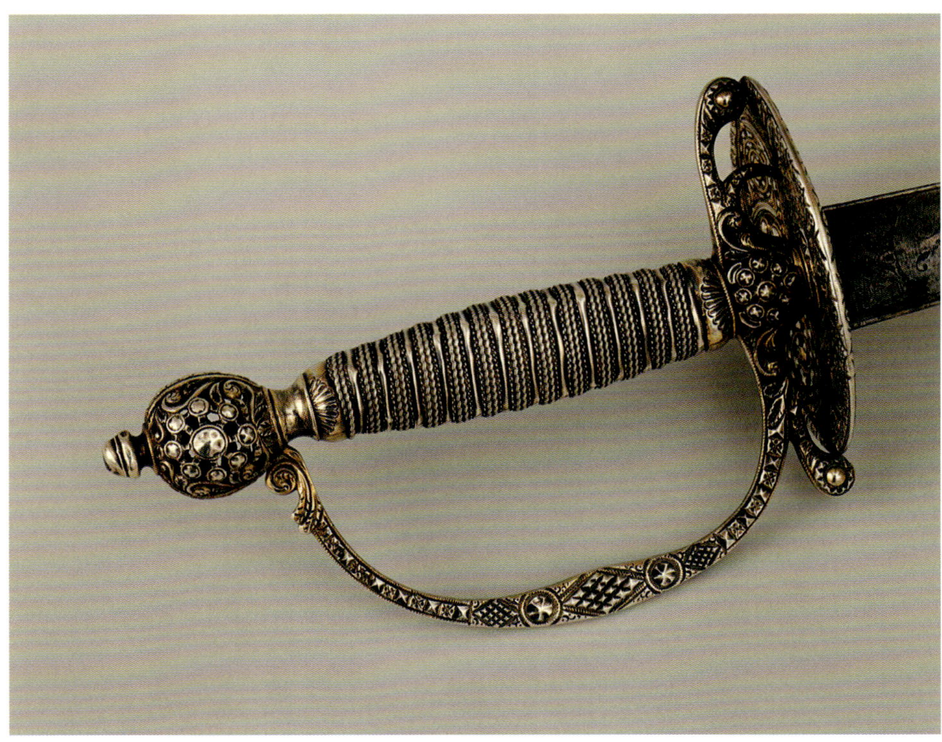

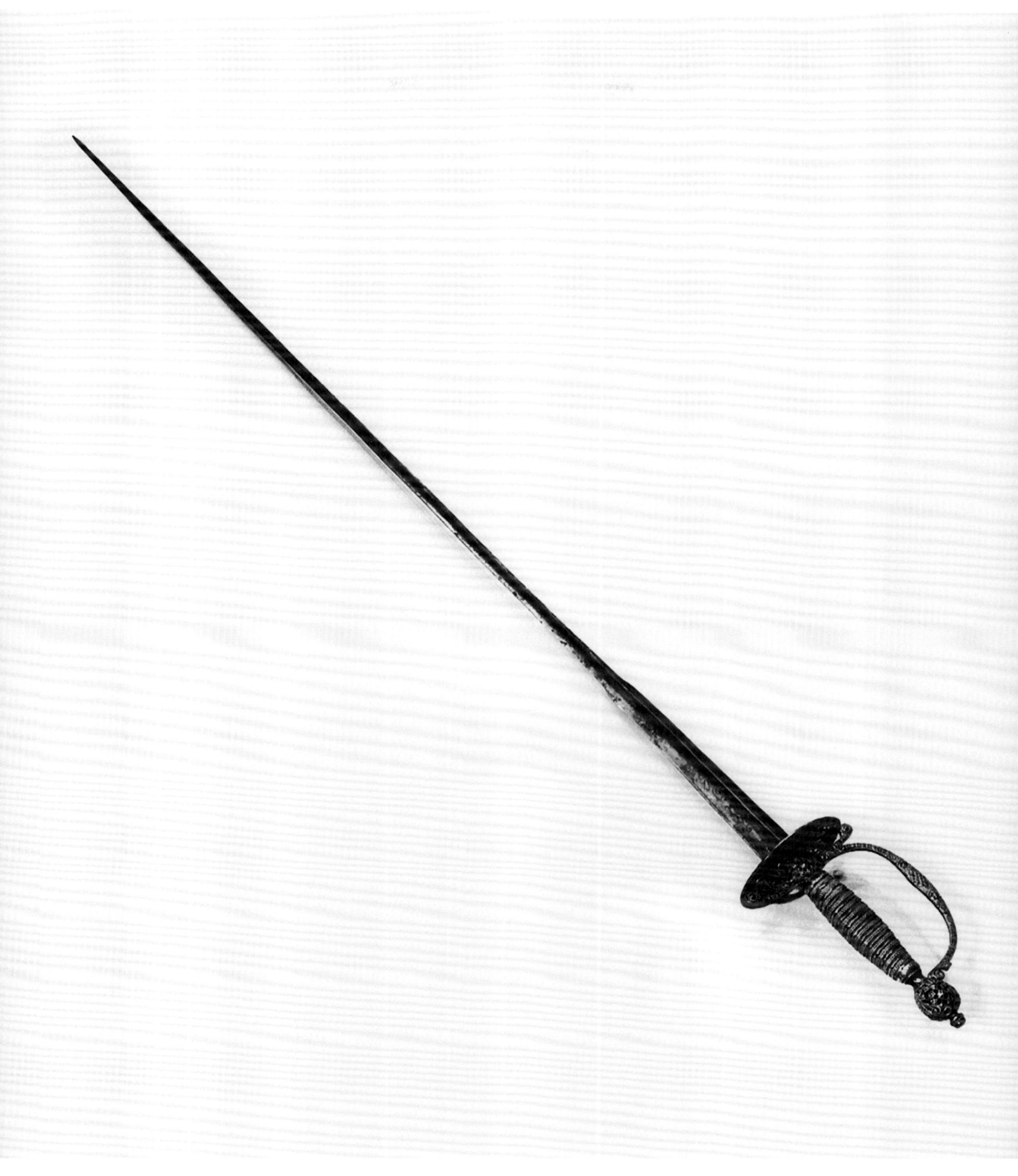

CAT. 71

Knee and Shoe Buckles

England or America, ca. 1760–1790
Colorless topaz, gilded silver, and steel:[44] Knee Buckle: H. 1⅝", W. 1½", D.¼";
Shoe Buckle: H. 2⅞", W. 3", D. ⅞"
Gift of Mrs. M. L. Shaffer and Mr. Charles C. Krumbhaar, Jr., 1955
W-617/A&B

In 1753 one observer of eighteenth-century gentleman's fashions opined, "His buckles, like diamonds, must glitter and shine. Should they cost fifty pounds they would not be too fine."[45] Shoe and knee buckles were an important indicator of an eighteenth-century gentleman's taste and social position, whether they were diamonds set in gold, made of paste, gilded, or plain metal.[46] George Washington followed the prevailing fashion and owned many sets of buckles that ranged from silver plate and paste varieties to "A Sett of Filligree Metal gilt Buckles"[47] and "Oval Stone knee Buckles,"[48] which were likely set with real gems.

These oval shoe and knee buckles set with topazes were originally part of a matched set containing one pair for Washington's shoes and one pair for the knee bands of his breeches. The shoe buckle is fitted with twenty-eight of the gemstones, whereas the knee buckle has twenty-two. The gold-foiled settings of the mounts provide a uniform yellow color to the otherwise colorless stones they secure. The steel chapes (or clasps) ensure a snug-fitting shoe and a safe mounting for the precious accessory.

Although he received from London a topaz seal engraved with his coat of arms in 1771,[49] Washington perhaps acquired these shoe and knee buckles locally. The stone was favored during the late eighteenth century, and many American jewelers made and advertised articles of "brazil topazees."[50] Despite their identification by later family members as buckles "frequently worn" by Washington, they were possibly the most valuable pair he owned and were likely reserved for dress occasions.[51] Washington's estate inventory listed in his study "1 Set of Shoe and knee buckles Paste in Gold" with a value of $250; these were likely the "Topaz shoe & knee buckles" Lawrence Lewis purchased for $232 at the private sales following Martha Washington's death.[52] They remained treasured family pieces among the descendants of Lawrence and Eleanor "Nelly" Custis Lewis, recorded in affidavits as each generation bequeathed them to the next. These reminders of the "glitter and shine" worn by George Washington were returned to Mount Vernon in 1893 and given to the Association by a subsequent generation of heirs.

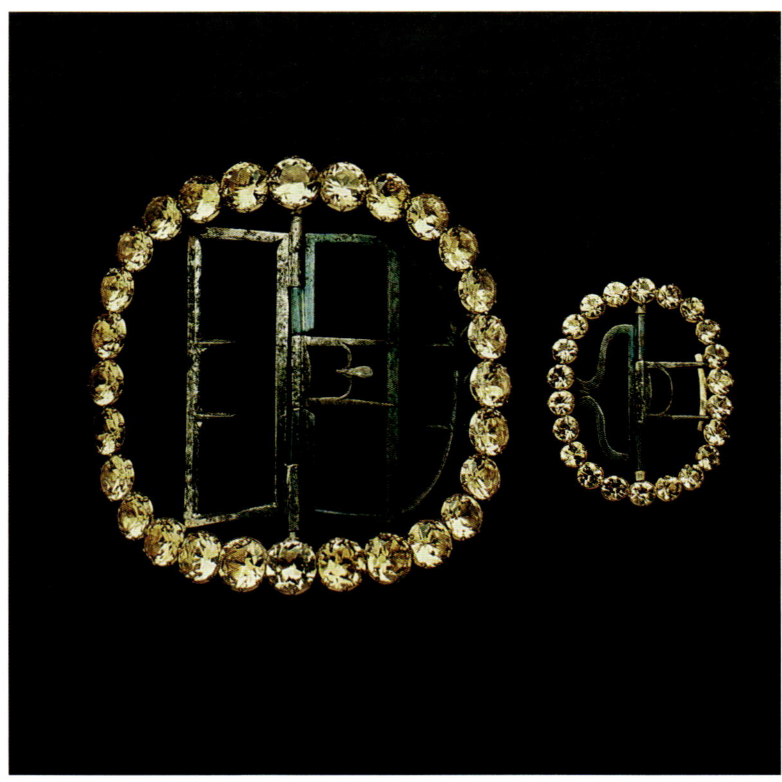

CAT. 72

Shoe Buckles

Probably England or France, ca. 1770–1790
Silver plate, copper, and steel, L. 3⅜", W. 2⅝"
Gift of Mary Mildred Sullivan and George Hammond Sullivan, 1917
W-458/A&B

Throughout his lifetime, George Washington purchased a variety of shoes that ranged from pairs of "Men's neatest shoes and Pumps" for dress occasions to "strong shoes" for everyday wear.[53] The buckles that accented and fastened the shoes also varied in accordance with the type of dress worn. While his paste and topaz buckles adorned Washington's shoes on more formal occasions, his "diam[on]d Cut Steel Buckles" and "Silv[e]r Plated Buckles" were those likely worn on a daily basis.[54]

These silver-plated shoe buckles are examples of the strong and practical yet elegant metal buckles that were worn by Washington and frequently highlighted in his portraits. The curved rectangular frames exhibit clean lines and are defined by a framed, beaded border that includes copper to contrast with the silver-plated background and refer to more expensive buckles set with faceted glass or stones.[55] By the time of Washington's presidency, buckles such as these were widely available in Philadelphia. The goldsmith and jeweler William Dawson advertised a "great variety of plated shoe and knee buckles," and the silversmith Joseph Anthony, Jr., informed the public that he carried "upwards of two hundred different patterns of plated shoe and knee buckles."[56] Washington may have bought his plated shoe buckles from one of these sources or from one of the many shops retailing silver-plated buckles in the urban areas he visited.

These buckles were likely among the "Shoe & knee buckles" purchased by family member Thomas Hammond shortly after Martha Washington's death.[57] They descended in the Hammond family, who carefully engraved "GW" on the sides of the buckles for proper identification before the buckles returned to Mount Vernon.[58]

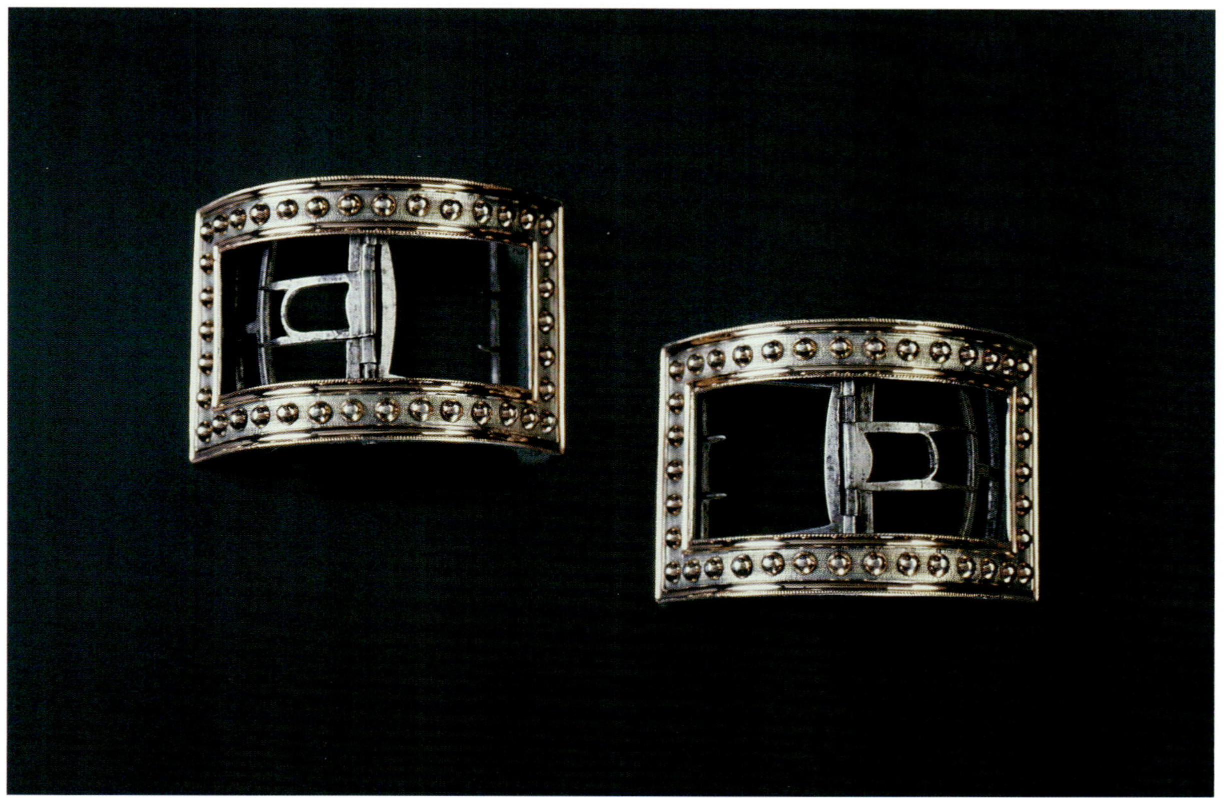

CAT. 73

Hair Bag

England or America, ca. 1760–1790
Silk and linen, L. 9¾", W. 5⅛"
Gift of Mrs. Lyttleton B. P. Gould, Jr., Mr. M. Chapin Krech, Dr. Shepard Krech, Mr. Alvin W. Krech, Mr. Peter Chapin, Mr. Charles Chapin, and Mrs. Charles Merrill Chapin III, in memory of Esther Maria Lewis Chapin, 1986
W-2976

Although many American gentlemen of his stature wore powdered wigs, George Washington did not and preferred to have his own hair powdered and dressed in a tightly braided queue. Once hair was in a queue, it was often wound with black ribbon and, for dress occasions, encased in a square black silk bag usually drawn closed by a tie concealed under a rosette or black bow of matching fabric. This solitaire style was generally associated with the military, and one observer noted Washington's preference for military hairstyle even when not in formal dress. When visiting Mount Vernon in 1785, Robert Hunter, Jr., recorded: "The General is six foot high, perfectly straight and well made. . . . His eyes are full and blue and seem to express an air of gravity. . . . His forehead is a noble one, and he wears his hair turned back, without curls (quite in the officer's style) and tied in a long queue behind."[59]

The wig or hair bag was an important accessory to complete a gentleman's attire, and George Washington's orders and invoices of the 1760s record his requests of "Wig or Hair Bags" and his receipt from London haberdashers of "Silk [or Rich] hair bags" and "Black Silk Wig Bags."[60] Even thirty years later as president, Washington continued his preference for the military fashion, and his secretary noted the purchase of "a dress bag, &c. for the President" in 1792.[61] Portraits record Washington's hair bag (see Cat. 52), as well as the hair powder that sometimes fell on his shoulders and collar. Others write that when attending presidential levees, "his hair was well powdered, with the queue in a black silk bag tied with a solitaire."[62]

Although a common component of eighteenth-century dress, relatively few hair bags survive today, and this rare example is the only one known of the many worn by George Washington. The imported black silk is seamed on three sides and supported by a lining of off-white plain-weave linen stiffening fabric.[63] A black grosgrain ribbon rosette is attached, and a paper label once sewn to the bag reads: "This black silk bag and rosette were General Washington's and the bag was used with the rosette attached [to] contain the General's queue . . . Tudor Place, Georgetown Feb. 5th 1849—Martha Peter." Martha Custis Peter, a granddaughter of Martha Washington, preserved many original Washington objects at her home in Georgetown, Tudor Place. In a demonstration of the way in which precious reminders of the Washingtons passed between descendants, this hair bag returned to Mount Vernon as part of a collection of Washington family artifacts owned by Esther Maria Lewis Chapin, a descendant of granddaughter Eleanor Parke Custis Lewis.

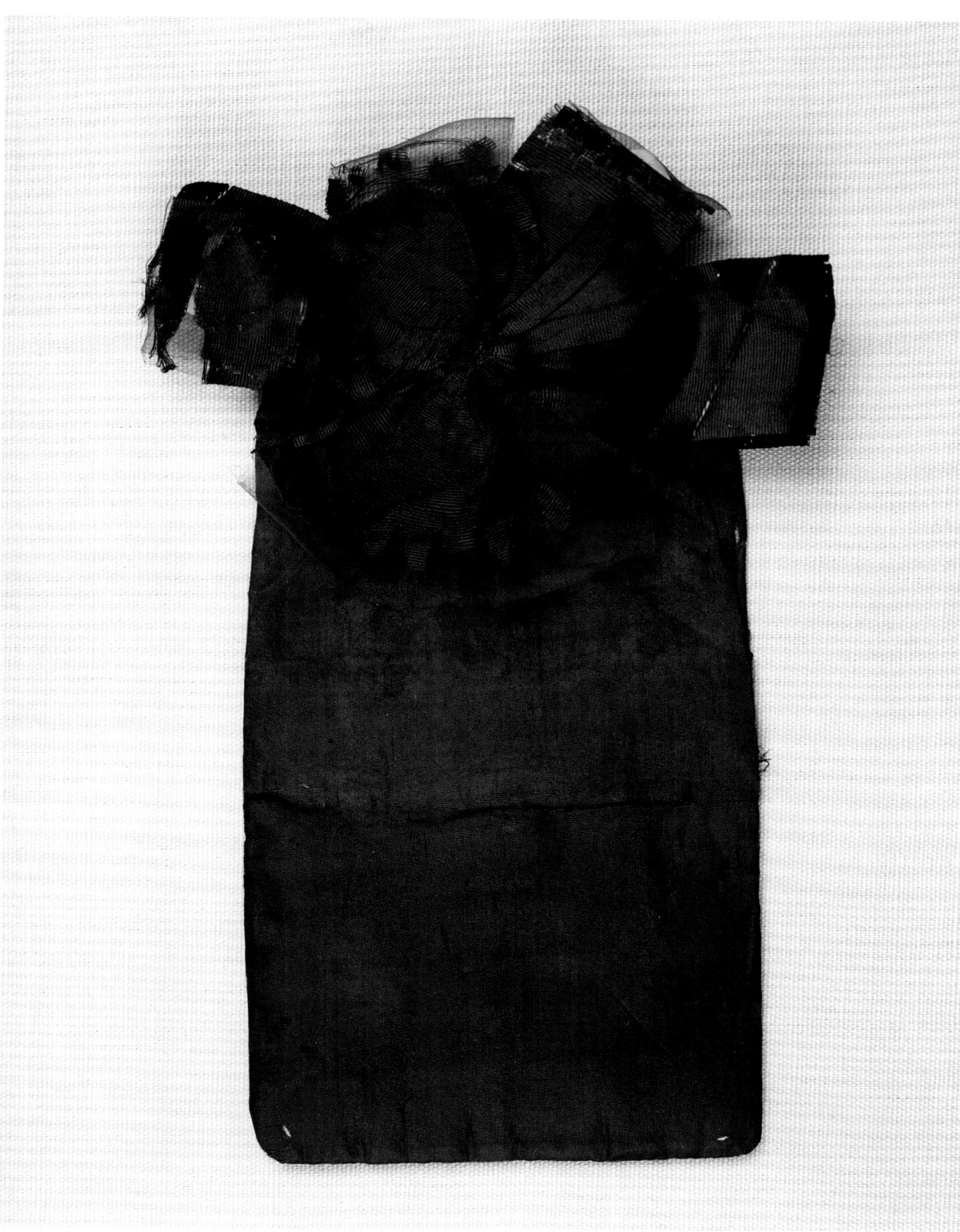

CAT. 74

Waistcoat

Probably England, ca. 1770–1790
Silk, cotton, and linen, L. 27¾", W. 20"
Gift of Miss Harriet V. Dykers, 1914
W-575

Eighteenth-century men's waistcoats varied widely in material and embellishment. Those of silk highlighted with silk embroidery were among the most costly and fashionable available and were typically reserved for dress or formal occasions. This silk embroidered and quilted waistcoat owned by George Washington was likely made in America from an imported English pattern that was subsequently cut, assembled, and lined by a tailor.[64] During his presidency, Washington probably took advantage of the milliners and merchants of New York and Philadelphia who stocked waistcoat patterns ready for embroidery. The presidential household accounts record payment to Jacob Cox "for a vest pattern for the President"[65] and to another person "for lacing the President's Vest."[66]

The cream satin-weave silk waistcoat front is quilted over cotton batting and embroidered in chain stitch with silk threads once shades of green, pink, and lavender (detail). The twelve cream silk-covered buttons are each embroidered with a floral sprig, and the two pocket flaps are also highlighted with embroidery. Similar waistcoat embroidery can be seen in Charles Willson Peale's miniature portrait of George Washington, painted in 1776,[67] and perhaps represents a preference by Washington for the light-colored and embroidered waistcoats fashionable in the latter half of the eighteenth century.[68]

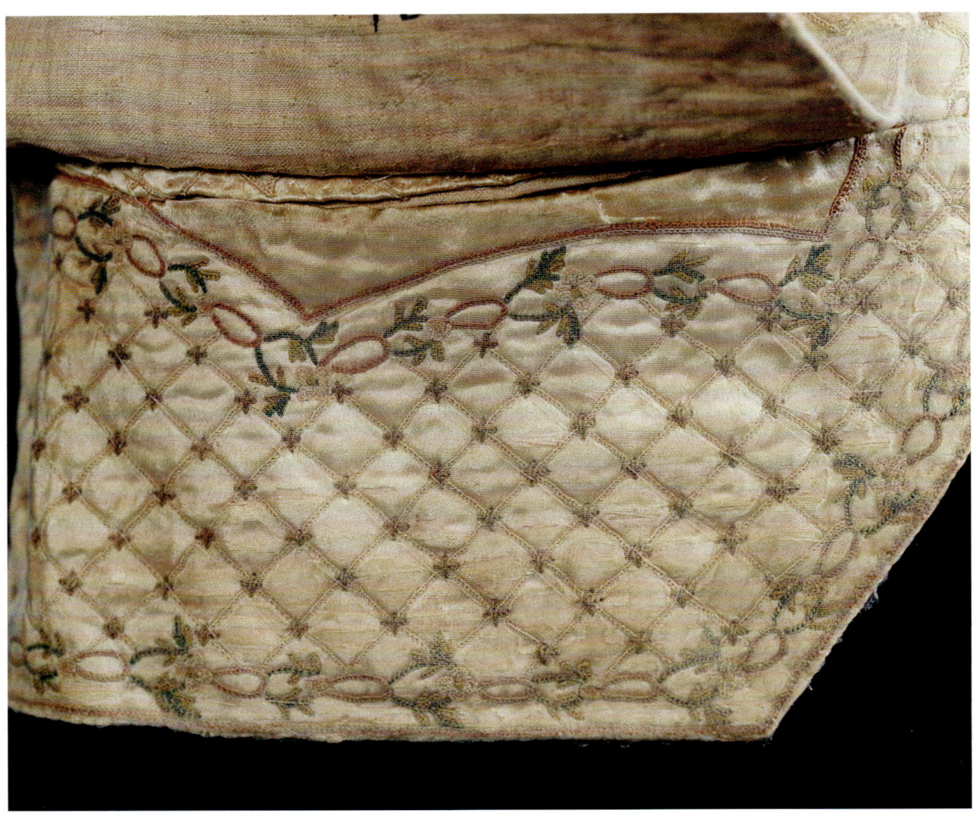

Portion of unfaded green, pink and lavender embroidery, preserved under one of the pocket flaps

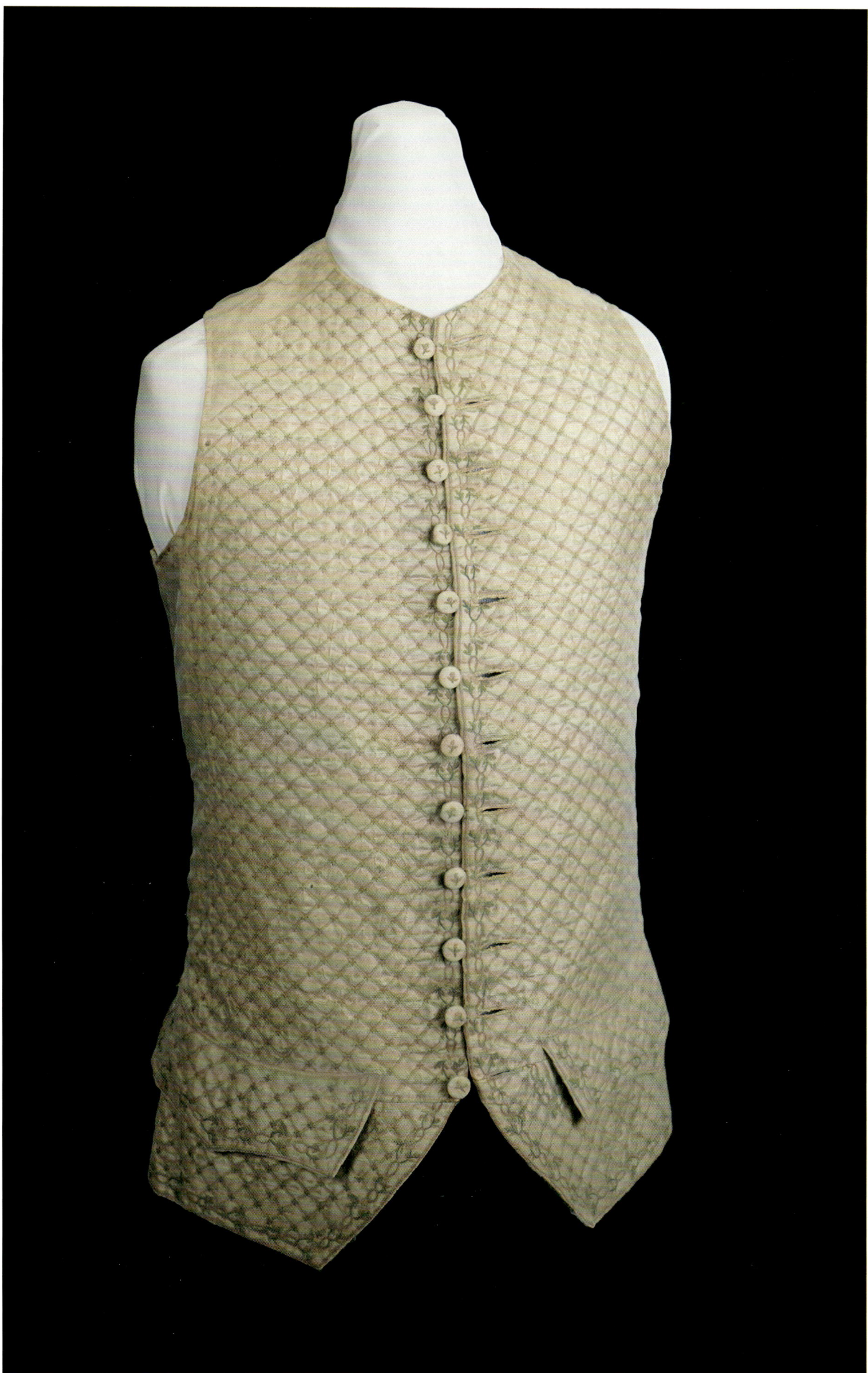

CAT. 75

Buttons

Probably England, ca. 1755–1795
Agate and silver, DIAM. 1¼"
Gift of Mary Walker Lee Bowman and Robert E. Lee IV, 1985
W-2344/A&B

During the second half of the eighteenth century the range of natural materials used for crafting articles of personal adornment expanded.[69] The New York silversmith Myer Myers purchased and resold "Aggat Buttons,"[70] while the Philadelphia goldsmith John Leacock advertised "white and brown chrystal stone buttons"[71] recently imported from London. Often, jewelers, silver- and gold smiths merely stated their importation and sale of "stone" goods, such as when the Philadelphia silversmith Philip Syng advertised his "variety of Stone Sleeve Buttons" and "stone Jacket" buttons all "set in silver."[72] George Washington likely purchased these agate buttons while passing through or residing in one of these urban centers where the articles were readily available. Agate, like amber, coral, and cornelian, was widely used in ancient Rome,[73] and it may have suited the Neoclassical taste for that reason. Washington and his contemporaries enjoyed references that connected the young American republic to its ancient predecessor, and he may have selected the buttons with that association in mind.

The convex surface of the agate is ornamented by a cast silver pin that continues on the reverse side as a stud. Examples in the Mount Vernon collection with a silver pin terminating in a loop suggest that Washington had two varieties of buttons: studs that held his garments and could be easily removed for laundering, and those that were sewn onto coats and sleeves more permanently. Given their materials, these buttons were likely worn on more formal or dress occasions and possibly on one of the black velvet suits Washington wore during the presidency.[74] Following George Washington's death in 1799, his agate buttons joined many others removed from his clothing and preserved by family members and admirers. Some were fashioned into memorial brooches and pendants, which offered an additional application of the classicizing material, while others retained their original appearance.

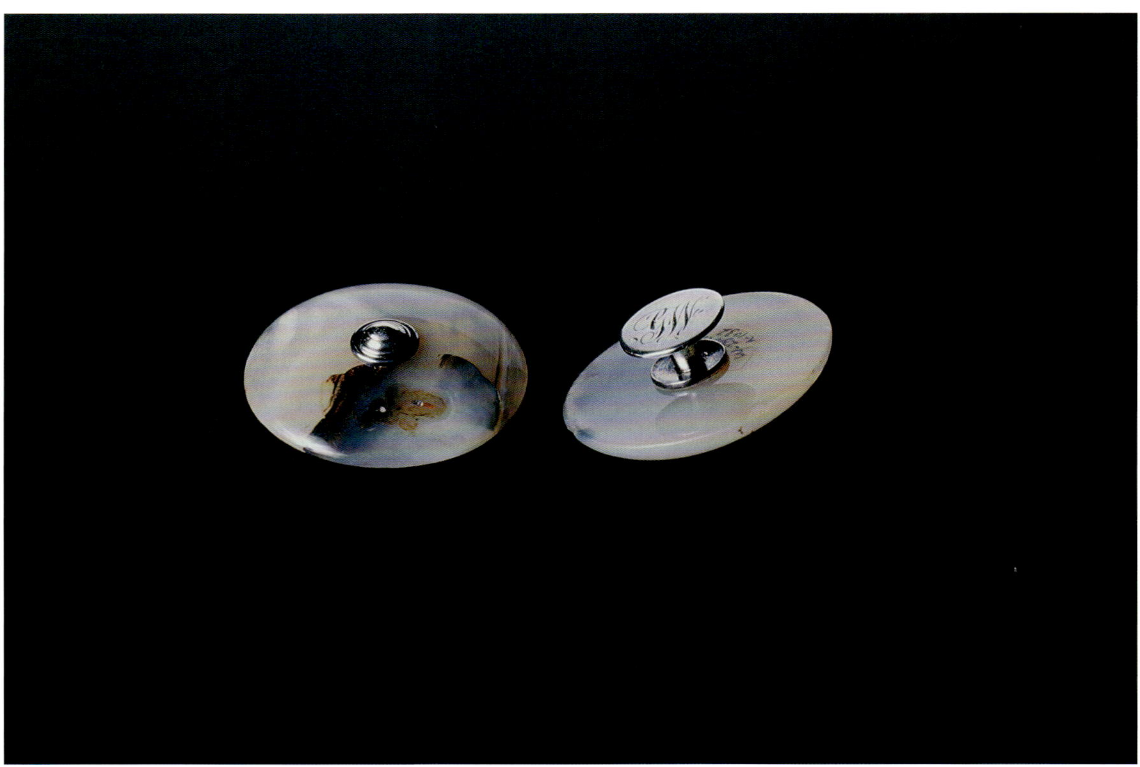

CAT. 76

Buttons

Probably American, ca. 1789–1797
Conch shell, silver, and gold, DIAM. 1¼"
Purchased with funds provided by R. Keith Kane, 1957
W-2080/A&B

By the time of George Washington's presidency, jewelers in New York and Philadelphia were advertising fancy buttons made from seashells.[75] In New York, the silversmith and jeweler James Byrne manufactured "all kinds of Conque shell work, in the most fashionable and elegant manner."[76] The Philadelphia jeweler, gold-, and silversmith Peter Geley advertised that he made and sold "Fancy Buttons of all kinds," including "Conck Shell, Clam Shell, or Mother of Pearl, ornamented with Gold, Silver or Plate."[77] Washington was very much in keeping with the current fashion when he acquired these buttons that combined the American interest in natural and sea materials with the jeweler's addition of gold and silver.

The presidential household account book for October 14, 1789, records payment to Mr. Lunt for "making conk shell buttons for Mrs. Washington,"[78] and it is possible that Lunt also supplied these conch-shell buttons owned and worn by George Washington. The concave front of the circular buttons is polished to a smooth s urface that enhances the light pink color of the shell. A central silver post secures a gold ten-pointed star and continues through to the back of the button, where it forms a loop by which to attach the button to a garment. Some of the additional seventeen examples in the Mount Vernon collection do not include the gold star and offer the possibility that George Washington owned two sets of nearly identical conch-shell buttons that adorned more than one suit of clothing.

In addition to George and Martha Washington, Eleanor "Nelly" Custis demonstrated an interest in the fashion for shell jewelry and buttons. Although she spent most of the presidency living with the Washingtons in New York and Philadelphia, Nelly was in Virginia in January 1796 when Mrs. Washington wrote to inform her, "I have also sent your conkshell clasp and six small buttons that I think you asked me for."[79]

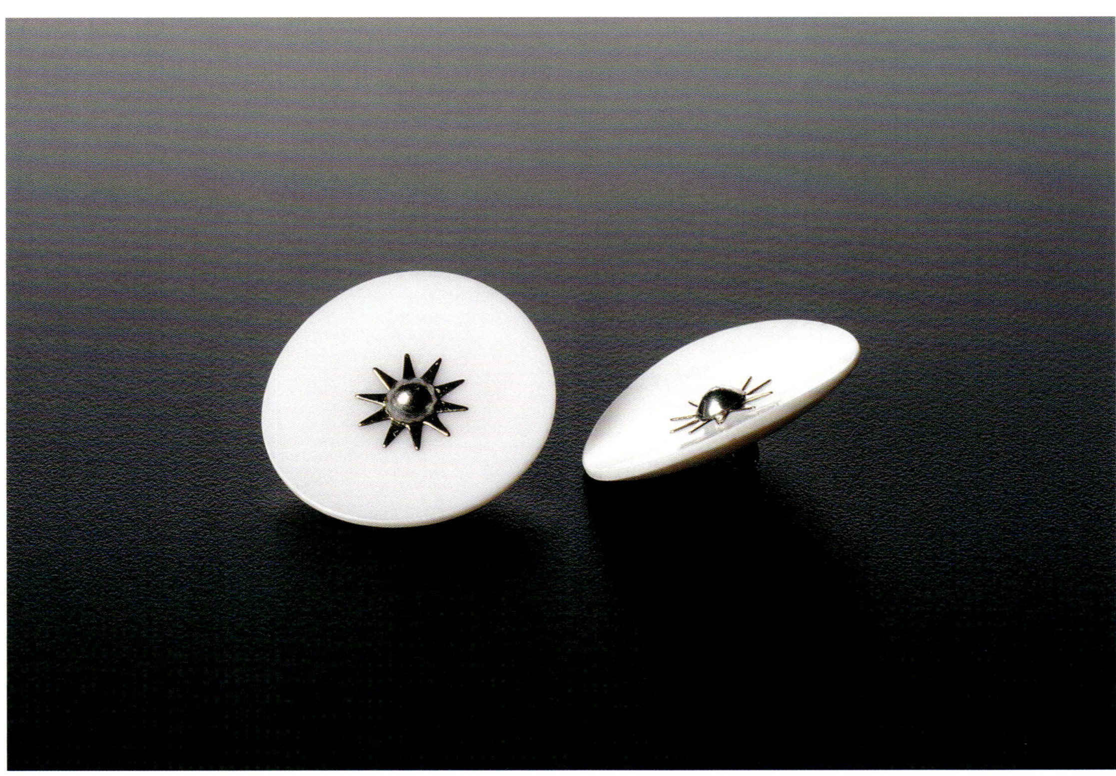

CAT. 77

Banyan

Probably Europe, ca. 1780–1795, possibly remade in the early nineteenth century
Cotton, OL. 5'3"
Purchase, 1962[80]
W-2407/A

Banyans, or loose gowns, offered eighteenth-century gentlemen comfortable and generous-fitting garments for leisure wear. They were made using a variety of imported textiles, from cotton and wool to heavily brocaded silks.[81] This cotton banyan owned by George Washington was perhaps worn by him during the warm Virginia summer months, when lightweight fabrics were preferable. Its red and blue check-printed cotton matched costly imported textiles with a casual garment of loose design.[82] Washington's wardrobe also contained summer-weight cotton waistcoats and breeches as well as "Morrocco Leather Slippers" that may have been worn with the banyan during warm weather or when less formally attired.[83]

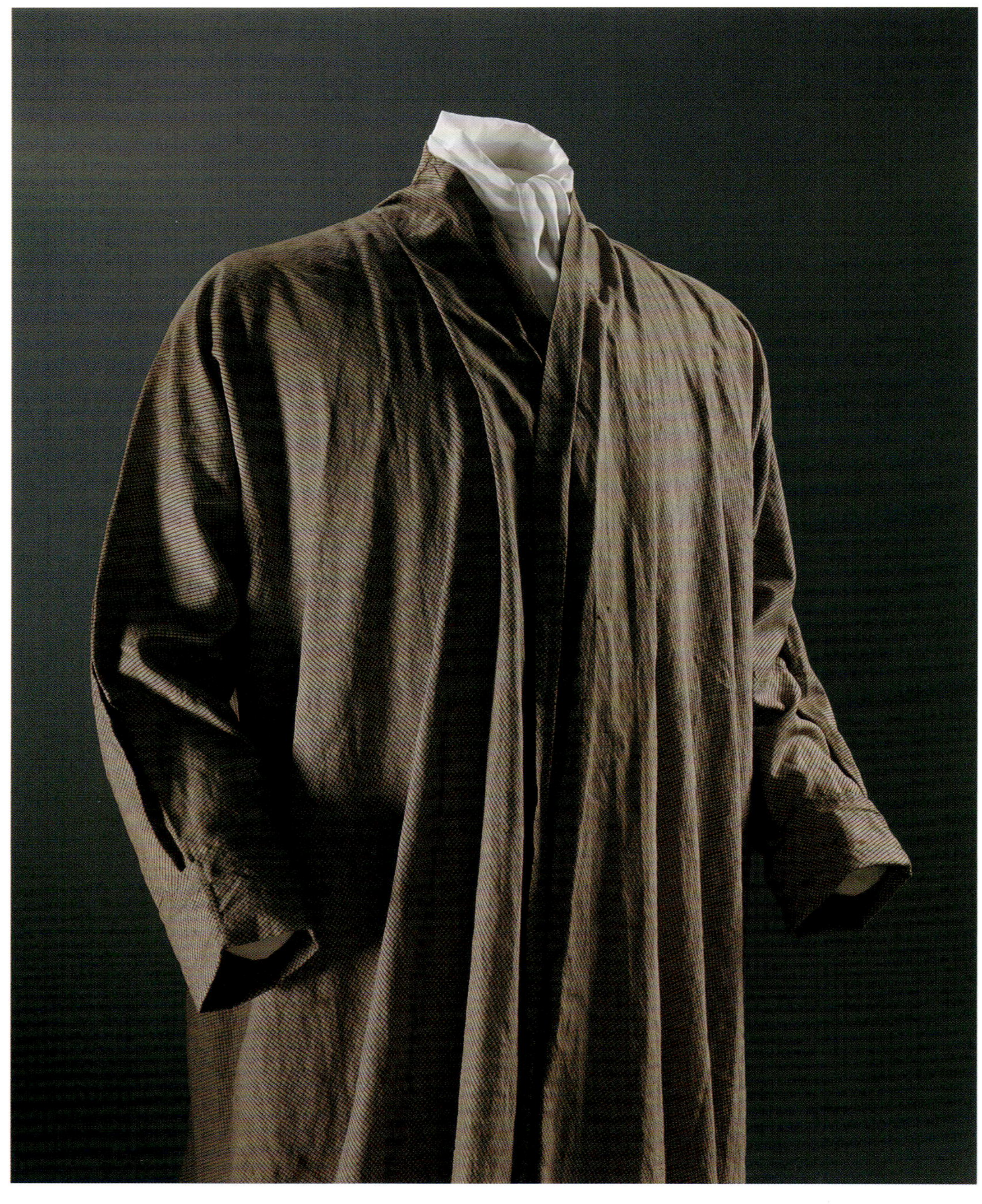

CAT. 78

Waistcoat

England or France, ca. 1785–1795
Silk, wool, and linen, L. 29", W. 19"
Purchase, 1958
W-2149

Eighteenth-century waistcoats brought color to a gentleman's dress and could be mixed with different fabrics and combinations of coat and breeches to create a blend of texture and color.[84] George Washington acknowledged his mixing of materials when he ordered "A Plain Coat for Riding, or Superfine blew broad Cloth" and requested an accompanying waistcoat "either of the same Cloth or otherwise as shall be thought most genteel."[85]

This voided silk velvet waistcoat offered variety to Washington's suits, for its now faded stripes were originally alternating bands of lavender, black, and cream. As president, Washington frequently appeared in black velvet at executive residence levees and for the opening of Congress. Present at the latter, Mrs. Henrietta Liston recorded that Washington "entered in full dress, as He always is on publick occasions, black velvet, sword, &c."[86] With construction and styling appropriate to Washington's presidential years, this velvet waistcoat may have complemented his signature black velvet suit when the circumstances merited a touch of color.[87]

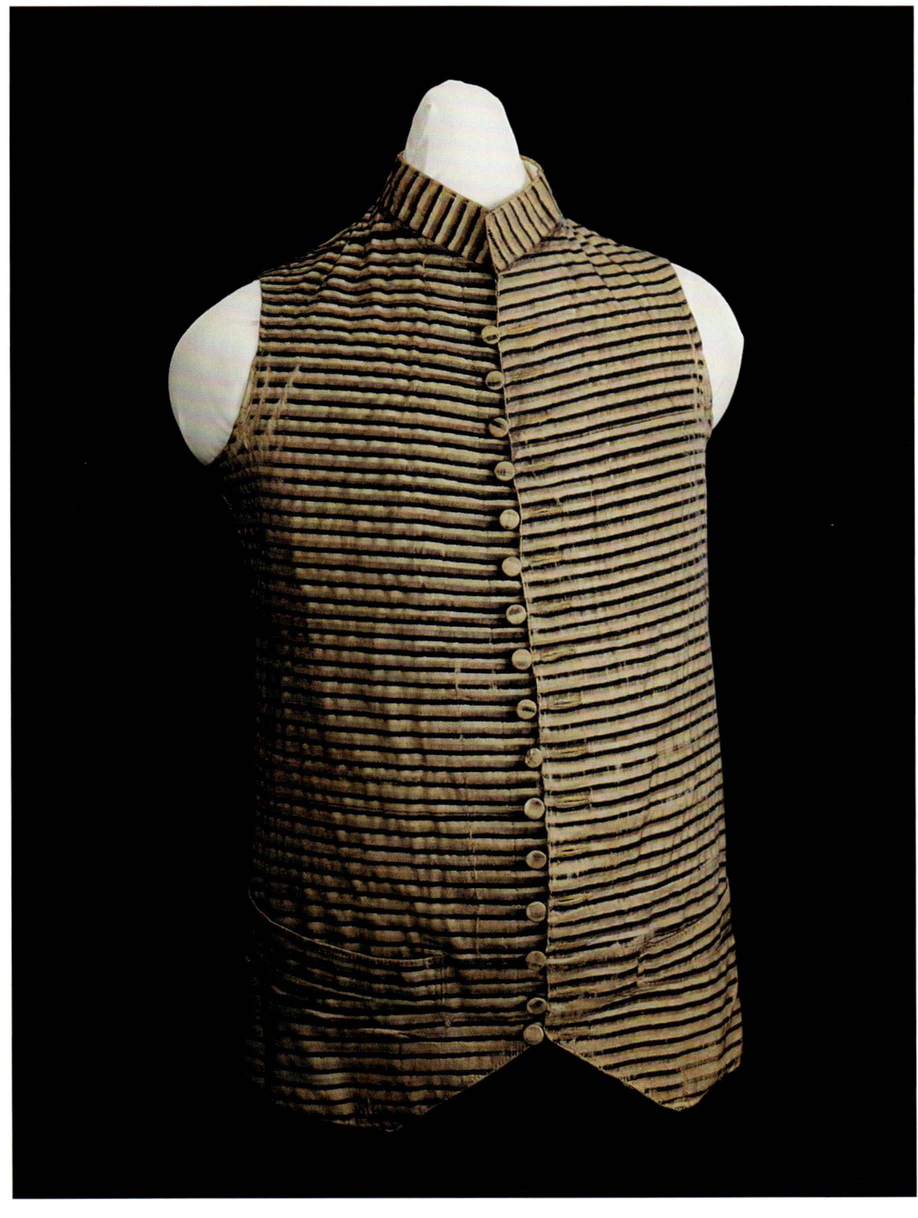

CAT. 79

Coat and Breeches

Possibly Hartford, Connecticut, ca. 1789
Wool, linen, and cotton-linen: Coat, overall back length 48⅛"[88];
Breeches: overall length from top of waistband to bottom of knee band 28"
Gift of John Murray Forbes with appreciation to William D. McGregor, 1877
W-574/ A&B

When George Washington stepped onto the balcony of Federal Hall in New York to be inaugurated as the first president of the United States, he set precedents for the new nation that he knew would be recorded and communicated around the globe. Well aware of the significance his attire would carry, Washington selected a suit of American-made cloth from the Woolen Manufactory at Hartford, Connecticut. His symbolic gesture did not go unnoticed by his constituents, and the *Maryland Journal and Baltimore Advertiser* reported:

> *We hear from New-York, that our beloved and illustrious President was proclaimed in a Suit of Broadcloth manufactured in the State of Connecticut. We hope, from this laudable Example in the first and best of Men, that we shall soon see industry and Economy fashionable in the United States. National Dresses and Manners, as well as Principles, are absolutely necessary to our becoming an independent People.*[89]

Foreign dignitaries present also took notice, including the representative from the Netherlands, Rudolph van Dorsten, who reported to his country that "His Excellency was dressed in plain brown clothes which had been presented to him by the mill at Hartford, Connecticut."[90]

A few months before the inauguration, George Washington had been considering the role American-made textiles should play in the new nation and wrote to the Marquis de Lafayette of his interest in procuring "homespun broad cloth, of the Hartford fabric, to make a suit of cloaths for myself," as he hoped "it will not be a great while, before it will be unfashionable for a gentleman to appear in any other dress. Indeed we have already been too long subject to British prejudices."[91] Congressman Jeremiah Wadsworth of Hartford, Connecticut, responded to Washington's interest by forwarding samples from the Woolen Manufactory, noting that the factory was finishing "a dark Brown" wool that was to be "superior in quallity to any yet made." Wadsworth wrote that he intended to wear a suit of this brown cloth on the opening day of Congress and offered to "preserve enough for one other suit" for Washington, for he hoped "it will be worn by one whose example will be worth more than any other encouragement that can be given to our infant Manufactueres."[92]

The newly manufactured fine brown cloth of which Wadsworth spoke, and perhaps that worn by Washington to his inauguration, reached Mount Vernon in early April 1789. Washington immediately wrote of his appreciation to Daniel Hinsdale, one of the principals of the manufactory:

> *I must beg you to accept of my best thanks for your agency in forwarding the Cloth to me—and likewise make my warmest acknowledgements acceptable to the Directors for this mark of their politeness and attention. I am extremely pleased to find that the useful manufactures are so much attended to in our Country, and with such a prospect of success—The patterns of Cloth which I have seen, and particularly the piece which I have lately received, exceed in fineness and goodness whatever the most sanguine expectation could have looked for at this period—I am fully persuaded that if the spirit of industry economy and patriotism, which seems now beginning to dawn, should exert itself to a proper latitude, that we shall very soon be able to furnish ourselves at least with every necessary and useful fabrick upon better terms than they can be imported without any extraordinary legal assistance.*[93]

Washington likely had the Hartford cloth fashioned into a suit of clothing in Virginia and took it with him to New York as president-elect.

This suit may be the one made of Hartford-manufactured wool worn by George Washington to his first inauguration on April 30, 1789. The partly lined coat and breeches are constructed of brown broadcloth, shrunk and napped in imitation of velvet, in what would have been a dressy daytime suit of clothing. The cut of the double-breasted coat and fall-front breeches is stylistically appropriate for 1789, and the coat retains evidence of metal buttons that could have been the gilt ones worn for the inauguration.[94]

After Washington's presidency and return to Mount Vernon, any association of his first inauguration with a particular suit of clothing appears to have been lost. Following his death, this brown broadcloth suit descended in the family of his niece Jane Washington Thornton.[95] The recent suggestion that the suit is a product of the Hartford Woolen Manufactory offers the possibility that this coat and breeches were those worn by our first president at his inauguration as a symbol of and hope for the development of American manufactures.

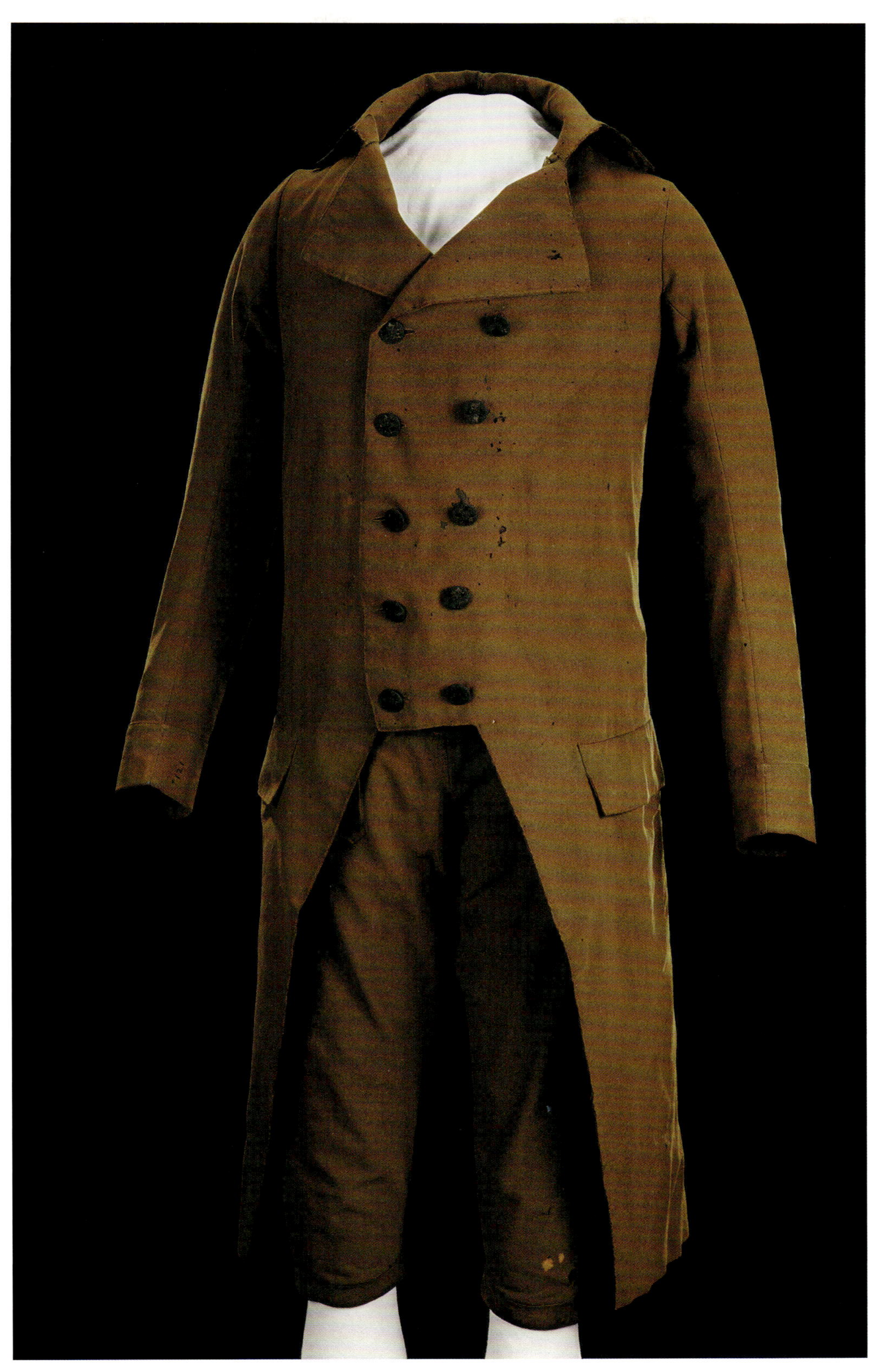

CAT. 80

Pocket Watch

James McCabe (ca. 1748–1811) and James Richards (active ca. 1796–1810)
London, England, 1793–1794
Gold, base metals, and porcelain, ow. 2"
Gift of Harrison Howell Dodge Heiberg, Jr.,
in memory of Harrison Howell Dodge, Mount Vernon Resident Director (1885–1937), 1976
W-446

George Washington was known for his punctuality and purchased several gold watches during his lifetime to assist him with keeping proper time. In 1788 he asked Gouverneur Morris to buy for him a French timepiece. Writing to Morris in Paris, Washington made clear the type of watch that would suit him:

> *I wish to have a gold watch procured for my own use (not a small trifling, nor finically ornamented one) but a watch* well *executed in point of Workmanship; and about the size & kind of that which was procured by Mr Jefferson for Mr Madison (which was large & flat) . . . I am told this species of watches, which I have described, can be found cheaper & better fabricated in Paris than at London . . . I enclose a Bill for Twenty five Guin[ea]s . . . Should the expense be greater (for I wish to have a good watch) I will take care to reimburse it to you. Nothing more is required with the Watch than a* plain handsome *key.*[96]

Morris responded by forwarding to Washington a timepiece made by Lépine, clockmaker to Louis XVI (1754–1793).[97]

Washington subsequently purchased this gold pocket watch during his presidency, perhaps from Ephraim Clark in Philadelphia. George Washington Parke Custis, Martha Washington's grandson who lived with them in the executive residence, identified Clark as Washington's watchmaker when he recalled: "So punctual a man delighted in always having about him a good timekeeper. In Philadelphia, the first president regularly walked up to his watchmaker's (Clarke, in Second street) to compare his watch with the regulator."[98] In 1793 Clark advertised "the best assortment of Gold, Silver, and Metal Watches, Ever offered at one time in this city,"[99] and that array could very well have included this pocket watch.

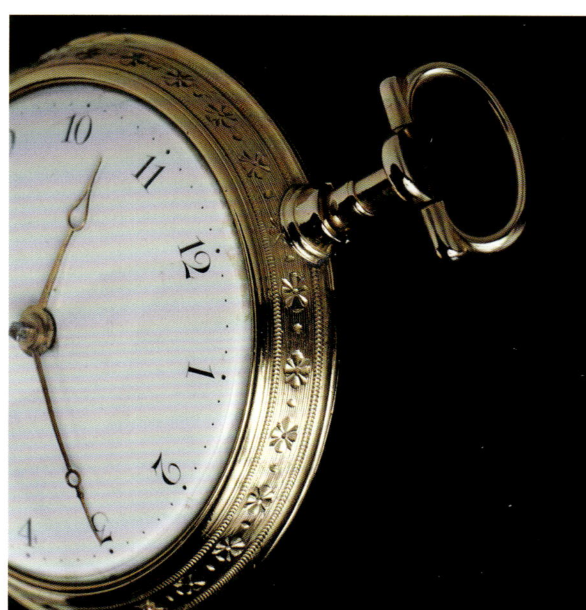

The watch was crafted by the Irish-born watchmaker James McCabe, who immigrated to London and operated a shop at 8 Ironmonger Lane in Cheapside.[100] The back of the watch is engraved "James McCabe No 3030 / London," identifying its maker and serial number. Arabic numerals on the white porcelain face mark the hours for the gold hands, and the only additional decoration is the carefully chased and engraved floral band on the circumference of the outer case (detail). The inner and outer gold cases are impressed with London hallmarks, assay marks, the date letter stamp identifying their crafting in 1793–1794, and the stamp of James Richards, the casemaker. Although they probably did not know they were supplying George Washington, McCabe and Richards crafted what no doubt blended well with Washington's preference for the neat and plain.

After Washington's death, this watch was inherited by Martha Washington's granddaughter Eliza Parke Custis Law, and it passed to her descendants, including Mrs. George R. Goldsborough. Mrs. Goldsborough also served as the Mount Vernon Ladies' Association Vice Regent for Maryland and gave the watch to Mount Vernon's Superintendent (or Resident Director) Harrison H. Dodge as a mark of gratitude for his stewardship of the property. Dodge placed the watch on loan to the Association in 1915 and stipulated in his will that it was to pass to each of his male successors when they reached the age of twenty-one. The chain of Dodge family ownership continued until great-grandson Harrison H. Dodge Heiberg, Jr., presented it to the Association in 1976.

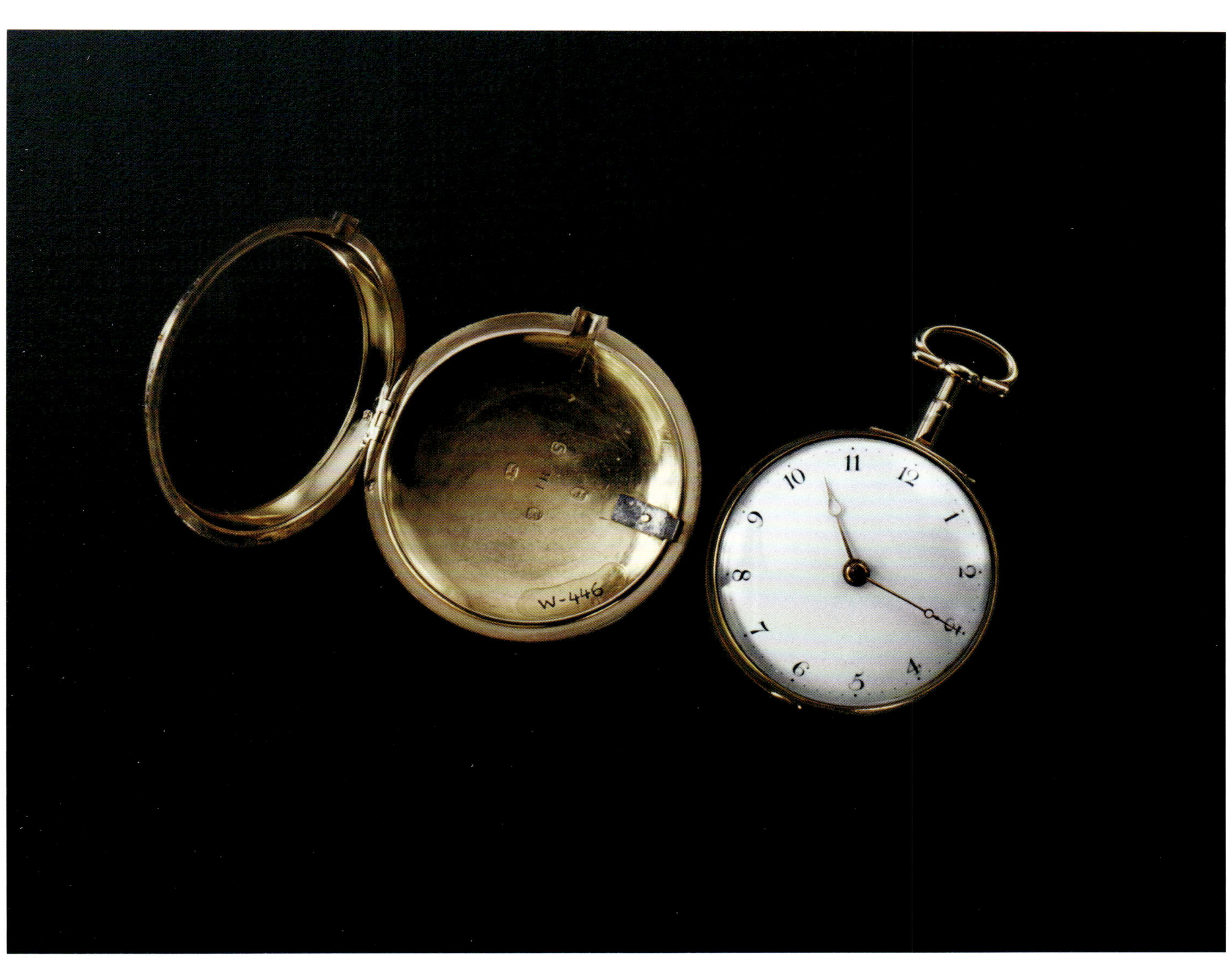
W-446

CAT. 81

Coat

Possibly Hartford, Connecticut, ca. 1790–1799
Wool, linen, and cotton, Overall length 50"
Purchase, 1949
W-1514

Besides the brown wool suit worn for his first inauguration, George Washington acquired several examples of the cloth produced by the Hartford Woolen Manufactory in Connecticut. In October 1789 the president visited the manufactory. He observed that it "seems to be going on with spirit" and recorded in his diary:

> *Their Broadcloths are not of the first quality, as yet, but they are certainly good; as are their Coatings, Cassimeres, Serges and Everlastings; of the first, that is, broad-cloth, I ordered a suit to be sent to me at New York—and of the latter a whole piece, to make breeches for my servants.*[101]

These purchases were not likely Washington's last from Hartford, for he retained an interest in American manufactured textiles that continued during his retirement.

When Joshua Brookes visited Mount Vernon in February 1799, he recalled:

> *About half past two the General returned. [He was] dressed in a blue great coat, large buttons, blue overalls and bespattered boots, a blue coat, coquelico cassimere wais[t]coat, blue small cloathes, [and] cocked hat with a cockade. In conversation he informed us his [clothes] were all of American manufacture.*[102]

Brookes described the former president in a combination of blue and red (coquelicot) clothing that declared his support of American industry to all who came to call upon him. Even on a routine day surveying his lands, Washington dressed in a manner that would have immediately conveyed his sentiments to anyone who saw him.

This blue wool cloth coat could very well be one of Washington's purchases from Hartford and perhaps the one he wore when Joshua Brookes visited Mount Vernon. The quality of the cloth suggests American manufacture, and the double-breasted styling with a high turndown collar dates from the last decade of the eighteenth century. Physical evidence exists for metal shank buttons that once secured the front of the coat as well as the back vents.[103] Martha Washington's granddaughter Eliza Parke Custis Law provided insight into the coat when she attached to it a paper label that reads: "This coat was made of the first American cloth sent to General Washington and much worn by him. My grandmother gave it to me as a relic. . . . The buttons were beg'd from me by many who prized them as relics of the father of our country." Eliza's words not only seem to confirm the American origin of the blue wool cloth, but they also explain why this coat (like so many of Washington's garments) does not survive with the buttons that once adorned it.

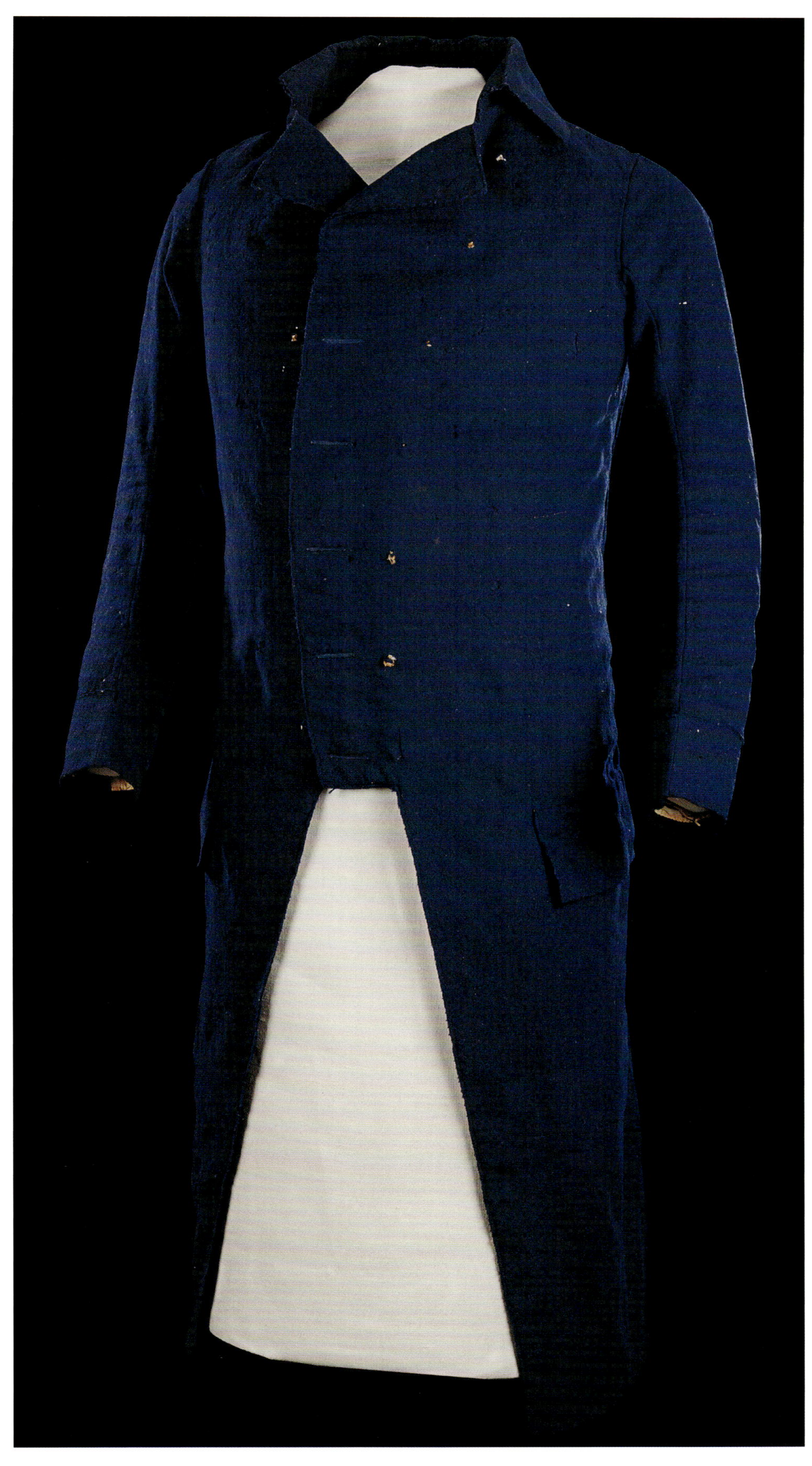

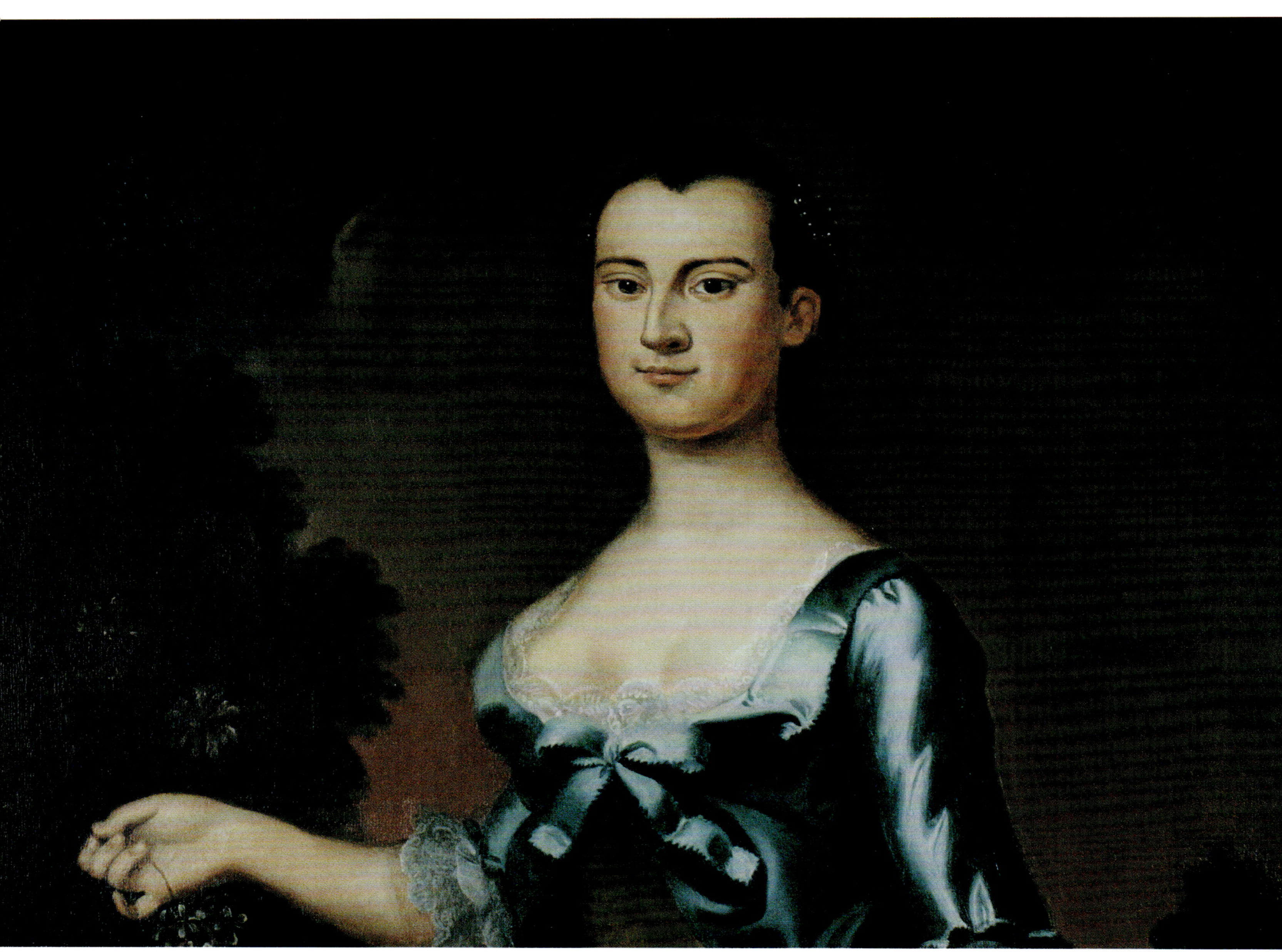

CHAPTER SEVEN

Seed Pearls to Silk Gowns
The Personal Style of Martha Washington

MARTHA WASHINGTON FULFILLED A VARIETY OF ROLES THROUGHOUT HER LIFE: a businesswoman and plantation mistress, wife to a general and a president, a mother and a grandmother. Whether in a social or national role, her appearance conveyed her ability to purchase the latest fashions that were nonetheless without ostentation. The attempt to fully understand her attire, the articles that surrounded her, and the way she conveyed her sentiments through them is somewhat frustrated by the era in which she lived. In an age before photography and a time when her legal and social roles were superseded by those of her husband, images of her from life are scarce, and those that are plentiful are often several generations removed. Except for a brief period when widowed by the death of her first husband, Daniel Parke Custis, her orders for personal articles were incorporated into those placed by George Washington.[1] Surviving personal articles, correspondence, and descriptions of Martha Washington, however, combine to offer the unfolding picture of a young woman mimicking the latest London fashions who became the nation's first First Lady, acutely conscious of how she represented a nation.[2]

In 1757 Martha Dandridge Custis (later Martha Washington) was widowed at the age of twenty-six (fig. 1). In addition to caring for two small children, she was left to manage the vast holdings of her late husband's estate, which involved dealing directly with the London mercantile community. During her husband's lifetime, Martha acquired her clothing and personal effects through orders placed by her husband to his London agent, Robert Cary and Company, and charged against his tobacco profits. In her widowhood she assumed the role of her deceased husband and wrote directly to Cary for those articles she wished to obtain. On August 20, 1757, Martha Custis wrote to Robert Cary, identifying herself and indicating, "I shall yearly ship a considerable part of the Tobacco I make to you which I shall take care to have made as good as possible and hope you will do your endeavor to get me a good Price." Against her tobacco, she noted, "I shall want some Goods this Year for my family which I have inclosed an Invoice of and hope you will take care they are well bot and sent me by your first Ship to this river."[3] Her enclosed request

Fig. 1. (opposite) Martha Dandridge Custis at age twenty-six, shortly before the death of her first husband, Daniel Parke Custis. Oil on canvas by Adrian Lamb (detail), MVLA

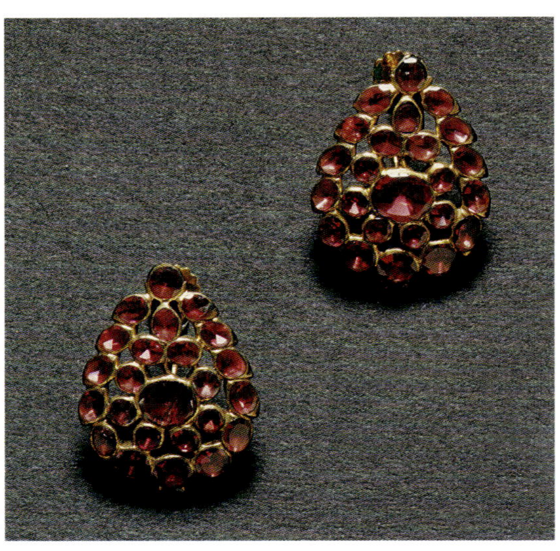

Fig. 2. (left) Garnet earrings worn by Martha Washington, and also perhaps by her daughter, Patsy, MVLA

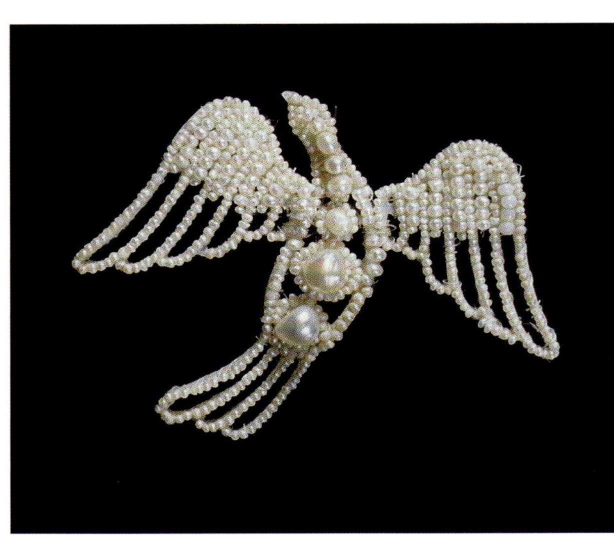

Fig. 3. (right) Martha Washington's seed pearl dove pin, ca. 1790, MVLA

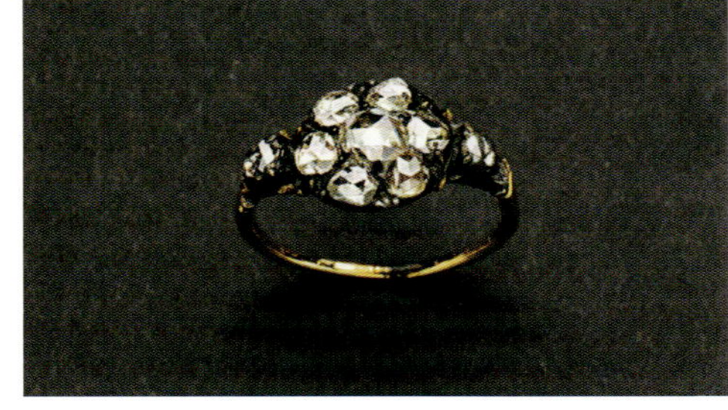

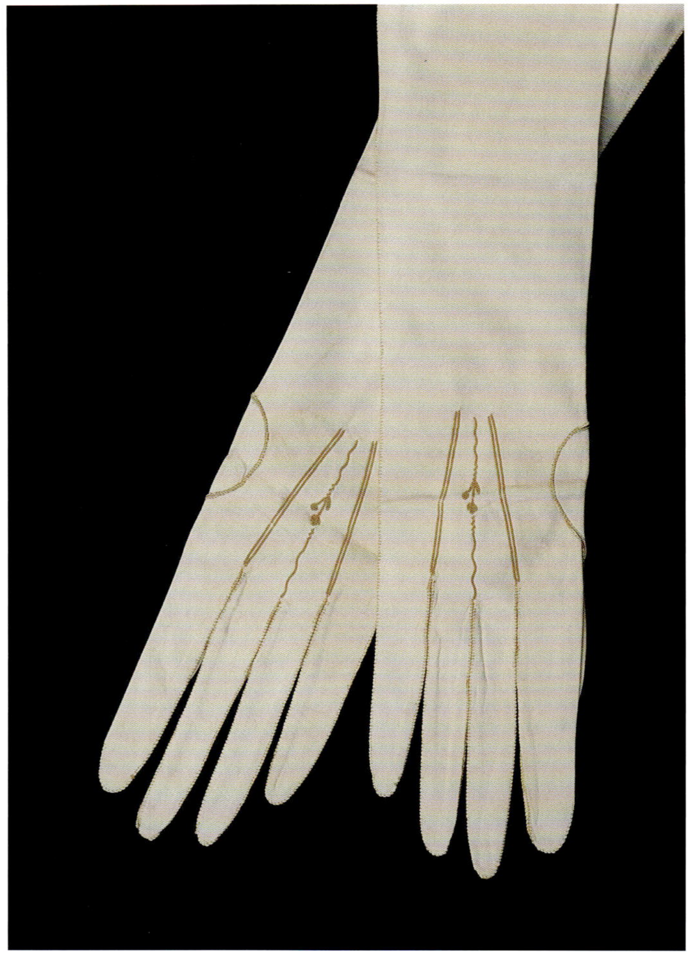

clockwise: Fig. 4. Gold-mounted diamond ring worn by Martha, possibly a gift from her first husband, Daniel Parke Custis, MVLA

Fig. 5. George Washington placed numerous orders to London for his wife's gloves in an array of colors and materials, most frequently for white kid leather like these survivals. MVLA

Fig. 6. Martha Washington's waist buckle, set with fashionable paste (artificial) stones, Courtesy of a private collection

included fashionable English laces, silks, jewelry, and footwear for herself. It is during the brief period of these requests that a portrait of the young Martha emerges.

In 1758 the future Mrs. Washington was direct about the kind and quality of goods she desired. She ordered "one Genteel suite of cloth[e]s for my self to be grave but not Extravagent nor to be in mourning," in addition to a variety of clothing and personal articles with wording that conveyed her preferences. For example, she requested two gowns of "the Best Indien" cloth, "silk hose of the smll 5s fashioned and of the Best silk," "a very handsome p[ai]r of Gold Shoe Buckles," and two "neck Laces" that were to be "very handsome." For her hair, she ordered "2 fine Ivory combes fine tooth[,] 2 large Tortis shell combs fine teeth[,] . . . [and] 2 pounds of fine perfumed powd[e]r for the hair."[4] As perhaps the wealthiest widow in the colony of Virginia, Martha Custis had ample means to support her requests for items that would meet her expectations for that which was "handsome," "fine," and "the Best."

By the time Martha Custis married George Washington in 1759, she already was established with Robert Cary and Company and his London merchant clientele. George Washington now assumed the role of placing orders for those articles of clothing the new Mrs. Washington wanted. His requests to London in their first years of marriage resulted in the shipment of dozens of yards of dress fabric, yards of ribbon, and pairs of shoes, in addition to a substantial number of fans, bonnets, and gloves. Paste and garnet buckles fastened her clothing and shoes; yards of lace trimmed her gowns; garnet, "gold wier" and "Silver Earings with Bobs" hung from her ears (figs. 2, 5, 6).[5]

In February 1764 George Washington suggested to Robert Cary that "Mrs. Washington would take it as a favor if you would direct Mr. Shelley to send her a pair of French bead earrings and necklace."[6]

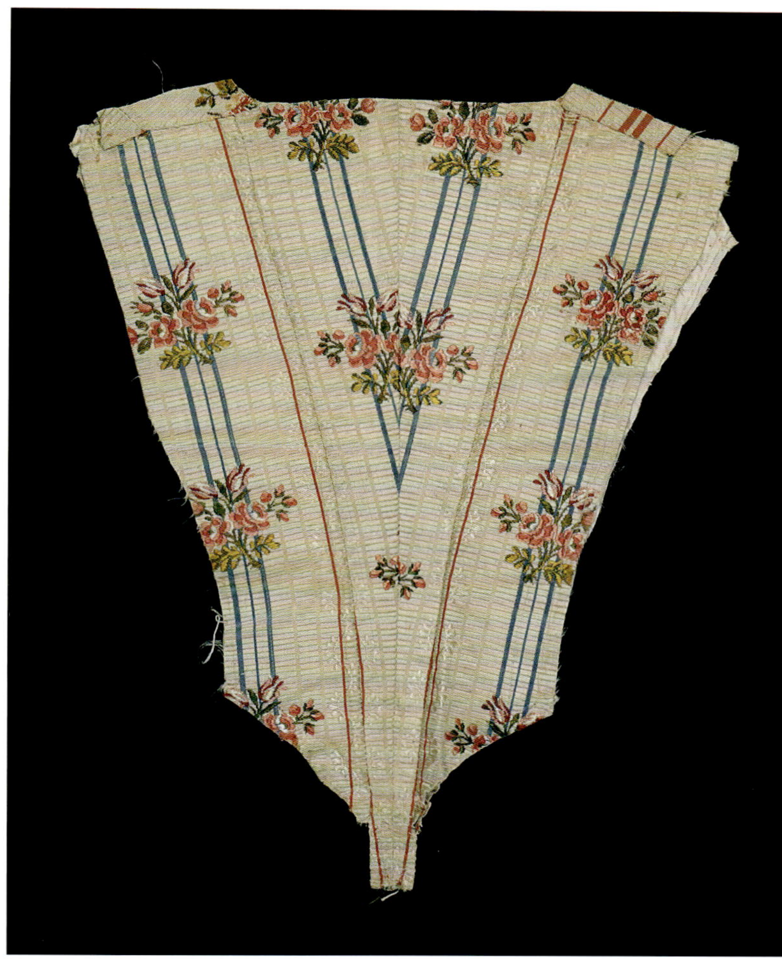

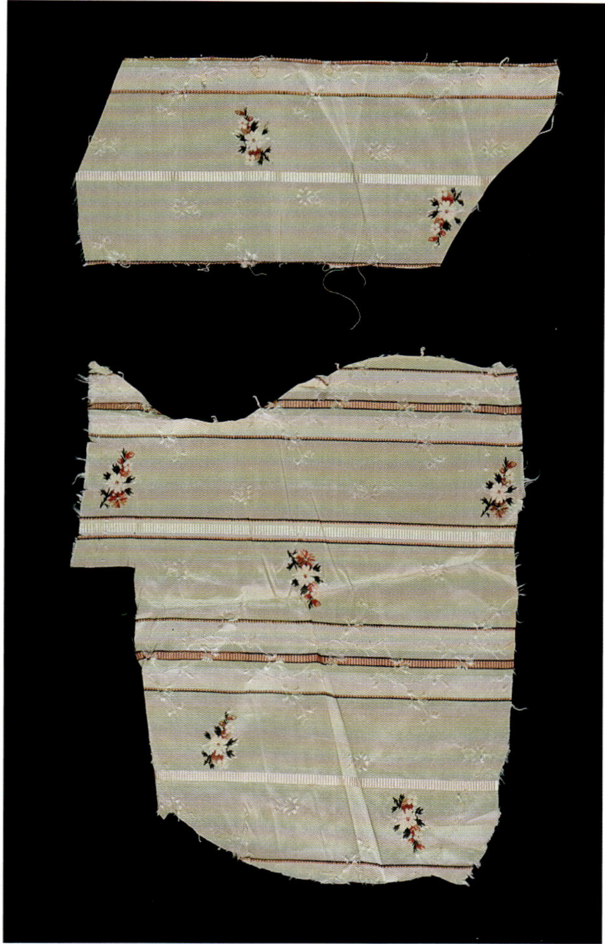

Fig. 7. (above left) Piece of a bodice from one of Martha Washington's gowns of imported silk, MVLA

Fig. 8. (above right) Woven silk fragments, probably English, from one of Martha Washington's gowns cut and distributed to her descendants, MVLA

Martha Washington already had examples of the glass beads that simulated pearls, for Cary and Company had shipped from London "2 four Row[e]d french Neck[lace]s" in 1762, and a pair of "french" earrings in 1760.[7] Perhaps a result of newly received word of the latest fashion, Mrs. Washington intervened after the order had been placed, and in August 1764 she wrote directly to the London milliner filling it: "Mr Washington wrote Mr Cary in February last to purchase of you a french necklace & earrings for me—if they are not already sent, I would rather choose a blew Turkey stone Necklace and Earrings sent in their place." In the same letter she added a request to the milliner regarding her young daughter, which revealed her continuing interest in fashion as well as practicality: "I have directed all the goods for Miss Custis's use to be got from you as I approvd of your last years choice . . . but if you can get those which may be more genteel and proper for her, I shall have no objections to it, provided it is done with frugality, for as she is only nine years old a superflutity, or expence in dress would be altogether unnecessary."[8] Her letter met with success: the jewelry order was changed, and "A Turkey Stone col[ore]d necklace and earrings" were sent the following February.[9]

As Martha Washington moved from widowhood to mistress of Mount Vernon, she acquired precisely the clothing and personal articles she wished, many of which represented some of the finest London goods available. When she took part in social engagements throughout Virginia and Maryland and accompanied George Washington to assemblies and balls, her attire conveyed wealth, refinement, and elegance. Her clothing and accompanying adornments did not, however, exhibit "the follies of luxury and ostentation."[10]

The orders to Robert Cary & Company and the shipments from London milliners and jewelers slowed to a halt when the Washingtons objected to unmerited taxation and adhered to nonimportation agreements. With Washington's election as commander in chief of the Continental Army, Martha Washington focused on providing clothing for the troops, assisting her husband where possible, and traveling to be with him at each winter encampment.[11] Near the end of the war, she lost her one remaining child, John Parke Custis, to camp fever at Yorktown and found herself again in mourning attire.

After the war, trade resumed, yet Martha Washington's purchases of English and European luxury goods were not quite on the level of her prewar consumption patterns. She was in her fifties and a grandmother, yet maintained an elegant appearance appropriate for a woman of her standing. When Olney Winsor dined with the Washingtons at Mount Vernon in March 1788, he noted, "Mrs. Washington is an elegant figure for a person of her years. . . . She was dressed in a plain black Sattin gown, with long Sleves, figured Lawn Apron & Hankdf, guaze French night Cap with black bowes—all very neat—but not gaudy."[12] Mr. Winsor's "neat" is telling in its contrast to "gaudy," for it shows that Martha Washington's attire was consonant with the neat and plain style, devoid of ostentation, preferred by her husband. Furthermore, her guest seems to have found her appearance to be in keeping with what one would expect of the wife of a victorious general.

With George Washington's election as the nation's first president, Martha Washington became the nation's first First Lady. She understood her position as a national figure and the meaning that would be conveyed by her personal appearance. Like her husband, she sought to remain true to the social and political principles of the new nation and to refrain from any appearance of court culture. She joined him in promoting American manufactures by wearing a riding dress of "fine Hartford brown Cloth."[13] From the goods readily available in the shops of New York and Philadelphia, she selected those appropriate for a president's wife that affirmed her regard for neat and plain items of high quality.

Shortly after joining her husband in New York in June 1789, Martha Washington sent to her niece Fanny at Mount Vernon, "two pair of shoes of a new fashioned kind those with Low Heels." In the accompanying note, Martha reported: "My Hair is set and dressed every day—and I have put on white muslin Habits for the summer—you would I fear think me a good deal in the fashion if you could but see me."[14] Less than three weeks later, Abigail Adams, wife of Vice President John Adams, wrote to her sister, "I took the earliest opportunity . . . to pay my respects to Mrs. Washington. . . . She received me with great ease & politeness. She is plain in her dress, but that plainness is the best of every article. . . . Her manners are modest and unassuming, dignified and feminine."[15] Mrs. Adams was pleased with the example Martha Washington was setting in appearance as well as countenance and found herself "much more deeply impressed than I ever did before their Majesties of Britain."[16]

On the occasion of a ball in honor of the president's birthday, Charlotte Chambers, too, approved of the example set by Mrs. Washington's attire:

> *She was dressed in a rich silk, but entirely without ornament, except the animation her amiable heart gives to her countenance. Next her were seated the wives of the foreign ambassadors, glittering from the floor to the summit of their headdress. One of the ladies wore three large ostrich-feathers. Her brow was encircled by a sparkling fillet of diamonds; her neck and arms were almost covered with jewels, and two watches were suspended from her girdle, and all reflecting the light from a hundred directions. Such superabundance of ornament struck me as injudicious. . . . However, it may not be in conformity to their individual taste thus decorating themselves, but to honor the country they represent.*[17]

Mrs. Chambers was likely not alone in her comparison of Martha Washington's attire to those of the foreign ambassadors' wives, and she was probably accurate in thinking that the women representing nations

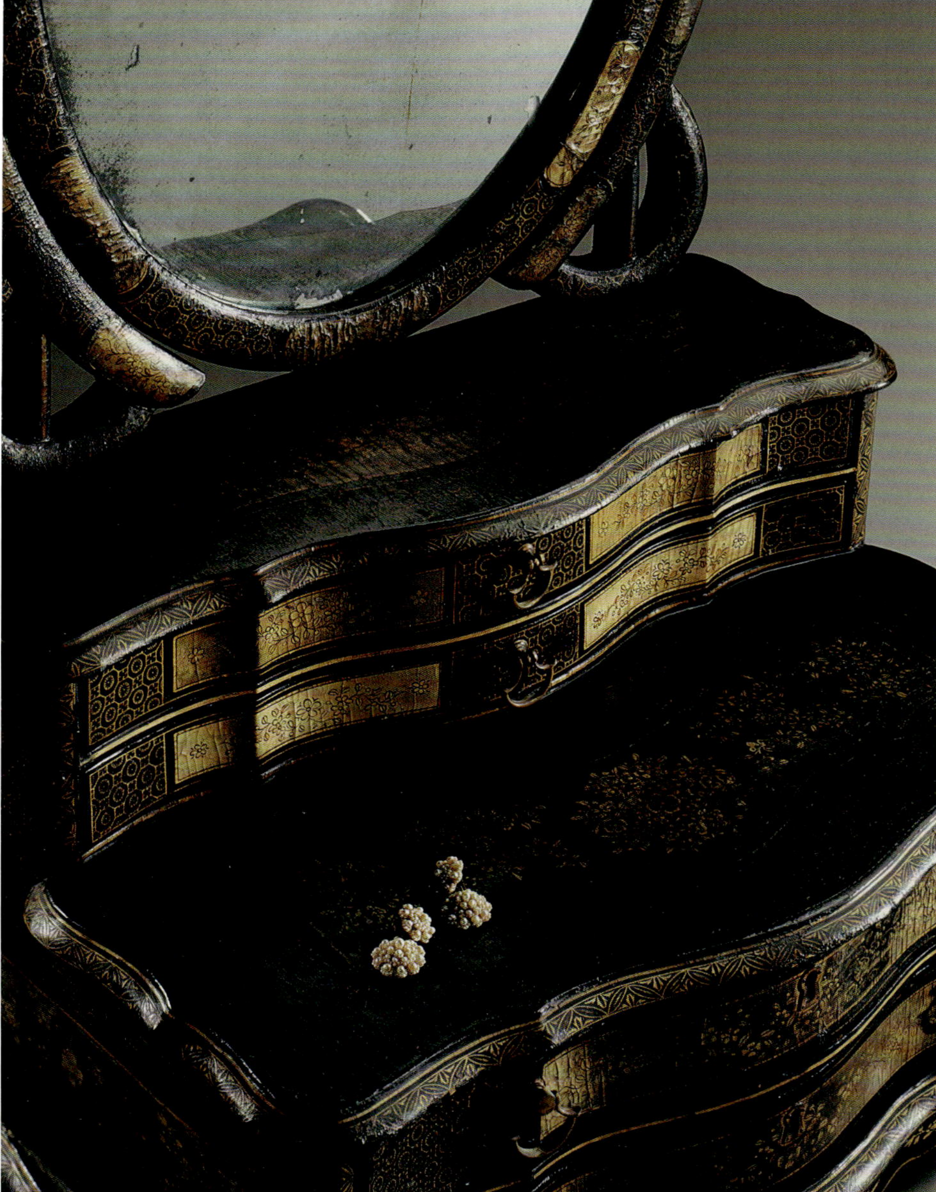

Fig. 9.
A pair of Martha Washington's seed pearl earrings on her Chinese lacquered dressing glass, MVLA

that evening wished to do so in a manner they felt did their country honor. For America's First Lady, that attire was plain, but "the best of every article."

The close of the presidential years offered Martha Washington relief from the national spotlight and a return to Mount Vernon. The many visitors that called on the Washingtons in retirement commented on Mrs. Washington's appearance. For example, Julian Niemcewicz of Poland recalled, "She had on a gown, with an even hem, of stiff white cotton. . . . A bonnet of white gauze, ribbons of the same color, encircling her head tightly, leaving the forehead completely uncovered and hiding only half of her white hair which in back was done up in a little pigtail."[18] The white, lightweight materials she wore on Niemcewicz's visit combined a Neoclassical aesthetic with summer-weight garments that presumably were most welcome in late May.

When Joshua Brookes visited for dinner the following February, he noted that Mrs. Washington was "dressed in a Mazareen blue satin gown with three belts over her handkerchief across the body."[19] The gown Brookes described was fitted with buttoned flaps that secured a fichu draped around her shoulders and was possibly the one she wore three years earlier when James Sharples rendered a pastel portrait

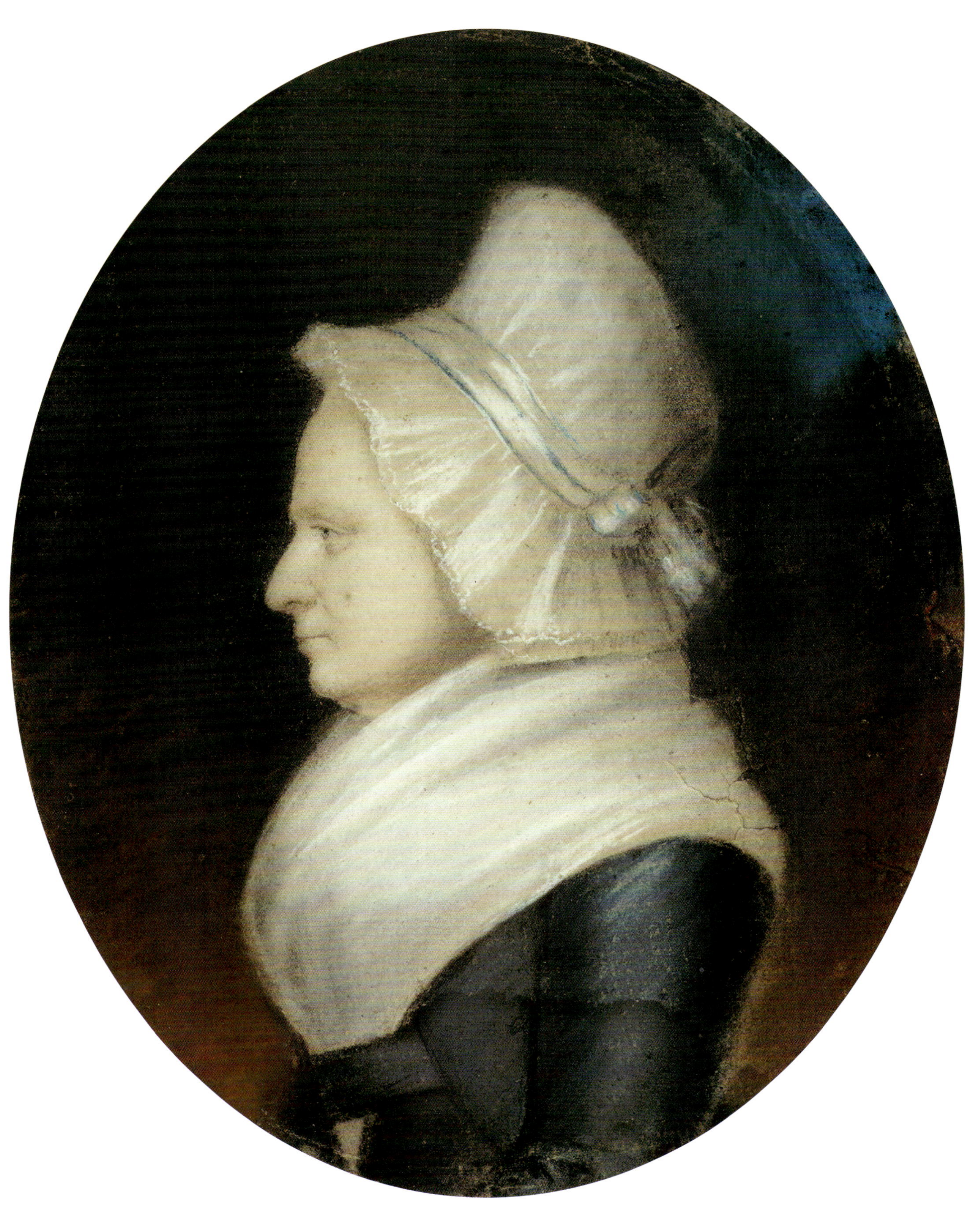

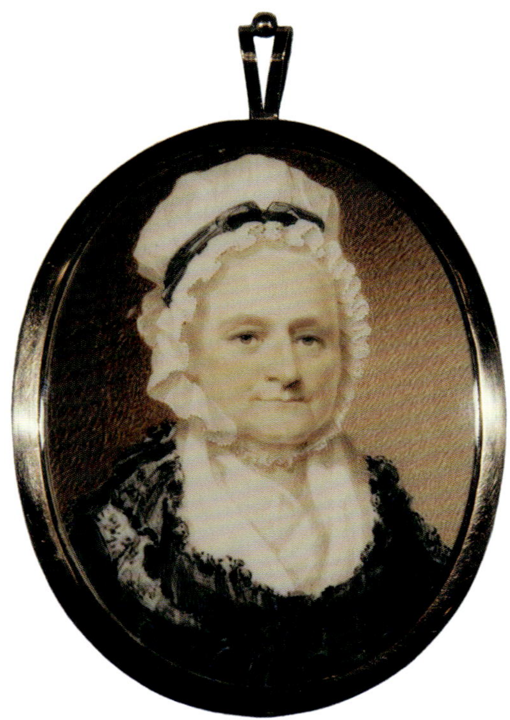

of her (fig. 10). In her final years, Mrs. Washington's overall appearance was perhaps recorded most accurately in a miniature portrait painted shortly before her death. Robert Field effected what was deemed a "striking likeness" of Mrs. Washington that was "drawn to please her grand children in the usual long laced cap & neckkershief, that they may see her as she affected it in her every day face" (fig. 11).[20]

Fig. 10.
Martha Washington, as rendered in pastel by James Sharples, ca. 1796, MVLA

Fig. 11.
Robert Field made this 1801 miniature of Martha Washington in "her every day face" at the request of her grandchildren, MVLA

Throughout her life, Martha Washington paid attention to the details of her appearance with an understanding of the ways in which her clothing and personal articles conveyed meaning. She avoided ostentation and maintained an elegance of appearance that was in keeping with her varied roles. She assisted in defining the role of First Lady and visibly represented the choice of simple elegance over an abundance of ornament. Martha Washington would perhaps prefer to be remembered as Pierre Étienne Du Ponceau described her. After "sitting in the parlour tete-à-tete with Mrs. Washington," his description did not include her attire but rather his impression that "she reminded me of the Roman matrons of whom I had read so much, and I thought that she well deserved to be the companion and friend of the greatest man of the age."[21]

CAT. 82

Shoes

England, ca. 1750–1760
Silk, leather, linen, and metallic lace, L. 9¼", W. 3", H. 4⅝" (heel)
Purchase, 1975
W-2667/A&B

When Martha Dandridge Custis married the young Colonel George Washington on January 6, 1759, she is said to have worn a "petticoat of white silk interwoven with silver," a gown of "deep yellow brocade with rich lace in the neck and sleeves," and "her shoes were purple satin with silver trimmings."[22] The combination of yellow and purple silks offered a stunning color combination as well as an exhibition of imported English finery that spoke of her elevated social and economic standing. These shoes are the most striking survival of the articles she wore that day.[23]

The shoes are made of purple satin-weave silk heavily embellished with silvered metal sequins and threads (detail). Small holes in the flaps indicate where the chapes (or clasps) of the buckles fastened the shoe closed, offering additional ornamentation. When worn by Martha Washington, they contrasted with her yellow silk gown, presenting a combination of purple and yellow she perhaps wore frequently. In March 1760 the London milliner Jane Backhouse sent "a purple & yellow Egret" as well as "A purple & yellow Honey Comb'd Stomacher" for one of the new Mrs. Washington's gowns.[24]

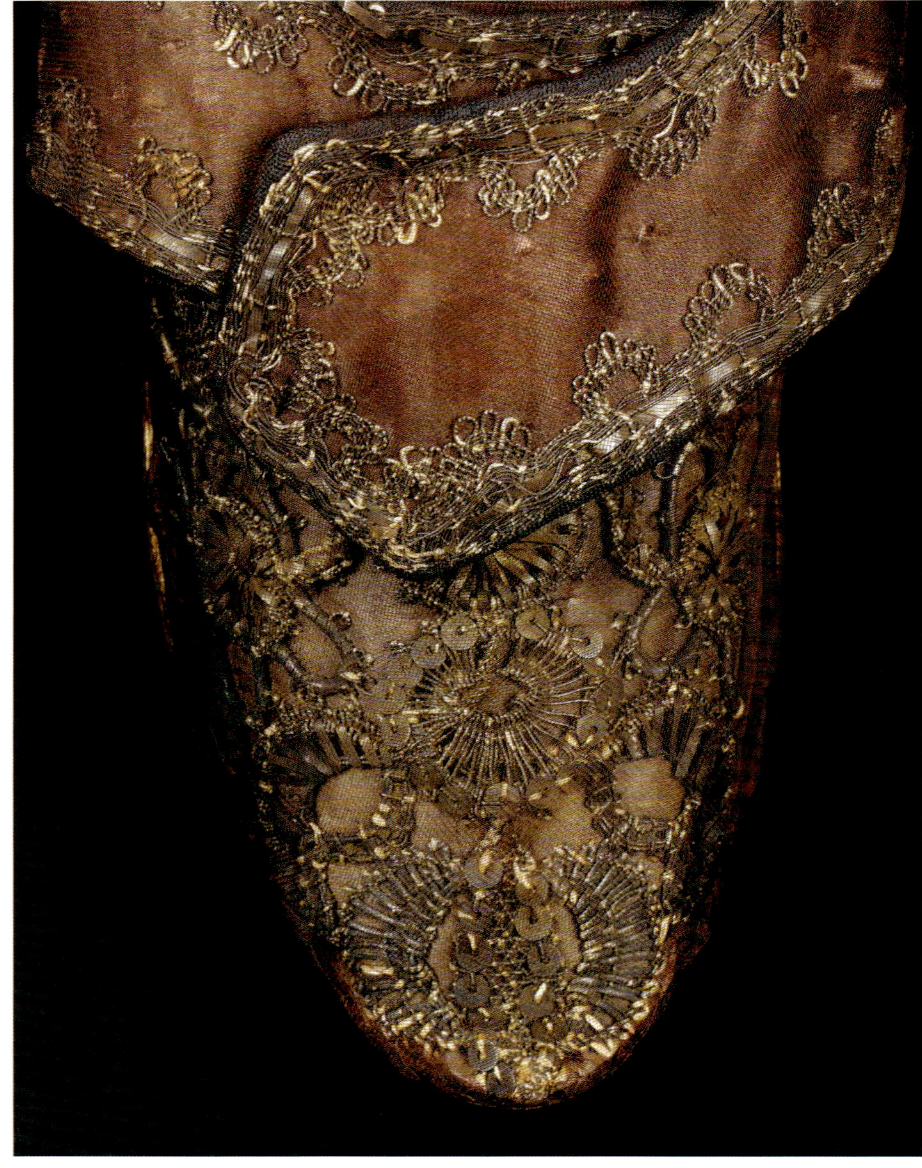

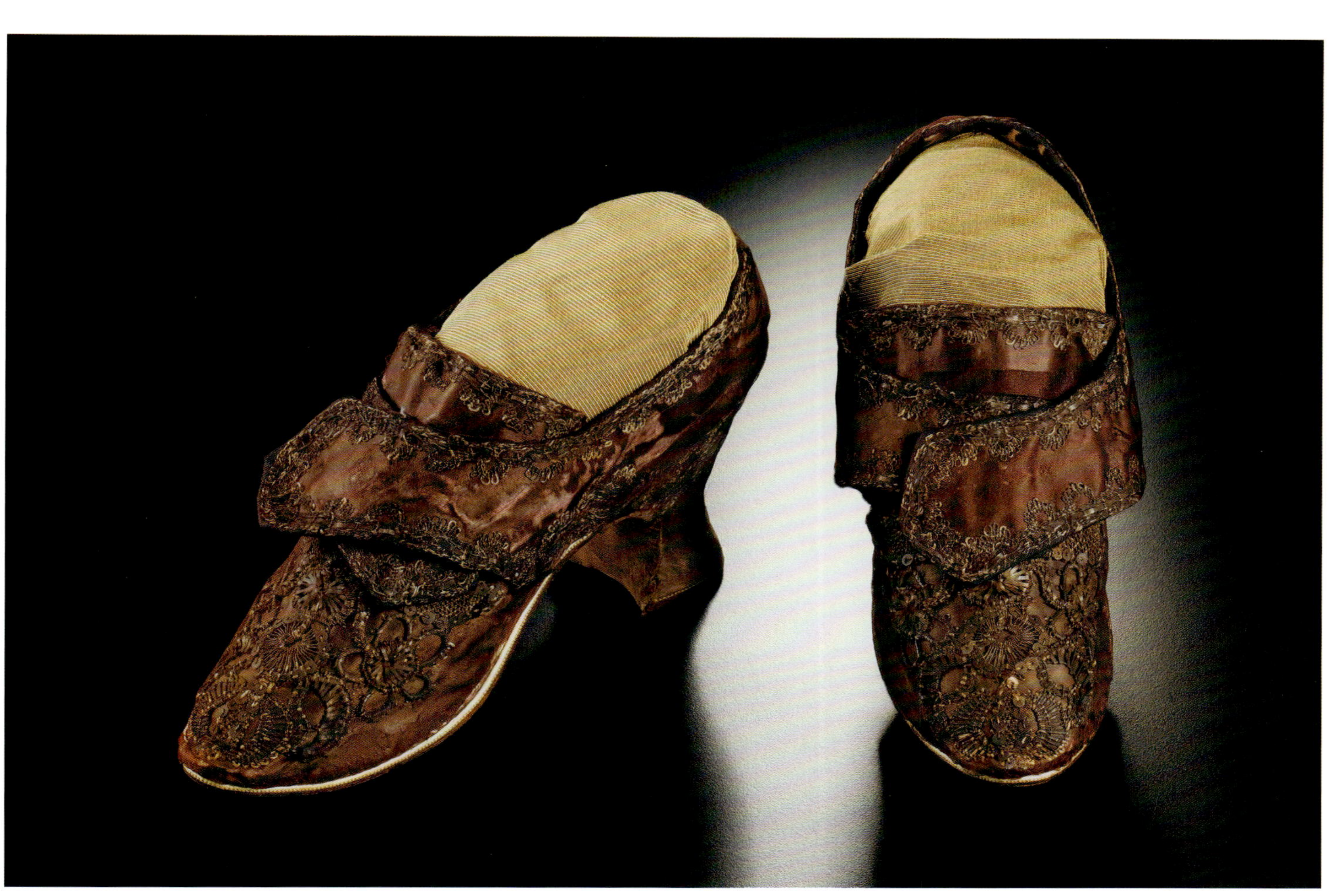

CAT. 83

Lace

Probably England, ca. 1730–1750
Linen, L. 17", W. 1¾"
Gift of Mrs. M. L. Shaffer and Mr. Charles C. Krumbhaar, Jr., 1955
W- 638/A

Of the many yards of lace owned and worn by Martha Washington, this fragment is distinguished by the history that it was worn on January 6, 1759, the day she married George Washington.[25] Known by both its Flemish name, Mechlin, and French name, point de Malines, this type of eighteenth-century bobbin lace was regarded as the "Queen of Laces."[26] A fine and costly favorite in European courts, its silky appearance belied a construction of loosely spun linen.[27] The delicately rendered floral motifs against a finely woven mesh ground provided an ethereal quality to the lace that trimmed Mrs. Washington's gown.

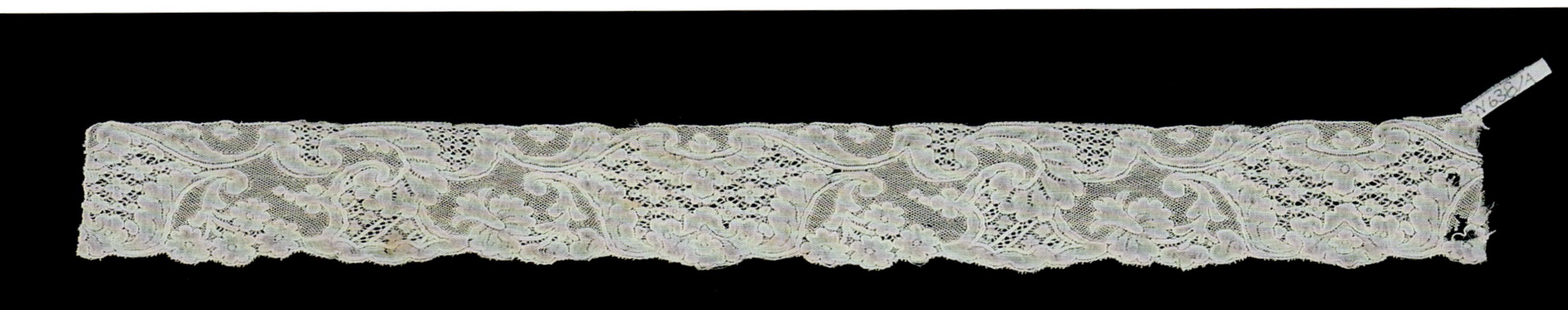

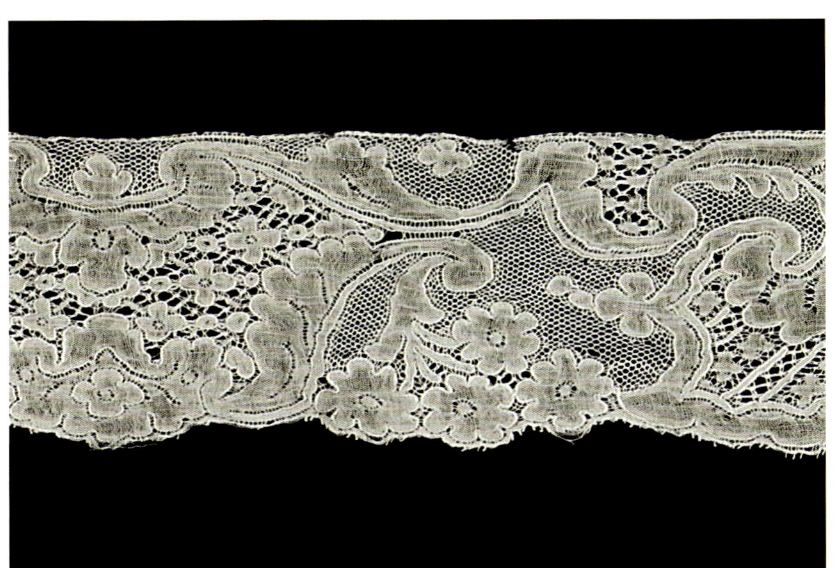

CAT. 84

Dressing Glass

China, ca. 1790–1795
Cypress, glass, and lacquer, H. 33⅛", W. 16½", D. 11⅞"
On deposit from Mrs. Lawrence Lewis Conrad, 1896
W-195

The American fascination with exotic and elegant Chinese imports was heightened after the Revolution by the onset of direct trading between China and the United States and the arrival of vessels laden with Chinese luxury goods in American ports.[28] During the presidency, the Washingtons took advantage of the variety of Chinese lacquer pieces available, and survivals include portable writing desks, dressing glasses, and dressing boxes. In 1795 Washington's household account book notes the purchase of "a Japan[ne]d toilet Glass for M[rs]. Washington" from the looking glass maker and retailer John McElwee.[29] Two years later, as George Washington drew up a list of public and private furnishings in the executive residence, he recorded seven privately purchased dressing glasses. Among them, one "Japan dress[g]" glass and one "Toilet" dressing glass noted with the name "McElwee" were the most costly.[30]

This dressing glass, with a history of use by Martha Washington, may very well be that purchased for her in 1795. The oval looking glass rests above tiered serpentine drawers in a frame supported by shaped bracket feet, and the overall surface decoration of gilded lacquer offers an elaborate array of elements of the Chinese design vocabulary. In addition to holding personal articles such as hair combs, pins, powders, and perfumes, the drawers were originally fitted with small similarly decorated lacquer dressing boxes that offered Mrs. Washington additional storage for her fashionable accessories.

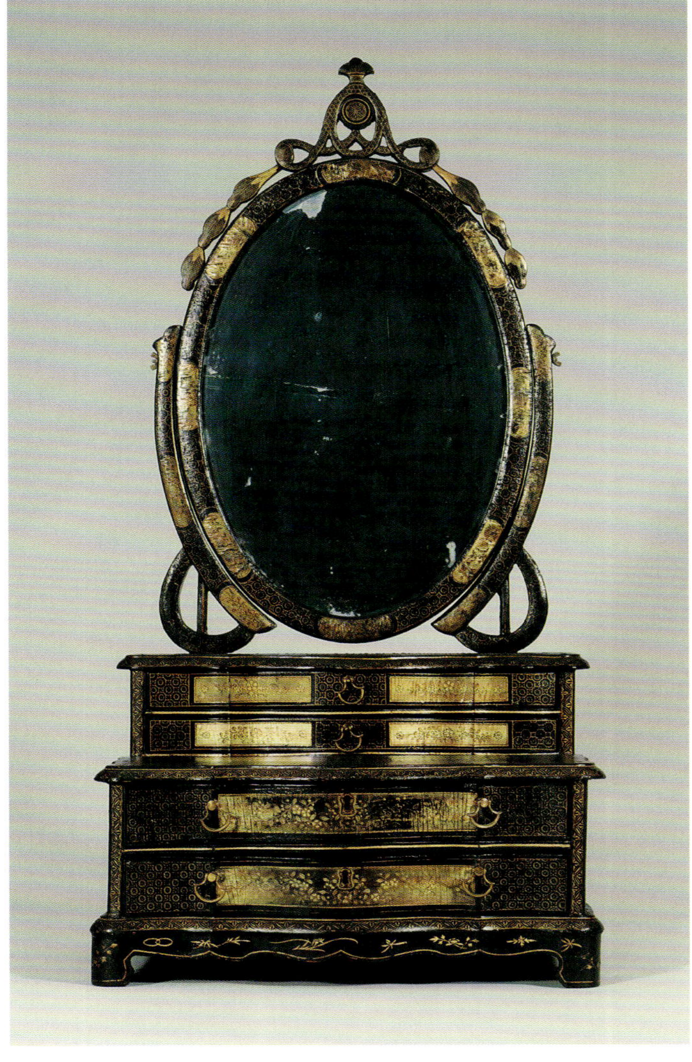

CAT. 85

Snuffbox

Maker unknown
Probably England, ca. 1755
Gold and agate, H. ¾", W. 1 15/16", D. 1½"
Gift of Mrs. Randall H. Hagner, Jr., Vice Regent for the District of Columbia, 1981
W-2810

The taking of snuff, a preparation of finely ground tobacco often enhanced by aromatic oils, herbs, or spices, became fashionable in the late seventeenth century, and its popularity continued into the eighteenth. It was enjoyed by both men and women and was considered by some to be medicinal. In colonial Virginia, snuff was an item often found on orders and invoices for goods shipped from England, and records indicate that the Washington household was no exception. "3 lb. Best Scotch Snuff [and] 3 lb. best violette Strasburg" were among the many items requested by George Washington in a September 1759 "Invoice of Sundries to be sent by Robt Cary Esq. and Company of London."[31] Violet Strasburg was a scented snuff particularly popular among women, and it is quite possible that this type of snuff was requested for Martha Washington's use with this snuffbox.

The Custis coat of arms, exquisitely engraved on the bottom, and the style of the snuffbox suggest that it was ordered before Martha Custis's marriage to George Washington in 1759. Settlement records of Daniel Parke Custis's estate indicate that Martha Washington obtained a number of items from a shipment from England that was ordered before Custis's death. The list of "Goods Mrs. Custis had out of those Shipped by Cary & Company" included snuff as well as a very costly snuffbox, the type that would correspond to this gold and agate example.[32]

This gold snuffbox with its agate lid is a beautiful example of the use of Rococo design to ornament a utilitarian object. Although no marks on the box attribute it to a specific artisan, the box is indicative of a high degree of craftsmanship. Each side is elaborately embossed and incised with asymmetric C-scrolls framing floral motifs, and the smooth, cool beauty of the polished agate lid contrasts with the chased work. Gold snuffboxes, requiring a significant amount of the precious metal, were a luxury item, not often found in eighteenth-century America, and Martha Washington's example is a particularly significant example of a rare form.[33]

Mrs. Washington likely continued to enjoy snuff well into her later years, for in a 1799 letter to George Washington, Thomas Law wrote, "I have to thank Mrs. Washington & to be angry at her sending snuff by Eliza—such an attention tho' it evinces her kindness yet it encourages a bad habit."[34] Perhaps not long after, Martha Washington gave the box itself to her granddaughter Eliza, for a note in Eliza's handwriting accompanies this snuffbox, identifying it as the "Gold snuff-box given to me by my beloved Grandmother."[35]

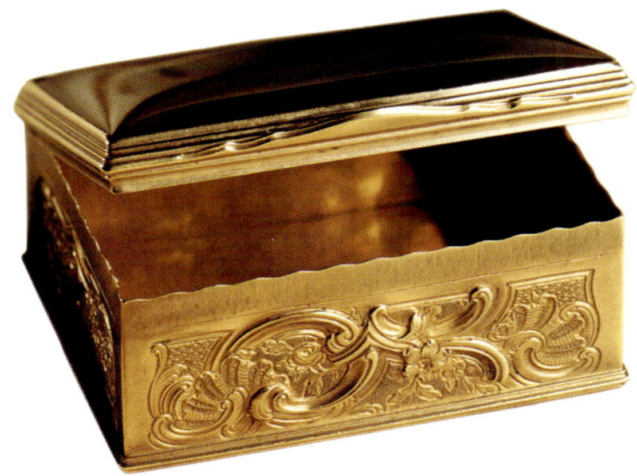

(Custis crest elaborately engraved on the bottom)

CAT. 86

Calling Card, Plate, and Case Covers

Card
Probably England, ca. 1780–1795
Laid paper
Gift of Mr. Basil Stevens, 1955
n.d. 134, RM-295, MS-2912

Engraving plate
England or America, ca. 1790–1795
Copper, H. 2⅜", W. 3 3/16"
Gift of Mr. and Mrs. Ralph G. Newman, 1985[36]
W-2993

Case Covers
Probably Europe, ca. 1790–1795
Silver, H. 2¼", W. 3⅜"
Courtesy of Arlington House, the Robert E. Lee Memorial
W-2594, IL-1250

As Martha Washington assumed the role of the nation's first president's wife, her title (for it seemed she should have one) was debated. Suggestions included the French and English aristocratic addresses of "Marquise" and "Lady," but she chose to remain "Mrs. Washington." The seemingly simple act kept to the philosophical premises of the new nation, avoided the appearance of an American aristocracy or court culture, and set a precedent that endures.[37]

The presidency also placed Martha Washington in an urban environment of established modes of social interaction that necessitated the formality of calling cards. Although she once confided to her niece, "there is certain bounds set for me which I must not depart from—and as I can not doe as I like I am obstinate and stay at home a great deal,"[38] nevertheless, Mrs. Washington dutifully performed the role assigned to her. This small handwritten calling card likely predates the engraving of this copperplate and the cards made from it. The larger engraved calling cards were perhaps stored in a case fitted with these silver filigree covers and used on those occasions when the president's wife represented the nation as Mrs. Washington.

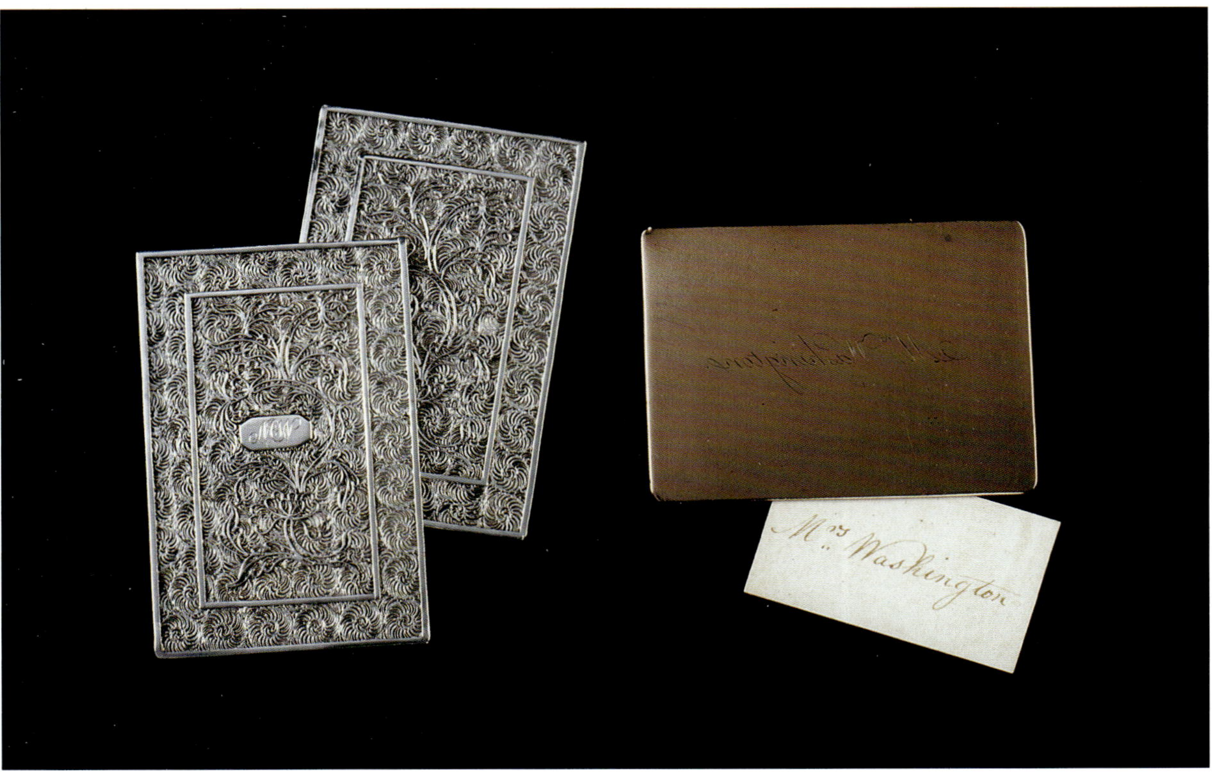

CAT. 87

Necklace

Probably England, ca. 1759
Garnet, silver, and gold, L. 17½", W. ⅝"
Gift of Barnaby Conrad, Jr., 1989
W-2212

Shortly after her marriage to George Washington, Martha Washington received a shipment of jewelry from the London shop of Susanna Passavant that included a variety of necklaces to complement the millinery sent by Frances Montague and Jane Backhouse. In addition to two garnet necklaces, Mrs. Washington received "A White Collar Necklace," "An Emerine Necklace," and "A long white Necklace."[39] Those set with garnets were among the most costly sent, and this necklace probably represents one of the two in this early invoice.

The deep red and pink rhodolite garnets are set in closed silver mounts originally washed in gold. The five floral rosettes of brilliant and oval-cut stones are linked by square cushion-cut garnets and united by a gold clasp. Although supplied through the Washingtons' London factor, its style and mountings offer the possibility that the necklace originated in Paris and was retailed in England by Susanna Passavant.[40]

Garnets were in high fashion when Martha Washington assembled an array of necklaces, earrings, pins, and rings for herself in the 1750s and 1760s. Mined in Bohemia, the range of red and deep pink stones were faceted and set by English and American jewelers with the same care afforded diamonds and could even outsparkle the more costly gem. Mrs. Washington's fondness for the stone was presumably shared by her young daughter, Martha "Patsy" Parke Custis, for whom a significant number of garnet pieces were ordered in the same years.[41] Many of the pieces of garnet jewelry enjoyed by Martha and her daughter were preserved by granddaughter Martha Custis Peter and her descendants before their return to Mount Vernon. A number of them were reworked in the nineteenth and early twentieth centuries, demonstrating generations of regard for the ruby-colored jewelry that spanned three centuries.

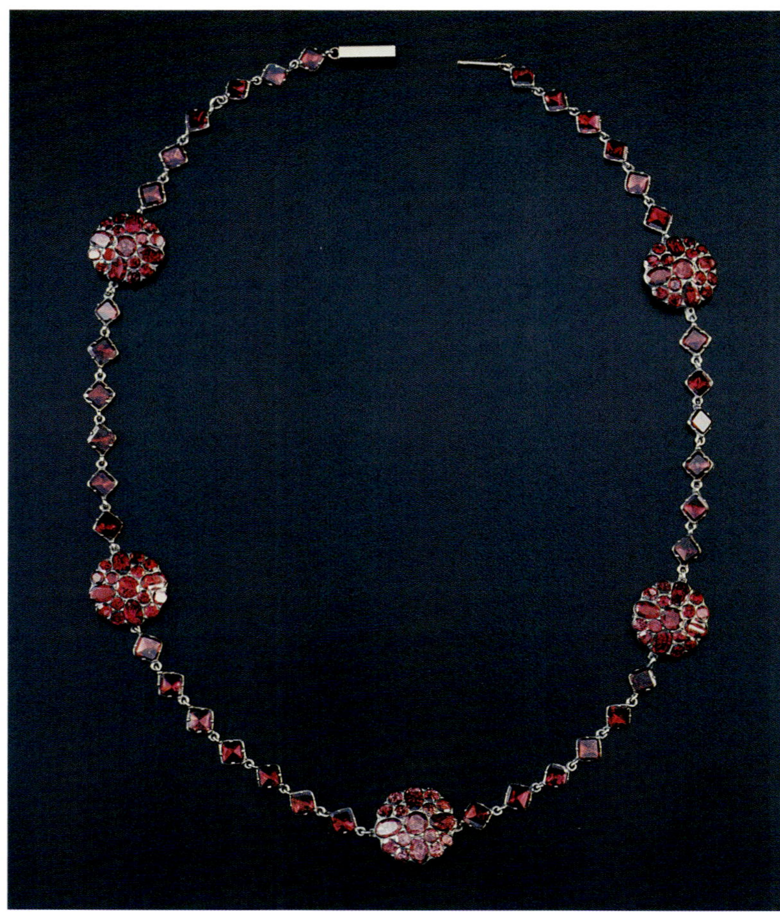

CAT. 88

Necklace

England or America, ca. 1789–1797
Pearl, gold, and silk, L. 12½", W. ½"
Gift of Colonel and Mrs. Edward Parke Custis Lewis Cumming, 1990
W-2369

With the onset of the neoclassical style, Martha Washington updated her jewelry as well as her clothing. Small seed pearls, imported from China and India and strung on horsehair or silk and fashioned into earrings, bracelets, necklaces, and hair ornaments, were widely popular in Federal America. Their smooth texture and white color melded with the Neoclassical aesthetic that referenced ancient Greece and Rome. Mrs. Washington perhaps selected them for their fashion as well as the philosophical principles of government to which they alluded.[42]

Seed pearl jewelry was readily available to Martha Washington during the presidential years. In Philadelphia, the shop of the goldsmith Jeremiah Boone offered a "neat assortment" of rings, bracelets, and lockets set with pearls, and the jeweler James Jacks advertised his recent importation from London of pearl rings, "pearl and diamond rings," and "diamond and pearl festooned necklaces with earrings."[43] In 1789 the New York presidential household account book recorded payment of sixteen pounds to "Mr M. Roberts for pearl pins & Earrings for Mrs. Washington."[44] Michael Roberts, who advertised "Pearl Devices" among his "just imported" goods "in the latest vessels from London,"[45] or one of the coterie of New York and Philadelphia jewelers and silversmiths importing and fashioning seed pearls into jewelry likely supplied this seed pearl necklace worn by the first lady.

The necklace is composed of three sizes of delicate pearls intricately woven onto a framework of two thin silk cords, to which is attached a surviving gold ring of the original clasp. Its simplicity and elegance accorded well with Martha Washington's attire and the prevailing neoclassical fashion. After her death, the necklace was preserved by her granddaughter Eleanor Parke Custis Lewis and her descendants until its donation to Mount Vernon.

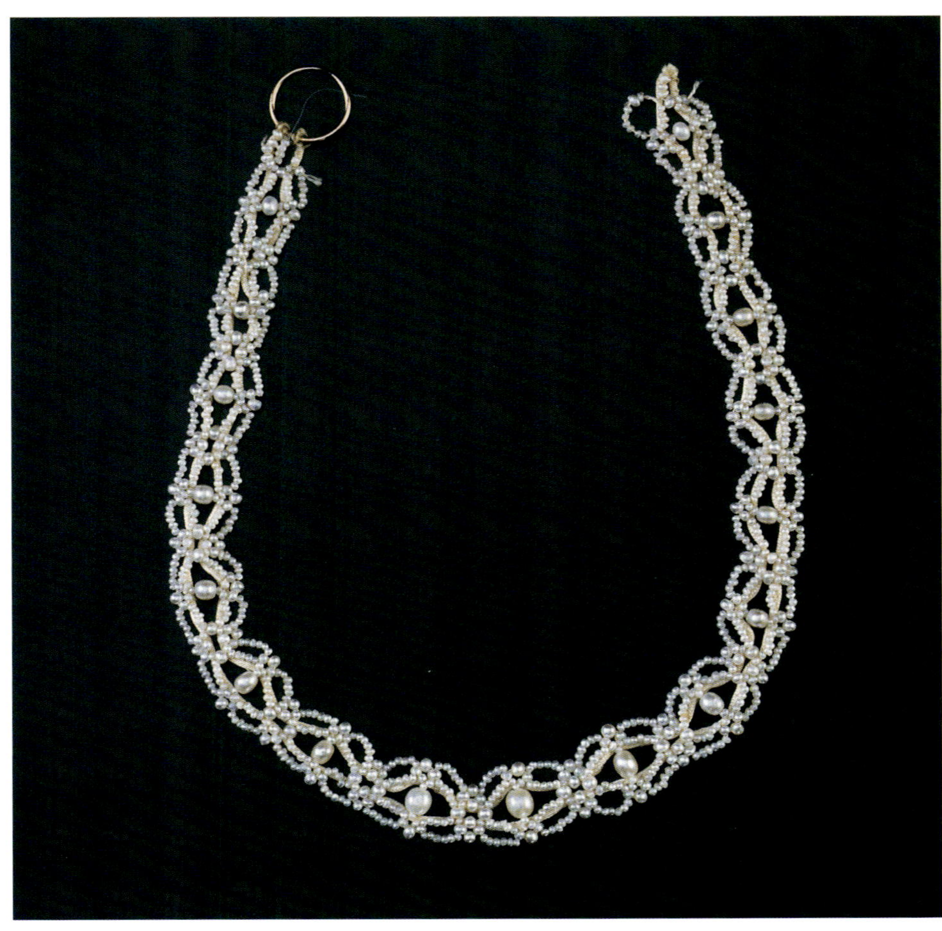

CAT. 89

Bathing Gown

America, ca. 1760
Linen, L. 46½"
Gift of Mrs. George R. Goldsborough, Vice Regent for Maryland, 1894
W-580

In July 1769 George and Martha Washington ventured to Berkeley Springs, Virginia, to take the mineral waters that they hoped would heal Martha's daughter, Patsy, then suffering from epileptic seizures. Bathing times and use of the bathhouse were assigned according to gender, and "the time set apart for the ladies was announced by a blast on a long tin horn, at which signal all of the opposite sex retired to a prescribed distance."[46] Martha Washington's attire for the bathing ritual would not have been witnessed by many and served the utilitarian function of protecting her modesty and perhaps providing a bit of warmth.

This bathing gown, identified by Eliza Parke Custis Law as "My Grandmothers bathing gown, in which [she] bathed at Berkeley Springs in Virginia," may be that worn by Mrs. Washington in 1769.[47] The gown is pieced of two varieties of blue and off-white homespun linen (detail). Circular lead weights sewn into the hem ensured that the gown did not rise improperly when she was in the water, and linen tape ties secured the front closure. The gown is a rare survival of both Martha Washington's clothing and eighteenth-century bathing garments. Fortunately, the respect, if not reverence, accorded all articles owned and used by Mrs. Washington ensured that this utilitarian gown was preserved by her descendants.

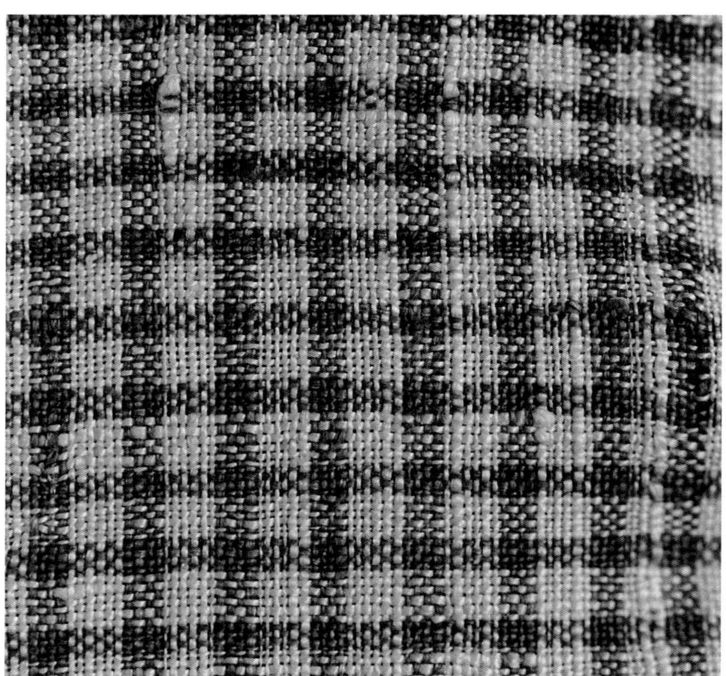

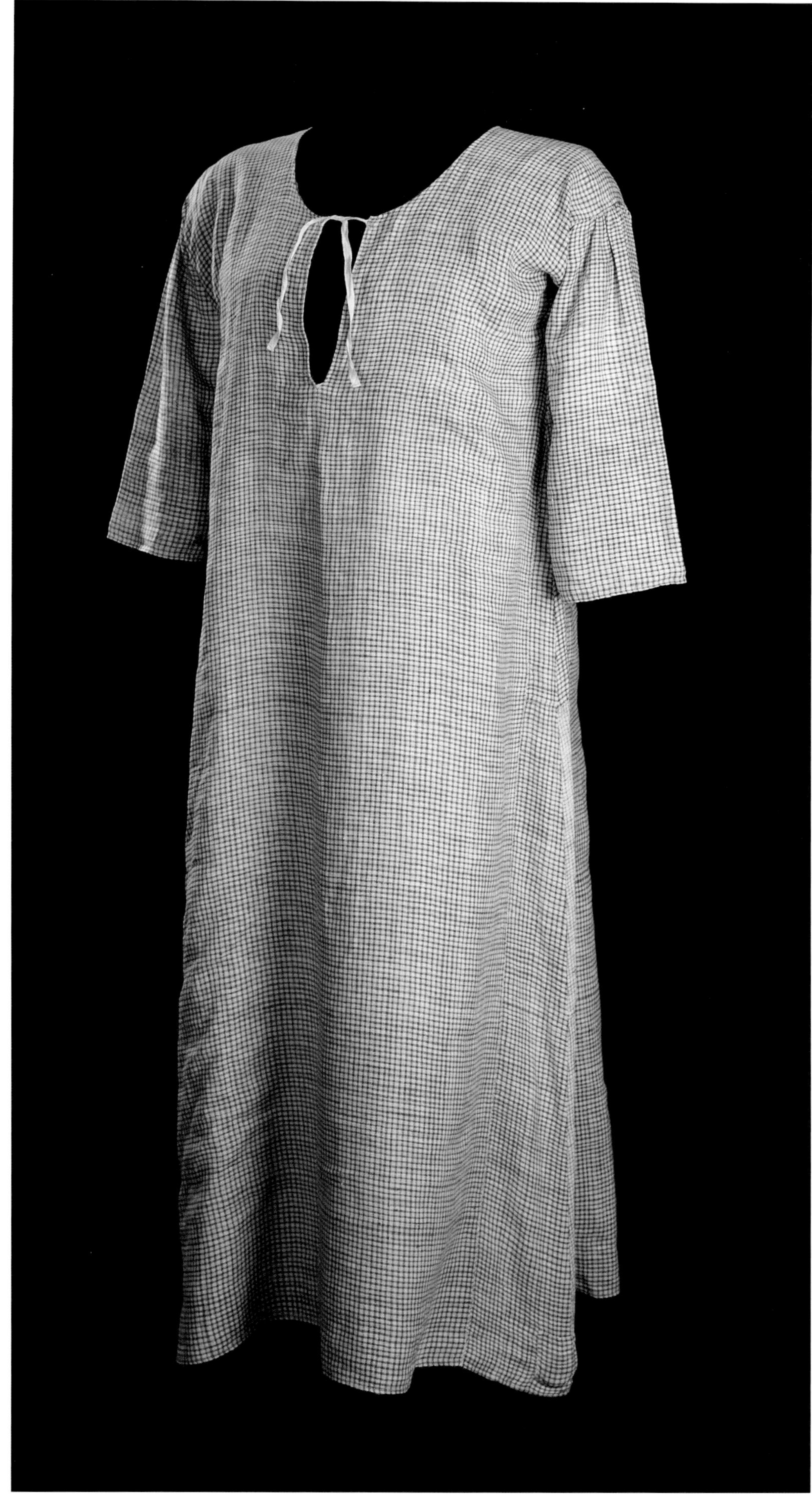

CAT. 90

Fragments of Silk Gowns

Yellow Lampas
Probably England, ca. 1740–1760
Purchased by the A. Alfred Taubman Fund and partial gift of an anonymous donor, 2004
W-2780/C

Cream Brocaded Lampas
England, probably Spitalfields, ca. 1740–1760
Purchase, 1956
W-2154/A–C

Striped Woven Silk
England or France, ca. 1780–1790
Purchased by the A. Alfred Taubman Fund and partial gift of an anonymous donor, 2004
W-2780/A

As a wealthy member of Virginia's elite planter class, Martha Washington had the opportunity and means to acquire fine European silks that represented some of the most costly luxury goods imported to the colonies. In the prewar years, when the Crown's legislation dictated colonial reliance on England, Mrs. Washington received large quantities of English silks shipped by Robert Cary and Company, secured from London milliners including Jane Backhouse. After the Revolution, direct trade routes with France and China were established, and the range of available imported silks widened.[48]

These fragments of Martha Washington's gowns provide a small picture of the variety of elaborately woven silks she wore. They survive only in fragment form because of the meaning they held for her descendants and the desire of many to have a piece of the attire of the beloved matriarch. In the beginning, whole dresses were inherited. Some fabrics, like this cream satin-ground silk with silk brocaded floral design, were "used to cover a chair which was at Mount Vernon" and later "taken from the chair and divided into five parcels" for the next generation of descendants.[49] Others, like the striped silk with delicate floral motif and the yellow lampas attributed to her wedding costume, represent fabrics cut and distributed to the successive generations.

If gathered and assembled, the silk fragments might exhibit evidence of Martha Washington's concern for the high value of imported textiles and the care she took to have dresses dyed, repaired, or remade into newly fashioned garments. As a wealthy widow in 1758, she wrote to Robert Cary & Company in London to specify the alterations she desired to a nightgown, or informal daytime dress, noting, "I have sent a night gown to be dide of fashanable couler fitt for me to ware . . . and beg you . . . have it dide better than that I sent Last year but was very badly done."[50] As Mrs. Washington in 1783, she enclosed a sample of dress fabric when writing to the New York merchant Daniel Parker with an order for "three yards of black silk like the enclosed; it is to repair old gowns, and consequently must be like them."[51] Whether complete or whole, these silk fragments offer insight into not only the types of silk gowns Martha Washington wore but also the appearance she presented to her contemporaries, and one of the ways she was memorialized by her descendants.

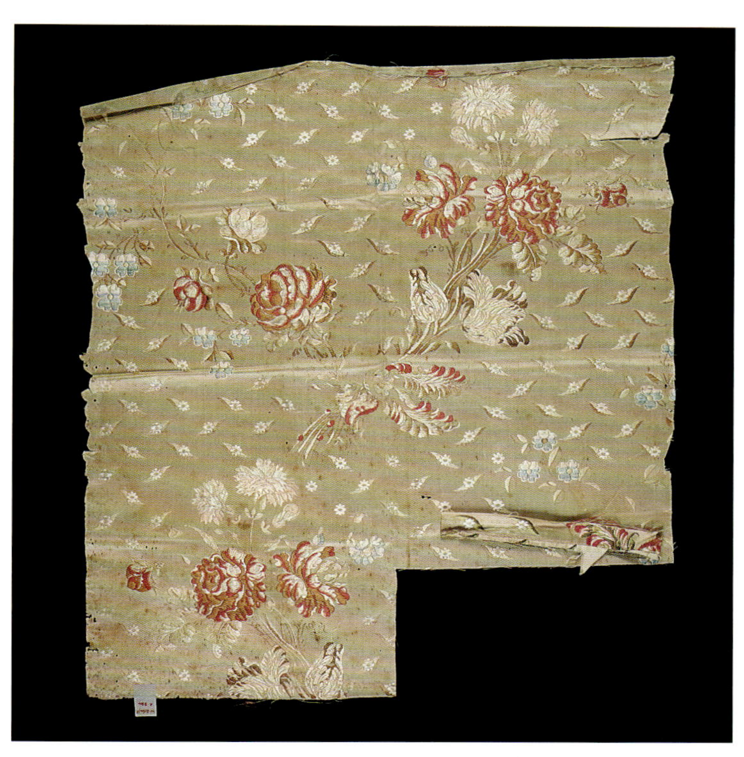

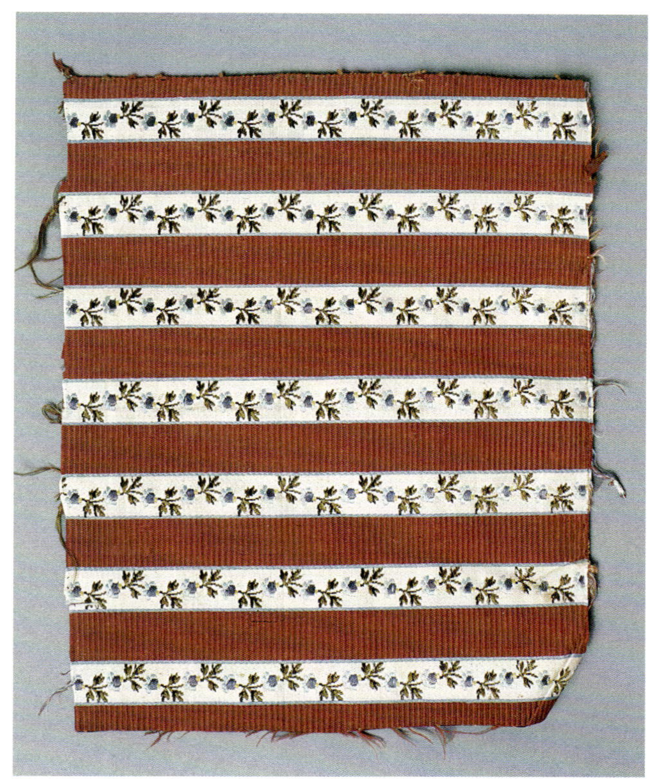

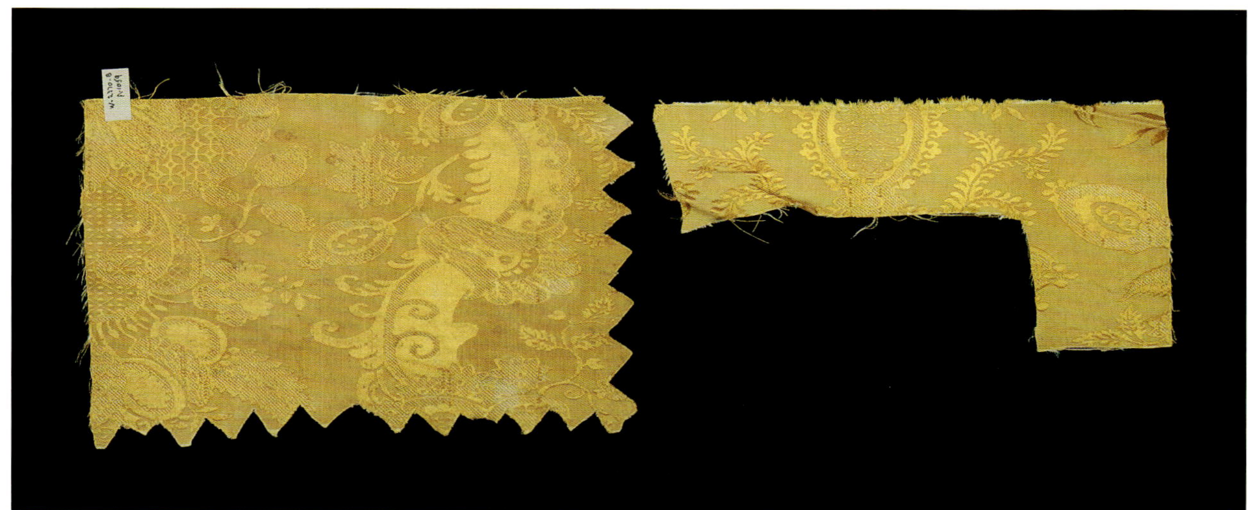

CAT. 91

Ring

England or America, 1750–1800
Gold, crystal, hair, and paper, L. ⅝", W. ½"
Gift of Mrs. Gertrude Hunt Knox, 1954
W-1976

Hairwork, or hair jewelry, became popular in both England and America by the middle of the eighteenth century. It not only served a decorative purpose but also provided a way to celebrate or memorialize a loved one. Produced by English jewelers or by newly developed workshops in America, hair jewelry was widely available to those who could afford such personalized objects of adornment.[52] The Washingtons took advantage of this elite practice, initially sending to England for "A Locket with the Inclosed hair in it" in 1770, and later delivering "a lock of both our hair" to the Poughkeepsie, New York, craftsman Andrew Billings.[53] During the presidency, the household accounts note payment to the New York jeweler Daniel van Voorhis for "hair work put into a breast pin for M^{rs} W^{n}" in 1789.[54]

Mourning rings were a popular method of incorporating hair into personal ornamentation and reached the height of fashion in the second half of the eighteenth century. Wills stipulated funds for the purchase of mourning rings for loved ones, and George Washington made such allowances in his will, providing five female family members and friends with "a mourning Ring of the value of one hundred dollars."[55] In her will, Martha Washington allotted ten guineas for memorial rings for her grandson, three granddaughters, and grandniece, as well as five guineas for a ring or "something in remembrance of me" for two other female relatives.[56]

Passed down through the family of granddaughter Martha Parke Custis Peter, this ring was perhaps worn by Martha Washington in remembrance of a close friend or relative.[57] George Washington's nephew, George Augustine Washington, for instance, bequeathed in his will "to my Aunt Martha Washington . . . a ring of 5 Guineas value to be wrought with some of my hair in token of my affectionate remembrance."[58] The ring features an oval symmetrical setting fitted with eighteen pearls encircling the bezel. The gold shank and body are cast in one piece, and the interior well contains a lock of hair and two paper backings under the crystal. The ring is a stylistic blend: the simple symmetrical design and gold-and-white color combination are in keeping with the late eighteenth-century Neoclassical aesthetic, while the rounded band suggests an earlier style.[59] It is one of many examples of fashionable hair jewelry owned by Martha Washington throughout her lifetime. In addition to rings, Mrs. Washington "always wore a locket" and "almost invariably her locket contained a miniature of her husband, generally with a lock of his hair set in the back, to which she attached a great deal of sentiment."[60]

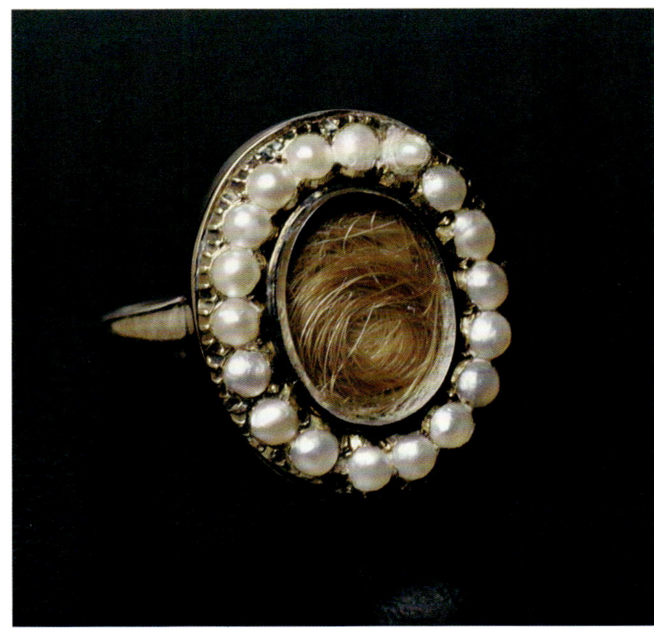

CAT. 92

Gown

England, ca. 1790–1800
Silk and linen, L. 58⅞"
Purchase, 1949
W-1523

Martha Washington owned and wore a variety of gowns that showcased imported silks that ranged from the simple to the elaborately designed. This brown silk satin gown is, however, the only intact example to survive in the Mount Vernon collection. Despite the later use of Mrs. Washington's silk gowns to upholster furniture and their disassembly and distribution among her descendants, this gown survived intact, stored in one of George Washington's military trunks (cat. 20). It was preserved by her granddaughter Eliza Parke Custis Law, who attached a note to the dress identifying it as "a favorite gown of my dear Grandmother Mrs. Washington."[61]

The gown is constructed of narrow brown satin-weave silk, likely of English manufacture. Three buttoned flaps secure the front closure, and boning sewn into the linen lining of the bodice provides definition and shaping. The open front was designed to accommodate a petticoat, and the wide scoop neckline would have been complemented by a fichu or kerchief. The gown's styling suggests it dates from the 1790s, when Mrs. Washington set an example for the nation and future president's wives to follow.[62]

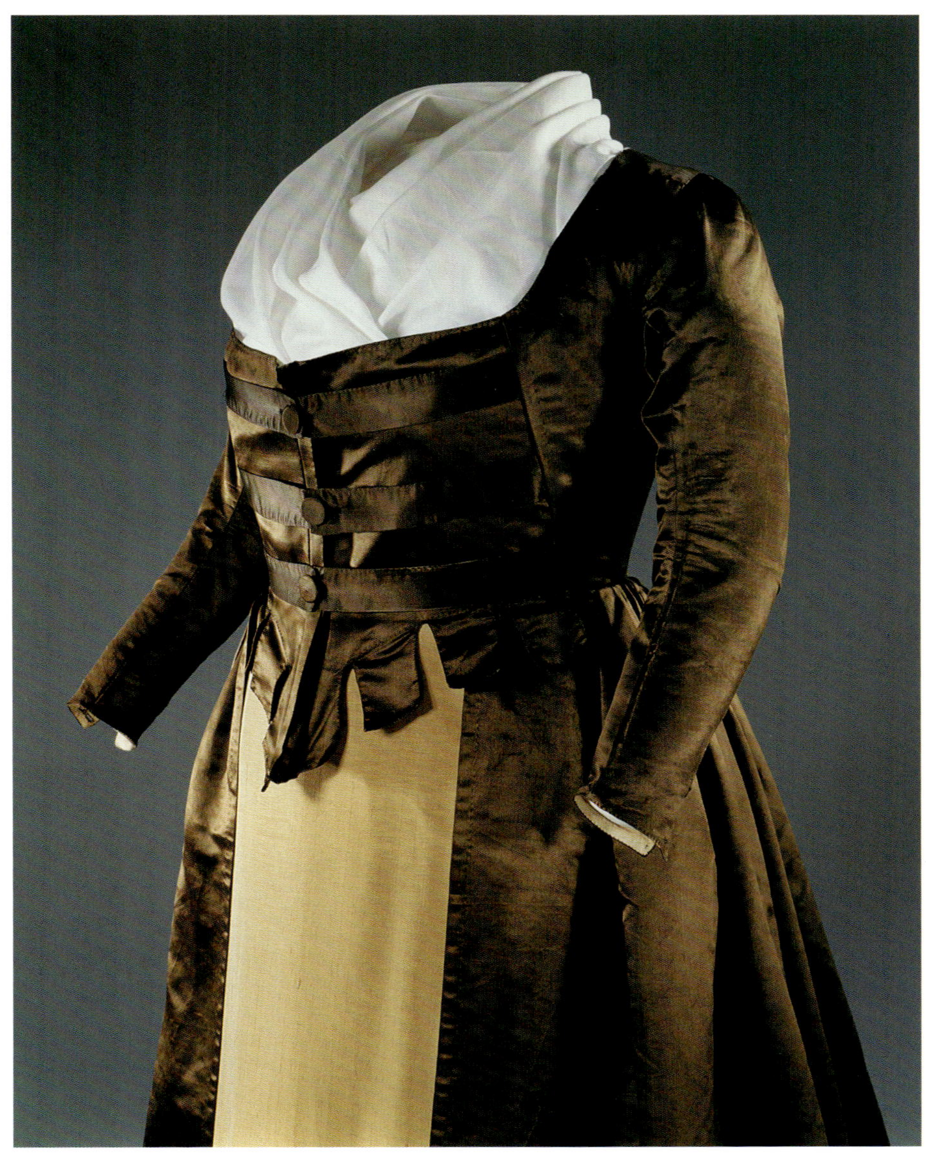

CAT. 93

Fan

China, ca. 1760–1795
Ivory, H. 7⅜", W. 12½" (open)
Given in memory of Lucy Ware Lewis McCormick, 1946
W-1441

Elegant and beautiful ivory fans made their way from China to America, initially via England, where they offered ladies' attire references to an exotic, faraway land. The first shipment of Chinese cargo aboard the *Empress of China* brought an assortment of fans to American consumers keen for the imported objects. The Dutch merchant Andreas Everardus van Braam Houckgeest brought Martha Washington at least one ivory fan as well as a gift of Chinese porcelains (cat. 43).[63] Purchase records indicate that Mrs. Washington was fond of the accessory, because she received "An Ivory Fan" from London in 1760, followed by shipments of "2 fash[ionable] Iv[or]y Fans" in 1761 and "1 fash[iona]ble Ivory fan & case" in 1764.[64]

This fan, of the brisé type, is constructed of twenty-four pierced and carved ivory sticks protected by two elaborately carved guards. The central medallion featuring a Chinese landscape is placed within a delicately carved floral ground bordered by a mixture of Eastern and Western design motifs. It survives as one of five ivory fans in the Mount Vernon collection with a history of having been owned by Martha Washington.[65]

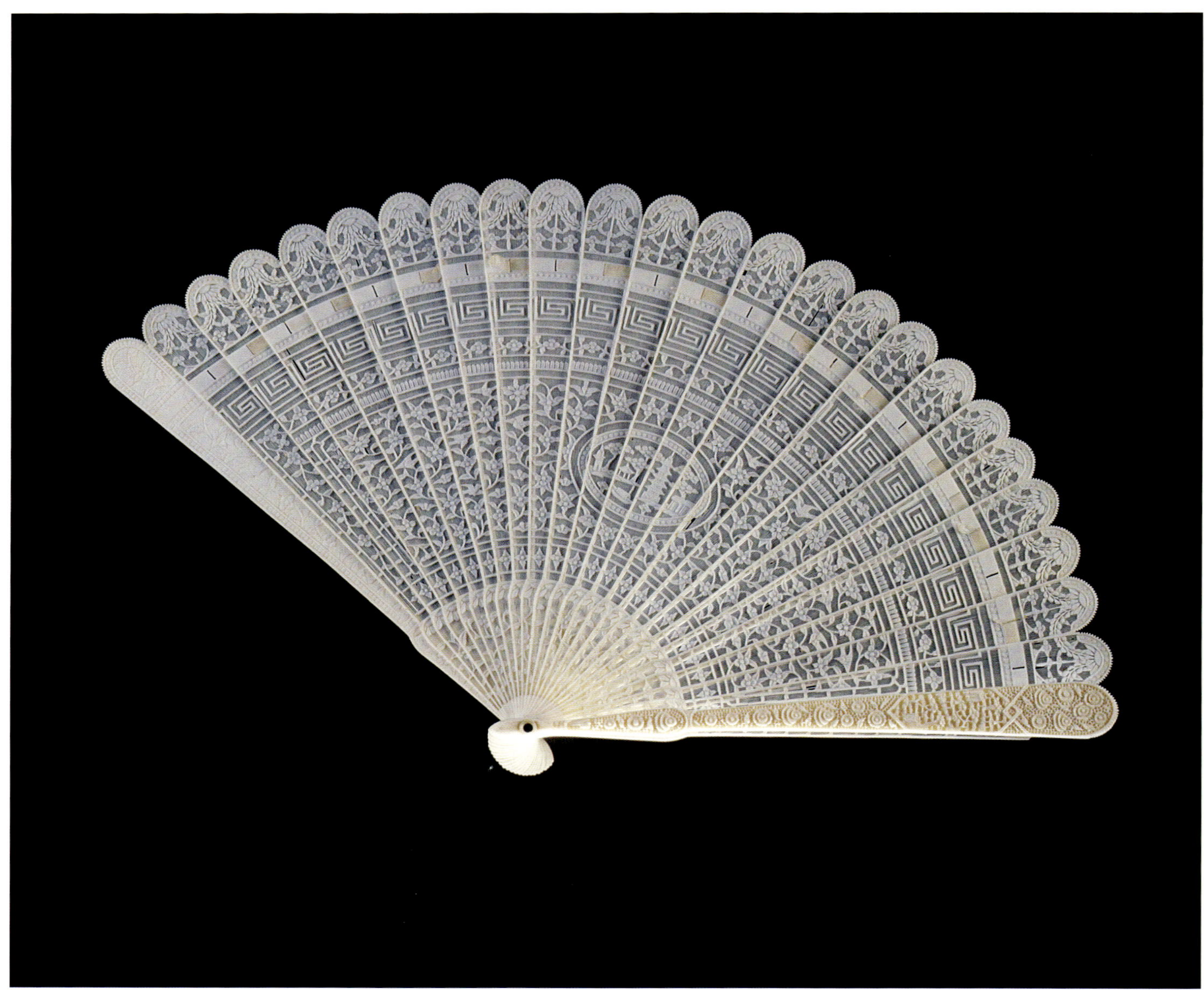

CAT. 94

Hair Comb

Probably America, ca. 1780–1795
Silver, L. 3½", W. 4½"
Given in memory of Lucy Ware Lewis McCormick, 1946
W-1442

Over her lifetime, Martha Washington utilized a variety of combs, pins, and ribbons to dress her hair properly. In the 1760s and 1770s arrivals from London included "A Garnet Comb for the Hair," paste "hair Combs," and "Paste and Garnet Pins for the hair," which were likely incorporated into her more formal hairstyles.[66] When the artist Charles Willson Peale painted Mrs. Washington in 1772, he included white French beads, or pearls, that may have adorned her dark brown hair on that occasion (cat. 12). Later portraits of Martha Washington often show her hair neatly tucked into a loose or mob cap, although she continued to pay close attention to hairstyles and have her hair dressed.

While First Lady, Mrs. Washington drew a distinction between hairstyles acceptable at Mount Vernon and those appropriate in the city. When writing from New York to her niece Fanny at Mount Vernon, Mrs. Washington noted, "all the genteel people say Crape cushing is not proper to send to you—but I think in the country where you cannot have a hair dresser they will do very well."[67] Martha Washington appears to have adhered to this advice herself. While her hair was professionally dressed throughout the presidential years in New York and Philadelphia, she seems to have been more relaxed in hairstyle at Mount Vernon, where one visitor recalled her hair only half-hidden by her bonnet and "done up in a little pigtail."[68]

Martha Washington probably obtained this silver hair comb during the presidency when she had access to shops offering a variety of combs. She may have even turned to the Philadelphia silversmith Joseph Anthony, already known for the coffeepot he provided (cat. 32), who advertised his assortment of "Silver, steel and tortoise shell slides for the hair" in 1790.[69] The shape of the gently curved comb enabled it to lie flat against her head, while its eleven long prongs secured her hair. According to her descendants who returned the comb to Mount Vernon, this silver comb was a gift from Martha Washington to her granddaughter Eleanor Parke Custis Lewis, who kept and preserved many of her grandmother's personal articles at her nearby home, Woodlawn Plantation.

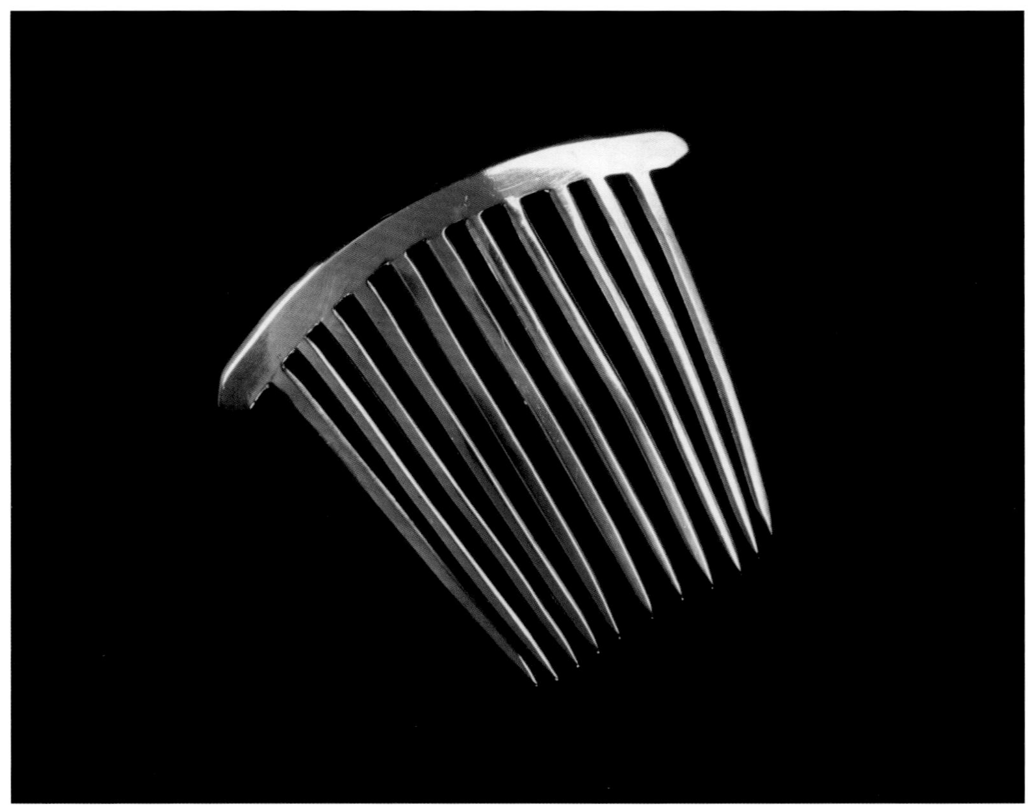

CAT. 95

Martha Washington (1731–1802)

1796
James Peale (1749–1831)
Philadelphia, Pennsylvania
Watercolor on ivory, 1⁹⁄₁₆ x 1¼"
Signed and dated lower left: I.P. 1796
Bequest of Miss Margaret B. Smith, 1910
W-624

In 1796 James Peale continued his family's practice of portraying the Washington family by painting this miniature portrait of Martha Washington as First Lady. Twenty-four years, a war, and the loss of her two remaining children had passed since Mrs. Washington sat for Charles Willson Peale, James' elder brother. Despite these years of hardship and the pressures she endured as First Lady, Peale portrays nearly the same pleasing expression that was captured in 1772. The similarity is perhaps due to Martha Washington's resolve to remain in positive spirits. At the beginning of the presidency, she expressed her outlook to her friend Mercy Otis Warren: "I am still determined to be cheerful and to be happy in whatever situation I may be, for I have also learnt from experianence that the greater part of our happiness or misary depends upon our dispositions, and not upon our circumstances."[70]

The miniature depicts Martha Washington in her sixty-fifth year, with her grayed hair tucked neatly in a white mob cap and a lace-accented fichu draped around her neck and shoulders. The portrait's gold mounting contains her plaited hair on the reverse, perhaps an inclusion requested by her granddaughter Eleanor "Nelly", the likely intended recipient of Peale's work.[71] In January 1796 Nelly was spending the Christmas season with her mother when her grandmother wrote, "I was in hopes my dear child to have had a picture drawn of me for you before this I have set several times—the picture is not yet done nor do I know when it will be ready to send to you as the painter beg[g]ed I would not hurry him—and as I know the only value of a picture is the likeness it bears to the person it is taken for—I shall wait till he brings it to me."[72] The portrait was still not ready when Mrs. Washington wrote again to Nelly on January 14, but its arrival seemed imminent.[73] The skill of the artist was not to be rushed, and the product was certainly worth the wait.

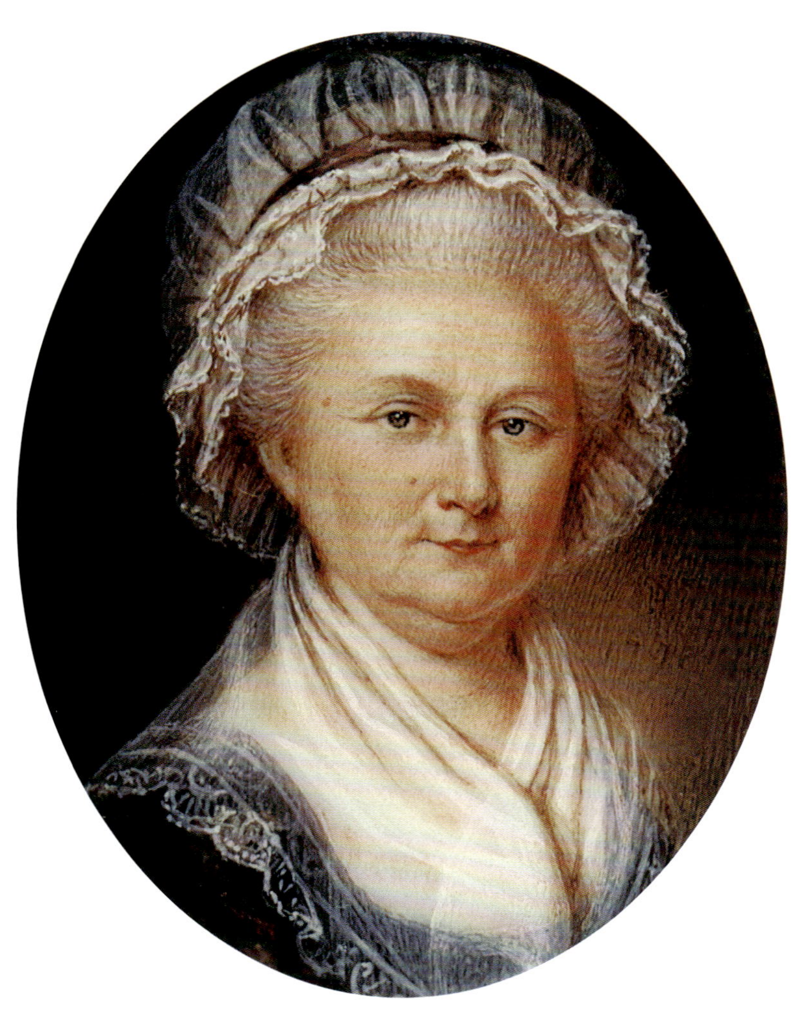

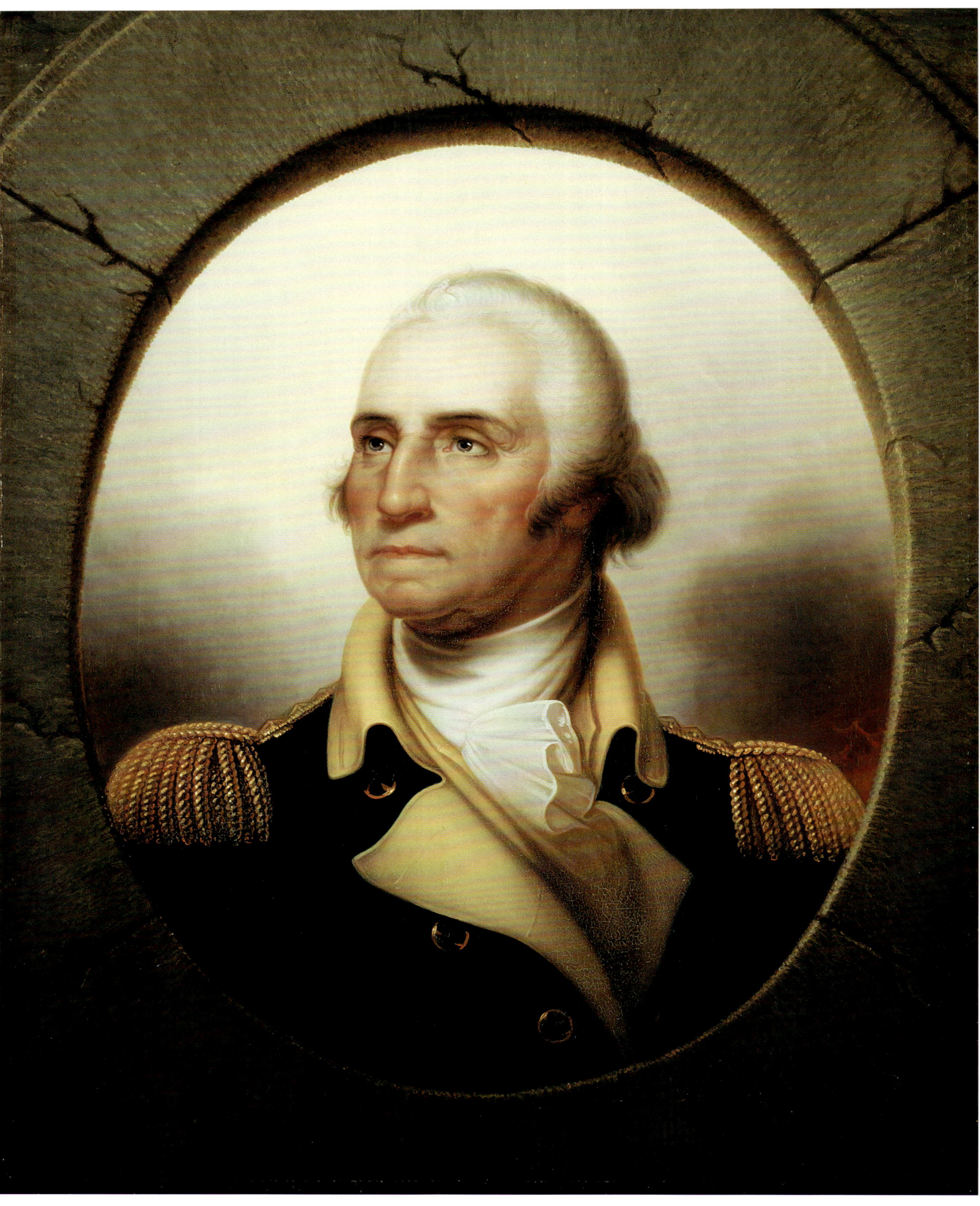

Afterword

THIS BOOK OFFERS A PORTRAIT OF GEORGE WASHINGTON through an illustrated narrative of the objects Washington selected to furnish the spaces where he lived, those owned and used by the people who surrounded him, and some of the clothing he chose to wear. Through events chosen to provide context for the objects he acquired, the narrative covers all too briefly Washington's journey from his early years through his retirement from public service. Nonetheless, they help us to appreciate George Washington's keen awareness of the power of objects to communicate and his wish to portray that which was appropriate for his roles as a Virginia gentry planter, a military general, and the president of a new nation. He deemed appropriate that which was in fashion but without ostentation. These attributes have also been applied to the many objects made in his memory that continue to tell the story of his life and legacy and to enrich the Mount Vernon collections.

George Washington has inspired the preservation of objects associated with him, the crafting of objects in his honor, and the collection of those objects at his home, Mount Vernon. Some of the early relics preserved and returned to Mount Vernon were short-lived, like the lemons plucked from one of Washington's trees and preserved in alcohol.[1] Others, like the "piece of Coffin in which Washington was buried" and the chair in which the father of our country was supposedly cradled as an infant, have endured to join more recent acquisitions.[2] Together, they symbolize the widespread esteem conferred on Washington and the continued interest in generating and preserving objects associated with him.

From the time of George Washington's victory over the British Crown to the present day, objects have

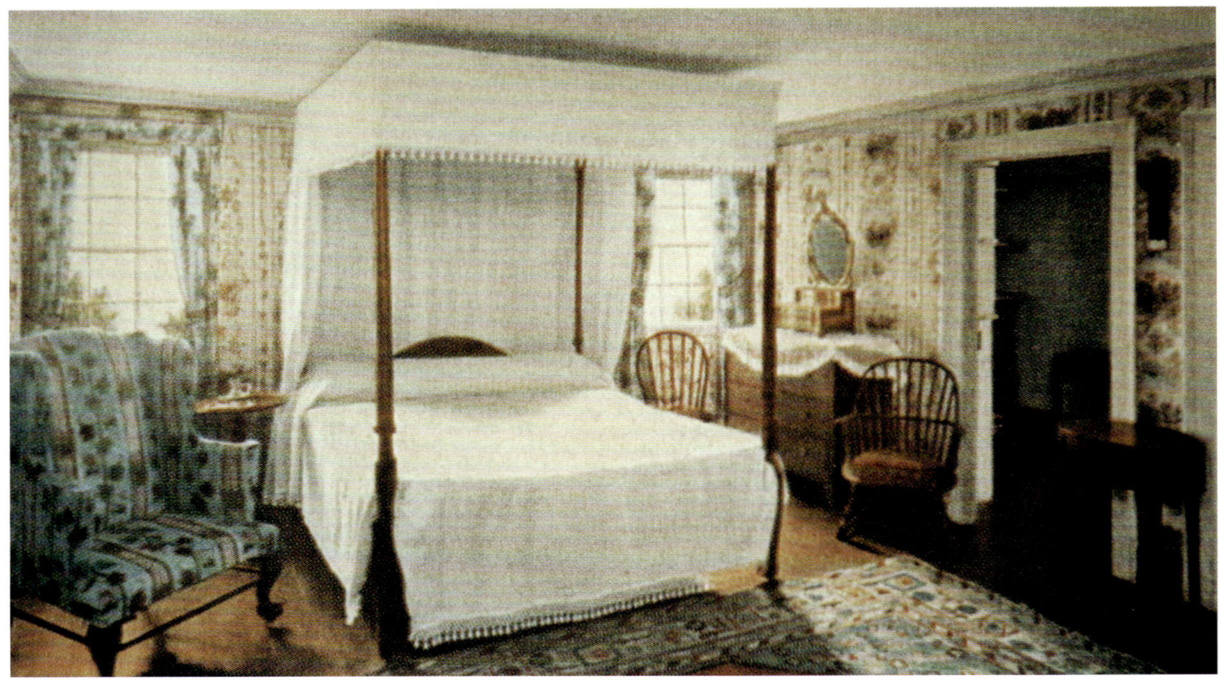

Fig. 1. (opposite) *George Washington,* by Rembrandt Peale, 1823, MVLA

Fig. 2. View of the Washington bedchamber when furnished with the Mary Ball Washington easy chair, ca. 1932

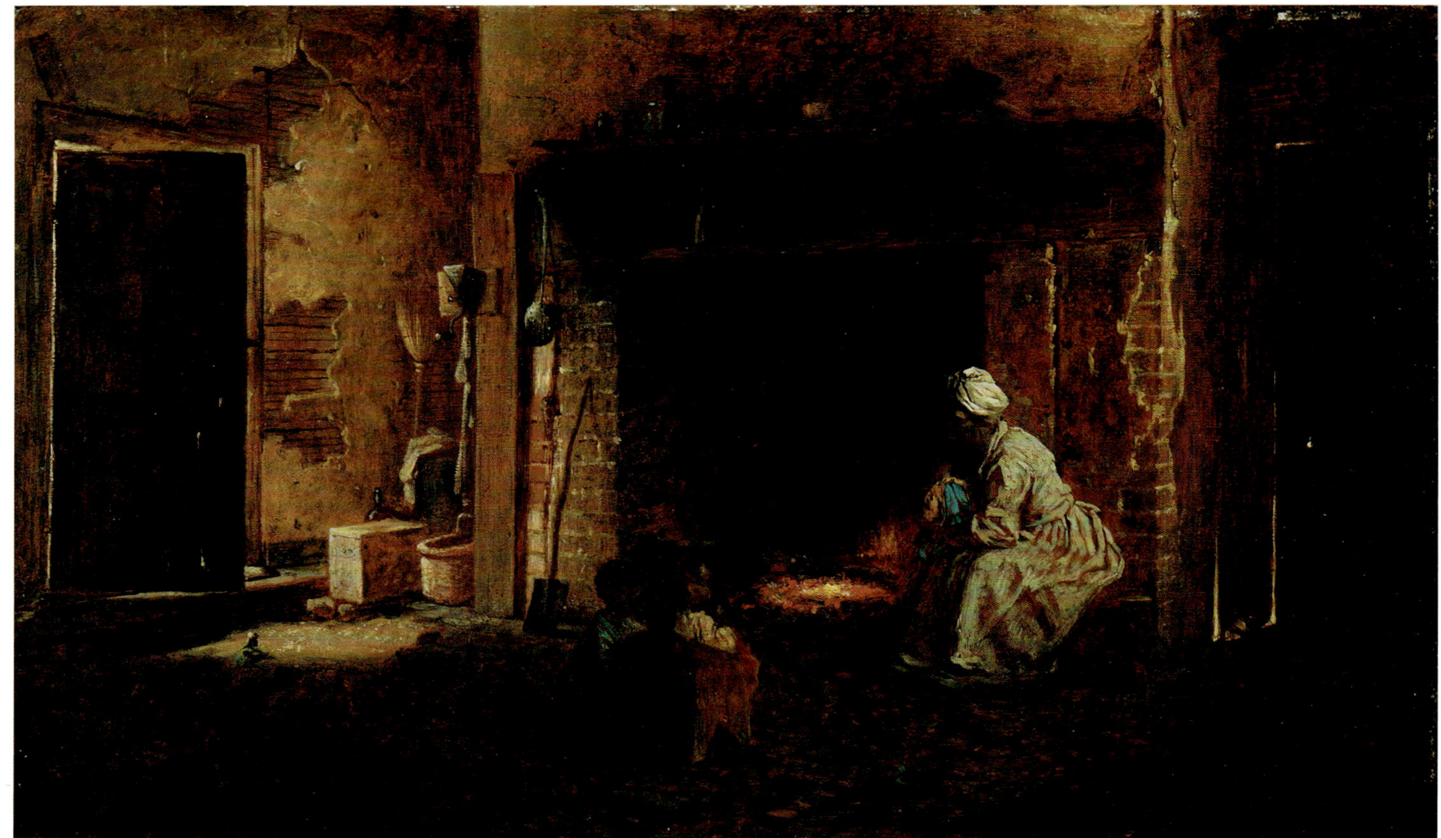

Fig. 3. Eastman Johnson was one of many artists to visit Mount Vernon, painting this view of the kitchen building and its slave inhabitants in 1864. *Washington's Kitchen at Mount Vernon*, by Eastman Johnson, oil on board, 1864, MVLA

been fashioned to memorialize and pay tribute to our nation's first president. At the war's end, American and imported European-manufactured goods were available to the consumer wishing to celebrate and honor the victorious general. In 1783 a Philadelphia shopkeeper "lately arrived from France" offered "all sorts of Jewelry and Modes of the highest taste and newest fashion" that included "Caps, half Caps, [&] Toques à la Washington" and "excellent fine Buttons à la Washington" of which some were "embroidered upon cloth, with the Liberty Tree."[3] With the resumption of trade, English textile mills were quick to produce and export for the American market yards of copperplated cottons emblazoned with Washington's image. The consumer's interest in objects featuring Washington continued throughout his lifetime.[4]

Washington's death on December 14, 1799, occasioned an outpouring of national grief and fueled the production of a wide range of prints, personal articles, and household goods. Less than three weeks after his funeral, the Philadelphia goldsmith Simon Chaudron advertised "Mourning Rings, With an elegant Portrait of the late illustrious General Washington."[5] Americans commissioned not only porcelains from China to memorialize Washington on their dining tables but also prints to hang on their walls.[6] The interest in objects heralding or memorializing Washington has not ceased.

As Washington's home, Mount Vernon has been included in the wealth of paintings and prints generated after his death. Some artists traveled to Mount Vernon, the "Mecca of the Western Hemisphere" as one artist termed it, to sketch and paint where Washington had lived.[7] Others have put brush to canvas in their studios to create posthumous portraits that are almost more remembered than those based on live sittings. The most sacred of objects crafted to memorialize the memory and legacy of George Washington, however, have been fashioned from true relics. They have preserved his hair in lockets, coffin fragments in elaborate cases, and buttons in gold mountings (fig. 4).

Although often overshadowed by her husband, Martha Washington's personal effects have also been treasured. Shortly after George Washington's death, a Society of Females wrote to the grieving widow to

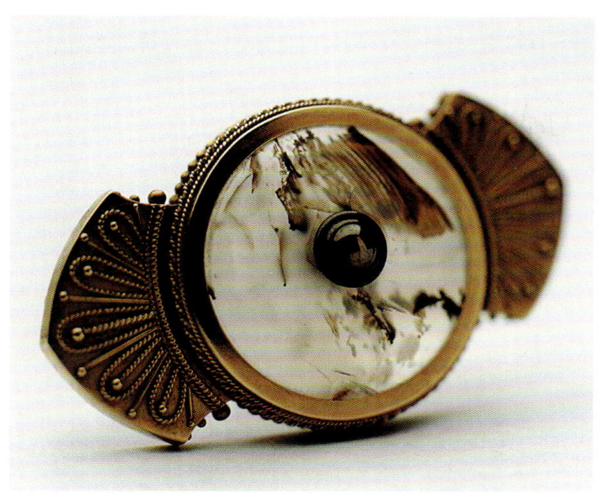

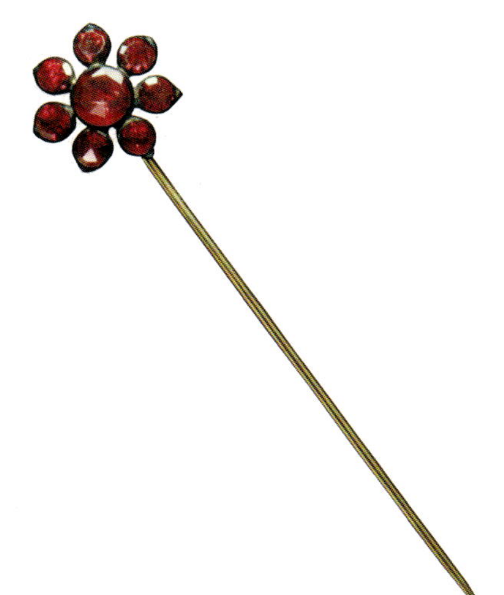

Fig. 4. (left) One of George Washington's agate buttons mounted as a gold brooch by one of George Washington Parke Custis' descendants, MVLA

Fig. 5. (right) Garnets from one of Martha Washington's necklaces fashioned into a pin by one of Martha Custis Peter's descendants, MVLA

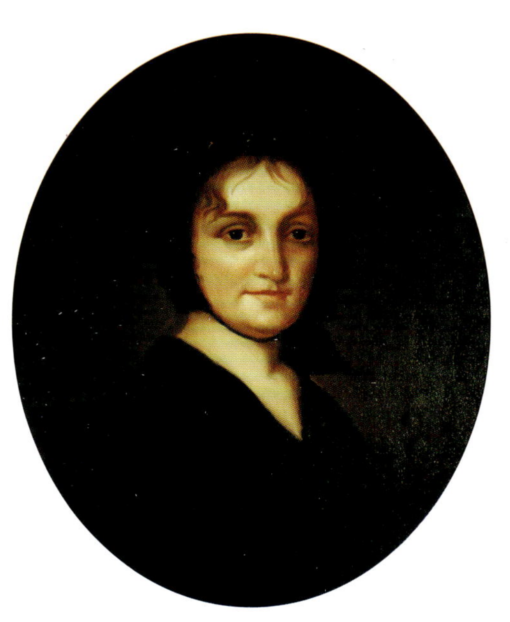

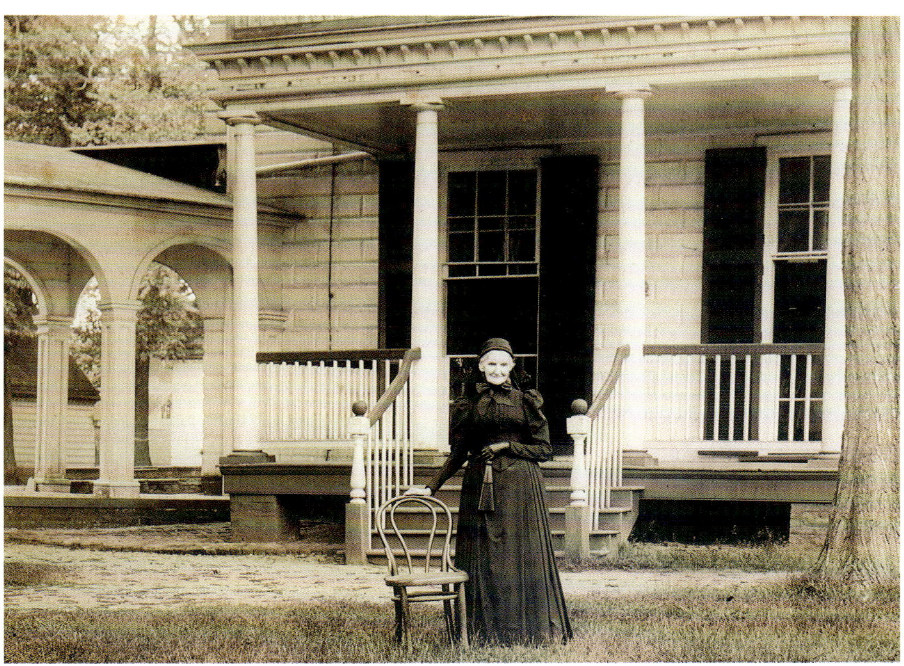

Fig. 6. (above left) Granddaughter Eleanor "Nelly" Parke Custis Lewis, who preserved numerous original Mount Vernon objects and personal articles, oil on canvas, MVLA

Fig. 7. (above right) Britannia Wellington Peter Kennon, Martha Washington's great-granddaughter, who preserved and catalogued treasured Washington articles.

request "some external remembrance of the Man 'first in War, first in Peace and first in the hearts of his Country'" in the form of "a lock, (however small) of his invaluable hair, while life remained we would wear it as a charm to deter us from ill and while gazing on it, think on the bright perfections of its former owner." But they also requested "a lock of your hair. Although we have not the happiness of being personally acquainted with you Madam, yet the chosen Friend of Washington, will ever be dear to our Hearts."[8] Whereas those who did not know her contented themselves with locks of her hair, her descendants divided and refashioned her jewelry to wear as tokens of remembrance and esteem for the family matriarch (fig. 5).

The George Washington Collection assembled at Mount Vernon includes a range of objects created to recall the lives and legacies of George and Martha Washington. These objects, like the ones Washington selected for his surroundings and attire, also have the power to communicate. They tell us that the individuals who made and owned them had an enduring appreciation of George Washington that spans four centuries, and that countless people desired to connect in a tactile way with the man regarded as "the embodiment of all that was noblest and best in the American people"[9] and remembered as "a wise, a good, & a great man."[10]

CAT. 96

Easy Chair

Attributed to Robert Walker
Virginia, ca. 1740–1760
Mahogany and beech, H. 46", W. 32", D. 31"
Purchase, 1910. Purchased with funds donated by the Detroit Mount Vernon Society.
Conservation courtesy of the Monica and Hermen Greenberg Foundation
W-152

Relics associated with the early life of George Washington were of particular interest to the Ladies' Association at the turn of twentieth century. This easy chair, with a history of ownership by Mary Ball Washington, caused a great deal of excitement when it was initially placed on loan to Mount Vernon in 1902, and later when it was offered for sale to the Association. The Vice Regent for Michigan, Elizabeth Rathbone, led the campaign to raise funds for the chair's purchase, noting its significance as "the oldest piece of furniture at Mount Vernon" and that it "was owned by his mother when George Washington was an infant."[11] With the assistance of the Detroit Mount Vernon Society,. Rathbone raised the money necessary to acquire the easy chair, and it was placed in the Washington bedchamber.

The chair's lofty associations and early introduction into the Mount Vernon collection no doubt helped to preserve what is now regarded as one of the most important pieces of Virginia seating furniture.[12] The chair has been attributed to the workshop of Robert Walker, a cabinetmaker from King George County, Virginia, whose clients included some of colonial Virginia's leading families.[13] Before his death in 1743, Augustine Washington, George's father, may have patronized Walker. In the years immediately following, it is doubtful that Mary Ball Washington could have afforded to do so or would have spent her limited resources for a purchase of this kind. Perhaps, then, the easy chair was a secondhand addition to Ferry Farm, George Washington's boyhood home or to Mary Ball Washington's later residence in Fredericksburg—both of which were situated in the general area of Walker's known patrons.

While it is not known when it entered the Washington household, the easy chair was no doubt a significant investment for the original owner. Upholstery research has identified the original foundation layers as well as the first generation of worsted wool upholstery fabric and linen tape trim. The original colors were dramatic, with the principal cloth a deep pink and mustard-colored damask outlined by blue-green trim.[14] Walker crafted an equally noteworthy frame, with all four mahogany cabriole legs adorned with scallop shell knee carving and claw-and-ball feet. A rare document of colonial upholstery, the easy chair is further distinguished as the only known eighteenth-century American example crafted with rear claw-and-ball feet.[15]

Although it was not in use at Mount Vernon and Washington was not likely held in it as an infant, this easy chair is a tangible example of the reverence shown for Mary Ball Washington and the type of relic that formed the base of the early Mount Vernon collection. Its preservation as an object with George Washington associations has also ensured the survival of an important link to understanding eighteenth-century Virginia craftsmen, upholstery, and interiors.

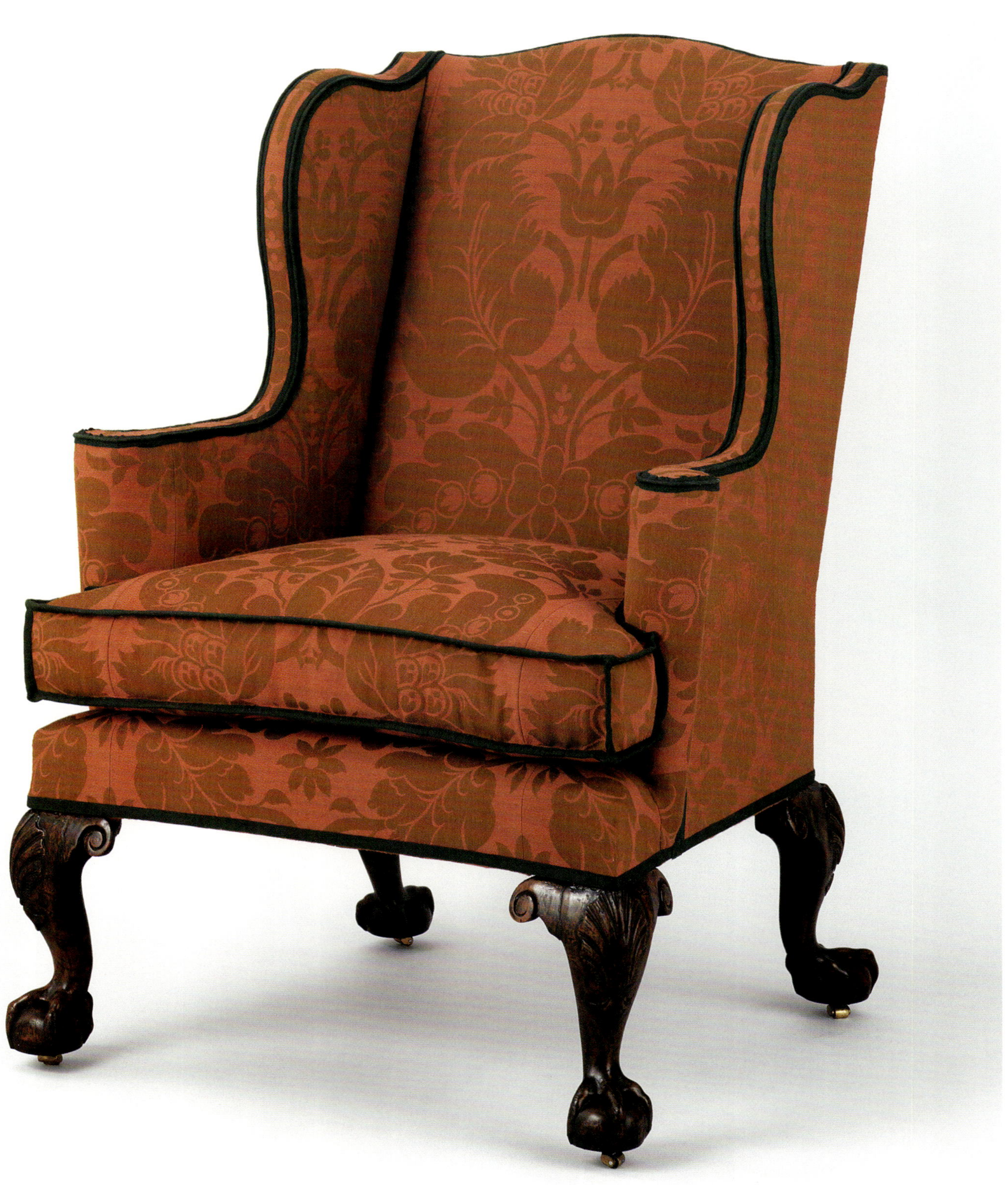

CAT. 97

Cross

America, ca. 1840–1860
Seed pearls and mother-of-pearl, H. 1 11/16", W. 15/16"
Gift of Mr. Barnaby Conrad, Jr., 1982
W-2831

Following Martha Washington's death, her descendants frequently refashioned jewelry so that each successive generation might wear a few of the stones, beads, or pearls that graced her ears or encircled her neck. In the mid-nineteenth century Katherine Williams Upshur, a great-great-granddaughter of Martha Washington, remade her inherited Martha Washington seed pearl necklace into a set of four cross pendants that could be equally shared among her four children.[16] As a deeply religious woman, Mrs. Washington would undoubtedly have approved of the selected form, and it may have been chosen with her sentiments in mind.[17]

This cross, like its three nearly identical counterparts, is composed of three sizes of seed pearls. The largest pearl rests atop a large rosette at the crossing, from which smaller vertical and horizontal rosettes emanate. The smallest pearls delicately encircle the rosettes and also form the pendant loop. With the exception of the loop, the cross is backed with thin pieces of mother-of-pearl to which the pearls are attached.

The American interest in seed pearl jewelry continued from Martha Washington's lifetime into the twentieth century.[18] For her descendants who wore this seed pearl cross, the prolonged period of fashion provided the ability to wear current styles while preserving the memory of Martha Washington and demonstrating an enduring appreciation of her legacy.

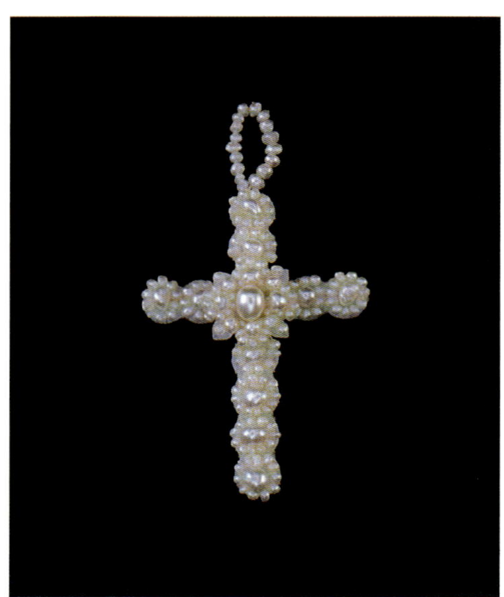

CAT. 98

Replica of George Washington's Sarcophagus

Robinson, Edkins and Aston
Birmingham, England, 1846
Silver and mahogany, L. 7½", W. 3½", H. 2½"
Purchased with funds donated by the Monica and Hermen Greenberg Foundation
2000.004

When the Philadelphia stonecutter John Struthers offered to supply a new marble sarcophagus for George Washington's remains at Mount Vernon, Lawrence Lewis replied on February 22, 1837, "The manner of making your offer, the delicacy with which it is proffered, forbids a refusal to accept it, and I tender you, in behalf of every relative of this distinguished man, a most cordial and sincere thanks for the kind of feeling which has actuated you upon this occasion." With respect to the form the sarcophagus should take, Lewis offered, "I leave it to your experience to make it in form and manner you think best."[19]

Struthers enlisted the help of the Philadelphia architect William Strickland for the design, which called for a sarcophagus "of the modern form" and a lid "emblazoned with the arms and insignia of the United States, beautifully sculpted in the boldest relief."[20] The completed sarcophagus arrived at Mount Vernon in October 1837, and Struthers was present for the transfer of Washington's remains when several pieces of the decaying coffin were kept as souvenirs. Struthers sent one fragment along with an engraving and description of the new marble sarcophagus to Jesse Hartley, a Liverpool businessman who had been instrumental in the stonecutter's immigration to the United States.

To house the precious relic, Hartley commissioned the Birmingham silversmiths Robinson, Edkins and Aston to craft this silver miniature replica of Washington's sarcophagus. The silversmiths combined the fragment and Struthers' engraving in a remarkably detailed and accurate replica of the marble original. The engraved exterior identifies the mahogany coffin fragment, the involvement of Struthers, and its ownership by Hartley.[21] The fragment itself rests in the gilded interior where it is secured to the lid and identified by the ink inscription "Washingtons Coffin" (detail). The replica survives today as an example of the great care taken on both sides of the Atlantic to preserve relics of George Washington and to fashion objects that express esteem for America's first president.

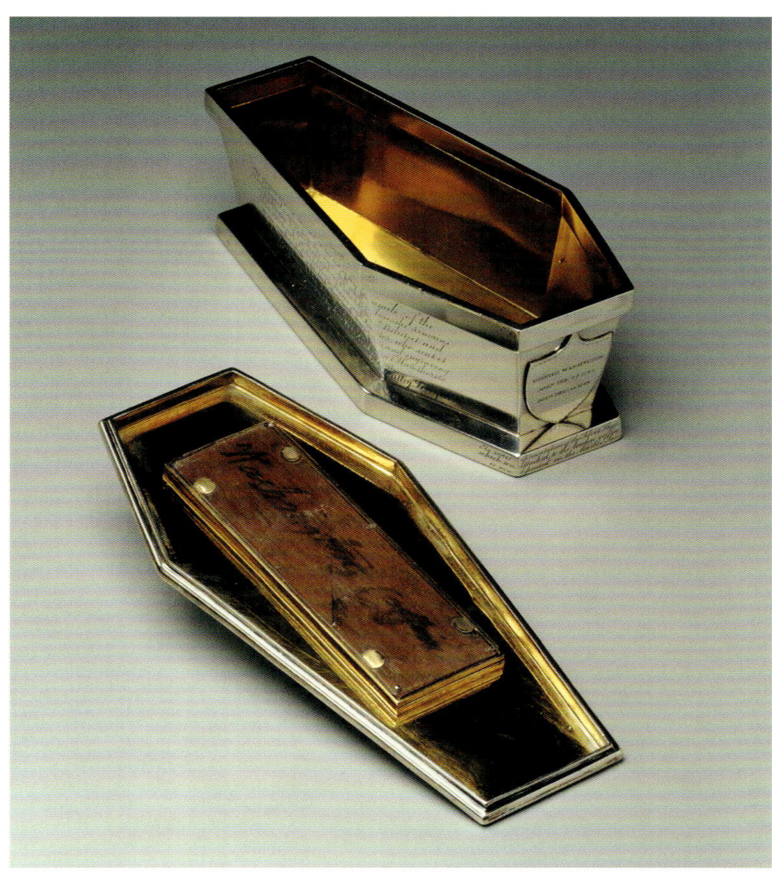

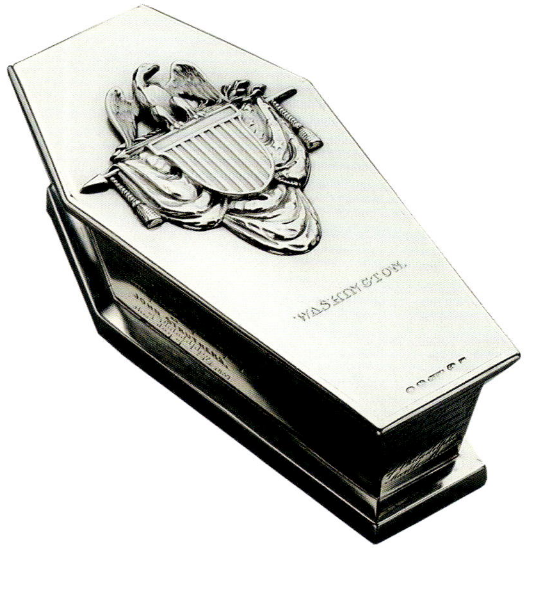

CAT. 99

Sewing Case

England and Europe, 1740–1800
Silk, wool, and metallic threads, L. 19", W. 4⅞"
Gift of Mrs. Marie Worthington Conrad Lehr in memory of Charles Angelo Conrad, 1915
W-588

Known for her needlework, Martha Washington regularly ordered needles, pins, thimbles, thread, and other sewing implements. In 1758, as a young widow overseeing the sewing needs of a large estate, she sent to London for "6 thousand Large pins," six thousand "short white" pins, "5 hundred of the Best White Chappel sorted neadles none Large, 5 hundred Large nedles to sew corse work . . . [and] 2 pound of Best Whited Brown thread."[22] Port cities such as Philadelphia also offered a ready supply of imported tools such as "White-chapel, blue point and common sewing and darning needles, Thimbles, scissars, sheers."[23] Small sewing cases were invaluable for storing the variety of needles, pins, thread, thimbles, and other sewing tools necessary for completing both basic and fancy needlework, and designs for them appeared in pattern books, where instructions allowed the use of any kind of fabric one had on hand.[24]

Designed to house the necessary tools of needlework, this sewing case features seven divisions, each utilizing a different fabric gleaned from various garments with a history of belonging to Martha Washington. At one end, five graduated semicircular layers of felted wool are trimmed with silver thread in a reticulated pattern, each flap sized for the storage of a wide variety of needles. Five pockets make up the body of the case in a combination of fabrics including white-bodied brocaded silks and a central blue-green silk damask.[25] Each pocket is lined with a pink satin-weave silk, with the exception of the damask fragment, for which a lining of the reversible fabric was not needed. A triangular flap of dark blue floral silk at the opposite end helped secure the contents of the sewing case after it was folded, and the entire case is trimmed with a small border of pink silk similar to that used to line the pockets.[26]

The dress fragments that were saved and used to make this sewing case are part of a continuing tradition of treasuring articles worn by Martha Washington. Small fragments of dress fabrics ranging in dates from the 1740s to the turn of the nineteenth century survive today in the Mount Vernon collection, other public collections, and in private hands.[27] Family members treasured these personal relics, cutting them into smaller and smaller pieces as they were distributed through the generations.[28] Passed down through the family of granddaughter Eleanor "Nelly" Custis Lewis, this sewing case combines the silks worn by Martha Washington in a utilitarian object that serves as a reminder of her personal style and skill with a needle.

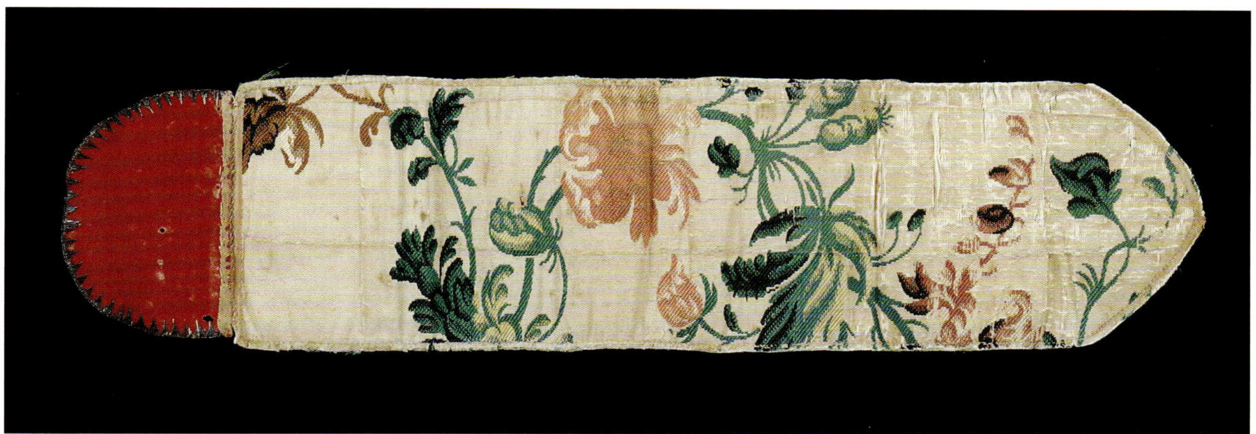
Exterior

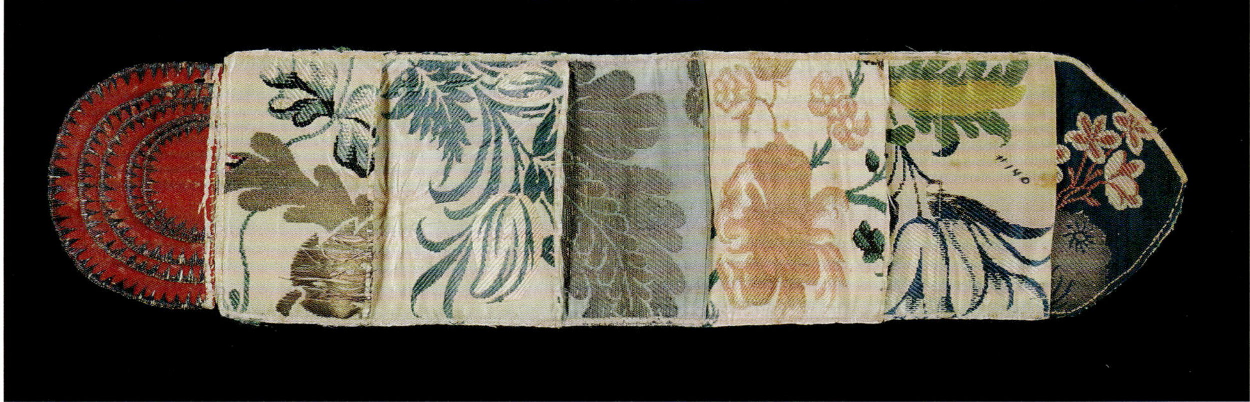
Interior

CAT. 100

George Washington and Family

ca. 1858–1860

Thomas P. Rossiter (1817–1871)[29]
New York
Oil on canvas, 15¼" x 26⅛"
Gift of Nanine Hilliard Greene, 2000
2000.16

In the 1850s the campaign of the Mount Vernon Ladies' Association to acquire and preserve George Washington's private residence spurred renewed interest in the Washington family. Artists, historians, and Washington enthusiasts had made the pilgrimage to Mount Vernon since Washington's lifetime, yet the official opening of Mount Vernon to the public transformed the once private Washington residence into a destination for Americans eager to connect with the founding father.

In 1857 the artist Thomas Rossiter began several large-scale historical compositions focused on the life of George Washington. He visited Mount Vernon in June 1858 and subsequently published a lengthy article detailing Washington's life and Mount Vernon. Rossiter's article demonstrated his deep admiration for "the great and good Washington" and his prediction that Mount Vernon would become "a shrine for coming generations."[30]

Rossiter's composition *George Washington and Family* bespeaks his visit to Mount Vernon as well as the influence of the author and historian Benson Lossing. In 1859 Lossing published *Mount Vernon and Its Associations*, which included numerous sketches of original Washington objects he had encountered during his research. Rossiter drew heavily on Lossing's volume, for his painting reflects the appearance and placement of the objects Lossing published. From the engraving of Louis XVI to the mantelpiece ornaments of "two small dark-blue vases, covered with flowers, delicately painted; and between . . . two bronze candelabra," the scene is filled with the objects included in Lossing's book (fig. 1).[31]

The painting is set in Washington's study, his most private of spaces, where the wall is lined with books in glass-fronted shelves, and his bust of French comptroller general Jacques Necker sits on the mantel. In addition to George and Martha Washington, Rossiter depicted Martha's granddaughters Eleanor and Elizabeth Custis, and an African American slave, perhaps the well-remembered Caroline. Martha, Nelly, and Eliza are romantically painted and their facial features appear nearly identical as they gaze at Washington, who reclines with one hand marking his place in a book while the other hand rests on what Lossing identified as "Washington's traveling writing-case."[32] The composition integrates the objects and people depicted and described by Lossing into a cohesive and pleasing composition that may deviate from historical accuracy but offers a portrait of the private side of Washington as well as the nineteenth-century admiration for a man Rossiter described as the nation's "Greatest and Best."[33]

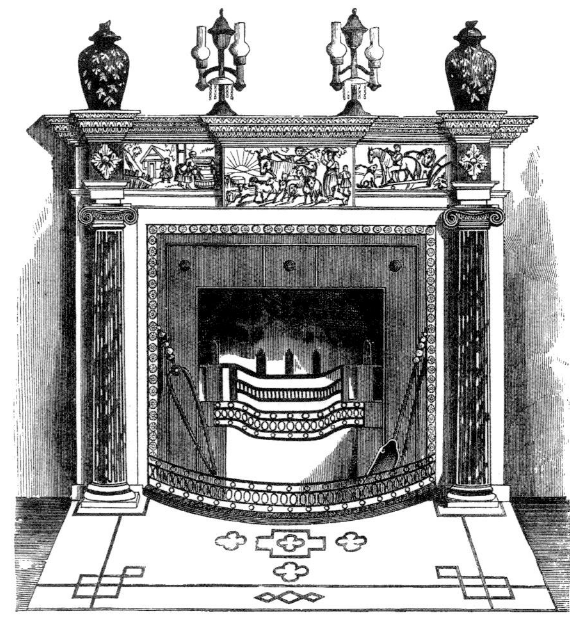

Fig. 1. Lossing's composition of Mount Vernon objects and mantlepiece, as published in 1859

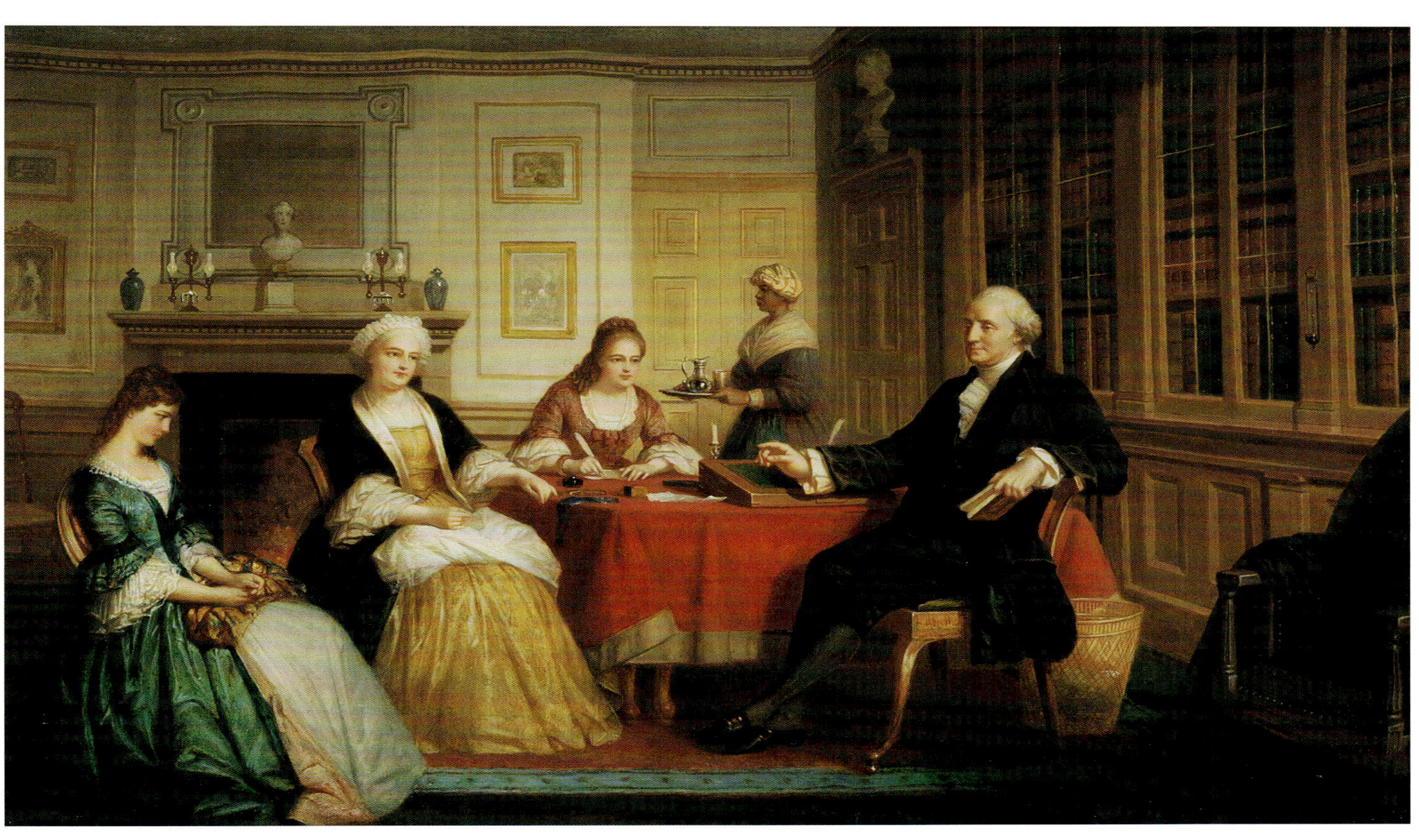

Photography Credits

Anonymous: introduction, figs. 1, 6, 7, 10, 11

ARPS: introduction, fig. 12

Gavin Ashworth: introduction, frontispiece, chap. 1, figs. 15, 17, 18, cats. 1–3, 6, 7–10, 13, 14, 17, 20, 23, 25, 26 and detail, 27 and details, chap. 3, fig. 3, cat. 28, fig. 1, cats. 30–32, cat. 33, fig. 1, cat. 35, chap. 3, fig. 9, cats. 36, 37, 39 and detail, 40, 42, 44, 46, 47, 49 and details, chap. 5 figs. 3, 4, cats. 53, 55, 56, 57 and detail, 58, 59, 61, cat. 62, fig. 1, 63, cats. 64 and detail, 65, 66, 67 and detail, 69, chap. 6 figs. 4, 6–9, cats. 72, 73, 74 and detail, 75, 78–80 and detail, 81, chap. 7, figs. 3, 4, 5, 7, 8, 12, cats. 83, 86–92, 94, 97, 99

Courtesy of The British Museum: cat. 7, fig. 1

Brooklyn Museum: cat. 23, fig. 1

Will Brown: chap. 1, fig. 9, cat. 4, cats. 22, 43

Harry Connolly: chap. 1, figs. 3, 19, 21, cat. 12, chap. 3, fig. 5, cat. 33, cats. 38, 47, 68, chap. 6 fig. 3, cats. 70, 71, chap. 7, figs. 4, 3, 6, cat. 84, afterword, fig. 8

Hal Conroy: chap. 3, figs. 6, 7, cat. 54, chap. 6 fig. 1

Conservation Center, Philadelphia: afterword, fig. 9

Cummins, Baltimore: introduction, fig. 8

Walter C. Densmore: cat. 23 detail, chap. 4, fig. 8, cat. 51 detail

Luke Dillon: introduction, fig. 5

Courtesy of Fairfax County Circuit Court: cat. 70, page from will

Mark Finkenstaedt: cat. 29, chap. 4, fig. 13, cat. 64 detail, chap. 6, fig. 2, cat. 90, red and cream striped floral, afterword, fig. 4

Robert B. Fisher: cats. 11, 20, chap. 5, fig. 1, cat. 70 (black & white)

Mark Gulezian: chap. 3, fig. 2, cat. 34, chap. 4, fig. 3, afterword, fig. 3, cats. 98, 100

Mark Hain: chap. 2, fig. 9

Carol Highsmith: chap 5. fig. 9

Courtesy of The Historical Society of Pennsylvania: chap. 4, fig. 11

Paul Kennedy: chap. 1, figs. 1, 14, chap. 4, figs. 2, 7, cats. 45, 50, 60. 95, afterword, fig. 5

Robert C. Lautman: introduction, fig. 13, chap. 1, fig. 4, chap. 3, figs. 1, 8, chap. 4, fig. 5, cat. 41, chap. 5 figs. 2, 5–8, 10, 11, afterword, fig. 6

Peter Leech: chap. 7, fig. 10

Leets Brothers: introduction, fig. 4

Marc LeFrancois: chap. 3, cat. 35

Taylor Lewis: cat. 23, fig. 2, cat. 82

Monte Markham: chap. 1, figs. 6, 8, chap. 2, fig. 1, chap. 3, fig. 9, chap. 4, fig. 1, chap 6, fig. 5

Howard Marler: introduction, fig. 2, cat. 5, chap. 7, fig. 11

MVLA: chap. 1, figs. 7, 16, chap. 2, figs. 3, 5, 10, 11, afterword, figs. 2, 7

Courtesy of the New-York Historical Society: chap. 4, fig. 4

Edward Owen: chap. 1, figs. 2, 11, 20, chap. 2, figs. 4, 7, cats. 18, 19, 24, chap. 4, figs. 6, 10, cats. 51, 52, 54 detail, 76, chap. 7, fig. 9, cats. 85, 92, afterword, figs. 1, 10

Smithsonian's National Museum of American History, Behring Center: chap. 1, fig. 10, chap. 4, fig. 12

Ted Vaughan: introduction, fig. 3, chap. 1, figs. 5, 12, chap. 2, figs. 2, 8, cats. 15, 16, 21, chap. 3, cat. 31. fig. 1, cat. 85 detail, chap. 7, fig. 1

Courtesy of the Washington-Custis-Lee Collection, Washington and Lee University, Lexington, Va.: chap. 1, figs. 13, 22, chap. 2, fig. 6

Frequently Cited Sources and Abbreviations

Buhler
Kathryn C. Buhler. *Mount Vernon Silver.* Mount Vernon, Va.: MVLA, 1957.

Decatur
Stephen Decatur, Jr. *Private Affairs of George Washington.* Boston: Houghton Mifflin, 1933.

Detweiler
Susan Gray Detweiler. *George Washington's Chinaware.* New York: Harry N. Abrams, 1982.

Fields
Joseph E. Fields, ed. *"Worthy Partner": The Papers of Martha Washington.* Westport, Conn.: Greenwood Press, 1994.

GW
George Washington

GWD
Donald Jackson and Dorothy Twohig, eds. *The Diaries of George Washington.* 6 vols. Charlottesville: University Press of Virginia, 1976–1979.

GWW
John C. Fitzpatrick, ed. *The Writings of George Washington.* 39 vols. Washington, D.C.: U.S. Government Printing Office, 1931–1944.

LWT
John C. Fitzpatrick, ed. *The Last Will and Testament of George Washington and Schedule of His Property to Which Is appended the Last Will and Testament of Martha Washington.* Rev. ed. Mount Vernon, Va.: MVLA, 1992.

MVI
Transcript of the Four Mount Vernon Estate Inventories, October 1973, MVLA Library.

MVLA
Mount Vernon Ladies' Association of the Union

MVLA AR
Mount Vernon Ladies' Association of the Union Annual Report

MW
Martha Washington

OED
Oxford English Dictionary. London: Oxford at the Clarendon Press, 1933.

PG
Pennsylvania Gazette. 4 fols. Malvern, Pa.: Accessible Archives, 1998. CD-ROM.

PGW Col.
W. W. Abbott, Dorothy Twohig, and Beverley H. Runge, eds. *The Papers of George Washington, Colonial Series.* 10 vols. Charlottesville: University of Virginia Press, 1983–95.

PGW Con.
W. W. Abbott, ed. *The Papers of George Washington, Confederation Series.* 6 vols. Charlottesville: University of Virginia Press, 1992–1997.

PGW Pres.
Dorothy Twohig, Mark Mastromarino, and Jack D. Warren, eds. *The Papers of George Washington, Presidential Series.* 12 vols. Charlottesville: University of Virginia Press, 1987–.

PGW Ret.
Dorothy Twohig, Philander D. Chase, Beverly H. Runge, Frank E. Grizzard, Jr., et al., eds. *The Papers of George Washington, Retirement Series.* 4 vols. Charlottesville: University of Virginia Press, 1998–1999.

PGW Rev.
W. W. Abbott, Dorothy Twohig, Philander D. Chase, and Beverly H. Runge, eds. *The Papers of George Washington, Revolutionary War Series.* 14 vols. Charlottesville: University of Virginia Press, 1985–.

NOTES TO THE INTRODUCTION

1. For a succinct overview of material culture and the value of its study, see Jules David Prown, "Mind in Matter: An Introduction to Material Culture Theory and Method," in *Material Life in America, 1600–1800*, ed. Robert Blair St. George (Boston: Northeastern University Press, 1988), 17–37.

2. For histories of the purchase and saving of Mount Vernon, see Elswyth Thane, *Mount Vernon Is Ours: The Story of Its Preservation* (New York: Duell, Sloan and Pearce, 1966); Elswyth Thane, *Mount Vernon, the Legacy: The Story of Its Preservation and Care since 1885* (Philadelphia: J. B. Lippincott, 1967); and Gerald W. Johnson, *Mount Vernon: The Story of a Shrine* (Mount Vernon, VA: MVLA, 1991).

3. The harpsichord (acc. no. W-16) was the Association's first acquisition. In 1859 Mrs. Robert E. Lee wrote from her home at Arlington House to John Augustine Washington III regarding the return of Nelly Custis Lewis's harpsichord to Mount Vernon. The harpsichord was transferred that year, and Mrs. Lee noted a wish to have the donation credited to Nelly Custis Lewis's widowed daughter-in-law, Mrs. Lorenzo Lewis.

4. Margaret J. M. Sweat, Vice Regent for Maine, Secretary, MVLA Minutes, 1870, 6.

5. In 1790 Gouverneur Morris wrote to the new president Washington, "I think it of very great Importance to fix the Taste of our Country properly, and I think your Example will go very far in that Respect." Gouverneur Morris to GW, January 24, 1790, PGW Pres., 5:48–49.

6. In a eulogy to George Washington on December 26, 1799, Henry "Light-Horse Harry" Lee proclaimed Washington "A citizen, first in war, first in peace, and first in the hearts of his countrymen." As cited in John Frederick Schroeder, *Maxims of George Washington* (Mount Vernon, VA: MVLA, 1989), 196.

7. Elswyth Thane, *Potomac Squire* (Mount Vernon, VA: MVLA, 1963), 413.

NOTES TO CHAPTER ONE

1. The property later became known as Wakefield, the name traditionally associated with George Washington's birthplace.

2. In 1732 England and the colonies were using the Julian calendar. When the Gregorian calendar was adopted in 1752, an adjustment of eleven days had to be made. Under the new system, dates were recorded with a single year, and Washington's birth date became February 22, 1732.

3. Augustine Washington's first wife, Jane Butler, died in 1729, leaving the widower with three children; Lawrence (1718–1752), Augustine (1720–1762), and Jane (1722–1734). In 1731 Augustine Washington married Mary Ball, with whom he had an additional six children: George (1732–1799), Betty (1733–1797), Samuel (1734–1781), John Augustine (1736–1787), Charles (1738–1799), and Mildred (1739–1740).

4. For more on the makeup of Virginia society at the time of Washington's youth, see Douglas Southall Freeman, *George Washington* (New York: Charles Scribner's Sons, 1948), 1:73–90.

5. Worthington Chauncey Ford, ed., *Wills of George Washington and His Immediate Ancestors* (Brooklyn, NY: Historical Printing Club, 1891), 42, 42n.

6. Washington's copy of *Rules of Civility and Decent Behaviour in Company and Conversation* was written about 1744 and is in the collection of the Library of Congress. For information on Washington's education, see William M. S. Rasmussen and Robert S. Tilton, *George Washington: The Man behind the Myths* (Charlottesville: University Press of Virginia, 1999), 9–12.

7. Lord Fairfax's extensive Virginia holdings were managed by his cousin, William, who lived with his family at Belvoir plantation. Lawrence Washington married William Fairfax's daughter, Anne.

8. GWD, 1:1–5.

9. Tuesday 15th [March 1748], GWD, 1:9–10.

10. Washington also presented his report orally to the Virginia legislature. See Commission from Robert Dinwiddie, October 30, 1753, PGW Col., 1:56–60, and Wednesday 31st [October 1753], GWD, 1:130–161.

11. Invoice, October 23, 1754, PGW Col., 1:217–219. The "1 Rich Crimson Ingr[ained] silk Sash" that Washington received may correspond to a survival in the Mount Vernon collection (acc. no. W-87).

12. Lease of Mount Vernon, December 17, 1754, PGW Col., 1:232–234.

13. Commission, August 14, 1755, PGW Col., 2:3–4.

14. Orders, October 6, 1755, PGW Col., 2:76.

15. George Washington had earlier conducted business with Anthony Bacon, a London merchant, and he wrote to Bacon on December 6, 1755, to alert him to the transfer of his business to Richard Washington. The young colonel thought that Richard Washington might be a relative and would be fair and careful. Richard Washington turned out not to be a relative.

16. GW to Richard Washington, December 6, 1755, PGW Col., 2:207–208.

17. Ibid., 2:207–209.

18. As quoted in Elswyth Thane, *Potomac Squire* (Mount Vernon, VA: MVLA, 1963), 17.

19. James Thomas Flexner, *Washington: The Indispensable Man* (Boston: Little, Brown and Co., 1974), 27–35.

20. GW to Richard Washington, April 15, 1757, PGW Col., 4:133.

21. Ibid., 132–134.

22. Richard Washington to GW, August 20, 1757, PGW Col., 4:376–381.

23. For more on George Washington's furniture purchases and his preference for the neat and plain, see Ronald L. Hurst, "From 'Neat and Plain' to Neoclassical," in *George Washington's Mount Vernon*, ed. Wendell Garrett (New York: Monacelli Press, 1998), 152–163.

24. Thomas Knox to GW, September 28, 1757, PGW Col., 4:427–428.

25. GW to Thomas Knox, January 1758, PGW Col., 5:87–88.

26. Dennis J. Pogue, "Mount Vernon: Transformation of an Eighteenth-Century Plantation System," in *Historical Archaeology of the Chesapeake*, ed. Paul A. Shackel and Barbara J. Little (Washington, DC: Smithsonian Institution Press, 1994), 103.

27. T. H. Breen, *Tobacco Culture: The Mentality of the Great Tidewater Planters on the Eve of the Revolution* (Princeton, NJ: Princeton University Press, 1985), 80–81.

28. Joseph J. Ellis, *His Excellency, George Washington* (New York: Alfred A. Knopf, 2004), 40.

29. GW to Robert Cary & Co., May 1, 1759, PGW Col., 6:315.

30. Ibid., 317–318.

31. GW to Robert Cary & Co., September 20, 1759, PGW Col., 6:348–358.

32. [May 1771], GWD, 3:25.

33. Fryday Feby. 15th [1760], GWD, 1:238.

34. GW to Robert Cary & Co., August 10, 1764, PGW Col., 7:323–326.

35. Breen, *Tobacco Culture*, 148.

36. Flexner, *Washington: The Indispensable Man*, 50.

37. GW to George Mason, April 5, 1769, PGW Col., 8:177–181.

38. GW to Robert Cary & Co., July 25, 1769, PGW Col., 8:229.

39. Ibid., 231–233. For more on GW's creamware purchase, see Detweiler, 53–60.

40. Breen, *Tobacco Culture*, 191.

41. [June 1771], GWD, 3:33.

42. GW to Robert Cary & Co., July 20, 1771, PGW Col., 8:506–507.

43. Invoice to Robert Cary & Co., July 18, 1771, PGW Col., 8:508–511. Martha Washington's copy of Hannah Glasse's book, likely the one specified in this order, survives in the Mount Vernon Archives.

44. [March 1772], GWD, 3:95.

45. [September 1771], GWD, 3:56.

46. [October 1772], GWD, 3:136–137.

47. [April–May 1773], GWD, 3:179–181.

48. [June 1773], GWD, 3:188.

49. GW to Burwell Bassett, June 20, 1773, PGW Col., 9:243–244. With Patsy's death, half of her estate went to Jacky and the other half to Martha Washington. George Washington used a portion of his wife's share to clear some of his debts with London agents and make improvements to Mount Vernon.

50. Eleanor Calvert was part of the distinguished Calvert family of Maryland. Her father, Benedict, was the illegitimate (but recognized) son of the fifth Lord Baltimore, Charles Calvert.

51. [May 1774], GWD, 3:251–252.

52. Invoice from Richard Washington, August 20, 1757, PGW Col., 4:379.

53. Samuel Wood was well known for cruet sets and individual casters and was likely engaged in a wholesale business. He trained Jabez Daniell in this specialty. Daniell was apprenticed to Wood on December 6, 1739, and was free from that apprenticeship on March 17, 1747. For further information on these two silversmiths, see Arthur G. Grimwade, *London Goldsmiths, 1697–1837* (London: Faber and Faber, 1976), 97, 190–191, 258, 483–484, 709.

54. The uniformity of the engraved griffins on the casters and bottle tops suggests the same shop or hand for engraving all three pieces of silver. This engraving is also similar to that found on the knives and forks that accompanied this shipment, thereby suggesting all were done at the same shop and perhaps by the same craftsman.

55. LWT, 56. In period terminology, *plate* referred to solid silver. *Plated ware* referred to silver plating over a base metal.

56. The maker's mark on this fork and on other elements of this flatware service is no longer decipherable. A script letter "D" is, however, legible and perhaps refers to a maker with that initial.

57. Mrs. Brown supplied the funds to purchase the fork at "The Final Sale of the Relics of General Washington" that took place in Philadelphia in 1891. See MVLA AR 1891, 10–11. The sale lots included items belonging to Lawrence Washington, Bushrod C. Washington, Thomas B. Washington, and J. R. C. Lewis. The owner of the fork at the time of the sale is not identified, but it could well have been Lewis, as the other surviving knives and forks of this kind descended in the Nelly Custis Lewis family before entering the collection of the Smithsonian Institution.

58. Invoice from Richard Washington, August 20, 1757, PGW Col., 4:376–380.

59. For additional information on early Chesapeake dining, see Barbara G. Carson, *Ambitious Appetites: Dining Behavior and Patterns of Consumption in Federal Washington* (Washington, DC: American Institute of Architects Press, 1990), 65–70.

60. Invoice from Thomas Knox, September 28, 1757, PGW Col., 4:427.

61. For additional information on Mount Vernon salt-glaze stoneware, see Detweiler, 21–30; and Ivor Noël Hume, *A Guide to Artifacts of Colonial America* (Philadelphia: University of Pennsylvania Press, 1969), 115–117.

62. The plates were supplied by the London Chinaman Richard Farrer. Invoice from Robert Cary & Co., March 31, 1761, PGW Col., 7:28.

63. For a discussion of press-molded plates and the use of stoneware at Mount Vernon, see Detweiler, 23–30.

64. Susan Gray Detweiler, "Table- and Teawares: Equipping the Washingtons' Table," in Garrett, *George Washington's Mount Vernon*, 194.

65. GW to Robert Cary & Co., July 25, 1769, PGW Col., 8:229–233. For further information, see Ann Smart Martin, "'Fashionable Sugar Dishes, Latest Fashion Ware': The Creamware Revolution in the Eighteenth-Century Chesapeake," in *Historical Archaeology of the Chesapeake*, ed. Paul A. Shackel and Barbara J. Little (Washington, DC: Smithsonian Institution Press, 1994), 174–177; and Detweiler, 53–60.

66. Dennis J. Pogue, "Slave Lifeways at Mount Vernon: An Archaeological Perspective," in *Slavery at the Home of George Washington*, ed. Philip J. Schwarz (Mount Vernon, VA: MVLA, 2001), 116–117. For additional information on archaeology at Mount Vernon, see Dennis J. Pogue, Esther C. White, and Eleanor E. Breen, "Digging for Trash and Finding Treasure at Mount Vernon," *Magazine Antiques* 168, no. 3 (September 2005): 88–95.

67. Lawyers representing the executors of Miss Margaret B. Smith of Washington, DC, effected the transfer of the tea service to Mount Vernon in May 1910. The bequest specified that the porcelain be identified as "Used by General and Mrs. Washington at Mount Vernon. To the Memory of Henrietta Elizabeth Smith, Grandniece of Martha Washington, Daughter of Commodore John Dandridge Henley, and Wife of J. Bayard H. Smith, Esq." MVLA AR 1910, 13–14.

68. George Washington's request for his set of "Fine Image China" is unknown. For his receipt, see Invoice from Richard Washington, August 20, 1757, PGW Col., 4:376–381. For further information on the tea service and its components, see Detweiler, 30–34.

69. PGW Col., 6:222.

70. PG, fol. 3 (1766–1783).

71. Mrs. George R. Goldsborough (née Eleanor Agnes Rogers) was born in Baltimore and died in 1906. A direct descendant of Martha Washington's granddaughter Eliza Parke Custis Law (1776–1831), Mrs. Goldsborough served as Vice Regent for Maryland of the MVLA from 1893 to 1904.

72. MVLA AR 1972, 19–22.

73. Louise Conway Belden, *The Festive Tradition: Table Decoration and Desserts in America, 1650–1900* (New York: W. W. Norton and Company, 1983), 77.

74. PGW Col., 6:315, 317.

75. Ibid., 336. For a complete list of items in the August 6, 1759, invoice from Robert Cary & Co., see ibid., 332. For additional information on Richard Farrer and this order, see Detweiler, 43–50.

76. For Euterpe, see Anton Gabszewicz, *Bow Porcelain: The Collection Formed by Geoffrey Freeman* (London: Lund Humphries, 1982), 128. For Clio, see Museum of Fine Arts, Boston, On-line Collections Database, acc. no. 1988.610.

77. As with the pair of Seasons, no maker's mark is evident on the Muses. They and other previously unknown and unlocated Washington objects sold at Christie's, New York, January 16, 2004.

78. The pair of Seasons were purchased by the Association in October 1974 from the estate of Stephen Decatur. According to Decatur, the Seasons were part of a gift sent by the Washingtons to the three children of Mary Lear Storer, sister of George Washington's secretary, Tobias Lear. See Stephen Decatur, "A Gift from Washington," *Magazine Antiques* (February 1937): 67. This provenance suggests that the porcelain figures left the Washingtons' possession in their lifetimes. The time span between the breaking up of the two pairs would, therefore, be over two hundred years.

79. The jelly glass is part of the G. Freeland Peter Collection, which contains objects that descended in the family of Martha Custis Peter of Tudor Place, one of Martha Washington's granddaughters. This jelly glass is listed as number 177 on the Peter Family List (PFL), a numbered listing of Washington objects in the Peter family, compiled by Britannia Wellington Peter Kennon.

80. GW Invoice to Robert Cary & Co., May 1, 1759, PGW Col., 6:317.

81. Invoice from Robert Cary & Co., August 6, 1759, PGW Col., 6:332–336.

82. G. Bernard Hughes, *English, Scottish and Irish Table Glass* (New York: Bramhall House, 1956), 273–293.

83. First Draft, 1802, MVI, 46. The "3 doz. Jelly Glasses" were valued at five dollars.

84. Hartshorne was derived from the horn of a male deer (hart) and was used as a jelling agent. For a further discussion, see Belden, *The Festive Tradition*, 161.

85. For a transcribed list of Martha Washington's jelly recipes, see Karen Hess, transcriber, *Martha Washington's Booke of Cookery* (New York: Columbia University Press, 1981), 358ff.

86. Charles F. Montgomery, *A History of American Pewter* (New York: Praeger Publishers, 1973), 1.

87. PGW Col., 6:326–328, 332–333.

88. Appraisers Inventory, 1800, MVI, 53.

89. Thomas Peter's list of items purchased at the 1802 sale list a "Lot Sundries" immediately before noting his purchase of "6 Water Plates." As Peter's purchase of Washington's pewter plates is not specified in his 1802 purchase list, it is possible that the plates were among the sundries noted. See *An Account of Sales of the Personal estate of Martha Washington (not specifically devised) late of Mount Vernon deceased—as rendered to me by Thomas Peter the Executor*, in MVLA AR 1959, 26–27. In 1956 George Washington's pewter plates and hot-water plates returned to Mount Vernon through G. Freeland Peter, a direct descendant of Thomas and Martha Peter. This plate is noted as number 113 on the Peter Family List, the numbered listing of Washington objects in the Peter family, created by Britannia Wellington Peter Kennon before her death.

90. This punch bowl is part of the G. Freeland Peter Collection at Mount Vernon which contains objects that descended in the family of Martha Custis Peter of Tudor Place, one of Martha Washington's granddaughters.

91. Rum was a product distilled from sugarcane (like molasses) of the great sugar plantations of the West Indies. For a discussion of the derivation of the word *punch*, see Belden, *The Festive Tradition*, 237.

92. GW to Thomas Knox, January 1758, PGW Col., 5:87–88. Invoice from Thomas Knox, August 18, 1758, PGW Col., 5:399–400.

93. Invoice from Robert Cary and Company, November 17, 1766, PGW Col., 7:475.

94. Detweiler, 28.

95. First Draft, 1802, MVI, 46.

96. Julian Ursyn Niemcewicz, *Under Their Vine and Fig Tree: Travels through America in 1797–1799, 1805*, trans. and ed. Metchie J. E. Budka (Elizabeth, NJ: Grassman Publishing Company, 1965), 96.

97. The maker's mark on the strainer, "S•M," can be identified as that of Samuel Meriton I, and his working dates agree with the 1750–1751 assay date letter. Samuel Meriton was apprenticed to William Wheat in 1731 and by 1739 was free and listed as a smallworker. For this and information noted in text, see Grimwade, *London Goldsmiths*, 186, 594.

98. To date, no invoice or record has surfaced to identify by whom this strainer was initially purchased. The 1750–1751 date stamp predates George Washington's earliest known receipt of English silver, and the strainer may therefore be part of the 187 pounds of "plate" that John "Jacky" Parke Custis inherited at the time of his father's death. That silver no doubt went with Jacky, his mother, and sister to Mount Vernon at the time of Martha Custis' marriage to George Washington. On the Peter Family List (a numbered listing of Washington objects in the Peter family compiled by Britannia Wellington Peter Kennon before her death), the strainer, number 35, is noted as "Custis plate," perhaps a reference to its Custis (as opposed to Washington) family origins.

99. Appraisers Inventory, 1800, MVI, 47.

100. For further information on Frank, his wife, Lucy (one of Martha Washington's slaves), and their children, see Mary V. Thompson, "Slaves at Mount Vernon in 1799," manuscript, 2005, Mount Vernon Library.

101. The spoon, one of three now in the Mount Vernon collection of the original two dozen ordered in 1762, was acquired by the donor's ancestor, Ann Eliza Coryton, from the property of Bushrod Washington, nephew of George Washington and heir to the Mount Vernon property in 1802.

102. GW to Robert Cary & Co., November 15, 1762, PGW Col., 7:167.

103. Invoice from Robert Cary & Co., April 13, 1763, PGW Col., 7:191–197.

104. Goldsmith John Payne was the son of an upwardly mobile goldsmith, Humphrey Payne, who had moved into the ranks of the merchants. He had followed in his father's footsteps after the elder Payne's death in 1751, succeeding to his father's fortune and his business, and therefore serving as a supplier rather than silversmith on this order. Ian Pickford, ed., *Jackson's Silver and Gold Marks of England, Scotland & Ireland*, 3rd rev. ed. (Woodbridge, Suffolk: Antique Collectors' Club, 1989), 253; Arthur G. Grimwade, *London Goldsmiths, 1697–1837, and Their Lives*, 2nd rev. ed (Trowbridge, Eng.: Redwood Burn, 1982), 196, 485.

105. Charles Willson Peale was born in Queen Anne's County, Maryland, and became a saddler's apprentice in Annapolis at the age of thirteen. Because of financial and political reasons, Peale abandoned the saddlers trade in 1764 and taught himself to paint with the assistance of John Hesselius. In 1767 a number of Peale's patrons financed his trip to England to study under Benjamin West. Peale returned to America in 1769 and lived in Annapolis until 1775. In 1775 Peale moved to Philadelphia and joined the city militia, where his regiment fought in the 1776 and 1777 battles at Trenton and Princeton. After the Revolutionary War, Peale remained in Philadelphia and served on a number of committees, including the General Assembly of Pennsylvania. As an artist, Peale made a deliberate effort to create a pictorial record of the Revolution and its leaders, creating many miniature portraits of his fellow officers while they were encamped. Peale is noteworthy for having painted Washington from life at least seven times over the course of twenty-three years (1772–1795) and is responsible for the first portrait of Washington, painted at Mount Vernon in 1772 at the same time these miniatures were rendered. Dumas Malone, ed., *Dictionary of American Biography* (New York: Charles Scribner's Sons, 1934), 14:345.

106. GWD, 3:108–109.

107. When George Washington extracted from his May 1772 ledger those items that were to be charged to his guardian accounts of John Parke Custis and Martha Parke Custis, he mistakenly transcribed the numbers. See GWW, 3:84, for a transcription of Washington's May 1772 ledger entry for the portrait and miniatures. For a transcription of the entry into John Parke Custis's accounts, see PGW Col., 9:367. For a transcription of the entry into Martha Parke Custis's accounts, see PGW Col., 9:370. These discrepancies, and the manner in which Washington described the portraits in his ledger, have led to the misunderstanding that the miniatures charged to the Custis accounts and that noted for Martha Washington were miniature portraits of George Washington.

108. Lillian B. Miller, ed., *The Selected Papers of Charles Willson Peale and His Family* (New Haven: Yale University Press, 1983), 1:120.

109. The miniature portrait of Martha Washington by Charles Willson Peale in the collection of the Yale University Art Gallery has traditionally been identified as this one, painted in 1772. See Miller, *The Selected Papers of Charles Willson Peale*, 1:120 n. 1; and Charles Coleman Sellers, *Portraits and Miniatures by Charles Willson Peale* (Philadelphia: American Philosophical Society, 1952), 42: part 1, 242. Mount Vernon's purchase of a miniature of Martha Washington in 1956 (postdating Sellers's volume) brought to light the miniature Sellers thought Peale painted in the summer of 1776 when Mrs. Washington was in Philadelphia. I believe that the Mount Vernon miniature is the one painted in 1772 and that the one at Yale was painted in 1776. Martha Washington appears older in the Yale miniature and more somber, perhaps owing to her daughter's death. Her more youthful appearance in Mount Vernon's miniature and the stylistic similarity of the miniature to those of Jacky and Patsy in 1772 suggest a 1772 date.

110. MW to Charles Willson Peale, December 26, 1780, Fields, 185.

111. Charles Willson Peale to MW, January 16, 1781, Fields, 185.

112. The miniature of Martha Washington was reset at a later date to include a replica miniature portrait of Jacky.

113. For additional information on this suite of silver and examples, see Buhler, 24–33.

114. Philippa Glanville, *Silver in England* (Winchester, MA: Allen & Unwin, 1987), 172.

115. Old Bailey Proceedings Online, May 1773, trial of David M'Lane (t17710515–10), www.oldbaileyonline.org (accessed August 10, 2005). This case gives details of John Carter and those who worked at his shop, located in Bartholomew Close in May 1773.

116. Grimwade, *London Goldsmiths*, 459. The four silver-plated candlesticks at Mount Vernon from the Custis suite (acc. no. W-2521/A-D) were initially stamped by John Winter & Co. of Sheffield.

117. Paul Davidson, *Antique Collector's Directory of Period Detail* (Hauppauge, NY: Barron's Educational Series, 2000), 99.

118. Replacing the teakettle and spirit lamp, this form appeared in England in the mid-eighteenth century (it was known afterward in France as a *forme anglaise*). Carl Hernmarck, *The Art of the European Silversmith, 1430–1830* (New York: Sotheby Parke Bernet, 1977), 1:149.

119. John Parke Custis's 1781 list survives as part of a scrapbook in the Mount Vernon Archives. For a transcript of the listing, see MVLA AR 1987, 48. Abingdon plantation, the home of Eleanor and John Parke Custis, was situated north of Mount Vernon along the Potomac River, on the site now occupied by Ronald Reagan National Airport.

120. GW to Robert Cary & Company, September 20, 1765, PGW Col., 7:402-404. Washington's requested hunting whip was supplied by "Davidson & Dennis Sadlery" and described as "A very best whole Hunter Whip, with a long silver Cap engravd George Washington." See Invoice from Robert Cary & Co., December 20, 1765, PGW Col., 7:418–420.

121. The core is visible at the narrower end of the crop, where the original leather loop was once located.

122. Rita Susswein Gottesman, *The Arts and Crafts in New York, 1726–1776* (New York: New-York Historical Society, 1938), 321. By 1780 Amory was advertising by himself as a manufacturer and seller of the "best and newest fashioned Horsewhips." See Rita Susswein Gottesman, *The Arts and Crafts in New York, 1777–1799* (New York: New-York Historical Society, 1954), 313. In 1787 Amory is listed in David C. Franks's New York City Directory as "Amery, John, whip-maker, No. 94 Broadway." Microfiche, MVLA Library.

NOTES TO CHAPTER TWO

1. GW to George William Fairfax, May 31, 1775, PGW Col., 10:367–368.

2. George Washington and fellow gentlemen volunteers of Fairfax County, Virginia, formed the Fairfax Independent Company in 1774–1775. For details of the blue and buff uniform they selected, see chapter 6.

3. William Spohn Baker, *Itinerary of General Washington from June 15, 1775 to December 23, 1783* (Philadelphia: J. B. Lippincott Co., 1892), 2.

4. Cash Accounts, PGW Col., 10:369–370.

5. Address to the Continental Congress, June 16, 1775, PGW Rev., 1:1–3.

6. GW to MW, June 18, 1775, PGW Rev., 1:3–6.

7. Washington also wrote to his stepson John Parke Custis, noting that he had "been called upon by the unanimous voice of the Colonies to take the command of the Continental Army—It is an honour I neither sought after, or was by any means fond of accepting, from a consciousness of my own inexperience, and inability to discharge the duties of so important a Trust." GW to John Parke Custis, June 19, 1775, PGW Rev., 1:15. He penned a similar letter to the officers of the five Virginia independent companies (gentlemen volunteers who organized themselves by county), claiming that he had been "launched into a wide & extensive field, too boundless for my abilities, & far, very far beyond my experience," and reiterated the sentiment in a letter to his brother, John Augustine Washington, June 20, 1775, PGW Rev., 1:16–17.

8. For further information on campaign furnishings, see Nicholas A. Brawer, *British Campaign Furniture: Elegance under Canvas, 1740–1914* (New York: Harry N. Abrams, 2001). For descriptions of those material comforts enjoyed by the Marquis de Lafayette and some of the British officers whose belongings were captured in July 1779, see Joseph M. Thatcher and Maurice H. O'Brien, *George Washington Slept Here . . . But Where Did He Sleep? A Furnishing Plan for Washington's Headquarters, State Historic Site, Newburgh, New York* (Waterford, NY: New York Office of Parks, Recreation and Historic Preservation, 1985).

9. Detweiler, 65.

10. His expense account notes them as "cash paid for Sadlery, a Letter Case, Maps, Glasses, etc., etc., for the use of my command." John C. Fitzpatrick, *George Washington's Accounts of Expenses while Commander-in-Chief of the Continental Army* (Boston: Houghton Mifflin, 1917), 2.

11. Invoice to His Excellency Genl Washington from William Vans, July 7, 1775, photostat, MVLA Library, original, Library of Congress. With the invoice, Vans apologetically noted that he "could procure only part of the Spoons now, the remainder will be made and sent next week." See William Vans to Colonel J. Reade, July 7, 1775, Washington Papers, Library of Congress.

12. Fitzpatrick, *George Washington's Accounts of Expenses*, 6–15.

13. Mabel Lorenz Ives, *Washington's Headquarters* (Upper Montclair, NJ: privately printed, 1932), 27–40.

14. For a listing of the types and number of stoneware items provided Washington, see Detweiler, 205.

15. Ives, *Washington's Headquarters*, 36–37.

16. GW to Lieutenant Colonel Joseph Reed, February 26–March 9, 1776, PGW Rev., 3:369–379.

17. Lieutenant Colonel Joseph Reed to GW, March 15, 1776, PGW Rev., 3:475.

18. Advertisement, October 19, 1769, PG, fol. 3 (1776–1783).

19. Advertisement, January 18, 1775, PG, fol. 3 (1776–1783).

20. Invoice, Plunket Fleeson to GW, May 4, 1776, photostat, MVLA Library, RM-244, FACS-2728. For more on Washington's military tents and images, see *General Washington's Military Equipment* (Mount Vernon, VA: MVLA, 1963), 21–22.

21. Fitzpatrick, *George Washington's Accounts of Expenses*, 23. Fitzpatrick mistakenly identifies Hollingshead as a Boston merchant, when he was, in fact, a Philadelphia silversmith. Hollingshead advertised in the *Pennsylvania Gazette* on January 5, 1774: "William Hollingshead, Silversmith, the lower corner of Arch and Second Streets." PG, fol. 3 (1776–1783). For a transcription of the purchase from Hollingshead, see Buhler, 34.

22. Fitzpatrick, *George Washington's Accounts of Expenses*, 23. Joseph Stanbury was an importer of glass and ceramics, whose shop on Second Street was next to that of Edmund Milne, the silversmith who fashioned Washington's silver camp cups in 1777. See Stanbury's advertisement of September 15, 1767, PG, fol. 3 (1776–1783).

23. Lieutenant Colonel Joseph Reed to GW, March 15, 1776, PGW Rev., 3:478 n. 6. Original invoices are in the Washington Papers, Library of Congress.

24. Invoices survive in the Washington Papers, Library of Congress, and are accessible online. See George Washington Papers at the Library of Congress, 1741–1799: Series 5. Financial Papers, http://rs6.loc.gov/ammem/gwhtml/gwhome.html. For transcriptions, see Detweiler, 205–206. For more on the types of ceramics represented, see Detweiler, 64–67.

25. As cited in John A. Garraty, *The American Nation*, 7th ed. (New York: Harper Collins, 1991), 111.

26. GW to Captain Caleb Gibbs, May 1, 1777, PGW Rev., 9:320–323.

27. "Historical Notes of Dr. Benjamin Rush," *Pennsylvania Magazine of History and Biography* 26, no. 2 (1903): 148. Rush notes that in March 1778 he found "the encampment dirty & stinking, no forage for 7 days—1500 horses died from ye want of it. 3 ounces of meal & pounds of flour in 7 days. Men dirty & ragged. The commander-in-chief and all ye Major Generals lived in houses out of ye Camp."

28. MW to Mercy Otis Warren, March 7, 1778, Fields, 177–178.

29. Gilbert Chinard, ed. and trans., *George Washington as the French Knew Him: A Collection of Texts* (Princeton, NJ: Princeton University Press, 1940), 13–16.

30. Ives, *Washington's Headquarters*, 192–197.

31. GW to John Mitchell, February 17, 1779, GWW, 14:127–128.

32. Detweiler, 67.

33. James Thacher, *Military Journal of the American Revolution* (Hartford, CT: Hurlbut, Williams and Company, 1862), 160.

34. Ibid., 162. Gérard consulted Washington about the operations of the Comte d'Estaing's fleet, while Marailles served as an unofficial agent to assist the King of Spain in his evaluation of Washington and the Americans.

35. Thacher, *Military Journal of the American Revolution*, 162.

36. Ibid., 163.

37. Baker, *Itinerary of General Washington*, 163.

38. GW to Doctor John Cochran, August 16, 1779, GWW, 16:116–117.

39. Chinard, *George Washington as the French Knew Him*, 38–39.

40. Ibid., 76.

41. GW to Colonel Elisha Sheldon, January 30, 1781, GWW, 21:162 n. 53.

42. GW to Colonel Samuel Miles, July 8, 1782, GWW, 24:404–405.

43. GW to Colonel Samuel Miles, August 15, 1782, GWW, 25:20–21.

44. Colonel Samuel Miles to GW, August 19, 1782, George Washington Papers at the Library of Congress, 1741–1799: Series 4. General Correspondence, 1697–1799, http://rs6.loc.gov/ammem/gwhtml/gwhome.html.

45. George Bennet to his mother, April 15, 1783, GWW, 26:321n.

46. Proclamation, November 4, 1783, GWW, 27:229–230.

47. Address to Congress on Resigning His Commission, December 23, 1783, GWW, 27:284–285.

48. The field bed descended in the family of George Washington's great-nephew, George Fayette Washington, until its return to Mount Vernon by Miss Birdie Washington. George Fayette Washington (1790–1867) was nine at the time George Washington died. He might have been given the bedstead or it could have been a gift to his father, George Augustine Washington (1763–1793), who was an officer in the Revolutionary War. The mahogany headboard, two tester frames, and two central hinged legs are not original.

49. For a history of campaign furnishings and their use, see Brawer, *British Campaign Furniture*.

50. Thomas Sheraton, *The Cabinet Dictionary* (London, 1803), 1:123.

51. Thomas Chippendale (active c. 1747–1779), George Hepplewhite (d. 1786), William Ince (active 1758–1804), John Mayhew (active c. 1758–1804), and Thomas Sheraton (active 1751–1805) all published designs for field beds. Brawer, *British Campaign Furniture*, 31–32.

52. Thomas Chippendale, *Gentleman and Cabinet-makers Director: Being a large collection of the most elegant and useful designs of Household Furniture, in the most fashionable taste* (London, 1762; repr., New York: Towse Publishing Company, 1938), pls. XLIX and XLIXa.

53. Ibid., pl. XLIX.

54. Fitzpatrick, *George Washington's Accounts of Expenses*, 4.

55. For additional campaign beds attributed to Washington's use, see Paula Deitz, "Design Notebook—Washington Slept Here, Often on a Camp Cot," *New York Times*, July 3, 1980, C10.

56. *Inventory of the Contents of Mount Vernon 1810* (Portland, OR: privately printed, 1909), 47.

57. See *General Washington's Swords and Campaign Equipment: An Illustrated Catalogue of Military Memorabilia in the Mount Vernon Collection* (Mount Vernon, VA: MVLA, 1948), 32–33; GW to Richard Washington, March 18, 1758, PGW Col., 5:105, and Invoice from Robert Cary & Co., December 3, 1771, PGW Col., 8:558–559.

58. The red-and-white trim is sometimes referred to as livery lace, elaborate edgings of the period that were woven in cut or uncut velvet using worsted wool or silk, and sometimes gold or silver. For a description of the red-and-white livery lace specified by George Washington, see Linda Baumgarten, *What Clothes Reveal: The Language of Clothing in Colonial and Federal America* (New Haven: Yale University Press, for the Colonial Williamsburg Foundation, 2002), 128–131.

59. GW to Robert Cary & Co., August 12, 1771, PGW Col., 8:516–517.

60. The pistol holders were part of a group of military items identified by the family as belonging to George Washington and left at Mount Vernon by John Augustine Washington III when he turned over the property to the Mount Vernon Ladies' Association in 1860.

61. GW to Nathaniel Woodhull, August 8, 1776, PGW Rev., 5:640–642.

62. GW to Colonel John Cox or John Mitchell, October 4, 1778, GWW, 13:23–24.

63. GW to Lieutenant Colonel John Laurens, January 30, 1781, GWW, 21:162n.

64. GW to Major General John Sullivan, June 17, 1777, PGW Rev., 10:64–65.

65. For additional information on Pyefinch, see E. G. R. Taylor, *The Mathematical Practitioners of Hanoverian England, 1714–1840* (Cambridge: Cambridge University Press, 1965), 270.

66. LWT, 17, 34.

67. As cited in Charles Coleman Sellers, *The Portraits and Miniatures by Charles Willson Peale* (Philadelphia: American Philosophical Society, 1952), 221.

68. As cited in Lillian B. Miller, ed., *The Selected Papers of Charles Willson Peale and His Family* (New Haven: Yale University Press, 1983), 1:191–192.

69. Charles Coleman Sellers, *Charles Willson Peale* (New York: Charles Scribner's Sons, 1969), 168–169. Sellers, *The Portraits and Miniatures by Charles Willson Peale*, 42: part 1, 225–226. Copies of the 1779 portrait painted by Peale for other patrons can be found in the collections of the United States Capitol, Princeton University, the Cleveland Museum of Art, Colonial Williamsburg Foundation, the Metropolitan Museum of Art, and the Yale University Art Gallery. Additional examples are held privately.

70. Elias Boudinot (1740–1821) of New Jersey served as commissary-general of prisoners with the rank of colonel. He served as a delegate from New Jersey to the Continental Congress from 1777 to 1778, and again from 1781 to 1784. In 1783, as president of the Continental Congress, he signed the Treaty of Paris and was for a time president of the United States in Congress Assembled. After the Constitution was ratified, he served as a U.S. representative from 1789 to 1795, then was appointed director of the United States Mint. Boudinot seems to have held an almost reverential regard for the general. Allen Johnson, ed., *Dictionary of American Biography* (New York: Charles Scribner's Sons, 1929), 2: 477–478.

71. Washington ordered and purchased many trunks during the Revolution. His war accounts for May 28, 1776, note payment "To Mr Jno Frazer a Trunk to pack my Papers in . . . 2/16/-." For this and other references to trunks, see *General Washington's Swords and Campaign Equipment: An Illustrated Catalogue of Military Memorabilia in the Mount Vernon Collection* (Mount Vernon, VA: MVLA, 1948), 44.

72. GW to Colonel John Cox or John Mitchell, October 4, 1778, GWW, 13:23–24.

73. *General Washington's Military Equipment*, 26.

74. Howard H. Wehmann, "To Major Gibbs With Much Esteem," *Prologue: The Journal of the National Archives* 4, no. 4 (Winter 1972): 229–230. Washington's letter to Gibbs, June 18, 1780, is in the pension application file of Gibbs's widow, Catherine Hall Gibbs (Mass., W24277), Revolutionary War Pension and Bounty-Land-Warrant Application Files, Records of the Veterans Administration, Washington, DC, RG 15, NA. A facsimile of the letter is reproduced in the article. For information on the role and duties of Major Caleb Gibbs, see *Pennsylvania Magazine of History and Biography* 38 (1914): 83–88.

75. GW to Daniel Parker, June 18, 1783, GWW, 27:20–21.

76. "Lutz, John, saddler" appears in *Washington Directories* of 1822 and 1827, *Georgetown Directory* of 1830, and *Directory for the District of Columbia* of 1834, but does not appear in succeeding directories. According to the District of Columbia's *Inventory of Historic Sites*, there is a John Lutz House (Aged Women's Home) at 1255 Wisconsin Avenue NW. It was built in 1750 with additions in 1870 and 1872.

77. Charles Pettit to GW, February 9, 1781, typescript, MVLA Library, original, Library of Congress.

78. GW to Charles Pettit, February 19, 1781, GWW, 21:249.

79. Harold Newman, *An Illustrated Dictionary of Silverware* (London: Thames and Hudson, 1987), 298.

80. http://genealogyfinds.com/documents/bostonlamb.htm. Source: *Other Merchants and Sea Captains of Old Boston* (Boston: State Street Trust Company, 1919).

81. At the time of Martha Washington's death in 1802, the Custine porcelain tea and coffee service, of which this waste bowl formed a part, was noted as a set of "GW" china in the "Sweet Meat Closset" (the third-floor room with bull's-eye window) with a value of 30 dollars. [Second Draft], 1802, MVI, 46. This waste bowl descended in the line of Martha Custis Peter, Martha Washington's granddaughter, until it entered the Mount Vernon collection in 1978.

82. Christine Meadows, "The Custine China," MVLA AR 1978, 26.

83. "A Visit to Mount Vernon from the Journal of Baron Ludwig von Closen," typescript, MVLA Library.

84. The Niderviller factory was founded in 1754 by Baron Jean-Louis de Bayerlé and sold to the Comte de Custine in 1770. See Rollo Charles, *Continental Porcelain of the Eighteenth Century* (London: University of Toronto Press, 1964), 150–151.

85. For additional information on the range of forms and decoration represented in the service, as well as its history, see Detweiler, 67–73.

86. "A Visit to Mount Vernon from the Journal of Baron Ludwig von Closen."

87. GW to the Comte de Custine-Sarreck, August 7, 1782, GWW, 24:485.

88. Detweiler, 72-73.

89. Ibid., 72.

90. Mrs. Wilfred Mustard is the granddaughter of Eliza Parke Custis Law. MVLA AR 1928, 21–22.

91. The full notation reads: "Washington July 4th 1830. My dear Brother who I love much George Washington Parke Custis has made me a present of this trunk. I prize it most dearly. It was that in which the cloaths of my Sainted Grandmother Mrs. Washington were always pack'd by her own hand when she went to visit, & spend sometime with the General, wherever the Army were in quarters. I have stood by it as she put in her cloaths sadly distress'd at her going away—& oh how joyfully when she returned did I look on to see her cloaths taken out, &the many gifts she always brought for her grandchildren!—no words can express how I loved her—she, & all else most fondly beloved are gone to their proper home among the Angels—my darling Grand children, three yet live, I leave this trunk to my Rosebud—it is fill'd with sacred Relics for my children—may God bless them! Eliza P. Custis."

92. Clement Biddle's *Philadelphia Directory 1791* lists "Sunnocks John, trunk maker 40, Chestnut St." The trunk label reads "JOHN SUNNOCKS, TRUNK-MAKER FROM LONDON, At his Shop, two Doors below *Second*, in Chesnut-Street, Philadelphia, makes and sells all Sorts of Trunks, viz. Strong Iron and Brass bound Trunks, for traveling either by Sea or Land; *Spanish* Sumters, flat Ditto, common Hair and Leather Trunks, Packing Ditto, of all Sorts; Stone Leather Trunks, Portmanteaus, Saddle Bags, Cloak Bags, Fire Buckets, Nests of Gilt Trunks and Caravans, in the neatest Manner; Horse Trunks, *English* Mails, Caravans, Bath-Boxes, etc. Ladies Hat Boxes, of all Sorts, made of Leather, Hair or Paper; Trunks for Plate, China, and Glass; strong Sea Chests, Liquor Cases, Packing Cases and Boxes, etc. etc. Retail, and for Exportation. *N. B.* Merchants, Captains of Vessels, and Storekeepers may be served on the shortest Notice, and most reasonable Terms."

93. "Washington's Household Account Book, 1793–1797," *Pennsylvania Magazine of History and Biography* 29, no. 4 (1905): 42, and account book entry for May 9, 1791, as cited in Decatur, 232.

94. John Hancock was a wealthy Boston merchant and president of the Continental Congress in 1776 when he commissioned Charles Willson Peale to paint life portraits of George and Martha Washington. According to some, Hancock hoped the portraits would make a favorable impression on General Washington and assure him a high military post. Hancock also wanted the general and Mrs. Washington to stay as guests in his home, but the Washingtons chose instead the accommodations of their old friend, Peyton Randolph. The Hancock portrait of George Washington is in the Brooklyn Museum. Sellers, *Charles Willson Peale*, 119.

95. The Marquis de Lafayette commissioned Peale to make a copy of the Hancock portrait, writing to Washington in September 1778, "Give me joy, my dear general, I schall have your picture, and M^r^Hancock has promis'd me a copy of that he has in Boston. He gave one to the Count d'Estaing, and I never saw a man so glad of possessing his sweet heart's picture, as the admiral was to receive yours." Lafayette initially requested a miniature version of the portrait, but Peale's records seem to indicate, because of the length of time he spent working on the piece, that it was a full-size or at least a cabinet-size replica. Peale made numerous painted copies of the Hancock portrait and prints after the painting, as did other artists. It is conceivable, then, that Le Paon first saw a lifelike portrait of Washington owned by another of his countrymen, because the Comte d'Estaing, the Comte de Grasse, and the French ambassador Conrad Alexandre Gérard are all known to have had copies of the Hancock portrait. Louis Gottschalk, *The Letters of Lafayette to Washington, 1777–1799* (New York: privately printed, 1944), 63; John Hill Morgan and Mantle Fielding, *The Life Portraits of Washington and Their Replicas* (Philadelphia: privately printed, 1931), 25–26.

96. For reasons unknown, Le Paon did not paint a background in the Washington portrait. In honor of his patron, Charles Willson Peale painted a detailed view of Boston in the background of the three-quarter length Hancock portrait. In later copies of the portrait, Peale would substitute various backgrounds, including Trenton and Yorktown. Sellers, *Charles Willson Peale*, 220.

97. The Prince de Condé, a member of the royal Bourbon family, was a celebrated military figure in France following his distinguished service as a commander in the Seven Years' War.

98. Publicly displaying artworks from royal collections was rare, and this particular venue was an interesting choice for the Prince de Condé's portrait of Washington since the Salon de la Correspondance was considered at odds with the French Royal Academy of Painting and Sculpture. The Salon's organizer, Pahin de la Blancherie, had a reputation not unlike that of the later P. T. Barnum and displayed fine art next to biological curiosities. Laura Auricchio, "Pahin de la Blancherie's Commercial Cabinet of Curiosity (1779–87)," *Eighteenth-Century Studies*, The Johns Hopkins University Press, 36, no. 1 (Fall 2002): 47–61.

99. Louis-Philippe and his two brothers, the Duc de Montpensier and the Comte de Beaujolais, traveled in America as young men, spending several days in April 1797 at Mount Vernon. Washington, recently retired from the presidency, gave the Frenchmen letters of introduction to facilitate their travels in Virginia. October 30, [1797], GWD, 4:265–266.

100. Fitzpatrick, *George Washington's Accounts of Expenses*, 23. Fitzpatrick mistakenly identifies Hollingshead as a Boston merchant, when he was, in fact, a Philadelphia silversmith. See his advertisement in the *Pennsylvania Gazette* of January 5, 1774, PG, fol. 3 (1766–1783). For a transcription of the Hollingshead purchase, see Buhler, 34.

101. Buhler, 34–35.

102. Richard Humphreys advertised himself as a Wilmington, Delaware, goldsmith in the *Pennsylvania Gazette* on November 7, 1771, noting that he had in his shop a shipment of "Dr. Hill's American Balsam." PG, fol. 3 (1766–1783). For details on Humphreys' working dates and marks, see Louise Conway Belden, *Marks of American Silversmiths in the Ineson-Bissell Collection* (Charlottesville: University Press of Virginia, 1980), 240.

103. Advertisement of Richard Humphreys, September 23, 1772, PG, fol. 3 (1766–1783). See also C. Louise Avery, *Early American Silver* (New York: Century Co., 1930), 190–192.

104. *Pennsylvania Evening Post*, September 3, 1779, as cited in Alfred Coxe Prime, *The Arts and Crafts in Philadelphia, Maryland and South Carolina, 1721–1785* (The Walpole Society, 1929), 73.

105. For a transcription of the order, see Buhler, 35–36. Colonel Clement Biddle, a Philadelphia merchant, served in a variety of roles during the war, including commissary-general of forage, a post he held until June 1780. For further information on Biddle, see Allen Johnson, ed., *Dictionary of American Biography* (New York: Charles Scribner's Sons, 1929), 2:239–240.

106. Howard C. Rice Jr., trans., *Travels in North America in the Years 1780, 1781, and 1782 by the Marquis De Chastellux* (Chapel Hill: University of North Carolina Press, 1963), 1:280.

107. At the time of his death in 1799, George Washington's will left his estate "real and personal" to Martha Washington for the remainder of her life. At her death in 1802, Martha Washington's will gave George Washington Parke Custis "all the silver plate of every kind of which I shall die possessed." That included both plate (silver) and plated ware (silverplate), although the majority of the plated ware went to his sister, Eleanor Parke Custis Lewis, as part of "all the plated ware not herein after otherwise bequeathed" in Martha Washington's will. LWT, 56, 58.

108. For information on the camp cup in the Yale collection, see Kathryn C. Buhler and Graham Hood, *American Silver: Garvan and Other Collections in the Yale University Art Gallery* (New Haven: Yale University Press, 1970), 209–210. For a photograph of the Edmund Milne cups in the Los Angeles County Museum of Art collection, see *Magazine Antiques* (February 1942): 110.

109. This urn has since become an icon of American silver as the first piece of Neoclassical style silver produced in America. Martha Gandy Fales, *Early American Silver*, rev. ed. (New York: Dutton, 1973), 28.

110. Buhler, 35–36.

111. Charles Truman, ed., *Sotheby's Concise Encyclopedia of Silver* (London: Conran Octopus, 1996), 197; Harold Newman, *An Illustrated Dictionary of Silverware* (London: Thames and Hudson, 1987), s.v. "Bright cutting."

112. Andrew Billing marked his work "A. Billing" and "A. Billings." See Belden, *Marks of American Silversmiths in the Ineson-Bissell Collection*, 61. This spoon is twice stamped "A. Billing," although Washington refers to the silversmith as "Billings" in his letter of January 22, 1783, GWW, 26:60.

113. *Journal of Congress*, October 29, 1781, as quoted in Baker, Itinerary of General Washington, 284.

114. GW to Rochambeau, February 9, 1782, GWW, 23:493.

115. See GW to the Superintendent of Finance, December 20, 1782, GWW, 25:453, and GW to Andrew Billings, January 22, 1783, GWW, 26:60.

116. LWT, 56.

NOTES TO CHAPTER THREE

1. *Quebec to Carolina in 1785–1786, Being the Travel Diary and Observations of Robert Hunter, Jr., a Young Merchant of London* (San Marino, CA: Huntington Library, 1943), as cited in MVLA AR 1945, 24.

2. GW to the Marquis de Lafayette, June 15, 1783, GWW, 27:14.

3. GW to Clement Biddle, August 13, 1783, GWW, 27:101.

4. GW to Daniel Parker, September 12, 1783, GWW, 27:150–151.

5. Ibid., 151.

6. GW to Daniel Parker, September 18, 1783, GWW, 27:155.

7. Detweiler, 77–80.

8. GW to Bushrod Washington, September 22, 1783, GWW, 27:160.

9. GW to the Marquis de Lafayette, February 1, 1784, GWW, 27:317–318. Washington's reference to his vine and fig tree is biblical; see 1 Kings 4:25, 2 Kings 18:31, and Micah 4:4.

10. GW to Clement Biddle, May 6, 1784, GWW, 27:397.

11. GW to Clement Biddle, May 7, 1784, GWW, 27:397–398.

12. GW to the Marchioness de Lafayette, November 25, 1784, GWW, 27:496–497.

13. GW to Mademoiselle de Lafayette, November 25, 1784, GWW, 27:497–498.

14. J. P. Brissot de Warville, *Nouveau Voyage dans les États Unis de l'Amérique Septentrionale, fait en 1788*, as cited in William Spohn Baker, *Washington after the Revolution, 1784–1799* (Philadelphia: J. B. Lippincott, 1898), 112–113.

15. Thursday 27th [January 1785], GWD, 4:80.

16. GW to George William Fairfax, February 27, 1785, PGW Con., 2:387–388.

17. GW to Samuel Vaughan, February 5, 1785, PGW Con., 2:326.

18. Chevalier de la Luzerne to Rayneveal, April 12, 1784, as cited in Baker, *Washington after the Revolution*, 7.

19. Winslow C. Watson, ed., *Men and Times of the Revolution; or Memoirs of Elkanah Watson*, 2nd ed. (New York: Dana and Company, 1856), 279–280.

20. Thursday 30th [June 1785], GWD, 4:157.

21. Lafayette to GW, February 6, 1786, PGW Con., 3:541.

22. GW to Adrienne, Marquise de Lafayette, May 10, 1786, PGW Con., 4:40.

23. *Quebec to Carolina in 1785–1786*, as cited in MVLA AR 1945, 22.

24. William M. S. Rasmussen and Robert S. Tilton, *George Washington: The Man behind the Myths* (Charlottesville: University Press of Virginia, 1999), 156.

25. GW to Mary Ball Washington, February 15, 1787, PGW Con., 5:35.

26. James Thomas Flexner, *Washington: The Indispensable Man* (Boston: Little, Brown and Company, 1974), 211.

27. Henry Knox (1750–1806), commissioned a major general in the Continental Army shortly after the British surrender at Yorktown, conceived of and organized the Society of the Cincinnati. He served as its first secretary under General Washington, first president of the society. Allen Johnson, ed., *Dictionary of American Biography* (New York: Charles Scribner's Sons, 1929), 10: s.v. "Knox, Henry." For the specific criteria for membership, see Minor Myers, Jr., *Liberty without Anarchy: A History of the Society of the Cincinnati* (Charlottesville: University Press of Virginia, 1983), 25–26.

28. Homer Eaton Keyes, "The Cincinnati and Their Porcelain," *Magazine Antiques* 17, no. 2 (February 1930): 132–133.

29. Martha Custis Williams, Arlington House, to Miss Wightt, April 1856, private collection.

30. http://www.wellesley.edu/NCH/Commontext/ Lowell/ lowellpoem.html, p. 3. For additional information on the society and its iconography, see Minor Myers, Jr., *The Insignia of the Society of the Cincinnati* (Washington, DC: The Society of the Cincinnati, 1998).

31. Detweiler, 17. For a further discussion on this advertisement and Washington's acquisition of Society of the Cincinnati porcelain, see ibid., 81–97.

32. Tench Tilghman (1744–1786), a Philadelphia merchant who liquidated his business before the Revolution, became Washington's aide-de-camp in 1776, serving in that capacity throughout the war. Performing both military and secretarial duties, he won Washington's confidence and gratitude. Washington selected him to carry the announcement of Cornwallis's surrender at Yorktown to the Continental Congress, a high honor. *Dictionary of American Biography* 18: s.v. "Tilghman, Tench."

33. GW to Tench Tilghman, August 17, 1785, GWW, 28:223–224.

34. Tench Tilghman to GW, October 13, 1785, typed transcript, MVLA Library, original, Library of Congress.

35. Henry Lee, Jr., to GW, July 3, 1786, PGW Con., 4:147–148.

36. GW to Henry Lee, Jr., July 26, 1786, PGW Con., 4:170–171.

37. GW to Henry Lee, Jr., October 31, 1786, PGW Con., 4:320.

38. OED, 4: s. v., "Fame," 1.b., 2. Although Fame was being relied on to spread positive reports on the members of the society, the dissemination of public infamy of others is attributed to her as well. Ibid., 4.

39. For a summary of Fitzhugh porcelains, see Jean McClure Mudge, *Chinese Export Porcelain for the American Trade: 1785–1835*, rev. ed. (Newark: University of Delaware Press, 1981), 161–166.

40. LWT, 56.

41. Benson J. Lossing, *Mount Vernon and Its Associations* (New York: W. A. Townsend & Co., 1859), 240.

42. W. Stephen Thomas, "Major Samuel Shaw and the Cincinnati Porcelain," *Magazine Antiques* (May 1935): 177.

43. GW to Daniel Parker, September 12, 1783, GWW, 27:151.

44. GW to Bushrod Washington, September 22, 1783, GWW, 27:160.

45. See Daniel Parker to GW, September 18, 1783, as cited in Detweiler, 208.

46. For examples in the Smithsonian collection mentioned in Parker's 1783 invoice, see Detweiler, 78–79.

47. LWT, 57–58.

48. Eleanor P. Lewis to Samuel Whitall, August 8, 1839, MVLA accession file.

49. GW to Bushrod Washington, September 22, 1783, GWW, 27:161.

50. Ibid.

51. GW to the Marquis de Lafayette, December 4, 1783, GWW, 27:258–259.

52. Buhler, 45. See also the Washington Papers, Library of Congress, vol. 230 (April 28–August 12, 1784). For details of the silver order and shipment, see Daniel Parker to GW, June 21, 1784, PGW Con., 1:467, and GW to Melancton Smith, December 20, 1784, PGW Con., 2:223–224.

53. Because of the volume of English silver plate exported to France, and that country's own production, it is difficult to determine if Washington received French- or English-made items (or a combination thereof) from Lafayette.

54. GW to the Marquis de Lafayette, October 30, 1783, GWW, 27:216.

55. Ibid., 217.

56. GW to the Marquis de Lafayette, April 4, 1784, GWW, 27:384.

57. The coffeepot is among thirty-three other pieces of silver placed on loan with the MVLA in 1936, thereby establishing the Dr. George Bolling Lee Collection. For a history of that collection, see cat. 1, "Cruet Stand, Bottles and Casters."

58. For a history of coffee consumption and equipage, see Pippa Shirley, "Tea, Coffee and Chocolate," in *Elegant Eating: Four Hundred Years of Dining in Style*, ed. Philippa Glanville and Hilary Young (London: V&A Publications, 2002), 108–111.

59. Invoice 8/1758, Ledger B, bound photostat, MVLA Library.

60. George Washington Cash Memoranda, October 1774–December 1784, bound photostat, MVLA Library.

61. GW to Clement Biddle, January 17, 1784, GWW, 27:304–305.

62. Joseph Anthony, Jr., worked as a silversmith in Philadelphia, advertising himself on Market Street from 1783 to 1796. In 1810 he admitted his sons, Michael and Thomas, to the business and the partnership of Joseph Anthony & Sons, which operated at 94 High Street until 1814. Stephen G. C. Ensko, *American Silversmiths and Their Marks III* (New York: Robert Ensko, 1948), 15.

63. GW to the the Marquis de Lafayette, October 30, 1783, GWW, 27:217.

64. Buhler, 45–46.

65. Both salvers attributed to Edward Sanford are on exhibit at Mount Vernon through the generosity of private collectors.

66. Thomas Jefferson to GW, December 10, 1784, PGW Con., 3:266. For more on the life and work of Jean-Antoine Houdon and his sculptures of George Washington, see Anne L. Poulet, *Jean-Antoine Houdon: Sculptor of the Enlightenment* (Chicago: University of Chicago Press, for the National Gallery of Art, 2003), 203. For the conservation of this bust, see Mary V. Thompson, "Houdon's Bust of Washington," MVLA AR 1998, 10–16.

67. Thomas Jefferson to GW, December 10, 1784, PGW Con., 3:266.

68. Benjamin Franklin to GW, September 20, 1785, PGW Con., 3:266.

69. Sunday 2d [October 1785], GWD, 4:200.

70. R. Walton Moore, "General Washington and Houdon," typescript, MVLA Library; see also MVLA AR 1967, 12.

71. Monday 10th [October 1785], GWD, 4:204.

72. Eleanor Parke [Custis] Lewis to [George Washington Parke Custis], December 3, 1849, MVLA, RM-185, NEWS-2571; see also MVLA AR 1967, 11-12.

73. Recent scientific investigation of the clay bust has prompted a reexamination of the process Houdon used to fashion the bust. It has traditionally been assumed that Houdon carved the bust of Washington at Mount Vernon and then made a life mask, which he carried back to France. Jeffrey Schwartz, Professor of Anthropology and History and Philosophy of Science at the University of Pittsburgh, made a comparison of digital scans of the life mask, preserved in the collection of the Pierpont Morgan Library in New York, and Mount Vernon's bust. His findings suggest that the dimensions of the two are so close that it is statistically impossible that they could derive from different creation processes, and that Houdon used the life mask of Washington to make the bust. At the time of this printing, art historians are attempting to reconcile Schwartz's theory with the written record and our traditional understanding of Houdon's work.

74. Appraisers Inventory, 1800, MVI, 13.

75. *Account of Sales of the Personal Estate of Martha Washington (not specifically devised) late of Mount Vernon deceased—as rendered to me by Thomas Peter the Executor*, MVLA AR 1959, 26.

76. For additional information on Joseph Rakestraw, see Sandra L. Tatman and Roger W. Moss, *Biographical Dictionary of Philadelphia Architects: 1700–1930* (Boston: G. K. Hall & Co., 1985), 641–642.

77. GW to George Augustine Washington, June 3, 1787, PGW Con., 5:217–219.

78. GW to Joseph Rakestraw, July 20, 1787, PGW Con., 5:267.

79. Cash Memoranda, May–September 1787, MVLA Library, photostat.

80. GW to George Augustine Washington, August 12, 1787, PGW Con., 5:286–289.

81. Early Christians used the dove, often with an olive branch in its beak, to denote "rest in peace." James Hall, *Illustrated Dictionary of Symbols in Eastern and Western Art* (Boulder, CO: Westview Press, 1996), 19, 152. At the conclusion of the biblical story of Noah, a dove returns to the ark carrying an olive branch signaling the restoration of peace between God and his people. Hans Biedermann, *Dictionary of Symbolism: Cultural Icons and the Meanings behind Them* (New York: Penguin Books, 1994), 245.

NOTES TO CHAPTER FOUR

1. Elswyth Thane, *Potomac Squire* (Mount Vernon, VA: MVLA, 1963), 291. These words are presumed to have come from Washington's diary entry of April 16, 1789. The diary entries from the spring and summer of 1789 are missing, but they were recorded by Jared Sparks before 1836 and were incorporated in Thane's text.

2. MW to John Dandridge, April 20, 1789, Fields, 213.

3. Decatur, 7.

4. GW to David Stuart, July 26, 1789, PGW Pres., 3:321.

5. Decatur, 15.

6. GW to James Madison, March 30, 1789, PGW Pres., 1:464.

7. Henry B. Hoffmann, "President Washington's Cherry Street Residence," *New-York Historical Society Quarterly Bulletin* 23, no. 1 (January 1939): 93.

8. The list of articles purchased, and from whom, is in the manuscript collection of the New-York Historical Society under the heading "Abstract Accounts of sundry persons for Goods furnished and Repairs done to the house occupied by the President of the United States. Also accounts for Marketing and Servants Wages." It is transcribed and published, in part, in Hoffmann, "President Washington's Cherry Street Residence," 95–98. I have rounded prices quoted in the present text to the nearest pound.

9. As quoted in Stephen Decatur, "George Washington and His Presidential Furniture," *American Collector* (February 1941): 8.

10. Early Descriptions Notebook, MVLA Library.

11. Benson J. Lossing, *Recollections and Private Memoirs of Washington, by his Adopted Son, George Washington Parke Custis* (New York: Derby & Jackson, 1860), 395.

12. GW to David Stuart, June 15, 1790, GWW, 31:53.

13. William Sullivan, *Public Men of the Revolution*, as cited in William Spohn Baker, *Washington after the Revolution, 1784–1799* (Philadelphia: J. B. Lippincott Co., 1898), 200.

14. Kenneth R. Bowling and Helen E. Veit, eds., *The Diary of William Maclay and Other Notes on Senate Debates*, vol. 9 of *Documentary History of the First Federal Congress of the United States of America, 4 March 1789–3 March 1791* (Baltimore: Johns Hopkins University Press, 1988), 137.

15. Ibid.

16. As cited in Stewart Mitchell, *New Letters of Abigail Adams, 1788–1801* (Boston: Houghton Mifflin Company, 1947), 19.

17. Fields, xxvi.

18. The Society of the Cincinnati porcelain must have been in use at one or both of the New York executive residences, for Tobias Lear writes of its transport to Philadelphia. Tobias Lear to GW, October 24, 1790, PGW Pres., 6:573–579.

19. Tobias Lear to Clement Biddle, as cited in Buhler, 49.

20. Tobias Lear to Clement Biddle, June 22, 1789, GWW, 30:348.

21. Alexander Macomb to Tobias Lear, January 31, 1790, PGW Pres., 5:71.

22. Wednesday 3d. [February 1790], GWD, 6:27–28.

23. "Articles purchased by the President of the United States from Monsr. Le Prince Agent for the Count de Moustier," MVLA Archives, acc. no. W-1310/a. See also Alexander Macomb to Tobias Lear, January 31, 1790, PGW Pres., 5:70–74.

24. Tobias Lear to Clement Biddle, February 10, 1790, PGW Pres., 5:72 n. 2.

25. Gouverneur Morris to GW, January 24, 1790, PGW Pres., 5:48–49.

26. Ibid., 48.

27. For a history of the Robert Morris House and its use as the executive residence in Philadelphia, see Edward Lawler, Jr., "The President's House in Philadelphia: The Rediscovery of a Lost Landmark," *Pennsylvania Magazine of History and Biography* 126, no. 1 (January 2002): 5–95.

28. GW to Tobias Lear, September 5, 1790, PGW Pres., 6:397.

29. GW to Tobias Lear, November 7, 1790, PGW Pres., 6:634.

30. Fields, 217.

31. List of Household Furniture, photostat, MVLA Library, original, Pennsylvania Historical Society.

32. [February] 17 [1797], GWD, 6:234. The rumor was incorrect. Mrs. Washington's last drawing room event was held on March 3, 1797.

33. [February] 22 [1797], GWD , 6:235.

34. George Washington Motier Lafayette (1779–1849) had been sent to America after his father's imprisonment during the French Revolution. See GWD, 6:236–237n for some details and additional sources covering the young Lafayette's stay in America.

35. [March] 12 [1797], GWD, 6:237.

36. [March] 15 [1797], GWD, 6:239.

37. See Rita Susswein Gottesman, *The Arts and Crafts in New York, 1777–1799* (New York: New-York Historical Society, 1954), 111.

38. The list of furniture supplied by Burling is part of the Congressional Account of 1789, National Archives, transcribed and excerpted in Susan G. Detweiler and Charles F. Hummel, "Two Philadelphia Mahogany Side Chairs from President Washington's Residence in Philadelphia," Appendix A, paper prepared for the Barra Foundation, MVLA curatorial files. Three of the six sets of mahogany chairs supplied by Burling for the executive residence have been identified to date. Of the set illustrated here, one chair survives at Mount Vernon, and two are in the White House collection. See Betty C. Monkman, *The White House: Its Furnishings and First Families* (New York: Abbeville Press, 2000), 20–21, 279.

39. For details of the yellow drawing room and its furnishings, see Lawler, "The President's House in Philadelphia," 37–41. The present slip seat cover reflects the chair's possible placement in the yellow drawing room.

40. Burling supplied "12 ditto [mahogany] chairs, 8 ditto [mahogany] plain ditto [chairs] . . . 24 Mahogany Chairs . . . 6 Plain Ditto [mahogany] chairs . . . 10 Mahogany Carved Chairs, 8 Mahogany Chairs" for the executive residence. The list of furniture supplied by Thomas Burling is part of the Congressional Account of 1789, National Archives, transcribed and excerpted in Detweiler and Hummel, "Two Philadelphia Mahogany Side Chairs from President Washington's Residence in Philadelphia."

41. An additional chair from the set in the Mount Vernon collection (acc. no. 2003.023) has "IIII" carved into the front seat rail and "M C IIII" carved into the front slip-seat rail. Another, in the collection of the Yale University Art Gallery, is catalogued and illustrated in Patricia E. Kane, *300 Years of American Seating Furniture: Chairs and Beds from the Mabel Brady Garvan and Other Collections at Yale University* (Boston: New York Graphic Society, 1976), 91. A chair from the set at the Maryland Historical Society is catalogued and illustrated in Gregory R. Weidman, *Furniture in Maryland, 1740–1940* (Baltimore: Maryland Historical Trust Press, 1993), 48–49.

42. George Washington's 1797 executive residence inventory notes "10 chairs cov'd with yellow damask" among the publicly owned "Cabinet Work." List of Household Furniture, photostat, MVLA Library, original, Pennsylvania Historical Society.

43. Lawler, "The President's House in Philadelphia: The Rediscovery of a Lost Landmark," 34.

44. Mrs. George R. Goldsborough (née Eleanor Agnes Rogers) was a direct descendant of Martha Washington's granddaughter Eliza Parke Custis Law (1776–1832). Mrs. Goldsborough served as Vice Regent for Maryland of the MVLA from 1893 to 1904.

45. John Fleming and Hugh Honour, *Dictionary of the Decorative Arts* (New York: Harper & Row, 1977), s.v., "Plateau": "An ornamental stand on a low plinth or feet for the centre of a dining table; usually made in parts so that it could be shortened or lengthened." French in origin, as its name suggests, the plateau was the successor to the *surtout* or silver centerpiece, a more vertical form, which, although highly decorative, could be fitted for candlesticks and containers for condiments. Carl Hernmarck, *The Art of the European Silversmith, 1430–1830* (New York: Sotheby Parke Bernet, 1977), 1:182–183.

46. Tobias Lear to Clement Biddle, as cited in Buhler, 49.

47. GW to Gouverneur Morris, October 13, 1789, GWW, 30:442. Washington subsequently revised his order to add "two pieces to the number of plateaux required, and ornaments equivalent," although he rescinded that direction when he received the first shipment and acknowledged that "[u]pon trial it need[ed] no addition." GW to Gouverneur Morris, March 1, 1790, PGW Pres., 5:192–193. GW to Gouverneur Morris, April 15, 1790, PGW Pres., 5:334.

48. Two additional center portions of the plateau survive in the Mount Vernon collection, and one is in the National Museum of American History at the Smithsonian Institution.

49. Edgar deN. Mayhew and Minor Myers, Jr., *A Documentary History of American Interiors from the Colonial Era to 1915* (New York: Scribners, 1986), 78. On the rise of French Neoclassicism, see Peter Thornton, *Authentic Décor: The Domestic Interior, 1620–1920* (New York: Random House, 1953), 138.

50. Theophilus Bradbury to his daughter Mrs. Hooper, December 26, 1795, as cited in *Christmas with George Washington, 1776–1799* (Philadelphia: Franklin Printing Co., 1954), [4–5]. When outfitted with its ornaments, the reflective surface surrounded by unpainted, unglazed, porcelain allegorical figures also suggested a reflecting pool flanked by statuary, such as the Baroque water garden at Versailles. Pierre Lemoine, *Guide to the Museum and National Domain of Versailles and Trianon*, trans. Mary Delahaye (Paris: Réunion des musées nationaux, 2002), 212, fig. 220.

51. GW to Gouverneur Morris, October 13, 1789, PGW Pres., 4:177–178.

52. For more on Morris's acquisition of Washington's table ornaments, see Detweiler, 108–118. The porcelain figures were a substitute for the traditional molded sugar, pastry, and almond paste decorations that had embellished royal European tables since the fifteenth century, sometimes configured into Baroque landscapes. Their porcelain composition was more desirable because they were less fragile and less attractive to vermin. Louise Conway Belden, *The Festive Tradition: Table Decoration and Desserts in America, 1650–1900* (New York: W. W. Norton, 1983), 63.

53. Gouverneur Morris to GW, January 24, 1790, PGW Pres., 5:48.

54.Ibid.

55. GW to Gouverneur Morris, April 15, 1790, PGW Pres., 5:334.

56. Gouverneur Morris to GW, January 24, 1790, PGW Pres., 5:57 n. 2.

57. Tobias Lear to GW, October 31, 1790, PGW Pres., 6:604.

58. GW to Gouverneur Morris, October 13, 1789, PGW Pres., 4:178.

59. Ibid.

60. Ibid.

61. Gouverneur Morris to GW, April 12, 1790, PGW Pres., 5:329.

62. Ibid.

63. GW to Gouverneur Morris, December 17, 1790, PGW Pres., 7:92–94.

64. GW to Tobias Lear, November 7, 1790, PGW Pres., 6:633.

65. Ibid., 633–634.

66. GW to the Secretary of War, August 14, 1797, GWW, 36:9.

67. GW to Clement Biddle, August 21, 1797, PGW Ret., 1:313.

68. The chair frame is stamped by Lelarge, a third-generation French cabinetmaker who became a master in 1775 and whose working dates were roughly 1775–1802.

69. "Articles purchased by the President of the United States from Monsr. Le Prince Agent for the Count de Moustier," MVLA Archives, acc. no. W-1310/a. See also Alexander Macomb to Tobias Lear, January 31, 1790, PGW Pres., 5:70–74.

70. Bertault is known to have worked with the Philadelphia cabinetmakers Adam and Ephraim Haines, and a Haines label exists on a surviving armchair from this suite in the collection of the Museum of Fine Arts, Boston. Additional extant examples of the initial French furniture purchase and the supplements acquired in Philadelphia are in the collections of the Historical Society of Delaware, the Connecticut Historical Society, Tudor Place, the White House, and Historic New England (formerly the Society for the Preservation of New England Antiquities).

71. In 1797 George Washington's list of those "Articles in the Green Drawing Room which will be sold" included "3 Green silk Window Curtains" and the French furniture noted as being "of Green Floured Damask." Typescript, MVLA Library, original, Pennsylvania Historical Society.

72. Tobias Lear to GW, March 15, 1797, PGW Ret., 1:36–37.

73. The discovery of the original green-and-white checked linen was made by Elizabeth Lahikainen of Historic Upholstery Conservation Services. A small sample was removed, while a larger portion remains under the present modern fabric. See Upholstery Conservation Treatment Report, EL no. 305-98, July 2001, MVLA curatorial files.

74. For more on this service and its varied elements, see Detweiler, 123–134.

75. For an overview of the coffee and tea wares produced at Sèvres, see Rosalind Savill, *The Wallace Collection Catalogue of Sèvres Porcelain* (London: Trustees of the Wallace Collection and the Westerham Press, 1988), 2:489–495.

76. Ibid., 564.

77. Ibid., 570.

78. Account of Sales of the Personal Estate of Martha Washington (not specifically devised) late of Mount Vernon deceased—as rendered to me by Thomas Peter the Executor, in MVLA AR 1959, 26–27.

79. Jean Gordon Lee, *Philadelphians and the China Trade, 1784–1844* (Philadelphia: Philadelphia Museum of Art, 1984), 81–89.

80. Detweiler, 154.

81. Eleanor H. Gustafson, "Collectors' Notes," *Magazine Antiques* 166, no. 4 (October 2004): 38-40.

82. LWT, 57.

83. For examples of these survivals and more information on this porcelain service, see Detweiler, 151-158.

84. GW to Gouveneur Morris, March 1, 1790, PGW Pres., 5:192–193.

85. Maureen Dillon, *Artificial Sunshine: A Social History of Domestic Lighting* (London: National Trust, 2002), 97.

86. GW to Gouveneur Morris, March 1, 1790, PGW Pres., 7:193.

87. Gouveneur Morris to GW, May 3, 1790, PGW Pres., 5:382.

88. GW to Gouverneur Morris, December 17, 1790, PGW Pres., 7:93–94.

89. GW to Gouverneur Morris, March 1, 1790, PGW Pres., 5:192.

90. See Gouverneur Morris to GW, August 30, 1790, PGW Pres., 6:376, and GW to Gouverneur Morris, December 17, 1790, PGW Pres., 7:93–94.

91. Dillon, *Artificial Sunshine*, 100.

92. Loris S. Russell, *A Heritage of Light* (Toronto: University of Toronto Press, 1981), 75–76.

93. Harold Newman, *An Illustrated Dictionary of Silverware* (New York: Thames and Hudson, 1987), 22.

94. Dillon, *Artificial Sunshine*, 100–101.

95. Ibid., 101.

96. List of Household Furniture, photostat, MVLA Library, original, Pennsylvania Historical Society.

97. The 1790 accounts of the Philadelphia City Commissioners identify the ninety-two chairs as "Elbow Chairs." Karie Diethorn, Associate Curator, Independence National Historical Park, to Dr. Joseph E. Fields, October 2, 1991, MVLA accession file. Affleck was also chosen to craft chairs for the Supreme Court chamber housed in Philadelphia's City Hall. For these chairs see William MacPherson Hornor, Jr., *Philadelphia Furniture* (Philadelphia: privately printed, 1935), 185.

98. Thomas Affleck, born in Aberdeen, Scotland, arrived in Philadelphia in 1763 after having apprenticed in Edinburgh and worked as a cabinetmaker in London. Using to his advantage both his connections with the influential Quaker community and the prime location of his shop on Second Street, Affleck quickly established himself as one of the top cabinetmakers in a city known for its excellent cabinetmakers, serving some of the city's most prominent families. For more information on Affleck, see *Philadelphia: Three Centuries of American Art* (Philadelphia: Philadelphia Museum of Art, 1976), 98–99, and Elizabeth Bidwell Bates and Jonathan L. Fairbanks, *American Furniture: 1620 to the Present* (New York: Richard Marek, 1981), 153, 204.

99. Diethorn to Fields, October 2, 1991.

100. Despite dispersal, thirty of the Congress Hall chairs survive in the collection of Independence National Park in Philadelphia. Additional examples are in the collections of the Brooklyn Museum, Dauphin County Historical Society in Harrisburg, PA, and in private collections.

101. Diethorn to Fields, October 2, 1991.

102. William H. Long's Museum was located on South Third Street in Philadelphia, where it highlighted a wide array of objects of interest and works of art. After Long's death in 1885, his widow sold many of the museum's holdings but retained possession of this chair. It subsequently sold at Parke-Bernet in New York in 1954. In 1991 Dr. and Mrs. Joseph E. Fields donated the chair to the MVLA.

103. Tobias Lear to Clement Biddle, July 18, 1790, GWW, 31:70.

104. Ephraim Brasher, a New York silversmith active between 1786 and 1807, was located in 1790 at 1 Cherry Street. See Ian M. G. Quimby, *American Silver at Winterthur* (Winterthur, DE: Henry Francis duPont Winterthur Museum, 1995), 207.

105. George Washington Accounts, photostat, MVLA Library, original, Winterthur Museum collection. See also Buhler, 57.

106. Martha Washington bequeathed to her grandson George Washington Parke Custis, "all the silver plate of every kind of which I shall die possessed." LWT, 56. This tray (acc. no. W-32) entered the Mount Vernon collection through George Washington Parke Custis descendants in 1932. Its mate (acc. no. W-2752) was also inherited by Custis and is currently at Mount Vernon through the generosity of an anonymous lender.

107. List of Household Furniture, photostat, MVLA Library, original, Pennsylvania Historical Society.

108. George S. McKearin and Helen McKearin, *American Glass* (New York: Bonanza Books, 1941), 64. The lozenge stopper may not be original.

109. In 1827 Robert Roberts, butler to Massachusetts Governor Christopher Gore, wrote, "If you don't use egg cups and stands, you must put on wine glasses." As quoted in Arlene Palmer, *Glass in Early America* (New York: W. W. Norton, 1993), 57.

110. GW to John Quincy Adams, September 12, 1796, GWW, 35:207-209.

111. John Quincy Adams to GW, February 11, 1797, PGW Ret., 1:212-213.

112. Theophilus Alte to GW, January 20, 1797, typescript, MVLA curatorial files, original, Library of Congress.

113. Theophilus Alte to GW, November 29, 1797, typescript, MVLA curatorial files, original, Library of Congress.

114. General Washington's Military Equipment (Mount Vernon, VA: MVLA, 1963), 39.

115. LWT, 18–19. George Washington bequeathed "To each of my Nephews, William Augustine Washington, George Lewis, George Steptoe Washington, Bushrod Washington and Samuel Washington, I give one of the Swords or Cutteaux of which I may die possessed; and they are to chuse in the order they are named. -These Swords are accompanied with an injunction not to unsheath them for the purpose of shedding blood, except it be for self defence, or in defence of their Country and its rights; and in the latter case to keep them unsheathed, and prefer falling with them in their hands, to relinquishment thereof." The swords inherited by George Lewis, George Steptoe Washington, and Bushrod Washington are in the Mount Vernon collection. The sword bequeathed to William Augustine Washington is part of the New York State Library holdings, and that given to Samuel Washington is at the Smithsonian Institution.

116. List of Household Furniture, photostat, MVLA Library, original, Pennsylvania Historical Society.

117. *Philadelphia Household Account Book*, bound photostat 36-A, MVLA Library, original, Historical Society of Pennsylvania.

118. Ernest M. Currier, *Marks of Early American Silversmiths* (Harrison, NY: privately published by Robert Alan Green, 1970), 110.

119. Peter Copy of Appraisers Inventory, MVI, 72.

120. The single candlestick identical to those illustrated here is held privately, but the pair that descended through the heirs of Eliza Parke Custis is in the Mount Vernon collection (acc. no. W-18/A&B) and illustrated in Buhler, 43.

121. Later, insurance companies provided them to their customers. John W. Waterer, *Leather in Life, Art and Industry* (London: Faber and Faber, 1946), 39-41.

122. Entry for March 10, 1797, in "Philadelphia Household Accounts Book, March 1793–March 1797," Pennsylvania Magazine of History and Biography 31 (1907): 347.

123. Stephens's *Philadelphia Directory* for 1796, 1, lists "Abel, Peter, shoemaker, Budd St. between Front and 2d streets."

124. The full label reads: "WILLIAM JONES / SADDLER, HARNESS, & / TRUNK-MAKER / No. 88, Chestnut, Four Doors / below Third-Street, near the / Cross-Keys, Philadelphia."

125. MVI, Appraisers Inventory, 1800, 61.

126. Ellen G. Miles, *George and Martha Washington: Portraits from the Presidential Years* (Washington, DC: National Portrait Gallery, 1999), 38.

127. As quoted in James Thomas Flexner, *Washington: The Indispensable Man* (Boston: Little, Brown and Company, 1974), 339-340.

128. Carrie Rebora Barratt and Ellen G. Miles, *Gilbert Stuart* (New Haven, CT: Yale University Press, for the Metropolitan Museum of Art, 2004), 133. On this page, Barratt and Miles also identify an impressive list of the thirty-two men who by 1795 had commissioned a total of thirty-nine portraits.

129. For this, and other details surrounding Stuart's paintings of George and Martha Washington, see Miles, *George and Martha Washington*, 38–47.

130. Ibid., 153.

131. Charles Henry Hart, "Original Portraits of Washington," *Century Magazine* 37, no. 6 (April 1889): 865.

NOTES TO CHAPTER FIVE

1. List of articles shipped aboard the *Salem*, signed by shipmaster Joshua Elkins, March 17, 1797, transcribed typescript, MVLA Library, original, Washington Papers, Library of Congress. See also Tobias Lear to GW, March 20, 1797, PGW Ret., 1:37–38 n. 1.

2. In a letter attributed to Martha Washington, she notes, "Our furniture and other things sent us from Philadelphia arrived safely, our plate we brought with us in the carriage." MW to Lucy Flucker Knox, Fields, 303.

3. GW to Tobias Lear, March 10, 1797, PGW Ret., 1:27.

4. GW to Tobias Lear, March 12, 1797, PGW Ret., 1:33.

5. GW to George Lewis, April 9, 1797, PGW Ret., 1:90.

6. GW to James McHenry, April 3, 1797, PGW Ret., 1:71–72.

7. GW to James McHenry, May 29, 1797, PGW Ret., 1:159–160.

8. Hamilton B. Staples, ed., "A Day at Mount Vernon in 1797," from a diary by Amariah Frost, Esq. (Worcester, MA, 1879), 8–11, as excerpted in Early Descriptions Notebook, MVLA Library.

9. Thomas G. Cary, *Memoir of Thomas Handasyd Perkins* (Boston: Little, Brown and Company, 1856), 199.

10. GW to Tobias Lear, July 31, 1797, facsimile, MVLA Library, original, private collection.

11. GW to Lawrence Lewis, August 4, 1797, PGW Ret., 1:288–289.

12. Julian Ursyn Niemcewicz , *Under Their Vine and Fig Tree: Travels through America in 1797–1799, 1805*, trans. and ed. Metchie J. E. Budka (Elizabeth, NJ: The Grassman Publishing Company, 1965), 97.

13. Ibid., 98.

14. Ibid., 102–103.

15. 21 [January 1799], GWD, 6:331. For the marriage, see [February], 22 [1799], GWD, 6:335.

16. As quoted in Elswyth Thane, *Potomac Squire* (Mount Vernon, VA: MVLA, 1963), 405.

17. GW to David Stuart, June 15, 1790, GWW, 31:54.

18. [December] 12, [1799], GWD, 6:378.

19. Account of the Last Illness and Death of Washington, December 14, 1799, Journal of Tobias Lear, typescript, MVLA Library, original, on deposit at the Historical Society of Pennsylvania.

20. Ibid.

21. Ibid.

22. LWT, 1.

23. LWT, 2.

24. Ibid. Daniel Parke Custis, Martha Washington's first husband, died without a will. By law, she was entitled to a life interest in one-third of his property, including slaves. At her death this property and slaves were to revert to his heirs, in this instance, the Custis grandchildren. For more on the difficulties encountered by Martha Washington on this matter, and a good account of Martha Washington's final years, see Mary V. Thompson, "To Follow Her Departed Friend: The Last Years of Martha Washington," *Virginia Cavalcade* (Spring 2002): 52–61.

25. GW to Arthur Young, December 12, 1793, GWW, 33:175–176.

26. George Washington began construction of the "New Room" or large dining room in 1775, and it was completed about 1787. The interior work, papering, and painting, though, were not finished until about 1789. For more on the architectural history of the room, see Mesick, Cohen, Waite Architects, "Mount Vernon Historic Structure Report," 3 vols. (1993), 2:349–373, MVLA Library.

27. Entry for February 21, 1797, Philadelphia Household Account Book, bound photostat, MVLA Library, [36-A]. The bill of lading for the goods Washington had shipped to Mount Vernon from Philadelphia aboard the sloop *Salem* is mentioned as an enclosure in Tobias Lear's letter to George Washington. See Tobias Lear to GW, March 20, 1797, PGW Ret., 1:37–38 n. 1. Aitken also supplied Washington with a secretary bookcase in 1797, MVLA acc. no. W-158. Research into the work of John Aitken, his shop, and related retail operations has not, to date, determined whether the chairs and case pieces sold by Aitken to Washington were of his own making or if they represent the hands of other craftsmen.

28. Advertisement of John Aitken, *Federal Gazette* (Philadelphia), June 9, 1790, as cited in Alfred Coxe Prime, ed., *The Arts and Crafts in Philadelphia Maryland and South Carolina, 1786–1800*, ser. 2 (The Walpole Society, 1932), 164–165.

29. While the 1797 edition of the *Philadelphia Directory* recorded John Aitken as a cabinetmaker located at 50 Chestnut Street, Aitken was also known for retailing furniture, and he noted the move of his "Cabinet Ware Room to No. 60, Union Street" in 1794. A few months later he published the dissolution of his co-partnership with John Hall & Co. Six years later Aitken advertised that he provided "A Large and General Assortment of Cabinet Furniture, Suitable for the home and exportation trade." See advertisments of John Aitken, *Federal Gazette* (Philadelphia), March 17, 1794, August 1, 1794, January 13, 1800, as cited in Prime, *The Arts and Crafts in Philadelphia Maryland and South Carolina*, 165.

30. During recent conservation work, non-Washington upholstery fabric was removed from a number of the original Aitken chairs at Mount Vernon to reveal tack holes in a swagged pattern on the side, front, and back seat rails. Silk threads with a satin weave structure were discovered inside the tack holes. Their green-blue color combined with green-blue silk and wool damask fragments in the Mount Vernon collection with a history of Washington upholstery use and Martha Washington's description of the chairs as "with green bottoms" suggest that the chairs may have been originally covered in a green silk worsted damask. The present upholstery reflects this possibility.

31. The Aitken side chairs were no doubt among the "27 Mahogany Chairs" listed "In the New Room" and valued at 270 dollars. "Appraisers Inventory," 1800, MVI, 1.

32. LWT, 57. Martha Washington's will of March 4, 1802, bequeathed to "my grand daughter Eleanor Parke Lewis . . . one of the new side board tables in the new room—also twelve chairs with green bottoms to be selected by herself." Twelve John Aitken side chairs were sold by descendants of Eleanor Lewis to the United States Government in 1878 and were later transferred to the Smithsonian Institution. Six of the twelve Smithsonian-owned chairs are on loan to Mount Vernon, as well as one chair owned by the Society of the Cincinnati. Additional chairs are owned by the Nelson-Atkins Museum of Art and Mount Vernon, and some are held privately.

33. The mahogany stretchers and brass supports are replacements.

34. GW to Wakelin Welch & Son, August 16, 1789, PGW Pres., 3:478.

35. Wakelin Welch & Son to GW, October 8, 1789, PGW Pres., 4:149.

36. PGW Pres., 4:150 n. 1.

37. A duplicate copy of the volume is in Washington's study at Mount Vernon today. For information on the original, and other books inventoried in Washington's study at the time of his death, see William Coolidge Lane, "The Inventory of Washington's Books Drawn up by the Appraisers of His Estate," in Appleton P. C. Griffin, *A Catalogue of the Washington Collection in the Boston Athenaeum* (Cambridge, MA: University Press, 1897), 549.

38. Wakelin Welch & Son to GW, February 14, 1790, PGW Pres., 5:139.

39. Sunday 2d. [November 1788], GWD, 5:417.

40. Monday 1st [February 1790], GWD 6:26.

41. For a complete list of purchases made by George Washington from the Comte de Moustier, see Alexander Macomb to Tobias Lear, January 31, 1790, PGW Pres., 5:70–71 n. 2. The original manuscript (W-838 m.s.) is in the Mount Vernon Archives.

42. LWT, 17.

43. These bowls were called wash-hand glasses or basins for most of the eighteenth century. Toward the end of the eighteenth and beginning of the nineteenth centuries they were referred to as finger cups and finger bowls. Arlene Palmer, *Glass in Early America: Selections from the Henry Francis duPont Winterthur Museum* (New York: W. W. Norton, 1993), 246.

44. Ibid.

45. Ibid., 247.

46. First Draft and Second Draft, 1802, MVI, 46. The cobalt blue glass wine rinser in the Mount Vernon collection (acc. no. W-2721) may have also been counted among the "28 blue glass bowls" stored in the "Sweet Meat Closset."

47. Harold Newman, *An Illustrated Dictionary of Glass* (London: Thames and Hudson, 1977), 72.

48. Palmer, *Glass in Early America*, 260.

49. GW to the Marquis de Lafayette, October 30, 1783, GWW, 27:217.

50. Humphreys also supplied Washington with tea- and dessert spoons. For an illustration of all four types of spoons, and the invoice for the tablespoons, see Buhler, 35–36.

51. For a comparison of Washington's Philadelphia-made salt spoon to John Parke Custis's English example, see ibid., 32.

52. Mrs. Richard Blackburn Tucker donated the ladle in honor of her mother-in-law, Mrs. Anna Maria Washington Tucker. The senior Mrs. Tucker (née Anna Maria Washington) was the daughter of John Augustine Washington III, the last private owner of Mount Vernon and was the last Washington family member born on the estate. The ladle entered the Mount Vernon collection in 1964 with a family history of George Washington ownership and use at Mount Vernon.

53. Niemcewicz , *Under Their Vine and Fig Tree*, 96.

54. T. Michael Miller, comp., *Artisans and Merchants of Alexandria, Virginia, 1780–1820* (Bowie, MD: Heritage Books, 1991), 1:293. For additional information on Adam Lynn, see George Barton Cutten, *The Silversmiths of Virginia* (Richmond, VA: Dietz Press, 1952), 14–17, and

Catherine B. Hollan, *Three Centuries of Alexandria Silver* (Alexandria, VA: Lyceum, 1994), 59.

55. Cutten, *The Silversmiths of Virginia*, 14.

56. The flowerpot descended in the family of Martha Washington's granddaughter Martha Custis Peter of Tudor Place before entering the Mount Vernon collection. It is listed as number 40 on the Peter Family List of Washington objects prepared by descendant Britannia Peter Kennon.

57. At Riversdale, the home of extended family members George and Rosalie Calvert, the hall was "ornamented with lemon-trees, geraniums, polianthusses, heliotropes, other plants." Margaret Law Callcott, ed., *Mistress of Riversdale: The Plantation Letters of Rosalie Stier Calvert, 1795–1821* (Baltimore: Johns Hopkins University Press, 1991), 234.

58. "Appraisers Inventory," 1800, MVI, 5. Martha Washington's 1802 estate inventory also lists "3 blue & White Flour Potts" in the "Sweet Meat Closset" valued at three dollars. First Draft, 1802, MVI, 46.

59. Gretchen Goodell, "Furnishing Plan for the Kitchen Building," manuscript, 2002, 9, MVLA Library. As Goodell notes, there has existed confusion in differentiating the midcentury saucepan from the stew pan. By the end of the eighteenth century, however, the bulbous saucepans of various sizes had become visually distinguishable from the popular French stew pan, with its cylindrical shape and shallow depth. See Donald L. Fennimore, *Metalwork in Early America: Copper and Its Alloys from the Winterthur Collection* (Winterthur, DE: Henry Francis duPont Winterthur Museum and the Antique Collectors' Club, 1996), 75–77.

60. George Washington, "NEGROES Belonging to George Washington in his own right and by Marriage," June 1799, GWW, 37:256–257. Lucy may also have been asked to prepare the meals for single hired white servants. GW to William Pearce, December 22, 1793, GWW, 33:200–201.

61. Martha Washington to Mrs. Elizabeth Powel, May 20, 1797, Fields, 302. Hercules, the head cook previously at Mount Vernon and later in the presidential household, ran away before returning to Virginia, leading Martha Washington to complain, "our cook Hercules went away so that I am . . . much at a loss for a cook." MW to Elizabeth Dandridge Henley, August 20, 1797, Fields, 307. Once back in Virginia, an attempt was made to find a cook to oversee the kitchen, and cash memoranda records for September 19, 1797, indicate that "Peter Gilling a French Cook came here on trial—no wages stipulated." Gilling must have remained at Mount Vernon for a short time, likely providing recipes and overseeing the work of Lucy and Nathan, for payments were made to him on September 23 and October 25 of the same year. "Cash Memoranda Book, September 1, 1797 to December 3, 1799," photostat, Mount Vernon Archives, original, John Carter Brown Library, Providence, RI.

62. Rupert Gentle and Rachael Field, rev. Belinda Gentle, *Domestic Metalwork, 1640–1820* (Woodbridge, Suffolk: Antique Collectors' Club, 1994), 452.

63. Hannah Glasse, *The Art of Cookery, Made Plain and Easy* (1747), 68. Martha Washington's original copy of this cookbook is in the Mount Vernon Archives.

64. Gentle and Field, *Domestic Metalwork*, 452, and Fennimore, *Metalwork in Early America*, 76.

65. "Philadelphia Household Account Book," August 31, 1793, and May 3, 1794. On May 25, 1796, George Washington's presidential household expenses include payment for "tinning stew pans." "Washington's Household Account Book," *Pennsylvania Magazine of History and Biography* 29, no. 4 (1905).

66. "Cash Memoranda Book, September 1, 1797, to December 3, 1799."

67. *Virginia Journal and Alexandria Advertiser*, March 30 and July 6, 1784. Records of purchases during the presidency indicate the frequency with which kitchen utensils were acquired. On July 6, 1795, George Washington bought "3 Stewpans & 2 pots with covers," and later expenses include a June 6, 1796, payment to Panwart & Walker for "sauce pans." Account books for the years following the presidency are not as detailed, but various purchases of "sundries" may indicate the acquisition of kitchen utensils as well as other necessary household tools.

68. January 17, 1787, PG, fol. 4 (1784–1800).

69. *Inventory of the Contents of Mount Vernon, 1810* (privately printed, 1909), 41–42.

70. LWT, 2.

71. In the *Account of Sales of the Personal Estate of Martha Washington (not specifically devised) late of Mount Vernon—as rendered to me by Thomas Peter the Executor*, MVLA AR, 1959, Thomas Peter, husband of Martha Parke Custis Peter, purchased two lots of "sundries," as well as "7 Cowes & five Calves and some kitchen furniture," 27.

72. This beaker vase descended through the Lewis family to the great-great-great-granddaughter of Martha Washington, Betty Washington Whiting. It was unknown to Mount Vernon before 2001 and was acquired at Christie's, New York, in January 2004, when a portion of Miss Whiting's estate was sold. The four complementing pieces of the garniture set similarly descended in the Lewis family and were sold to the Smithsonian Institution in the late nineteenth century. They are in the Lewis Collection of the Political History Division of the Smithsonian's National Museum of American History, Behring Center. For an illustration and description of these pieces, see Detweiler, 169.

73. Jean McClure Mudge, *Chinese Export Porcelain for the American Trade, 1785–1835* (Newark: University of Delaware Press, 1962), 228.

74. See Jean McClure Mudge, *Chinese Export Porcelain in North America* (New York: Riverside Book Company, 1986), 202.

75. H. A. Crosby Forbes, *Hills and Streams: Landscape Decoration on Chinese Export Blue and White Porcelain* (Washington, DC: International Exhibitions Foundation, 1982), 7.

76. Eight known shipments came from London (1762, 1763, 1765, 1766, and 1772), New York (1783), and Philadelphia (1790). Detweiler, 163. See Mudge, *Chinese Export Porcelain in North America*, 85–109.

77. First Draft, 1802, MVI, 6, 46.

78. LWT, 58.

79. See OED, 4:276, and David S. Howard, *The Choice of the Private Trader: The Private Market in Chinese Export Porcelain Illustrated from the Hodroff Collection* (London: Philip Wilson, 1994), 205.

80. "Appraisers Inventory," 1800, MVI, 21, 25, 27. Peter family tradition suggests that this guglet and basin were used by Martha Washington, although that use is impossible to document at this time.

81. The guglet and basin were likely part of the "3 Jugs and Bason" purchased by Thomas Peter at the sale of Martha Washington's effects in 1802. See MVLA AR 1959, 26–27. They are identified as numbers 81 and 82 on the Peter Family List, a numbered listing of Washington objects in the Peter family compiled by Britannia Wellington Peter Kennon before her death. The pair remained in the Peter family until their return to Mount Vernon in 1959.

82. Washington's accounts record the purchase from Burling of a "Table for Mrs. Washington" on November 20, 1789, at just over three pounds. See "Sundries bo[t] on account of GW," Henry Francis duPont Winterthur Museum, Winterthur, DE.

83. "Congressional Account of 1789," National Archives, Washington, DC. This transcription is from part of the account excerpted in Susan G. Detweiler and Charles F. Hummel, "Two Philadelphia Mahogany Side Chairs from President Washington's Residence in Philadelphia," Appendix A, paper prepared for the Barra Foundation, MVLA curatorial files.

84. See Margaret Van Cott, "Thomas Burling of New York City, Exponent of the New Republic Style," *Furniture History* 37 (2001): 32–47.

85. Although not identified as a Burling or breakfast table, the table is listed as Mrs. Washington's and at the same price paid to Burling in 1789. See List of Household Furniture, February 1797, photostat, MVLA Library, original, Pennsylvania Historical Society.

86. George Washington Parke Custis purchased "1 Breakfast table" for "$2.50." Fields, 413.

87. GW to Robert Cary & Co., October 25, 1765, PGW Col., 7:409–410.

88. Invoice from Robert Cary & Co., March 27, 1766, PGW Col., 7:432.

89. In an era before the manufacture of preprinted canvases, needlewomen drew their own designs. For more on eighteenth-century canvas work, see Susan Burrows Swan, *A Winterthur Guide to American Needlework* (New York: Crown Publishers, 1976), 26–63.

90. MW to Fanny Bassett Washington, June 2, 1794, Fields, 267.

91. MW to Fanny Basset Washington, July 14, 1794, Fields, 271.

92. "Dinner at Mount Vernon—1799, from the Unpublished Journal of Joshua Brookes (1773–1859)," *New-York Historical Society Quarterly* 31, no. 2 (1947): 72–85.

93. The Mount Vernon collection also contains a needlecase made from a fragment of one of the shell-patterned seat cushions. It returned to Mount Vernon through a descendant of Eliza Parke Custis Law.

94. Maya Hambly, *Drawing Instruments, 1580–1980* (London: Sotheby's Publications, 1988), 115.

95. *Virginia Journal and Alexandria Advertiser*, August 18, 1784.

96. April 7, 1784, PG, fol. 4 (1784–1800).

97. "Private sales, which took place upstairs among the Legatees, to be settled on the final adjustment without interest—22 July 1802," photostat, Mount Vernon Archives, original, Manuscript Division, Library of Congress. In this private sale, Doctor Peyton purchased "one box plotting instruments . . . [$]20"; Mr. Peter purchased "a case with a rule . . . 5"; and L. Washington purchased "a box of instruments . . . 20."

98. *Inventory of the Contents of Mount Vernon*, 27, 33.

99. Accompanying documentation for the accession is now in the Mount Vernon Archives. In addition to the handwritten note by Eliza, another note, likely in the hand of Eliza Parke Custis Law's granddaughter, Eleanor Agnes Goldsborough, identifies the rule as "Martha Washington rule which was always in her work basket." Regardless of where it was stored while at Mount Vernon, the connection between the rule and Martha Washington remains constant.

100. *The Workwoman's Guide, Containing Instructions to the Inexperienced in Cutting Out and Completing Those Articles of Wearing Apparel, &c., Which Are Usually Made At Home; Also, Explanations on Upholstery, Straw-Platting, Bonnet-making, Knitting, &c. By A Lady* (London: Simpkin, Marshall, and Co., 1838), 15, 213.

101. Gowns and stomachers with such ornamental detailing survive in the collections of the Museum of Fine Arts, Boston (stomacher, acc. no. 49.918; dress, acc. no. 50.494) and Colonial Williamsburg Foundation (gown and stomacher, acc. nos. 1985-117, 1–2; gowns, acc. nos. G1946-133, 1951-150, 1983-233). Portraits of the period, such as John Singleton Copley's *Mary and Elizabeth Royall*, ca. 1758 (Museum of Fine Arts, Boston), also illustrate such garments. A pair of surviving breeches (Museum of Fine Arts, Boston, acc. no. 99.664.9) indicates that gentlemen's waistcoats and other garments also received the decorative treatment.

102. Linda Baumgarten, John Watson, and Florine Carr, *Costume Close-Up: Clothing Construction and Pattern, 1750–1790* (Williamsburg, VA: Colonial Williamsburg Foundation, 2000), 14.

103. GW to the Secretary of the Treasury, September 1, 1796, GWW 35:201.

104. MW to Fanny Bassett Washington, June 5, 1791, Fields, 231.

105. Despite the number of entries for "Knight" in period census records and advertisements, the maker of the pinking iron remains unknown.

106. "Account of Sales of the Personal Estate of Martha Washington," MVLA AR, 1959, 27.

107. The numbers on the paper labels of the pinking iron (330) and lead plank (517) correspond to the Peter Family List prepared by Britannia Wellington Peter Kennon of Tudor Place before the Peter family belongings were divided in 1911.

108. According to the donor, Mrs. A. W. Bryan of Lambertville, New Jersey, this fishing tackle box and its contents were a gift from George Washington to his longtime friend and physician Dr. James Craik. Dr. Craik apparently then presented the box to George Coryell of Alexandria, and it descended in the Coryell family to the donor, a great-great-grandniece of George Coryell.

109. Sunday 6th [1751-1752], GWD,1:45.

110. [September 1770], GWD, 2:269.

111. Monday, 30th [July 1787], GWD, 5:178.

112. Monday 2d. [November 1789], GWD, 5:488-489.

113. Pennsylvania Packet, June 12, 1790, as cited in William Spohn Baker, *Washington after the Revolution, 1784–1799* (Philadelphia: J. B. Lippincott Co., 1898), 183.

114. Invoice to Robert Cary & Co., November 15, 1762, PGW Col., 7:166. Washington also received from London "500 very best Kirby hooks sorted from a perch to a large Cod" and "1 fishing Reel compleat." Invoice from Robert Cary & Co., April 13, 1763, PGW Col., 7:195.

115. The hook maker has not, to date, been identified. A 1774 list of London merchants in the Winterthur Library (DA 690 S54 s 1774) identifies Ann Sharp as a "needle and fish hook maker," indicating the involvement of women in the crafting of these small articles and offering the possibility that George Washington's fishing hooks were made by a female maker. No tie between Ann Sharp and the stamp "IS" is known. The author is grateful to Winterthur Museum Curators Donald Fennimore and Ann Wagner for providing these insights.

116. Joseph Willard to GW, November 7, 1789, PGW Pres., 4:280. GW to Joseph Willard, December 23, 1789, PGW Pres., 4:432. Washington recorded in his diary sitting for Savage. See Monday December 21st [1789], GWD, 5:509; Monday December 28th [1789], GWD, 5:511; Wednesday January 6th [1790], GWD, 6:2.

117. Savage was working on a portrait of Mary Brewton Motte Alston when Washington spent the night of April 29, 1791, with William Alston and his family. See GWD, 6:123-124.

118. The paintings are numbers 123 and 136 in the listing of paintings exhibited at the Columbian Gallery, New York, April 6, 1802. Photocopy, MVLA curatorial files, original, Ryerson Library, Art Institute of Chicago. Savage also exhibited the paintings in Philadelphia (1795–1800) and Boston (1812–1817).

119. A similar pair of east and west front views of Mount Vernon, also attributed to Edward Savage, sold at Christie's, New York, January 18, 1997.

120. For a more detailed explanation of this color change and analysis of other details of the paintings, see MVLA AR 1964, 14-17.

121. GW to Richard Chichester, August 8, 1792, PGW Pres., 10:641.

122. GW to William Pearce, December 28, 1794, GWW, 34:74.

123. Joseph H. Jones, *The Life of Ashmel Green, V.D.M* (New York: Robert Carter and Brothers, 1849), 266–267.

124. Fennimore, *Metalwork in Early America*, 294.

125. Cash Accounts, February 1770, PGW Col., 8:305.

126. Charles Turner was an Alexandria, Virginia, silversmith originally from Scotland. He mended a pair of knee buckles and a pair of spurs for John Parke Custis in January 1769 and mended George Washington's silver salt spoons in 1775. See Cash Accounts, January 1769, PGW Col., 8:156, and Miller, *Artisans and Merchants of Alexandria, Virginia*, 200.

127. Friday May 13 [1785], GWD, 4:137-138.

128. MVLA Minutes, 1939, 46.

NOTES TO CHAPTER SIX

1. PGW Col., 1:39.

2. GW Memorandum, ca. 1748, typed transcript, original, Washington Papers, Library of Congress, GW Personal Items Research Notebook, MVLA Library.

3. GW to Thomas Knox, January 1758, PGW, 5:78–88.

4. GW to Charles Lawrence, September 28, 1760, GWW, 2:352.

5. GW to Charles Lawrence, April 26, 1763, GWW, 2:396.

6. GW to Charles Lawrence, June 20, 1768, GWW, 2:492.

7. GW to Robert Cary & Co., November 30, 1759, GWW, 2:339.

8. GW to John Didsbury, October 12, 1761, GWW, 2:369.

9. GW to Richard Washington, October 20, 1761, GWW, 2:372.

10. Ibid.

11. Ibid.

12. Robert A. Rutland, ed., *The Papers of George Mason, 1725–1792*, 3 vols. (Chapel Hill: University of North Carolina Press, 1970), 1:211.

13. James L. Kochan, "'as plain as blue and buff could make it': George Washington's Uniforms as Commander-in-Chief and President, 1775–1799, *44th Washington Antiques Show Catalogue*, 1999, 94.

14. William Milnor to GW, November 29, 1774, PGW Col., 10:191 n. 6.

15. Cash Accounts, June 1775, PGW Col., 10:370.

16. As cited in James Thomas Flexner, *George Washington* (Boston: Little, Brown and Co., 1972), 4:416.

17. James Thacher, *Military Journal of the American Revolution* (Hartford, CT: Hurlbut, Williams & Co., 1862), 30.

18. General Orders, July 14, 1775, PGW Rev., 1:115.

19. Gilbert Chinard, ed. and trans., *George Washington as the French Knew Him* (Princeton, NJ: Princeton University Press, 1940), 75.

20. GW to Daniel Parker, January 22, 1783, GWW, 26:60.

21. GW to Daniel Parker, March 19, 1783, GWW, 26:243.

22. Ibid.

23. George Benet to his mother, April 15, 1783, GWW, 26:321n.

24. *Quebec to Carolina in 1785–1786, Being the Travel Diary and Observations of Robert Hunter, Jr., a Young Merchant of London*, November 15, 1785, 191–198, as excerpted in "Early Descriptions Notebook," MVLA Library.

25. GW to George Augustine Washington, June 10, 1787, PGW Con., 5:225.

26. GW to Daniel Hinsdale, PGW Pres., 2:42.

27. "New York Presidential Household Account Book," October 14, 1789, photostat, MVLA Library, original, Yale University.

28. "New York Presidential Household Account Book," February 9, 1790, photostat, MVLA Library, original, Yale University.

29. The household account book for October 14, 1789, notes payment to "Ann Ball for mak'g Shirts." Cited in Decatur, 72.

30. The household account book for January 24, 1791, notes payment to "Mrs. Clark for a pc. Cotton for Shirts for the President 28½ yds." Cited in Decatur, 191.

31. The household account book for April 27, 1792, notes payment "to Mrs. Emerson to pay for ruffling 4 shirts for the Prest." Cited in Decatur, 250.

32. Entries for June 8, 1793, January 21, 1794, January 7, 1795, and March 16, 1797, "Philadelphia Household Account Book," bound photostat, MVLA Library.

33. William Sullivan, *Public Men of the Revolution*, as cited in William Spohn Baker, *Washington after the Revolution, 1784–1799* (Philadelphia: J. B. Lippincott, 1898), 200–201.

34. As cited in Decatur, 67–68.

35. GW to George Steptoe Washington, March 23, 1789, GWW, 30:247.

36. GW to Bushrod Washington, January 15, 1783, GWW, 26:40.

37. GW to Catherine Macaulay Graham, January 9, 1790, GWW, 30:498.

38. The lion passant is stamped on the oval guard, while the knuckle guard marks include those of London assay, the date letter "M" in an incuse shield, and a maker's mark that appears to be "A R." The accompanying scabbard, not on display, has a throat mount engraved "Fesey, Cutler to His Majesty." Fesey was likely the retailer of the sword. Sarah Bevan Meschutt, manuscript, February 2, 2002, MVLA curatorial files.

39. George C. Neumann, *Swords and Blades of the American Revolution* (Harrisburg, PA: Promontory Press, 1973), 55. Michael D. Coe et al., *Swords and Hilt Weapons* (New York: Barnes and Noble, 1993), 70.

40. Richard Washington to GW, November 10, 1757, PGW Col., 5:49–52.

41. Sarah Bevan Meschutt, manuscript, February 2, 2002, MVLA curatorial files.

42. "Appraisers Inventory," 1800, MVI, 13.

43. LWT, 19. The swords inherited by George Lewis, George Steptoe Washington, and Bushrod Washington are in the collection at Mount Vernon. The sword bequeathed to William Augustine Washington is part of the New York State Library holdings, and that given to Samuel Washington is at the Smithsonian Institution.

44. Previously misidentified as paste, the buckles were confirmed as containing natural colorless topaz stones by the gemologist Richard Zemlo in August 2005, when he conducted multiple tests using a refractometer that consistently yielded a reading indicating the stones are topaz.

45. As quoted from *Monsieur à la Mode*, in Martha Gandy Fales, *Jewelry in America, 1600–1900* (Woodbridge, Suffolk: Antique Collectors' Club, 1995), 49.

46. Joan Evans, *A History of Jewellery, 1100–1870* (Boston: Boston Book and Art, 1970), 163. Paste, or glass that could be cut and faceted in the same manner as gemstones, received widespread popularity, and the Paris jeweler Georges Frédéric Strass contributed to its success with his development in the 1730s of transparent and highly refractive lead glass for this purpose. Although glass paste required great skill in the setting, its inexpensiveness allowed for experimentation in jewelry design and was utilized for a wide range of forms such as brooches, rings, earrings, bracelets, and all types of buckles. Glass paste rapidly became an alternative to diamonds and other precious gems, and its popularity produced a large market for the relatively inexpensive jewelry. For an extensive description of paste jewelry, including a discussion of other known Washington examples, see Fales, *Jewelry in America, 1600–1900*, 45–51, 115–117.

47. Invoice from Robert Cary & Co., November 17, 1766, PGW Col., 7:473.

48. Invoice from Robert Cary & Co., February 13, 1764, PGW Col, 7:287–288.

49. Invoice from Robert Cary & Co., December 3, 1771, PGW Col., 8:564.

50. Advertisement of Edmond Milne, December 15, 1763, in the *Pennsylvania Journal*, as cited in Alfred Coxe Prime, *The Arts and Crafts in Philadelphia Maryland and South Carolina, 1721–1785* (The Walpole Society, 1929), 81. For additional information on topaz in American jewelry, see Fales, *Jewelry in America, 1600–1900*, 113–114.

51. Frances Parke Butler, the first child of Martha Washington's granddaughter and George Washington's adopted daughter (Eleanor Parke Custis Lewis), was born at Mount Vernon on November 27, 1799, and was later married to Colonel E. G. W. Butler. On January 7, 1867, she signed an affidavit identifying these knee and shoe buckles as those belonging to George Washington and frequently worn by him. She further stated her ownership of the "companion buckles" in 1867, but their location is at present unknown. The affidavit is in the MVLA curatorial files.

52. "Appraisers Inventory," 1800, MVI, 13. "Private sales, which took place upstairs among the legatees," July 22, 1802, photostat, MVLA Library, original, Manuscript Division, Library of Congress.

53. In 1759 Washington requested of Robert Cary & Co. "Half a dozn. Pair of Men's neatest Shoes and Pumps." GW to Robert Cary & Co.,

May 1759, GWW, 2:321. The same year, he ordered "1 pair strong Shoes" from John Didsbury of London. GW to John Didsbury, November 30, 1759, GWW, 2:340. For a good listing and overview of the shoes and buckles George Washington purchased for himself, his family members, servants and slaves, see Mary V. Thompson, "Shoes Purchased/Owned by the Washingtons," manuscript, MVLA curatorial files.

54. For Washington's topaz shoe and knee buckles, see cat. 71. In 1765 Washington received "2 Setts diamd Cut Steel Buckles" from London. Invoice from Robert Cary & Co., December 20, 1765, PGW Col., 7:422. In 1771 John Didsbury of London sent Washington "2 pr Silvr Plated Buckles" when shipping "3 pr dress & 3 pr Neat Str Shoes." Invoice from Robert Cary & Co., December 3, 1771, PGW Col., 8:564.

55. American silversmiths carved the buckles to simulate the appearance of those set with stones. Fales, *Jewelry in America, 1600–1900*, 147–148. The same may hold true for these silver-plated buckles and the "diamd Cut Steel Buckles" Washington purchased in 1765.

56. Advertisements of William Dawson, April 26, 1793, and Joseph Anthony, Jr., December 7, 1790, *Pennsylvania Packet*, as cited in Alfred Coxe Prime, *The Arts and Crafts in Philadelphia Maryland and South Carolina, 1786–1800*, ser. 2 (The Walpole Society, 1932), 86, 112.

57. "Private sales, which took place upstairs among the Legatees," July 22, 1802, photostat, MVLA Library, original, Manuscript Division, Library of Congress.

58. The engraved "GW" on the buckles matches the "GW" on the barrels of a pair of pistols owned by George Washington and purchased by Thomas Hammond at the sale of his effects. When the pistols (acc. no. W-480/A&B) entered the Mount Vernon collection, the Hammond family noted in an affidavit that they had "engraved on the barrels later on (about 1858) for the purpose of identification, at a time when the true value of such mementos was becoming better recognized, and similar articles were found to be mislaid and lost." The presumption that the engraved initials "GW" on the buckles were made by the Hammond family is based on that affidavit. The buckles are also marked "LPC" and "F," but the maker or source of those marks has not yet been identified.

59. *Quebec to Carolina in 1785–1786*, as cited in MVLA AR 1945, 21. For descriptions of various hairstyles for men in the eighteenth century, see C. Willett and Phillis Cunnington, *Handbook of English Costume in the Eighteenth Century* (London: Faber and Faber, 1957), 94, 248–257, and R. Turner Wilcox, *Five Centuries of American Costume* (New York: Charles Scribner's Sons, 1963), 46–47.

60. See Washington's order in September 1760 of "2 wig, or Hair Bags," and invoices in March 1761 from Lardner & Company, Haberdashers, for "2 Black Silk Wig Bags" and in April 1762 from Stephen Heath, Haberdasher for "2 Silk [or Rich] hair bags." Invoice to Robert Cary & Co., September 28, 1760, PGW Col., 6:464; Invoice from Robert Cary & Co., March 31, 1761, PGW Col., 7:25; and Invoice from Robert Cary & Co., April 10, 1762, PGW Col., 7:125.

61. Decatur, 327.

62. Ibid., 73.

63. The stiffening fabric is inserted between two layers of fabric that have been stitched together to form the back of the bag. Loreen B. Finkelstein, report, June 6, 2005, Textile and Costume Conservatory, LLC, Williamsburg, VA.

64. During an examination of the waistcoat in 1993, Colonial Williamsburg Textile and Costume Curator Linda Baumgarten identified its probable origin as an example of a pattern. These patterns were textile panels with pre-embroidered or woven waistcoat decorations already completed. For additional information on and examples of these types of waistcoats, see Linda Baumgarten, *Eighteenth-Century Clothing at Williamsburg* (Williamsburg, VA: Colonial Williamsburg Foundation, 1988), 57–58, Linda Baumgarten, *What Clothes Reveal: The Language of Clothing in Colonial and Federal America* (New Haven: Yale University Press, for Colonial Williamsburg Foundation, 2002), 193, and Avril Hart and Susan North, *Historical Fashion in Detail: The Seventeenth and Eighteenth Centuries* (London: V&A Publications, 1998), 106.

65. Account of January 31, 1791, as cited in Decatur, 194.

66. Account of June 2, 1792, as cited in Decatur, 264.

67. See cat. 18.

68. The second half of the eighteenth century witnessed a popularity of lighter silk waistcoats with scattered designs and embroidery. Anne Buck, *Dress in Eighteenth-Century England* (New York: Holmes & Meier, 1979), 29.

69. Fales, *Jewelry in America, 1600–1900*, 121–127.

70. David L. Barquist, *Myer Myers, Jewish Silversmith in Colonial New York* (New Haven: Yale University Press, 2001), 42.

71. *Pennsylvania Gazette*, January 25, 1759, as excerpted in Prime, *The Arts and Crafts in Philadelphia, Maryland and South Carolina, 1721–1785*, 77.

72. *Pennsylvania Journal*, March 17, 1763, as excerpted in Prime, *The Arts and Crafts of Philadelphia Maryland and South Carolina 1721–1785*, 92.

73. Harold Newman, *An Illustrated Dictionary of Jewelry* (London: Thames and Hudson, 1981), 15.

74. Mary Custis Lee's probate inventory identifies the agate buttons she inherited as "taken from the black velvet coat of General George Washington." They were later incorporated into a pendant and sold at Sotheby's, New York, May 19, 2005.

75. Fales, *Jewelry in America, 1600–1900*, 126.

76. *New-York Daily Adversitser*, January 3, 1793, as cited in Rita Susswein Gotesman, comp., *The Arts and Crafts in New York, 1777–1799* (New York: New-York Historical Society, 1954), 65.

77. Pennsylvania Packet, January 25, 1793, as cited in Prime, *The Arts and Crafts in Philadelphia Maryland and South Carolina, 1786-1800*, ser. 2, 116.

78. "New York Presidential Household Account Book," 1789, photostat, MVLA Library, original, Yale University. While the entry indicates payment to Mr. Lunt, it is possible that it refers to the New York jeweler, gold-, and silversmith John Lent. See Gottesman, *The Arts and Crafts in New York*, 69-70.

79. MW to Eleanor Parke Custis, January 3, 1796, Fields, 289.

80. After George Washington's death, the banyan was owned by George Washington Parke Custis. Authenticity statements have identified it as the gown worn by George Washington at the time of his death and that the stain on it is his blood. To date, no verification of either of these assertions has been made.

81. For additional information on banyans, see Baumgarten, *What Clothes Reveal*, 110–112, 139, 196.

82. The banyan's shawl collar, high neckline, and sloping shoulders suggest an early nineteenth-century date. Notes and report of Colonial Williamsburg Textile and Costume Curator Linda Baumgarten, 1993, MVLA curatorial Files. The inclusion of identically printed cotton squares in a quilt (acc. no. W-365) worked by Martha Washington suggest the fabric dates to the Washingtons' lifetimes and offers the possibility of the garment's reworking after George Washington's death.

83. A pair of lightweight white cotton breeches (acc. no. W-1515) and a waistcoat (acc. no. W-2673) survive in the Mount Vernon collection. In 1772 George Washington ordered and received "1 pr. of Morrocco Leather Slippers." GW to John Didsbury, July 17, 1772, GWW, 3:94. Invoice, September 29, 1772, PGW Col., 9:107.

84. Buck, *Dress in Eighteenth-Century England*, 95.

85. GW to Thomas Gibson, July 18, 1771, PGW Col., 8:501.

86. Mrs. Henrietta Liston to her uncle, December 9, 1796, in Bradford Perkins, "A Diplomat's Wife in Philadelphia: Letters of Henrietta Liston, 1796–1800," *William and Mary Quarterly*, 3rd ser., 11, no. 4 (October 1954): 606.

87. Physical examination by Colonial Williamsburg Textile and Costume Curator Linda Baumgarten in October 2004 confirmed the original colors of purple, buff-cream, and black-brown. At the same

time, Baumgarten clarified the waistcoat's dating and subsequent alterations.

88. In October 2004 Colonial Williamsburg's Textile and Costume Curator Linda Baumgarten and Textile Conservator Loreen Finkelstein took detailed measurements of the coat and breeches. At the same time, they recorded the measurements of nine additional articles of Washington's clothing in the Mount Vernon collection. Based on the measurements of the clothing, in Baumgarten's report (October 19, 2004, MVLA curatorial Files), she suggested "that George Washington's posture was typical for an upper-class man of his era: narrow, sloped shoulders, back relatively flat with arms drawn back, and chest prominent. His arms were not especially muscular or thick, as the paintings of him suggest." She further noted that Washington's "waist was probably around 35 to 36 inches in the last quarter of the 18th century (the breeches waistbands were adjustable from 33 up to 39 inches)."

89. GW to Daniel Hinsdale, April 8, 1789, PGW Pres., 2:42 n. 1.

90. As cited in Decatur, 9.

91. GW to the Marquis de Lafayette, January 29, 1789, GWW, 30:187.

92. Jeremiah Wadsworth to Tobias Lear, February 15, 1789, as cited in Decatur, 9–10.

93. GW to Daniel Hinsdale, April 8, 1789, PGW Pres., 2:41–42.

94. The suit was examined by Colonial Williamsburg Textile and Costume Curator Linda Baumgarten in October 2004, and this analysis is derived from notes taken by the author at that time. Washington supposedly wore gilt buttons at his inauguration that were engraved with the United States coat of arms by William Rollinson, examples of which survive at the Valley Forge Historical Society. Decatur, 11.

95. Jane Washington Thornton was the daughter of George Washington's half brother Augustine. She married Colonel John Thornton, and one of their daughters, Frances Gregory Thornton, married George Alexander Thornton. Their son, Alfred Augustine Thornton, inherited the clothes. His brother-in-law, John Murray Forbes, later verified the history of the clothing in a written statement to the MVLA, Minutes, 1877, 12–13. As an heir of George Washington, Jane Thornton was qualified to participate in the private sales held following Martha Washington's death in 1802. Although no record of her purchase of the suit at those sales has surfaced, Mrs. Thornton could have come into possession of it in 1802 or later, through a trade or gift with/from a relative.

96. GW to Gouverneur Morris, November 28, 1788, PGW Pres., 1:135.

97. George Washington's Lépine pocket watch is in the collection of the Historical Society of Pennsylvania, Atwater Kent Museum, Philadelphia.

98. George Washington Parke Custis, *Recollections and Private Memoirs of Washington* (New York: Derby & Jackson, 1860), 454.

99. Advertisement in the *Federal Gazette*, November 7, 1793, as cited in Prime, *The Arts & Crafts in Philadelphia Maryland and South Carolina, 1786–1800*, ser. 2, 244.

100. James McCabe's shop was at several locations throughout his working career. He was situated at 8 Ironmonger Lane at the time he crafted George Washington's watch. For further information on McCabe and listings of the other locations of his shop, see Paul E. Hackamack, "James McCabe," *National Association of Watch and Clock Collectors Bulletin* (Columbia, PA: privately printed, 1978), 601–615.

101. Tuesday 20th [October 1789], GWD, 5:468.

102. "Dinner at Mount Vernon-1799, from the Unpublished Journal of Joshua Brookes (1773–1859)," *New-York Historical Society Quarterly* 31, no. 2 (April 1947): 74.

103. The coat was examined by Colonial Williamsburg Textile and Costume Curator Linda Baumgarten in June 1993 and October 2004. This analysis derives from her written report of 1993 and the author's notes taken during the 2004 visit. MVLA curatorial files.

NOTES TO CHAPTER SEVEN

1. For Martha Custis's correspondence with her London factors during her brief widowhood, see Fields, chap. 1. Evidence of articles purchased at her request also appear in the "Philadelphia Household Account Book," photostat, MVLA Library, excerpts of which are published in Decatur.

2. The term *First Lady* as a way of referring to the president's wife was not used during Martha Washington's lifetime, coming into usage only much later. It is used here for the modern reader's convenience.

3. MW to Robert Cary and Company, August 20, 1757, Fields, 5.

4. MW to Robert Cary and Company, 1758, Fields, 26–27.

5. In 1763 Robert Cary & Co. shipped "1 pr. gold wier Earrings" and "2 pr Silver Earings with Bob" that were supplied by John Payne of London. "Invoices and Letters, 1755–1766," bound photostat, 49, MVLA Library.

6. GW to Robert Cary & Co., February 13, 1764, GWW, 2:414.

7. In 1760 the London Jeweler D. Grymes provided "A pair French Earings." "Invoices and Letters, 1755–1766," bound photostat, 28, MVLA Library. In 1761 Washington ordered "2 french Necklaces" which were supplied by Stephen Heath of London and invoiced as "2 four Row'd French Necks." Invoice to Robert Cary & Co., October 12, 1761, PGW Col., 7:79. Invoice from Robert Cary & Co., April 10, 1762, PGW Col., 7:125. For additional information on French jewelry, see Martha Gandy Fales, *Jewelry in America, 1600–1900* (Woodbridge, Suffolk: Antique Collectors' Club, 1995), 39–42.

8. MW to Mrs. Shelbury, August 1764, Fields, 148.

9. Invoice from Robert Cary & Co., February 13, 1765, PGW Col., 7:355.

10. GW to Catherine Macaulay Graham, January 9, 1790, GWW, 30:498.

11. Mary V. Thompson, "'As if I had Been a Very Great Somebody': Martha Washington in the American Revolution; Becoming the New Nation's First Lady," manuscript, 2002, MVLA Library.

12. John P. Kaminski and Gaspare J. Saladino, eds., *The Documentary History of the Ratification of the Constitution* (Madison: State Historical Society of Wisconsin, 1988), 8:523.

13. The New York presidential account book notes payment to Colonel Wadsworth on May 23, 1789, for "6½ yds fine Hartford brown Cloth for a riding dress for M[rs] Washington." Cited in Decatur, 18.

14. MW to Fanny Bassett Washington, June 8, 1789, Fields, 215.

15. Abigail Adams to her sister, June 28, 1789, in Stewart Mitchell, ed., *New Letters of Abigail Adams, 1788–1801* (Boston: Houghton Mifflin Co., 1947), 13.

16. Abigail Adams to her sister, July 12, 1789, in ibid., 15.

17. Charlotte Chambers to her mother, February 25, 1795, as cited in William Spohn Baker, *Washington after the Revolution, 1784–1799* (Philadelphia: J. B. Lippincott Co., 1898), 300–301.

18. Julian Ursyn Niemcewicz, *Under Their Vine and Fig Tree: Travels through America in 1797–1799, 1804, with Some Further Account of Life in New Jersey*, trans. and ed., Metchie J. E. Budka (Elizabeth, NJ: Grassman Publishing Co., 1965), 85.

19. "Dinner at Mount Vernon—1799, from the Unpublished Journal of Joshua Brookes (1773–1859)," MVLA AR 1947, 20.

20. Diary of John Pintard, July 31, 1801, as excerpted in "Early Descriptions Research Notebook," MVLA Library.

21. Pierre Étienne Du Ponceau to his daughter, Anna L. Garasche, September 9, 1837, in James L. Whitehead, "Notes and Documents: The Autobiography of Peter Stephen Du Ponceau," *Pennsylvania Magazine of History and Biography*, July 1939, 312–313.

22. Recollection of Britannia Wellington Peter Kennon, ca. 1899, MVLA curatorial files.

23. Lace fragments with a history of trimming Martha Washington's wedding gown survive in the Mount Vernon collection (for an exam-

ple, see cat. 83), and fragments of yellow silk with the same provenance have returned through descendants of all three of her granddaughters (for an example, see cat. 90). The shoes appear as number 53, "Mrs. Washington's wedding slippers," on the Peter Family List, the numbered listing of Washington objects in the Peter family, drawn up by Britannia Wellington Peter Kennon before her death.

24. Invoice from Robert Cary & Co., March 15, 1760, PGW Col., 6:395.

25. This history was conveyed by the original lender, a descendant of Martha Washington's granddaughter Eleanor Parke Custis Lewis, at the time of its deposit at Mount Vernon in 1893. It matches examples of lace that descended in the line of granddaughter Martha Custis Peter with the attribution of having been worn by Martha Washington on her wedding day.

26. Elizabeth A. Lonze, *The Secrets of Real Lace* (Kalamazoo, MI: privately printed, 1994), 39.

27. Margaret Simeon, *The History of Lace* (London: Stainer & Bell, 1979), 86.

28. The first American ship, the *Empress of China*, made her voyage in 1784. For further insight into the trade of luxury goods, see Crossman, *The Decorative Arts of the China Trade*.

29. Entry for February 28, 1795, "Philadelphia Household Account Book," bound photostat, MVLA Library. For advertisements of the variety of goods sold by McElwee (M'Elwee) at his shops, see Prime, *The Arts and Crafts in Philadelphia Maryland and South Carolina, 1786–1800*, ser. 2, 211–214.

30. "List of Household Furniture," photostat, MVLA Library, original, Historical Society of Pennsylvania.

31. Invoice to Robert Cary & Co., September 20, 1759, PGW Col., 6:352–355. Snuff of various types appear on invoices, although John C. Fitzpatrick indicates that the last order for snuff was placed in 1775. See Fitzpatrick, *George Washington Himself: A Common-Sense Biography Written from His Manuscripts* (Indianapolis: Bobbs-Merrill Co., 1933), 146, 521.

32. See an accounting of the Custis estate, ca. 1759, in Fields, 113.

33. See Morrison H. Heckscher and Leslie Greene Bowman, *American Rococo, 1750–1775: Elegance in Ornament* (New York: Abrams, for the Metropolitan Museum of Art, 1992), 119.

34. Thomas Law to GW, August 10, 1799, PGW Ret., 4:232. Thomas Law was married to Eliza Parke Custis in 1796, although they separated and divorced a few years later.

35. Undated note, Eliza Parke Custis, MVLA accession file. For information on Eliza Custis, see Christine Meadows, "Eliza Custis in Miniature," MVLA AR 1992.

36. Before its purchase and donation to the MVLA, the engraving plate descended in the family of Martha Washington's granddaughter Martha Custis Peter. The reverse of the plate demonstrates Martha Peter's reuse of it for her calling cards and is engraved "M[rs] Peter / of / Tudor Place."

37. Ellen McCallister Clark, "The Life of Martha Washington," in Fields, xxvii.

38. MW to Fanny Bassett Washington, October 23, 1789, Fields, 220.

39. Invoice of Goods Shipped by Robert Cary & Co., March 1759, "Invoices and Letters, 1755–1766," bound photostats, MVLA Library.

40. The gemologist Richard Zemlo examined the necklace in August 2005, identifying the stones as rhodolite garnets and suggesting their possible Paris origin based on the style and mounts of comparable period pieces from that city.

41. For additional information on eighteenth-century garnet jewelry and those examples worn by Martha "Patsy" Parke Custis, see Martha Gandy Fales, "The Jewelry," in *Magazine Antiques* 135, no. 2 (February 1989): 513, and Fales, *Jewelry in America*, 35–38.

42. For additional information on seed pearl jewelry and its popularity in Federal period America, see Fales, *Jewelry in America*, 108–111.

43. Advertisement of Jeremiah Boone, *Federal Gazette* (Philadelphia), March 1, 1796, advertisement of James Jacks, *Federal Gazette* (Philadelphia), November 27, 1797, as cited in Prime, *The Arts and Crafts in Philadelphia Maryland and South Carolina 1786-1800*, ser. 2, 90, 123.

44. Account book entry for December 5, 1789, as cited in Decatur, 98.

45. Advertisement of Michael Roberts, October 7, 1786, *Independent Journal: or, the General Advertiser*, as cited in Gotesman, *The Arts and Crafts in New York, 1777–1799*, 90.

46. John C. Moorman, *The Virginia Springs* (Richmond, VA: J. W. Randolph, 1854), 259–260. For additional information on eighteenth-century bathing ritual and dress, including this bathing dress, see Claudia B. Kidwell, "Women's Bathing and Swimming Costume in the United States," *United States National Museum Bulletin 250* (1968): 3–32.

47. The handwritten note that accompanied the gown when it entered the Mount Vernon collection reads: "This is a much honored relic—My Grandmothers bathing gown, in which bathed at Berkeley Springs in Virginia soon after her marriage with Genl Washington—she gave it to me [illegible] leave it to my darling Rosebud—EPCustis," MVLA accession file.

48. Surviving fragments from Martha Washington's dresses in the Mount Vernon Collection suggest she wore silks from France and China as well as England. For additional information on the legislation surrounding imported textiles in America and silks worn by Martha Washington's contemporaries, see Linda Baumgarten, *What Clothes Reveal: The Language of Clothing in Colonial and Federal America* (New Haven: Yale University Press, for Colonial Williamsburg Foundation, 2002), 75–86. For examples similar to those worn by Martha Washington, see Natalie Rothstein, *The Victoria and Albert Museum's Textile Collection: Woven Textile Design in Britain from 1750 to 1850* (New York: Abbeville and the Victoria and Albert Museum, 1994), and Natalie Rothstein, *Silk Designs of the Eighteenth Century in the Collection of the Victoria and Albert Museum, London with a Complete Catalogue* (Boston: Bulfinch Press, Little, Brown and Co., 1990).

49. Recollection of G. Freeland Peter on the history of this textile and its division at Tudor Place, the home of Martha Washington's granddaughter Martha Custis Peter, MVLA accession file.

50. MW to Robert Cary and Company, 1758, Fields, 25–26. For a definition of nightgowns and insight into other alterations requested by the Washingtons and their contemporaries, see Baumgarten, *What Clothes Reveal*, 182–207.

51. GW to Daniel Parker, June 18, 1783, GWW, 27:20. For a discussion of the value of fabrics and the habit of reworking and altering clothing in the eighteenth century, see Susan Burrows Swan, *Plain and Fancy: American Women and Their Needlework, 1650–1850* (Austin, TX: Curious Works Press, 1995), 18–19, and Baumgarten, *What Clothes Reveal*, 182–207.

52. For additional information on hairwork, see Fales, *Jewelry in America*, 98–107.

53. Invoice, August 20, 1770, GWW, 3:24, and GW to Major Andrew Billings, June 17, 1783, GWW, 27:19.

54. Entry for December 28, 1789, as cited in Decatur, 104–105. For additional information on the goods advertised by van Voorhis, see Rita Susswein Gotesman, comp., *The Arts and Crafts in New York, 1777–1799* (New York: New-York Historical Society, 1954), 74–78.

55. LWT, 18.

56. LWT, 58.

57. A handwritten note in the hand of Elizabeth Hunt Tayloe, a descendant of Martha Peter, identifies the ring: "This ring was Mrs. Washingtons. My mother inherited it (a 3rd gr-granddaughter). My mother has many times worn it & she gave it to me in 1943. Eliz. Hunt Tayloe," MVLA accession file.

58. Will of George Augustine Washington, 1795, MVLA Archives (RM-530, MS-4533), 2–3. The ring stipulated in George Augustine Washington's will has not been identified to date and may refer to this example.

59. The transition from rococo to neoclassical design eventually broadened the hoop band and flattened its profile, a change not seen in the band of this ring. For a discussion of this stylistic evolution, see Diana Scarisbrick, *Rings: Symbols of Wealth, Power and Affection* (London: Thames and Hudson, 1993), 117–125.

60. Decatur, 66.

61. The full note reads: "This was a favorite gown of my dear Grandmother Mrs. Washington-she gave it to me after the Genl's death-I leave it to my grandchild Eliz. L. Rogers my darling Rosebud," MVLA curatorial files.

62. The author is grateful for the comments of Colonial Williamsburg Textile and Costume Curator Linda Baumgarten, whose examination of the gown in 1993 and 2004 provided insights into its dating, construction, and origin. Notes and reports, MVLA curatorial files.

63. For additional information on Chinese fans in America and an example of van Braam's presumed gift, see Carl L. Crossman, *The Decorative Arts of the China Trade: Paintings, Furnishings and Exotic Curiosities* (Woodbridge, Suffolk: Antique Collectors' Club, 1991), 322–337.

64. "Invoices and Letters, 1755–1766," bound photostat, MVLA Library, 26, 58. Invoice of goods from Robert Cary & Co., March 31, 1761, PGW Col., 7:25.

65. Additional ivory fans in the Mount Vernon collection with a history of Martha Washington ownership include acc. nos. W-610, W-1857, W-2704, and W-2791.

66. In 1770 George Washington requested "A Garnet Comb for the Hair to be bought of Benja. Gurdon & Son to Suit a Sett of Necklace and Earings sent by them in Septr. 1768" and "A Complt. Sett of Paste Necklace, Earings; Sprig; and hair Combs, together with Pins, and buttons for the Stomacher." Invoice, August 20, 1770, GWW, 3:23. While these were perhaps purchased for the use of sixteen-year-old Martha Parke Custis, it is likely they remained at Mount Vernon and were used by Martha Washington after her daughter's death in 1773. The "Paste and Garnet Pins for the hair" were requested by Washington in 1772. Invoice of Goods to be Shipped by Robert Cary & Co., July 15, 1772, GWW, 3:91.

67. MW to Fanny Bassett Washington, June 8, 1789, Fields, 215.

68. Niemcewicz, *Under Their Vine and Fig Tree*, 85.

69. Advertisement of Joseph Anthony, Jr., *Pennsylvania Packet*, December 7, 1790, as cited in Alfred Coxe Prime, ed., *The Arts and Crafts in Philadelphia Maryland and South Carolina, 1786–1800*, ser. 2 (The Walpole Society, 1932), 86.

70. MW to Mercy Otis Warren, December 26, 1789, Fields, 223–224.

71. In June 1791 George Washington's accounts note payment to "M[r]. Peale for taking a miniature of Mrs. Washington for Miss Custis." Decatur, 240. That miniature remains unidentified but was probably intended for Eliza Parke Custis. The miniature referred to in Martha Washington's 1796 correspondence to Eleanor "Nelly" Parke Custis has previously been noted as missing, probably due to the fact that this James Peale miniature returned to Mount Vernon through descendants of Martha Washington's sister, Elizabeth Dandridge Henley, and not through descendants of Nelly. The considerable number of Washington objects that passed between family members and Nelly's frequent gifts to others, however, should be taken into account. For more thoughts on this and other miniatures of Martha Washington, see Robert G. Stewart, "Portraits of George and Martha Washington," *Magazine Antiques* 135, no. 2 (February 1989): 474–479. For additional renderings of Martha Washington during the presidency, see Ellen G. Miles, *George and Martha Washington: Portraits from the Presidential Years* (Washington, DC: Smithsonian Institution, 1999).

72. MW to Eleanor Parke Custis, January 3, 1796, Fields, 289.

73. MW to Eleanor Parke Custis, January 14, 1796, Fields, 290.

NOTES TO THE AFTERWORD

1. In 1886 Mount Vernon Superintendent Harrison H. Dodge asked the Vice Regent for Connecticut if she would like the lemons in alcohol sent "some years ago" by Mrs. Wright of Connecticut transferred from the Massachusetts Room to the Connecticut Room, or if they should be placed in the relics case in the West Virginia Room. H. H. Dodge to Susan E. J. Hudson, October 14, 1886, Superintendent's Letters, 20 (1904–1905), MVLA Archives.

2. Mount Vernon inventory, ca. 1900, MVLA curatorial files. The inventory for the "Banquet Hall (New York Room—Relic Case)" lists "3—Piece of Coffin in which Washington was buried." Numerous coffin fragments survive in the MVLA collection, and the precise fragment recorded here has yet to be identified.

3. Advertisement of Pn. Lefebure, *Pennsylvania Packet*, September 13, 1783, as cited in Alfred Coxe Prime, ed., *The Arts and Crafts in Philadelphia Maryland and South Carolina, 1721–1785* (The Walpole Society, 1929), 78.

4. For additional information on the array of those objects made during and after George Washington's lifetime, see William Ayres, "At Home with George: Commercialization of the Washington Image, 1776–1876," in *George Washington American Symbol*, ed. Barbara J. Mitnick (New York: Hudson Hills Press, 1999), 91–107. For textiles, see Ayres, "At Home with George," 92–94.

5. Advertisement of Simon Chaudron, January 4, 1800, *Federal Gazette* (Philadelphia), as cited in Alfred Coxe Prime, ed., *The Arts and Crafts in Philadelphia Maryland and South Carolina, 1786–1800*, ser. 2 (The Walpole Society, 1929), 98.

6. For published examples of memorial porcelains, see Thomas V. Litzenburg, Jr., and Ann T. Bailey, *Chinese Export Porcelain in the Reeves Center Collection* (London: Third Millennium Publishing, 2003), 265, and Ronald W. Fuchs II, *Made in China: Export Porcelain from the Leo and Doris Hodroff Collection at Winterthur* (Winterthur, DE: Henry Francis du Pont Museum, 2005), 100–101. For prints, see Wendy C. Wick, *George Washington, an American Icon: The Eighteenth-Century Graphic Portraits* (Charlottesville: University Press of Virginia and the Barra Foundation, 1982), 66–73.

7. For some of these works of art, see Barbara J. Mitnick, "Parallel Visions: The Literary and Visual Image of George Washington," Raymond H. Robinson, "The Marketing of an Icon," and Mark Thistlethwaite, "Hero, Celebrity and Cliché: The Modern and Postmodern Image of George Washington," in *George Washington American Symbol*.

8. A Society of Females to MW, February 14, 1800, Fields, 351–352.

9. Samuel Eliot Morison and Henry Steele Commager, *The Growth of the American Republic* (New York: Oxford University Press, 1950), 1:203.

10. Thomas Jefferson to Walter Jones, January 2, 1814. The original manuscript in the Virginia Historical Society contains an ampersand, although many publications of the letter substitute the word *and*. See John Frederick Schroeder, *Maxims of George Washington* (Mount Vernon, VA: MVLA, 1989), 200.

11. Report of the Vice Regent for Michigan (Elizabeth B. A. Rathbone) at the meeting of Council, as recorded in the Minutes of the Council of the Mount Vernon Ladies' Association of the Union, May 1910, MVLA Library.

12. Ronald L. Hurst to Christine Meadows, April 21, 1987, MVLA curatorial files.

13. A recent reevaluation of Virginia furniture by Colonial Williamsburg curators Ronald L. Hurst, Tara Gleason Chicirda, and Robert Leath has occasioned a reattribution of a number of pieces traditionally attributed to the workshop of Peter Scott. Through that investigation, this easy chair has been attributed to Robert Walker, who served such illustrious clients as the Carters, Fitzhughs, and Lees. Robert Leath, "A Receipt, a Court Case and a Bureau Table: Rethinking Colonial Furniture II," lecture, Colonial Williamsburg Antiques Forum, February 2005. Publication of the findings and reattributions made by Hurst, Chicirda, and Leath is forthcoming in *American Furniture, 2006*.

14. In 2004–2005 Colonial Williamsburg Upholstery Conservator Leroy Graves investigated the original upholstery of the chair, which

revealed evidence of the first show cloth. An evaluation of this original upholstery is included in his forthcoming publication. At the same time, Colonial Williamsburg curators Linda Baumgarten and Tara Gleason Chicirda and Historic Furnishing Textile Specialist Natalie Larson identified the likely original colors of the fabric as well as a worsted damask in the Colonial Williamsburg collection (acc. no. G1966-411.1) appropriate as a source for the reproduction fabric. Mount Vernon is grateful to these, and all Colonial Williamsburg colleagues, who have furthered an understanding of this chair.

15. Wallace B. Gusler, *Furniture of Williamsburg and Eastern Virginia, 1710–1790* (Richmond: Virginia Museum, 1979), 31.

16. All four crosses have returned to Mount Vernon through gift and loan (acc. nos. W-1873, W-2006, W-3103).

17. For additional information on the religious beliefs of George and Martha Washington, see manuscript prepared by Mount Vernon Research Specialist Mary V. Thompson, "In the Hands of a Good Providence: Religion in the Family of George Washington." For examples of seed pearl crosses that incorporate gemstones, see Martha Gandy Fales, *Jewelry in America, 1600–1900* (Woodbridge, Suffolk: Antique Collectors' Club, 1995) 109–111.

18. Fales, *Jewelry in America*, 110.

19. Lawrence Lewis to John Struthers, February 22, 1837, as cited in John Struthers, *Tomb of Washington at Mount Vernon* (Philadelphia: Cary & Hart, 1840), 11–12. Lawrence Lewis was George Washington's nephew and last surviving executor of his estate at the time of the correspondence.

20. Ibid., 37–38.

21. The exterior inscriptions read: "The portion of wood inserted in the lid of this facsimile of the Sarcophagus, was cut from the inner shell which encloses the remains of Washington, by Wm. Strickland, of Philadelphia, Architect, and John Struthers, of Philadelphia, Mason and Sculptor, who sent it to me, together with a printed historical description and engraving of the Sarcophagus, etc. John Struthers was born at Hawthorns in the Parish of Irvine, in Ayrshire, 22nd November, 1786, Jesse Hartley, Liverpool / This Sarcophagus containing the remains of George Washington, First President of the United States, was made and presented for the purpose by John Struthers, of Philadelphia this day of A.D. 1837 / George Washington, Born Feb. 22, 1732, died Decr. 14, 1799 / An Exact Representation of the Silver Shield or Escutcheon which was attached to the leaden coffin and which is now deposited in the Marble Sarcophagus / By the permission of Lawrence Lewis, Esq. This Sarcophagus of Washington was presented by John Struthers, of Philadelphia, Marble Mason."

22. MW to Robert Cary and Company, 1758, Fields, 27.

23. September 1, 1790, PG, fol. 4 (1784–1800).

24. *The Workwoman's Guide, Containing Instructions to the Inexperienced in Cutting Out and Completing Those Articles of Wearing Apparel, &c., Which Are Usually Made At Home; Also, Explanations on Upholstery, Straw-Platting, Bonnet-making, Knitting, &c. By A Lady* (London: Simpkin, Marshall, and Co., 1838), 212–213, pl. 24.

25. Although difficult to determine owing to the small size of the fragments, the sewing case appears to combine fabrics featuring the larger-than-life flowers of the 1740s to 1750s and the asymmetrical natural motifs of the 1760s and 1770s. The triangular blue silk brocade fragment may date to later in the eighteenth century. For a brief overview of mid-eighteenth-century fabric fashions, see Linda Baumgarten, *What Clothes Reveal: The Language of Clothing in Colonial and Federal America* (New Haven: Yale University Press, for Colonial Williamsburg Foundation, 2002), 84.

26. This system of storage is confirmed by the large amount of abrasion evident on this end of the exterior fabric, which is a larger fragment of one of the fanciful silk brocades featured on the interior.

27. A sewing case also made of fragments with a history of being Martha Washington's gowns survives in the Colonial Williamsburg collection (acc. no. G1971-1419). See Baumgarten, *What Clothes Reveal*, 213.

28. A variety of dress fabric fragments survive in the Mount Vernon collection, including almost one dozen fragments believed to be from the dress Martha Dandridge Custis wore when she married George Washington in 1759.

29. Thomas Rossiter, a portrait and historical painter, was born in New Haven, Connecticut, in 1817. He studied in London and Paris, opening a studio in New York in 1846. The artist died in Cold Spring, New York, in 1871. Mantle Fielding, *Dictionary of American Painters, Sculptors and Engravers*, enl. ed., ed. Genevieve C. Doran (Greens Farms, CT: Modern Books and Crafts, 1974), 309.

30. Thomas P. Rossiter, "Mount Vernon, Past and Present: What Shall Be Its Destiny?" *Crayon* 5, pt. 9 (September 1858): 243, 252.

31. Benson J. Lossing, *Mount Vernon and Its Associations, Historical, Biographical and Pictoral* (New York: W. A. Townsend & Co., 1859), 188.

32. Ibid.,139.

33. Rossiter, *Mount Vernon*, 252.

Index

Numbers in italics reference pages with illustrations. Numbers following n. or nn. are Note numbers.